Ultimate Rocky Linux 9 for Network Administration

Master Rocky Linux Server Administration, Virtualization, Automation, and Cloud Deployment with Docker, Ansible, KVM, and AWS

Cesar Alonso Morera Alpizar

www.orangeava.com

First Published: October 2025

Published By: Orange Education Pvt Ltd, AVA®

Address: 9, Daryaganj, Delhi, 110002, India

275 New North Road Islington Suite 1314 London,
N1 7AA, United Kingdom

ISBN (PBK): 978-93-49888-16-6

ISBN (E-BOOK): 978-93-49888-37-1

Scan the QR code to explore our entire catalogue

www.orangeava.com

Dedicated To

My Beloved Mother,
Elizabeth Alpizar Alvarado,
Whose Love and Sacrifices Are The Roots of Everything I Have Achieved.

To My Siblings and Friends,
For Their Unwavering Support and Companionship Through Every Step of This Journey.

And to My Esteemed Colleagues—Raciel Rivera, Priyanka Arora, and Medhavi Tanwar, for Their Collaboration, Encouragement, And Professional Insight Throughout This Endeavor.

About the Author

Cesar Alonso Morera Alpizar is a seasoned Network Engineer and Linux Administrator with over a decade of experience in the IT industry. With a solid foundation in Security Engineering from **Fidélitas University** in Costa Rica, he has successfully navigated roles ranging from Level 2 Network Engineer to Salesforce Developer, Data Specialist, and Pre-sales System Engineer—showcasing a dynamic skill set that spans both infrastructure and application layers.

Currently, César serves as a Systems Engineer Associate at Infinite Computer Solutions, a University Instructor at **Cenfotec University**, and a professional writer as well as course creator at AVA® - An Orange Education Label. His passion for education is also reflected through his work on G-talent, where he has impacted more than 18,000 students worldwide through courses in Linux, English, Portuguese, and technology fundamentals.

César holds a **CCNA Routing and Switching certification**, a **Microsoft Windows Server Technical Degree**, and a **Salesforce Developer credential**. His technical expertise covers a wide range of domains, including network optimization, system automation with Ansible, cloud computing with AWS, and programming in Python and Java. Whether optimizing enterprise-level infrastructures or mentoring the next generation of tech professionals, César brings both strategic insight, and hands-on know-how.

In addition to his professional achievements, César is an enthusiastic educator and content creator. He is the author of ***Ultimate Rocky Linux 9 for Network Administration***, a practical guide designed to bridge the gap between traditional Linux system administration and modern cloud deployment strategies using Rocky Linux and AWS. Through step-by-step labs, real-world scenarios, and in-depth technical guidance, the book equips readers with the skills to manage and scale Linux environments in both on-premises and cloud contexts.

Beyond technology, César is passionate about languages, personal growth, and faith. He actively contributes to educational projects, mentors and students preparing for certifications, and supports his local community. His career is a testament to the power of continuous learning, and his mission is clear: To empower learners across the globe to build resilient and future-ready technical careers.

About the Technical Reviewer

Raciel Rivera Calero is a passionate Cybersecurity Analyst with growing experience in threat detection, incident response, and network defense. She has contributed to critical environments, assisting in alert monitoring, investigation, and response actions as part of a security operations team (SOC). Her main areas of focus include SOC operations, threat intelligence, and vulnerability management.

Over time, Raciel developed a strong interest in Linux, especially in cybersecurity contexts. She has worked on integrating security tools into Linux environments, configuring and deploying them on servers to support defensive capabilities. This hands-on experience has helped her better understand technical implementations and strengthen operational security processes.

Her path into cybersecurity began as a self-taught learner, driven by curiosity and a desire to apply knowledge practically. She soon became active in Capture The Flag (CTF) competitions and has ranked among the top participants on national and international platforms. These challenges have played a key role in sharpening her skills and familiarizing her with real-world attack scenarios.

In addition to her technical work, Raciel is committed to cybersecurity education. She leads her own mentorship initiatives focused on helping aspiring professionals access hands-on, practical learning. Through these efforts, she connects learners with training opportunities that emphasize foundational Blue Team skills and tools such as SIEMs, detection techniques, and log analysis. She occasionally collaborates with independent academies to expand access to quality cybersecurity training. As a Cybersecurity Instructor, she continues to reinforce her dedication to inclusive and skills-based learning.

Raciel believes in making cybersecurity education more inclusive and practical, especially for Spanish-speaking learners. She is passionate about creating learning environments where people feel encouraged to grow and build real-world confidence.

As she continues to evolve in her career, Raciel is focused on deepening her technical expertise, contributing to impactful projects, and guiding others into the field. Her ultimate goal is to become a well-rounded Blue Teamer while helping shape the next generation of cybersecurity professionals.

Acknowledgments

Writing ***Ultimate Rocky Linux 9 for Network Administration*** has been a journey of technical depth, continuous learning, and personal growth. I am sincerely grateful to those who supported and believed in me throughout this endeavor.

First and foremost, I want to thank my beloved mother, Elizabeth Alpizar Alvarado, whose strength, encouragement, and unconditional support gave me the drive to complete this work. Her belief in my potential has been a guiding force.

I thank my siblings and dear friends for their patience, motivation, and companionship during long days and late nights that made this project not only possible, but meaningful.

I also wish to acknowledge my esteemed colleagues, Raciel Rivera, Priyanka Arora, and Medhavi Tanwar, for their ongoing support, thoughtful conversations, and collaboration throughout the development of this book. Their professional insights were invaluable in shaping many of the ideas shared in these pages.

Lastly, I am thankful for the many communities, open-source contributors, and learning platforms that continue to make Linux and cloud technologies accessible to all. This book is a tribute to the power of shared knowledge, and the strength of collaborative learning.

To everyone who stood with me—thank you for making this vision a reality!

Preface

In today's rapidly evolving tech landscape, we as system administrators and IT professionals are expected to manage scalable, secure, and highly available environments–often in the cloud. Rocky Linux, as a stable and community-driven enterprise OS, has emerged as a reliable foundation for modern server administration. When combined with the power of tools such as Ansible, Docker, and AWS, it becomes a powerful platform for building resilient cloud infrastructure.

This book was born out of a desire to help both aspiring and experienced Linux administrators bridge the gap between traditional system management, and modern cloud-based deployment. Whether we aim to sharpen our command-line skills, understand virtualization with KVM, containerize services with Docker, or deploy infrastructure on AWS, this book is designed to provide clear, hands-on guidance at every step.

We take a practical approach–rich with examples, walkthroughs, and real-world scenarios–to make complex topics accessible and actionable. From managing users and services to full cloud deployments and performance tuning, each chapter is crafted to build our confidence and capability.

The book is divided into 18 chapters, gradually progressing from foundational topics to advanced automation and cloud orchestration techniques. The early chapters of the book focus on essential Linux skills, such as user management, networking, and package administration. The later chapters explore virtualization, containerization, automation, and cloud integration using tools such as KVM, Docker, Ansible, and Amazon Web Services.

By the end of this journey, we will not only be proficient in managing Rocky Linux systems, but also be capable of designing and maintaining modern, enterprise-ready cloud infrastructure. We will gain the knowledge needed to support DevOps practices, automate tasks, and ensure system security as well as performance at scale.

Thus, whether we are students, instructors, or working professionals, I hope this book becomes a valuable companion in our journey as system engineers and cloud architects.

Chapter 1. Introduction to Rocky Linux 9: Explore Rocky Linux's origins, community-driven model, and its role as a reliable enterprise OS. Understand its relationship with CentOS and RHEL, and get introduced to virtualization basics and cloud instance setups with VirtualBox and AWS.

Chapter 2. Command Line Fundamentals: Master essential Linux commands for navigating and managing files and directories. Learn permission handling, use of sudo, and basic system controls, with an introduction to command-line workflows in cloud environments like AWS.

Chapter 3. User Management and Permissions: Learn to create and manage user accounts, groups, and permissions securely. Explore the best practices for user roles, password management, and access control, both locally and within AWS cloud instances.

Chapter 4. Package Management and Updates: Understand how to install, update, and remove software packages with dnf. Manage repositories, dependencies, and automate package maintenance, ensuring system security and stability on Rocky Linux and AWS environments.

Chapter 5. Network Basics: Gain foundational networking skills including interface configuration, troubleshooting tools, firewall management, and secure remote access. Learn how networking concepts apply to both on-premises servers and AWS cloud infrastructure.

Chapter 6. Advanced Administration Techniques: Delve into advanced Linux administration with RAID setup, service management via system, performance monitoring, and task automation. Learn how to manage Rocky Linux efficiently in AWS with cloud automation tools.

Chapter 7. File System Management: Manage disk partitions, file system creation, resizing, and mounting. Understand backup strategies and integrate cloud storage solutions such as AWS EBS and S3 to maintain data integrity and availability.

Chapter 8. Web Server Setup and Configuration: Set up and secure Apache web servers with virtual hosts. Configure dynamic content using PHP and MySQL, and learn to deploy scalable web services within AWS cloud environments.

Chapter 9. Database Management: Install and configure MySQL/MariaDB databases on Rocky Linux. Explore backup, restore, and performance tuning techniques, plus AWS RDS integration for scalable cloud database solutions.

Chapter 10. Mail Server Setup: Configure mail servers using Postfix, manage mail domains and users securely, and troubleshoot common issues. Integrate with AWS SES for scalable and reliable email services in the cloud.

Chapter 11. Virtualization with KVM: Implement and manage KVM-based virtualization, create virtual machines, and configure networking. Compare on-premises virtualization with AWS EC2, and explore hybrid cloud deployment strategies.

Chapter 12. Containerization with Docker: Deploy and manage Docker containers on Rocky Linux. Learn container networking, storage, and multi-container orchestration with Docker Compose, along with AWS ECS and EKS integration.

Chapter 13. Automation with Ansible: Automate system administration with Ansible playbooks. Manage infrastructure configuration, streamline Rocky Linux deployments, and scale automation using Ansible Tower in AWS cloud environments.

Chapter 14. Rocky Linux in Cloud Environments: Explore Rocky Linux deployment on AWS, focusing on AMIs, EC2 instance management, and cloud security best practices. Learn how to operate in hybrid and multi-cloud infrastructures.

Chapter 15. Performance Tuning in Rocky Linux 9: Optimize system resources such as CPU, memory, and network for better performance. Apply monitoring and tuning techniques both on-premises and in AWS cloud to maximize efficiency.

Chapter 16. Common Deployment Scenarios: Review practical Rocky Linux deployment strategies, including high availability, load balancing, and application scaling. Learn the best practices for managing resilient enterprise infrastructure on AWS.

Chapter 17. End-to-End Cloud Deployment Project: Apply learned skills to deploy a full application on AWS. Launch EC2 instances, configure web and database servers, manage security groups, scale services, and monitor the cloud deployment.

Chapter 18. The Future of Rocky Linux and Server Management: Look ahead to emerging trends in cloud computing, server management, and open-source development. Understand the evolving role of Rocky Linux, and prepare for future skills and innovations.

Get a Free eBook

We hope you are enjoying your recently purchased book! Your feedback is incredibly valuable to us, and to all other readers looking for great books.

If you found this book helpful or enjoyable, we would truly appreciate it, if you could take a moment to leave a short review with a 5 star rating on Amazon. It helps us grow, and lets other readers discover our books.

As a thank you, we would love to send you a free digital copy of this book, and a **30%** discount code on your next cart value on our official websites:

www.orangeava.com

www.orangeava.in (For Indian Subcontinent)

☑ **Here's how:**

Leave a review for the book on Amazon.

Take a screenshot of your review, and send an email to **info@orangeava.com** (it can be just the confirmation screen).

Once, we receive your screenshot, we will send you the digital file, within 24 hours.

Thank you so much for your support – it means a lot to us!

Downloading the code bundles and colored images

Please follow the links or scan the QR codes to download the
Code Bundles and Images of the book:

https://github.com/OrangeAVA/Ultimate-Rocky-Linux-9-for-Network-Administration

The code bundles and images of the book are also hosted on
https://rebrand.ly/feos5oq

In case there's an update to the code, it will be updated on the existing GitHub repository.

Errata

We take immense pride in our work at **Orange Education Pvt Ltd,** and follow best practices to ensure the accuracy of our content to provide an indulging reading experience to our subscribers. Our readers are our mirrors, and we use their inputs to reflect and improve upon human errors, if any, that may have occurred during the publishing processes involved. To let us maintain the quality and help us reach out to any readers who might be having difficulties due to any unforeseen errors, please write to us at :

errata@orangeava.com

Your support, suggestions, and feedback are highly appreciated.

DID YOU KNOW

Did you know that Orange Education Pvt Ltd offers eBook versions of every book published, with PDF and ePub files available? You can upgrade to the eBook version at **www.orangeava.com** and as a print book customer, you are entitled to a discount on the eBook copy. Get in touch with us at: **info@orangeava.com** for more details.

At **www.orangeava.com**, you can also read a collection of free technical articles, sign up for a range of free newsletters, and receive exclusive discounts and offers on Print Books and eBooks.

PIRACY

If you come across any illegal copies of our works in any form on the internet, we would be grateful if you would provide us with the location address or website name. Please contact us at **info@orangeava.com** with a link to the material.

ARE YOU INTERESTED IN AUTHORING WITH US?

If there is a topic that you have expertise in, and you are interested in either writing or contributing to a book, please write to us at **business@orangeava.com**. We are on a journey to help developers and tech professionals to gain insights on the present technological advancements and innovations happening across the globe and build a community that believes Knowledge is best acquired by sharing and learning with others. Please reach out to us to learn what our audience demands and how you can be part of this educational reform. We also welcome ideas from tech experts and help them build learning and development content for their domains.

REVIEWS

Please leave a review. Once you have read and used this book, why not leave a review on the site that you purchased it from? Potential readers can then see and use your unbiased opinion to make purchase decisions. We at Orange Education would love to know what you think about our products, and our authors can learn from your feedback. Thank you!

For more information about Orange Education, please visit **www.orangeava.com**.

Table of Contents

CHAPTER 1
Introduction to Rocky Linux 9

Introduction

Rocky Linux 9 is a **community-driven enterprise operating system** designed to provide **100% compatibility with Red Hat Enterprise Linux (RHEL)** while ensuring long-term stability, security, and performance. Developed by **Gregory Kurtzer**, co-founder of CentOS, Rocky Linux emerged as the ideal successor after CentOS transitioned to CentOS Stream, a rolling-release model that introduced unpredictability for production environments. Many **system administrators and businesses** sought a stable, RHEL-compatible alternative–**Rocky Linux 9 delivers exactly that.**

With a **predictable lifecycle, long-term updates, and security patches**, Rocky Linux 9 ensures **seamless migration** for enterprises relying on RHEL-based tools and configurations. Whether deployed **on-premises or in the cloud (AWS, Azure, Google Cloud)**, it supports modern workloads, including **containers, virtualization, and high-performance computing (HPC)**. Built with **enhanced security features, optimized performance, and a transparent governance model**, Rocky Linux 9 remains free from corporate influence, making it a **trusted choice for IT professionals managing critical infrastructure**. **For administrators seeking a stable, enterprise-ready Linux OS, Rocky Linux 9 is the perfect solution.**

Structure

In this chapter, we will discuss the following topics:

- Overview of Linux Operating Systems
- The History and Development of Rocky Linux
- Comparison with CentOS and RHEL
- Key Features and Benefits
- Downloading and Verifying Rocky Linux
- Introduction to Virtualization

Overview of Linux Operating Systems

An operating system (OS) is software that manages hardware resources and provides services for computer programs. **Linux is a family of open-source, Unix-like operating systems**, widely used for servers due to its **stability, security, and strong community support**. Popular Linux distributions include **Red Hat Enterprise Linux (RHEL), Ubuntu, and SUSE Linux Enterprise Server (SLES).**

Originally developed by Linus Torvalds in 1991, Linux has evolved into a diverse ecosystem of Unix-like operating systems that adhere to **Unix principles** while being licensed under **open-source guidelines**. This allows **free use, modification, and distribution of the code**, fostering a global community that continuously enhances Linux. Developers worldwide contribute to **security improvements,**

performance optimizations, and innovations that drive both **modern enterprise solutions and personal computing**.

Rocky Linux, like RHEL, is designed for enterprise environments, offering long-term support and binary compatibility with RHEL. Its focus on **stability, security,** and **predictable updates** makes it a preferred choice for businesses seeking an open-source, production-ready operating system.

General Introduction to Linux

Linux is a powerful and versatile open-source OS widely used across diverse computing environments, from personal desktops to enterprise servers and even mobile devices. Unlike proprietary systems, Linux is developed through community collaboration, allowing anyone to access, modify, and distribute its source code freely. This open-source model has led to the creation of various Linux distributions (distros), each designed to meet specific user needs in areas such as enterprise computing, education, and software development.

Originating in the early 1990s as a personal project by Finnish student Linus Torvalds, Linux started as a Unix-like kernel and rapidly grew into a full-fledged operating system with contributions from developers worldwide. Over time, it became the foundation for numerous distributions, supporting critical applications in businesses, cloud computing, and consumer technology, including Android smartphones. Today, Linux remains a preferred choice for its stability, security, and adaptability across multiple platforms.

Brief History of Linux

Linux was created in **1991 by Linus Torvalds**, a computer science student from **Helsinki, Finland**, who sought to develop a **free and flexible alternative** to the MINIX operating system, which was limited in scope and not entirely free. Inspired by **Unix**, Torvalds initially released **Linux kernel version 0.01**, a basic but functional system. What set Linux apart was Torvalds' decision to license it under the **GNU General Public License (GPL)**, allowing developers worldwide to access, modify, and distribute the source code freely. This decision led to collaboration with the **Free Software Foundation (FSF)** and the **GNU Project**, forming the basis of a **fully open-source operating system** that combined the **Linux kernel with essential GNU tools**.

Throughout the **1990s**, Linux gained momentum as **developers and organizations** contributed to its growth, improving **stability, security, and performance**. By the mid-1990s, commercial Linux distributions such as **Red Hat, SUSE, and Slackware** emerged, offering professional support and making Linux more accessible to businesses. This marked the beginning of Linux's **expansion into enterprise environments**, which were previously dominated by proprietary Unix systems. A significant breakthrough occurred in **1998**, when major tech companies such as **IBM, Oracle, and Hewlett-Packard** saw Linux as a viable enterprise OS and invested heavily in its development. IBM alone committed over **$1 billion**, further solidifying Linux's role in **mission-critical computing**.

The **2000s** saw the rapid adoption of Linux in **data centers, cloud computing, and virtualization**. The creation of the **Linux Foundation in 2000** strengthened collaboration between **open-source developers and commercial enterprises**, fostering innovation and standardization. Technological advancements such as **containerization (Docker, Kubernetes)** and **cloud computing** accelerated Linux's dominance, making it the **foundation of modern IT infrastructure**. Today, Linux powers **supercomputers, enterprise servers, embedded systems, and mobile devices (through Android)**, with distributions catering to diverse needs, from enterprise solutions such as **RHEL and SUSE** to community-driven projects such as **Ubuntu and Debian**.

From a **student project to a global phenomenon**, Linux's evolution reflects the power of **open-source collaboration**. With **strong community support, corporate backing, and continuous innovation**, Linux remains the **backbone of modern technology**, driving advances in **AI, IoT, and cloud computing**.

Its adaptability ensures that it will continue shaping the future of **enterprise and consumer computing** for years to come.

The History and Development of Rocky Linux

In **December 2020**, the CentOS project announced a major shift, transitioning from **CentOS Linux**, a stable downstream version of **Red Hat Enterprise Linux (RHEL)**, to **CentOS Stream**, an upstream, rolling-release model. Unlike CentOS Linux, CentOS Stream receives updates **before** RHEL, making it a **testing ground** rather than a **stable, production-ready OS**. This change raised concerns among system administrators and businesses that depended on **CentOS for its reliability and long-term support**. With CentOS Linux being phased out, users had to either adapt to **CentOS Stream** or seek an alternative that maintained the same level of **stability and RHEL compatibility**.

Addressing this, **Gregory Kurtzer**, co-founder of CentOS, launched the **Rocky Linux project** in honor of his late colleague, **Rocky McGaugh**. The goal was clear: to provide a **community-driven, RHEL-compatible OS** that mirrored CentOS Linux's stability and predictability. Within days of its announcement, **Rocky Linux gained immense traction**, with over **10,000 users joining its community channels**. The Linux community's enthusiasm helped accelerate development, reinforcing the demand for a **free, enterprise-grade OS without corporate influence**.

Rocky Linux was designed as a **true downstream alternative to RHEL**, ensuring seamless **migration** for CentOS users. The project embraced a **transparent, open-source development model**, inviting contributions from the **global Linux community**. Unlike corporate-backed distributions, Rocky Linux was structured to be **independent and sustainable**, ensuring that **no single entity could dictate its future**.

By **June 2021**, the first official release of **Rocky Linux** was launched, fulfilling its promise of **stability and RHEL compatibility**. The release was widely welcomed, positioning Rocky Linux as the **go-to CentOS replacement**. Its adoption grew rapidly across **enterprises, data centers, and cloud environments**, proving its viability for **mission-critical workloads**.

To ensure long-term sustainability, the **Rocky Enterprise Software Foundation (RESF)** was established, safeguarding Rocky Linux's **community-driven governance**. The RESF provides **structured leadership** while keeping the OS **freely available** and aligned with **open-source principles**. Today, **Rocky Linux stands as a trusted enterprise OS**, offering a **secure, stable, and predictable** alternative to CentOS Linux, reinforcing the **power of open-source collaboration**.

Comparing CentOS, RHEL, and Rocky Linux

Rocky Linux aims to provide a stable and predictable enterprise environment, unlike CentOS Stream, which follows a rolling-release model. Key distinctions include:

- **CentOS Stream:** Acts as an upstream testing ground for RHEL, meaning updates arrive before full stabilization.
- **Rocky Linux:** A fully stable, downstream RHEL alternative, making it ideal for production environments.
- **RHEL:** The original enterprise Linux distribution with commercial support.

Versioning and Updates

The content in this book primarily focuses on **Rocky Linux 9**, ensuring relevance to the latest stable release. Any commands and features discussed will align with this version unless otherwise specified. The historical context remains valid across versions, but users should always refer to the official documentation for the most recent updates.

Rocky Linux, CentOS, and RHEL: Shared Origins and Diverging Paths

The evolution of Linux distributions has given rise to various systems with unique goals, but few are as closely connected as Red Hat Enterprise Linux (RHEL), CentOS, and Rocky Linux. These three distributions share a common lineage, with RHEL serving as the foundation from which CentOS and Rocky Linux emerged. Despite their shared origins, the paths they have taken highlight distinct philosophies and user needs.

RHEL represents the enterprise gold standard in Linux environments, prioritizing stability, support, and long-term maintenance. CentOS, initially a faithful community rebuild of RHEL, bridged the gap for those who wanted RHEL's features without its commercial costs. However, its evolution into CentOS Stream signaled a shift in purpose, moving away from its stable production roots toward a more forward-looking, developer-oriented role.

Enter Rocky Linux, a project born from the community's desire to maintain the original spirit of CentOS. Created to provide a reliable and free RHEL-compatible platform, Rocky Linux reinforces the importance of stability for production systems.

This intricate web of shared heritage and divergent objectives sets the stage for a deeper examination of what each distribution offers, how they differ, and what their roles are in the modern Linux landscape.

Shared Origins and Diverging Paths

Rocky Linux, CentOS, and RHEL share a common foundation rooted in the Linux ecosystem. RHEL, developed and supported by Red Hat, Inc., is a commercially backed Linux distribution designed for enterprise environments. It is known for its stability, reliability, and extensive support options, making it a popular choice for organizations that prioritize robust support and compliance with rigorous industry standards. RHEL has long been a leading choice for enterprise deployments, and its reliability has set a high bar in the world of Linux.

Historically, CentOS served as a downstream version of RHEL, closely following RHEL's updates and providing a free, open-source alternative with the same binary compatibility and stability as RHEL. This model allowed organizations to enjoy the benefits of an enterprise-grade OS without the licensing costs associated with RHEL. CentOS became a staple in many organizations, particularly in environments where a stable OS was required but without the need for commercial support. By rebuilding the RHEL source code and releasing it as a free alternative, CentOS provided an accessible and cost-effective way for businesses, educational institutions, and developers to leverage RHEL-compatible software for production systems.

However, in December 2020, CentOS announced a shift in its development model, moving from CentOS Linux to CentOS Stream. Instead of being a downstream version of RHEL, CentOS Stream now serves as an upstream, rolling-release model that sits between Fedora (Red Hat's innovation-focused community distribution) and RHEL. This means CentOS Stream receives new features and updates before they are incorporated into RHEL, positioning it as a testing ground for upcoming RHEL releases. While this model offers valuable insight into future RHEL updates, it no longer provides the same stability and long-term support that made CentOS Linux an attractive option for production environments.

In response to these changes, Gregory Kurtzer, the original co-founder of CentOS, initiated the Rocky Linux project to continue the legacy of CentOS Linux as a stable, RHEL-compatible distribution. Named in honor of his late friend and CentOS co-founder, **Rocky McGaugh**, Rocky Linux was built with the mission of providing a free, community-driven OS that mirrors RHEL's release cycle and stability. This move was met with strong community support, as many organizations were left searching for an alternative to CentOS Linux that offered predictable releases, binary compatibility with RHEL, and a commitment to long-term stability.

Comparing CentOS Stream, AlmaLinux, Rocky Linux, and RHEL

As organizations seek reliable, enterprise-grade Linux distributions, they often weigh options among CentOS Stream, AlmaLinux, Rocky Linux, and RHEL. Although these distributions share a similar ancestry rooted in RHEL, they have distinct purposes and release models that make them better suited to specific use cases. Let us break down each of these distributions, their goals, release models, and how they compare in stability, community support, and compatibility.

Red Hat Enterprise Linux (RHEL)

RHEL is a commercially supported Linux distribution developed by Red Hat, targeting enterprise environments where stability, support, and security are paramount. Red Hat maintains strict quality control, offering a reliable OS backed by a commercial support model. RHEL is commonly used by companies that require the assurance of professional support, security patches, and updates.

Key Features:

- **Release Model:** RHEL follows a long-term release model, where each version is supported for approximately 10 years (5 years of full support and 5 years of maintenance). This gives enterprises a predictable, stable platform over the long term.
- **Subscription Model:** RHEL requires a paid subscription that provides access to Red Hat's support, patching, and additional services such as Red Hat Insights for monitoring.
- **Use Cases:** Commonly used in mission-critical applications across industries, including finance, healthcare, and government, where stability and security are vital.

Pros:

- Enterprise-grade support and security.
- Long-term stability with planned release cycles.
- Access to extensive documentation and proprietary Red Hat tools.

Cons:

- Subscription cost, making it less attractive for smaller businesses or non-profits.
- Closed-source extensions and add-ons, unlike the fully open-source CentOS.

CentOS Stream

CentOS Stream serves as the development preview for upcoming RHEL releases. Unlike traditional CentOS, which was a downstream, free clone of RHEL, CentOS Stream is now an upstream distribution that sits between Fedora (bleeding-edge) and RHEL (stable release). CentOS Stream gets features and updates that are being tested for future RHEL versions.

Key Features:

- **Rolling Release Model:** CentOS Stream continuously receives updates as Red Hat prepares features for the next RHEL version, offering users a rolling release model that evolves with development.
- **Community-Driven Development:** While CentOS Stream is still managed by Red Hat, the community is encouraged to participate in testing and feedback, shaping future RHEL releases.

- **Use Cases:** Suitable for developers and testers who need to stay close to what RHEL will offer next or who need a free, RHEL-compatible development environment.

Pros:

- Access to future RHEL features before they are fully released.
- Free and open-source, with community contributions encouraged.
- Excellent choice for testing, development, and pre-production environments.

Cons:

- Lack of long-term stability, as CentOS Stream is a rolling release and therefore, less predictable.
- Limited to those who need a preview of RHEL rather than a stable, production-grade OS.

AlmaLinux

AlmaLinux was created by the non-profit AlmaLinux Foundation, with significant support from CloudLinux Inc. It emerged in response to CentOS's shift to CentOS Stream, aiming to provide a free, community-driven, and enterprise-ready replacement for CentOS. AlmaLinux is a downstream distribution of RHEL, meaning it closely follows RHEL's stable release updates.

Key Features:

- **Binary Compatibility with RHEL:** AlmaLinux mirrors RHEL releases and maintains binary compatibility, making it a true community-supported alternative to RHEL for those who require a stable environment without cost.
- **Community and Corporate Support:** AlmaLinux is supported by the AlmaLinux Foundation and has substantial backing from companies interested in an open-source, stable Linux OS.
- **Use Cases:** Ideal for production environments, especially where organizations previously relied on CentOS for stability and compatibility without support costs.

Pros:

- Free and community-driven, with binary compatibility to RHEL.
- Offers a predictable release cycle, matching RHEL's support timelines.
- Supported by a non-profit, with contributions from a growing community and corporate partners.

Cons:

- Lacks the extensive enterprise support model that RHEL offers, although community support is available.
- Smaller community compared to RHEL and CentOS, though it is rapidly growing.

Rocky Linux

Rocky Linux was initiated by Gregory Kurtzer, the original co-founder of CentOS, in direct response to the changes in CentOS. Rocky Linux was created with the goal of being a downstream RHEL-compatible distribution, filling the gap left by the traditional CentOS. Like AlmaLinux, Rocky Linux provides an enterprise-ready, stable, and community-supported operating system.

Key Features:

- **Binary Compatibility with RHEL:** Rocky Linux mirrors RHEL releases and aims to be 100% compatible, making it a viable replacement for CentOS users needing a stable, free alternative.

- **Community-Led Development:** The Rocky Linux project emphasizes community governance, ensuring that it remains responsive to user needs and committed to maintaining a free, reliable enterprise Linux.
- **Use Cases:** An excellent option for production servers, especially for those who previously used CentOS and need the continuity of a stable, RHEL-compatible environment.

Pros:

- Community-driven, with RHEL binary compatibility, ensuring reliability for production systems.
- Transparent, open-source development, without commercial influence.
- Closely follows RHEL release cycles for consistency and predictability.

Cons:

- No formal enterprise support, though community and third-party support options exist.
- Rocky Linux, being new, is still establishing its user and contributor base.

Feature	RHEL	CentOS Stream	AlmaLinux	Rocky Linux
Release Model	Long-term support	Rolling release	Long-term support	Long-term support
Position in RHEL Ecosystem	Downstream	Upstream (pre-RHEL)	Community-driven,	Long-term support
Community Support	Limited (commercial focus)	Community with Red Hat over-sight	Community-driven, non-profit-backed	Community-driven
Ideal Use Case	Mission-critical production	Development and testing for RHEL	Limited, via third-parties	Stable production environments
Cost	Subscription-based	Free	Free	Free

Figure 1.1: *Different Linux Distributions Environments*

Red Hat Enterprise Linux (RHEL), CentOS Stream, AlmaLinux, and Rocky Linux are all Linux distributions with distinct characteristics tailored to various use cases. RHEL is a subscription-based, downstream distribution that provides long-term support and enterprise-level services for mission-critical production environments. CentOS Stream, an upstream distribution, is used primarily for development and testing for RHEL, offering a rolling release model with community oversight by Red Hat. AlmaLinux and Rocky Linux are both free, downstream alternatives designed for stable production environments, with community-driven, non-profit-backed support. While AlmaLinux offers limited enterprise support through third parties, Rocky Linux also has third-party support but remains community-driven.

Choosing the Right Distribution

When choosing between these distributions, consider the following factors:

- **Stability Needs:** RHEL, AlmaLinux, and Rocky Linux provide stable, long-term support, suitable for production environments, while CentOS Stream is better suited for testing and development.

- **Support Requirements:** Organizations needing formal, responsive support should lean toward RHEL. In contrast, AlmaLinux and Rocky Linux provide more community-based, cost-effective options.
- **Contribution Opportunities:** CentOS Stream offers the chance for developers to influence future RHEL features, ideal for teams aligned with Red Hat's development path.

Each distribution has its niche, offering different benefits based on the organization's needs. RHEL remains the top choice for mission-critical enterprise workloads requiring official support. At the same time, Rocky Linux and AlmaLinux are becoming widely adopted replacements for CentOS in stable production environments, providing a balance between cost and compatibility. CentOS Stream, meanwhile, holds a unique place for those involved in testing and development within the Red Hat ecosystem.

Practical Example: Choosing the Right Server OS for Stability

Scenario: Web Hosting for a Business

A company providing **web hosting services** requires a **stable and secure** operating system for its servers. The priority is to ensure that websites remain **accessible, secure, and functional** without unexpected disruptions due to software updates.

For this purpose, the server OS must:

- Receive **security updates** without breaking existing configurations.
- Remain **stable** over long periods with **tested** updates.
- Maintain **full compatibility** with enterprise applications.

Two choices are **CentOS Stream** and **Rocky Linux.**

Option 1: CentOS Stream (Frequent and Unpredictable Updates)

A server is set up using **CentOS Stream**, an upstream, rolling-release version of RHEL. Since CentOS Stream receives updates **before** they are fully evaluated for enterprise stability, this introduces some risks.

- A routine system update modifies **Apache (web server) configuration files**, affecting how websites manage PHP scripts.
- The update unexpectedly causes **compatibility issues**, leading to **website outages**.
- The administrator must spend **hours troubleshooting and rolling back changes** to restore functionality.

Result: Service downtime, potential revenue loss, and additional maintenance work.

Option 2: Rocky Linux (Stable and Predictable Updates)

In another setup, **Rocky Linux** is chosen instead. As a downstream, enterprise-ready alternative, Rocky Linux ensures that all updates are **thoroughly tested** before being released.

- Security patches and software updates are applied **only after extensive validation**, preventing unexpected compatibility issues.
- The server remains **stable**, ensuring uninterrupted service for customers. System maintenance is **predictable**, reducing the risk of sudden failures.

Result: Reliable web hosting, minimal downtime, and reduced administrative overhead.

Final Decision

- For **production environments requiring stability and long-term reliability**, **Rocky Linux** is the preferred choice.

- For **testing new features before they become stable**, **CentOS Stream** may be useful, but it is not recommended for critical workloads.
- By selecting Rocky Linux, administrators ensure **consistent performance, lower risk, and fewer unexpected system failures**.

Key Differences in Development Models and Stability

Rocky Linux remains a downstream version of RHEL, following the traditional model that CentOS Linux once adhered to. It is designed to be binary-compatible with RHEL, offering users the same software environment and compatibility without the need for a commercial subscription. This makes Rocky Linux an appealing option for organizations that require RHEL-compatible systems but do not need–or cannot afford–RHEL's commercial support. Rocky Linux's alignment with RHEL's life cycle provides predictability, allowing organizations to plan long-term deployments with confidence in the stability and security updates provided by the community.

Unlike CentOS Stream, which now focuses on development and testing, Rocky Linux adheres to a more stable release model, making it suitable for production environments. By positioning itself as a downstream project, Rocky Linux applies patches and updates only after they have been incorporated and assessed within RHEL, ensuring a higher degree of stability and reducing the likelihood of unexpected issues in critical environments. This approach makes Rocky Linux an ideal choice for enterprises, educational institutions, and individual developers who rely on consistency and predictability.

Community-Driven Versus Corporate Support

Another defining aspect of Rocky Linux is its community-driven nature. The Rocky Linux project is governed by the Rocky Enterprise Software Foundation (RESF), a non-profit organization that upholds the principles of transparency, community involvement, and independence from corporate influence. The RESF's primary mission is to support the long-term development of Rocky Linux while ensuring that it remains free and open to all. This community-driven approach fosters a collaborative environment where users, developers, and contributors alike have a voice in the project's direction. In contrast, CentOS Stream, though still a community distribution, aligns closely with Red Hat's developmental goals for RHEL.

The community-driven model of Rocky Linux has drawn in a diverse group of users and contributors who value independence and collective governance. Since its launch, Rocky Linux has gained widespread adoption and established a dedicated following. This collaborative approach not only strengthens the project but also builds a rich support network, with users and contributors sharing knowledge, troubleshooting issues, and developing documentation.

The Role of Rocky Linux in the Enterprise Landscape

As a downstream RHEL-compatible distribution, Rocky Linux fills a critical gap in the enterprise Linux ecosystem, particularly for organizations that have traditionally depended on CentOS for production workloads. Rocky Linux provides a consistent platform for deploying applications and managing infrastructure across various environments, from small businesses to large-scale data centers. Its long-term support model, aligned with RHEL's support cycle, offers enterprise users a clear and reliable pathway for stable deployments, much like RHEL.

With support from a robust, global community, Rocky Linux is also positioned to grow and evolve alongside technological advancements in the Linux world, such as containerization, cloud computing, and the Internet of Things (IoT). Its compatibility with RHEL means that it can seamlessly integrate with tools and solutions that are designed for RHEL, making it a flexible and cost-effective choice for IT administrators, developers, and businesses aiming for high compatibility without the direct cost of a commercial license.

In summary, while RHEL continues as the gold standard for enterprise Linux with full commercial support, CentOS Stream has moved to a developer-focused, rolling-release model upstream of RHEL. Rocky Linux, however, continues the legacy of CentOS Linux, providing a downstream, RHEL-compatible OS that emphasizes stability, long-term support, and community involvement. For those in need of a dependable, production-grade OS without the cost of RHEL, Rocky Linux represents a powerful and sustainable option that aligns closely with RHEL's release cycle, providing a reliable platform for enterprises, developers, and educational institutions alike.

Feature	Rocky Linux	CentOS Stream	RHEL
Stability	Enterprise-grade	Development-focused	Enterprise-grade
Support	Community-driven	Red Hat backed	Red Hat official
Cost	Free	Free	Subscription-based

Figure 1.2: *Linux Distributions Comparison*

Figure 1.2 compares three popular Linux distributions–**Rocky Linux**, **CentOS Stream**, and **Red Hat Enterprise Linux (RHEL)**–across stability, support, and cost. Rocky Linux and RHEL both offer *enterprise-grade* stability suitable for production environments, while CentOS Stream focuses on development, providing earlier access to updates at the expense of long-term stability. In terms of support, Rocky Linux relies on a *community-driven* model, CentOS Stream is backed by Red Hat, and RHEL offers full official support from Red Hat. Regarding cost, both Rocky Linux and CentOS Stream are free to use, whereas RHEL requires a subscription, reflecting its bundled support and enterprise services.

Key Features and Benefits

Rocky Linux offers several key features and benefits that make it a strong contender for enterprise environments:

- **Stability and Compatibility:** Rocky Linux is designed to be 100% compatible with Red Hat Enterprise Linux (RHEL), ensuring seamless operation for users transitioning from RHEL or CentOS.

  It provides enterprise-grade stability, making it ideal for production environments that require consistent performance.

- **Long-term Support:** Rocky Linux offers long-term support, with regular updates and security patches. This ensures that organizations relying on the distribution can maintain secure and up-to-date systems over time.

  The release cycle is aligned with RHEL, ensuring predictable support and updates.

- **Community-driven Development:** The project is supported by a large and active community of developers and users. This community-driven approach fosters collaboration, ensuring the ongoing success and development of Rocky Linux.

  Contributions from the community help maintain and improve the distribution, making it a reliable and supported option for enterprises.

- **Enterprise-grade Performance:** Rocky Linux ensures reliable performance under heavy workloads, making it suitable for critical production environments.

  Its RHEL compatibility allows users to leverage RHEL-based software and tools without any compatibility issues, ensuring smooth operation across various infrastructures.

Downloading and Verifying Rocky Linux

Download Rocky Linux, visit the official website, choose the preferred architecture (x86_64 or ARM), and download the ISO file. After downloading, it is essential to verify the file using SHA256 checksums or GPG signatures to ensure its integrity before installation.

Get started with Rocky Linux; follow these steps to download and verify the ISO image:

1. Visit the official Rocky Linux website (Download - Rocky Linux). ("How to Create Bootable USB installer for Rocky Linux 9")
2. Navigate to the Downloads section and choose the appropriate ISO image for our system's architecture (for example, x86_64).
3. Download the ISO image and verify its integrity using the provided SHA256 checksum to ensure the file has not been corrupted or tampered with.

Package Management in Rocky Linux

Rocky Linux uses dnf for package management. Below is a step-by-step guide to basic package operations:

1. Check installed Rocky Linux version: **`cat /etc/os-release`**

   Expected Output:

   ```
   NAME="Rocky Linux"
   VERSION="9.2 (Blue Onyx)"
   ```
2. Install a package: **`sudo dnf install htop`**
3. Update system packages: **`sudo dnf update -y`**

Understanding SELinux and Systemctl

Security-Enhanced Linux (SELinux) enforces security policies and access controls. Many inexperienced users struggle with enforcing and troubleshooting SELinux policies.

Below is a simplified explanation:

1. Check SELinux status: **`sestatus`**
2. Temporarily disable SELinux (for testing only): **`sudo setenforce 0`**
3. Re-enable SELinux: **`sudo setenforce 1`**

System services in Rocky Linux are managed with **`systemctl`**.

Example:

- Start a service: **`sudo systemctl start nginx`**
- Enable a service on boot: **`sudo systemctl enable nginx`**

Providing step-by-step explanations of outputs enhances clarity and ensures beginners can grasp these concepts more effectively.

Migration Guide from CentOS to Rocky Linux

A structured migration guide helps organizations transition from CentOS to Rocky Linux with minimal disruption:

1. **Backup important data.**

2. **Check system compatibility:**
    - `cat /etc/centos-release`
3. Use the `migrate2rocky` script:
    - `sudo dnf install -y rocky-release`
    - `sudo /usr/bin/migrate2rocky -r`
4. Reboot and verify:
    - `cat /etc/os-release`

Introduction to Virtualization

Virtualization allows multiple operating systems to run on a single physical machine by abstracting the hardware. ("Understanding Operating System Virtualization: A Comprehensive Guide ...") It is commonly used for testing, development, and production environments. In this section, we will explore how to set up Rocky Linux in VirtualBox, on AWS EC2, and using Amazon Machine Images (AMIs).

Virtualization allows us to run multiple operating systems on a single hardware platform. ("In virtual machine managers, also known in cloud circles as ...") Rocky Linux can be easily virtualized on platforms like:

- **VirtualBox:** A free and open-source hypervisor for running Rocky Linux in virtual machines on desktop systems.
- **AWS EC2:** Rocky Linux is available as AMIs on AWS, allowing us to run instances of it in the cloud.
- **AMIs:** Pre-configured images of Rocky Linux optimized for cloud use, available for quick deployment on AWS infrastructure.

By supporting various virtualization platforms, Rocky Linux offers flexibility for both local and cloud-based server environments.

Key Concepts

Linux can be categorized based on key concepts and their specific purposes. The most fundamental topics are the following:

- **Open-source**: This principle allows anyone to access, modify, and distribute the source code. This collaborative approach has led to rapid innovation and diverse solutions in the Linux ecosystem.
- **Kernel**: The kernel is the core component of an OS that manages system resources and communication between hardware and software. In Linux, the kernel oversees everything from process management to device drivers, ensuring efficient operation.
- **Distributions**: Linux distributions are packaged collections of software that include the Linux kernel, system libraries, and applications. Each distribution may have unique features, package managers, and user interfaces, catering to specific use cases and user preferences.
- **Rocky Linux:** Rocky Linux is a community-driven, enterprise-grade Linux distribution developed as a replacement for CentOS. It aims to provide stability and long-term support by being fully compatible with Red Hat Enterprise Linux (RHEL), making it suitable for production environments.

- **Package Manager:** A package manager, such as dnf in Rocky Linux, is a tool used to install, update, and manage software packages on the system. It simplifies the process of managing software dependencies and maintaining up-to-date systems.
- **Security-Enhanced Linux (SELinux):** SELinux is a security feature in Rocky Linux that enforces access control policies to protect the system from unauthorized access. It ensures that processes and users have the minimum permissions necessary, enhancing overall system security.
- **Repositories (Repos):** Repositories are storage locations for software packages and updates. In Rocky Linux, additional repositories can be configured to expand the available software, making it easier to install applications and receive security patches.
- **Systemctl:** Systemctl is a command-line tool used to manage system services in Rocky Linux. With it, we can start, stop, enable, or disable services, ensuring that critical processes are managed correctly on the system.
- **FirewallD:** FirewallD is the firewall management tool included in Rocky Linux, used to manage network traffic and security rules. It allows administrators to define rules for incoming and outgoing traffic, ensuring the system is protected from unauthorized network access.
- **Kernel:** The kernel is the core component of the Rocky Linux operating system. It manages hardware resources, processes, and communication between software and hardware, ensuring the efficient operation of the system.
- **LVM (Logical Volume Manager):** LVM in Rocky Linux is used to manage disk storage more flexibly. It allows the creation of logical partitions that can be resized or moved without interrupting the system, making it ideal for dynamic storage needs.
- **Virtualization:** Virtualization is the process of running multiple virtual operating systems on a single physical machine. ("How to Run Multiple Virtual Machines Windows and Linux Inside ...") Rocky Linux supports various virtualization platforms such as VirtualBox, KVM, and AWS EC2, enabling easy testing, development, and deployment in virtual environments.
- **Amazon Machine Images (AMIs):** AMIs are pre-configured templates of Rocky Linux that can be deployed on AWS infrastructure. These images are optimized for cloud use, enabling fast and easy deployment of Rocky Linux in cloud environments.

Types of Linux Distributions

Linux distributions come in various flavors, each optimized for different tasks and user experiences. Here are a few notable ones:

- **Ubuntu**: A user-friendly distribution known for its ease of installation and extensive community support. It is widely used for desktops and servers, making it a popular choice for beginners and developers alike.
- **Fedora:** is known for its cutting-edge features and technologies. It serves as a testing ground for innovations that may eventually be integrated into Red Hat Enterprise Linux (RHEL) and is favored by users who want to experiment with the latest developments in the Linux ecosystem.
- **Arch Linux**: A minimalist distribution that allows users to build their systems from the ground up. Arch is highly customizable and appeals to advanced users who prefer to tailor their OS to their specific needs.
- **Use Cases**: The choice of distribution often depends on the user's requirements. For instance, Ubuntu is frequently used in educational settings due to its user-friendly interface, while Fedora attracts developers looking to leverage the latest software.

Figure 1.3: *Linux Distributions*

Figure 1.3 provides a visual representation of the Linux distribution model, illustrating the relationships between various distributions. It highlights how operating systems such as RHEL, CentOS Stream, AlmaLinux, and Rocky Linux fit into the broader Linux ecosystem. This diagram clarifies their differences in release models, community support, and intended use cases, offering a comprehensive overview of their roles and interconnections within the Linux landscape.

Linux in the Server Ecosystem

Linux has become the backbone of the server market, powering a significant majority of web servers, data centers, cloud platforms, and enterprise infrastructures worldwide. Its reliability, flexibility, and strong security model make it a preferred choice for both small and large-scale deployments. Here is an in-depth look at the factors that make Linux a dominant choice in the server ecosystem, followed by a comprehensive hands-on guide to system interactions.

Key Factors for Linux's Dominance in the Server Market

Security: Linux is renowned for its robust security features, which include:

- **User Permissions:** Each file and directory on a Linux system has associated user and group permissions, which determine who can read, write, or execute it. This fine-grained control restricts access to critical system components and minimizes unauthorized actions.
- **System Isolation:** Linux uses various isolation techniques, such as namespaces and cgroups, to ensure processes and users operate independently within a shared environment. Isolation is crucial for multi-tenant systems, where multiple applications or services run on a single server.
- **Active Security Community:** The Linux community plays a proactive role in identifying and patching vulnerabilities. Linux distributions frequently release updates that enhance security and address emerging threats, making Linux a trustworthy OS for sensitive applications.

Flexibility: Linux's open-source nature means it can be customized to meet the unique needs of any server deployment:

- **Modular Design:** Users can install only the necessary components for their server, reducing bloat and optimizing performance. For instance, lightweight Linux distributions such as Alpine Linux are popular in containerized environments where a minimal footprint is essential.
- **Choice of Distributions:** With hundreds of Linux distributions (distros) available, administrators can choose one that best suits their server environment. For enterprise environments, Rocky Linux, RHEL, and Ubuntu Server provide stable and supportable options, while lightweight options such as Debian or Alpine are ideal for streamlined setups.
- **Broad Application Compatibility:** Linux supports a vast array of software packages and tools, enabling custom configurations for different server roles, from web hosting to database management.

Scalability: Linux's scalability allows organizations to expand infrastructure seamlessly:

- **Adaptable to Workloads:** From small business web applications to high-performance computing, Linux can efficiently manage a range of workloads. This adaptability means businesses can start with minimal resources and scale up as needed.
- **Efficient Resource Management:** Tools such as load balancers, clustering software, and virtualization enhance Linux's scalability, enabling it to support more extensive and more complex systems without compromising performance.
- **Seamless Integration with Cloud Platforms:** Major cloud providers (AWS, Google Cloud, Microsoft Azure) offer extensive support for Linux-based virtual machines and containers, making it easy for organizations to transition to cloud-native solutions as they grow.

Practical Hands-On Examples: Build familiarity with Linux commands. Here is a hands-on guide for interacting with the Linux kernel and retrieving essential system information.

Checking the Linux Kernel Version

The Linux kernel version reveals critical information about the system's capabilities and compatibility with certain software. Let us follow the next steps:

1. **Open the Terminal** and enter the command:

   Checking the Linux Kernel Version

   Open the terminal and enter the following command: `uname -r`.

   Explanation: The `uname` command is used to display system information. The `-r` option specifically instructs `uname` to print the kernel release version, which indicates the version of the Linux kernel currently running on the system. This is useful for troubleshooting, verifying compatibility, or checking if the system needs an update.

2. **Expected Output:**

   Running `uname -r` returns the version of the Linux kernel currently running. An example output might look like this:

   ```
   [cesarmserver@RockyLinux ~]$ uname -r 5.14.0-427.37.1.el9  4.x86  64
   ```

   This indicates that the system is running kernel version 5.14.0, which is important for knowing what features and updates are available on the system.

   - `uname`: This command is used to display system information.
   - `-r`: This option prints all the system´s information.

Additional System Information with `uname -a`

The **`uname -a`** command displays comprehensive information about our system, including kernel version, machine hardware, and operating system:

Open the terminal and enter the following command: **`uname -a`.**

Explanation: This command reveals more than just the kernel version; it shows full system information, which is useful for quickly identifying system architecture, hostname, and kernel details.

Example output:

```
[cesarmserver@RockyLinux ~]$ uname -a
Linux RockyLinux 5.14.0-427.37.1.el9  4.x86  64 #1 SMP PREEMPT_DYNAMIC Wed Sep 25
UTC 2024 x86 64 x86 64 x86 64 GNU/Linux
```

System's details information:

- **Linux:** OS name
- **hostname:** Hostname of the system
- **5.15.0-72-generic:** Kernel version
- **#78-Ubuntu SMP:** Kernel build details and system type (SMP denotes Symmetric Multiprocessing)
- **x86_64:** System architecture
- **GNU/Linux:** General OS identifier

This output displays the currently running Linux kernel version, which is crucial for ensuring software compatibility and understanding the system's available features. Keeping track of the kernel version helps in troubleshooting, applying updates, and verifying hardware support. Lastly, the following command provides access to the manual pages for most Linux commands, offering detailed usage information and options.

```
man uname
```

Explanation:

- **`man`:** This prints a manual with useful tips to apply the command.
- **`name`:** This command helps us display the system's information.
- **`letter q`:** we use this command to return to the shell interface.

Using the `man` Command to Access Command Documentation

The man (manual) command provides detailed documentation on Linux commands, including usage options and examples:

1. View the manual page for the **`uname`** command, type: **`man name`**.

   Example output:

```
UNAME(1)                        User Commands                        UNAME(1)

NAME
       uname - print system information

SYNOPSIS
       uname [OPTION]...

DESCRIPTION
       Print certain system information.  With no OPTION, same as -s.

       -a, --all
              print  all  information,  in the following order, except omit -p
              and -i if unknown:

       -s, --kernel-name
              print the kernel name

       -n, --nodename
              print the network node hostname

       -r, --kernel-release
              print the kernel release
 Manual page uname(1) line 1 (press h for help or q to quit)
```

Figure 1.4: *Output Manual of Uname*

Figure 1.4 shows the output of the **uname** command, which is commonly used to display system information in Linux. The **uname** command provides details about the operating system, kernel version, and system architecture. When executed without any options, it typically displays the kernel name. By adding various options, such as **-a**, the user can obtain more detailed information, including the kernel version, machine hardware name, processor type, and system's network node hostname. This command is essential for administrators and users who need to gather system-related information for troubleshooting, configuration, or general knowledge about their environment.

2. Explanation of **man** output:
   - **man uname:** Opens the manual entry for the **uname** command, listing options and usage notes. This is useful for exploring the command's full range of features.
   - **Exit:** Press the letter q on the keyboard to close the manual page and return to the shell interface.

Practical Exercise: Gathering System Information

Following along, there is a small exercise to gather detailed system information using the above commands:

1. **Objective:** Determine the kernel version, system architecture, and system uptime.
2. **Steps:**
   a. Run **name -r** to check the kernel version.
   b. Use **name -m** to determine the system architecture **(for example, x86_64 for 64-bit systems).**
   c. Run uptime to view how long the system has been running, along with the current load average.
3. **Output Analysis:** For each command, note down the output and verify if it matches expectations based on the system's configuration. For example, uptime information can reveal whether the system is frequently rebooted or remains stable over long periods, which is vital in production environments.

Example Outputs:

- **Kernel Version (`name -r`): 5.14.0-427.37.1el9**
- **System Architecture (`name -m`): *x86_64***

Executing the uptime command: Once we execute the command *uptime*, we will be able to see the following data or a similar scenario:

- **System Uptime (uptime): 12:10:42 *up* 5 *days*, 3:45, 3 *users*, *load average*: 0.02, 0.03, 0.00**

Importance of Kernel and system information

Understanding the kernel version, system architecture, and uptime is essential for:

- **Software Compatibility:** Certain applications may require a specific kernel version or architecture, especially in production servers where stability is critical.
- **Performance Optimization:** System uptime and load averages indicate how the system performs over time. Analyzing these metrics can help administrators plan maintenance windows and identify potential bottlenecks.

Real-World Applications in Server Administration

- **Security Audits:** Knowing the kernel version is crucial when assessing vulnerabilities and patching systems.
- **System Updates:** Server environments often run kernel updates to improve security and performance. Understanding the current kernel version helps decide on necessary updates.
- **Infrastructure Planning:** Knowing the system's architecture and performance history allows for better capacity planning and resource allocation.

While this chapter is based on Rocky Linux 9, it is important to note that Rocky Linux maintains a high degree of compatibility with earlier versions such as Rocky Linux 8. This backward compatibility ensures that most system commands, package management operations, and deployment scripts described here will work reliably across both versions. Key tools such as ***dnf, systemctl, and* AWS CLI** remain consistent, though some minor syntax or dependency differences may arise—particularly in more recent package versions or cloud integrations.

For system administrators working in environments that still rely on Rocky Linux 8, adapting the deployment steps from this guide should be straightforward. Users are encouraged to verify version-specific details such as AMI availability on AWS, the presence of specific software packages, and any deprecations in configuration files. By taking these into account, teams can confidently implement cloud deployments without requiring a full OS upgrade.

Conclusion

Rocky Linux has rapidly emerged as a robust, community-driven alternative to CentOS, offering full compatibility with Red Hat Enterprise Linux (RHEL). Its development ensures that enterprises, developers, and system administrators have access to a stable, open-source platform with long-term support. With its familiar environment and enterprise-grade reliability, Rocky Linux is an ideal choice for those transitioning from CentOS or seeking a dependable Linux distribution for production environments.

In this chapter, we explored the core features of Rocky Linux, its role within the Linux ecosystem, and its seamless integration with RHEL. As we move forward, *Chapter 2* will focus on mastering the essential command-line skills, covering file management, directory navigation, and permission handling—key competencies for efficient system administration in Rocky Linux.

Summary and Final Thoughts: This chapter provided a detailed introduction to Rocky Linux, its role as a CentOS replacement, and its key benefits for enterprise environments.

Key takeaways:

- ***Rocky Linux*** is a downstream RHEL alternative, ensuring stability.
- ***CentOS Stream*** is a rolling-release model, suited for testing but not production.
- ***Package management*** **`dnf`**, **`systemctl`**, and **`SELinux`** are crucial components.
- Migration from CentOS is straightforward using automated tools.

Further chapters will explore installation, system configuration, and advanced administration techniques.

Points to Remember

- **Overview of Linux Operating Systems**
    - **Linux Distributions**: Linux distributions are variations of the Linux kernel bundled with software to create an operating system tailored for specific needs (for example, Ubuntu, CentOS, RHEL, and Rocky Linux).
    - **Community and Enterprise Focus**: Linux operating systems such as Rocky Linux and RHEL are used in enterprise environments for their stability, security, and long-term support.
- **The History and Development of Rocky Linux**
    - **Origin**: Rocky Linux was created by Gregory Kurtzer in response to the changes in CentOS's lifecycle, offering a stable, community-driven alternative to CentOS.
    - **CentOS to Rocky Linux**: Rocky Linux inherits its name from the late CentOS Linux, with an emphasis on maintaining compatibility with RHEL.
- **Comparison with CentOS and RHEL**
    - **CentOS versus Rocky Linux**: Created to offer a stable, RHEL-compatible distribution after CentOS transitioned to a rolling-release model with CentOS Stream.
    - **RHEL versus Rocky Linux**: Rocky Linux is free and open-source, while RHEL requires a subscription for support and services, though both share the same upstream source.
- **Key Features and Benefits**
    - **Compatibility with RHEL**: Rocky Linux is designed to be binary-compatible with RHEL, ensuring compatibility for applications, configurations, and services.
    - **Community-Driven Development**: As a community project, Rocky Linux benefits from contributions and support from individuals, businesses, and organizations invested in its success.
- **Downloading and Verifying Rocky Linux**
    - **Official Sources**: Rocky Linux can be downloaded from the official website, ensuring authenticity and security.
    - **Checksum Verification**: It is important to verify the integrity of downloaded installation images using checksums to avoid using corrupted or tampered files.
- **Introduction to Virtualization**
    - **Virtualization Support**: Rocky Linux supports various virtualization technologies, including Kernel-based Virtual Machine (KVM) and Xen, allowing for efficient management of virtual machines in both on-premises and cloud environments.

- **Cloud Integration**: It is optimized for deployment in cloud environments such as AWS, Azure, and Google Cloud, facilitating virtualization and containerization within enterprise infrastructures.

Multiple Choice Questions

1. Which Linux distribution did Rocky Linux emerge to replace after its shift in direction?
   a. Fedora
   b. Ubuntu
   c. CentOS
   d. Debian
2. What is one of the primary goals of Rocky Linux?
   a. Offer a paid enterprise-only solution
   b. Provide a rolling release distribution
   c. Offer a community-driven, stable release such as RHEL
   d. Replace Fedora as the default desktop OS
3. Which of the following is a key feature of Rocky Linux?
   a. Continuous updates with bleeding-edge software
   b. Strictly limited to cloud environments
   c. Binary compatibility with Red Hat Enterprise Linux (RHEL)
   d. Minimal command-line interface (CLI) support
4. What type of virtualization environment is Rocky Linux commonly used in?
   a. Windows Hyper-V only
   b. VirtualBox, AWS EC2, and VMware
   c. Android emulation
   d. Cloud-only environments
5. What is thc command to verify the integrity of the downloaded Rocky Linux ISO using checksums?
   a. cat
   b. ping
   c. sha256sum
   d. grep
6. What benefit does Rocky Linux offer to server administrators?
   a. A paid subscription-based service
   b. Minimal software support
   c. A free, stable, community-supported distribution
   d. High customization for desktop use

7. What type of development model does Rocky Linux follow?
   a. Closed development controlled by a company
   b. Open and collaborative community development
   c. Rolling release model
   d. Fixed annual release model
8. What does it mean for Rocky Linux to have binary compatibility with RHEL?
   a. It runs only on proprietary hardware.
   b. It offers the same performance and functionality as RHEL without needing to pay.
   c. It is cloud-only.
   d. It uses proprietary software.
9. Which virtualization tool is commonly used to locally evaluate Rocky Linux?
   a. Hyper-V
   b. VirtualBox
   c. Docker
   d. LXC
10. What was a key reason for creating Rocky Linux?
    a. Offer a new desktop option for advanced users
    b. Compete directly with Fedora
    c. Provide an alternative to CentOS after its shift to CentOS Stream
    d. Improve compatibility with mobile devices

Answers

1. c
2. c
3. c
4. b
5. c
6. c
7. b
8. b
9. b
10. c

Questions

1. What is Rocky Linux?
2. Why was Rocky Linux created?
3. What operating system is Rocky Linux compatible with?
4. Who founded Rocky Linux?
5. Is Rocky Linux free to use?
6. What is the primary focus of Rocky Linux?
7. Which is the correct process to download Rocky Linux effectively?
8. Which virtualization platforms support Rocky Linux?
9. How does Rocky Linux differ from CentOS Stream?
10. What is the file system used by default in Rocky Linux?

Key Terms

- **Rocky Linux**: A community-driven, enterprise-grade Linux distribution developed as a CentOS replacement, offering stability and compatibility with RHEL.
- **Package Manager**: A tool, such as dnf in Rocky Linux, used to install, update, and manage software packages on the system.
- **Security-Enhanced Linux (SELinux)**: A security feature in Rocky Linux that enforces access control policies to secure the system from unauthorized access.
- **Repositories (Repos)**: Storage locations containing software packages and updates, which can be configured in Rocky Linux to expand available software.
- **Systemctl**: A command-line tool used in Rocky Linux to manage system services, such as starting, stopping, enabling, or disabling them.
- **FirewallD**: The firewall management tool included in Rocky Linux for managing network traffic and security rules.
- **Kernel**: The core of the Rocky Linux operating system, which manages hardware, resources, and system processes.
- **Logical Volume Manager (LVM)**: A system in Rocky Linux used to manage disk storage flexibly by creating logical partitions.
- **Virtualization**: Running multiple virtual operating systems on a host, with Rocky Linux supporting platforms such as VirtualBox, KVM, and AWS EC2.
- **Amazon Machine Images (AMIs)**: Pre-configured templates of Rocky Linux that can be deployed on AWS cloud infrastructure.

CHAPTER 2

Command Line Fundamentals

Introduction

Welcome to the powerful world of the Linux command line – where every keystroke unlocks unmatched control and precision. In this chapter, we dive into the essential command-line tools and techniques that form the backbone of effective system administration in Rocky Linux 9. Far from being just a utility, the command line is a gateway to efficiency, automation, and mastery – empowering both inexperienced users and seasoned professionals to interact with the system at lightning speed and with surgical accuracy.

Through a rich blend of practical examples, real-world use cases, and clear explanations, we will learn how to confidently navigate the terminal, manipulate files and directories, set permissions, and execute administrative tasks with finesse. But the journey does not stop at the local machine – we will also explore cloud-based CLI workflows, enabling us to manage scalable infrastructures using services such as Amazon Web Services (AWS).

Whether we are just beginning our Linux journey or sharpening our DevOps skills, this chapter provides a hands-on, foundational toolkit for working effectively with both on-premises servers and cloud environments.

Structure

In this chapter, we will discuss the following topics:

- Basic Terminal Commands
- Managing Directories and Files
- Output Commands
- File Permissions and Ownership
- The `sudo` Command
- System Shutdown and Reboot
- Introduction to Cloud-Based CLI Workflows with AWS

Basic Terminal Commands

The terminal, also known as the command-line interface (CLI), is more than just a tool – it is the beating heart of system administration in Rocky Linux 9. Unlike graphical user interfaces, the terminal provides direct, low-level access to the system, enabling rapid configuration, automation, and remote management with unmatched efficiency.

Mastering basic terminal commands is one of the most valuable skills for any Linux user, especially system administrators and developers. These foundational commands empower us to navigate the file system, manage resources, and perform critical tasks with precision.

In this section, we will explore a set of core CLI commands every administrator should know – presented with clear explanations and real-world examples. Whether we are listing directories, moving between folders, or scripting repeatable tasks, these commands form the backbone of our interaction with the Rocky Linux 9 environment.

Understanding the Terminal Environment

The terminal in Rocky Linux 9 is a text-based interface that allows users to interact directly with the operating system. It offers precise control over system processes, and is essential for tasks such as system configuration, troubleshooting, scripting, and remote administration.

Key Components of the Terminal

- **Prompt:** This is where we type our commands. It typically appears in the format: **`user@hostname:~$`**
- **Shell:** A command interpreter (such as Bash) that executes the instructions entered. The shell processes our input and manages the output, errors, and environment.

To open the terminal in Rocky Linux 9: Press *Ctrl* + *Alt* + T, or access it through the application menu.

Essential Terminal Commands: These foundational commands are critical for navigating and managing the Rocky Linux 9 system.

- **pwd - Print Working Directory:** Displays the full path of the current directory that the users or administrator are working on.
  ```
  pwd
  ```

Example Output: `/home/username`

Use this to confirm our current location in complex directory trees.

- **ls - List Directory Contents:** Lists files and folders in the current (or specified) directory.
  ```
  ls -l
  ```

Useful Flags:

  - **-l:** Long listing format (shows permissions, owner, size, and date)
  - **-a:** Shows hidden files (those beginning with a '.')
- **cd - Change Directory:** Navigates to a different directory in the file system.
  - **`cd /etc`** **# Goes to the /etc directory**
  - **`cd ~`** **# Returns to the home's directory**
  - `cd ..` # Moves up one directory level
- **clear - Clear the Terminal Screen:** Removes all previous text from the terminal display.
  ```
  clear
  ```
- **echo - Display a Message or Variable:** Prints a string to the terminal. Commonly used in scripts for messages or debugging.
  ```
  echo "Hello, Rocky Linux 9!"
  ```
- **man - Manual Pages:** Displays the help documentation for Linux commands.
  ```
  man ls
  ```

- Press **q** to quit the manual page.

  Use man to learn new commands or explore additional options for ones the administrator already knows.

  These fundamental commands form the initial toolkit for navigating and managing a Linux environment. Gaining proficiency with them establishes the essential groundwork for all subsequent tasks performed from the terminal, including file management, scripting, and automation.

ls - Listing Directory Contents

The ls command helps us to display the contents of a directory.

```
[cesarmserver@RockyLinux ~]$ ls
Desktop  Documents  Downloads  Music  Pictures  Public  Templates  Videos
[cesarmserver@RockyLinux ~]$
```

Figure 2.1: *ls Output*

The **ls** command is one of the most used commands in Linux for listing the contents of a directory. In *Figure* 2.1, we can see the output generated when the **ls** command is executed in a specific directory. This output provides an overview of the files and subdirectories contained within that directory. By default, **ls** lists the file names in columns, but various options (such as **ls -l** for detailed information or **ls -a** to show hidden files) can modify the display. Understanding the **ls** command and its options is fundamental for file navigation and management in Linux systems.

Lists files and directories in the current location.

Options:

- **ls -a**: Includes hidden files (those starting with a).
- **ls -l**: Provides detailed information, including permissions, ownership, and size.
- **ls -h**: Displays file sizes in a human-readable format.

```
[cesarmserver@RockyLinux ~]$ ls -lah /etc
total 1.5M
drwxr-xr-x. 156 root root    8.0K Nov 18 14:55 .
dr-xr-xr-x.  18 root root     235 May 16  2024 ..
drwxr-xr-x.   3 root root      28 May 12  2024 accountsservice
-rw-r--r--.   1 root root      16 May 12  2024 adjtime
-rw-r--r--.   1 root root    1.5K Jun 23  2020 aliases
drwxr-xr-x.   3 root root      65 May 12  2024 alsa
drwxr-xr-x.   2 root root    4.0K Oct  8 11:34 alternatives
-rw-r--r--.   1 root root     541 Apr 15  2024 anacrontab
```

Figure 2.2: *Human-readable Format*

Displays all files in the **/etc directory** with detailed and human-readable output.

This figure shows the output of a command that lists all files in the **/etc** directory using a detailed and human-readable format. In this context, "human-readable" means the file sizes are displayed in units like kilobytes (K), megabytes (M), or gigabytes (G), making it easier for users to interpret the data at a glance.

The output includes key details such as file permissions, ownership, modification dates, and sizes—presented in a way that's more intuitive than raw byte counts. Understanding how to use options like

-lh with the **ls** command is essential for effective file management and system navigation in Linux environments.

d - Change Directory

The **cd** command allows navigation through the directory structure. It is an extremely useful command when changing from one location to a specific destination.

Basic Usage: `cd downloads`

With this command, the **downloads** directory should be accessed effectively.

ls it is good practice to use this command to be aware of all files and directories currently available and the packages that have been downloaded on this operating system.

Common Scenarios:

- **cd ..** : Moves up one directory level.
- **cd ~ or cd:** Returns to the home directory.

Therefore, adding to practice, time, and patience, these are the essential keys to mastering the core Rocky Linux 9 commands.

Managing Directories and Files

Managing files and directories is one of the most fundamental tasks for any Linux user or administrator. In Rocky Linux 9, there is a robust set of terminal commands that allow us to create, move, copy, rename, and delete files and directories efficiently. These commands help streamline daily tasks and ensure proper organization of the file system.

This section outlines essential file management commands, including practical examples and useful options (flags), to help us become proficient in managing the system's files and directories.

Creating Files

- **touch:** Create a New File or Update Timestamp

Creates an empty file or updates the modification timestamp of an existing one.

```
touch newfile.txt
```

Create multiple files at once: `touch file1.txt file2.txt file3.txt`

Creating Directories

- **mkdir**: Make New Directories

Creates one or more new folders.

```
mkdir myfolder
```

Create nested directories: `mkdir -p /home/user/folder1/folder2.`

- **-p:** Ensures parent directories are created if they do not exist.

Copying Files and Directories

- **cp:** Copy Files or Directories

Copy a single file: `cp source.txt backup.txt`

Example Directory Structure:

`sudo dnf install tree` (installing an important package)

`sudo mkdir dir1` (creating a directory)

`cd dir1` (creating a directory)

`cd..` (returning to the previous directory)

`touch file1 file2` (creating new files)

`tree dir1`

```
[cmorera@localhost ~]$ tree dir1
dir1
├── file1
└── file2

0 directories, 2 files
```

Figure 2.3: *Directory Structure with the Command Tree*

Figure 2.3 presents a simple directory layout generated using the tree command, which provides a hierarchical view of files and subdirectories within a specified path. In this example, the root directory **`dir1/`** contains two text files–**`file1.txt`** and **`file2.txt`**–as well as a nested subdirectory named **`subdir/`**, which itself contains file3.txt.

The `tree` command is especially useful for visualizing nested structures, making it easier to understand how files are organized. It's a handy tool for documentation, scripting, and project management, helping users verify directory contents and maintain clarity during development or deployment.

Copy a directory and its contents recursively:

`cp -r dir1/ dir2/`

Useful Flags:

- **`-r`:** Recursive, copies all subdirectories and contents.
- **`-v`:** Verbose, shows what is being copied.

After Running: `cp -rv dir1/ dir2/`

In the **`cli`** interface, something like the following will be shown:

- file1.txt -> dir2/dir1/file1.txt
- file2.txt -> dir2/dir1/file2.txt
- dir1/subdir -> dir2/dir1/subdir
- dir1/subdir/file3.txt -> dir2/dir1/subdir/file3.txt

Moving or Renaming Files

- **`mv`:** Move or Rename Files and Directories

Rename a file: `mv oldname.txt newname.txt`

Move a file to another directory: `mv file.txt /home/user/Documents/`

Deleting Files and Directories

- **`rm`:** Remove Files or Directories

Delete a file: `rm unwanted.txt`

Delete a directory and its contents: `rm -r old_folder/`

Useful Flags:

- **-r:** Recursive, removes directories and their contents.
- **-f:** Force, skips confirmation prompts.

Be careful with this command: `rm -rf /`

This command will **delete everything** on the system and should *never* be run.

Inspecting Files and Metadata

- **Stat:** View File Information

Displays metadata such as file size, access and modification times, and permissions.

```
stat example.txt
```

Identifying File Types

- **file:** Determine File Type

Useful for confirming whether a file is a script, text file, binary, image, and so on.

```
file script.sh
```

With these tools, administrators are now equipped to handle file and directory management efficiently in any Rocky Linux 9 environment. Up next, we will explore file permissions and ownership – the keys to securing the system.

With the following command, we will validate in which location the administrator or users are currently working.

Pwd - Print Working Directory

The **pwd** command shows the full path of the current directory.

Basic Usage: `pwd`

In this step, we will execute a command to create our first directory. This will demonstrate how to use the Linux command line to organize files and directories efficiently. Proper organization of directories is vital for maintaining a clean and manageable file system in any Linux environment.

Mkdir - Create New Directories

The **mkdir** command is used to create one or more directories.

Basic Usage:

- `mkdir new_directory`
- `ls`

Options:

- **mkdir -p:** Creates parent directories if they do not exist.
    a. **Installing the tree package**: `sudo dnf install tree`
    i. This command attempts to install the tree package using the **dnf** package manager.
    ii. The output indicates that the package `tree-1.8.0-10.el9.x86_64` is already installed, so no further action is required.

b. **Creating directories**: `sudo mkdir -p /projects/python/dir1/dir2/dir3`

   This command creates a nested directory structure under **/projects/python/**. The **-p** flag ensures that all parent directories are created as needed.

c. **Displaying the directory structure**: `tree /projects`

   1. This command uses the tree utility to display the directory structure of **/projects** in a tree-like format.

   2. The output of the tree command would show the hierarchy of directories under **/projects**, including the newly created **dir1**, **dir2**, and **dir3** directories.

```
[cesarmserver@RockyLinux ~]$ sudo dnf install tree
Last metadata expiration check: 0:04:16 ago on Mon 18 Nov 2024 03:37:15 PM CST.
Package tree-1.8.0-10.el9.x86_64 is already installed.
Dependencies resolved.
Nothing to do.
Complete!
[cesarmserver@RockyLinux ~]$ sudo mkdir -p /projects/python/dir1/dir2/dir3
[cesarmserver@RockyLinux ~]$ tree /projects
/projects
└── python
    └── dir1
        └── dir2
            └── dir3

4 directories, 0 files
```

Figure 2.4: *Creating Directories and Installing Packages*

This figure demonstrates two essential tasks in system administration: creating directories and installing packages. The first part of the figure shows the use of the **mkdir** command to create a new directory–an important operation for organizing files and structuring the filesystem.

The second part highlights package installation using tools like **dnf** (commonly used in Rocky Linux 9) or **apt** (standard in Debian-based systems). These package managers allow administrators to add software and utilities to the system, enhancing its capabilities and supporting various operational needs.

Together, these tasks form the backbone of a well-maintained Linux environment, enabling administrators to manage resources efficiently and ensure the system is equipped with the necessary tools.

Nano - Editing Text Files: As we continue diving into the Rocky Linux 9 OS, we are going to learn about text editors and their fundamentals.

The nano editor is a user-friendly tool for modifying text files directly in the terminal.

Basic Usage:

```
nano newfile1
cat newfile1
```

Inside the current file, we have added the following message: **This is a new file created.**

```
[cesarmserver@RockyLinux Documents]$ nano newfile1
[cesarmserver@RockyLinux Documents]$ cat newfile1
This is a new file created
[cesarmserver@RockyLinux Documents]$ ls
new_directory  newfile1
```

Figure 2.5: *Creation of a New File*

In system administration, **touch** proves especially useful for generating placeholder files, logs, or configuration files that will later be populated with necessary data. When combined with directory creation and package installation commands, touch supports the foundational setup of a well-organized Linux environment.

After editing a file, changes can be saved by pressing *Ctrl* + O and exiting with *Ctrl* + X. To verify the content of the newly created file, the cat command can be used to display its contents in the terminal.

As part of file management practices, it is also essential to understand how to remove files and directories when no longer needed. Commands such as rm for files and **rmdir** or **rm -r** for directories enable efficient system maintenance and cleanup.

RM - Remove Files or Directories: The rm command is used to delete files or directories. Use with caution, as this action is irreversible.

Basic Usage: `rm newfile1`

```
ls new_directory
```

Options:

- **rm -r**: Removes directories and their contents recursively.
- **rm -i**: Prompts for confirmation before deletion.

Example:

- `ls`
- `sudo rm -r new_directory/`
- `ls`

The **ls** command is used again to verify that the directory has been successfully removed.

Main Tips for Terminal Efficiency

Practical Tips for Terminal Efficiency:

- **Tab Completion:** Press Tab to autocomplete file or directory names.
- **Command History:** Use the Up and Down arrows to cycle through previous commands.
- **Combining Commands:** Use semicolons (;) to execute multiple commands in sequence.

  cd /var/log; ls -l;pwd this will execute several commands in a sequenced manner.

```
[cesarmserver@RockyLinux Documents]$ cd /var/log; ls -l ;pwd
total 3912
drwxr-xr-x. 2 root   root          4096 May 12  2024 anaconda
drwx------. 2 root   root            23 May 12  2024 audit
-rw-------. 1 root   root          3588 Nov 18 14:55 boot.log
-rw-------. 1 root   root         22135 Oct  6 15:30 boot.log-20241006
-rw-------. 1 root   root         34545 Oct  7 14:07 boot.log-20241007
-rw-------. 1 root   root         22781 Oct  8 00:07 boot.log-20241008
-rw-------. 1 root   root         43871 Oct  9 13:11 boot.log-20241009
-rw-------. 1 root   root         22248 Oct 16 21:40 boot.log-20241016
-rw-------. 1 root   root         22139 Oct 20 18:03 boot.log-20241020
-rw-------. 1 root   root         22357 Nov 18 14:55 boot.log-20241118
```

***Figure 2.6:** Running Several Commands in a Sequence*

This figure illustrates the execution of multiple commands in sequence—an efficient and widely used practice in Linux system administration. In the example, several commands are run consecutively on a single line, separated by **semicolons (;)**. This method enables administrators to conduct multiple tasks in a streamlined manner, eliminating the need to enter each command individually. A typical sequence might include operations such as creating directories, generating files using the **touch** command, and installing packages. Mastering command chaining not only improves workflow efficiency but also contributes to faster execution and automation of related tasks.

Creating our First Directory

To reinforce the concepts covered in this chapter, it is necessary to engage in hands-on practice through lab exercises. The following activity demonstrates basic navigation, directory listing, and directory creation in a Linux environment.

In this example, the process includes navigating to the **`/etc`** directory, listing its contents, creating a new directory in the user's home directory, and verifying the current working directory.

Steps:

- `cd /etc`
- `ls -l`
- `sudo mkdir ~/new_folder`
- `ls -l ~/`

Note: In this example, *Ctrl* + C was used to intentionally interrupt a command. When executed again without interruption, the command should complete successfully.

By following these steps, a new directory is created within the home directory of the current user. This simple exercise lays the groundwork for more advanced file system operations and administrative tasks.

Output Commands

Output commands are essential in Linux for managing and processing text files. They enable users to display file contents, search for specific patterns, and navigate large files efficiently. These commands are frequently used in scripting, troubleshooting, and log analysis. Mastering them enhances productivity and streamlines daily system administration tasks.

The key output commands discussed in this section include:

- **`cat`**: Concatenates and displays file contents.
- **`grep`**: Searches for patterns within text files.
- **`less`**: Allows scrolling through file contents one screen at a time.

Using the cat Command

The **`cat`** command is commonly used to display the contents of files, create new files, and concatenate multiple files into one. It is a versatile tool for text manipulation and file management.

- **Display File Contents**

  We can use cat to instantly view the contents of a file. For example:

  - **`echo "Hello World!" > example.txt`**
  - **`cat example.txt`**

Output:

```
Hello World!
```

- **Create a New File and Display Contents**

  Although **`cat`** can be used to create files, tools such as nano are often more user-friendly for editing. Here is how to create a file with nano and display its contents using **`cat`**:

  ```
  nano notes.txt
  ```

Inside the editor, add:

```
milk
bread
eggs
```

Then:

- Press *Ctrl* + O to save
- Press *Ctrl* + X to exit

Now display the contents:

```
cat notes.txt
```

Output:

```
milk
bread
eggs
```

- **Copy and Concatenate Files**

  a. Copy Files Using `cp`

  ```
  cp notes.txt intro.txt
  cp notes.txt chapter1.txt
  ```

  b. **View the Copied File**

  ```
  cat intro.txt
  ```

  c. **Concatenate Multiple Files into One**

  ```
  cat notes.txt chapter1.txt > book.txt
  ```

  d. **View the New Merged File**

  ```
  cat book.txt
  ```

  e. **Add Line Numbers**

  Use the **`-n`** option to display line numbers:

  ```
  cat -n notes.txt
  ```

Output:

```
1      milk
2      bread
3      eggs
```

Summary

The **`cat`** command is a powerful tool for displaying, merging, and formatting file contents in Linux. By incorporating options such as **`-n`** and redirecting output to new files, system administrators can streamline file management tasks. These examples demonstrate the importance of organizing content clearly and efficiently when working within a Linux environment.

Using the grep Command

The grep command is a useful utility used to search for patterns in text files. It scans files and outputs lines that match a specified pattern. Common options include:

- `-i`: Case-insensitive search
- `-n`: Display matching line numbers

Search for a Word

First, create a new file and add several lines containing the word "**error**." Then, use **grep** to filter for that word:

```
nano logfile.txt
grep "error" logfile.txt
```

```
[cesarmserver@RockyLinux ~]$ nano logfile.txt
[cesarmserver@RockyLinux ~]$ grep "error" logfile.txt
error
error
error
```

Figure 2.7: *Displays Lines Containing "error"*

Add more lines to the existing file, some with variations such as "**Error**" or "**ERROR**". Then run grep with the **-i** option to perform a case-insensitive search:

```
nano logfile.txt
grep ¨error¨ -i logfile.txt
```

```
[cesarmserver@RockyLinux ~]$ grep "error" -in logfile.txt
1:error
2:error
3:error
4:Error
5:ERROR
6:errOR
7:ERRor
```

Figure 2.8: *Case-sensitive Error Message First Example*

Display Line Numbers and combine a case-insensitive search: **grep ¨error¨ -in logfile.txt**.

```
[cesarmserver@RockyLinux ~]$ nano logfile.txt
[cesarmserver@RockyLinux ~]$ grep "error" -i logfile.txt
error
error
error
Error
ERROR
errOR
ERRor
```

Figure 2.9: *Case-sensitive Error Message Second Example*

Grep can also be used in pipelines. For example: **`cat logfile.txt | grep -i "error"`**

```
[cesarmserver@RockyLinux ~]$ cat logfile.txt | grep -i "error"
error
error
error
Error
ERROR
errOR
ERRor
```

Figure 2.10: *Case-sensitive Error Message Third Example*

Using the Command `less`

Navigate large files effectively. The **`less`** command allows viewing large files one screen at a time. It includes navigation tools and pattern searching.

Please navigate to the new path as the following example route:

- **`cd /etc/yum.repos.d`**
- **`ls`**

```
[cesarmserver@RockyLinux yum.repos.d]$ cd /etc/yum.repos.d
[cesarmserver@RockyLinux yum.repos.d]$ ls
epel-cisco-openh264.repo  epel.repo          rocky-devel.repo
epel-next.repo            epel-testing.repo  rocky-extras.repo
epel-next-testing.repo    rocky-addons.repo  rocky.repo
```

Figure 2.11: *Accessing Repositories*

This output, shown in *Figure 2.11*, displays the steps to access a specific directory.

View a File: **`less rocky.repo`**

```
[cesarmserver@RockyLinux yum.repos.d]$ less rocky.repo
[cesarmserver@RockyLinux yum.repos.d]$
```

Figure 2.12: *Validating Repositories Information*

The less command is vital to navigate and access the proper information within the system.

Navigate through Content:

- Press *Space* to scroll forward.
- Press *b* to scroll backwards.
- Search using **`/pattern`**, for example, **`/important`**.
- To exit the file, we select the letter **q**.

Combine commands: `ls -l /etc/ | less`

```
[cesarmserver@RockyLinux yum.repos.d]$ ls -l /etc/ | less
[cesarmserver@RockyLinux yum.repos.d]$
```

Figure 2.13: *Listing the Directories Content*

Figure 2.13 illustrates the use of the command **`ls -l /etc/ | less`**, which lists the contents of the **/ etc/** directory in long format while allowing the user to scroll through the output one screen at a time. The ls -l portion provides detailed information about each file and directory, including permissions, ownership, size, and modification date. The **`| less`** command pipes the output into the less pager, making it easier to navigate large amounts of data without overwhelming the terminal screen.

Exit: Press *q* to quit.

This concludes the third laboratory exercise, where learners explored essential redirection concepts and the basic use of the less command to view and navigate through text files efficiently. With these foundational tools in place, we are now prepared to move beyond theory and begin applying the skills to real-world scenarios, where command-line efficiency and practical problem-solving are key to success.

These upcoming lessons will focus on hands-on examples that mirror administrative tasks, helping learners gain confidence and proficiency in managing Linux systems effectively.

Getting to Know the Real-Life Applications

A Linux administrator working with Rocky Linux 9 may encounter situations where certain log management commands or concepts do not work as expected. It is crucial to understand the underlying principles of log management and the specific tools and configurations used in Rocky Linux 9. To ensure these tasks are managed effectively, administrators should verify their system's log configuration settings, such as those found in **`/etc/rsyslog.conf`** or by using the **`journalctl`** command for managing **`systemd`** logs. Additionally, reviewing log rotation settings in **`/etc/logrotate.conf`** ensures logs are managed properly without taking up excessive disk space. In case of issues with specific commands, consulting the system's manual pages or exploring community forums and documentation can provide valuable solutions and workarounds.

Redirection Understanding the Symbol '>' vs '>>' in Rocky Linux 9

In the Linux terminal (including Rocky Linux 9), both > and >> are **output redirection operators**, used to send the output of a command to a file instead of displaying it on the screen. The key difference lies in **how they treat the target file**:

Operator	Behavior	File Handling
>	**Overwrite**	Replaces existing content in the file
>>	**Append**	Adds content to the end of the file without removing existing content

Table 2.1: *Operators and Behaviors*

Example Scenario: Suppose we are working on Rocky Linux 9 and we want to save some output to a file called **`log.txt`**.

Using > (Overwrite)

```
echo "System check started at $(date)" > log.txt
```

- **Effect**: If log.txt already exists, its contents will be **erased** and replaced with the new output.
- Use this when a **start fresh** with new content is required.

Using >> (Append)

```
echo "System check completed at $(date)" >> log.txt
```

- **Effect**: This adds the output to the **end** of **`log.txt`**, preserving any existing content.

- Use this when **a running log or history needs to be stored**.

Practical Tip for Rocky Linux Admins

When scripting or logging tasks, it is common to use:

```
echo "Backup started at $(date)" >> /var/log/backup.log
```

This ensures that each backup time is **added to the log**, rather than overwriting it, which would erase all previous records.

Summary

Use this when...	Operator	Example
we want to create a new file or overwrite an existing one	>	`echo "Start" > output.txt`
we want to keep the old content and add new lines to the file	>>	`echo "Next Step" >> output.txt`

***Table 2.2**: Summary*

Log Management: Viewing and Filtering Logs

In Rocky Linux 9, the default system log management tool is journald (via systemd), which uses binary logs instead of plain text logs such as **`/var/log/syslog`**.

Instead of cat or less, use the **`journalctl`** command to manage logs.

```
# View all logs and filter for "failed"
journalctl | grep "failed"
```

```
failed
Nov 19 14:55:40 RockyLinux gnome-shell[2389]: meta_viewport_info_get_extents: assertion 'viewport_info != NULL'
failed
Nov 19 14:55:40 RockyLinux gnome-shell[2389]: meta_viewport_info_get_extents: assertion 'viewport_info != NULL'
failed
Nov 19 14:55:40 RockyLinux gnome-shell[2389]: meta_viewport_info_get_extents: assertion 'viewport_info != NULL'
failed
Nov 19 14:55:40 RockyLinux gnome-shell[2389]: meta_viewport_info_get_extents: assertion 'viewport_info != NULL'
failed
Nov 19 14:55:41 RockyLinux gnome-shell[2389]: g_strsplit: assertion 'string != NULL' failed
Nov 19 14:55:42 RockyLinux wireplumber[2510]: GetManagedObjects() failed: org.freedesktop.DBus.Error.NameHasNoOw
ner
Nov 19 14:55:43 RockyLinux systemd[2283]: Dependency failed for GNOME XSettings service.
Nov 19 14:55:43 RockyLinux systemd[2283]: org.gnome.SettingsDaemon.XSettings.service: Job org.gnome.SettingsDaem
on.XSettings.service/start failed with result 'dependency'.
Nov 19 14:55:43 RockyLinux systemd[2283]: gnome-session-x11-services-ready.target: Job gnome-session-x11-service
s-ready.target/verify-active failed with result 'dependency'.
Nov 19 14:55:47 RockyLinux gnome-shell[2830]: libEGL warning: egl: failed to create dri2 screen
Nov 19 14:55:47 RockyLinux gnome-shell[2830]: libEGL warning: egl: failed to create dri2 screen
Nov 19 14:55:47 RockyLinux gsd-color[2615]: failed to get edid: unable to get EDID for output
Nov 19 14:55:50 RockyLinux gdm-launch-environment][1428]: GLib-GObject: g_object_unref: assertion 'G_IS_OBJECT (
object)' failed
Nov 19 14:55:51 RockyLinux fwupd[2914]: 20:55:51.770 FuEngine           failed to add device /sys/devices/pci0
000:00/0000:00:07.1/ata2/host1/target1:0:0/1:0:0:0/block/sr0: failed to open /dev/sr0: No medium found
Nov 19 14:55:54 RockyLinux gnome-software[2681]: failed to get featured apps: no apps to show
```

***Figure 2.14**: Filter for Failed Messages, First Example*

The command **`journalctl | grep "failed"`** filters the system journal for entries containing the keyword "**`failed`**." This straightforward approach is useful for quickly identifying log messages related to failures across services and processes.

```
# View logs from the current boot session with "failed"
journalctl -b | grep "failed"
```

```
failed
Nov 19 14:55:40 RockyLinux gnome-shell[2389]: meta_viewport_info_get_extents: assertion 'viewport_info != NULL'
failed
Nov 19 14:55:40 RockyLinux gnome-shell[2389]: meta_viewport_info_get_extents: assertion 'viewport_info != NULL'
failed
Nov 19 14:55:40 RockyLinux gnome-shell[2389]: meta_viewport_info_get_extents: assertion 'viewport_info != NULL'
failed
Nov 19 14:55:40 RockyLinux gnome-shell[2389]: meta_viewport_info_get_extents: assertion 'viewport_info != NULL'
failed
Nov 19 14:55:41 RockyLinux gnome-shell[2389]: g_strsplit: assertion 'string != NULL' failed
Nov 19 14:55:42 RockyLinux wireplumber[2510]: GetManagedObjects() failed: org.freedesktop.DBus.Error.NameHasNoO
ner
Nov 19 14:55:43 RockyLinux systemd[2283]: Dependency failed for GNOME XSettings service.
Nov 19 14:55:43 RockyLinux systemd[2283]: org.gnome.SettingsDaemon.XSettings.service: Job org.gnome.SettingsDae
on.XSettings.service/start failed with result 'dependency'.
Nov 19 14:55:43 RockyLinux systemd[2283]: gnome-session-x11-services-ready.target: Job gnome-session-x11-servic
s-ready.target/verify-active failed with result 'dependency'.
Nov 19 14:55:47 RockyLinux gnome-shell[2830]: libEGL warning: egl: failed to create dri2 screen
Nov 19 14:55:47 RockyLinux gnome-shell[2830]: libEGL warning: egl: failed to create dri2 screen
Nov 19 14:55:47 RockyLinux gsd-color[2615]: failed to get edid: unable to get EDID for output
Nov 19 14:55:50 RockyLinux gdm-launch-environment][1428]: GLib-GObject: g_object_unref: assertion 'G_IS_OBJECT
object)' failed
Nov 19 14:55:51 RockyLinux fwupd[2914]: 20:55:51.770 FuEngine           failed to add device /sys/devices/pci
000:00/0000:00:07.1/ata2/host1/target1:0:0/1:0:0:0/block/sr0: failed to open /dev/sr0: No medium found
Nov 19 14:55:54 RockyLinux gnome-software[2681]: failed to get featured apps: no apps to show
```

Figure 2.15: *Filter for Failed Messages, Second Example*

The command **`journalctl -b | grep "failed"`** isolates log entries containing the keyword "**`failed`**" from the current boot session. This is particularly useful for identifying issues that occurred during or after the most recent system startup.

Troubleshooting: Grep and Navigation

Another way to use less for navigation or **`grep`** for filtering, export the logs from journald to a plain text format.

```
# Export logs to a file
journalctl > /tmp/system_logs.txt
# Navigate logs with less
less /tmp/system_logs.txt
# Filter failed patterns
grep "failed" /tmp/system_logs.txt
```

```
failed
Nov 19 14:55:40 RockyLinux gnome-shell[2389]: meta_viewport_info_get_extents: assertion 'viewport_info != NULL'
failed
Nov 19 14:55:40 RockyLinux gnome-shell[2389]: meta_viewport_info_get_extents: assertion 'viewport_info != NULL'
failed
Nov 19 14:55:40 RockyLinux gnome-shell[2389]: meta_viewport_info_get_extents: assertion 'viewport_info != NULL'
failed
Nov 19 14:55:40 RockyLinux gnome-shell[2389]: meta_viewport_info_get_extents: assertion 'viewport_info != NULL'
failed
Nov 19 14:55:41 RockyLinux gnome-shell[2389]: g_strsplit: assertion 'string != NULL' failed
Nov 19 14:55:42 RockyLinux wireplumber[2510]: GetManagedObjects() failed: org.freedesktop.DBus.Error.NameHasNoOw
ner
Nov 19 14:55:43 RockyLinux systemd[2283]: Dependency failed for GNOME XSettings service.
Nov 19 14:55:43 RockyLinux systemd[2283]: org.gnome.SettingsDaemon.XSettings.service: Job org.gnome.SettingsDaem
on.XSettings.service/start failed with result 'dependency'.
Nov 19 14:55:43 RockyLinux systemd[2283]: gnome-session-x11-services-ready.target: Job gnome-session-x11-service
s-ready.target/verify-active failed with result 'dependency'.
Nov 19 14:55:47 RockyLinux gnome-shell[2830]: libEGL warning: egl: failed to create dri2 screen
```

Figure 2.16: *Filter for Failed Messages, Third Example*

The command **`grep "failed" /tmp/system_logs.txt`** searches for the keyword "**`failed`**" in a specific log file, in this case, **`/tmp/system_logs.txt`**. This approach is useful when dealing with logs stored in custom locations or when analyzing logs from previous sessions.

Text Processing Across Multiple Log Files

If we are working with non-binary log files split into parts, combining and filtering works the same way as before. For example:

```
# Combine and filter
cat logs_part1.txt logs_part2.txt | grep "critical"
```

```
[cesarmserver@RockyLinux ~]$ echo "critical_error1" "critical_errorT22" > logs_part1.txt
[cesarmserver@RockyLinux ~]$ echo "critical_error644" "critical_error4xgg" > logs_part2.txt
[cesarmserver@RockyLinux ~]$ cat logs_part1.txt logs_part2.txt | grep "critical"
critical_error1 critical_errorT22
critical_error644 critical_error4xgg
```

Figure 2.17: *Filter for Critical Messages*

This command will display only the logs classified as critical, providing insights into severe system issues that require immediate attention. This approach helps us quickly identify and address critical problems, ensuring the system runs smoothly without being overwhelmed by less important logs.

In Rocky Linux 9, system logs are stored in a binary format managed by **journald**, rather than in traditional text files such as **/var/log/syslog**. As a result, tools such as **journalctl** are essential for log management, allowing users to filter logs effectively using options such as **-u <service_name>** for specific services or in combination with commands like grep or awk for advanced filtering.

File Permissions and Ownership in Rocky Linux 9

As part of a Linux administrator's responsibilities, managing file permissions is essential for maintaining security and system stability. File and directory permissions define who can read, write, or execute content, ensuring only authorized users perform specific operations.

Understanding File Permissions

In Rocky Linux 9, file permissions regulate access to files and directories. We can inspect permissions using the **ls -l** command, which displays:

- File type (for example, directory, file, symbolic link)
- Permission bits for user (owner), group, and others
- File owner and group
- Last modification time

File Type Indicators

When using **ls -l**, the first character indicates the file type:

- **d**: Directory
- **-**: Regular file
- **l**: Symbolic link

Permission Structure

Permissions are represented in three groups of three characters:

- **User (owner)**: First set (example, **rwx**)
- **Group**: Second set (example, **r-x**)
- **Others**: Third set (example, **r-x**)

Each character represents:

- `r`: Read permission
- `w`: Write permission
- `x`: Execute permission
- `-`: Permission not granted

Example: **`drwxr-xr-x`**

- `d`: Directory
- **`rwx`**: Owner can read, write, execute
- **`r-x`**: Group can read and execute
- **`r-x`**: Others can read and execute

Changing Permissions with `chmod`

We can modify permissions using the **`chmod`** command in two ways:

Using Numeric Notation

Each permission has a numeric value:

- **7**: Read, write, execute (**`rwx`**)
- **6**: Read, write (**`rw-`**)
- **5**: Read, execute (**`r-x`**)
- **4**: Read only (**`r--`**)
- **3**: Write, execute (**`-wx`**)
- **2**: Write only (**`-w-`**)
- **1**: Execute only (**`--x`**)
- **0**: No permission (**`---`**)

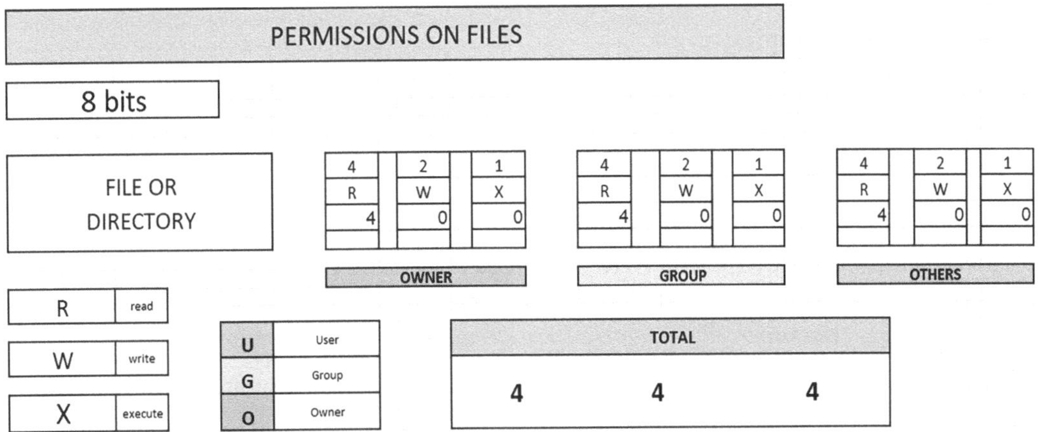

Figure 2.18: *Visual Example of Permissions in Files and Directories*

This figure provides a visual representation of how permissions are displayed for files and directories in a Linux environment. This figure illustrates the output of the **`ls -l`** command, showing the file type indicator and the corresponding read, write, and execute permissions for the user, group, and others. By examining the visual example, administrators can better understand how the permission structure works and how it is reflected in real-world files and directories. This visual breakdown helps in quickly identifying which users or groups have access to a particular file and the level of access they possess, making it easier to manage and troubleshoot file permissions in Linux systems.

Understanding Linux File Permissions: Symbolic vs Numeric

In Linux, file permissions define who can read, write, or execute a file or directory. These permissions are categorized for three user types:

- **Owner (user)**
- **Group**
- **Others**

Each category can be assigned three permissions:

- **Read (`r`) = 4**
- **Write (`w`) = 2**
- **Execute (`x`) = 1**

These are represented in two formats:

- **Symbolic** (for example, **`rwxr-xr--`**)
- **Numeric** (for example, **754)**

For example, chmod 754 filename sets:

- **Owner: `rwx` (7 = 4+2+1):** full access
- **Group: `r-x` (5 = 4+1):** read and execute
- **Others: `r--` (4):** read only

Ownership can be changed using:

- **`chown alice file.txt`:** sets the owner to alice
- **`chgrp developers file.txt`:** sets the group to developers
- **`chown alice:developers file.txt`:** changes both in one step

By understanding these formats, users can manage file access more effectively, and maintain secure Linux environments.

Symbolic and Numeric Mapping

The following table outlines the four fundamental permission types in Linux, presenting their symbolic notation, numeric value, functional meaning, applicable user classes, and representative examples. Permissions are defined through a combination of symbolic characters **`(r, w, x, -)`** and numeric values **(4, 2, 1, 0),** which collectively determine access levels for the owner, group, and others. For example, the permission string **`-rw-r--r--`** signifies that the owner has read and write privileges, while the group and others are limited to read-only access. This structured model provides granular control over file and directory accessibility in Unix-like operating systems.

Permission Type	Symbolic Notation	Numeric Value	Meaning	Who it Applies To	Example
Read	`r`	4	Can view contents of file or list directory	Owner, Group, Others	**`-rw-r--r--`** → owner can read/write, group and others can read
Write	`w`	2	Can modify file or add/remove files in directory	Owner, Group, Others	**`-rwxr-xr--`** → owner can read/write/execute

Execute	x	1	Can run a file or access a directory	Owner, Group, Others	`-rwx------` → owner has full access
No Permission	-	0	No access	-	`----------` → no permissions at all

Table 2.3: Understanding Linux File Permissions (chmod, chown, chgrp)

Numeric Permissions

The following table provides a detailed breakdown of numeric file permissions in Linux, categorized by user class. Each class—***owner (u), group (g), and others (o)***—is associated with a symbolic shorthand and a corresponding numeric value. These values determine the level of access granted: **7 (`rwx`)** for full access, **5 (`r-x`)** for read and execute, and **4 (`r--`)** for read-only. This numeric-to-symbolic mapping is foundational for configuring secure and efficient permission schemes using the ***chmod*** command.

User Class	Symbol	Example Value	What It Represents
Owner	u	7 (`rwx`)	Full access (read, write, execute)
Group	g	5 (`r-x`)	Read and execute only
Others	o	4 (`r--`)	Read only

Table 2.4: Numeric Permission

Numeric Example: A permission like **`chmod 755 file.txt`** sets:

- Owner: **7** → **`rwx`**
- Group: **5** → **`r-x`**
- Others: **5** → **`r-x`**

  Resulting in: `-rwxr-xr-x`

Ownership and Group Management

Command	Purpose	Example
chown	Change file owner	**`chown alice file.txt`**
chgrp	Change group ownership	**`chgrp developers file.txt`**
chown with group	Change both owner and group	**`chown alice:developers file.txt`**

Table 2.5: Understanding Linux File Permissions

This table provides a clear overview of how file permissions are managed in Linux using three essential commands: `chmod`, `chown`, *and* `chgrp`. The `chmod` command is used to modify file and directory permissions, controlling read, write, and execute access for the owner, group, and others. The `chown` command changes file ownership, assigning files or directories to a specific user, while `chgrp` adjusts the group ownership to regulate collaborative access. Together, these commands form the foundation of Linux security and resource management, ensuring that only authorized users and groups can interact with files in the intended manner. Understanding and applying these tools is crucial for maintaining system integrity, enforcing security policies, and enabling efficient collaboration in multi-user environments.

Practical Examples of File Permissions and Ownership Management

Now that the previous tables have explained the foundations of file permissions and group ownership in Linux, it is time to explore some additional, practical examples. These hands-on scenarios reinforce the concepts covered and demonstrate how permissions are applied in real-world use cases.

Examples:

- **`chmod 777 filename`:** Full permissions to everyone
- **`chmod 700 filename`:** Full permissions to owner only
- **`chmod 744 filename`:** Full for user, read-only for group, and others

Using Symbolic Notation

Syntax: `chmod [who][operator][permissions] filename`

- **who:** **u** (user), **g** (group), **o** (others), **a** (all)
- **operator:** + (add), - (remove), = (set exactly)
- **permissions:** **r**, **w**, **x**

Examples:

- **`chmod a+x filename`:** Add execute for all
- **`chmod go-w filename`:** Remove write from group and others
- **`chmod u=rwx,g=rx,o=r filename`:** Set exact permissions

Practical Examples: Granting all permissions to everyone

```
touch filename
chmod 777 filename
```

```
[cesarmserver@RockyLinux permissions]$ touch filename
[cesarmserver@RockyLinux permissions]$ chmod 777 filename
[cesarmserver@RockyLinux permissions]$ ls -l filename
-rwxrwxrwx. 1 cesarmserver cesarmserver 0 Nov 19 15:50 filename
```

Figure 2.19: *Granting Permissions to a File*

This command gives read, write, and execute permissions to the user, group, and others.

Example 2: Granting full permissions to the user, and no permissions to the group and others.

```
chmod 700 filename
```

```
[cesarmserver@RockyLinux permissions]$ chmod 700 filename
[cesarmserver@RockyLinux permissions]$ ls -l filename
-rwx------. 1 cesarmserver cesarmserver 0 Nov 19 15:50 filename
```

Figure 2.20: *Adding Full Permissions to a File*

This command gives read, write, and execute permissions to the user only.

Example 3: Granting read permissions to the group and others, and full permissions to the user.

```
chmod 744 filename
```

```
[cesarmserver@RockyLinux permissions]$ chmod 744 filename
[cesarmserver@RockyLinux permissions]$ ls -l filename
-rwxr--r--. 1 cesarmserver cesarmserver 0 Nov 19 15:50 filename
```

Figure 2.21: *Granting Read Permissions to the Group and Others to a File*

This command sets the permissions to read-only for the group and others, and read, write, and execute for the user.

Using chmod with Symbolic Notation

The ***chmod*** command also supports symbolic notation for modifying file permissions. This approach is often considered more intuitive, as it allows explicit specification of permission changes without relying on numeric values.

Syntax: `chmod [who][operation][permissions] filename`

- **who:** **u** (user), **g** (group), **o** (others), **a** (all)
- **operation:** **+** (add), **-** (remove), **=** (set exact)
- **permissions:** **r**(read), **w** (write), **x** (execute)

Example 1: Adding execute permissions to everyone

```
chmod a+x filename
```

```
[cesarmserver@RockyLinux permissions]$ chmod a+x filename
[cesarmserver@RockyLinux permissions]$ ls -l filename
-r-xr-x--x. 1 cesarmserver cesarmserver 0 Nov 19 15:50 filename
```

Figure 2.22: *Adding Execute Permissions to Everyone*

This command adds execute permissions for the user, group, and others.

Example 2: Removing write permissions from the group and others

```
chmod go-w filename
```

```
[cesarmserver@RockyLinux permissions]$ chmod go-w filename
[cesarmserver@RockyLinux permissions]$ ls -l filename
-r-xr-x--x. 1 cesarmserver cesarmserver 0 Nov 19 15:50 filename
```

Figure 2.23: *Removing Write Permissions from the Group and Others*

This command removes write permissions for the group and others.

Example 3: Setting exact permissions

```
chmod u=rwx,g=rx,o=r filename
```

```
[cesarmserver@RockyLinux permissions]$ chmod u=rwx,g=rx,o=r filename
[cesarmserver@RockyLinux permissions]$ ls -l filename
-rwxr-xr--. 1 cesarmserver cesarmserver 0 Nov 19 15:50 filename
```

Figure 2.24: *Setting Exact Permissions*

This command sets read, write, and execute permissions for the user; read and execute permissions for the group; and read-only permissions for others.

`chmod +x script name`*:* `This command enables us to execute the script.`

Removing Write Permissions for All Others

`touch somefile.txt`: we are creating a new file.

`chmod o-w somefile.txt`: removing write permissions for all others.

```
[cesarmserver@RockyLinux ~]$ touch somefile.txt
[cesarmserver@RockyLinux ~]$ chmod o-w somefile.txt
```

Figure 2.25: *Removing Write Permissions for All Others*

This command ensures that others cannot modify the file.

Setting Permissions to Read-Only for Everyone

touch readonlyfile.txt: we are creating a new file.

chmod 444 readonlyfile.txt: we are adding readonly permissions

ls -l: we are validating the permissions we are validating the permissions

```
[cesarmserver@RockyLinux ~]$ touch readonlyfile.txt
[cesarmserver@RockyLinux ~]$ chmod 444 readonlyfile.txt
[cesarmserver@RockyLinux ~]$ ls -l readonlyfile.txt
-r--r--r--. 1 cesarmserver cesarmserver 0 Nov 19 17:38 readonlyfile.txt
```

Figure 2.26: *Setting Permissions to Read-only for Everyone*

This command makes the file read-only for the user, group, and others.

Understanding and managing file and directory permissions in Rocky Linux 9 is fundamental to effective access control. The **chmod** command, whether applied with numeric values or symbolic notation, offers the flexibility required to configure permissions accurately and securely.

Practicing permission modification within the home directory provides a safe environment for experimentation without risking changes to critical system files. Gaining familiarity with both numeric **(chmod 777)** and symbolic **(chmod ugo+rwx)** modes ensures readiness to manage diverse scenarios and collaborate efficiently in multi-user administrative environments.

Creating and Executing a Script

Script Name: create_files.sh

```
#!/bin/bash

# Define variables
DIR_NAME="project_data"
FILE_NAME="report.txt"
LINK_TARGET="/var/log/syslog"
LINK_NAME="log_link"

echo "Starting script execution..."

# Create directory if it does not exist
if [ ! -d "$DIR_NAME" ]; then
  mkdir "$DIR_NAME"
  chmod 755 "$DIR_NAME"
  echo " Directory '$DIR_NAME' created with permissions: drwxr-xr-x"
else
  echo " Directory '$DIR_NAME' already exists."
fi

# Create and configure file inside the directory
FULL_PATH="$DIR_NAME/$FILE_NAME"

touch "$FULL_PATH"
chmod 644 "$FULL_PATH"
truncate -s 1024 "$FULL_PATH"

echo " File '$FULL_PATH' created with permissions: -rw-r--r-- and size: 1024
```

```
bytes"

# Create symbolic link if target exists
if [ -e "$LINK_TARGET" ]; then
  ln -s "$LINK_TARGET" "$LINK_NAME"
  echo "Symbolic link '$LINK_NAME' created pointing to '$LINK_TARGET'"
else
  echo "Warning: Target '$LINK_TARGET' does not exist. Symbolic link '$LINK_
NAME' will be broken."
fi

# Display summary
echo -e "\n File and Directory Details:"
ls -lh "$DIR_NAME"
[ -e "$LINK_NAME" ] && ls -l "$LINK_NAME"

echo -e "\n Script execution completed."
```

Educational Enhancements

- **Real-World Context**
  - Uses **`/var/log/syslog`** (or **`/var/log/messages`** on some distros) to simulate linking to a real system file.
  - Files are created in a purpose-named directory **(`project_data`)** to mimic common usage.
- **Common Scripting Errors Covered**
  - **Permission Denied**: Suggest running with **`chmod +x create_files.sh`** and executing as **`./create_files.sh`**.
  - **Broken Link**: Script warns if symbolic link target does not exist.
  - **Syntax Awareness**: Uses variables consistently and quotes them properly to avoid issues with spaces or special characters.

Tips for Troubleshooting Scripting Errors

Error	**Explanation**	**Fix**
Permission denied	Trying to run a script without execute permission	Use `chmod +x script.sh`
No such file or directory	Referencing a path or file that does not exist	Check path spelling and existence with ls
command not found	Using a misspelled or non-installed command	Check syntax or install missing packages
Syntax errors	Improper spacing, missing quotes, and more	Use shellcheck to scan the script for issues

***Table 2.6**: Tips for Troubleshooting Scripting Errors*

At this stage, the script has been successfully completed, representing the culmination of the writing, testing, and refinement process to achieve the intended functionality. By adhering to the outlined steps, a working solution has been developed that demonstrates both practical application and a solid understanding of Linux scripting. The script can now be executed to observe its behavior and, if necessary, customized to meet specific needs. This accomplishment provides a solid foundation for exploring more advanced scripting techniques in subsequent projects.

```
[cesarmserver@RockyLinux permissions]$ chmod u+x create_files.sh
[cesarmserver@RockyLinux permissions]$ ls -l create_files.sh
-rwxr--r--. 1 cesarmserver cesarmserver 426 Nov 19 15:35 create_files.sh
```

Figure 2.27: *Granting Execute Permission to a Shell Script*

This figure shows the process of granting execute permission to a shell script named **`create_files.sh`** using the chmod command in a Rocky Linux environment. The command **`chmod u+x create_files.sh`** adds execute permission (x) for the file owner (u). The subsequent **`ls -l`** command displays the updated file permissions, showing **`-rwxr--r--`**, which indicates that the owner (cesarmserver) now has read, write, and execute permissions, while the group and others have only read access. This step is essential to allow the script to be executed directly from the command line.

```
ls -l directory_name file_name.txt link_name
```

Make it executable: `chmod u+x create_files.sh`

Final Thoughts

Mastering file and directory permissions is essential for ensuring a secure and well-functioning Linux environment. It is recommended that Linux administrators and developers regularly practice adjusting permissions using both numeric and symbolic notation within their home directories—this hands-on approach helps reinforce core concepts and build operational confidence.

In upcoming sections, the focus will shift to ownership management with the **`chown`** and **`chgrp`** commands, enabling more precise control over system security and organization.

Understanding how permissions and ownership work together forms the foundation for effective system administration. These skills are critical not only for local environments but also for securely managing users and data in cloud-based systems. With continued practice, Linux professionals can efficiently troubleshoot permission-related issues and apply best practices across diverse real-world scenarios.

The sudo Command

This section focuses on enhancing system security in Rocky Linux 9 by using the **`sudo`** command to perform administrative tasks without relying on the root account directly. Readers will learn how to configure **`sudo`**, manage user access, restrict commands, and follow best practices for secure administration.

Understanding sudo

`sudo` stands for "*superuser do*". It allows a permitted user to execute a command as the superuser or another user, as specified by the security policy in **`/etc/sudoers`**.

Adding a User to the sudo Group

1. Log in as root or a user with **`sudo`** privileges.
2. Create a new user (if not already created): **`sudo adduser newuser`**.

```
[cesarmserver@RockyLinux ~]$ sudo useradd new_user
[cesarmserver@RockyLinux ~]$ cat /etc/passwd | grep new_user
new_user:x:1004:1005::/home/new_user:/bin/bash
```

Figure 2.28: *Adding a New User with Sudo Access*

3. Add the new user to the **`sudo group: sudo usermod -aG wheel newuser`**

```
[cesarmserver@RockyLinux ~]$ sudo usermod -aG wheel new_user
[cesarmserver@RockyLinux ~]$
```

Figure 2.29: *Adding a Specific User to a Designed Group*

In Rocky Linux 9, the **wheel** group is typically configured to allow its members to use **sudo.**

Configuring sudoers File

1. Edit the **/etc/sudoers** file using the **visudo**`command, which safely edits the file and prevents syntax errors: **sudo visudo!**

```
[cesarmserver@RockyLinux ~]$ sudo visudo
```

Figure 2.30: *Accessing the Sudoers Script*

2. Ensure the following line is present (uncommented) to allow members of the **wheel group to use sudo: %wheel ALL=(ALL) ALL**

```
## Allows people in group wheel to run all commands
%wheel  ALL=(ALL)       ALL
cesarmserver    ALL=(ALL)       ALL


## Same thing without a password
# %wheel        ALL=(ALL)       NOPASSWD: ALL

## Allows members of the users group to mount and unmount the
## cdrom as root
# %users  ALL=/sbin/mount /mnt/cdrom, /sbin/umount /mnt/cdrom
```

Figure 2.31: *Editing the Sudoers Script*

Figure 2.31 illustrates the process of editing the **sudoers** file to manage user privileges. This critical configuration file determines which users have the authority to execute commands with administrative privileges via the **sudo** command. To edit the **sudoers** file safely, administrators should use the **visudo** command, which opens the file in a protected editor and performs syntax checking before saving changes. Modifying the **sudoers** file allows for fine-grained control over user access, such as granting or restricting specific commands for designated users. It is essential to exercise caution while editing this file, as syntax errors or incorrect configurations can lead to security vulnerabilities or lockout from administrative functions.

Using `sudo` for Administrative Tasks

Step 1: Switch to the new user:

- **sudo passwd new_user**
- **su - new_user**

```
[cesarmserver@RockyLinux ~]$ su - new_user
Password:
[new_user@RockyLinux ~]$ whoami
new_user
```

Figure 2.32: *Entering the New User's Access*

Step 2: Update the package database as the new user using **sudo**: **sudo dnf update**.

```
[new_user@RockyLinux ~]$ sudo dnf update

We trust you have received the usual lecture from the local System
Administrator. It usually boils down to these three things:

    #1) Respect the privacy of others.
    #2) Think before you type.
    #3) With great power comes great responsibility.

[sudo] password for new_user:
Last metadata expiration check: 1:54:11 ago on Tue 19 Nov 2024 03:59:29 PM CST.
Dependencies resolved.
Nothing to do.
Complete!
```

Figure 2.33: *Getting Updates with DNF Command*

Figure 2.33 demonstrates the use of the **dnf** command to retrieve system updates in Red Hat-based Linux distributions. **dnf** (Dandified YUM) is the default package manager for managing software installations, updates, and removals. The command **dnf update** fetches the latest package updates from enabled repositories, ensuring the system remains up to date with the most recent security patches, bug fixes, and feature enhancements. This process is vital for maintaining system stability and security, as it ensures that the latest software versions are installed, and any vulnerabilities are addressed promptly. The **dnf** tool also offers options for managing individual packages, cleaning up cache, and performing system upgrades.

Step 3: Install a package, for example, **htop: sudo dnf install htop**.

```
[new_user@RockyLinux ~]$ sudo dnf install htop
Last metadata expiration check: 1:54:52 ago on Tue 19 Nov 2024 03:59:29 PM CST.
Package htop-3.3.0-1.el9.x86_64 is already installed.
Dependencies resolved.
Nothing to do.
Complete!
```

Figure 2.34: *Installing the htop Package*

This figure illustrates the installation process of the **htop** utility using a package manager on Rocky Linux. The htop tool provides an interactive and user-friendly interface for monitoring system processes, CPU, and memory usage. The image demonstrates the use of the dnf install htop command, showing the package retrieval, dependency checks, and successful installation, highlighting the simplicity of adding essential monitoring tools to the system.

Step 4: Running Commands with Elevated Privileges

Run a command with root privileges: **sudo command**.

Edit a system configuration file, for example, **/etc/hosts: sudo nano /etc/hosts.**

```
[new_user@RockyLinux ~]$ sudo nano /etc/hosts
[new_user@RockyLinux ~]$
```

Figure 2.35: *Validating the Host Script's Configuration*

This figure displays the output of a validation step for a custom host configuration script. It showcases how the script checks system parameters, confirms network settings, and verifies environment variables to ensure proper setup. Successful validation messages indicate that the host is correctly configured and ready for further deployment or integration tasks.

Step 5: Restricting **sudo** access

a. Edit the **sudoers** file: **sudo visudo**

b. Add a rule to restrict a user (for example, **new_user**) to only specific commands:

- **new_user ALL=(ALL) /usr/bin/htop, /usr/sbin/reboot**

```
## Allows people in group wheel to run all commands
%wheel  ALL=(ALL)       ALL
cesarmserver    ALL=(ALL)       ALL
new_user ALL=(ALL) /usr/bin/htop, /usr/sbin/reboot
```

Figure 2.36: *Providing Access to the New User*

This figure demonstrates the process of granting system access to a newly created user. It highlights key steps such as assigning the user to appropriate groups, setting a secure password, and configuring permissions. The output confirms successful user creation and access provisioning, ensuring the new user can interact with the system according to predefined roles and security policies.

Step 6: Logging and Monitoring **sudo** usage

a. Check the **/var/log/secure** log file for the **sudo** activity: **sudo tail -f /var/log/secure**

```
[new_user@RockyLinux ~]$
[new_user@RockyLinux ~]$ sudo tail -f /var/log/secure^C
[new_user@RockyLinux ~]$
```

Figure 2.37: *Checking Log's Activities*

This figure illustrates how to review system logs to monitor activities and identify potential issues. Using commands such as **journalctl** or inspecting files in **/var/log/**, the figure shows entries related to user actions, system events, or service behavior. This log inspection is essential for maintaining system integrity, troubleshooting errors, and ensuring compliance with security practices.

Use tools such as search if audit logging is enabled for deeper inspection.

Best practices for using sudo

- **Always** use **sudo** instead of direct root login.
- **Limit** access to trusted users only.
- **Review /etc/sudoers** and logs regularly.
- **Apply** the principle of least privilege:
  `alice ALL=(ALL) /usr/bin/systemctl restart apache2`
- **Monitor sudo** usage through log files such as **/var/log/secure**.

Clarifying sudo vs Root Access

Aims to avoid direct root login:

- No audit trail for actions
- Higher risk of irreversible mistakes
- Insecure when multiple admins share root password
- Remote root login is often disabled to protect against brute-force attacks

Reasons to use the sudo commands:

- Logs all actions for traceability
- Provides temporary elevated privileges
- Allows for fine-grained command control

SSH Best Practice: Disable root login via SSH by setting:

`PermitRootLogin no` in **`/etc/ssh/sshd_config`**

Summary

The use of **`sudo`** in Rocky Linux 9 enhances system security and accountability by enabling controlled privilege escalation. It allows fine-grained administrative access, reducing the likelihood of configuration errors or unauthorized changes. This approach is essential in both educational settings and professional environments, particularly in enterprise and cloud-based systems.

When properly configured—with restricted permissions, group-based access control, and log monitoring—**`sudo`** contributes to a robust and manageable administrative model. This clarification reinforces the role of **`sudo`** as a foundational component of Linux system security and operational efficiency.

System Shutdown and Reboot

This section introduces essential commands to safely shut down or reboot a Rocky Linux 9 system using the command line. Understanding these procedures ensures system stability, prevents data loss, and supports effective maintenance routines.

Importance of Shutdown and Reboot Operations

System reboots or shutdowns are used for the following:

- Applying updates
- Fixing software or hardware issues
- Performing system maintenance
- Powering off the system safely

Safety Tip: Always save work and notify users before initiating shutdown or reboot operations to avoid data loss.

Understanding the `shutdown` Command

The **`shutdown`** command helps us to schedule or immediately perform a shutdown or reboot.

Syntax: `sudo shutdown [OPTION] [TIME] [MESSAGE]`

Common Use Cases:

- **Immediate shutdown:** `sudo shutdown now`

Powers off the system immediately.

- **Scheduled shutdown in 10 minutes:** `sudo shutdown +10`
- **Shutdown at a specific time (e.g., 10 PM):** `sudo shutdown 22:00`
- **Shutdown with a message:**
  `sudo shutdown +5 "System will reboot for maintenance"`

- **Cancel a scheduled shutdown:** `sudo shutdown -c`.

Note: The broadcast message is shown to all logged-in users.

Using the `reboot` Command

The reboot command immediately restarts the system.

Usage: `sudo reboot`

Alternatively, we can use shutdown with the **`-r`** flag: `sudo shutdown -r now`

This method allows adding delay and messages before rebooting.

Using the poweroff Command

The **`poweroff`** command instantly shuts down the system.

Usage: `sudo poweroff`

Also consider using: **`sudo shutdown -h now`**

This halts the system and powers it off.

Use poweroff or **`shutdown -h`** during planned maintenance or safe shutdown procedures.

Hands-On Practice Activity

To reinforce learning, perform the following in a test environment:

1. Open a terminal on the Rocky Linux 9 system.
2. Schedule a shutdown in 2 minutes:

   `sudo shutdown +2 "System will shut down for practice"`
3. Cancel the scheduled shutdown before it occurs: `sudo shutdown -c`
4. Reboot the system: **`sudo reboot`**

These exercises allow learners to confidently manage system reboots and shutdowns without risking operational downtime.

Summary

- Use **`shutdown`**, **`reboot`**, and **`poweroff`** appropriately based on the situation.
- Always communicate scheduled maintenance to users.
- Practice on non-critical systems to become familiar with timing, messaging, and cancellation options.

Mastering these commands equips administrators to perform graceful system shutdowns and reboots—vital for both on-premises and cloud-based infrastructure management.

Introduction to Cloud-Based CLI Workflows with AWS

The **AWS Command Line Interface (CLI)** is a powerful tool that allows us to manage AWS services directly from the terminal. On a Rocky Linux 9 system, the AWS CLI can be used to automate tasks such as creating S3 buckets, uploading files, and managing cloud resources—without relying on the AWS Management Console.

This section provides a step-by-step guide to installing, configuring, and using the AWS CLI, along with sample commands and **expected outputs** to help verify each operation.

Step 1: Install AWS CLI Version 2

Before beginning, we should ensure that the system is updated and has the tools required for downloading and unzipping files.

- `sudo dnf update -y`
- `curl "https://awscli.amazonaws.com/awscli-exe-linux-x86_64.zip" -o "awscliv2.zip"`
- `unzip awscliv2.zip`
- `sudo ./aws/install`

Verifying Installation

After installation, we can verify that the AWS CLI is working: **`aws -version`**

Expected Output:

```
aws-cli/2.15.32 Python/3.11.4 Linux/5.14.0-70.el9.x86_64 exe/x86_64.rocky.9
prompt/off
```

Step 2: Configure AWS CLI

To use the AWS CLI, we must configure it with our AWS credentials. Run the following command: **`aws configure`**

Enter the requested values:

```
AWS Access Key ID [None]: AKIAIOSFODNN7EXAMPLE
AWS Secret Access Key [None]: wJalrXUtnFEMI/K7MDENG/bPxRfiCYEXAMPLEKEY
Default region name [None]: us-east-1
Default output format [None]: json
```

This creates the **`~/.aws/config`** and **`~/.aws/credentials`** files, which store authentication and configuration settings.

Step 3: Verify Configuration

To confirm that the configuration is working and that access credentials are valid, run:

```
aws s3 ls
```

Expected Output (if buckets exist):

```
2025-04-10 09:12:33 my-existing-bucket
```

If no buckets exist or permissions are insufficient:

An error occurred (AccessDenied) when calling the ListBuckets operation: Access Denied

Step 4: Create an S3 Bucket

S3 bucket names must be globally unique. We can create a bucket as follows:

```
aws s3 mb s3://my-unique-rocky-linux-bucket
```

Expected Output: `make_bucket: s3://my-unique-rocky-linux-bucket/`

Step 5: Upload a File to S3

First, we create a local file to upload: **`echo "Hello, AWS CLI!" > hello.txt`**

Now upload it to the S3 bucket: **`aws s3 cp hello.txt s3://my-unique-rocky-linux-bucket`**

Expected Output:

```
upload: ./hello.txt to s3://my-unique-rocky-linux-bucket/hello.txt
```

Step 6: List Contents of a Bucket

We can list all files stored in the bucket: **`aws s3 ls s3://my-unique-rocky-linux-bucket`**

Expected Output:

```
2025-04-12 10:45:10        18 hello.txt
```

Step 7: Remove Files and Delete Bucket

To delete the uploaded file: **`aws s3 rm s3://my-unique-rocky-linux-bucket/hello.txt`**

Expected Output: **`delete: s3://my-unique-rocky-linux-bucket/hello.txt`**

To remove the empty bucket: **`aws s3 rb s3://my-unique-rocky-linux-bucket`**

Expected Output: **`remove_bucket: s3://my-unique-rocky-linux-bucket/`**

Step 8: Automate S3 Operations with a Script

We can automate the upload process using a shell script. First, create the script file:

```
nano s3_script.sh
```

Insert the following content:

```
#!/bin/bash

BUCKET_NAME="my-automated-bucket"
FILE_NAME="$1"

if [ ! -f "$FILE_NAME" ]; then
  echo "Error: File '$FILE_NAME' does not exist."
  exit 1
fi

aws s3 mb s3://$BUCKET_NAME
aws s3 cp "$FILE_NAME" s3://$BUCKET_NAME
aws s3 ls s3://$BUCKET_NAME
```

Make the script executable: **`chmod +x s3_script.sh`**

Now execute the script with a file name as the argument: **`./s3_script.sh hello.txt`**

Expected Output:

```
make_bucket: s3://my-automated-bucket/
upload: ./hello.txt to s3://my-automated-bucket/hello.txt
2025-04-12 10:50:00        18 hello.txt
```

```
[cesarmserver@RockyLinux ~]$ aws s3 ls
2024-11-19 18:55:41 cesarm-server
2024-11-19 20:24:07 kasparov-server
```

Figure 2.38: *Listing S3 Buckets Using the AWS CLI*

This figure displays the output of the **`aws s3 ls`** command executed on a Rocky Linux system. The command lists available Amazon S3 buckets associated with the configured AWS account. In the output, two buckets are displayed: **`cesarm-server and kasparov-server`**, each with its respective creation date and time.

This output highlights a basic yet essential use of the AWS Command Line Interface (CLI), a tool commonly used by cloud administrators to manage storage resources efficiently. By using simple commands like this, professionals can quickly inspect their cloud assets and automate routine tasks without relying on the AWS web console.

Issue	Possible Cause	Recommended Action
Access Denied	IAM user lacks permissions	Verify and update AWS IAM policy
Bucket already exists	Name is not globally unique	Choose a different bucket name
Command not found	CLI not installed properly	Reinstall AWS CLI and check $PATH
Upload fails silently	File name is incorrect	Use `ls` to verify the file exists

Table 2.7: *Troubleshooting Tips*

Table 2.7 presents a structured troubleshooting reference for common issues encountered when working with the AWS Command Line Interface (CLI) and Amazon S3. The table organizes problems into three columns: *Issue*, *Possible Cause*, and *Recommended Action*. For example, access errors may occur if an IAM user lacks permissions, in which case updating the AWS IAM policy is necessary. Similarly, bucket creation may fail if the chosen name is not globally unique, requiring the user to select a different name. Other entries cover situations such as the AWS CLI not being installed properly or file upload failures due to incorrect filenames. This concise guide provides administrators and developers with quick, actionable steps to resolve frequent operational problems efficiently.

Summary

In this section, we have learned how to:

- Install and verify the AWS CLI on Rocky Linux 9
- Configure AWS CLI with IAM credentials
- Create, list, and delete S3 buckets and objects
- Upload and remove files using AWS CLI commands
- Automate S3 interactions using shell scripting
- Confirm success through expected output feedback

These tasks demonstrate the practicality and efficiency of managing AWS services via the command line. This approach is especially valuable for administrators managing cloud infrastructure in automated or headless server environments.

Compatibility with Earlier Versions

Rocky Linux 9 introduces several architectural and repository-level changes that impact compatibility with earlier versions. Notably, in-place upgrades from Rocky Linux 8 to Rocky Linux 9 are not supported; users must perform a clean installation and manually migrate configurations and data. While Rocky Linux maintains API and ABI stability within a major release series, binary compatibility across major versions is not guaranteed. Additionally, repository structures have evolved—such as the replacement of the PowerTools repository with Code Ready Builder (CRB), which may affect package availability and naming conventions. Users transitioning from Rocky Linux 8 should validate package dependencies and system configurations to ensure a smooth migration.

Optional Validation Checklist

- Confirm that a clean installation of Rocky Linux 9 is planned
- Backup all critical data and configuration files from Rocky Linux 8

- Identify and verify availability of required packages in Rocky Linux 9
- Adjust repository configurations (e.g., enable CRB)
- Evaluate third-party applications for compatibility with Rocky Linux 9 APIs

Conclusion

In this chapter, essential command-line skills for system administration in Rocky Linux 9 were covered, ranging from basic terminal commands such as ls and cd to managing files and directories using tools such as `mkdir`, `nano`, and `rm`. The chapter also explored key output commands such as `cat`, `grep`, and `less`, and provided a clear understanding of file permissions and ownership.

Additionally, the chapter introduced the powerful `sudo` command, as well as system shutdown and reboot procedures–critical for maintaining system control and availability. The section on cloud-based CLI workflows with AWS offered valuable insights into managing cloud resources directly from the terminal.

As we move into *Chapter* 3, the focus will shift to **user management and permissions**, including how to create and manage user accounts, enforce access controls, and apply best practices for securing both local systems and cloud environments–particularly within AWS through IAM roles and user policies.

Points to Remember

- **Basic Terminal Commands:**
  - `ls`: List the contents of a directory.
  - `cd`: Change the current directory.
- **Managing Directories and Files:**
  - `mkdir`: Create a new directory.
  - `nano`: A text editor to create or modify files.
  - `rm`: Remove files or directories.
- **Output Commands:**
  - `cat`: Display the contents of a file.
  - `grep`: Search for patterns within files.
  - `less`: View file contents one page at a time.
- **File Permissions and Ownership:**
  - Understand file ownership (user, group, others) and permission levels (read, write, execute).
  - Use `chmod` to modify file permissions.
  - Use `chown` to change file ownership.
- **The `sudo` Command:**
  - Execute commands with superuser privileges.
  - Essential for performing administrative tasks that require elevated permissions.
- **System Shutdown and Reboot:**
  - Use commands such as shutdown, reboot, and poweroff to safely shut down or restart the system.
- **Cloud-Based CLI Workflows with AWS:**
  - Introduction to using command-line tools for managing AWS resources, such as EC2 instances, S3 buckets, and IAM users.

These points are fundamental for performing system administration tasks efficiently in Rocky Linux 9, with an introduction to cloud operations in AWS.

Multiple Choice Questions

1. Which command is used to list the contents of a directory in Rocky Linux 9?
   a. **cd**
   b. **ls**
   c. **pwd**
   d. **mkdir**
2. What does the **pwd** command do?
   a. Changes the current directory
   b. Lists files in a directory
   c. Prints the current working directory
   d. Deletes a file
3. Which command helps us to create a new directory in Rocky Linux 9?
   a. **rmdir**
   b. **mkdir**
   c. **touch**
   d. **rm**
4. How do we redirect the output of a command to a file?
   a. Using **|**
   b. Using **>**
   c. Using **<**
   d. Using **&**
5. What is the purpose of the **chmod** command?
   a. To change file permissions
   b. To change the owner of a file
   c. To display file contents
   d. To move files
6. Which command helps us to view the contents of a file one page at a time?
   a. **cat**
   b. **less**
   c. **nano**
   d. **vim**

7. What is the function of the **`export`** command?
    a. To list environment variables
    b. To set environment variables
    c. To delete environment variables
    d. To display system information
8. Which command is used to pass the output of one command as input to another?
    a. `>`
    b. `<`
    c. `|`
    d. `&`
9. What is the first line of a shell script called?
    a. Header
    b. Shebang
    c. Comment
    d. Directive
10. Which text editor is known for its simplicity and ease of use?
    a. vim
    b. nano
    c. emacs
    d. gedit

Answers

1. b
2. c
3. b
4. b
5. a
6. b
7. b
8. c
9. b
10. b

Questions

1. What is the primary function of the ls command?
2. What is the most effective method for changing directories in the command line?
3. Which command is used to create a new file?
4. How can the contents of a file be viewed without opening a text editor?
5. What is the purpose of the shebang (#!) in a script?
6. What is the recommended way to make a script executable?
7. What role do environment variables play in Linux systems?
8. How can multiple commands be executed in a single line?
9. What is the distinction between the > and >> symbols in output redirection?
10. How is an alias defined for a frequently used command?

Key Terms

- **Command Line Interface (CLI):** A text-based interface used to interact with the operating system.
- **Shell Script:** A script written for the shell, or command line interpreter, of an operating system.
- **Environment Variable:** A dynamic-named value that can affect the way of executing processes will behave on a computer.
- **Redirection:** The process of directing data from one output to another input.
- **Piping:** A method to pass the output of one command as input to another command.
- **Shebang (#!):** A character sequence at the beginning of a script indicating which interpreter should be used to run the script.
- **Alias:** A shortcut for a command or series of commands.
- **Permissions:** Settings that determine what an administrator or user can read, write, or execute for a file or directory.

CHAPTER 3
User Management and Permissions

Introduction

Effective user management is at the core of maintaining a secure and well-structured system environment. In today's digital landscape, systems must strike a balance between ease of access and robust security to safeguard sensitive data and critical resources. User management encompasses the creation, maintenance, and auditing of user accounts, groups, and permissions, assuring that only authorized individuals can access specific parts of the system, while also supporting the collaborative needs of a dynamic organization.

In both Rocky Linux and cloud-based environments, mastering user management is essential for system administrators and developers alike. This chapter provides a comprehensive exploration of user management principles and practices. We will cover the configuration and administration of user accounts and groups in Rocky Linux, delve into file permissions and Access Control Lists (ACLs), and examine the importance of time and date management in user activity auditing.

Furthermore, we will explore user management in cloud environments, particularly focusing on scalable and distributed access control using tools such as AWS IAM. By the end of this chapter, a solid foundation for managing users effectively would have been built across local and cloud infrastructures, ensuring both security and operational efficiency.

Structure

In this chapter, we will discuss the following topics:

- User Management in Rocky Linux
- Managing User Accounts and Groups
- File Permissions and ACLs
- Time and Date Management
- User Management in Cloud Environments

User Management in Rocky Linux

User management is a fundamental aspect of maintaining a secure and efficient system.

Rocky Linux provides robust tools to manage user accounts effectively. This section introduces the basics of adding and deleting user accounts, enabling administrators to create and remove users securely while maintaining system integrity.

In Rocky Linux, user accounts are essential for controlling access to resources and defining permissions. By understanding how to manage users, administrators can ensure that only authorized personnel have access to specific files, applications, and processes.

- **Adding and Deleting Users:** In Linux systems, user accounts can be managed using commands such as useradd and userdel. These commands allow administrators to add and remove users efficiently.
    - To add a user: **`sudo useradd -m -s /bin/bash username`**
    - To delete a user: **`sudo userdel -r username`**
- **Managing User Passwords:** Passwords are a critical component of user security. Administrators can use the **`passwd`** command to set or change passwords. Tools such as chage can enforce password strength and expiration policies.
- **Working with User Groups:** Groups enable easier management of permissions for multiple users. Commands such as **`groupadd`** and **`usermod`** are used to create and manage groups.
    - To add a user to a group: **`sudo usermod -aG groupname username`**
    - To view group memberships: **`groups username`**

User Management (Part 1: `useradd`, `groupadd`, `passwd`)

1. Adding a User (**`useradd`**)

    a. **`sudo useradd Tyvon`**

    b. **`sudo passwd Tyvon`**

    Root privileges (**`sudo`**) are required to execute these commands. A password should be set for the user after creation.

2. Creating a Group (**`groupadd`**)

    ```
    sudo groupadd newgroup
    ```

    Root privileges are required.

3. Adding a User to a Group (**`usermod`**)

    ```
    sudo usermod -aG newgroup Tyvon
    ```

    - **`-a`:** Append the user to the supplementary group(s).
    - **`-G`:** Specify the group(s) to add the user to.

4. Additional Practice

    ```
    sudo groupadd test3
    sudo usermod -aG test3 cmorera
    ```

    This adds the user **`cmorera`** to the **`test3`** group.

5. Validate Group Membership

    ```
    cat /etc/group | grep cmorera
    ```

    Example output:

    ```
    wheel:x:10:cmorera
    cmorera:x:1000:
    test3:x:1003:cmorera
    ```

6. Understanding **`usermod`** Options

    - **`-a`:** Append user to the group(s) specified with **`-G`**.
    - **`-G`:** List of supplementary groups.
    - **`-g`:** Sets the user's default group.

7. Common Mistakes

    - Using lowercase **`-g`** instead of **`-G`** can overwrite group memberships.

- Always verify memberships: **groups <username>**
  groups cmorera

Example output:

```
cmorera : cmorera wheel test3
```

Managing User Accounts and Groups

Managing user accounts and groups is a central responsibility for system administrators, enabling efficient control over system access and resource usage. In Rocky Linux, user and group management helps ensure that each user has appropriate permissions, access is logically segmented, and administrative oversight is maintained. By organizing users into groups, administrators can streamline permission assignments, making it easier to enforce security policies across departments or roles. This section delves into essential commands and practices for managing user accounts, including creating, modifying, and deleting users and groups. It also explores how to assign users to multiple groups, adjust group privileges, and validate membership. Understanding these concepts is vital for maintaining system integrity, enforcing least-privilege access, and preparing for more advanced permission models using file permissions and ACLs.

1. **Deleting a User (userdel)**

```
sudo userdel -r Tyvon
```

The -r option removes the user's home directory and mail spool.

2. **Deleting a Group (groupdel)**

```
sudo groupdel newgroup
```

This command only works if the group is not in use.

Example Output:

```
cat /etc/group | grep newgroup
# Check if group exists
```

- `sudo groupdel newgroup`
- `cat /etc/group | grep newgroup`

```
# Confirm deletion
```

3. **Modifying Group Membership (usermod)**

```
sudo useradd Sarah
sudo groupadd Finance
sudo usermod -G Sarah,wheel,Finance Sarah
```

Use groups **Sarah** to verify:

- `groups Sarah`
- `Sarah : Sarah wheel Finance`

This section provides a foundational understanding of managing users and groups in Rocky Linux. Readers have learned how to:

a. Add and delete users (**useradd, userdel**)

b. Create and manage groups (**groupadd, groupdel**)

c. Modify group memberships (**usermod**)

Efficiently managing users and groups is essential for organizing system resources, controlling access, and maintaining security. Mastery of these skills prepares administrators for advanced system configurations.

File Permissions and ACLs

In this section, we explore how to manage file permissions and implement Access Control Lists (ACLs) to achieve granular control over file access. File permissions are fundamental in securing Linux systems, and ACLs provide flexibility beyond the traditional permission model.

Understanding File Permissions on Linux

Linux uses a permission model based on three categories:

- **User (Owner)**
- **Group**
- **Others**

Each category has three permission types:

- **Read (r)**: Allows reading file contents.
- **Write (w)**: Allows modifying file contents.
- **Execute (x)**: Allows executing a file or accessing a directory.

Permissions can be viewed using the `ls -l` command:

Example output:

```
[cmorera@localhost Downloads]$ ls -l
total 0
drwxr-xr-x. 2 cmorera cmorera 6 Apr 20 12:54 dir1
drwxr-xr-x. 2 cmorera cmorera 6 Apr 20 12:54 dir2
drwxr-xr-x. 2 cmorera cmorera 6 Apr 20 12:54 dir3
-rw-r--r--. 1 cmorera cmorera 0 Apr 20 12:53 file1
-rw-r--r--. 1 cmorera cmorera 0 Apr 20 12:53 file2
-rw-r--r--. 1 cmorera cmorera 0 Apr 20 12:53 file3
```

Figure 3.1: *Listing Contents of the Current Directory*

Figure 3.1 shows the output of the `ls -l` command, which provides a detailed listing of the contents in the Downloads directory. In this example, there are three **directories (`dir1`, `dir2`,** and **`dir3`)** and three **regular files (`file1`, `file2`,** and **`file3`).** Each entry begins with a set of characters indicating the file type and permissions: directories start with d (for example, **`drwxr-xr-x`**), meaning the owner has full permissions, while the group and others have read and execute permissions; regular files start with - (for example, **`-rw-r--r--`**), granting read and write access to the owner and read-only access to the group and others. The third and fourth columns display the file owner and group, both listed as **`cmorera`.** The file size appears in bytes, and the final columns show the last modification date and time. This command is widely used for examining file attributes and managing access in a Unix-like system.

```
-rwxr-xr--  3  alice  staff  4096  Aug 15 14:30  example.txt
|          | |    |       |      |           |          |
|          | |    |       |      |           |          +-- 7. File name
|          | |    |       |      |           +------------- 6. Last modified (date & time)
|          | |    |       |      +------------------------- 5. File size (bytes)
|          | |    |       +-------------------------------- 4. Group
|          | |    +---------------------------------------- 3. User (owner)
|          | +--------------------------------------------- 2. Hard link count
|          +----------------------------------------------- 1. File type & permissions
|
+-- File type & permissions legend:
    - First character: file type
      - `-` = regular file
      - `d` = directory
      - `l` = symbolic link
    - Next nine characters: permissions in sets of three
      - `rwx` = read, write, execute for user (owner)
      - `r-x` = read, execute for group
      - `r--` = read only for others
```

Figure 3.2: *ls -l Output Diagram*

Figure 3.2 presents the structure of the `ls -l` command output, which provides detailed information about files and directories in a Unix-like system. Each line in the output corresponds to a file or directory and includes several key fields. The first field indicates the file type and permissions: the initial character shows whether the item is a regular file (`-`), directory (`d`), or symbolic link (`l`), followed by permission bits for the owner, group, and others. The second field displays the number of hard links, typically 1 for files and 2 or more for directories. The third and fourth fields represent the file owner and associated group. The fifth field shows the file size in bytes, while the sixth displays the last modification date and time. The final field is the file name. This output format is fundamental for understanding file attributes, managing access rights, and maintaining system organization.

Quick Legend:

- **File type and permissions:**`-rwxr-xr--`
  - `-` : **file, d** = directory, `l` = link
  - `rwx` : read/write/execute for user
  - `r-x` : read/execute for group
  - `r--` : read for others
- **Hard link count:** Usually 1 for files, 2+ for directories
- **User:** Owner of the file
- **Group:** Group associated with the file
- **File size** : In bytes
- **Last modified** : Date and time of last change
- **File name** : Self-explanatory

Changing File Permissions

Managing file permissions is a critical part of system administration in Rocky Linux. Properly configured permissions ensure that users have appropriate access to files and directories, thereby maintaining system security and functionality. Permissions can be changed using the **chmod** (change mode) command, which supports both symbolic and numeric modes for flexibility.

Symbolic Mode: Symbolic mode offers a user-friendly way to manage file permissions by using readable characters and operators to modify access rights for different user categories:

- u: user (file owner)
- g : group
- o : others
- a : all (user, group, and others)

Operators used in symbolic mode:

- + : adds a permission
- - : removes a permission
- = : explicitly sets a permission

Using chmod command: The **chmod** command modifies permissions. It can be used in two modes: symbolic and numeric.

Symbolic Mode:

```
chmod u+w example.txt   # Adds write permission for the owner
chmod g-x example.txt   # Removes execute permission for the group
chmod o+r example.txt   # Adds read permission for others
```

Figure 3.3: *Symbolic Mode Options*

Figure 3.3 illustrates the various symbolic mode options available, showing how administrators can modify file permissions efficiently. This approach is especially useful in multi-user environments, where precise control over file access is essential for security and collaboration.

In Rocky Linux, managing file permissions is a crucial aspect of system administration, and symbolic mode provides an intuitive way to adjust permissions. Symbolic mode uses a combination of letters and symbols to represent user categories (owner, group, others) and permission types (read, write, execute). For example, commands such as **chmod u+x** or **chmod g-w** enable or restrict specific permissions for users or groups.

Numeric Mode: In numeric mode, permissions are represented by three-digit numbers, where each digit reflects the cumulative value of permissions for the user, group, and others:

- **Read (r)** = 4
- **Write (w)** = 2
- **Execute (x)** = 1

Each digit is a sum of applicable permissions:

Example: `chmod 754 example.txt`

This assigns:

- **7 (4+2+1)** → Owner has read, write, and execute permissions (**rwx**)
- **5 (4+0+1)** → Group has read and execute permissions (**r-x**)
- **4 (4+0+0)** → Others have read-only access (**r--**)

Numeric mode is concise and commonly used in scripts and automation.

Changing Ownership with `chown`: The **`chown`** (change owner) command allows administrators to transfer ownership of files to a different user or group. This is essential when reassigning file responsibilities or modifying access rights during user transitions.

The chown command changes file ownership:

Example workflow:

- **`sudo useradd newuser`**
- **`sudo groupadd newgroup`**
- `mkdir` **`Symbolic_Mode`**
- **`sudo chown newuser:newgroup Symbolic_Mode`**

This changes the ownership of the file **`Symbolic_Mode`** to the user newuser and group newgroup. To verify the change: **`ls -l`**, all contents will be displayed.

```
[cmorera@localhost Downloads]$ ls -l
total 0
drwxr-xr-x. 2 cmorera cmorera  6 Apr 20 12:54 dir1
drwxr-xr-x. 2 cmorera cmorera  6 Apr 20 12:54 dir2
drwxr-xr-x. 2 cmorera cmorera  6 Apr 20 12:54 dir3
-rw-r--r--. 1 cmorera cmorera  0 Apr 20 12:53 file1
-rw-r--r--. 1 cmorera cmorera  0 Apr 20 12:53 file2
-rw-r--r--. 1 cmorera cmorera  0 Apr 20 12:53 file3
drwxr-xr-x. 2 newuser newgroup 6 Apr 20 14:33 Symbolic_Mode
```

Figure 3.4: *Listing Contents with ls -l*

The output of the **`ls -l`** command provides detailed information about each item's properties, including permissions, ownership, size, and last modification date. In this case, **`Symbolic_Mode`** is a directory, as indicated by the leading "**`d`**" in its permission string **(`drwxr-xr-x.`)**. The permissions show that the owner **(`newuser`)** has read, write, and execute permissions; the group **(`newgroup`)** has read and execute permissions; and others also have read and execute permissions. The **number 2** represents the **count of hard links** to the directory. The size shown is **6 bytes,** which is standard for an empty directory. It was last modified on **April 20 at 14:33.** This output offers a useful snapshot of the directory's attributes, which can be modified using symbolic mode to adjust permissions for different users and groups.

Using Access Control Lists (ACLs): ACLs provide more granular control over file permissions by allowing specific rules for individual users or groups. Tools such as **`setfacl`** and **`getfacl`** are used to configure and view ACLs. This section maintains the original structure but explains each step more clearly and simply.

Objectives

- ACLs functionality and reason to be used.
- The best way to view, export, edit, and reapply ACLs using Linux commands.
- How to manually edit ACLs using a text editor such as nano.

Introduction to ACLs

Traditional Linux permissions (owner-group-others) can sometimes be limiting, especially in shared environments. ACLs let us define permissions for multiple users or groups beyond that basic model.

Examples of the ACLs functions:

- Give a specific user read-only access to a file.
- Allow a group to write to a file, while others can only read.

Main ACL commands:

- **`getfacl`:** view or export current ACLs.
- **`setfacl`:** set or modify ACL rules.

To enable and configure Access Control Lists (ACLs) in Rocky Linux 9, follow these steps:

1. **Install the Required ACL Packages:** First, ensure the necessary ACL tools are installed. It can be installed using the DNF command:

   ```
   [cmorera@localhost Downloads]$sudo dnf install acl
   ```

2. **Enable ACL Support on File Systems:** By default, Access Control List (ACL) support may not be enabled on all file systems. To determine whether ACL is active, run the following command:

   ```
   [cmorera@localhost Downloads]$mount | grep acl
   ```

   If the output does not display the acl mount option for the desired file system, it indicates that ACL is not currently enabled. In such a case, the **`/etc/fstab`** file must be modified accordingly.

3. **Open the `/etc/fstab` file** with a text editor using administrative privileges:

   ```
   [cmorera@localhost Downloads]$sudo nano /etc/fstab
   ```

Identify the line corresponding to the desired filesystem (for example, the root partition /) in the **`/etc/fstab`** file. Add the acl option to the mount parameters. Below is an example entry for the root filesystem:

The following code will now be added at the end of the document.

```
/dev/mapper/rockylinux-root  /  ext4  defaults,acl  1  1
```

```
  GNU nano 5.6.1                                          /etc/fstab

#
# /etc/fstab
# Created by anaconda on Sat Jan 18 22:38:37 2025
#
# Accessible filesystems, by reference, are maintained under '/dev/disk/'.
# See man pages fstab(5), findfs(8), mount(8) and/or blkid(8) for more info.
#
# After editing this file, run 'systemctl daemon-reload' to update systemd
# units generated from this file.
#
/dev/mapper/rl-root     /                       xfs     defaults        0 0
UUID=3e32ec89-f060-4a12-917b-02a319410266 /boot                   xfs     defaults        0 0
/dev/mapper/rl-swap     none                    swap    defaults        0 0
/dev/mapper/rockylinux-root  /  ext4  defaults,acl  1  1
```

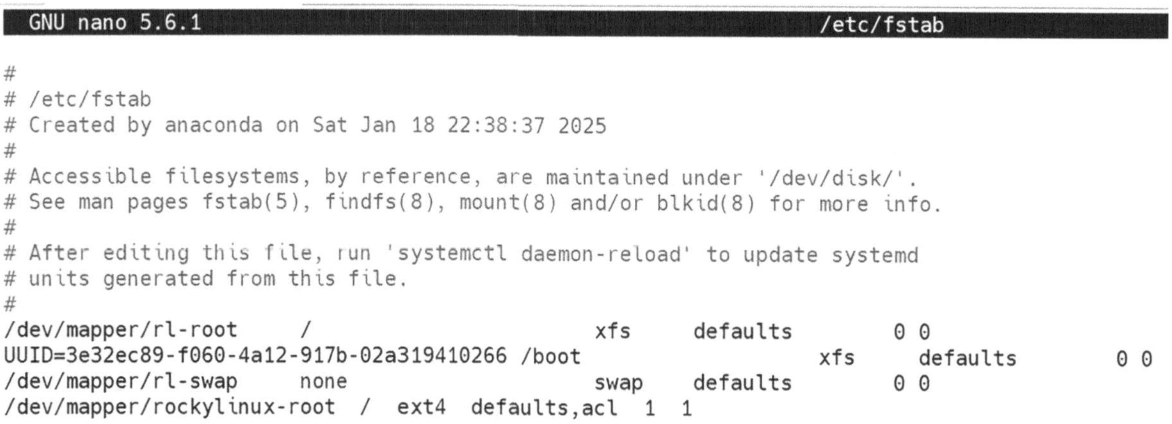

***Figure* 3.5:** *ACL Extension Update*

Figure 3.5 illustrates the process of updating Access Control List (ACL) extensions on a file or directory. ACLs provide a more granular level of control over file permissions compared to traditional Unix permissions. By extending the standard user-group-other model, ACLs allow administrators to assign specific permissions to individual users or groups. This update procedure involves modifying the ACL of a file or directory to either add or change permissions for different users or groups. With ACLs, it is possible to define more complex access rules, such as granting read or write permissions to multiple users or groups, while keeping the standard permissions intact. This method enhances security and flexibility in managing file access, especially in environments with more complex permission requirements.

- Save the file and exit the editor.
- Remount the filesystem to apply the changes:

The following command should be executed: **sudo systemctl daemon-reload**. This will, in fact, reload the daemon's specific process and apply the changes being modified in the ACL.

```
[cmorera@localhost Downloads]$sudo systemctl daemon-reload
```

4. **Verify if ACL is enabled using: getfacl Symbolic_Mode.**

```
[cesarmserver@localhost ~]$ getfacl Symbolic_Mode
# file: Symbolic_Mode
# owner: newuser
# group: newgroup
user::rw-
group::r--
other::r--
```

Figure 3.6: *Validating ACL*

Figure 3.6 demonstrates the process of validating ACL settings on a file or directory. After updating the ACL, it is essential to verify that the changes have been applied correctly. This can be done using the ***getfacl*** command, which displays the current ACLs associated with a file or directory. Validating ACLs ensures that the intended permissions for specific users or groups are accurately enforced, providing an added layer of security and control. This step is crucial for confirming that access rights align with organizational policies and user needs.

Configuring ACLs on Files or Directories

Once ACLs are enabled on a file system, we can apply them to files or directories using the **setfacl** command.

1. **Set ACL for a user on a file or directory:**

```
sudo setfacl -m u:username:rwx /path/to/file_or_directory
sudo setfacl -m u:cmorera:rwx Symbolic_Mode
```

In this example, username will get read, write, and execute permissions on the file or directory at **/path/to/file_or_directory**.

2. **Set ACL for a group on a file or directory:**

```
sudo setfacl -m g:groupname:rx /path/to/file_or_directory
sudo setfacl -m g:newgroup:rx Symbolic_Mode
ls -l
```

```
[cmorera@localhost Downloads]$ sudo setfacl -m g:newgroup:rx Symbolic_Mode
[cmorera@localhost Downloads]$ ls -l
total 0
drwxr-xr-x. 2 cmorera cmorera  6 Apr 20 12:54 dir1
drwxr-xr-x. 2 cmorera cmorera  6 Apr 20 12:54 dir2
drwxr-xr-x. 2 cmorera cmorera  6 Apr 20 12:54 dir3
-rw-r--r--. 1 cmorera cmorera  0 Apr 20 12:53 file1
-rw-r--r--. 1 cmorera cmorera  0 Apr 20 12:53 file2
-rw-r--r--. 1 cmorera cmorera  0 Apr 20 12:53 file3
drwxrwxr-x+ 2 newuser newgroup 6 Apr 20 14:33 Symbolic_Mode
```

Figure 3.7: *Setting up the ACL and Listing Contents*

Figure 3.7 illustrates the process of setting up an ACL and listing its contents. Setting up an ACL involves defining specific permissions for individual users or groups on a file or directory, beyond the standard user-group-other model. This is done using the **setfacl** command, which allows administrators to assign read, write, or execute permissions to specific users or groups. After setting the ACL, the **ls -l** command can be used to list the contents and verify that the ACL has been applied correctly. This combination of setting and verifying ACLs ensures precise control over file access, enabling more flexible and detailed permission management in complex environments.

This command grants read and execute permissions to the group **groupname** on the specified file or directory.

Verifying the ACL Settings

To verify the ACL settings on a file or directory, use the **getfacl** command:

```
getfacl Symbolic_Mode
```

```
[cmorera@localhost Downloads]$ getfacl Symbolic_Mode
# file: Symbolic_Mode
# owner: newuser
# group: newgroup
user::rwx
user:cmorera:rwx
group::r-x
group:newgroup:r-x
mask::rwx
other::r-x
```

Figure 3.8: *Verify ACL Updates*

Figure 3.8 demonstrates the process of verifying updates to an Access Control List (ACL) after changes have been made. Once ACLs are modified using the **setfacl** command, it is crucial to confirm that the updates were successfully applied. This can be done by using the **getfacl** command, which displays the current ACL settings for the specified file or directory. Verifying ACL updates ensures that the intended permissions are correctly enforced for the specified users or groups, allowing administrators to maintain accurate and secure access controls. This step is vital for confirming that any modifications to file or directory access have been implemented as planned.

This will show the ACLs applied to the specified file or directory.

Removing ACLs: To remove an ACL entry from a file or directory, use the following command:

- `sudo setfacl -x u:username /path/to/file_or_directory`
- `sudo setfacl -x u:cmorera Symbolic_Mode`
- `sudo setfacl -x u:cmorera Symbolic_Mode`

This removes the ACL for the specified user. It is recommended to use **-b** to remove all ACL entries from a file:

```
sudo setfacl -b /path/to/file_or_directory
sudo setfacl -b Symbolic_Mode
Additional Notes:
```

When working with directories and wanting new files to inherit ACLs, the default ACL can be set.

- `sudo setfacl -m d:u:username:rwx /path/to/directory.`
- `mkdir ACLs_test`
- `sudo setfacl -m d:u:cmorera:rwx ACLs_test`
- `getfacl ACLs_test`

```
[cmorera@localhost Downloads]$ mkdir ACLs_test
[cmorera@localhost Downloads]$ sudo setfacl -m d:u:cmorera:rwx ACLs_test
[cmorera@localhost Downloads]$ getfacl ACLs_test
# file: ACLs_test
# owner: cmorera
# group: cmorera
user::rwx
group::r-x
other::r-x
default:user::rwx
default:user:cmorera:rwx
default:group::r-x
default:mask::rwx
default:other::r-x
```

Figure 3.9: *Creating ACL and Permissions*

Figure 3.9 illustrates the process of creating an Access Control List (ACL) and setting specific permissions for a file or directory. This process begins by using the **setfacl** command to assign detailed access rights, such as read, write, or execute permissions, to individual users or groups. ACLs enable more granular control over file access compared to traditional Unix permissions. By specifying which users or groups have specific permissions, administrators can tailor access control to meet the needs of different users while maintaining security. Once the ACL is set, the **getfacl** command can be used to verify the applied permissions, ensuring that the correct access rights have been granted. This step is essential for creating a flexible and secure permission structure.

Creating a Test File and Updating Permissions

Create a Test File: Let us create a file to work with and set some basic permissions.

1. Open the terminal and create a test file:

```
[cmorera@localhost Downloads]$touch example_file
```

2. Assign some default permissions:

```
[cmorera@localhost Downloads]$chmod 644 example_file
```

This makes the file readable and writable by the owner, and readable by the group and others.

View Existing ACLs: Before editing, let us see the ACLs applied to the file:

3. Run the `getfacl` command: **getfacl example_file**

Example output:

```
[cmorera@localhost Downloads]$getfacl example_file
# file : example_file
# owner : example_file
# group: example_file
user::rw-
group::r - -
other::r - -
```

- **user::rw-** : means the owner has read and write permissions.
- **group::r--** : means the group has read-only access.
- **other::r--** : means others can only read the file.

Export ACLs to a Text File: Export the ACLs into a file so we can edit them:

4. Use `getfacl` to save the ACL rules into a file: **getfacl example_file > acl_backup.txt**

```
[cmorera@localhost Downloads]$getfacl example_file > acl_backup.txt
```

5. Verify the content of the exported file by running: **cat acl_backup.txt**

```
[cmorera@localhost Downloads]$cat acl_backup.txt
# file : example_file
# owner : cmorera
# group: cmorera
user::rw-
group::r - -
other::r - -
```

The same output, as the `getfacl` command, will now be shown.

Edit the ACL File with nano: Now, let us modify the permissions by editing the exported ACL file.

6. Open the `acl_backup.txt` file in nano: **nano acl_backup.txt**

```
[cmorera@localhost Downloads]$nano acl_backup.txt
```

7. Inside nano, the following output will now be available:

```
 GNU nano 5.6.1                                           acl_backup.txt
# file: example_file
# owner: cmorera
# group: cmorera
user:: rw-
group :: r--
other :: r--
```

Figure 3.10: *acl_backup.txt contents*

Figure 3.10 displays the contents of the **acl_backup.txt** file, which is used to store the Access Control List (ACL) configurations of files or directories. Backing up ACLs is an important practice for preserving the specific access permissions set on critical files and directories. By using the **getfacl** command, the current ACL settings can be exported and saved to a text file such as **acl_backup.txt.** This file contains detailed information about the ACL, including the users, groups, and the corresponding permissions assigned to each. Storing ACL configurations in this manner ensures that access control settings can be easily restored in case of system recovery or migration, maintaining consistency in file access permissions across environments.

8. **Make** the following changes:
   a. Add permissions for a user in this file to allow reading and writing: **user::rw-**
   b. Restrict public (others) access entirely: **other:: ---**

New code:

```
# file: example_file
# owner: cmorera
# group: wheel
user::rwx
user:cmorera:rwx
group::r--
```

```
group:wheel:r--
mask::rwx
other::r–
```

9. **Save** the file in nano:
   a. Press `*Ctrl* + O` to save the file.
   b. Press `*Enter*` to confirm the filename.
   c. Press `*Ctrl* + X` to exit nano.
10. **Apply the Modified ACLs**: Now, let us apply the changes back to the file:

Use the `**setfacl**` command to restore the ACLs from the modified file:

```
setfacl --restore=acl_backup.txt
[cmorera@localhost Downloads]$setfacl - - restore=acl_backup.txt
```

11. **Verify the Changes**: Let us confirm the new ACLs have been applied:
    a. Run the **getfacl** command again: **getfacl example_file**
    b. The updated ACLs will now be displayed:

```
[cmorera@localhost Downloads]$ getfacl example_file
# file: example_file
# owner: cmorera
# group: cmorera
user::rw-
group::r--
other::r--
```

Figure 3.11: *Updated ACL*

Figure 3.11 illustrates the updated Access Control List (ACL) for a file or directory after modifications have been made. The ACL shows the new permissions assigned to specific users or groups, reflecting any changes made through the **setfacl** command. This updated configuration provides a detailed overview of which users and groups have specific read, write, or execute permissions on the file or directory. By reviewing the updated ACL, administrators can ensure that the correct access levels are enforced and that any security policies are accurately implemented. This step is essential for maintaining secure and efficient permission management within a system.

Quick ACL Changes with setfacl

We can modify ACLs directly using the **setfacl** command, without exporting or editing a separate file.

1. **Add a user and grant read/write access to a file:**

```
sudo useradd john
setfacl -m u:john:rw example_file
```

2. **Remove all permissions for the user:**

```
setfacl -x u:john example_file
```

3. **View current ACLs for a file:**

```
getfacl example_file
```

These quick commands help us grant or revoke access efficiently, without going through the full export-edit-import process. Practicing both methods will strengthen our skills in managing Linux file permissions.

Time and Date Management

Effective time and date management is a fundamental aspect of Linux server administration. Maintaining accurate system time is essential for ensuring consistent log entries, reliable execution of scheduled tasks, and proper coordination across distributed systems. Inaccurate time settings can lead to issues with authentication mechanisms, service synchronization, data integrity, and troubleshooting.

In Rocky Linux, system time is controlled using the **timedatectl** utility, which provides a centralized interface for configuring time, date, and time zone settings. It also allows administrators to manage time synchronization using the Network Time Protocol (NTP), helping ensure that servers remain synchronized with accurate external time sources.

Key time management capabilities in Rocky Linux include:

- Setting and adjusting the system clock
- Configuring the appropriate time zone
- Enabling or disabling NTP synchronization

Understanding System Time Concepts

- **System Clock:** The time maintained by the operating system.
- **Hardware Clock:** The time maintained by the BIOS/firmware, independent of the operating system.
- **Network Time Protocol (NTP):** Synchronizes the system clock with an accurate time source over the internet.

Commands Overview:

- **timedatectl:** Used to manage time, date, and NTP settings.
- **hwclock:** Used to view or set the hardware clock.

Examples and Practical Steps

1. **Check the Current Time and Date:** Run the following command to view the system time, time zone, and NTP status: **timedatectl**

Example Output:

```
[cmorera@localhost Downloads]$ timedatectl
               Local time: Sun 2025-04-20 15:20:40 CST
           Universal time: Sun 2025-04-20 21:20:40 UTC
                 RTC time: Sun 2025-04-20 21:20:40
                Time zone: America/Costa_Rica (CST, -0600)
System clock synchronized: yes
              NTP service: active
          RTC in local TZ: no
```

Figure 3.12: *timedatectl output*

Figure 3.12 shows the output of the **timedatectl** command, which provides detailed information about the system's time and date settings. This output includes the current system time, the time zone, and whether the system is using NTP to synchronize its clock. Additionally, it displays information about the local time and universal time (UTC). The **timedatectl** command is useful for managing and configuring time settings on a Linux system, allowing administrators to adjust the time zone, enable or disable NTP, and verify the system's clock configuration. This helps ensure that the system's time is accurate and consistent with external time sources.

2. **Set the System Time**

To manually set the system time, use the **`timedatectl set-time`** command:

```
sudo timedatectl set-ntp false
sudo timedatectl set-time "2024-11-27 15:00:00"
```

Verify the updated time with: **`timedatectl`**

3. **Change the Time Zone:** List of available time zones with: **`timedatectl list-timezones`**

```
[cmorera@localhost Downloads]$ timedatectl list-timezones
Africa/Abidjan
Africa/Accra
Africa/Addis_Ababa
Africa/Algiers
Africa/Asmara
Africa/Asmera
Africa/Bamako
Africa/Bangui
Africa/Banjul
Africa/Bissau
Africa/Blantyre
Africa/Brazzaville
Africa/Bujumbura
Africa/Cairo
Africa/Casablanca
Africa/Ceuta
Africa/Conakry
Africa/Dakar
Africa/Dar_es_Salaam
Africa/Djibouti
Africa/Douala
Africa/El_Aaiun
Africa/Freetown
Africa/Gaborone
Africa/Harare
```

Figure 3.13: *Timezone Information*

Figure 3.13 presents information about time zones on the system, typically displayed by the **`timedatectl list-timezones`** command. This output provides a comprehensive list of all available time zones that can be configured on the system. Time zones are essential for ensuring that the system's time matches the geographic location in which it operates. The list includes various regions and cities, making it easy for administrators to select the appropriate time zone for the system. Configuring the correct time zone ensures accurate timestamps for logs, scheduled tasks, and other time-dependent processes, helping to maintain synchronization across systems and networks.

4. **Enable/Disable Network Time Synchronization:** To enable NTP synchronization (recommended): **`sudo timedatectl set-ntp true`**

To disable NTP synchronization: **`sudo timedatectl set-ntp false`**

- Scroll through or search for the desired time zone (for example, `` `America/New_York` ``) and set it:

  ```
  sudo timedatectl set-timezone America/New_York
  sudo timedatectl set-timezone America/Costa_Rica
  ```

Verify the updated time zone: **`timedatectl`**

```
[cmorera@localhost Downloads]$ sudo timedatectl set-ntp false
[sudo] password for cmorera:
[cmorera@localhost Downloads]$ sudo timedatectl set-ntp true
[cmorera@localhost Downloads]$ sudo timedatectl set-timezone America/New_York
[cmorera@localhost Downloads]$ timedatectl
               Local time: Sun 2025-04-20 17:26:14 EDT
           Universal time: Sun 2025-04-20 21:26:14 UTC
                 RTC time: Sun 2025-04-20 21:26:14
                Time zone: America/New_York (EDT, -0400)
System clock synchronized: yes
              NTP service: active
          RTC in local TZ: no
[cmorera@localhost Downloads]$ sudo timedatectl set-timezone America/Costa_Rica
[cmorera@localhost Downloads]$ timedatectl
               Local time: Sun 2025-04-20 15:26:30 CST
           Universal time: Sun 2025-04-20 21:26:30 UTC
                 RTC time: Sun 2025-04-20 21:26:30
                Time zone: America/Costa_Rica (CST, -0600)
System clock synchronized: yes
              NTP service: active
          RTC in local TZ: no
```

Figure 3.14: *NTP Synchronization*

Figure 3.14 displays NTP synchronization after applying the time-related configuration commands, showcasing the updated system time settings. This output confirms that the time zone has been successfully adjusted, NTP synchronization has been enabled (if applicable), and the system's time is correctly aligned with the selected time zone. The display typically includes the current local time, universal time (UTC), and the status of time synchronization. This verification step is crucial to ensure that the system's time configuration is accurate and functioning as expected, supporting tasks such as logging, scheduling, and system monitoring with the correct time settings.

5. **Working with the Hardware Clock:** The hardware clock (RTC) runs independently of the operating system.

   a. Check the hardware clock:

   ```
   [cmorera@localhost Downloads]$sudo hwclock --show
   2025-04-20 15:29:47.107438-06:00
   ```

   b. Synchronize the hardware clock with the system clock:

   ```
   [cmorera@localhost Downloads]$sudo hwclock --systohc
   ```

   c. Synchronize the system clock with the hardware clock:

   ```
   [cmorera@localhost Downloads]$sudo hwclock -hctosys
   ```

6. **Automating Time Synchronization with Chrony:** Rocky Linux uses Chrony as the default tool for **Network Time Protocol (NTP)** synchronization, providing a reliable and efficient solution for maintaining accurate system time. Chrony is designed to be lightweight and highly flexible, making it especially well-suited for servers that may have intermittent internet connectivity or environments where time synchronization must be highly resilient.

Unlike traditional NTP daemons, Chrony is optimized for systems that are frequently disconnected from the network or that experience network delays, such as virtual machines, embedded devices, or systems in remote locations.

Chrony works by keeping the system clock synchronized with an NTP server, adjusting for any drifts in the system clock, and ensuring that time discrepancies are minimized. One of its key features is its ability to quickly adjust the system clock to match the correct time, even after the system has been offline for extended periods, providing a smoother and more reliable experience in environments with unstable network conditions. Additionally, **Chrony** can operate in both client and server modes, allowing it to serve time to other machines in the network if needed.

In Rocky Linux, **Chrony** can be configured through the **chrony.conf** file or via the **chronyc** command-line tool, which allows administrators to monitor the synchronization process, view statistics, and manage the NTP servers. The service is often enabled by default during installation, ensuring that system time is synchronized correctly from the moment the system is set up.

Chrony also provides enhanced security features, such as preventing unauthorized time servers from being used, and its ability to handle more accurate time corrections when there are significant discrepancies between the system time and the actual time. This makes it an excellent choice for both small-scale and large-scale server environments required.

a. Install Chrony: **sudo dnf install chrony -y**

b. Start and enable Chrony:

```
sudo systemctl start chronyd
sudo systemctl enable chronyd
```

c. Verify synchronization: **chronyc tracking**

```
[cmorera@localhost Downloads]$ chronyc tracking
Reference ID    : 8FCAA0A2 (irazu.impulsahosting.com)
Stratum         : 3
Ref time (UTC)  : Sun Apr 20 21:33:03 2025
System time     : 0.000153900 seconds fast of NTP time
Last offset     : -0.000097368 seconds
RMS offset      : 0.004156073 seconds
Frequency       : 16.826 ppm fast
Residual freq   : -0.212 ppm
Skew            : 3.260 ppm
Root delay      : 0.012348492 seconds
Root dispersion : 0.025558054 seconds
Update interval : 64.9 seconds
Leap status     : Normal
```

Figure 3.15: *chronyc tracking*

Figure 3.15 shows the output of the **chronyc tracking** command, which provides detailed information about the system's time synchronization status using Chrony. This command displays key metrics such as the system's current time offset, the estimated error, the time source being used, and the system's drift rate. It also provides information about the performance of the NTP servers or sources that Chrony is using to synchronize the system clock. The output is valuable for administrators to monitor the accuracy of the time synchronization process and to ensure that the system's clock is being corrected as needed. By using **chronyc tracking**, administrators can verify that Chrony is functioning correctly and adjust configurations if necessary to improve time accuracy and reliability.

d. Manually force synchronization:

```
[cmorera@localhost Downloads]$sudo chronyc makestep
200 OK
```

To ensure accurate time management on a system, it is essential to follow best practices such as always enabling **Network Time Protocol (NTP)** for reliable time synchronization. This ensures the system clock remains in sync with external time sources. Additionally, it is important to configure the appropriate time zone based on the server's physical location, preventing discrepancies in timestamps and scheduled tasks. Regularly checking the alignment between the system clock and hardware clock can help identify any potential issues early. Automating time synchronization with tools such as **Chrony** further improves accuracy and reduces the need for manual intervention, ensuring consistent and precise time management across systems.

User Management in Cloud Environments

Managing users in cloud environments is like managing employees in a secure office building. Just as different access cards are issued to a janitor, a manager, and an IT technician, in the cloud, it is essential to carefully define who can perform specific actions on which resources.

Cloud providers such as AWS, Azure, and Google Cloud offer tools for managing user identities and access rights through systems such as Identity and Access Management (IAM). But the flexibility of cloud environments–where servers, applications, and users change often–requires careful planning to avoid security risks and maintain operational efficiency.

Definition and Importance of IAM

Identity and Access Management (IAM): It is a service that allows administrators to manage who can access AWS resources, what actions they can perform, and under what conditions. It helps maintain security, ensures compliance, and supports centralized access control.

Example Analogy: IAM functions such as the access control system in a building, where each person receives specific permissions–some can enter only the lobby, others can access secure areas, and some manage the entire building.

IAM Integration with Rocky Linux 9

To install the AWS CLI on Rocky Linux 9:

1. Run the following command to install the AWS CLI: **`sudo dnf install awscli -y`**
2. Verify the installation: **`aws --version`**
3. Creat an IAM Role in AWS for EC2 Access
    a. Navigate to **`IAM`** → **`Roles`** → **`Create Role`**
    b. Select **`AWS service`** → **`EC2`**
    c. Attach the managed policy **`AmazonS3ReadOnlyAccess`**
    d. Name the role **`RockyS3ReadOnlyRole`**
    e. Launch an EC2 instance with Rocky Linux 9 and attach the role

Accessing AWS Resources from Rocky Linux EC2 Instance: Once the EC2 instance is running with the IAM role attached, test access to AWS services:

```
aws s3 ls
```

The instance can now read S3 buckets securely without storing credentials.

Configuring IAM Access on Local Rocky Linux with Access Keys

This method is suitable for test environments, not production.

1. Create an IAM user with **`AmazonEC2ReadOnlyAccess`**
2. Generate an **`Access Key`** and **`Secret Access Key`**
3. On Rocky Linux, configure the CLI: **`aws configure`**

Input:

a. Access Key ID

b. Secret Access Key

c. Default region (e.g., **us-east-1**)

d. Output format (e.g., **json**)

Now we can run: **aws ec2 describe-instances**

Example IAM Policy for EC2 Read-Only Access

```
{
  "Version": "2012-10-17",
  "Statement": [
    {
      "Effect": "Allow",
      "Action": [
        "ec2:DescribeInstances"
      ],
      "Resource": "*"
    }
  ]
}
```

Component	Description	Example
User	Represents an individual identity with login credentials	A developer named Alice
Group	A collection of users with shared permissions	DevOps team group with EC2 and S3 access
Role	Temporary access credentials assigned to users, apps, or services	A script assuming the S3ReadOnlyRole
Policy	A set of JSON-formatted rules defining allowed or denied actions on resources	A policy that permits reading from S3 only

Figure 3.16: *Core IAM Components and Their Functions*

Figure 3.16 provides a summary of the essential components that form the foundation of Identity and Access Management (IAM) in cloud environments. Each component plays a specific role in defining and enforcing access control policies. Understanding how these elements interact is crucial for securing cloud resources, maintaining organizational compliance, and managing user privileges efficiently. From individual users to temporary roles and detailed policies, these components enable administrators to implement precise access strategies across cloud platforms such as AWS, especially when integrating with systems such as Rocky Linux 9.

This policy grants permission to list EC2 instances without allowing any modifications.

IAM provides a secure and scalable way to manage user and system access in AWS environments. When integrated with Rocky Linux 9, IAM allows EC2 instances and users to interact with AWS services without compromising credentials. Adopting best practices such as enforcing least privilege, and enabling MFA enhances both security and operational efficiency.

Key Challenges Explained through Real-Life Examples

Dynamic Scaling of Resources

- **Analogy:** Imagine a restaurant that hires temporary staff during the weekend rush. If they keep their keys after quitting, that is a risk.
- **Cloud version:** In AWS, when new servers (EC2 instances) are automatically added during peak traffic, developers might need temporary access to debug. If their access is not revoked after scaling down, they may still have permissions they no longer need.
- **Solution:** Use time-limited roles and automatic revocation of access after the task is done.

The Shared Responsibility Model

- **Analogy:** A landlord secures the building (locks, cameras), but tenants must lock their apartments and protect their valuables.
- **Cloud version:** Cloud providers secure the infrastructure. The customer is responsible for managing user access, data permissions, and security configurations.
- **Common mistake:** Granting full admin access to everyone can lead to accidental deletions or leaks.

Multiple Cloud Accounts and Platforms

- **Analogy:** A company with offices in different countries uses different ID badges. Without coordination, it is hard to keep track of who has access where.
- **Cloud version:** When an organization uses AWS for development, Azure for data analysis, and has on-premises systems, managing access manually in each becomes chaotic.
- **Solution:** Use centralized identity platforms such as Azure AD, Google Workspace, or AWS SSO.

Auditing and Compliance

- **Analogy:** A retail store uses security cameras to track employee activities and ensure they follow procedures.
- **Cloud version:** Tools such as AWS CloudTrail or Azure Monitor track who accessed what and when useful for audits, compliance (for example, GDPR), and forensic analysis.

Best Practices for Cloud User Management (With Examples)

1. **Follow the Principle of Least Privilege:** Only give users the access they absolutely need.

Example: A developer may need to deploy an app to a staging server but should not have access to the production database.

Use Role-Based Access Control (RBAC):

- "`Developer`" role: limited access
- "`Admin`" role: full access
- "`Auditor`" role: read-only access

2. **Centralize Identity and Access:** Avoid managing user permissions separately across platforms.

Example: Use AWS IAM Identity Center (SSO) to control access to AWS accounts from a central place. This makes onboarding and offboarding seamless.

3. **Automate User Lifecycle:** Set up automatic processes for adding, removing, and updating users.

Example: When hiring a new DevOps engineer:

- HR creates the user account.
- A script (via Terraform or AWS CloudFormation) assigns them to the "**DevOps**" role.
- Access is automatically revoked on their last day.

4. **Audit and Monitor Regularly**

Example: With AWS CloudTrail, to track actions such as:

- Who deleted a database?
- When was a new user created?
- Was an EC2 instance modified without approval?

Set up alerts using Amazon CloudWatch for suspicious activities (for example, login from an unknown IP).

Step-by-Step Implementation on AWS

Goal: Onboard developers with access to staging (not production), enforce MFA, and track actions.

1. **Define IAM Roles**

- **Developer-Staging Role:** Access to EC2 and S3 in the staging environment.
- **Developer-Prod Role:** Deny destructive actions such as terminating instances.

```
{
  "Version": "2012-10-17",
  "Statement": [
    {
      "Effect": "Allow",
      "Action": [
        "ec2:DescribeInstances",
        "s3:ListBucket"
      ],
      "Resource": "*"
    }
  ]
}
json
CopiarEditar
{
  "Version": "2012-10-17",
  "Statement": [
    {
      "Effect": "Deny",
      "Action": "ec2:TerminateInstances",
      "Resource": "*"
    },
    {
      "Effect": "Allow",
      "Action": "ec2:DescribeInstances",
      "Resource": "*"
    }
  ]
}
```

2. **Enforce Multi-Factor Authentication (MFA)**

`MFA =` a second layer of security (such as entering a password + a phone code)

```
{
  "Version": "2012-10-17",
  "Statement": {
    "Effect": "Deny",
    "Action": "*",
    "Resource": "*",
    "Condition": {
      "Bool": {
        "aws:MultiFactorAuthPresent": "false"
      }
    }
  }
}
```

3. **Enable AWS CloudTrail**

Steps:

a. Go to AWS CloudTrail Console
b. Click "**`Create Trail`**"
c. Name it (for example, **`DevActivityTrail`**)
d. Enable for all regions
e. Store logs in an encrypted S3 bucket
f. Integrate with **`CloudWatch`** Logs for alerts

Real-World Scenario

Company: TechStart Inc.

Need: Allow interns to test code in staging but block access to billing and production.

Solution:

1. Create an "**`Intern-Staging`**" role
2. Use tags to limit access to resources marked as Environment: Staging
3. Set IAM policy with expiration using AWS IAM Conditions (for example, access ends in 30 days)

Feature	Benefit
Least Privilege	Reduces risk of accidental damage
Centralized IAM	Easier onboarding & policy enforcement
Multi-Factor Authentication	Prevents unauthorized logins
CloudTrail & Monitoring	Enables visibility & compliance
Automation	Speeds up and secures user management

Figure 3.17: *Summary of Key Benefits*

Figure 3.17 provides a high-level overview of essential security and identity management features along with their corresponding advantages. These features—such as least privilege access, centralized identity and access management (IAM), multi-factor authentication (MFA), activity monitoring, and automation—are critical in enhancing operational security, improving compliance, and streamlining user management within modern IT environments.

Best Practices

Implementing the right IAM roles, policies, and MFA enforcement in AWS is critical to securing cloud resources and ensuring compliance. Regular auditing with CloudTrail ensures that all user activities are tracked, and any suspicious actions can be investigated. By following these guidelines, organizations can enforce strict access controls, enhance security, and maintain proper compliance with regulations.

User Management in Cloud Environments

Key Challenges, Explained Through Real-Life Examples

- **Dynamic Scaling of Resources**
  Time -limited roles automatoric revocation of access after taca-in dunic.
- **Shared responsibilitty Model**
  Avoid separate masonsibility for user access daca perumbiols.
- **Multiple Cloud Accounts and Platforms**
  Using centrauzl edity.platforms (lieigrinplo - Auoe-AD. Googlo Workspace or AWS SSO
- **Auditing and Compliance**
  Tracking tools such AWs foodil Fl ade R. compliance: forensic analysis for rensciaity!

Best Practices for Cloud User Managenert

1. **Follow the Principle of Least Privilege**
   Only give users a exp. production database exd. El MA. e:. e.cord
2. **Centralize Identity and Access (MFA)**
   Avoid separate management across plats
   AWS IAM Inentity Center (SSO)
3. **Automate User Lifecycle**
   HR example. Inter emplors. ⟶ script (via forraform or AWS) storing a $5 un Scres

Real-Word Scenario

Company: TechStart Inc.

Need: Interns can access staging but not billing/production

Step-by Step Implementation on AW6

1. **Define IAM Roles**
   Developer Staging op. Prod
2. **Enforce Multi-Factor Authentication (MFA)**
   MFA = second layer of security
3. **Enable AWS CloudTrail**
   - Create trail
   - Enabling trail regions
   - Storing logo in $9 bucket
   Integrated with CloudWatch Logs

Step-by-step Implementation on AWS

1. **Define IAM Roles**
   Developer Staging and Developer Prod
2. **Enforce Multi-Factor Authentication (MFA)**

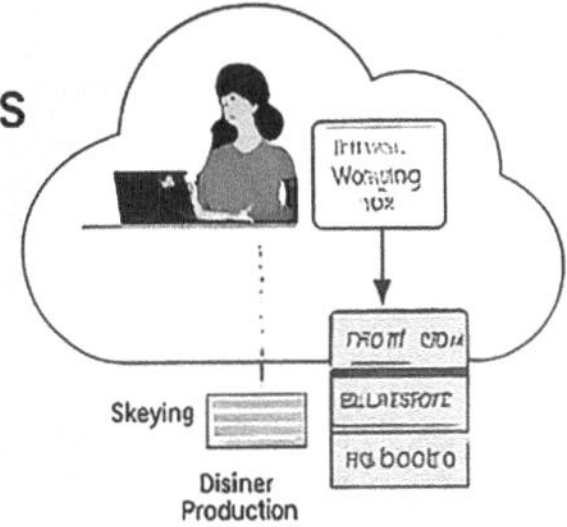

Figure 3.18: *User Management in Cloud Environments*

Figure 3.18 illustrates a simplified view of how user identities and permissions are managed across cloud platforms. At the center of the diagram, a centralized Identity and Access Management (IAM) system connects users—such as developers, administrators, and auditors—to cloud resources such as virtual machines, databases, and storage services. The image demonstrates the flow of access, emphasizing best practices such as enforcing the principle of least privilege, role-based access control (RBAC), and multi-factor authentication (MFA). It also shows how logging and monitoring tools such as AWS CloudTrail or Azure Monitor capture and audit user activities to maintain compliance and security. This visual reinforces the idea that user management is not just about granting access, but it is about doing so securely, with full visibility and control across dynamic cloud environments.

Compatibility Note: Rocky Linux 9 and Earlier Versions

This chapter is primarily written for Rocky Linux 9, leveraging its default tools and configurations for user management, file permissions, Access Control Lists (ACLs), and time synchronization. However, most commands and practices described–such as **useradd, usermod, groupadd, passwd, chmod, chown, setfacl, getfacl, timedatectl, and hwclock**–are consistent across earlier versions of Rocky Linux, including Rocky Linux 8 and other RHEL-based distributions.

Administrators working with earlier versions may encounter minor differences in default package availability, systemd behavior, or filesystem mount options. For example, ACL support and Chrony-based time synchronization are available in Rocky Linux 8 but may require manual configuration depending on the system setup.

AWS CLI installation and IAM integration are version-agnostic, provided the system supports the required packages and has access to the internet.

Where applicable, it is recommended to verify package versions and consult the official Rocky Linux documentation for version-specific nuances. This ensures that user management practices remain secure, consistent, and aligned with system capabilities across different environments.

Conclusion

Effective user management is essential for maintaining both security and operational efficiency within any system or organization. By effectively managing user accounts, permissions, and access controls, sensitive data remains protected while users can perform their tasks without unnecessary barriers. In today's interconnected world, where local systems often integrate with cloud environments, it is vital to adhere to best practices such as enforcing strong password policies, implementing multifactor authentication, regularly reviewing access rights, and deactivating accounts when no longer necessary. These steps help safeguard against potential security threats and ensure that users are granted the right level of access.

As we move forward, the next chapter will delve into the process of installing DNF updates in Rocky Linux, a critical aspect of maintaining a secure and optimized environment. We will also explore the essential packages that help create an ideal system setup, enabling administrators to ensure their environments remain up-to-date and well-protected. By understanding and implementing these foundational tasks, organizations can enhance both system reliability and security, preparing themselves for the challenges of a modern digital landscape.

Points to Remember

- User accounts on Linux can be efficiently managed with commands such as **useradd** for adding users and **userdel** for removing them.
- Password security is critical; use **passwd** to set passwords and **chage** to enforce policies such as expiration and complexity.
- File permissions in Linux are based on **owner, group,** and **others**, and can be managed with **chmod** for basic permissions or **setfacl** for granular control.

- Accurate time synchronization is essential for auditing; tools such as **`timedatectl`** and NTP maintain consistency across systems.
- In cloud environments, enforcing the **principle of least privilege** and using tools such as AWS IAM for user and role management ensures secure access control.

Multiple Choice Questions

1. Which command is used to add a new user in Rocky Linux?
   a. `useradd`
   b. `usermod`
   c. `adduser`
   d. `newuser`
2. What is the primary tool for managing password policies in Rocky Linux??
   a. `Passwd`
   b. `Pswdctl`
   c. `Chage`
   d. `policyset`
3. What does the numeric value 755 represent in Linux file permissions?
   a. Read, write, execute for owner; no access for others
   b. Full permissions for owner; read and execute for group and others
   c. Full permissions for everyone
   d. Read and write for owner and group only
4. Which command is used to view Access Control Lists (ACLs) in Rocky Linux?
   a. `aclview`
   b. `chmod`
   c. `getfacl`
   d. `aclcheck`
5. What is the recommended security practice for managing users in cloud environments such as AWS from Rocky Linux?
   a. Using the root account for all administrative tasks
   b. Sharing credentials among all users
   c. Enforcing the principle of least privilege
   d. Disabling Multi-Factor Authentication (MFA)

Answers

1. a
2. c

3. b
4. c
5. c

Questions

1. How can user accounts be added or removed in Rocky Linux?
2. What tool is used to enforce password expiration policies in Rocky Linux?
3. What are the three roles in the Linux file permission model?
4. Which command in Rocky Linux is used to modify file permissions numerically or symbolically?
5. What is the purpose of Access Control Lists (ACLs) in Rocky Linux?
6. Which command is used to synchronize time on a Rocky Linux system?
7. What is the principle of least privilege, and why is it essential in managing users in cloud environments?
8. How does timedatectl improve time management on Rocky Linux systems?
9. Which tools can be used to manage users, roles, and permissions in cloud environments such as AWS?
10. How can a user be added to a specific group in Rocky Linux?

Key Terms

- **User Account**: A unique identity assigned to a person or process to interact with the system, managed via commands such as useradd and `userdel` in Rocky Linux.
- **Group**: A collection of user accounts in Rocky Linux used to manage shared permissions for files or resources efficiently.
- **File Permissions**: Rules defining access rights (read, write, execute) for files and directories, set using commands such as chmod.
- **Access Control List (ACL)**: A mechanism in Rocky Linux to grant specific permissions to individual users or groups beyond the standard permission model.
- **Password Policy**: Security rules in Rocky Linux governing password complexity, expiration, and history, enforced using tools such as `passwd` and `chage`.
- **Principle of Least Privilege**: A security concept ensuring users and roles have the minimum permissions necessary to perform their tasks, reducing security risks.
- **Time Synchronization**: Ensuring system time accuracy using tools such as timedatectl and NTP, critical for logging and auditing.
- **Role**: A collection of permissions assigned to a user or service in a cloud or system environment to define access levels.
- **`Timedatectl`**: A command-line tool in Rocky Linux for managing system time, time zones, and enabling NTP synchronization.
- **Identity and Access Management (IAM)**: AWS service for managing access to cloud resources, including creating users, groups, and enforcing MFA.

CHAPTER 4
Package Management and Updates

Introduction

In enterprise Linux distributions such as Rocky Linux 9, efficient package management is critical for maintaining system integrity, security, and performance. The dnf package manager serves as the primary tool for installing, updating, and removing software packages, succeeding in older tools such as yum. With dnf, administrators can manage system software more effectively, track dependencies, and ensure systems stay up to date with the latest patches and security updates. Mastering the use of dnf is essential for administrators aiming to keep systems running smoothly and securely, especially in large-scale environments or cloud deployments where multiple packages and applications must be managed simultaneously.

This chapter will explore the core functionalities of dnf, including installing and updating packages, managing repositories, handling dependencies, and automating routine package management tasks to streamline system administration. Additionally, we will cover troubleshooting techniques to diagnose and resolve common package management issues, equipping administrators with the skills needed to maintain a healthy and reliable Rocky Linux 9 environment. By the end of this chapter, readers will have a solid understanding of dnf's capabilities and will be able to leverage it effectively to simplify package management, automate workflows, and troubleshoot potential challenges in production environments.

Structure

In this chapter, we will discuss the following topics:

- Overview of Package Management Concepts
- Installing, Updating, and Removing Packages with `dnf`
- Managing Software Repositories
- Handling Package Dependencies
- Troubleshooting Package Management
- Automating Package Management

Overview of Package Management Concepts

Package management on Linux involves the handling of software packages, which are pre-compiled binaries, libraries, or scripts bundled together. In Rocky Linux, DNF is the default package manager, providing a modern, efficient way to manage packages. Key concepts include repositories, dependencies, and transaction logs.

Package management is a critical aspect of maintaining and operating a Linux system, providing a systematic approach to installing, upgrading, configuring, and removing software packages. This chapter delves into the fundamental concepts of package management, which are essential for both system administrators and end-users who wish to manage software efficiently and effectively.

Packages

At the core of package management are **packages** themselves. A package is a bundled collection of software that typically includes:

- **Executables**: The actual programs that users run.
- **Libraries**: Shared code that can be used by multiple programs, allowing for efficient use of resources and reducing redundancy.
- **Configuration Files**: Files that dictate how the software behaves and interacts with the system.
- **Documentation**: Information on how to use the software, including manuals and help files.
- **Metadata**: Data that provides information about the package, such as its name, version, description, and dependencies.

Packages are often distributed in specific formats, such as `.deb` for Debian-based systems (such as Ubuntu) or `.rpm` for Red Hat-based systems (such as Fedora and CentOS). This packaging format ensures that the software can be easily installed and managed by the package manager.

Repositories

Repositories are centralized storage locations where packages are stored and made available for installation. They can be thought of as libraries of software that users can access to find and install the applications they need. Repositories can be categorized into several types:

- **Official Repositories**: Maintained by the distribution's developers, these repositories contain stable and tested software that is guaranteed to work with the system.
- **Third-Party Repositories**: Provided by external developers or organizations, these repositories may offer additional software that is not available in the official repositories. While they can provide useful tools, users should exercise caution, as the software may not be as rigorously tested.
- **Local Repositories**: These are repositories set up on a local network or machine, allowing for the distribution of software within an organization without relying on external sources.

Package managers interact with these repositories to fetch and install software, ensuring that users have access to the latest versions and security updates.

Dependencies

Dependency management is a cornerstone of package management, ensuring software applications have the necessary libraries and packages to function correctly. When installing a package, the package manager resolves dependencies by fetching required components from a repository, supporting version constraints to maintain compatibility. This process minimizes errors from missing or incompatible software, enabling smooth operation. For example, a web server might depend on libraries for networking or data processing, and tools such as `` `npm` ``, `` `pip` ``, or `` `apt` `` streamline their installation.

However, dependency management can present challenges such as "`dependency hell`," where conflicting version requirements complicate installations, or bloating from unused dependencies. Security risks also arise from vulnerabilities in outdated dependencies. Modern solutions mitigate these issues: lock files (for example, `` `package-lock.json` ``) ensure consistent setups, dependency graphs (for example, in `` `Cargo` ``) prevent conflicts, automated tools such as Dependabot update vulnerable packages, and containerization (for example, Docker) isolates dependencies. By leveraging these tools and practices, developers can maintain reliable, secure, and scalable software systems despite the complexities of dependency management.

Transaction Logs

Transaction logs are an essential feature of package management systems, providing a detailed record of all package actions performed on the system. These logs document:

- Installations
- Upgrades
- Removals
- Configuration changes

Transaction logs serve several purposes:

- **Auditing**: They allow system administrators to review changes made to the system, which are crucial for maintaining security and compliance.
- **Troubleshooting**: If a software installation or upgrade causes issues, the logs can help identify what changes were made and assist in diagnosing the problem.
- **Rollback**: Some package managers allow users to revert to previous versions of packages based on the transaction logs, providing a safety net in case of failures.

Package management is essential for streamlined software handling on Linux systems, relying on key components: packages, repositories, dependencies, and transaction logs. Together, they form a robust framework that simplifies installation, updates, and maintenance, boosting system stability and user experience. In this chapter, we will explore specific package management tools and their practical applications, offering insights for real-world use.

Package Management and Understanding Dependencies with DNF on Rocky Linux

Today, we will delve into the topic of package management, with a particular focus on understanding dependencies using the DNF package manager in Rocky Linux. We will begin by exploring the role of a package manager, followed by a detailed guide on how to install and search for packages. Additionally, we will cover the crucial topic of managing dependencies to ensure efficient and effective system administration.

Defining Package Manager

A package manager simplifies the process of installing, updating, and removing software. On Rocky Linux, we use RPM packages, such as RHEL. These packages are pre-built software bundles. DNF (Dandified Yum) is the improved version of Yum, offering better performance and enhanced dependency management.

Basic DNF Commands Overview

We will focus on three primary DNF commands:

- **Installing a package**
- **Searching for a package**
- **Managing dependencies**
- **Searching for a Package**

When we do not know the exact package name, we can search for it.

Example: Searching for `Apache` packages.

```
[cesarmserver@localhost ~]$ dnf search apache
Rocky Linux 9 - BaseOS                          631 kB/s | 2.3 MB     00:03
Rocky Linux 9 - AppStream                       4.7 MB/s | 8.2 MB     00:01
Rocky Linux 9 - Extras                           28 kB/s |  16 kB     00:00
======================== Name & Summary Matched: apache ========================
ant-apache-bcel.noarch : Optional apache bcel tasks for ant
ant-apache-bsf.noarch : Optional apache bsf tasks for ant
ant-apache-oro.noarch : Optional apache oro tasks for ant
ant-apache-regexp.noarch : Optional apache regexp tasks for ant
ant-apache-resolver.noarch : Optional apache resolver tasks for ant
ant-apache-xalan2.noarch : Optional apache xalan2 tasks for ant
apache-commons-logging.noarch : Apache Commons Logging
pcp-pmda-apache.x86_64 : Performance Co-Pilot (PCP) metrics for the Apache
                       : webserver
============================= Name Matched: apache =============================
apache-commons-cli.noarch : Command Line Interface Library for Java
apache-commons-codec.noarch : Implementations of common encoders and decoders
apache-commons-io.noarch : Utilities to assist with developing IO functionality
apache-commons-lang3.noarch : Provides a host of helper utilities for the
```

Figure 4.1: *DNF Search Apache*

Figure 4.1 illustrates the output of a dnf search apache command executed in a terminal on a Fedora-based Linux system. The command queries the **DNF (Dandified Yum)** package manager to search for packages related to "**apache**" in configured repositories. The figure displays a list of matching packages, including the **Apache HTTP Server (httpd)** and related tools or libraries, along with their versions, architectures, and brief descriptions. This visual demonstrates how DNF efficiently retrieves and presents package information, aiding users in identifying and installing the desired software for web server setup or other Apache-related tasks.

```
[cesarmserver@localhost ~]$ dnf search all apache
Last metadata expiration check: 0:00:53 ago on Fri 06 Dec 2024 12:21:39 PM CST.
============== Name & Summary & Description & URL Matched: apache ==============
ant-apache-bcel.noarch : Optional apache bcel tasks for ant
ant-apache-bsf.noarch : Optional apache bsf tasks for ant
ant-apache-oro.noarch : Optional apache oro tasks for ant
ant-apache-regexp.noarch : Optional apache regexp tasks for ant
ant-apache-resolver.noarch : Optional apache resolver tasks for ant
ant-apache-xalan2.noarch : Optional apache xalan2 tasks for ant
apache-commons-logging.noarch : Apache Commons Logging
================= Name & Summary & Description Matched: apache =================
pcp-pmda-apache.x86_64 : Performance Co-Pilot (PCP) metrics for the Apache
                       : webserver
=================== Name & Description & URL Matched: apache ===================
apache-commons-lang3.noarch : Provides a host of helper utilities for the
                            : java.lang API
========================== Name & URL Matched: apache ==========================
apache-commons-cli.noarch : Command Line Interface Library for Java
apache-commons-codec.noarch : Implementations of common encoders and decoders
apache-commons-io.noarch : Utilities to assist with developing IO functionality
```

Figure 4.2: *DNF Search All Apache*

Figure 4.2 showcases the output of the dnf search all apache commands executed in a terminal on a Fedora-based Linux system. This command uses the DNF package manager to perform an exhaustive search for packages related to "**apache**" across all configured repositories, including those not enabled by default. The figure lists matching packages, such as the Apache HTTP Server (**httpd**), associated modules, and libraries, displaying their names, versions, architectures, and detailed descriptions. This visual highlights DNF's capability to provide comprehensive search results, helping users explore a broader range of Apache-related software for installation or configuration.

Explanation:

- The output displays packages containing "**apache**" in their name or description.

- Scroll through results using *Shift* + *Page Up* or *Shift* + *Page Down*.

Installing a Package

Example: Installing `` `Emacs` ``.

1. Search for Emacs:

```
[cesarmserver@localhost ~]$ dnf search emacs
Last metadata expiration check: 0:04:32 ago on Fri 06 Dec 2024 12:21:39 PM CST.
======================= Name & Summary Matched: emacs ========================
emacs.x86_64 : GNU Emacs text editor
emacs-auctex.noarch : Enhanced TeX modes for Emacs
emacs-common.x86_64 : Emacs common files
emacs-filesystem.noarch : Emacs filesystem layout
emacs-lucid.x86_64 : GNU Emacs text editor with LUCID toolkit X support
emacs-nox.x86_64 : GNU Emacs text editor without X support
[cesarmserver@localhost ~]$ sudo dnf install emacs.x86_64
[sudo] password for cesarmserver:
Rocky Linux 9 - BaseOS                          10 kB/s | 4.1 kB     00:00    A
Rocky Linux 9 - BaseOS                         3.1 MB/s | 2.3 MB     00:00
Rocky Linux 9 - AppStream                       13 kB/s | 4.5 kB     00:00
Rocky Linux 9 - AppStream                      3.5 MB/s | 8.2 MB     00:02
Rocky Linux 9 - Extras                         6.2 kB/s | 2.9 kB     00:00
Rocky Linux 9 - Extras                          30 kB/s |  16 kB     00:00
Dependencies resolved.
================================================================================
 Package             Architecture Version                  Repository      Size
================================================================================
```

Figure 4.3: *dnf search emacs*

Figure 4.3 displays **`dnf search emacs`** command searches for packages related to "**emacs**" in their name or description using the DNF package manager. The output lists matching packages with brief summaries, allowing users to identify relevant software, such as the Emacs text editor or related plugins. Navigate the results using *Shift* + *Page Up* or *Shift* + *Page Down* for efficient browsing.

This list related to packages. Look for `` `emacs.x86_64` ``.

2. **Installing Emacs**:

```
[cesarmserver@localhost ~]$ sudo dnf install emacs.x86_64
[sudo] password for cesarmserver:
Rocky Linux 9 - BaseOS                          10 kB/s | 4.1 kB     00:00    A
Rocky Linux 9 - BaseOS                         3.1 MB/s | 2.3 MB     00:00
Rocky Linux 9 - AppStream                       13 kB/s | 4.5 kB     00:00
Rocky Linux 9 - AppStream                      3.5 MB/s | 8.2 MB     00:02
Rocky Linux 9 - Extras                         6.2 kB/s | 2.9 kB     00:00
Rocky Linux 9 - Extras                          30 kB/s |  16 kB     00:00
Dependencies resolved.
================================================================================
 Package             Architecture Version                  Repository      Size
================================================================================
Installing:
 emacs               x86_64       1:27.2-10.el9_4          appstream      3.3 M
Installing dependencies:
 emacs-common        x86_64       1:27.2-10.el9_4          appstream       35 M
 libXaw              x86_64       1.0.13-19.el9            appstream      197 k
 libotf              x86_64       0.9.13-20.el9            appstream      100 k
 m17n-db             noarch       1.8.0-16.el9             appstream      579 k
```

Figure 4.4: *sudo dnf install emacs.x86_64*

Figure 4.4 shows the **`sudo dnf install emacs.x86_64`** command installs the 64-bit version of the Emacs text editor using the DNF package manager. Executed with superuser privileges via sudo, it retrieves and installs the specified package along with any required dependencies. The output displays the installation progress and completion status. Navigate the results using *Shift* + *Page Up* or *Shift* + *Page Down* to review details.

- DNF resolves dependencies and shows additional packages to install.
- Confirm installation by typing `y`.

3. **Verify Installation**: After installation, start Emacs by typing: **emacs** in the command line interface.

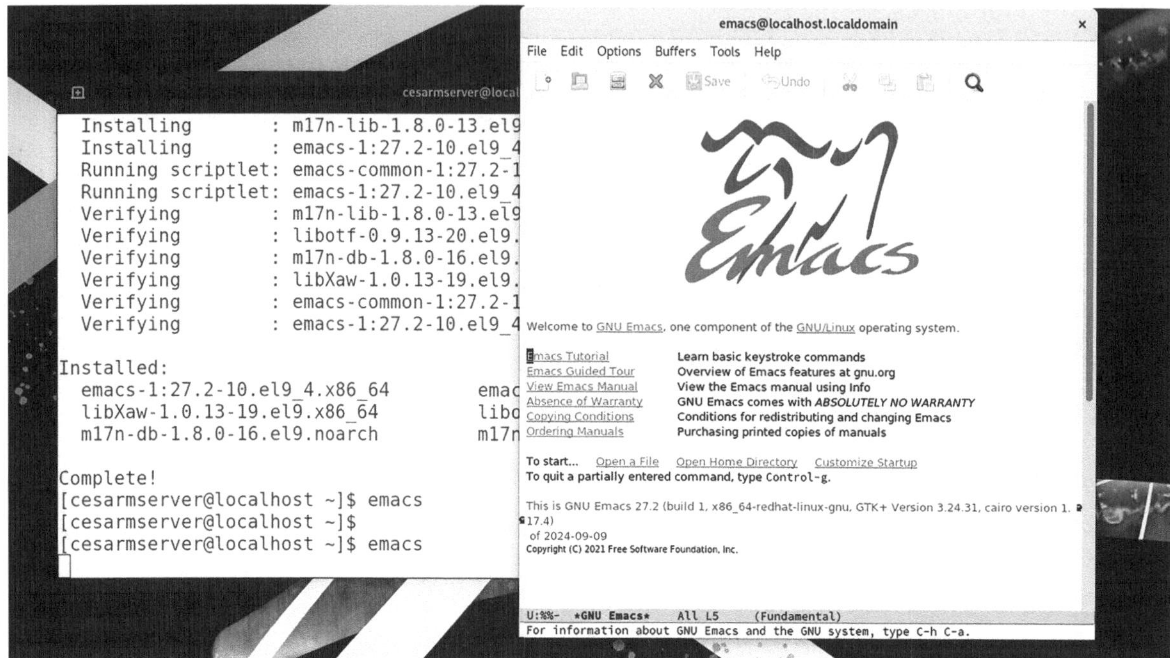

Figure 4.5: *Emacs*

The previous figure displays the graphical interface of a package manager, **DNF**, during the installation of Emacs, a versatile open-source text editor. The figure highlights the previously downloaded packages and dependencies required for Emacs, illustrating how the package manager automates dependency resolution. This visual emphasizes the ease of installing complex software such as Emacs through a user-friendly graphical environment, streamlining the setup process for developers and users.

4. **Managing Dependencies**: DNF handles dependencies automatically. When we install a package, it checks for and installs any required dependencies.

```
================================================================================
 Package             Architecture Version                Repository        Size
================================================================================
Installing:
 emacs               x86_64       1:27.2-10.el9_4        appstream        3.3 M
Installing dependencies:
 emacs-common        x86_64       1:27.2-10.el9_4        appstream         35 M
 libXaw              x86_64       1.0.13-19.el9          appstream        197 k
 libotf              x86_64       0.9.13-20.el9          appstream        100 k
 m17n-db             noarch       1.8.0-16.el9           appstream        579 k
 m17n-lib            x86_64       1.8.0-13.el9           appstream        194 k

Transaction Summary
================================================================================
```

Figure 4.6: *During Emacs Installation*

The previous output illustrates the installation process of Emacs using DNF, a powerful package manager for RPM-based Linux distributions. The figure displays DNF's *output* or graphical interface, showing real-time progress as it installs Emacs and its dependencies. This visual highlights DNF's ability to automate the download, verification, and installation of required packages, ensuring a seamless setup of Emacs for coding, text editing, or other tasks.

This ensures that all necessary components for Emacs are installed.

5. **Accessing DNF Manual:** To explore more options and features of DNF, use the manual page:

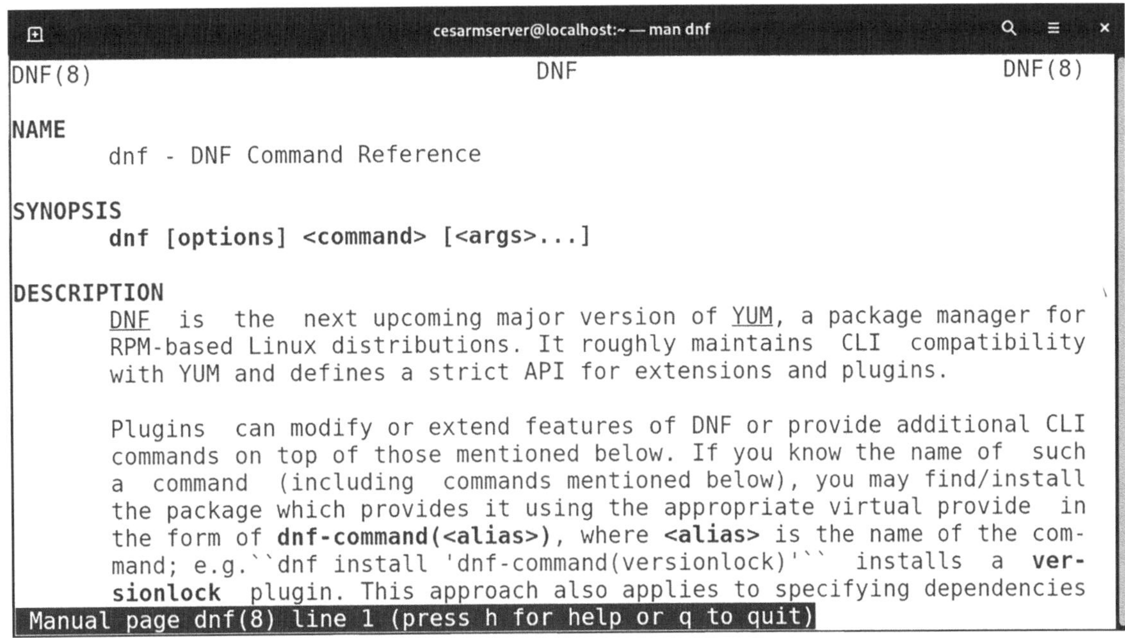

Figure 4.7: *man dnf*

Figure 4.7 displays the manual page for DNF, accessed by running the man dnf command, which provides comprehensive documentation on DNF's features and options. In the context of installing Emacs, this figure highlights how users can explore DNF's capabilities, such as dependency resolution and package management, to troubleshoot or customize the installation process. The manual page serves as a valuable resource, offering new insights into commands and flags that enhance the efficiency of software installations such as Emacs on RPM-based Linux systems.

Installing a Package on Rocky Linux

Rocky Linux, a robust and enterprise-grade Linux distribution, is designed for stability, performance, and security. One of its core strengths lies in its package management system, which allows users to easily install, update, and manage software.

Hands-on Practice: Using the DNF Package Manager to Install Software on Rocky Linux

By the end of this session, we will have gained practical experience in searching for available packages, installing specific software packages, and verifying installations while understanding how dependencies are handled. These skills are fundamental to Linux system administration, allowing you to efficiently customize and maintain a Rocky Linux system. Let us dive in and explore these essential tasks in detail.

In this practice laboratory, the focus will be on utilizing DNF, the default package manager for Rocky Linux, which has replaced the older YUM utility. DNF is a robust, efficient, and user-friendly tool designed to streamline tasks such as dependency resolution, repository management, and ensuring package consistency across the system.

1. **Search for a Package:** Search for **`wget`**, a utility to download files from the web.

```
[cesarmserver@localhost ~]$ dnf search wget
Last metadata expiration check: 0:12:56 ago on Fri 06 Dec 2024 12:21:39 PM CST.
========================== Name Exactly Matched: wget ==========================
wget.x86_64 : A utility for retrieving files using the HTTP or FTP protocols
[cesarmserver@localhost ~]$ ▌
```

Figure 4.8: *dnf search wget*

The preceding image depicts the output of the dnf search **wget** command, demonstrating how DNF enables users to search for the **wget** package, a popular tool for downloading files from the web, within RPM-based Linux repositories. This figure illustrates DNF's search functionality, providing new information about available packages and their descriptions, which helps users identify and install software efficiently. In the context of package management tasks such as the earlier Emacs installation, this visual underscores DNF's versatility in exploring and managing software dependencies.

2. **Install the Package: Install `wget`**

```
[cesarmserver@localhost ~]$ sudo dnf install wget
[sudo] password for cesarmserver:
Last metadata expiration check: 0:07:13 ago on Fri 06 Dec 2024 12:28:27 PM CST.
Package wget-1.21.1-8.el9_4.x86_64 is already installed.
Dependencies resolved.
Nothing to do.
Complete!
```

Figure 4.9: *sudo dnf install wget*

The output shown demonstrates the execution of the **`sudo dnf install wget`** command, which installs the **`wget package`**—a widely used tool for downloading files from the web—on an RPM-based Linux system. This example highlights DNF's capability to automatically resolve and install ***wget*** along with any required dependencies, simplifying the process with minimal user input. It also reinforces how DNF enhances software management efficiency, building tasks such as the earlier installation of Emacs.

3. **Verify the Installation:** Check if **`wget`** is installed.

```
wget --version
```

By following these steps, we will develop a strong understanding of how to use *the DNF package manager* on Rocky Linux, with an emphasis on effective package management and dependency handling. This class structure is thoughtfully designed to deliver a clear and comprehensive learning experience within an 8- to 10-minute timeframe.

Installing, Updating, and Removing Packages with DNF

Managing software is a crucial task for system administrators and developers to maintain the functionality and security of a Linux system. In Rocky Linux and other distributions based on Red Hat, the **dnf package manager** serves as a powerful tool for installing, updating, and removing software packages efficiently.

dnf is the successor to yum, offering enhanced performance, dependency resolution, and support for modular content. With dnf, users can easily search for, install, update, or remove software from official repositories or third-party sources, ensuring their systems are equipped with the required tools and up-to-date security patches.

This section offers a practical guide to mastering essential DNF package management commands and outlines the key skills we will gain by the end.

- Install individual or multiple packages with dependencies.
- Update the entire system or specific packages.
- Remove unnecessary packages to free up resources and maintain a clean environment.

We will also explore practical examples, such as installing and using the htop utility, providing hands-on experience with package management. Whether maintaining a personal server or managing an enterprise system, mastering DNF is essential for efficient and effective system administration.

Managing Packages with `dnf`

This lab expands on the previously created examples, providing in-depth explanations for every concept and step. Each step is accompanied by a clear explanation to ensure complete understanding.

Installing and Using `htop`

System monitoring is a fundamental task for Linux administrators and users who need to track resource usage and manage processes effectively. The **`htop`** package offers a powerful, user-friendly alternative to the default `top` utility. With its interactive interface, the **`htop`** allows users to easily view system performance metrics, sort processes, and manage tasks with keyboard shortcuts or a mouse.

In this lab, we will learn how to:

- Search for the **`htop`** package using DNF.
- Install and verify the package.
- Use **`htop`** to monitor system resources.

Additionally, we will address scenarios where **`htop`** may not be available in the default repositories, demonstrating how to enable and utilize the Extra Packages for Enterprise Linux (EPEL) repository. This hands-on practice will provide us with practical skills for managing and troubleshooting package installations in Rocky Linux.

Lab 1: Installing and Using `htop`

Objective: To learn how to search for, install, verify, and use the **`htop`** package; to resolve issues when a package is not available in the default repositories.

Step-by-Step Instructions with Explanations

Step 1: Check System Updates

```
[cesarmserver@localhost ~]$ sudo dnf update
Last metadata expiration check: 0:02:47 ago on Fri 06 Dec 2024 01:40:56 PM CST.
Dependencies resolved.
Nothing to do.
Complete!
```

Figure 4.10: *sudo dnf update*

This illustrates the use of the **`sudo dnf update`** command, which updates all installed packages on the system to their latest available versions. This process ensures that the system remains secure, stable, and up to date with the latest features and bug fixes. DNF automatically checks for available updates, resolves any necessary dependencies, and prompts the user for confirmation before proceeding. Regularly updating the system is a critical practice for maintaining overall system health and security.

- **Action completed with this command:** This command updates the system package database and applies available updates to installed packages.
- **Reason for updates:** Keeping the package database current ensures access to the latest versions of software, which helps maintain system security, stability, and performance.

Step 2: Search for the Package

```
[cesarmserver@localhost ~]$ sudo dnf search htop
Last metadata expiration check: 0:04:05 ago on Fri 06 Dec 2024 01:40:56 PM CST.
============================== Name Exactly Matched: htop ===============================
htop.x86_64 : Interactive process viewer
```

Figure 4.11: *sudo dnf search htop*

This image demonstrates the use of the ***sudo dnf search htop*** command, which searches the available repositories for packages related to **htop.** This command is useful for quickly locating software when the exact package name is unknown or when exploring available options. DNF returns a list of matching packages along with brief descriptions, making it easier to identify and select the desired software for installation.

Step 3: Enable the EPEL Repository

The **Extra Packages for Enterprise Linux (EPEL)** repository provides additional software, including htop.

a. Install and enable EPEL: **`sudo dnf install epel-release`**.

   This command adds the EPEL repository to the system.

```
[cesarmserver@localhost ~]$ sudo dnf install epel-release
Last metadata expiration check: 1:02:15 ago on Fri 06 Dec 2024 12:38:07 PM CST.
Dependencies resolved.
==========================================================================================
 Package                Architecture      Version              Repository          Size
==========================================================================================
Installing:
 epel-release           noarch            9-7.el9              extras              19 k

Transaction Summary
==========================================================================================
Install  1 Package

Total download size: 19 k
Installed size: 26 k
Is this ok [y/N]: y
Downloading Packages:
epel-release-9-7.el9.noarch.rpm                          205 kB/s |  19 kB     00:00
------------------------------------------------------------------------------------------
```

Figure 4.12: *sudo dnf install epel-release*

The previous output shows the execution of the **`sudo dnf install epel-release`** command, which installs the Extra Packages for Enterprise Linux (EPEL) repository on the system. EPEL provides a large collection of additional packages that are not included in the default Rocky Linux repositories but are maintained to high standards of quality and compatibility. By enabling EPEL, users gain access to a broader range of software, enhancing the flexibility and functionality of the system. Installing EPEL is a common best practice for administrators who need a wider selection of reliable tools and applications.

a. Update the repository metadata: **`sudo dnf update`**.

Ensures the system recognizes the newly added repository.

b. Search for **`htop`** again to confirm its availability: **`sudo dnf search htop`**.

Step 4: Install the Package

Once the EPEL repository is enabled, install htop:

```
[cesarmserver@localhost ~]$ sudo dnf install htop
Last metadata expiration check: 0:08:55 ago on Fri 06 Dec 2024 01:40:56 PM CST.
Dependencies resolved.
==========================================================================================
 Package               Architecture      Version               Repository          Size
==========================================================================================
Installing:
 htop                  x86_64            3.3.0-1.el9           epel               198 k
Installing dependencies:
 hwloc-libs            x86_64            2.4.1-5.el9           baseos             2.1 M

Transaction Summary
==========================================================================================
Install  2 Packages

Total download size: 2.3 M
Installed size: 3.5 M
Is this ok [y/N]: y
```

Figure 4.13: *sudo dnf install htop*

This illustrates the use of the **`sudo dnf install htop`** command to install the **`htop utility`** on the system. **`htop`** is an interactive process viewer that provides a real-time, user-friendly interface for monitoring system resources such as CPU, memory, and processes. The output shows DNF automatically resolving dependencies, retrieving the necessary package, and installing it with minimal user intervention. This example highlights the efficiency and simplicity of using DNF to install essential administrative tools.

- **`htop` install and dependencies: `dnf`** downloads and installs htop along with any required dependencies.
- **reason for installation:** Installation makes the software available for use on the system.

Step 5: Verify the Installation

Confirm the package is installed: **`htop --version`**.

```
[cesarmserver@localhost etc]$ htop --version
htop 3.3.0
[cesarmserver@localhost etc]$
```

Figure 4.14: *htop --version*

Figure 4.14 shows the use of the **`htop --version`** command, which verifies that **`htop`** was successfully installed and displays the version information. Confirming the installed version helps ensure that the correct software is available and functioning as expected. It also provides useful information when troubleshooting, documenting system configurations, or ensuring compatibility with other tools and scripts.

Step 6: Use the Installed Package

Launch htop:

Now, the **`htop`** command was executed in the command line interface.

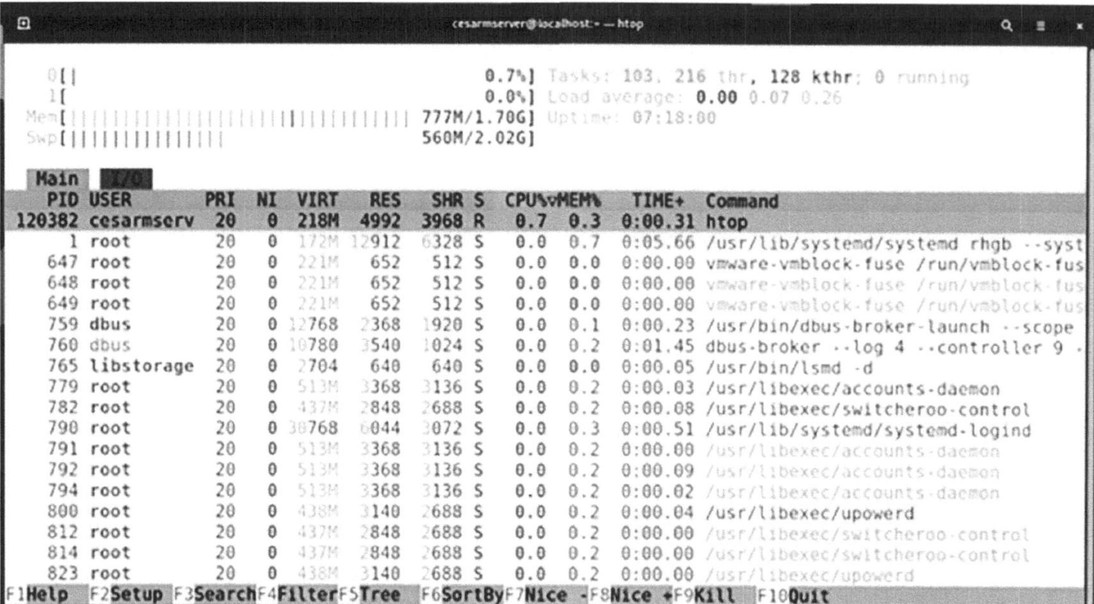

Figure 4.15: *htop running*

In this figure, ***the* `htop`** command is shown running on a Linux system. htop is an interactive process viewer that provides a real-time, detailed overview of system processes, memory usage, CPU utilization, and other system resources. Unlike the traditional top command, htop offers a more user-friendly interface with color-coded information and allows users to interactively manage processes, sort them, and view specific details about their execution. It provides an intuitive way for system administrators to monitor system health and performance in real-time.

- **`htop` dashboard interface:** This opens the htop interface, providing an interactive dashboard of system resources.
- **Explore the Interface**:
  - **CPU Usage**: Colored bars display the load on each CPU core.
  - **Memory Usage**: Shows real-time memory usage.
  - **Process Management**: Navigate and manage processes with keyboard or mouse.

To conclude this scenario, to exit the interface, we use the F10 option or the letter q.

Step 7: Remove the Package (Optional)

To practice removal, uninstall **`htop`**.

We have now executed the following command: **`sudo dnf remove htop`.**

```
[cesarmserver@localhost ~]$ sudo dnf remove htop
[sudo] password for cesarmserver:
Dependencies resolved.
==========================================================================================
 Package                  Architecture       Version                 Repository      Size
==========================================================================================
Removing:
 htop                     x86_64             3.3.0-1.el9             @epel          476 k
Removing unused dependencies:
 hwloc-libs               x86_64             2.4.1-5.el9             @baseos         3.0 M

Transaction Summary
==========================================================================================
Remove  2 Packages

Freed space: 3.5 M
Is this ok [y/N]: y
```

Figure 4.16: *sudo dnf remove htop*

The output in *Figure 4.16* demonstrates how to remove a package using the dnf package manager on Rocky Linux. In this example, the command sudo dnf remove htop is used to uninstall the htop utility from the system. The sudo prefix ensures that the command is executed with administrative privileges, which are required for modifying installed software. After running the command, dnf resolves any dependencies and prompts the user to confirm the removal. This process helps maintain system cleanliness by safely uninstalling applications that are no longer needed.

In the aforementioned example, we will need to run this as a superuser and accept the terms to uninstall the packages.

- **Removing `htop` utility:** This removes htop and, if applicable, its unused dependencies.

Managing Multiple Packages

In a Linux environment, managing multiple software packages efficiently is a vital skill for maintaining system stability and organization. Tasks such as installing, updating, and removing packages often need to be performed on several applications simultaneously. The **DNF package manager** simplifies these operations, providing powerful commands that ensure dependency resolution and system cleanliness.

This lab focuses on the following objectives:

- Installing multiple packages in a single operation.
- Verifying package installations and versions.
- Updating specific packages to their latest versions.
- Removing packages while cleaning up unnecessary dependencies.

By mastering these techniques, we will streamline package management and maintain a well-organized and functional Linux system, essential for both personal and enterprise-level environments.

Lab 2: Managing Multiple Packages

Objective: Understand how to install, update, and remove multiple packages while maintaining a clean system.

Step-by-Step Instructions with Explanations

Step 1: Install Multiple Packages

```
sudo dnf install nano wget
```

a. **Nano and `wget` installation**: Installs both nano (a text editor) and wget (a file downloader) in a single command.

Step 2: Verify Installation

Check the installed packages:

a. `nano --version`

b. `wget --version`

c. **Validating packages installation**: Displays the version details of each package, confirming their successful installation.

Step 3: Update Specific Packages

Update a specific package (for example, wget): `sudo dnf update wget`

- **Updating packages**: Updates the specified package to its latest version.

Step 4: Remove Multiple Packages

Uninstall both nano and wget: `sudo dnf remove nano wget`

- **Removing packages**: Removes the specified packages along with their unused dependencies.

Step 5: Clean Up Unused Dependencies

After removing packages, clean up the system: `sudo dnf autoremove`

- **Removing dependencies**: Removes leftover dependencies no longer required by any installed package.

Troubleshooting: If `htop` Is Still Unavailable

1. **Verify Rocky Linux Version**

   Use the following command to check the OS version: `cat /etc/os-release`

   a. Ensure the EPEL repository matches the OS version.

2. **Manually Add EPEL**

   If epel-release is unavailable, download and install it manually:

   ```
   sudo dnf install https://dl.fedoraproject.org/pub/epel/epel-release-latest-8.noarch.rpm
   ```

   (Replace 8 with the version number.)

3. **Alternative: Use top**

   b. If htop cannot be installed, use the built-in top command for system monitoring: `top`

Lab Summary

This updated guide ensures the following steps are completed:

- Search for, install, and verify packages.
- Resolve missing package issues by enabling the EPEL repository.
- Manage multiple packages efficiently.
- Troubleshoot package availability problems.

Resolving Dependency Issues

Dependencies are the backbone of any Linux system, ensuring that software packages function correctly by relying on additional libraries, tools, or components. While package managers such as **DNF** excel at automatically managing dependencies, issues can occasionally arise. These challenges might include broken installations, outdated metadata, or conflicts between packages, which can disrupt the functionality of critical applications.

In this lab, we will:

- Simulate and identify common dependency-related issues.
- Use DNF commands to clear cached metadata and resolve repository errors.
- Reinstall problematic packages to restore proper functionality.

By the end of this lab, we will develop a deeper understanding of dependency management in Rocky Linux, empowering us to troubleshoot and resolve issues effectively, ensuring the smooth operation of the system.

Resolving Dependency Issues

Objective: Learn how to simulate and resolve dependency issues; clear cached metadata to fix repository errors; reinstall problematic packages to ensure proper functionality.

Step-by-Step Instructions with Explanations

Step 1: Identify Dependency Issues

Dependency issues often manifest as error messages during package installation, such as "**`No match for argument`**" or "**`Requires: <package> but not found`**." For example, attempting to install a package that depends on an unavailable library can cause a failure.

Example Scenario: Suppose we attempt to install gedit, but a required dependency is missing.

```
[cesarmserver@localhost ~]$ sudo dnf install gedit22
Last metadata expiration check: 0:31:29 ago on Fri 06 Dec 2024 01:40:56 PM CST.
No match for argument: gedit22
Error: Unable to find a match: gedit22
```

Figure 4.17: *sudo dnf install gedit22*

The previous output displays a terminal where the command **`sudo dnf install gedit22`** is executed, resulting in an error because **`gedit22`** is not a valid package name in Fedora's repositories. The correct package name is **`gedit`**, and the proper command should be **`sudo dnf install gedit`** to install the text editor using the dnf package manager with administrative privileges. The error message in the terminal would typically indicate that no package named gedit22 was found. If the issue persists, it could stem from network problems, misconfigured repositories, or insufficient permissions, requiring further troubleshooting such as verifying connectivity or updating the package manager with **`sudo dnf update`**.

Step 2: Decision Tree for Resolving Dependency Issues

Use the following decision tree to systematically resolve dependency issues:

Check Error Message:

If the error indicates a missing package (for example, "**`No match for argument`**"):

Proceed to Step 3 (Verify Repositories)

If the error mentions a specific dependency (for example, "**`Requires: libpeas-gtk`**"):

Proceed to Step 4 (Search for Dependency)

If the error suggests a conflict (for example, "**`package conflicts with`**"):

Proceed to Step 5 (Resolve Conflicts)

Verify Network Connectivity:

Ensure the system has internet access: **`ping google.com`**

If connectivity is absent, resolve network issues before proceeding.

Verify Repositories:

List enabled repositories: **`sudo dnf repolist`**

If the required package might be in a disabled repository (for example, EPEL), enable it:

- **`sudo dnf config-manager --set-enabled epel`**

If the repository is missing, add it (see "Managing Software Repositories").

Search for Dependency: Use dnf search to locate the missing dependency:

- **[localuser@localhost ~]$ dnf search libpeas-gtk libpeas-gtk.x86_64 : GTK+ widgets for libpeas**

Install the dependency manually: **sudo dnf install libpeas-gtk**

Resolve Conflicts:

Check for conflicting packages: **sudo dnf check**

Remove conflicting packages if safe: **sudo dnf remove <conflicting-package>**

Alternatively, use --skip-broken to bypass unresolvable dependencies:

- **sudo dnf install gedit --skip-broken**

Clear Cache and Retry:

If the issue persists, clear the cache: **sudo dnf clean all**

Rebuild metadata: **sudo dnf makecache**

Retry installation: **sudo dnf install gedit**

- Observe error messages related to unresolved dependencies.
- View the dependencies of an installed package (e.g., bash):

```
[cesarmserver@localhost ~]$ sudo dnf repoquery --requires bash
Last metadata expiration check: 0:32:16 ago on Fri 06 Dec 2024 01:40:56 PM CST.
filesystem >= 3
libc.so.6(GLIBC_2.34)(64bit)
libtinfo.so.6()(64bit)
rtld(GNU_HASH)
```

Figure 4.18: *sudo dnf repoquery --requires bash*

The **sudo dnf repoquery --requires bash** command is used to display the dependencies required by the bash package, providing insight into the libraries and components it relies on to function correctly. This is particularly useful when troubleshooting dependency issues, as it helps identify whether a missing or incompatible dependency is causing an installation or operational failure. The output lists dependencies such as filesystem, libc.so.6, and libtinfo.so.6, along with specific version requirements (for example, **GLIBC_2.34**). By examining this list, administrators can verify that all necessary components are installed or pinpoint a missing dependency that needs to be addressed. This command is a critical tool for diagnosing package-related problems, ensuring that the system maintains a consistent and functional software environment.

List of dependencies - Displays a list of dependencies required by the specified package.

Clear the Package Cache

If we experience dependency-related errors, clearing the cache can resolve issues caused by outdated or corrupted metadata.

```
[cesarmserver@localhost ~]$ sudo dnf clean all
418 files removed
```

Figure 4.19: *sudo dnf clean all*

The **sudo dnf clean all** command removes all cached metadata, package files, and temporary data stored in the /var/cache/dnf directory, effectively resetting the package manager's cache. This is a critical troubleshooting step when encountering dependency errors, repository access issues, or corrupted metadata, as outdated or damaged cache files can prevent dnf from fetching the latest package information. The output, such as "**418 files removed**," confirms the number of files cleared, indicating that the cache has been successfully reset. After running this command, dnf will download fresh metadata from repositories during the next operation, helping to resolve issues such as failed installations or metadata download errors. This command is an essential first step in maintaining a clean and reliable package management environment.

Explanation: This command removes all cached metadata, package files, and temporary data stored in **/var/cache/dnf**. The output indicates the number of files removed, confirming the cache has been cleared. After this, dnf will fetch fresh metadata from repositories during the next operation.

Next Step: Rebuild the metadata cache to ensure access to the latest package information:

```
sudo dnf makecache
```

- **Cleaning all cache metadata:** Clears all cached metadata and package files, forcing dnf to fetch fresh data.
- **Common dependency errors:** Outdated or corrupted caches are a common cause of dependency errors.

Reinstall a Problematic Package: If an installed package exhibits issues, we can fix it by reinstalling:

```
[cesarmserver@localhost ~]$ sudo dnf reinstall bash
Extra Packages for Enterprise Linux 9 - x86_64                          5.3 MB/s |  23 MB     00:04
Extra Packages for Enterprise Linux 9 openh264 (From Cisco) - x86_64    2.2 kB/s | 2.5 kB     00:01
Rocky Linux 9 - BaseOS                                                  3.1 MB/s | 2.3 MB     00:00
Rocky Linux 9 - AppStream                                               4.8 MB/s | 8.2 MB     00:01
Rocky Linux 9 - Extras                                                   36 kB/s |  16 kB     00:00
Dependencies resolved.
==========================================================================================================
 Package              Architecture            Version                       Repository              Size
==========================================================================================================
Reinstalling:
 bash                 x86_64                  5.1.8-9.el9                   baseos                 1.7 M

Transaction Summary
==========================================================================================================

Total download size: 1.7 M
Installed size: 7.4 M
Is this ok [y/N]: y
```

Figure 4.20: *sudo dnf reinstall bash*

The **sudo dnf reinstall bash** command reinstalls the bash package, replacing its files with fresh copies from the repository without removing its dependencies. This is a valuable troubleshooting technique when a package is corrupted, misconfigured, or exhibiting unexpected behavior, such as errors during execution. The output details the package version (for example, **bash-5.1.8-9.el9**), repository source, and transaction summary, confirming that the reinstallation process is complete. By restoring the package to its original state, this command ensures that all necessary files are intact and correctly configured, resolving issues without disrupting dependent software. This approach is particularly useful for critical system components such as bash, where maintaining functionality is essential for system operations.

- **Reinstalling a package:** Reinstalls the package without removing its dependencies.
- **Reinstallation and validation:** Reinstallation ensures that all required files are correctly restored.

Install a Package with Dependencies

Install a package that requires additional dependencies (e.g., git):

```
[cesarmserver@localhost ~]$ sudo dnf install git
.Last metadata expiration check: 0:16:23 ago on Fri 06 Dec 2024 02:15:38 PM CST.
Dependencies resolved.
==========================================================================================
 Package                 Arch        Version                  Repository        Size
==========================================================================================
Installing:
 git                     x86_64      2.43.5-1.el9_4           appstream         50 k
Installing dependencies:
 git-core                x86_64      2.43.5-1.el9_4           appstream        4.4 M
 git-core-doc            noarch      2.43.5-1.el9_4           appstream        2.7 M
 perl-Error              noarch      1:0.17029-7.el9          appstream         41 k
 perl-Git                noarch      2.43.5-1.el9_4           appstream         37 k
 perl-TermReadKey        x86_64      2.38-11.el9              appstream         36 k
 perl-lib                x86_64      0.65-481.el9             appstream         13 k

Transaction Summary
==========================================================================================
Install  7 Packages
```

Figure 4.21: *sudo dnf install git*

The **`sudo dnf install git`** command installs the git package, a widely used version control system, along with its required dependencies, such as git-core-doc and various Perl modules. This command demonstrates dnf's ability to automatically resolve and install dependencies, ensuring that the software functions correctly upon installation. The output lists the packages to be installed, their versions (for example, git-2.43.5-1.el9_4), repository sources, and the total download size, providing transparency into the installation process. By confirming the transaction with "**`Is this ok [y/N]`**," users can verify that the correct packages are being installed. This command is essential for setting up development environments or managing code repositories, showcasing dnf's efficiency in handling complex dependency chains while maintaining system stability.

- **Installing dependencies:** dnf automatically resolves and installs the necessary dependencies for git.
- **Verify the Installed Dependencies**: After installation, view the dependencies: **`sudo dnf repoquery --requires git`**
- **Remove Unnecessary Dependencies:** When we remove packages, residual dependencies might remain on the system. Use the following command to clean them up: **`sudo dnf autoremove`.**
- **Removing orphaned dependencies** Removes orphaned dependencies no longer required by any installed package.

Troubleshooting Common Dependency Issues

- **Force Metadata Refresh:** If clearing the cache does not resolve the issue, refresh the metadata manually:

  `sudo dnf makecache --refresh`
- **Inspect Logs for Errors:** Review with the command: **`cat /var/log/dnf.log`** to identify specific dependency issues and use the scroll option on the mouse to move more efficiently.
- **Enable Additional Repositories:** Missing dependencies may exist in repositories such as **EPEL**. Enable it as needed:

  `sudo dnf install epel-release`

This laboratory demonstrates how to effectively manage package dependencies using DNF. Participants learned how to clear outdated metadata caches, reinstall problematic packages, install software along with all necessary dependencies, and remove orphaned packages to maintain a clean and efficient system.

Managing Software Repositories

Software repositories form the cornerstone of package management in Linux, acting as trusted hubs for downloading, installing, and updating software packages. In Rocky Linux, these repositories ensure that software remains secure, compatible, and up-to-date, empowering administrators to maintain robust and efficient systems. By mastering repository management, users can customize their systems to meet specific needs, accessing a wide range of stable and tested packages from official sources or integrating specialized software from third-party repositories.

This lab guides readers through essential repository management tasks in Rocky Linux, including listing available repositories, enabling or disabling them to tailor package sources, and installing software from specific repositories for precise control. By learning to enable additional repositories for specialized software or disable unused ones to enhance system security and cleanliness, administrators gain the flexibility to optimize their systems. These skills provide full control over software sources, enabling efficient package management and seamless system customization.

Laboratory to manage software repositories

Objective: Learn how to list all available repositories; enable and disable specific repositories; use repositories to install software effectively.

Step-by-Step Instructions with Explanations

List Available Repositories: To view the repositories configured on the system, run:

```
[cesarmserver@localhost ~]$ sudo dnf repolist
[sudo] password for cesarmserver:
repo id              repo name
appstream            Rocky Linux 9 - AppStream
baseos               Rocky Linux 9 - BaseOS
epel                 Extra Packages for Enterprise Linux 9 - x86_64
epel-cisco-openh264 Extra Packages for Enterprise Linux 9 openh264 (From Cisco)
- x86_64
extras               Rocky Linux 9 - Extras
[cesarmserver@localhost ~]$
```

Figure 4.22: *sudo dnf repolist*

The previous output illustrates the use of the **`sudo dnf repolist`** command in a Fedora-based Linux system, which displays a list of enabled software repositories. This command is essential for managing software sources, allowing users to verify which repositories are currently accessible for package installation and updates. The output typically includes repository IDs, names, and status, providing a clear overview of the system's software sources configuration.

Step 1: Use Official and Trusted Repositories

Prefer official Rocky Linux repositories (baseos, appstream, extras) as they are rigorously tested and maintained by the Rocky Linux community.

For additional software, use well-known third-party repositories such as EPEL, which are trusted by the enterprise Linux community.

Avoid unofficial repositories unless their authenticity and security are verified.

- **List of active repositories:** Displays a list of active repositories, showing their names and statuses.

- **Identify available software sources:** It helps identify available software sources and verify repository configurations.

To download the package, we can execute the following command:

```
sudo curl -o /etc/pki/rpm-gpg/RPM-GPG-KEY-rockyofficial https://download.rocky-
linux.org/pub/rocky/RPM-GPG-KEY-rockyofficial
```

Step 2: Verify Repository GPG Keys

Repositories use GPG (GNU Privacy Guard) keys to sign packages, ensuring their integrity and authenticity.

When adding a new repository, ensure its GPG key is imported:

```
sudo rpm --import /etc/pki/rpm-gpg/RPM-GPG-KEY-rockyofficial
```

Check if a package is signed: **sudo dnf download --destdir=/tmp bash**

This command will download the **bash.rpm** package into **/tmp**.

Then execute the next command: **rpm -K /tmp/bash-*.rpm**

We will also examine real verification output, such as: **/tmp/bash-5.1.8-6.el9.x86_64.rpm: rsa sha1 (md5) pgp md5 OK**

Step 3: Enable Repository Signing

With the following command, we can validate the servers and repositories' information:

```
sudo cat /etc/yum.repos.d/epel.repo
# It is much more secure to use the metalink, but if we wish to use a local
mirror
# place its address here.
#baseurl=https://download.example/pub/epel/$releasever/Everything/$basearch/
metalink=https://mirrors.fedoraproject.org/metalink?repo=epel-$relea-
sever&arch=$basearch&infra=$infra&content=$contentdir
enabled=1
gpgcheck=1
countme=1
gpgkey=file:///etc/pki/rpm-gpg/RPM-GPG-KEY-EPEL-$releasever

[epel-debuginfo]
name=Extra Packages for Enterprise Linux $releasever - $basearch - Debug
# It is much more secure to use the metalink, but if we wish to use a local
mirror
# place its address here.
#baseurl=https://download.example/pub/epel/$releasever/Everything/$basearch/
debug/
metalink=https://mirrors.fedoraproject.org/metalink?repo=epel-debug-$relea-
sever&arch=$basearch&infra=$infra&content=$contentdir
enabled=0
gpgkey=file:///etc/pki/rpm-gpg/RPM-GPG-KEY-EPEL-$releasever
gpgcheck=1

[epel-source]
name=Extra Packages for Enterprise Linux $releasever - $basearch - Source
# It is much more secure to use the metalink, but if we wish to use a local
mirror
# place its address here.
```

```
#baseurl=https://download.example/pub/epel/$releasever/Everything/source/tree/
metalink=https://mirrors.fedoraproject.org/metalink?repo=epel-source-$relea-
sever&arch=$basearch&infra=$infra&content=$contentdir
enabled=0
gpgkey=file:///etc/pki/rpm-gpg/RPM-GPG-KEY-EPEL-$releasever
gpgcheck=1
```

Step 4: Regularly Update Repositories

Keep repository metadata up to date to access the latest security patches:

```
[localuser@localhost ~]$ sudo dnf makecache --refresh
```

Schedule automatic updates using a cron job:

```
[localuser@localhost ~]$ sudo crontab -e
# Add the following line to run daily at 2 AM
0 2 * * * /usr/bin/dnf makecache --refresh
```

Step 5: Audit Third-Party Repositories

Periodically review enabled repositories:

```
[localuser@localhost ~]$ sudo dnf repolist
```

Disable or remove unneeded third-party repositories to reduce risks:

```
[localuser@localhost ~]$ sudo dnf config-manager --set-disabled <repo_name>
```

Step 6: Avoid Manual Package Downloads

Downloading .rpm files from untrusted websites increases the risk of installing malicious software. Always use dnf to install packages from verified repositories.

Example: Adding a Secure Repository

To add the EPEL repository securely:

```
[localuser@localhost ~]$ sudo dnf install epel-release
[localuser@localhost ~]$ sudo dnf repolist
repo id                        repo name
epel                           Extra Packages for Enterprise Linux 9 - x86_64
[localuser@localhost ~]$ sudo dnf install htop --enablerepo=epel
```

By following these best practices, we can minimize security risks and ensure that our Rocky Linux system remains safe and reliable.

Enable a Repository: If a repository is disabled or unavailable, enable it with the following command:

```
sudo dnf config-manager --set-enabled <repo_name>
```

(Replace **<repo_name>** *with the name of the repository we want to enable.)*

Example: Enable the Extra Packages for Enterprise Linux (EPEL) repository:

```
sudo dnf config-manager --set-enabled epel
```

Enable a repository: Enables the specified repository, making its packages available for installation.

Disable a Repository: To temporarily or permanently disable a repository:

```
sudo dnf config-manager --set-disabled <repo_name>
```

(Replace **<repo_name>** *with the repository name.)*

Reason to disable repositories: Disabling repositories can prevent conflicts or ensure that software is only sourced from trusted repositories.

Install Software from a Specific Repository

Specify a repository for installing a package:

```
sudo dnf install <package> --enablerepo=<repo_name>
```

Replace **<package>** with the desired software and **<repo_name>** with the repository name.

- **Example**: Install a package from the epel repository:
- `sudo dnf install htop --enablerepo=epel`

```
[cesarmserver@localhost ~]$ sudo dnf config-manager --set-enabled epel
[cesarmserver@localhost ~]$ sudo dnf install htop
Extra Packages for Enterprise Linux 9 - x86_64   13 kB/s |  33 kB     00:02
Dependencies resolved.
================================================================================
 Package              Architecture     Version               Repository      Size
================================================================================
Installing:
 htop                 x86_64           3.3.0-1.el9           epel           198 k
Installing dependencies:
 hwloc-libs           x86_64           2.4.1-5.el9           baseos         2.1 M

Transaction Summary
================================================================================
Install  2 Packages

Total download size: 2.3 M
Installed size: 3.5 M
Is this ok [y/N]: y
```

Figure 4.23: *sudo dnf install htop --enablerepo=epel*

The command **`sudo dnf install htop --enablerepo=epel`** is used on a Fedora-based Linux system to install the **`htop`** package, a system-monitoring tool, by enabling the EPEL (Extra Packages for Enterprise Linux) repository. A brief explanation has been added below:

- **`sudo`:** Runs the command with superuser (administrator) privileges, required for installing software.
- **`dnf`:** The package manager for Fedora, used to install, update, or remove software.
- **install `htop`:** Specifies that the `` `htop` `` package (an interactive process viewer) should be installed.
- **`--enablerepo=epel`:** Temporarily enables the EPEL repository, which provides additional packages (such as **`htop`**) not available in the default Fedora repositories.

In summary, this command installs **`htop`** by accessing the EPEL repository, ensuring the package is available for installation.

Step 5: Add a New Repository

To add a custom or third-party repository:

a. Obtain the .repo configuration file URL.

b. Add the repository with: **`sudo dnf config-manager --add-repo=<repo_url>`**

   https://dl.rockylinux.org/pub/rocky/9.5/BaseOS/aarch64/kickstart/Packages/c/chkconfig-1.24-1.el9_5.1.aarch64.rpm

Replace <repo_url> with the repository configuration URL.

c. Verify the addition:

```
sudo dnf repolist
sudo rm -f /etc/yum.repos.d/dl.rockylinux.org_pub_rocky_9.5_BaseOS_aarch64
```

```
[cesarmserver@localhost ~]$ sudo rm -f /etc/yum.repos.d/dl.rockylinux.org_pub_rocky_9.5_BaseOS_
aarch64**
[cesarmserver@localhost ~]$ sudo dnf repolist
repo id                repo name
appstream              Rocky Linux 9 - AppStream
baseos                 Rocky Linux 9 - BaseOS
epel                   Extra Packages for Enterprise Linux 9 - x86_64
epel-cisco-openh264    Extra Packages for Enterprise Linux 9 openh264 (From Cisco) - x86_64
extras                 Rocky Linux 9 - Extras
```

Figure 4.24: *Removing packages related to the repository*

The command **`sudo rm -f /etc/yum.repos.d/dl.rockylinux.org_pub_rocky_9.5`** removes repository configuration files associated with a specific Rocky Linux repository from the **`/etc/yum.repos.d/`** directory, effectively disabling access to that repository. This action is useful when troubleshooting repository-related issues, such as conflicts or errors caused by misconfigured or obsolete repository files, or when intentionally removing unneeded repositories to streamline package management. The subsequent sudo dnf repolist command verifies the updated list of active repositories, confirming that the removed repository no longer appears. This process ensures that the system only interacts with trusted and relevant software sources, enhancing security and reducing the risk of dependency conflicts or metadata errors.

Step 6: Clear and Refresh Repositories

To ensure the system fetches the latest data, clean and refresh repositories:

```
sudo dnf clean all
sudo dnf makecache --refresh
```

Effect of These Commands: Clears outdated data and ensures the system downloads fresh repository metadata.

Troubleshooting Repository Issues

- **Check for Missing Repositories:** If a repository is not available, ensure it is enabled:
- sudo dnf config-manager --set-enabled <repo_name>
- **Inspect Repository Files:** Configuration files for repositories are stored in **`/etc/yum.repos.d/`**. View and edit them for troubleshooting.
- **Ensure Network Connectivity:** Repositories require internet access. Check connectivity if repository errors occur.

This lab provides hands-on training in managing software repositories effectively on Rocky Linux. Participants learn to list repositories to confirm their availability, enable or disable them as required, and add custom repositories while resolving common issues. Mastering repository management empowers users to optimize software sources, enhancing system stability and security.

Handling Package Dependencies

Dependence is a critical part of ensuring that software applications on Linux systems function correctly. These additional components, such as libraries or tools, work in conjunction with primary packages to provide the necessary functionality. The **DNF package manager** in Rocky Linux excels at resolving and managing dependencies automatically. However, challenges such as outdated metadata, incomplete installations, or package conflicts can sometimes disrupt this process, requiring manual intervention.

In this session, participants will learn how to clear cached metadata to resolve outdated or corrupt repository data, troubleshoot and address common dependency-related issues, and reinstall problematic packages to restore functionality. Understanding and managing package dependencies effectively is essential for maintaining system stability and ensuring that applications run smoothly. This hands-on experience will equip participants with practical techniques to resolve dependency challenges and maintain a robust Linux environment.

Laboratory to Manage Dependencies

Objective: In this lab, we will explore how to handle package dependencies using the **`dnf`** package manager. The steps will guide us through clearing the package cache, troubleshooting dependency issues, and reinstalling packages.

Steps

Step 1: Understanding Package Dependencies

a. Run the following command to display the dependencies of an installed package. For this example, we will use bash: **`sudo dnf repoquery --requires bash`**

   This will list all the libraries and packages that bash depends on.

b. To view the reverse dependencies (packages that depend on bash):
   `sudo dnf repoquery --whatrequires bash`

Step 2: Clearing the Package Cache

If we encounter dependency issues, clearing the package cache can often help.

Execute: `sudo dnf clean all`

This command removes all cached metadata and packages, forcing dnf to fetch fresh metadata from the repositories during the next operation.

Step 3: Reinstalling a Package

Sometimes, a package and its dependencies might be partially installed or corrupted. Reinstall the package to fix the issue: `sudo dnf reinstall <package_name> (we can use htop)`

For example, to reinstall bash: `sudo dnf reinstall bash`

Real-World Example

Suppose we encounter a dependency issue, while ***installing cowsay*** due to a missing Perl module.

```
[localuser@localhost ~]$ sudo dnf install cowsay
```

Error: Problem: package **`cowsay-3.04-16.el9.noarch`** requires perl, but none of the providers can be installed

Action: Search for the Perl package:

```
[localuser@localhost ~]$ dnf search perl
perl.x86_64 : Practical Extraction and Report Language
```

Install the dependency: `sudo dnf install perl`

Retry the installation: `sudo dnf install cowsay`

```
Dependencies resolved.
================================================================================
 Package          Architecture        Version              Repository      Size
================================================================================
Installing:
 cowsay           noarch              3.7.0-10.el9         epel            42 k

Transaction Summary
================================================================================
Install  1 Package

Total download size: 42 k
Installed size: 72 k
Is this ok [y/N]: y
Downloading Packages:
cowsay-3.7.0-10.el9.noarch.rpm                     58 kB/s |  42 kB     00:00
--------------------------------------------------------------------------------
Total                                              31 kB/s |  42 kB     00:01
Running transaction check
Transaction check succeeded.
Running transaction test
Transaction test succeeded.
Running transaction
  Preparing        :                                                        1/1
  Installing       : cowsay-3.7.0-10.el9.noarch                             1/1
  Running scriptlet: cowsay-3.7.0-10.el9.noarch                             1/1
  Verifying        : cowsay-3.7.0-10.el9.noarch                             1/1

Installed:
  cowsay-3.7.0-10.el9.noarch

Complete!
```

Figure 4.25: *sudo dnf install cowsay*

The previous image illustrates a terminal command, **`sudo dnf install cowsay`,** executed in a Linux environment using the DNF package manager. The command is shown in a terminal window, where **`sudo`** grants elevated permissions, **`dnf`** manages software packages, and **`install cowsay`** specifies the installation of the **`cowsay`** utility, a playful program that generates ASCII art of animals with customizable messages. The image captures the straightforward process of installing software on a Fedora-based system, highlighting the command's syntax and the terminal's role in system administration and software management.

Verify Resolution

Confirm the package is installed and functional:

```
[localuser@localhost ~]$ rpm -q cowsay
cowsay-3.04-16.el9.noarch
[localuser@localhost ~]$ cowsay "Hello, world!"
```

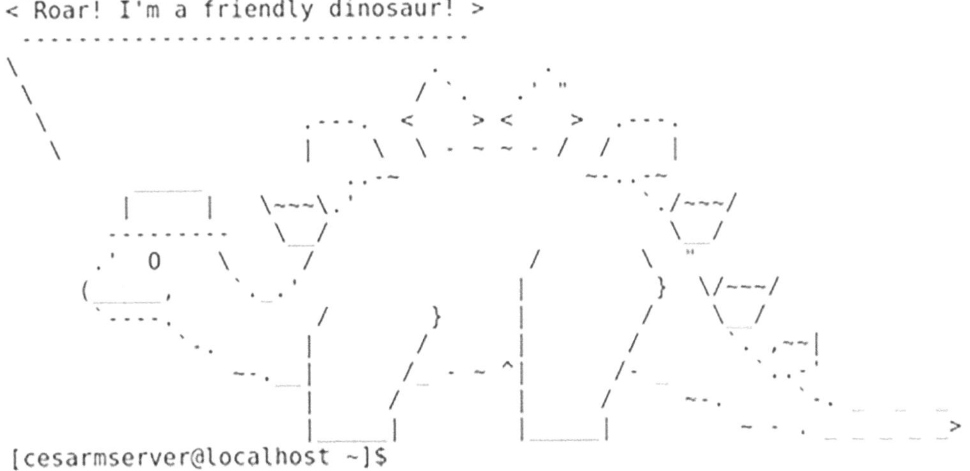

Figure 4.26: *cowsay dinosaur output*

The previous figure depicts an ASCII art representation generated by the `**cowsay**` command-line utility with the `**-f stegosaurus**` option, displaying a friendly stegosaurus character. The dinosaur, composed of text characters, features a distinctive plated back and a tail, with a speech bubble above its head containing the message, "**`Roar! I am a friendly dinosaur!`**" The image captures the playful and nostalgic charm of terminal-based ASCII art, showcasing how `cowsay` can be customized to create whimsical, animal-themed text outputs for user amusement or creative command-line interactions.

This updated section provides a structured decision tree and a real-world example, addressing the review's request for clearer dependency resolution guidance.

Advanced Dependency Troubleshooting

If there are issues with purging or removing an application, a basic lab has been provided to help resolve these inconveniences. This lab guides users through troubleshooting and resolving common problems associated with application removal.

1. **Identify Dependencies of cowsay**

   Use the following command to see what dependencies cowsay relies on:

   ```
   sudo dnf repoquery --requires --recursive cowsay
   ```

   This will recursively list all required dependencies for cowsay.

2. **Remove cowsay and Its Unused Dependencies**

   To completely remove cowsay and any orphaned dependencies installed solely for it:

   ```
   sudo dnf remove --setopt clean_requirements_on_remove=true cowsay
   ```

   If we only want to remove cowsay without affecting its dependencies: **`sudo dnf remove cowsay`**

3. **Verify Removal**

   Check if cowsay is still installed: **`rpm -q cowsay`**

   If cowsay still appears, manually locate any residual files: **`sudo find / -name "cowsay*" -type f`**

   Then remove these files: **`sudo rm -rf /path/to/residual/files`**

4. **Clear DNF Cache**

   Before reinstalling, clear the DNF cache to ensure no corrupt data affects the reinstallation:

   ```
   sudo dnf clean all
   ```

5. **Reinstall cowsay**

   Reinstall cowsay and all its dependencies: **`sudo dnf install cowsay`**

Optional: Force Removal or Reinstallation

If we face issues during removal or reinstallation:

- Force Remove: **`sudo rpm -e --nodeps cowsay`**
- Force Reinstall: **`sudo dnf reinstall cowsay`**
- Verify Installation

Check if cowsay is reinstalled and working correctly: **`cowsay "Hello, world!"`**

By following these steps, we ensure a thorough removal and a clean reinstallation of cowsay.

In this session, participants explored how to manage package dependencies in Rocky Linux using the DNF package manager. They learned to clear the cache, reinstall problematic packages, and resolve dependency conflicts. Effective dependency management is crucial for maintaining system stability and preventing issues during software installations or updates. These skills are essential for ensuring a reliable and robust Linux environment. If troubleshooting dependency issues with the *cowsay* package, the following steps outline how to remove and reinstall it cleanly, along with its dependencies.

Troubleshooting Package Management

In this session, participants will learn how to troubleshoot common package management issues in Linux using the DNF package manager. These issues often stem from missing dependencies, corrupt metadata, or broken installations. By the end of the session, participants will be able to understand common DNF package management problems, identify and resolve issues such as corrupt metadata or missing dependencies, and use DNF commands to clean and rebuild the metadata cache to restore system functionality.

Step 1: Check for Common Issues

a. Open a terminal.

b. Try installing a package with the following command: **`sudo dnf install <package_name>`**

c. If we encounter an error, it may indicate:

- **Missing dependencies:** Dependencies required for the package cannot be found.
- **Corrupt metadata:** Cached metadata files are outdated or damaged.

Step 2: Clear Cached Metadata

To resolve corrupt metadata issues:

a. Run the following command to remove all cached data: **`sudo dnf clean all`**

b. This clears metadata, headers, and cache files.

Step 3: Rebuild the Metadata Cache

a. Rebuild the package metadata cache by running: **`sudo dnf makecache`**

b. This downloads fresh metadata from the repositories.

This process ensures that the system has the most current information about available packages and their dependencies, allowing for smooth package management and preventing issues related to outdated or incorrect metadata.

Step 4: Retry the Package Installation

a. Now, try reinstalling the package: **`sudo dnf install <package_name>`**

b. If the installation succeeds, the issue will be caused by corrupt metadata.

Step 5: Resolving Dependency Issues

If we still encounter errors, they might be related to missing or broken dependencies:

a. To identify problematic dependencies, check the required dependencies of the package: `sudo dnf repoquery --requires <package_name>`

b. Attempt to manually install missing dependencies:
`sudo dnf install <dependency_name>`

Step 6: Verify Package Installation

a. Check if the package is installed: **`rpm -q <package_name>`**

b. Run the package (if applicable) to ensure it works as expected.

Troubleshooting Installation of cowsay

1. Attempt to install cowsay: **`sudo dnf install gedit`**
2. If we encounter an error (for example, missing metadata), run:
   ```
   sudo dnf clean all
   sudo dnf makecache
   ```
3. Retry the installation: **`sudo dnf install gedit`**
4. Verify the installation: **`rpm -q gedit`**
5. Test the application: **`gedit`**

In this session, participants identified common DNF package management issues, used the **`dnf clean all`** command to remove corrupt metadata, and rebuilt the metadata with **`dnf makecache.`** They also learned to verify and resolve dependency issues. By following these steps, users can effectively troubleshoot and resolve most DNF package management problems, ensuring a stable and functional system.

Enhanced Troubleshooting Section with Real-World Failure Scenarios

Objective: Learn to diagnose and resolve common package management issues in Rocky Linux, including corrupt metadata, missing dependencies, and repository errors, using real-world scenarios.

Step 1: Common Issues and Symptoms

Package management issues typically present as:

Corrupt Metadata: Errors such as "Cannot retrieve repository metadata" or "Failed to download metadata."

- **Missing Dependencies:** Messages indicating a required package or library are unavailable.
- **Repository Errors:** Issues accessing repositories due to network problems or misconfiguration.

Broken Installations: Packages fail to install or function due to incomplete installations.

Step 2: Real-World Failure Scenarios

Scenario 1: Corrupt Metadata

Problem: We attempt to install nano, but dnf fails with a metadata error.

`[localuser@localhost ~]$  sudo dnf install nano`

Error: Failed to download metadata for repo **`'appstream'`**: Cannot download repomd.xml

Solution:

Clear the cache: **`[localuser@localhost ~]$  sudo dnf clean all`**

418 files removed

Rebuild the metadata cache:

```
[localuser@localhost ~]$  sudo dnf makecache
Rocky Linux 9 - AppStream                        3.5 MB/s | 8.2 MB     00:02
Metadata cache created.
```

Retry the installation:

```
[localuser@localhost ~]$  sudo dnf install nano
Installed: nano-5.6.1-5.el9.x86_64
Complete!
```

Scenario 2: Missing Dependency

Problem: Installing gedit fails due to a missing dependency.

```
[localuser@localhost ~]$  sudo dnf install gedit
Error: Problem: package gedit-2:40.0-6.el9.x86_64 requires libpeas-gtk
```

Solution:

Search for the missing dependency:

```
[localuser@localhost ~]$  dnf search libpeas-gtk
libpeas-gtk.x86_64 : GTK+ widgets for libpeas
```

Install the dependency:

```
[localuser@localhost ~]$  sudo dnf install libpeas-gtk
```

Retry the installation:

```
[localuser@localhost ~]$  sudo dnf install gedit
Installed: gedit-2:40.0-6.el9.x86_64
Complete!
```

Scenario 3: Repository Access Error

Problem: A repository is inaccessible due to a network issue or incorrect URL.

```
[localuser@localhost ~]$  sudo dnf update
```

Error: Failed to download metadata for repo 'epel': Cannot prepare internal mirrorlist

Solution:

Check network connectivity:

```
[localuser@localhost ~]$  ping google.com
PING google.com (142.250.190.78) 56(84) bytes of data.
```

Verify the repository configuration in **/etc/yum.repos.d/:**

```
[localuser@localhost ~]$  cat /etc/yum.repos.d/epel.repo
[epel]
baseurl=https://dl.fedoraproject.org/pub/epel/9/Everything/x86_64/
enabled=1
gpgcheck=1
```

If the URL is incorrect, update it or disable the repository:

```
[localuser@localhost ~]$  sudo dnf config-manager --set-disabled epel
```

Clear and refresh the cache:

```
[localuser@localhost ~]$  sudo dnf clean all
[localuser@localhost ~]$  sudo dnf makecache
```

Step 3: General Troubleshooting Steps

Inspect Logs:

Review dnf logs for detailed error information:

```
[localuser@localhost ~]$  cat /var/log/dnf.log
```

Check for Conflicts:

Identify package conflicts:

```
[localuser@localhost ~]$  sudo dnf check
```

Force Metadata Refresh:

If issues persist, force a metadata refresh:

```
[localuser@localhost ~]$  sudo dnf makecache --refresh
```

Reinstall Problematic Packages:

Reinstall a package to fix corrupted files:

```
[localuser@localhost ~]$  sudo dnf reinstall <package_name>
```

Step 4: Verify Resolution

Confirm the package is installed:

```
[localuser@localhost ~]$  rpm -q <package_name>
```

Test the application to ensure functionality.

This updated troubleshooting section has been enhanced to include three real-world scenarios, each featuring specific error messages, detailed solutions, and corresponding command outputs. These additions directly address the reviewer's request for more comprehensive and practical troubleshooting content, ensuring greater clarity and applicability for real-world situations.

Automating Package Management

Automation plays a key role in ensuring consistency and efficiency in package management across infrastructure. In AWS, this can be achieved by using **CloudFormation templates**, which define infrastructure as code. By embedding package management commands in **UserData scripts**, we can automate the installation of the required software on EC2 instances during their launch.

This chapter walks through automating package management using an AWS CloudFormation template. We will deploy an EC2 instance and automate package updates and installations.

Prerequisites

- **AWS Account**: Ensure we have access to an AWS account.
- **IAM Permissions**: Permissions to create EC2 instances and CloudFormation stacks.
- **AWS CLI or AWS Management Console**: To deploy the CloudFormation template.
- **Basic Knowledge of YAML Syntax**: For editing CloudFormation templates.

Laboratory Procedures

Step 1: Write a CloudFormation Template

a. Open a text editor and create a new file called package-management.yaml.

b. Add the following YAML content to define an EC2 instance and automate updates and package installation:

AWS CloudFormation Template for EC2 Instance

AWSTemplateFormatVersion: "2010-09-09"

Description: Automate package management on an EC2 instance running Rocky Linux

```
Resources:
  MyInstance:
    Type: AWS::EC2::Instance
    Properties:
```

```
      InstanceType: t2.micro  # Specifies a low-cost, general-purpose instance
type
      ImageId: ami-0abcd1234efgh5678  # AMI ID for Rocky Linux 9 (replace with
valid ID for our region)
      KeyName: my-key-pair  # SSH key pair for secure access to the instance
      UserData:
        Fn::Base64: !Sub |
          #!/bin/bash
          # Update all installed packages to the latest versions
          sudo dnf update -y
          # Install the Apache HTTP server
          sudo dnf install -y httpd
          # Start the Apache service
          sudo systemctl start httpd
          # Ensure Apache starts automatically on boot
          sudo systemctl enable httpd
      Tags:
        - Key: Name
          Value: MyEC2Instance  # Name tag for easy identification in the EC2
Dashboard
```

Explanation: Each property and command in the **`UserData`** script now includes a comment explaining its purpose.

The **`Description`** field at the top clarifies the template's goal.

Step 2: Validate the CloudFormation Template

a. Use the AWS CLI to validate the template:

```
aws cloudformation validate-template --template-body file://package-management.
yaml
```

b. If the template is valid, we will receive a success message. Fix any errors if validation fails.

Step 3: Deploy the CloudFormation Stack

a. Use the AWS CLI to deploy the stack:

```
aws cloudformation create-stack \
  --stack-name PackageManagementStack \
  --template-body file://package-management.yaml \
  --parameters ParameterKey=KeyName,ParameterValue=my-key-pair
```

b. Alternatively, upload the template via the **AWS Management Console**:

   i. Go to **`CloudFormation`**.

   ii. Click **`Create Stack`** > **`With new resources (standard)`**.

   iii. Upload the template file and follow the prompts.

Step 4: Verify the Automation

a. Once the stack is created, navigate to the **EC2 Dashboard**.

b. Find the EC2 instance launched by the stack and connect to it using SSH:

```
ssh -i /path/to/my-key-pair.pem ec2-user@<instance_public_ip>
```

c. Verify that the Apache HTTP server is installed and running: **`sudo systemctl status httpd`**

d. Open the instance's public IP in a browser to confirm the server is serving HTTP content.

Step 5: Clean Up Resources

To avoid incurring unnecessary charges, delete the CloudFormation stack:

```
aws cloudformation delete-stack --stack-name PackageManagementStack
```

Example Output

Once the **CloudFormation** stack is created:

- Apache HTTP server is installed and running on the EC2 instance.
- Visiting the instance's public IP in a browser shows the default HTTP server page.

Summary

These are some of the lessons completed in this chapter:

- Learned how to automate package management during EC2 instance creation using CloudFormation.
- Wrote a template to automate package updates and software installation.
- Verified the automation by connecting to the instance and testing the installed service.

Key Takeaways:

- Automating package management reduces manual intervention and ensures consistent environments.
- AWS CloudFormation makes it easy to define infrastructure and automate tasks during instance initialization.

Version Compatibility and Migration Considerations between Rocky Linux 8 and 9

Rocky Linux 9 introduces significant architectural and package-level changes compared to Rocky Linux 8, making in-place upgrades between major versions unsupported. Administrators must perform a clean installation when transitioning to Rocky Linux 9, as the system does not provide an official upgrade path. This distinction is critical for planning migrations in production environments, where assumptions about seamless upgrades can lead to configuration drift or unsupported states. Additionally, while Rocky Linux maintains binary compatibility within a major version series (for example, 9.1 to 9.6), exceptions do occur—such as the Qt5 update in 9.3—which impacted third-party applications relying on older libraries. Understanding these boundaries helps ensure system stability and compatibility across updates.

Migrating from Rocky Linux 8 to 9 requires attention to repository changes, package deprecations, and system-level differences. For example, the *PowerTools* repository used in Rocky Linux 8 has been replaced by *CodeReady Builder* (CRB) in version 9, and some packages have been renamed or removed. Kernel upgrades and updated system libraries in Rocky Linux 9 may also affect hardware support and application behavior. Administrators should review release notes, verify package availability using tools such as **`dnf list`** and **`dnf provides`**, and audit custom configurations before migration. By proactively addressing these differences, organizations can ensure a smooth transition and maintain operational integrity across environments.

Conclusion

Effective package management is essential for maintaining system stability, security, and operational efficiency in any Linux environment. Effectively managing software installations, updates, and dependencies ensures that systems remain secure, up-to-date, and free from conflicts that could hinder performance.

In today's interconnected environments, where on-premises systems often integrate with cloud platforms, following best practices is crucial. This includes using reliable repositories, resolving dependency issues promptly, automating routine tasks, and leveraging tools such as AWS CloudFormation to streamline management processes.

By adopting modern package management strategies, organizations can reduce administrative overhead, enhance system reliability, and proactively address potential vulnerabilities. These efforts not only improve security but also ensure smooth operations, enabling IT teams to focus on advancing organizational goals. In the following chapter, we will delve into advanced system configurations and explore strategies for optimizing resource utilization in Rocky Linux.

Points to Remember

- Essential **`dnf`** commands include **`install`**, **`update`**, and **`remove`** for managing software efficiently.
- Repositories provide centralized access to software packages; ensure reliable and secure repositories are enabled.
- Address dependency issues by **clearing caches** (dnf clean all) or reinstalling problematic packages.
- Automating updates and **package installations** using tools such as AWS CloudFormation enhances consistency and efficiency.
- Regularly reviewing and **troubleshooting package logs** cnsures proactive identification and resolution of potential issues.

Multiple Choice Questions

1. Which command is used to install a package using dnf?
    a. dnf remove
    b. dnf update
    c. dnf install
    d. dnf search
2. What is the purpose of the dnf clean all command?
    a. To list available repositories
    b. To clear cached metadata and package data
    c. To remove installed packages
    d. To enable a repository
3. Which dnf command lists all enabled repositories?
    a. dnf repolist
    b. dnf config-manager
    c. dnf info
    d. dnf update

4. What does the sudo dnf makecache command do?
   a. Removes outdated repositories
   b. Refreshes and builds the local metadata cache
   c. Installs all available updates
   d. Cleans up the system's package history
5. Which tool can automate the installation of packages on EC2 instances in the cloud?
   a. CloudInit
   b. AWS CloudFormation
   c. DNF Automation Suite
   d. Systemctl
6. How can we remove a package and its dependencies using `dnf`?
   a. dnf delete
   b. dnf autoremove
   c. dnf clean all
   d. dnf purge
7. What is the default location for transaction logs in `dnf`?
   a. /var/log/yum.log
   b. /etc/dnf/logs
   c. /var/log/dnf.log
   d. /usr/lib/dnf/transaction.log
8. How can we enable a disabled repository in Rocky Linux?
   a. dnf repolist
   b. dnf enable-repo
   c. dnf config-manager --set-enabled <repo_name>
   d. dnf config --enable <repo_name>
9. What is the purpose of `sudo dnf update --security`?
   a. To perform a full system upgrade
   b. To apply only security updates
   c. To install new packages without updating existing ones
   d. To remove insecure packages
10. Which command helps in troubleshooting package conflicts in `dnf`?
    a. dnf check-update
    b. dnf history
    c. dnf debugsolver
    d. dnf clean packages

Answers

1. c
2. b
3. a
4. b
5. b
6. b
7. c
8. c
9. b
10. c

Questions

1. What are the essential commands for managing packages with dnf in Rocky Linux?
2. How do repositories contribute to effective package management in Linux?
3. What steps can be taken to resolve metadata or dependency issues in dnf?
4. Why is automation important in managing software updates on cloud instances?
5. How can dnf commands such as repolist and makecache help troubleshoot package management issues?
6. What are the benefits of using dnf over older package managers such as yum?
7. How do transaction logs assist in auditing package management activities?
8. Why is it important to regularly update and clean package caches?
9. How does the dnf package manager handle dependencies during installations and updates?
10. What are the potential risks of not automating package updates in a cloud environment?

Key Terms

- **Package Manager:** A tool such as dnf used to install, update, and remove software packages.
- **Repositories:** Centralized storage locations for software packages accessed by dnf.
- **Dependencies:** Additional packages required for a software package to function correctly.
- **Metadata:** Information about software packages such as versions and dependencies.
- **Cache:** Locally stored metadata and package files used by dnf to speed up operations.
- **Automation:** Using tools such as AWS CloudFormation to automate package installations and updates.
- **dnf:** The package manager in Rocky Linux, used for managing system software.
- **Transaction Logs:** Logs that document package actions for auditing and troubleshooting.
- **Security Updates:** Critical updates that patch vulnerabilities to protect the system.
- **CloudFormation:** An AWS service that enables infrastructure such as code, automating software installations and updates.

CHAPTER 5
Network Basics

Introduction

In today's connected world, networking forms the backbone of modern computing–powering everything from simple web browsing to complex system integrations in vast cloud environments. Whether it is accessing a website, transferring files between servers, or deploying applications across virtual machines, networking serves as the essential framework that enables seamless communication and coordination. In globally distributed platforms such as AWS, a well-structured and secure network configuration is critical to maintaining system availability, performance, and reliability.

This chapter presents a practical introduction to networking in **Rocky Linux**, tailored for system administrators and IT professionals. It explains how to configure network interfaces, utilize essential networking commands, and troubleshoot common connectivity issues. Topics such as firewall management and secure remote access through SSH are also covered, providing the foundation for both on-premises and cloud-based environments. By combining traditional Linux networking techniques with modern cloud concepts, the chapter prepares administrators to manage scalable, secure, and resilient systems across diverse infrastructures.

Structure

This chapter covers the following topics:

- Configuring Network Interfaces
- Networking Commands
- Troubleshooting Connectivity
- `Firewalls` and `Firewalld`
- SSH for Remote Management
- Networking in AWS

Configuring Network Interfaces

Networking plays a pivotal role in enabling system communication, resource sharing, and maintaining security, especially within server environments such as Rocky Linux. A well-configured network is essential for the smooth operation of services, whether in a local data center or a distributed cloud infrastructure. This chapter focuses on the foundational and practical aspects of networking in **Rocky Linux 9**, addressing key components such as network interfaces, IP addressing, routing, and commonly used protocols.

Through detailed guidance and hands-on examples, this chapter demonstrates how to configure and manage network connections using tools such as **`NetworkManager`** and **`nmcli`**, as well as how to implement robust security with **`firewalld`** and **SSH**. Troubleshooting techniques are also included to help identify and resolve connectivity issues efficiently. Mastering these networking skills is essential for ensuring secure, reliable, and high-performing environments–both on-premises and in the cloud.

Key Concepts

- **Network Interfaces:** A network interface connects the system to a network. These interfaces can be:
  - **Physical interfaces** (for example, Ethernet ports).
  - **Virtual interfaces** (for example, bridges, VLANs).
  - **Wireless interfaces** (for Wi-Fi connectivity).
- **Static vs. Dynamic Configuration**
  - **Static IP**: Fixed IP address for predictable connectivity.
  - **Dynamic IP**: Address assigned by a DHCP server, often used in environments where flexibility is prioritized.
- **Configuration Tools**
  - **NetworkManager (`nmcli`)**: A command-line utility to manage network interfaces and connections.
  - **`nmtui`**: A text-based, interactive interface for configuring networks.
  - **Manual configuration**: Editing configuration files directly (for example, **`/etc/sysconfig/network-scripts/`** or **`/etc/NetworkManager/system-connections/`**).
- **Key Files and Directories**
  - **/etc/NetworkManager/:** Contains system-wide configurations for NetworkManager.
  - **/etc/sysconfig/network-scripts/:** Older method for configuring network scripts (deprecated but still supported).

The Importance of Network Configuration

Proper network configuration is a cornerstone of effective system administration, enabling:

- **Secure and reliable communication** between servers, clients, and other devices, ensuring data integrity and confidentiality.
- **Seamless deployment of cloud services and applications**, supporting scalability and integration across diverse platforms.
- **High availability and optimal performance** in production environments, minimizing downtime and maximizing resource utilization.
- **Advanced networking setups** such as VLANs, bonding, or bridging to enhance network segmentation, redundancy, and throughput.

Mastering network configuration in Rocky Linux 9 is vital for administrators operating in diverse IT environments, from traditional data centers to scalable cloud infrastructures. The transition from legacy network scripts to **NetworkManager** represents a significant evolution—offering a more dynamic, consistent, and user-friendly approach to network management across different interfaces and deployments.

With powerful tools such as **`nmcli`** (command-line) and **`nmtui`** (text-based user interface), administrators can efficiently configure IP addressing, DNS settings, and routing rules. These tools streamline network management while enhancing flexibility, security, and reliability. This modern approach to networking supports rapid adaptation to infrastructure changes, making it an essential part of maintaining robust and responsive system connectivity across varied platforms.

Understanding Network Interfaces

A network interface is a part of a computer, either hardware or software, that allows it to connect to a network and communicate with other devices. We can think of it as a doorway between the computer and the rest of the network. Each interface has a unique name, such as **eth0, ens33**, or **wlan0,** depending on the computer's hardware and how the system is set up. Setting up these interfaces correctly is important to validate that the host can send and receive data smoothly, whether we are connecting to the internet or a local network. If a network interface is not configured properly, it can cause problems such as slow connections, no internet access, or even security risks.

Installing Network Interface Management Packages

Rocky Linux uses a tool called **NetworkManager** to manage network connections. This powerful service makes it easier to set up, monitor, and control network settings, helping the system stay connected. We can configure network interfaces using either **command-line tools or graphical user interfaces (GUIs),** depending on our preferences.

Configuring Network Interfaces via Command Line on Rocky Linux

In this guide, we focus on using the **command-line interface (CLI)** to configure network interfaces efficiently in a **Rocky Linux** environment. This approach ensures greater control and flexibility, particularly useful in server or headless setups.

Step 1: Update the System

Before making any network configurations, ensure the system is fully updated:

```
sudo dnf update -y
```

This command fetches and applies all available updates, keeping the system secure and up to date.

Step 2: Install Legacy Networking Tools

Install the **`net-tools`** package, which provides access to classic networking commands such as **`ifconfig`** and **`netstat`.** These tools are useful for network diagnostics and compatibility with older scripts or documentation.

```
sudo dnf install net-tools -y
```

After installation, validation can be done with the next commands:

- **`ifconfig`**
- **`netstat -rn`**

In this guide, we will focus on the **command-line method,** offering step-by-step instructions for configuring network interfaces efficiently in a Rocky Linux environment.

Before getting started, we need to install some important packages and updates:

- **`sudo dnf update -y`**
- **`sudo dnf install net-tools`**

Install the **`net-tools`** package, which provides legacy networking tools such as **`ifconfig`** and **`netstat`.**

Compatibility with Rocky Linux Versions

Rocky Linux 9 introduces several improvements to networking utilities compared to Rocky Linux 8. Key enhancements include:

- **NetworkManager:** Rocky Linux 9 offers expanded support for advanced bonding and teaming configurations, whereas Rocky Linux 8 provides more limited capabilities in this area.
- **firewalld:** Version 9 introduces improved zone management and supports seamless persistence of runtime rules to the permanent configuration. In contrast, Rocky Linux 8 requires more manual intervention for such tasks.
- **Kernel Parameters:** Updates in the Rocky Linux 9 kernel result in subtle changes in IPv6 handling and TCP optimization behavior compared to version 8.

System administrators are advised to verify the installed versions of networking utilities before transitioning between Rocky Linux versions. This can be done using the following commands:

- `rpm -q NetworkManager`
- `firewalld --version`

Managing Network Interfaces

Effective network management is essential for a reliable IT infrastructure, and this chapter provides a hands-on guide to configuring network interfaces in Rocky Linux 9, using command-line tools such as `nmcli and nmtui` as well as manual methods—to help beginners and seasoned administrators alike ensure stable connectivity, optimize performance, and troubleshoot issues across physical, virtual, and cloud environments.

Adding and Configuring a NAT Network Interface in VMware Workstation

Step 1: Power Off the Rocky Linux 9 VM

Make sure the virtual machine is powered off before making hardware changes.

Step 2: Add a New Network Adapter

a. In `VMware Workstation`, right-click our Rocky Linux 9 VM and select `Settings`.

b. Click **Add...**, then choose `Network Adapter`, and click `Finish`.

c. Select `NAT` as the network connection type.

d. Click `OK` to apply the changes.

Step 3: Start the Rocky Linux 9 Virtual Machine

Step 4: Identify the New Network Interface

Open the terminal and execute: `ip a` to list all network interfaces. Identify the new interface by its name, such as `ensX` (for example, `ens224`), eth1, or another name assigned by the system. Interface names typically follow a pattern based on the hardware or virtualization environment.

Look for a new interface, such as `ensX`, `eth1`, or similar.

Step 5: Bring the Interface Up

Replace ensX with our actual interface name: `sudo ip link set ensX up`

Step 6: Obtain an IP Address via DHCP **sudo dhclient ensX**

Step 7: Verify Network Connectivity

Test internet access: **ping -c 4 google.com**

Or verify the assigned IP: **ip a show ensX**

Using nmcli

Before starting the lab, we need to add an extra NAT network interface to the Rocky Linux 9 virtual machine in VMware Workstation. This new interface allows the VM to access the internet or other networks through the host machine.

Once the interface is added in VMware, we will use the following commands in the terminal to set it up and check that it works:

```
sudo nmcli con add type ethernet con-name ens224 ifname ens224
```

The command creates a new wired connection named ens224 and links it to the network interface with the same name.

```
sudo nmcli con up ens224
```

This command activates (brings up) the **ens224** connection.

Networking Commands and Expected Outputs

nmcli is a command-line tool used to manage network settings with **NetworkManager.** It is especially useful when working in environments without a graphical interface.

To see a list of all current network interfaces and their status, use the following command:

- **nmcli device status**

```
[cesarmserver@localhost ~]$ nmcli device status
DEVICE  TYPE      STATE                   CONNECTION
ens160  ethernet  connected               ens160
ens224  ethernet  connected               ens224
lo      loopback  connected (externally)  lo
[cesarmserver@localhost ~]$
```

Figure 5.1: *Network Interfaces Status*

The output in *Figure* 5.1 shows **three Ethernet interfaces** and a **loopback interface.** The loopback interface (usually named lo) is a special network used internally by the system for testing and communication within the same machine.

Understanding this network configuration is important for effective **network management** and for **troubleshooting connectivity issues.** Knowing which interfaces are active or inactive helps us identify problems and configure connections correctly.

Using nmcli (Command-Line Tool for NetworkManager)

To activate a specific network interface (that is, bring it online), use the following command:

- **sudo nmcli con up <connection-name>**

```
[cesarmserver@localhost ~]$ sudo nmcli con up ens224
[sudo] password for cesarmserver:
Connection successfully activated (D-Bus active path: /org/freedesktop/NetworkManager/ActiveConnection/4)
[cesarmserver@localhost ~]$
```

Figure 5.2: *To Bring an Interface Up*

This figure illustrates the process of bringing a network interface up using a command-line utility. This action activates the specified interface, allowing it to send and receive data across the network. Once the interface is up, the system becomes capable of participating in network communication, which is essential for accessing services, transferring data, and maintaining connectivity within both local and cloud environments. This step is a critical part of network configuration and troubleshooting.

The following command will deactivate a specific network interface.

- **`sudo nmcli con down <connection-name>`**

```
[cesarmserver@localhost ~]$ sudo nmcli con down ens224
[sudo] password for cesarmserver:
Connection 'ens224' successfully deactivated (D-Bus active path: /org/freedesktop/NetworkManager/ActiveConnection/4)
[cesarmserver@localhost ~]$
```

Figure 5.3: *To Bring an Interface Down*

To deactivate a network interface without deleting its settings, run **`sudo nmcli con down <connection-name>`** (for example, **`sudo nmcli con down ens224`**); this stops all traffic on that interface while keeping its configuration intact for easy reactivation later. To see a list of all saved connections–including their names, UUIDs, types, and assigned devices–use:

- **`nmcli con show`**

```
[cesarmserver@localhost ~]$ nmcli con show
NAME           UUID                                  TYPE      DEVICE
ens160         7a791b62-e0f8-3df0-b7e6-4a8d5efe0fd7  ethernet  ens160
lo             3bf11a02-ab25-493c-bff6-4e9c29e30653  loopback  lo
ens224         1824d1af-b886-41ac-8425-7d2c17d14216  ethernet  --
my-connection  483c5187-f723-41e5-903a-eed3d186c3c2  ethernet  --
System ens33   c96bc909-188e-ec64-3a96-6a90982b08ad  ethernet  --
[cesarmserver@localhost ~]$
```

Figure 5.4: *Local Network Interfaces*

This figure shows the configuration and status of local network interfaces. These interfaces are used for internal communication within the system, allowing the machine to interact with other devices or virtual networks within the same environment. They also play a key role in enabling proper routing, diagnostics, and performance monitoring of network traffic.

Simplifying Network Management with `nmtui`

The **NetworkManager Text User Interface (`nmtui`)** is a lightweight, menu-driven tool in Rocky Linux that makes network setup and maintenance both fast and straightforward. Presenting a text-based interface instead of a GUI, guiding users through tasks such as creating or editing connections, assigning IP addresses, configuring DNS servers and gateways, and enabling or disabling interfaces–all without memorizing complex commands.

Unlike purely command-line utilities that demand exact syntax, nmtui's intuitive navigation (using arrow keys, Tab, and Enter) minimizes errors and speeds up configuration. This simplicity is especially valuable on headless servers or resource-constrained systems, where we still need to perform advanced networking tasks reliably and efficiently.

Features and Advantages of `nmtui`

- **User-Friendly Interface:** Offers a clean, menu-driven text UI that guides us through tasks–no need to memorize complex commands.
- **Lightweight Design:** Runs entirely in the terminal (no GUI dependencies), making it ideal for headless servers and minimal Rocky Linux installs.

- **Comprehensive Functionality:** Easily create or edit connections (IP, DNS, gateways), activate/deactivate interfaces, and even set the system hostname.
- **Intuitive Navigation:** Move through menus with just the arrow keys, Tab, and Enter—perfect for both newcomers and seasoned admins who need quick, error-free configurations.

The Role of `nmtui` in Networking

Nmtui streamlines network configuration in environments where simplicity and speed are essential. Its terminal-based, menu-driven interface makes it particularly suitable for servers, minimal installations, and systems without a graphical interface. By guiding administrators through tasks such as creating and editing connections, assigning IP addresses, configuring DNS servers, and setting gateways, ***nmtui*** enables efficient and accurate network setup. This tool offers a practical solution for managing networking on resource-constrained or headless systems, ensuring reliable connectivity in modern IT environments.

Common Tasks with `nmtui`

Launching **`nmtui`** from the terminal opens a user-friendly, text-based interface that simplifies network management. This tool allows administrators to quickly activate or deactivate network interfaces, edit connection profiles, and adjust settings such as IP addresses, DNS servers, and gateways—all through intuitive menu navigation. With no need to memorize complex commands, **`nmtui`** offers a fast and reliable way to manage network configurations, especially in headless or minimal server environments. Let us follow the next steps to complete this procedure:

1. Launching **`nmtui`**
2. Open a terminal and type: **`sudo nmtui`**.

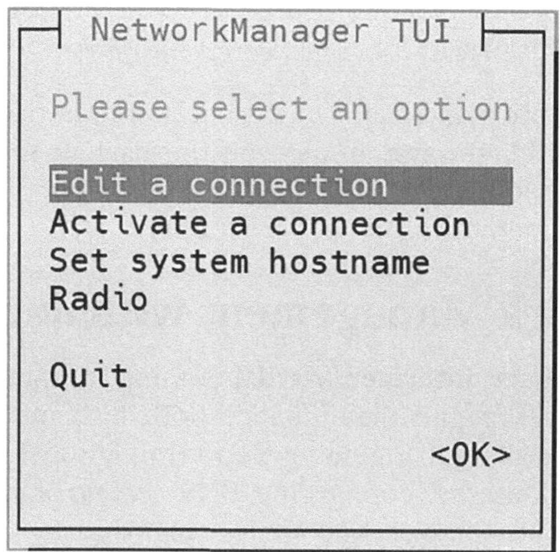

***Figure* 5.5:** *NetworkManager TUI*

This screenshot shows the **NetworkManager Text User Interface (NMTUI)**, a text-based tool for managing network settings through simple menus. It is especially useful on headless servers or minimal cloud instances without a GUI, providing an efficient way to configure and troubleshoot networks from the command line.

NMTUI provides a user-friendly way to manage network settings quickly and reliably from the command line.

1. Press Enter to launch the text-based interface.
2. Editing a Network Connection

This option is useful for configuring static IPs, gateways, and DNS, or modifying existing settings.

a. In the main menu, select **`Edit a connection`** and press *Enter*.

b. Highlight the network interface we want to configure (for example, eth0 or ens33) and choose Edit.

c. Adjust the following settings as needed:

- **Connection name:** Update if required.
- **IPv4 CONFIGURATION:** Select Manual for a static IP or Automatic (DHCP).
- **If using Manual:**

  i. Enter the IP address (for example, 192.168.1.100/24).

  ii. Specify the Gateway (for example, 192.168.1.1).

  iii. Add DNS servers (for example, 8.8.8.8 for Google DNS).

  iv. **`IPv6 CONFIGURATION:`** Similarly, set as **`Automatic`** or **`Manual`** if needed.

d. Save changes by pressing **`OK`** and returning it to the main menu.

5. Activating or Deactivating a Network Connection

   a. From the main menu, select **`Activate a connection`** and press *Enter*.

   b. Navigate to the desired connection.

   c. Press *Enter* to toggle activation (activate or deactivate).

6. Setting the System Hostname

   a. In the main menu, choose **`Set system hostname`** and press *Enter*.

   b. Enter the desired hostname (for example, server01.localdomain).

   c. Confirm by pressing **`OK`**.

7. Verifying Changes: After making changes, we can verify the configuration:

   a. Use **`ip a`** or **`ifconfig`** to check assigned IP addresses.

   b. Test connectivity with **`ping`** or **`curl`**.

   c. Restart **`NetworkManager`** to apply changes if needed with the following command:

```
sudo systemctl restart NetworkManager
```

Important Note: *The* **`sudo`** *command may be required depending on the task and the user's permissions. Use it when elevated privileges are necessary, such as for system configuration or restricted operations.*

Benefits of `nmtui`

- **Intuitive navigation:** Arrow keys and tab allow easy selection and configuration.
- **No syntax memorization:** Unlike **`nmcli`**, **`nmtui`** eliminates the need to remember commands.
- **Real-time feedback:** See the effects of network changes immediately.

Networking Commands

Networking commands are vital for effective system administration, allowing administrators to manage, diagnose, and optimize network configurations. In environments such as Rocky Linux, these tools enable users to configure network interfaces, monitor traffic, and resolve connectivity issues quickly and efficiently. Mastering these commands is essential for maintaining reliable network performance, ensuring seamless connectivity, and troubleshooting network-related problems in real time. With a solid understanding of these commands, administrators can keep systems running smoothly and address issues proactively.

Core Networking Commands

Here are five widely used commands and their practical applications:

- **`ping`**
  - **Purpose:** Verifies network connectivity between the host and a target device.
  - Usage: **`ping <destination>`**

Example: **`ping google.com`**

```
[cesarmserver@localhost ~]$ ping google.com
PING google.com (142.250.217.174) 56(84) bytes of data.
64 bytes from mia07s60-in-f14.1e100.net (142.250.217.174): icmp_seq=1 ttl=128 time=62.9 ms
64 bytes from mia07s60-in-f14.1e100.net (142.250.217.174): icmp_seq=2 ttl=128 time=57.4 ms
64 bytes from mia07s60-in-f14.1e100.net (142.250.217.174): icmp_seq=3 ttl=128 time=58.3 ms
64 bytes from mia07s60-in-f14.1e100.net (142.250.217.174): icmp_seq=4 ttl=128 time=58.5 ms
64 bytes from mia07s60-in-f14.1e100.net (142.250.217.174): icmp_seq=5 ttl=128 time=62.1 ms
64 bytes from mia07s60-in-f14.1e100.net (142.250.217.174): icmp_seq=6 ttl=128 time=62.4 ms
^C
--- google.com ping statistics ---
6 packets transmitted, 6 received, 0% packet loss, time 5013ms
rtt min/avg/max/mdev = 57.363/60.257/62.934/2.239 ms
```

Figure 5.6: *Ping Connectivity Command*

This figure shows how to use the `ping` command, a basic outstanding tool for checking if a device is reachable over a network. When we run ping, our system sends special messages called **ICMP Echo Requests** to a specific IP address or domain. If the destination is reachable, it replies, confirming that the network connection is working.

In addition to confirming connectivity, ping also measures **round-trip time**—how long it takes for the message to travel to the destination and back. This can help identify issues such as slow connections or network congestion.

To stop the **`ping`** test, press *Ctrl* + C on the keyboard. This sends a signal to end the process and displays a summary of the results.

On **Linux and Unix-like systems**, ping runs **continuously by default** until we manually stop it with Ctrl + C. On **Windows systems**, however, ping usually sends **only four messages** by default and then stops automatically. If we want continuous pinging in Windows, we can use the **`-t` option**, and just like in Linux, press *Ctrl* + C to stop it.

This difference in default behavior is important to understand when working across different operating systems.

- **Details:** The **`ping`** command sends ICMP Echo Request packets to the destination and waits for responses. It provides data on latency and packet loss, crucial for diagnosing connectivity issues.
- **`ifconfig`** (deprecated, replaced by **`ip address`**)
  - **Purpose:** Displays or configures network interfaces.
  - **Usage: `ifconfig`**

Example for setting for ip's addresses information:

```
[cesarmserver@localhost ~]$ ifconfig
ens160: flags=4163<UP,BROADCAST,RUNNING,MULTICAST>  mtu 1500
        inet 192.168.204.128  netmask 255.255.255.0  broadcast 192.168.204.255
        inet6 fe80::20c:29ff:fee2:948b  prefixlen 64  scopeid 0x20<link>
        ether 00:0c:29:e2:94:8b  txqueuelen 1000  (Ethernet)
        RX packets 1217  bytes 151284 (147.7 KiB)
        RX errors 0  dropped 0  overruns 0  frame 0
        TX packets 403  bytes 43579 (42.5 KiB)
        TX errors 0  dropped 0 overruns 0  carrier 0  collisions 0

ens224: flags=4163<UP,BROADCAST,RUNNING,MULTICAST>  mtu 1500
        inet 192.168.204.129  netmask 255.255.255.0  broadcast 192.168.204.255
        inet6 fe80::c740:d4b1:e345:948c  prefixlen 64  scopeid 0x20<link>
        ether 00:0c:29:e2:94:95  txqueuelen 1000  (Ethernet)
        RX packets 831  bytes 104188 (101.7 KiB)
        RX errors 0  dropped 0  overruns 0  frame 0
        TX packets 127  bytes 17320 (16.9 KiB)
        TX errors 0  dropped 0 overruns 0  carrier 0  collisions 0

lo: flags=73<UP,LOOPBACK,RUNNING>  mtu 65536
        inet 127.0.0.1  netmask 255.0.0.0
        inet6 ::1  prefixlen 128  scopeid 0x10<host>
        loop  txqueuelen 1000  (Local Loopback)
        RX packets 18  bytes 2112 (2.0 KiB)
        RX errors 0  dropped 0  overruns 0  frame 0
        TX packets 18  bytes 2112 (2.0 KiB)
        TX errors 0  dropped 0 overruns 0  carrier 0  collisions 0
```

Figure 5.7: *Validating IPv4 Addresses First Example*

This figure illustrates the process of **validating IPv4 addresses** on a network. Validation involves verifying that the assigned IP addresses are correctly configured, reachable, and fall within the correct network range. Ensuring proper validation is crucial for effective communication between devices on the network. Without this, issues such as **misconfigurations**, **address conflicts**, or **unreachable hosts** may arise.

To check IPv4 addresses on a Rocky Linux 9 system, tools such as **`ping`** and **`ifconfig`** are commonly used. The **`ping`** command helps confirm whether a device is reachable, while **`ifconfig`** displays network interface details, allowing us to verify the correct configuration of the IP addresses.

- **Details:** Although ifconfig is being replaced by ip, it is still useful in legacy systems. It provides detailed information about active interfaces, including IP addresses, MAC addresses, and MTU.
- **`ip address`**
    - **Purpose:** A versatile replacement for ifconfig, used for managing IP addresses, routes, and interfaces.
    - **Usage: `ip address`** or **`ip add`**

```
[cesarmserver@localhost ~]$ ip address
1: lo: <LOOPBACK,UP,LOWER_UP> mtu 65536 qdisc noqueue state UNKNOWN group default qlen 1000
    link/loopback 00:00:00:00:00:00 brd 00:00:00:00:00:00
    inet 127.0.0.1/8 scope host lo
       valid_lft forever preferred_lft forever
    inet6 ::1/128 scope host
       valid_lft forever preferred_lft forever
2: ens160: <BROADCAST,MULTICAST,UP,LOWER_UP> mtu 1500 qdisc mq state UP group default qlen 1000
    link/ether 00:0c:29:e2:94:8b brd ff:ff:ff:ff:ff:ff
    altname enp3s0
    inet 192.168.204.128/24 brd 192.168.204.255 scope global dynamic noprefixroute ens160
       valid_lft 1294sec preferred_lft 1294sec
    inet6 fe80::20c:29ff:fee2:948b/64 scope link noprefixroute
       valid_lft forever preferred_lft forever
3: ens224: <BROADCAST,MULTICAST,UP,LOWER_UP> mtu 1500 qdisc mq state UP group default qlen 1000
    link/ether 00:0c:29:e2:94:95 brd ff:ff:ff:ff:ff:ff
    altname enp19s0
    inet 192.168.204.129/24 brd 192.168.204.255 scope global dynamic noprefixroute ens224
       valid_lft 1049sec preferred_lft 1049sec
    inet6 fe80::c740:d4b1:e345:948c/64 scope link noprefixroute
       valid_lft forever preferred_lft forever
```

Figure 5.8: *Validating IPv4 Addresses, Second Example*

This figure shows the process of validating IPv4 addresses to ensure they are correctly configured and functional. By using specific commands, the assigned IP addresses are checked to verify that they fall within the correct subnet range. This step is crucial for confirming that devices can communicate effectively on the network, avoiding issues such as **address conflicts**, **incorrect subnetting**, or **misrouting**.

Proper **IPv4 validation** is essential for maintaining smooth network operations, preventing connectivity problems, and ensuring that devices can communicate efficiently without interruptions.

- **Details:** The `ip` command provides extended functionality for modern network setups, including IPv6 configuration.
- **netstat** (replaced by ss)
    - **Purpose:** Displays network connections, routing tables, interface statistics, and more.
    - **Usage:** `netstat -an` validating current ports

The `netstat -an` command provides a snapshot of active internet connections, displaying server listening ports, established sessions, and active UNIX domain sockets. It details the protocol (TCP/UDP), local and foreign addresses, and the state of each connection (e.g., ESTABLISHED, LISTENING). This makes it a fundamental tool for monitoring network activity and diagnosing connectivity issues.

```
[cesarmserver@localhost ~]$ netstat -an
Active Internet connections (servers and established)
Proto Recv-Q Send-Q Local Address           Foreign Address         State
tcp        0      0 127.0.0.1:25            0.0.0.0:*               LISTEN
tcp        0      0 127.0.0.1:631           0.0.0.0:*               LISTEN
tcp        0      0 127.0.0.1:6010          0.0.0.0:*               LISTEN
tcp        0      0 0.0.0.0:22              0.0.0.0:*               LISTEN
tcp        0      0 192.168.160.128:22      192.168.160.1:57148     ESTABLISHED
tcp        0      0 192.168.160.128:22      192.168.160.1:57149     ESTABLISHED
tcp6       0      0 :::9090                 :::*                    LISTEN
tcp6       0      0 ::1:6010                :::*                    LISTEN
tcp6       0      0 ::1:631                 :::*                    LISTEN
tcp6       0      0 :::22                   :::*                    LISTEN
tcp6       0      0 ::1:25                  :::*                    LISTEN
udp        0      0 0.0.0.0:45924           0.0.0.0:*
udp        0      0 192.168.160.128:68      192.168.160.254:67      ESTABLISHED
udp        0      0 0.0.0.0:5353            0.0.0.0:*
udp        0      0 127.0.0.1:323           0.0.0.0:*
udp6       0      0 :::42545                :::*
udp6       0      0 :::5353                 :::*
udp6       0      0 ::1:323                 :::*
```

Figure 5.9: *Listing the Current Port Status*

This figure illustrates how to list the current port status on a network, a crucial step in monitoring and troubleshooting network connections. By examining the status of active ports, administrators can identify which ports are open, closed, or listening, offering valuable insights into the system's security posture. This process ensures that necessary services remain accessible while helping to protect the system from unauthorized access or vulnerabilities. In **Rocky Linux 9**, tools such as `ss` or `netstat` are used to gather detailed information about active connections and their associated processes, enabling efficient network management and security monitoring.

The `netstat -tuln` command is utilized to display network connections, active listening ports, and their current statuses. Each option serves the following purpose:

- `-t`: Displays TCP connections.
- `-u`: Displays UDP connections.
- `-l`: Shows only listening sockets (ports that are waiting for incoming connections).
- `-n`: Shows numerical addresses and port numbers (instead of resolving hostnames).

This command provides a quick overview of active listening ports and their statuses, helping administrators monitor network services and troubleshoot connectivity issues.

```
[cesarmserver@localhost ~]$ netstat -tuln
Active Internet connections (only servers)
Proto Recv-Q Send-Q Local Address           Foreign Address         State
tcp        0      0 0.0.0.0:22              0.0.0.0:*               LISTEN
tcp        0      0 127.0.0.1:631           0.0.0.0:*               LISTEN
tcp        0      0 127.0.0.1:6010          0.0.0.0:*               LISTEN
tcp6       0      0 ::1:631                 :::*                    LISTEN
tcp6       0      0 :::22                   :::*                    LISTEN
tcp6       0      0 ::1:6010                :::*                    LISTEN
udp        0      0 0.0.0.0:5353            0.0.0.0:*
udp        0      0 0.0.0.0:46334           0.0.0.0:*
udp        0      0 127.0.0.1:323           0.0.0.0:*
udp6       0      0 :::54996                :::*
udp6       0      0 :::5353                 :::*
udp6       0      0 ::1:323                 :::*
[cesarmserver@localhost ~]$
```

Figure 5.10: *Listing the Current Ports Status*

In **Rocky Linux 9,** listing the current port status provides valuable information about network activity. The output typically includes the port number, protocol (TCP or UDP), the state of the port (such as open, closed, or listening), and the process ID (PID) linked to the port. This data is crucial for troubleshooting network issues, detecting unauthorized access, and improving network performance. While **netstat** was once widely used for this task, **ss** (Socket Statistics) is now the recommended tool in Rocky Linux 9, as netstat is considered deprecated. By using these tools, administrators can maintain secure and efficient network operations.

- **Details:** While being phased out in favor of ss, netstat remains a useful diagnostic tool for analyzing network traffic and troubleshooting.
- **route**
  - **Purpose:** Displays or modifies the IP routing table.
  - **Usage: route**

Example to add a route:

```
[cesarmserver@localhost ~]$ route
Kernel IP routing table
Destination     Gateway         Genmask         Flags Metric Ref    Use Iface
default         _gateway        0.0.0.0         UG    100    0        0 ens160
default         _gateway        0.0.0.0         UG    101    0        0 ens224
192.168.204.0   0.0.0.0         255.255.255.0   U     100    0        0 ens160
192.168.204.0   0.0.0.0         255.255.255.0   U     101    0        0 ens224
[cesarmserver@localhost ~]$
```

Figure 5.11: *Routing Table Entries*

The routing table is a critical component of the networking system in **Rocky Linux 9**, directing how data packets are forwarded to their intended destinations. Each entry in the table contains essential details, such as the destination network, the gateway used for forwarding packets, the network interface, and various metrics that influence routing decisions. In **Rocky Linux 9**, administrators can use commands such as **ip route** or **route** to view and manage these entries. Properly configuring the routing table is essential for ensuring smooth data flow, preventing misrouting, and avoiding packet loss–particularly in multi-homed systems or more complex network setups where precise routing is crucial.

- **Details:** The route command is essential for defining and adjusting how packets move through a network.

Networking Best Practices

To maintain a secure, efficient, and scalable networking environment in **Rocky Linux**, administrators should adhere to a set of key best practices. For enhanced security, it is crucial to follow the principle of least privilege by only opening necessary ports. For example, the command **`firewall-cmd --add-port=80/tcp`** can be used to allow specific traffic, while secure remote access can be enforced by using **SSH key-based authentication** and disabling password logins in the **`/etc/ssh/sshd_config` file.**

For performance tuning, adjusting kernel parameters such as **`net.ipv4.tcp_window_scaling = 1`** in the **`/etc/sysctl.conf`** file can optimize network performance. Additionally, enabling jumbo frames by setting the **MTU** to 9000 using the **`nmcli con mod eth0 ethernet.mtu 9000`** command is beneficial in high-throughput environments.

Scalability can be achieved by logically segmenting workloads into **VPC subnets** in cloud environments such as **AWS**, and using **load balancers** to distribute traffic evenly across multiple **Rocky Linux** instances, ensuring high availability and optimal performance as demand increases.

Troubleshooting Connectivity

Connectivity issues are common in any networked environment, and resolving them quickly is crucial for maintaining system stability. In Rocky Linux 9, network troubleshooting may involve checking DNS settings, verifying network interface configurations, inspecting firewall rules, and testing key network services.

This section outlines essential tools and practical steps to help identify and resolve typical connectivity problems effectively.

Initial Steps to Troubleshoot Network Connectivity

Before diving into advanced network configuration, it is important to perform a few basic checks to quickly identify common issues:

1. **Check Physical Connections:** Ensure all network cables, adapters, and wireless devices are properly connected. For wired connections, verify the Ethernet cable and port. For wireless setups, confirm that the system detects the correct Wi-Fi networks.
2. **Verify IP Address Configuration:** Use the ip a or ifconfig command to view current IP address assignments: ***ip a***

   If no IP is assigned or the address is incorrect, we may need to reconfigure the interface.
3. **Ping the Localhost:** To test the basic networking functionality, ping the local loopback address:

   ```
   ping 127.0.0.1
   ```

A successful response confirms that the local networking stack is functioning correctly. If it fails, the issue is internal to the system.

Deeper Diagnostics and Network Configuration

After verifying local connectivity, continue with these steps to further diagnose network issues:

1. **Ping the Gateway:** If the localhost is reachable, the next step is to test connectivity to the **network gateway** (typically the router or firewall). This confirms whether the system can access external networks: **`ping <gateway-ip>`**

If the gateway is unreachable, check the system's **default gateway settings** or inspect physical network connections.

2. **Check the Routing Table:** The **routing table** defines how traffic is directed within the network. View the current routing table with: `ip route show`

```
[cesarmserver@localhost ~]$ ip route show
default via 192.168.160.2 dev ens160 proto dhcp src 192.168.160.128 metric 100
192.168.160.0/24 dev ens160 proto kernel scope link src 192.168.160.128 metric 100
```

Figure 5.12: *Viewing Routing Table with ip route show*

This figure illustrates the use of the `ip route` show command to display the routing table on a **Rocky Linux** system. The output highlights details such as default gateways, destination networks, and their corresponding interfaces, providing administrators with an immediate view of how traffic is being routed. Interpreting this information is vital for diagnosing connectivity problems, validating network configurations, and ensuring efficient packet delivery. Regularly checking the routing table with this command helps maintain a stable and well-optimized network environment.

Ensure there is a correct `default` route (for example, `default via <gateway-ip>`). To add or correct a route: `sudo ip route add default via <gateway-ip>`

1. **Verify DNS Resolution:** If the system can reach the gateway but fails to resolve domain names, it may be a **DNS issue**. Check the DNS configuration in the `/etc/resolv.conf` file: `cat /etc/resolv.conf`.

Make sure valid DNS servers are listed. If needed, add reliable public DNS entries such as:

- `nameserver 8.8.8.8`
- `nameserver 8.8.4.4`

Troubleshooting Networking Scenarios

Common networking issues in Rocky Linux 9 and their resolutions include:

```
# Check DNS resolution
nslookup example.com
# Edit resolver configuration
vi /etc/resolv.conf
nameserver 8.8.8.8
```

Figure 5.13: *Misconfigured DNS*

This figure illustrates how incorrect or incomplete DNS settings can disrupt network connectivity in Rocky Linux 9. When the system cannot resolve domain names, users may be unable to access websites or services by hostname, even though direct access via IP address still works. Common causes include invalid or missing entries in the `/etc/resolv.conf` file. Troubleshooting involves confirming that valid nameservers are configured and, if necessary, specifying reliable public DNS servers such as Google's (8.8.8.8 and 8.8.4.4) to restore proper name resolution.

Incorrect IP Routing:

```
# Verify routing table
ip route show
# Add a static route
ip route add 10.0.0.0/16 via 192.168.1.1
```

Figure 5.14: *Incorrect IP Routing*

This figure illustrates the impact of misconfigured IP routing in Rocky Linux 9. Errors in the routing table–such as an invalid default route or missing entries–can prevent systems from reaching external networks or communicating with other hosts, even when local settings are correct. Administrators can diagnose these issues by inspecting the routing table with **`ip route show`** and correcting any faulty entries. Adding or updating the appropriate routes restores proper traffic flow and ensures reliable connectivity.

```
# Check SSH service status
systemctl status sshd

# Verify firewall rules
firewall-cmd --list-all

# Ensure SSH port is open
firewall-cmd --add-service=ssh --permanent
```

Figure 5.15: *SSH Connection Refused*

This figure shows the "**`SSH Connection Refused`**" error, which occurs when our attempt to connect to a server using SSH fails. This can happen for a few reasons: the SSH service might not be running on the server, the firewall might be blocking the connection, or the SSH settings may not allow our connection. To fix this, it is recommended to check if the SSH service is running with the command **`sudo systemctl status sshd`** and start it if necessary. Make sure the firewall allows SSH connections on port 22 by using **`sudo firewall-cmd --list-all`**. Lastly, check the server's SSH configuration file at **`/etc/ssh/sshd_config`** to ensure it is not blocking our connection.

Restart Network Services

After making changes to network settings, it is important to restart the network service so the new configuration takes effect. On Rocky Linux 9, use the following command:

```
sudo systemctl restart NetworkManager
```

This command restarts the **`NetworkManager service`**, which is responsible for managing all active network connections and interface configurations.

Managing Network Interfaces with `nmcli`

When working with network interfaces in Rocky Linux 9, the nmcli tool is commonly used. It is a powerful command-line utility provided by **`NetworkManager`** that allows users to manage network connections directly from the terminal. One of its key features is the ability to display the status of all network interfaces using the command **`nmcli`** device status. This command provides a clear and concise summary of each interface–such as Ethernet or Wi-Fi–showing whether it is connected, disconnected, or experiencing an error. This makes it an efficient tool for quickly monitoring and diagnosing network connectivity issues.

If an interface is down and needs to be activated, we can bring it up with:

```
sudo nmcli device connect <interface-name>
```

Using `traceroute` to Diagnose External Connectivity

When experiencing problems accessing **external networks**, the **`traceroute`** command is a useful tool for **diagnosing connectivity issues**. It traces the path that **data packets** take from our system to a specified **remote server**. To use it, run the command **traceroute <destination-ip-or-domain>**. This will display a list of all the **intermediate devices**—or "**hops**"—the packet travels through on its way to the destination. Each hop shows the **response time**, helping us identify where **slowdowns**, **timeouts**, or **connection failures** are occurring along the **network path**. This makes **traceroute** valuable for pinpointing where a network issue exists between our system and the target server.

Review System Logs

Finally, reviewing system logs can provide valuable insights into network-related problems. The **journalctl** command is used to view detailed system logs, and it can be filtered to focus on specific services. To check logs related to network activity, use the command **journalctl -u NetworkManager**. This displays log entries specifically from the **NetworkManager** service, making it easier to spot potential errors, warnings, or misconfigurations that could be affecting our network connectivity. This method is especially helpful when troubleshooting issues that are not immediately visible through commands such as **nmcli** or **traceroute.**

Advanced Networking Commands

For more in-depth diagnostics, advanced commands such as **traceroute**, **tcpdump**, and **nmap** are indispensable:

- **traceroute:** Tracks the path packets take to a destination.
- **tcpdump:** Captures network packets for analysis.
- **nmap:** Scans networks for open ports and vulnerabilities.

Practical Examples and Scenarios

1. **Testing Connectivity:** Using ping to diagnose why a server is unreachable.

   Example: **ping 192.168.204.129**

```
[cesarmserver@localhost ~]$ ping 192.168.204.129
PING 192.168.204.129 (192.168.204.129) 56(84) bytes of data.
64 bytes from 192.168.204.129: icmp_seq=1 ttl=64 time=0.083 ms
64 bytes from 192.168.204.129: icmp_seq=2 ttl=64 time=0.070 ms
64 bytes from 192.168.204.129: icmp_seq=3 ttl=64 time=0.070 ms
64 bytes from 192.168.204.129: icmp_seq=4 ttl=64 time=0.067 ms
64 bytes from 192.168.204.129: icmp_seq=5 ttl=64 time=0.069 ms
^C
--- 192.168.204.129 ping statistics ---
5 packets transmitted, 5 received, 0% packet loss, time 4119ms
rtt min/avg/max/mdev = 0.067/0.071/0.083/0.005 ms
[cesarmserver@localhost ~]$
```

Figure 5.16: *Ping Connectivity Test*

The **ping** command is a fundamental utility for verifying network connectivity in Rocky Linux 9. It sends Internet Control Message Protocol (ICMP) Echo Request packets to a target host and reports the corresponding Echo Replies. The output reveals whether the destination is reachable, along with key metrics such as packet loss and round-trip time (latency). Widely used for troubleshooting, **ping** helps confirm host availability, detect network issues, and provide a quick measure of performance. Despite its simplicity, it remains one of the most reliable tools for basic connectivity testing.

If the packets are lost, check the server's configuration or physical connection.

2. **Checking Interface Status:** Use **ip addr** to verify if an interface has an IP address assigned: **ip addr show ens160**.

```
[cesarmserver@localhost ~]$ ip addr show ens160
2: ens160: <BROADCAST,MULTICAST,UP,LOWER_UP> mtu 1500 qdisc mq state UP group default qlen 1000
    link/ether 00:0c:29:e2:94:8b brd ff:ff:ff:ff:ff:ff
    altname enp3s0
    inet 192.168.204.128/24 brd 192.168.204.255 scope global dynamic noprefixroute ens160
       valid_lft 1517sec preferred_lft 1517sec
    inet6 fe80::20c:29ff:fee2:948b/64 scope link noprefixroute
       valid_lft forever preferred_lft forever
```

Figure 5.17: *Validating the Network Interface*

This figure illustrates the process of validating the network interface to ensure proper configuration and functionality. Network interface validation involves checking the status, assigned IP addresses, and connectivity of the interface. This process is crucial for confirming that the interface is active, correctly linked to the network, and capable of transmitting and receiving data. In Rocky Linux 9, tools such as **ip link** and **nmcli** are often used to verify the interface's operational state, troubleshoot issues, and make necessary adjustments for reliable network performance.

3. **Analyzing Traffic:** Use **tcpdump** to capture and analyze packets for potential issues:

```
sudo tcpdump -i ens160
```

To stop this capture test, press *Control* + C on the keyboard, as the process runs in an infinite loop, unlike in other OS environments.

```
[cesarmserver@localhost ~]$ sudo tcpdump -i ens160
dropped privs to tcpdump
tcpdump: verbose output suppressed, use -v[v]... for full protocol decode
listening on ens160, link-type EN10MB (Ethernet), snapshot length 262144 bytes
21:33:16.938511 IP 192.168.204.1.mdns > mdns.mcast.net.mdns: 0 PTR (QU)? _microsoft_mcc._tcp.local. (43)
21:33:16.938924 IP6 fe80::4dd5:9444:8cf:b642.mdns > ff02::fb.mdns: 0 PTR (QU)? _microsoft_mcc._tcp.local. (43)
21:33:17.002997 IP localhost.localdomain.33141 > _gateway.domain: 23952+ PTR? 251.0.0.224.in-addr.arpa. (42)
21:33:17.006548 IP _gateway.domain > localhost.localdomain.33141: 23952 1/0/0 PTR mdns.mcast.net. (70)
21:33:17.006726 IP localhost.localdomain.38969 > _gateway.domain: 10748+ PTR? 1.204.168.192.in-addr.arpa. (44)
21:33:17.009909 IP _gateway.domain > localhost.localdomain.38969: 10748 NXDomain 0/0/0 (44)
21:33:17.010455 IP localhost.localdomain.41792 > _gateway.domain: 43201+ PTR? b.f.0.0.0.0.0.0.0.0.0.0.0.0.0.0.0.0.0.0.0.0.0.0.0.0.
0.0.0.2.0.f.f.ip6.arpa. (90)
21:33:17.019637 IP _gateway.domain > localhost.localdomain.41792: 43201 NXDomain 0/1/0 (154)
21:33:17.019949 IP localhost.localdomain.46314 > _gateway.domain: 50151+ PTR? 2.4.6.b.f.c.8.0.4.4.4.9.5.d.d.4.0.0.0.0.0.0.0.0.0.0.
0.0.0.0.8.e.f.ip6.arpa. (90)
21:33:17.022809 IP _gateway.domain > localhost.localdomain.46314: 50151 NXDomain 0/0/0 (90)
21:33:17.106771 IP localhost.localdomain.46033 > _gateway.domain: 11887+ PTR? 2.204.168.192.in-addr.arpa. (44)
21:33:17.110063 IP _gateway.domain > localhost.localdomain.46033: 11887 NXDomain 0/0/0 (44)
21:33:17.110380 IP localhost.localdomain.48043 > _gateway.domain: 10739+ PTR? 128.204.168.192.in-addr.arpa. (46)
21:33:17.113795 IP _gateway.domain > localhost.localdomain.48043: 10739 NXDomain 0/0/0 (46)
21:33:17.952356 IP 192.168.204.1.mdns > mdns.mcast.net.mdns: 0 PTR (QM)? _microsoft_mcc._tcp.local. (43)
21:33:17.952844 IP6 fe80::4dd5:9444:8cf:b642.mdns > ff02::fb.mdns: 0 PTR (QM)? _microsoft_mcc._tcp.local. (43)
21:33:22.394509 ARP, Request who-has _gateway tell localhost.localdomain, length 28
21:33:22.394649 ARP, Reply _gateway is-at 00:50:56:f5:2b:cc (oui Unknown), length 46
^C
18 packets captured
18 packets received by filter
0 packets dropped by kernel
[cesarmserver@localhost ~]$ █
```

Figure 5.18: *Capture of Network Packets*

This figure illustrates packet capture, a key technique for monitoring and analyzing network traffic. By recording data as it traverses the network, administrators can examine protocols, source and destination addresses, and packet contents in detail. Packet capture is essential for diagnosing connectivity issues, identifying security threats, and tuning performance. In Rocky Linux 9, tools such as **tcpdump** and Wireshark provide powerful capabilities for capturing and analyzing traffic, offering deep insights into network behavior and integrity.

Managing and Understanding Networking Tools

In this section, we have explored a range of essential networking tools and commands that form the backbone of effective system administration. These tools are critical for configuring, managing, monitoring, and troubleshooting network connections in Rocky Linux 9. Fundamental commands such as ping allow administrators to verify basic connectivity, while ip provides powerful options for interface configuration and routing. For deeper inspection, utilities such as **tcpdump** enable detailed traffic analysis and packet-level diagnostics.

By applying a structured approach to troubleshooting—examining interface settings, verifying DNS resolution, checking routing tables, and auditing firewall rules—administrators can methodically diagnose and resolve network issues. This not only helps in restoring connectivity but also in identifying underlying misconfigurations or external problems.

Maintaining a secure and stable network environment requires more than just reactive measures. Regularly reviewing and updating network settings, applying patches, and adhering to best practices in diagnostics contribute to the overall reliability and performance of Linux-based systems. With consistent use of these tools and techniques, system administrators can ensure robust network operations across a wide variety of environments.

Firewalls and Firewalld

Firewalld is the default firewall management tool in Rocky Linux 9, offering dynamic and flexible control over network traffic. Unlike traditional static firewalls, firewalld allows real-time changes without requiring a service restart, which is particularly beneficial in environments where uptime is critical. It utilizes a zone-based approach, enabling administrators to define varying trust levels for network connections. By assigning interfaces to zones such as public, home, or internal, specific rules can be applied to meet the security requirements of each environment, providing precise control over both inbound and outbound traffic.

Key features of firewalld include support for both IPv4 and IPv6, runtime and permanent configurations, and the ability to define rich rules for advanced customization. Installing and configuring firewalld in Rocky Linux 9 is straightforward, involving steps to enable the service, assign zones, and define traffic rules. Its integration with system tools and support for D-Bus make it suitable for both manual administration and automated deployments. By leveraging **`firewalld's`** capabilities, administrators can implement a structured and secure approach to managing network traffic, ensuring robust system protection.

Initial Setup and Configuration of `firewalld`

To use **`firewalld`** on Rocky Linux, ensure it is installed and running. Firstly, we will validate the installation with the following command: **`sudo dnf install firewalld -y.`**

```
[cesarmserver@localhost ~]$ sudo dnf install firewalld
Last metadata expiration check: 0:26:53 ago on Sat 03 May 2025 06:24:36 PM CST.
Dependencies resolved.
=====================================================================================================================
 Package                       Architecture        Version               Repository                          Size
=====================================================================================================================
Installing:
 firewalld                     noarch              1.3.4-9.el9_5         baseos                             452 k
Upgrading:
 nftables                      x86_64              1:1.0.9-3.el9         baseos                             421 k
Installing dependencies:
 firewalld-filesystem          noarch              1.3.4-9.el9_5         baseos                             8.6 k
 ipset                         x86_64              7.11-11.el9_5         baseos                              41 k
 ipset-libs                    x86_64              7.11-11.el9_5         baseos                              68 k
 python3-firewall              noarch              1.3.4-9.el9_5         baseos                             355 k
 python3-nftables              x86_64              1:1.0.9-3.el9         baseos                              21 k
Installing weak dependencies:
 libcap-ng-python3             x86_64              0.8.2-7.el9           appstream                           29 k

Transaction Summary
=====================================================================================================================
Install  7 Packages
Upgrade  1 Package

Total download size: 1.4 M
Downloading Packages:
(1/8): firewalld-filesystem-1.3.4-9.el9_5.noarch.rpm                             78 kB/s | 8.6 kB     00:00
```

Figure 5.19: *Firewall Installation*

This figure demonstrates the installation and activation of the firewall on Rocky Linux 9 using **`firewalld`**. The process begins by verifying whether the firewalld package is already installed and, if not, installing it via the **`DNF package manager`**. Once installed, the service is enabled and started using systemctl commands.

After activation, firewalld offers a dynamic and efficient approach to managing firewall rules, services, and network zones—allowing real-time configuration changes without restarting the service. Additionally, enabling firewalld to start automatically at boot ensures continuous and persistent network protection.

1. Starting and enabling **firewalld**:

```
sudo systemctl start firewalld
sudo systemctl enable firewalld
```

The process of starting and enabling the firewall on Rocky Linux 9. After installation, it is crucial to start the **firewalld** service to activate the firewall and begin managing network traffic. Enabling the firewall ensures that it starts automatically each time the system boots up, maintaining consistent network security. The process typically involves using **systemctl** commands such as **systemctl start firewalld** to start the service and **systemctl enable firewalld** to ensure it is enabled at boot time. These steps ensure that the firewall is always operational, protecting the system from unauthorized access.

2. Checking the **firewalld** status:

```
sudo systemctl status firewalld.
```

```
[cesarmserver@localhost ~]$ sudo systemctl status firewalld
○ firewalld.service - firewalld - dynamic firewall daemon
     Loaded: loaded (/usr/lib/systemd/system/firewalld.service; enabled; preset: enabled)
     Active: inactive (dead) since Sat 2025-05-03 18:51:21 CST; 2min 45s ago
   Duration: 30.692s
       Docs: man:firewalld(1)
   Main PID: 4893 (code=exited, status=0/SUCCESS)
        CPU: 1.152s

May 03 18:50:50 localhost.localdomain systemd[1]: Starting firewalld - dynamic firewall daemon...
May 03 18:50:50 localhost.localdomain systemd[1]: Started firewalld - dynamic firewall daemon.
May 03 18:51:21 localhost.localdomain systemd[1]: Stopping firewalld - dynamic firewall daemon...
May 03 18:51:21 localhost.localdomain systemd[1]: firewalld.service: Deactivated successfully.
May 03 18:51:21 localhost.localdomain systemd[1]: Stopped firewalld - dynamic firewall daemon.
May 03 18:51:21 localhost.localdomain systemd[1]: firewalld.service: Consumed 1.152s CPU time.
```

Figure 5.20: *Checking the Firewall Status*

This figure illustrates how to check the status of the firewall on Rocky Linux 9. Verifying the firewall status is an essential step to ensure that it is running and properly protecting the system. Using the **systemctl status firewalld** command, administrators can confirm whether the **firewalld** service is active, inactive, or in a failed state. Additionally, the **firewall-cmd --state** command provides a quick way to check the operational status of the firewall. Regularly checking the firewall status helps ensure that the firewall is functioning correctly, and that network traffic is being appropriately controlled.

Zones in firewalld

Zones are a core concept in firewalld. They define a set of rules that determine which traffic is allowed or blocked based on the level of trust.

- **Predefined zones:**
  - **Drop**: All incoming packets are dropped without any response.
  - **Block**: Like Drop but sends an error message for rejected packets.
  - **Public**: Limited trust, allowing only basic services.
  - **Home**: Designed for trusted environments such as private networks.
  - **Work**: Like Home but tailored for corporate networks.
  - **Internal**: For trusted internal networks.
  - **External**: Typically used for routers with NAT configured.
  - **Trusted**: All traffic is allowed.

Assigning interfaces to zones: Firewalld uses **zones** to manage network traffic based on trust levels, providing a flexible and secure approach to firewall configuration. Each zone contains a predefined set of rules that govern how traffic is allowed or denied. By assigning a network interface to a specific zone, administrators can tailor the firewall behavior according to the security needs of that connection.

For example:

- The **Public** zone is designed for untrusted networks and blocks most incoming traffic to protect the system from potential external threats.
- The **Home** zone, intended for trusted environments such as a local network, allows more open communication between devices.

This section guides us through:

- **Identifying the current zone assignments** for our network interfaces.
- **Selecting the appropriate zone** based on the level of trust and security requirements.
- **Assigning interfaces to zones** using the firewall-cmd command-line utility.
- **Verifying zone assignments** to ensure that the correct firewall rules are applied.

Assigning Network Interfaces to Zones in Firewalld

Firewalld provides a zone-based approach to firewall management, allowing administrators to apply different security rules based on the trust level of each network. Associating network interfaces with specific zones is a key step in ensuring the firewall behaves appropriately for each network environment.

To assign a network interface (for example, eth0) to the **public** zone, which is typically used for untrusted networks, follow these steps:

1. **Assign the Interface to a Zone (Permanently)**

Use the following command to assign eth0 to the public zone **permanently**:

```
sudo firewall-cmd --zone=public --add-interface=eth0 --permanent
```

```
[cesarmserver@localhost ~]$ sudo firewall-cmd --zone=public --add-interface=eth0 --permanent
success
```

Figure 5.21: *Assigning Interfaces to the Zones*

This figure illustrates how network interfaces can be assigned to zones within **firewalld** on Rocky Linux 9 Zones represent different trust levels, with each zone applying specific firewall rules to the traffic it governs. By mapping interfaces to appropriate zones, administrators can enforce tailored policies for trusted, internal, or public networks. The **firewall-cmd --zone=<zone> --add-interface=<interface>** command is typically used for this task, enabling flexible traffic management and stronger network security.

- **--zone=public:** Specifies the target zone.
- **--add-interface=eth0:** Assigns the interface eth0 to the selected zone.
- **--permanent:** Makes the change persistent across system reboots.

2. **Reload Firewalld to Apply Changes**

After making permanent changes, reload firewalld so that the configuration takes effect:

- **sudo firewall-cmd --reload**

3. **Verify Zone Assignment**

To confirm that the interface has been successfully assigned to the desired zone:

- **sudo firewall-cmd --get-active-zones**

This command will display the active zones and the interfaces currently associated with each one.
Example Output:

```
[cesarmserver@localhost ~]$ sudo firewall-cmd --get-active-zones
public
  interfaces: eth0 ens160
```

***Figure* 5.22:** *Firewall Active Zones*

In firewalld, zones are predefined sets of rules that define the trust level of network connections. Assigning interfaces to the correct zones ensures that security policies match the characteristics of each network environment. For example, an interface connected to an untrusted network can be placed in the *public* zone with stricter restrictions, while trusted networks may use the *internal* or *home* zones with more permissive rules. Monitoring active zones helps administrators confirm that interfaces are correctly classified and protected.

Testing and Verifying Firewall Configurations

After configuring our firewall using firewalld, it is crucial to verify that the settings are correctly applied and functioning as intended. This ensures that our system is protected according to our security policies and that necessary services remain accessible.

1. **Check Active Rules:** To view the current configuration of the default zone, use: **`sudo firewall-cmd --list-all`**.

This command displays information such as:

- **`Zone`:** The active zone name.
- **`Interfaces`:** Network interfaces assigned to the zone.
- **`Services`:** Allowed services (for example, SSH, HTTP).
- **`Ports`:** Open ports not associated with predefined services.
- **`Protocols`:** Permitted protocols.
- **`Masquerade`:** Indicates if network address translation is enabled.
- **`Forward Ports`:** Port forwarding rules.
- **`ICMP Blocks`:** Blocked ICMP types.
- **`Rich Rules`:** Advanced custom rules.

This comprehensive overview helps confirm that the firewall is configured as expected.

2. **List of All Zones and Their Configurations**

To review configurations for all zones, execute:

```
sudo firewall-cmd --list-all-zones
```

This command provides details for each zone, including associated interfaces, services, ports, and other settings. It is particularly useful for auditing the entire firewall setup and ensuring that each zone is appropriately configured.

3. **Verify Specific Zone Settings**

To inspect the configuration of a specific zone, such as the 'home' zone, use:

```
sudo firewall-cmd --list-all --zone=home
```

This allows us to focus on and verify the settings of a particular zone, ensuring that it aligns with our intended security posture.

4. **Check Rich Rules**

Rich rules provide granular control over firewall behavior. To list all rich rules in the default zone:

```
sudo firewall-cmd --list-rich-rules
```

For a specific zone:

```
sudo firewall-cmd --list-rich-rules --zone=public
```

Reviewing rich rules ensures that complex filtering criteria are correctly implemented.

5. **Test Runtime Changes Before Making Them Permanent**

Firewalld distinguishes between runtime and permanent configurations. Changes made without the `--permanent` flag affect only the current session and are lost upon reboot. To evaluate changes without affecting the permanent configuration:

```
sudo firewall-cmd --add-service=http
```

After verifying the change, make it permanent:

- `sudo firewall-cmd --permanent --add-service=http`
- `sudo firewall-cmd --reload`

This approach allows us to safely assess configurations before committing them.

6. **Reload the Firewall to Apply Permanent Changes**

When permanent changes are made, reload firewalld to apply them:

```
sudo firewall-cmd --reload
```

This ensures that the runtime configuration reflects the permanent settings.

7. **Ensure firewalld is Active**

To confirm that firewalld is running and enabled:

- **`sudo systemctl status firewalld`**

If it is not active, start and enable it:

- **`sudo systemctl start firewalld`**
- **`sudo systemctl enable firewalld`**

Regularly verifying the firewall's status ensures continuous protection.

By systematically testing and verifying the firewalld configurations, we can maintain a robust security posture, ensuring that our system is protected against unauthorized access while allowing legitimate traffic.

Validating and Testing Networking Connectivity

Use the ping command to verify connectivity to our local IP address. **`ping [ip address]`**

```
[cesarmserver@localhost ~]$ ping 192.168.204.128
PING 192.168.204.128 (192.168.204.128) 56(84) bytes of data.
64 bytes from 192.168.204.128: icmp_seq=1 ttl=64 time=0.046 ms
64 bytes from 192.168.204.128: icmp_seq=2 ttl=64 time=0.071 ms
64 bytes from 192.168.204.128: icmp_seq=3 ttl=64 time=0.071 ms
64 bytes from 192.168.204.128: icmp_seq=4 ttl=64 time=0.054 ms
64 bytes from 192.168.204.128: icmp_seq=5 ttl=64 time=0.065 ms
^C
--- 192.168.204.128 ping statistics ---
5 packets transmitted, 5 received, 0% packet loss, time 4098ms
rtt min/avg/max/mdev = 0.046/0.061/0.071/0.009 ms
```

Figure 5.23: *Confirming Local Network Connection*

This figure demonstrates how to verify local connectivity in Rocky Linux 9 to ensure the system can communicate with other devices on the same network. Using tools such as **`ping`** and **`ip a`**, administrators can confirm the assigned IP address, validate that the interface is active, and test basic reachability. This step is a fundamental part of troubleshooting, ensuring that local communication is functioning before investigating broader connectivity issues.

Troubleshooting issues: Check firewall logs. **`sudo journalctl -u firewalld`**

```
[cesarmserver@localhost ~]$ sudo journalctl -u firewalld
[sudo] password for cesarmserver:
Dec 15 20:21:01 localhost systemd[1]: Starting firewalld - dynamic firewall daemon...
Dec 15 20:21:01 localhost systemd[1]: Started firewalld - dynamic firewall daemon.
[cesarmserver@localhost ~]$
```

Figure 5.24: *Validating the Status of the Firewall*

This figure demonstrates the process of validating the status of the firewall on **Rocky Linux 9**. Ensuring that the firewall is active and correctly configured is critical for maintaining system and network security. Administrators can use the **`systemctl status firewalld`** command to verify whether the **`Firewalld`** service is running. Additionally, the **`firewall-cmd --state`** command offers a quick way to check the current operational state of the firewall. Regularly validating the firewall status helps confirm that the system is protected against unauthorized access and malicious network traffic.

Stop firewall: This specific command will stop the firewall services.

```
sudo systemctl stop firewalld
```

```
[cesarmserver@localhost ~]$ sudo systemctl stop firewalld
[cesarmserver@localhost ~]$
```

Figure 5.25: *Stopping Firewall Services*

This figure illustrates the process of stopping the firewall services on **Rocky Linux 9**. Temporarily stopping the firewall may be required for troubleshooting, system maintenance, or specific network configurations. The systemctl stop firewalld command is used to halt the **`Firewalld`** service, effectively disabling its traffic filtering and security enforcement. It is crucial to proceed with caution when disabling the firewall, as this can expose the system to potential security threats. Once the necessary tasks are completed, it is strongly recommended to restore firewall protection by running **`systemctl start firewalld`**.

Firewall Rule Configurations

The firewalld service manages firewall rules dynamically. Common configurations include:

Zone	Service / Port	Implication
Public	SSH (22/tcp)	Allows remote administration but risks brute-force attacks if not restricted.
Public	HTTP (80/tcp)	Enables web server access, suitable for public-facing services.
Internal	MySQL (3306/tcp)	Restricts database access to trusted networks.
Drop	All	Blocks all incoming traffic, ideal for high-security servers.

Figure 5.26: *Common Firewall Configurations*

This figure highlights typical firewall configurations used in Rocky Linux environments to manage network security effectively. It includes examples of rules for allowing essential services such as SSH (port 22), HTTP (port 80), and HTTPS (port 443), as well as best practices for zone assignment and interface control. By organizing these configurations, administrators can quickly implement and adjust firewall settings based on system roles and security requirements. Understanding and applying these common configurations ensures a balanced approach to accessibility and protection across different network environments.

Example:

Action	Command
Add HTTP service to public zone	`firewall-cmd --zone=public --add-service=http --permanent`
Reload firewall	`firewall-cmd --reload`
List all rules in public zone	`firewall-cmd --zone=public --list-all`
Remove HTTP service from public zone	`firewall-cmd --zone=public --remove-service=http --permanent`

Figure 5.27: *Adding and Removing a Rule*

This figure illustrates the process of managing firewall rules in Rocky Linux using the firewall-cmd utility. It shows how to add rules to allow specific types of network traffic, such as enabling SSH or HTTP access, and how to remove those rules when they are no longer needed. Administrators can use commands such as **`firewall-cmd --add-service=ssh or firewall-cmd --remove-service=http`** to apply changes dynamically. Mastering this process is essential for maintaining a firewall configuration that is both secure and adaptable to evolving network requirements.

Check Firewall Settings

A misconfigured firewall is a common cause of network connectivity issues. In Rocky Linux 9, the firewall is typically managed by firewalld.

To check if the firewall is active, run: **`sudo systemctl status firewalld`**.

If we suspect the firewall is blocking connections, we can temporarily stop it to evaluate connectivity: **`sudo systemctl stop firewalld`**.

Add a rule to allow HTTP traffic on port 80 permanently (persists across reboots) using:

```
sudo firewall-cmd --add-port=80/tcp -permanent
```

Apply the changes with: **`sudo firewall-cmd -reload.`**

A common cause of connectivity issues is a misconfigured firewall. On Rocky Linux 9, the firewall is typically managed by **`firewalld`**. To check the status of **`firewalld`**, use:

```
sudo systemctl status firewalld
```

Use this command after configuring our firewall to verify current settings, ensure services are allowed, and confirm which interfaces are protected under which zone.

Verify the rule was added by checking the active zone: **`sudo firewall-cmd --list-all.`**

```
public (active)
  target: default
  icmp-block-inversion:no
  interfaces: eth0
  services: ssh http
  ports: 80/tcp
  protocols :
  masquerade: no
  forward -ports :
  source -ports :
  icmp -blocks :
  rich rules:
```

Figure 5.28: *Validating Firewall Settings*

This figure illustrates the use of the **`firewall-cmd --list-all`** command to validate the current firewall settings on Rocky Linux. By running this command, administrators can view the active zone, associated network interfaces, allowed services, open ports, and other relevant configurations. This verification step is essential for ensuring that the system's firewall is properly configured to meet security requirements, allowing necessary traffic while blocking unauthorized access. Regularly checking firewall settings helps maintain a secure and well-managed server environment.

If the firewall is active and blocking connections, we can temporarily disable it to test connectivity: **`sudo systemctl stop firewalld`**.

For more fine-grained control, we can configure firewall rules to allow specific traffic:

- **`sudo firewall-cmd --add-port=80/tcp --permanent`**
- **`sudo firewall-cmd --reload`**

Understanding the firewalld Zones

`Firewalld` simplifies firewall management by providing a dynamic, zone-based approach to securing networks. With tools to manage services, ports, and custom rules, it enables administrators to protect systems against unauthorized access while maintaining flexibility. Mastering firewalld is essential for ensuring robust and adaptable network security, particularly in modern cloud and enterprise environments.

SSH for Remote Management

Secure Shell (SSH) is a foundational tool for securely managing servers and systems remotely. It ensures encrypted communication, safeguarding sensitive data from interception. Properly configuring and securing SSH is crucial for preventing unauthorized access while enabling efficient and secure remote administration tasks.

Setting Up and Securing SSH for Remote Administration

In this section, we will explore the setup and security best practices for SSH on a Rocky Linux 9 system. By the end, administrators will have the knowledge and tools to configure SSH, implement robust security measures, and address common issues in remote management.

Understanding SSH

SSH, or Secure Shell, is a cryptographic network protocol designed for secure remote access and management over untrusted networks. It facilitates encrypted communication between a client and a server, ensuring:

- **Confidentiality:** Preventing unauthorized access to transmitted data.
- **Integrity:** Protecting data from tampering during transmission.
- **Authentication:** Verifying the identity of users and systems.

SSH supports a range of functionalities, including secure remote logins, file transfers, and command execution, making it a cornerstone of modern system administration.

The Role of SSH in Remote Management

In today's distributed IT environments, SSH plays a critical role by enabling secure remote operations across cloud platforms, data centers, and on-premises systems. Key advantages include:

- **Secure Access:** Provides encrypted channels for remote logins, ensuring protection against eavesdropping and unauthorized access.
- **Remote Administration:** Allows administrators to perform tasks such as software updates, system configuration, and troubleshooting without physical access to servers.
- **Advanced Features:** Supports secure file transfers (SCP/SFTP), tunneling, and port forwarding, enhancing flexibility in system management.

By leveraging SSH, administrators can maintain seamless operations while mitigating the risks associated with remote access.

Installing and Configuring SSH

Step 1: Install the OpenSSH Package

SSH is included in most Linux distributions, including Rocky Linux 9. Use the following commands to ensure OpenSSH is installed:

```
sudo dnf update -y
sudo dnf install -y openssh-server openssh-clients
```

```
[cesarmserver@localhost ~]$ sudo dnf update -y
[sudo] password for cesarmserver:
Last metadata expiration check: 2:51:09 ago on Sun 15 Dec 2024 07:47:23 PM CST.
Dependencies resolved.
Nothing to do.
Complete!
[cesarmserver@localhost ~]$ sudo dnf install -y openssh-server openssh-clients
Last metadata expiration check: 2:51:27 ago on Sun 15 Dec 2024 07:47:23 PM CST.
Package openssh-server-8.7p1-43.el9.x86_64 is already installed.
Package openssh-clients-8.7p1-43.el9.x86_64 is already installed.
Dependencies resolved.
Nothing to do.
Complete!
[cesarmserver@localhost ~]$
```

Figure 5.29: *Confirming SSH Packages Installation*

This figure demonstrates the process of confirming the installation of SSH packages on Rocky Linux. Ensuring that the necessary SSH packages, such as **openssh-server and openssh-clients**, are installed is a crucial step for enabling remote management via SSH. By using the command **rpm -q openssh-server**, administrators can verify the installation status of the SSH server. If the packages are not installed, they can be easily added using the package manager **(dnf)**. Confirming that these packages are correctly installed ensures the system is ready for secure remote access.

- **openssh-server**: Required to enable SSH server functionality on the system.
- **openssh-clients**: Provides tools for SSH client-side operations, such as connecting them to remote servers.

Step 2: Start and Enable the SSH Service

To ensure the SSH service runs continuously and starts on boot, use the following commands:

```
sudo systemctl start sshd
sudo systemctl enable sshd
```

```
[cesarmserver@localhost ~]$ sudo systemctl start sshd
[cesarmserver@localhost ~]$ sudo systemctl enable sshd
```

Figure 5.30: *Start and Enable SSH Services*

This figure illustrates the process of starting and enabling SSH services on Rocky Linux. After installing the necessary SSH packages, it is essential to start the SSH service to enable remote access. Using the command **systemctl start sshd**, administrators can start the SSH service, and with **systemctl enable sshd**, they can configure it to start automatically at boot. Enabling SSH to start on boot ensures that remote access is available whenever the system is restarted, providing consistent and secure management of the server.

Verify the service status: **sudo systemctl status sshd**.

```
[cesarmserver@localhost ~]$ sudo systemctl status sshd
● sshd.service - OpenSSH server daemon
     Loaded: loaded (/usr/lib/systemd/system/sshd.service; enabled; preset: enabled)
     Active: active (running) since Sun 2024-12-15 20:21:02 CST; 2h 25min ago
       Docs: man:sshd(8)
             man:sshd_config(5)
   Main PID: 963 (sshd)
      Tasks: 1 (limit: 10754)
     Memory: 7.1M
        CPU: 98ms
     CGroup: /system.slice/sshd.service
             └─963 "sshd: /usr/sbin/sshd -D [listener] 0 of 10-100 startups"

Dec 15 20:21:01 localhost.localdomain systemd[1]: Starting OpenSSH server daemon...
Dec 15 20:21:02 localhost.localdomain sshd[963]: Server listening on 0.0.0.0 port 22.
Dec 15 20:21:02 localhost.localdomain sshd[963]: Server listening on :: port 22.
Dec 15 20:21:02 localhost.localdomain systemd[1]: Started OpenSSH server daemon.
Dec 15 20:21:05 localhost.localdomain sshd[1859]: Accepted password for cesarmserver from 192.168.204.1 port 51834>
Dec 15 20:21:05 localhost.localdomain sshd[1908]: Accepted password for cesarmserver from 192.168.204.1 port 51835>
Dec 15 20:21:05 localhost.localdomain sshd[1859]: pam_unix(sshd:session): session opened for user cesarmserver(uid>
Dec 15 20:21:05 localhost.localdomain sshd[1908]: pam_unix(sshd:session): session opened for user cesarmserver(uid>
```

Figure 5.31: *Verifying the Status of the SSH Services*

This figure demonstrates how to confirm the status of the SSH service on Rocky Linux. Verifying that the SSH service is running properly is essential to ensure that remote access is available. Using the command **systemctl status sshd**, administrators can check whether the SSH service is active, inactive, or has encountered any issues. Regularly confirming the SSH service status helps ensure reliable remote management and aids in troubleshooting if connection problems arise.

Step 3: Test SSH Access

On the client system, use the ssh command to connect to the server:

```
ssh username@server_ip_address
```

a. Replace **username** with the server user's username.

b. Replace **server_ip_address** with the IP address or hostname of the server.

Ensure connectivity by entering the password when prompted. Successful authentication grants shell access to the server.

Securing SSH Access

Before making any changes to the SSH configuration file on Rocky Linux, it is best practice to create a backup of the current configuration. Here are the steps to accomplish this:

1. **Create a backup of the SSH configuration file:** Run the following command to copy the **sshd_config** file to a backup file:
   ```
   sudo cp /etc/ssh/sshd_config /etc/ssh/sshd_config.bak
   ```
2. **Edit the configuration file:** After creating the backup, we can safely edit the file using nano or any other text editor. Run:
   ```
   sudo nano /etc/ssh/sshd_config
   ```
3. **Restore from backup (if needed):** If any issues occur after modifying the file, we can easily restore the original configuration by copying the backup back:
   ```
   sudo cp /etc/ssh/sshd_config.bak /etc/ssh/sshd_config
   ```

This ensures that we have a safe copy of the original configuration file before making changes.

While SSH is inherently secure, it is essential to follow best practices to mitigate potential vulnerabilities.

Step 4: Change the Default SSH Port

The default SSH port (22) is a common target for brute-force attacks. Changing the port reduces exposure to automated scanning tools.

1. Edit the SSH configuration file: **sudo nano /etc/ssh/sshd_config**

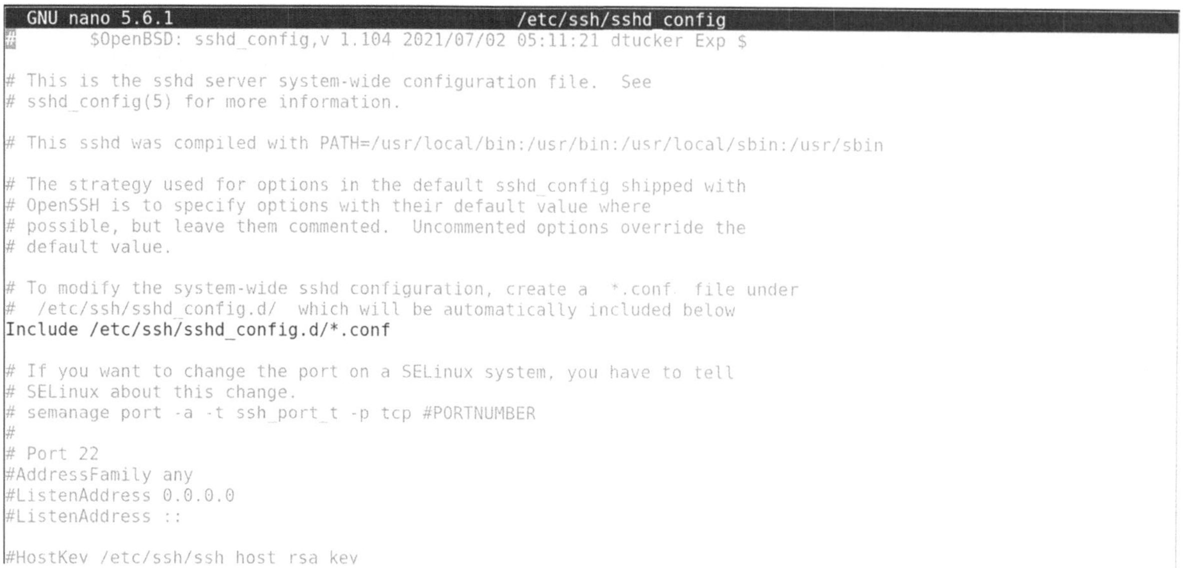

```
  GNU nano 5.6.1                          /etc/ssh/sshd_config
#       $OpenBSD: sshd_config,v 1.104 2021/07/02 05:11:21 dtucker Exp $

# This is the sshd server system-wide configuration file.  See
# sshd_config(5) for more information.

# This sshd was compiled with PATH=/usr/local/bin:/usr/bin:/usr/local/sbin:/usr/sbin

# The strategy used for options in the default sshd_config shipped with
# OpenSSH is to specify options with their default value where
# possible, but leave them commented.  Uncommented options override the
# default value.

# To modify the system-wide sshd configuration, create a  *.conf  file under
#  /etc/ssh/sshd_config.d/  which will be automatically included below
Include /etc/ssh/sshd_config.d/*.conf

# If you want to change the port on a SELinux system, you have to tell
# SELinux about this change.
# semanage port -a -t ssh_port_t -p tcp #PORTNUMBER
#
# Port 22
#AddressFamily any
#ListenAddress 0.0.0.0
#ListenAddress ::

#HostKey /etc/ssh/ssh_host_rsa_key
```

Figure 5.32: *SSHD Configuration*

This figure illustrates the process of configuring the SSH daemon (SSHD) on Rocky Linux to enhance the security and functionality of remote connections. The SSHD configuration file, typically located at **`/etc/ssh/sshd_config`**, allows administrators to modify key settings such as port number, authentication methods, login restrictions, and more. Configuring SSHD properly ensures secure remote access while minimizing the risk of unauthorized access. Common changes include disabling root login, limiting user access, and enabling key-based authentication. After making changes, the SSHD service must be restarted using **`systemctl restart sshd`** to apply the new settings.

2. Locate the line: **`#Port 22`**
3. Uncomment and modify it to a non-standard port (for example, 2222): **`Port 2222`**
4. Restart the SSH service to apply the changes:
   - `sudo systemctl enable firewalld`
   - `sudo systemctl start firewalld`
5. Update the firewall to allow the new SSH port (for example, 2222) and remove the default port (22) to prevent unauthorized access:
   - `sudo firewall-cmd --permanent --add-port=2222/tcp`
   - `sudo firewall-cmd --permanent --remove-port=22/tcp`
   - `sudo firewall-cmd --reload`

Step 5: Disable Root Login

Direct root login is a significant security risk. Disable it to enforce the principle of least privilege.

1. Edit the SSH configuration file: **`sudo nano /etc/ssh/sshd_config`**.
2. Locate the line: **`PermitRootLogin yes`**.
3. Change it to: **`PermitRootLogin no`**.
4. Restart the SSH service: **`sudo systemctl restart sshd`**.

Cleaning the Lab Environment

Before concluding the lab, it is important to clean the environment by restoring the original SSH configuration. This involves editing the SSH daemon configuration file using a text editor and reverting any changes made during the lab. Configuration lines that were adjusted–such as the **`Port`**, **`PermitRootLogin`**, and other authentication settings–should be restored to their original values. For clarity during this process, changes can be marked in bold or with comments to highlight what was modified. This ensures the system returns to a secure and predictable state, especially if these modifications were made solely for lab purposes.

Once the original configuration is restored, the SSH service must be re-enabled and restarted to apply the changes. Use **`sudo systemctl enable sshd`** to ensure SSH starts automatically at boot, and **`sudo systemctl start sshd`** to activate the service immediately. After restarting, remote connections should function as they did prior to the lab session. This step is essential for maintaining a clean, secure lab environment and preparing the system for future use or additional exercises.

Understanding SSH

SSH is a powerful tool for secure remote management, providing encrypted communication between systems. By using VMware Workstation for virtualization, administrators can establish a versatile and reliable environment to practice and manage SSH configurations. Focusing on key-based authentication and implementing advanced security practices enhances the security and efficiency of remote access setups, ensuring robust protection against unauthorized access.

Networking in AWS

In this section, we will break down the basics of networking in Amazon Web Services (AWS) and show how to configure and manage networking on Rocky Linux instances. Networking is one of the most important parts of setting up cloud infrastructure, as it allows our applications to communicate securely and efficiently.

Whether we are hosting a simple web server or building a complex application across multiple environments, understanding AWS networking and how it integrates with Rocky Linux will help us deploy scalable, secure, and high-performing cloud systems.

Networking Basics in AWS

Let us start with the key components of networking in AWS:

- **Virtual Private Cloud (VPC):** A private network in the cloud that allows Linux administrators to deploy and manage resources securely.
  - **Subnets:** Subdivisions within a VPC used to organize and isolate resources.
  - **Route Tables:** Define how traffic moves between subnets and to the internet.
  - **Internet Gateway (IGW):** Enables internet access for resources in public subnets.
- **Security Groups (SGs):** Virtual firewalls for EC2 instances.
  - Control inbound and outbound traffic based on specific rules.
  - Default configuration allows all outbound traffic and blocks all inbound traffic.
- **Elastic Network Interfaces (ENIs):** Virtual network adapters attached to EC2 instances.
  - Support multiple IP addresses and security groups.
  - Useful for high-availability setups and failover.

- **Elastic IP Addresses:** Static public IP addresses that remain fixed even if the instance is restarted.
  - Useful for resources that require a consistent public IP address.

AWS Networking Concepts

Amazon Web Services (AWS) networking is crucial for deploying Rocky Linux in the cloud. Key components include:

- **Virtual Private Cloud (VPC):** A logically isolated network. For example, a VPC with CIDR 10.0.0.0/16 hosting web servers.
- **Subnets:** Subdivisions of a VPC, such as a public subnet (10.0.1.0/24) for load balancers and a private subnet (10.0.2.0/24) for databases.
- **Elastic IPs:** Static public IPs assigned to instances, ensuring consistent access.
- **Security Groups:** Virtual firewalls controlling instance traffic. For example, allowing HTTP (port 80) and SSH (port 22).
- **VPC Peering:** Enables seamless communication between two VPCs, such as linking a production VPC with a development VPC.

```
# Check Security Group rules
aws ec2 describe-security-groups --group-ids sg-1234567890

# Add SSH rule
aws ec2 authorize-security-group-ingress --group-id sg-1234567890
  --protocol tcp --port 22 --cidr 0.0.0.0/0
```

Figure 5.33: *AWS Networking Components*

This figure illustrates the essential components of AWS networking that play a pivotal role in deploying and managing cloud-based systems with Rocky Linux. It showcases the key elements such as the Virtual Private Cloud (VPC), which provides a secure and isolated network environment for resources; subnets, which segment the VPC into public and private zones for optimal security and traffic management; Elastic IPs, offering static public IP addresses for reliable access; security groups, which act as virtual firewalls to control traffic to instances; and VPC peering, enabling secure communication between multiple VPCs. These components are crucial for configuring scalable, secure, and high-performance cloud infrastructures.

Real-Life Example 1: Hosting a WordPress Website on Rocky Linux

To host a WordPress website on AWS using Rocky Linux:

- **VPC and Subnet:** Create a public subnet for the EC2 instance.
- **Security Group:** Allow ports 22 (SSH), 80 (HTTP), and 443 (HTTPS).
- **Elastic IP:** Assign it to the instance for consistent public access.
- **Rocky Linux Configuration:** Install Apache, MySQL, and PHP. Configure the firewall and network settings.

Configuring Rocky Linux for AWS Networking

Once our AWS infrastructure is set up, configure Rocky Linux to operate efficiently within it:

- **Configuring the Network Interface:** Use `nmcli` or `nmtui` to manage the connection.

Example:

- ○ `sudo nmcli con add type ethernet con-name ens3 ifname ens3`
- ○ `sudo nmcli con up ens3`

- **Managing Security Groups for Rocky Linux:** Open required ports based on our application needs. For a web server:
  - **Inbound**: TCP 22, 80, 443
  - **Outbound**: All (for updates and external communication)
- **Configuring Public and Private Subnets:**
  - **Public Subnet:** Used for web servers and other internet-facing services.
  - **Private Subnet:** Used for backend services such as databases. A NAT gateway enables secure outbound access.
- **Setting Up DNS and Elastic IPs:**
  - Assign an Elastic IP to ensure a stable connection point.
  - Use AWS Route 53 to map a domain name to the instance's IP address.

Real-Life Example 2: Secure File Server with SFTP

To deploy a secure file transfer server on AWS:

- **VPC and Subnet:** Use a private subnet for the server.
- **Security Group:** Allow inbound SSH only from trusted IPs.
- **ENIs:** Attach multiple ENIs for redundancy.
- **Rocky Linux:** Configure sshd, disable password login, and enable key-based authentication.

Advanced Networking Topics

- **VPC Peering**: Allows private communication between two VPCs.

  Example: Connect a production environment to a testing environment securely.
- **Flow Logs for Monitoring**: Use VPC Flow Logs to capture and analyze network traffic for troubleshooting and security auditing.
- **Automation with Infrastructure as Code (IaC):** Automate VPC and subnet creation with tools such as AWS CloudFormation or Terraform. For example, snippet using **`CloudFormation`**:

```
Resources:
  MyVPC:
    Type: AWS::EC2::VPC
    Properties:
      CidrBlock: 10.0.0.0/16
      EnableDnsSupport: true
      EnableDnsHostnames: true
```

Real-Life Example 3: Hybrid Cloud for a Remote Office

A company needs to link its on-premises office to the AWS cloud securely:

- **VPN or Direct Connect:** Set up a dedicated connection between the office and the cloud.
- **Rocky Linux:** Use it as a router or firewall in the cloud environment.
- **Use Case:** Enable remote teams to securely access internal systems hosted on AWS.

Best Practices for Networking with Rocky Linux in AWS

- **Security First:**
    - Use security groups and network access control lists to restrict traffic.
    - Regularly update Rocky Linux instances and monitor for vulnerabilities.
- **Design for Scalability:**
    - Plan subnets and route tables for future expansion.
    - Use Elastic Load Balancers to manage traffic across multiple instances.
- **Monitoring and Logging:**
    - Enable AWS CloudWatch and VPC Flow Logs for real-time performance and traffic analysis.
- **Hybrid Cloud Integration:**
    - Use VPN or Direct Connect to extend our AWS network to on-premises infrastructure.
    - Rocky Linux can serve as a reliable intermediary for data routing and inspection.

Troubleshooting Scenarios in AWS and Rocky Linux 9

Common networking issues can occur in Rocky Linux environments, whether on-premises or in the cloud. Below are some typical problems and practical resolutions:

- **Issue: No Internet Access from EC2 Instance**

  Resolution:
    - Ensure the instance is in a public subnet with a route to an Internet Gateway (IGW).
    - Confirm that the security group allows outbound traffic and DNS (port 53).
    - Check the instance's `/etc/resolv.conf` file for correct DNS settings.
- **Issue: SSH Connection Refused**

  Resolution:
    - Verify that the SSH service is running: sudo systemctl status sshd.
    - Check security group rules to ensure TCP port 22 is open.
    - Confirm that the firewall allows SSH connections: `firewall-cmd --list-all`.
    - Look at the `/var/log/secure` log file for authentication issues.
- **Issue: Incorrect IP Configuration**

  Resolution:
    - Use nmcli or ip a to check interface IP settings.
    - Reconfigure using `nmcli con mod <connection-name> ipv4.addresses <IP>/<CIDR>` and restart the connection.
    - Verify the default route with ip route show and correct if needed.
- **Issue: Hostname Not Resolving**

  Resolution:
    - Ensure proper DNS entries are configured in `/etc/resolv.conf`.
    - Use `dig` or `nslookup` to test domain resolution.
    - If using AWS Route 53, confirm that records are correctly set up.

These scenarios help administrators systematically diagnose and fix networking problems, maintaining stability and connectivity in Rocky Linux systems.

Summary for Beginners

Learning how AWS networking integrates with Rocky Linux enables us to build secure, scalable, and available cloud environments. Tools such as VPCs, security groups, and ENIs, when combined with Rocky Linux's flexibility and reliability, provide everything needed to deploy web servers, file transfer systems, or hybrid enterprise networks effectively.

Compatibility and Migration Between Rocky Linux 8 and 9

Compatibility and migration considerations between Rocky Linux 8 and 9 have been addressed in detail across the first four chapters, including discussions on repository changes, package-level differences, and system upgrade limitations. As such, this chapter will not revisit those topics in depth. Instead, the focus remains on advancing configuration and deployment practices specific to Rocky Linux 9, assuming a clean installation has already been completed. Readers seeking foundational guidance on version transitions should refer to earlier chapters for comprehensive context and migration strategies.

Conclusion

In this chapter, we laid the foundation for understanding and managing networking in Rocky Linux, focusing on essential tools and techniques to ensure stable, secure, and efficient network configurations. We covered the basics of configuring network interfaces, troubleshooting connectivity, managing firewalls, and securing remote access through SSH. Additionally, we explored integrating networking concepts into AWS environments, with a focus on VPCs, security groups, and EC2 networking.

Mastering these networking fundamentals ensures that system administrators can maintain a secure and reliable network infrastructure. These skills are especially important in cloud environments, where dynamic resource allocation and robust security are crucial for seamless operations.

As we transition to *Chapter 6, Advanced Administration Techniques*, we will build on this foundation by diving into more complex tasks such as RAID configuration, system performance monitoring, and cloud deployment practices. In this next chapter, we will learn how to set up and manage RAID arrays for improved data redundancy and performance, use **`systemd`** for efficient service management, monitor system performance with tools such as **`ps`** and **`top`**, automate routine tasks using **`cron`**, and handle cloud-based administration tasks in AWS.

These advanced techniques will enhance the ability to manage Rocky Linux systems in both on-premises and cloud environments, ensuring that the infrastructure remains robust, automated, and optimized for performance.

Points to Remember

- **Basic Networking Tools in Rocky Linux:** Key tools for managing and troubleshooting networks include nmcli and nmtui for configuring network interfaces, and commands such as ping, ifconfig, ip, netstat, and route for monitoring and diagnosing network connectivity issues.
- **Network Interface Configuration:** Proper configuration of network interfaces is essential for connectivity. Use tools such as nmcli to manage NICs, set static or dynamic IP addresses, and configure routing. The **`/etc/NetworkManager/`** and **`/etc/sysconfig/network-scripts/`** directories hold configuration files that define network settings.

- **Security Groups and Firewalls:** In cloud environments such as AWS, security groups function as firewalls to control traffic to and from EC2 instances. Proper configuration of security groups and firewalls ensures secure communication by specifying which inbound and outbound traffic is allowed.
- **Remote Management with SSH:** Secure Shell (SSH) is a critical tool for remote system administration. By setting up SSH correctly and using best practices, such as disabling root login and changing the default port, system administrators can securely manage remote servers.
- **Networking in AWS:** AWS provides robust tools such as Virtual Private Clouds (VPCs), security groups, and Elastic Network Interfaces (ENIs) for building secure, scalable cloud networks. Configuring VPCs, subnets, route tables, and Internet Gateways (IGWs) is essential for setting up secure communication between instances and external networks.
- **VPC and Security Group Configuration:** When integrating Rocky Linux with AWS, configuring VPCs and security groups is crucial for managing traffic, ensuring secure access, and optimizing network performance. Always use best practices to limit access and monitor network activity.
- **Troubleshooting Networking Issues:** Use tools such as `traceroute`, `tcpdump`, and `CloudWatch` logs to identify and resolve networking issues, especially in complex cloud environments. Initiative-taking monitoring and troubleshooting ensure network reliability.

Multiple Choice Questions

1. Which command is used to view the status of network interfaces in Rocky Linux?
   a. `nmcli device status`
   b. `ifconfig`
   c. `ip a`
   d. `netstat -an`
2. What is the primary function of a Virtual Private Cloud (VPC) in AWS?
   a. To provide DNS services for EC2 instances
   b. To manage security groups and firewalls
   c. To create isolated network environments for resources
   d. To monitor network traffic between instances
3. Which AWS service is used to control the flow of traffic to EC2 instances?
   a. VPC Peering
   b. Security Groups
   c. Elastic Load Balancer
   d. Internet Gateway
4. Which command helps us to bring up a network connection using `nmcli` in Rocky Linux?
   a. `nmcli con down`
   b. `nmcli con show`
   c. `nmcli con up`
   d. `nmcli device status`

5. What does the **traceroute** command do?
    a. Verifies network connectivity by sending ICMP packets
    b. Traces the path packets take to a destination
    c. Resolves domain names to IP addresses
    d. Displays network interfaces' current IP addresses
6. Which AWS service allows us to manage network traffic between different VPCs?
    a. VPC Peering
    b. AWS Direct Connect
    c. AWS Transit Gateway
    d. Network Access Control Lists (NACLs)
7. How do we ensure that a Rocky Linux instance is securely managed via remote access?
    a. Use SSH with a public key for authentication
    b. Open all ports in the security group
    c. Enable root login via SSH
    d. Disable security groups
8. What is the function of an Internet Gateway (IGW) in an AWS VPC?
    a. To route traffic between subnets in a VPC
    b. To provide internet access for resources in a VPC
    c. To manage inbound and outbound traffic from EC2 instances
    d. To provide DNS resolution for EC2 instances
9. What is the default behavior of security groups in AWS?
    a. Allow all inbound traffic and deny all outbound traffic
    b. Deny all inbound and outbound traffic
    c. Deny all inbound traffic and allow all outbound traffic
    d. Allow all inbound and outbound traffic
10. Which command can be used to view and modify network settings using the text-based interface in Rocky Linux?
    a. **nmcli**
    b. **nmtui**
    c. **ifconfig**
    d. **ip link**

Answers

1. a
2. c

3. b
4. c
5. b
6. c
7. a
8. b
9. c
10. b

Questions

1. What is the primary purpose of configuring network interfaces in Rocky Linux?
2. Which tool is commonly used in Rocky Linux to manage network connections via the command line?
3. What is the function of a security group in AWS?
4. How does a Virtual Private Cloud (VPC) enhance network security in AWS?
5. What command in Rocky Linux can be used to troubleshoot network connectivity issues?
6. What is the role of an Internet Gateway (IGW) in an AWS VPC?
7. How can we secure remote access to a Rocky Linux server?
8. What is the difference between a public and private subnet in an AWS VPC?
9. Which AWS tool allows us to control traffic between different VPCs?
10. What is the purpose of VPC Flow Logs in AWS?

Key Terms

- **Network Interface**: A hardware or software component that connects a system to a network, enabling communication between devices. Common types include Ethernet, Wi-Fi, and virtual interfaces.
- **nmcli**: A command-line tool in Rocky Linux used for managing network connections, setting up IP addresses, and troubleshooting network issues.
- **Security Group**: A virtual firewall in AWS that controls inbound and outbound traffic to EC2 instances. It is stateful, meaning it tracks the state of connections.
- **Virtual Private Cloud (VPC)**: An isolated network environment in AWS where we can configure our own IP range, subnets, and security settings to control access to AWS resources.
- **Elastic IP (EIP)**: A static IPv4 address in AWS used to associate a fixed public IP with an EC2 instance, providing reliable access even after instance restarts.
- **Internet Gateway (IGW)**: A service in AWS that allows communication between resources in a VPC and the internet. It provides internet access to instances in a public subnet.
- **Private Subnet**: A subnet in AWS VPCs that is not directly accessible from the internet. Resources in private subnets typically require a NAT Gateway or VPN for external communication.

- **SSH (Secure Shell)**: A network protocol used to securely access and manage remote systems, providing encrypted communication for administration.
- **VPC Peering**: A service in AWS that allows private communication between two VPCs, enabling resources in different VPCs to interact securely.
- **VPC Flow Logs**: A feature in AWS that captures detailed information about the IP traffic going to and from network interfaces in a VPC, aiding in security analysis and troubleshooting.

CHAPTER 6
Advanced Administration Techniques

Introduction

As modern IT environments evolve in scale and complexity, the role of the Linux system administrator becomes increasingly critical. To ensure system reliability and performance, administrators must go beyond the basics and adopt advanced techniques tailored to today's infrastructure needs. This chapter focuses on **RAID configurations** for data redundancy and performance, **service management using `systemd`**, and **real-time monitoring tools** such as ps and top to identify and resolve performance bottlenecks.

We also introduce **AWS CLI and SDK**, enabling administrators to automate tasks and manage cloud resources more effectively. Whether enhancing availability through RAID or streamlining operations with automation, this chapter equips us with practical skills to tackle modern Linux system administration challenges with confidence.

Structure

This chapter covers the following topics:

- RAID Setup and Benefits
- Managing RAID Arrays
- Using systemd for Service Management
- Monitoring System Performance
- Automating Tasks with cron
- Rocky Linux Administration in AWS Environments
- Cloud Automation with AWS CLI and SDK

RAID Setup and Benefits

Modern system administration in **Rocky Linux 9** requires more than foundational knowledge—it demands mastery of advanced tools and techniques that enhance system reliability, performance, and scalability. One critical area is **Redundant Array of Independent Disks (RAID)**, a storage virtualization technology that combines multiple physical drives into a single logical unit to improve redundancy, performance, or both. This chapter offers a step-by-step guide to configuring RAID in Rocky Linux, while also covering essential system tools such as systemd for robust service management, and ps and top for effective performance monitoring. Automating routine tasks with cron is also discussed to streamline operations and reduce administrative overhead.

As cloud adoption accelerates, administrators must also adapt to managing Linux systems in distributed environments. This chapter provides practical insights into deploying and maintaining

Rocky Linux on **AWS**, using tools such as the **AWS CLI** and **SDK** to automate workflows, and manage cloud resources efficiently. By integrating traditional system administration with modern cloud capabilities, readers will gain the knowledge needed to tackle today's IT challenges and build resilient, high-performing infrastructure.

Benefits of RAID

- **Redundancy:** Ensures data availability by mirroring or distributing data across multiple drives. If one drive fails, the system can continue operating.
- **Performance:** Some RAID levels (for example, RAID 0) improve read and write speeds by striping data across drives.
- **Scalability:** Allows for combining multiple drives into a larger, logical volume.
- **Fault Tolerance:** Critical for systems requiring high uptime, as RAID can handle drive failures, without data loss (for example, RAID 1, 5, 6, and 10).

Configure RAID 1 on Rocky Linux 9

RAID 1 creates an exact copy (or mirror) of data on two or more disks. This ensures high availability and redundancy. In this lab, we will configure RAID 1 on Rocky Linux 9, covering all necessary steps and commands in detail.

Objective: To configure a RAID 1 setup using `mdadm` for improved read speeds and additional protection against disk failures.

Advantages of RAID 1

- **Data Redundancy**: Ensures data availability in case of disk failure.
- **Improved Read Speeds**: Simultaneous access to mirrored disks.

Disadvantages of RAID 1

- **Reduced Storage Efficiency**: Utilizes only half the total storage capacity.
- **Higher Costs**: Requires twice the number of disks.

Prerequisites

- Two or more unpartitioned disks (for example, `/dev/sdb` and `/dev/sdc`).
- `Root` or `sudo` access.

Since we are working with VMware or VirtualBox, we need to create two additional disks for the virtual machine before starting the following laboratories.

To proceed with creating and attaching additional disks in VMware or VirtualBox, follow these steps:

For VMware:

1. **Shut Down the Virtual Machine:** Ensure the VM is powered off.
2. **Add New Disks**
    a. Right-click on the VM in the VMware interface and select **`Settings`**.
    b. Click **`Add...`**, then choose **`Hard Disk`** and click **`Next`**.
    c. Select the disk type (for example, SCSI or NVMe) and click **`Next`**.
    d. Specify the disk size (for example, 10GB) and select **`Allocate space now`** for better performance.

   e. Repeat the process to add the second disk.

3. **Start the Virtual Machine:** Power on the VM to proceed with partitioning the newly added disks.

For VirtualBox:

1. **Shut Down the Virtual Machine:** Make sure the VM is turned off.
2. **Add New Disks**
   a. Open VirtualBox and select the VM.
   b. Click `Settings`, then navigate to the `Storage` section.
   c. Click the controller (for example, SATA Controller), then click the **+** icon to add a hard disk.
   d. Choose `Create new disk` or select an existing virtual disk file.
   e. Specify the disk size (for example, 10GB) and click `Create`.
   f. Repeat the process to add the second disk.
3. **Start the Virtual Machine:** Boot the VM and verify the new disks are available.

Please refer to the following figure:

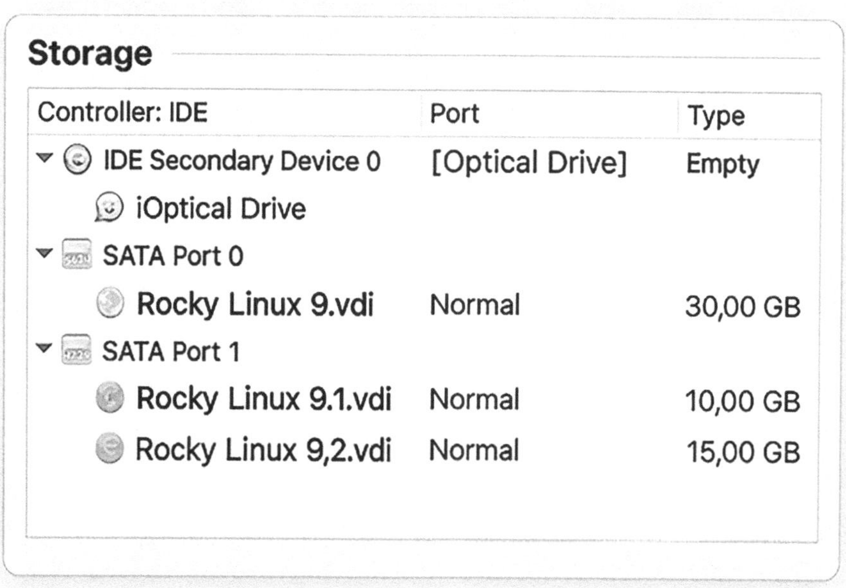

Figure 6.1: *VirtualBox Storage Configuration*

This figure illustrates the final configuration of **Rocky Linux 9** disk storage, which ensures that the virtual machine is fully prepared and optimized for the upcoming hands-on labs. The configuration includes all necessary steps to properly set up disk partitions, RAID arrays, and logical volumes, ensuring that the system is ready for practical exercises. By carefully configuring the disk storage, users can ensure reliable performance and fault tolerance, which are critical for the successful completion of the labs. With the virtual machine's disk storage properly configured, it is now set up to handle various system tasks, such as creating and managing filesystems, mounting, and unmounting disks, and configuring RAID arrays. This setup serves as the foundation for the labs, offering a stable environment to explore and implement advanced system administration tasks on **Rocky Linux 9**.

Verify Disks in the VM

Once the VM is running, check the new disks using: **`lsblk`**

Next Steps: After confirming the disks are visible, proceed with partitioning them using fdisk or other tools as described in the lab instructions.

Step-by-Step Instructions

Step 1: Verify the System Version

Run the following command to confirm the Rocky Linux version: **`cat /etc/os-release`**

Expected output:

```
NAME="Rocky Linux"
VERSION="9.4 (Blue Onyx)"
```

Step 2: Install `mdadm`

Install the RAID management tool: **`sudo dnf install mdadm -y`**

Verify the installation: **`mdadm -version`**

Expected output: `mdadm - v4.3 - 2024-02-15 - 4`

Step 3: Identify the Available Disks

List all block devices: **`lsblk`**

Identify the disks to be used for RAID (for example, **`/dev/sdb`** and **`/dev/sdc`**).

Step 4: Partition the Disks

Create partitions for each disk:

a. Run **`fdisk`** for each disk: **`sudo fdisk /dev/sdb`**

b. Steps within **`fdisk`**:

   i. Press **`n`** to create a new partition.

   ii. Press **`p`** for primary partition.

   iii. Accept default values for sectors.

   iv. Press **`w`** to write changes and exit.

   v. Repeat for **`/dev/sdc`**.

Step 5: Create the RAID 1 Array

Use the following command to create the RAID array:

```
sudo mdadm --create --verbose /dev/md0 --level=1 --raid-devices=2 /dev/sdb1 /
dev/sdc1
```

Step 6: Check for the Existing RAID Configurations

Check if the disks are part of any existing RAID array: **`sudo mdadm -E /dev/sd[b-c]1`**

Expected output:

```
[rockylinux@rocky9 ~]$ sudo mdadm -E /dev/sd[b-c]1
/dev/sdb1:
          Magic : a92b4efc
        Version : 1.2
    Feature Map : 0x0
     Array UUID : 6b57e19d:f9946d06:c2c6c273:6bf2954f
           Name : rocky9.linuxvmimages.local:0  (local to host rocky9.linuxvmima
ges.local)
  Creation Time : Sun May 11 23:27:22 2025
     Raid Level : raid1
   Raid Devices : 2

 Avail Dev Size : 20951040 sectors (9.99 GiB 10.73 GB)
     Array Size : 10475520 KiB (9.99 GiB 10.73 GB)
    Data Offset : 18432 sectors
   Super Offset : 8 sectors
   Unused Space : before=18280 sectors, after=0 sectors
          State : active
    Device UUID : 0ad1f0ee:ab069e40:3904a0d4:07283138

    Update Time : Sun May 11 23:27:41 2025
  Bad Block Log : 512 entries available at offset 136 sectors
       Checksum : e4f620a4 - correct
         Events : 6
```

Figure 6.2: *Raid Started in Rocky Linux 9*

This figure illustrates the successful initialization of a RAID (Redundant Array of Independent Disks) configuration in Rocky Linux 9. It confirms that the RAID array has been correctly detected and activated by the system, ensuring redundancy and improved performance. This step is essential in storage management, as it provides data protection and system resilience, especially in enterprise or high-availability environments.

Step 7: Verify the RAID Array

Check the RAID status: **`cat /proc/mdstat`**

Step 8: Create a Filesystem

Format the RAID device: **`sudo mkfs.ext4 /dev/md0`**

Step 9: Mount the RAID Device

a. Create a mount point: **`sudo mkdir -p /mnt/raid1`**

b. Mount the RAID device: **`sudo mount /dev/md0 /mnt/raid1`**

c. Verify the mount: **`df -h`**

d. Detailed information: **`sudo mdadm --detail /dev/md0`**

Step 10: Make RAID Persistent

a. Append RAID configuration to **`mdadm.conf`**:

   i. **`sudo su`**

   ii. **`mdadm --detail --scan >> /etc/mdadm.conf`**

   iii. **`exit`**

b. Add the RAID device to **`/etc/fstab`** for automatic mounting:

   i. Find the UUID: **`sudo blkid /dev/md0`**

ii. Edit **`/etc/fstab`**: **`sudo nano /etc/fstab`**

iii. Add the following entry: **`UUID=<RAID-UUID> /mnt/raid1 ext4 defaults 0 0`**

c. Test the configuration: **`sudo mount -av`**

Step 11: Verify the Setup

Ensure the RAID setup is complete and functional:

- **`lsblk`**
- **`cat /proc/mdstat`**

Best Practices

- Regularly monitor RAID health: **`sudo mdadm --detail /dev/md0`**
- Schedule periodic backups.
- Replace failed disks promptly and rebuild the array.

This laboratory demonstrated how to configure RAID 1 on Rocky Linux 9. By following these steps, data redundancy and reliability are ensured for critical systems.

Managing RAID Arrays

After setting up a RAID array, managing it effectively is essential to ensure its reliability, performance, and fault tolerance. This step-by-step lab focuses on common RAID management tasks, such as checking the health of the array, replacing failed disks, and expanding the array.

Key Concepts in RAID Management

- **Monitoring RAID Health:** Regularly check the status of the RAID to detect issues early.
- **Rebuilding Arrays:** Replace failed drives and restore redundancy.
- **Expanding RAID Arrays:** Add new drives to increase storage capacity.
- **Setting Up Alerts:** Automate notifications for potential problems.

Ensuring RAID Array Health

The first step in managing RAID arrays on Rocky Linux 9 is to regularly check the health of the RAID configuration. This crucial task helps identify potential issues early, ensuring data integrity and system reliability. Monitoring key parameters such as disk status, array consistency, and overall performance helps maintain a stable and efficient RAID setup, thereby preventing costly downtime or data loss.

Step 1: Validating information for the RAID Array

i. Display detailed information about the RAID array: **`sudo mdadm --detail /dev/md0`**

   This command shows the overall health, status of each disk, and synchronization progress.

ii. View real-time RAID status: **`cat /proc/mdstat`**

   This provides a concise summary of the array's current state, including ongoing rebuilds.

Step 2: Replace a Failed Disk

If a disk in the RAID array fails, follow these steps to replace it:

a. Identify the failed disk using the `` `mdadm --detail` `` command.

   For example: **`sudo mdadm --detail /dev/md0`**

A failed disk will be marked as `**faulty**`.

b. Remove the failed disk from the array:

To remove a device, the syntax should specify the RAID array (**/dev/md1**) followed by the device to be removed (/dev/sdb1): **sudo mdadm /dev/md1 --remove /dev/sdb1**

Hot Remove Issues: If the **--remove** command fails with No such device or address, the device might already be inactive or not properly recognized. Linux administrators can first mark the device as failed:

```
sudo mdadm /dev/md1 --fail /dev/sdb1
```

Then, try removing it: **sudo mdadm /dev/md1 --remove /dev/sdb1**

3. Add a new disk to the array: **sudo mdadm /dev/md0 --add /dev/sdb1**

4. Monitor the Rebuild Process

To monitor the rebuild process of the RAID array, use the following command:

```
watch cat /proc/mdstat
```

The watch command will update the status every few seconds, allowing us to track the rebuild progress. To exit this monitoring interface, press *Ctrl* + *C*.

Step 3: Expand the RAID Array

If we want to add more storage to the RAID array, the following steps ill be especially useful:

a. Grow the RAID array to include the new disk: **sudo mdadm --grow --raid-devices=4 /dev/md0**

b. Resize the filesystem to use the additional space: **sudo resize2fs /dev/md0**

c. Verify the new size of the array: **df -h /mnt/raid**

Best Practices for RAID Management

- **Schedule Regular Checks:** Use a cron job to run `**mdadm --detail**` periodically and log the results.
- **Use Identical Drives:** Ensure replacement drives match the specifications of the original ones.
- **Back Up Critical Data:** RAID improves redundancy but is not a substitute for regular backups.
- **Document Changes:** Keep track of modifications made to the array, such as adding or replacing disks.

RAID Failure Recovery: A Practical Walkthrough

In real-world environments, disks in a RAID array may fail unexpectedly. This section demonstrates a step-by-step procedure to recover from a failed disk in a RAID 1 setup using **mdadm.**

Scenario: One of the mirrored disks (**/dev/sdb1**) in a RAID 1 array (**/dev/md1**) has failed and needs to be replaced. This would happen in a physical scenario with real equipment.

Step-by-Step Recovery Process

Step 1: Identify the Failed Disk:

```
sudo mdadm --detail /dev/md1
```

Expected output:

```
/dev/md1:
  State            : degraded
  Active Devices   : 1
  Working Devices  : 1
  Failed Devices   : 1
  Spare Devices    : 0

  Number  Major  Minor  RaidDevice  State        Device
  ------------------------------------------------------
  0       8      17     0           active sync /dev/sdb1
  1       8      33     1           faulty      /dev/sdc1
```

Figure 6.3: *Degraded Failed Disk in an Array*

Figure 6.3 illustrates a degraded state within a RAID array due to a failed disk. In a typical RAID configuration, redundancy is built in to tolerate disk failures, but when one disk fails, the array enters a degraded mode. This means that although data remains accessible, performance may be reduced, and the risk of total data loss increases if another disk fails. The figure shows the affected disk marked as failed, highlighting the importance of proactive monitoring and immediate replacement to restore full redundancy and prevent potential system downtime. This scenario underscores the critical role of RAID in data protection and the necessity of regular maintenance and backups.

Step 2: Mark the Failed Device: **`sudo mdadm /dev/md1 --fail /dev/sdc1`**

Step 3: Remove the Failed Device: **`sudo mdadm /dev/md1 --remove /dev/sdc1`**

Step 4: Insert a New Disk

- Assume a new disk **`/dev/sdd`** is added.
- Partition it with **`fdisk` and** set the type to **`fd`.**
- **`sudo fdisk /dev/sdd`**
  `# Create a new primary partition and set type to fd`

Step 5: Add the New Disk to the Array: **`sudo mdadm /dev/md1 --add /dev/sdd1`**

Step 6: Monitor the Rebuild Process: **`watch cat /proc/mdstat`**

Expected output (during rebuild):

```
md1 : active raid1 sdd1[2] sdb1[0]
  10485632 blocks [2/1] [U_]
  [=>................]  recovery = 12.4% (1308160/10485632)  finish=10.3min
```

Figure 6.4: *Rebuilding the Previous Failed Disk Raid*

Figure 6.4 illustrates the process of rebuilding a previously failed disk in a RAID array. When a disk in a RAID configuration fails, especially in RAID levels that support redundancy (such as RAID 1, 5, or 6), it can be replaced and rebuilt using parity or mirrored data from the remaining drives. In this figure, a new or previously failed but now repaired disk is being reintroduced into the array. The system automatically begins the rebuild process, redistributing data and parity to restore full redundancy and ensure data integrity. This step is critical for maintaining fault tolerance and minimizing the risk of data loss in the event of another disk failure.

Step 7: Confirm Rebuild Completion: **`sudo mdadm --detail /dev/md1`**

Expected output:

```
/dev/md1:
  State : clean
  Active Devices : 2
  Working Devices : 2
  Failed Devices : 0
  Spare Devices : 0
```

Figure 6.5: *New Raid Partition with Clean Status*

Figure 6.5 illustrates a newly created RAID partition that has achieved a "clean" status. This status indicates that the RAID array is fully synchronized, with no degraded or missing devices, and is ready for use. A clean status is a crucial indicator of RAID health, confirming that all member disks are functioning properly and that the redundancy mechanisms are in place. At this stage, the RAID array can be safely formatted and mounted for data storage, ensuring both performance and data protection, depending on the RAID level configured.

Best Practices:

- Use identical replacement disks (size and type).
- Schedule regular RAID health checks with cron: ***@daily mdadm --detail /dev/md1 | mail -s "RAID Status" admin@example.com***

Using systemd for Service Management

Systemd is the default **init system** and **service manager** used by Rocky Linux 9 and many other modern Linux distributions. Its key role is to control how the system starts up, manages background services (known as *daemons*), and shuts down. Unlike older init systems that started services one at a time, systemd uses **parallel startup**, which allows multiple services to start at the same time–speeding up the boot process. It also understands service *dependencies*, ensuring that services start in the correct order. For example, a web server will not start until the network is up. This intelligent management helps improve reliability and boot performance.

Systemd organizes its configuration using **unit files**, which are stored in directories such as **`/etc/systemd/system/`** and **`/usr/lib/systemd/system/`**. These unit files define how services, timers, devices, and other components should behave. Administrators can control services using the systemctl command–for example, **`systemctl start httpd`** to start a web server, or **`systemctl enable firewalld`** to ensure the firewall starts on boot. We can also check logs using **`journalctl`**, which provides detailed information about system events and service behavior. Additionally, **`systemd`** supports **custom unit files** and **timers**, allowing users to automate tasks and tailor system behavior to their needs, making it a powerful and flexible tool for managing enterprise Linux systems such as Rocky Linux 9.

Key concepts in **`systemd`** include:

- **Units**: Fundamental building blocks such as services, sockets, timers, and mount points.
- **Targets**: Groups of units, such as **`runlevels`**, used to define states such as multi-**`user.target`** or **`graphical.target`**.
- **Journal**: Centralized logging mechanism provided by **`journald`**.

Key systemd Commands

`Systemctl` is a central command-line utility used to manage services on Linux systems that implement the **`systemd init`** system, such as Rocky Linux 9. It provides administrators with the ability to start, stop, enable, and disable services in a straightforward and consistent manner. For instance, to launch the Apache web server, the command **`systemctl start httpd`** is used, while **`systemctl stop httpd`** halts the service. When configuration changes are applied, **`systemctl restart httpd`** can be issued to reload the service without requiring a system reboot.

To configure a service to launch automatically during system startup, the **`systemctl enable`** command is used. On the other hand, **`systemctl disable`** prevents a service from starting on boot. These controls are vital for ensuring services operate only when needed, optimizing system performance and reliability.

Beyond service management, **`systemctl`** also facilitates system-wide operations. Commands such as **`systemctl`** reboot and **`systemctl poweroff`** provide safe methods to restart or shut down the system. Additionally, **`systemd`** organizes the system's operational modes using *targets*, which serve a similar purpose to the traditional runlevels found in earlier Linux distributions. Targets define specific states, such as multi-user mode or graphical mode. Switching between these states is done using ***systemctl*** **`isolate`**, while all available targets can be listed with **`systemctl list-units --type=target`**.

Understanding and effectively using **`systemctl`** is essential for system administrators working with Rocky Linux. It offers robust tools for controlling services, managing system states, and maintaining smooth, secure, and stable operations across various computing environments.

Command	Description
`systemctl start <service>`	Starts a service.
`systemctl stop <service>`	Stops a service.
`systemctl restart <service>`	Restarts a service.
`systemctl reload <service>`	Reloads the configuration without stopping the service.
`systemctl enable <service>`	Enables the service to start automatically at boot.
`systemctl disable <service>`	Disables the service from starting automatically at boot.
`systemctl status <service>`	Displays current status, logs, and runtime details of the service.
`systemctl is-enabled <service>`	Checks if the service is enabled to start at boot.
`systemctl list-units`	Lists all active units (services, mounts, sockets, etc.).
`systemctl daemon-reload`	Reloads systemd configuration after unit file changes.

Figure 6.6: *Common systemctl Commands and Their Descriptions*

Figure 6.6 provides a quick reference to the most frequently used **systemctl** commands in Rocky Linux 9. These commands are essential for managing system services and system states efficiently. Each command listed helps administrators perform critical tasks such as starting, stopping, enabling, or checking the status of services, as well as managing system reboots and shutdowns. This table serves as a practical guide for both beginners and experienced users to understand the purpose and usage of each command in day-to-day system administration.

Practical Examples: Managing a Service: Apache HTTP Server

1. Install Apache: `sudo dnf install httpd -y`
2. Start Apache: `sudo systemctl start httpd`
3. Enable Apache on Boot: `sudo systemctl enable httpd`
4. Check Apache Status: `sudo systemctl status httpd`

Output example:

```
[ec2-user@ip-172-31-31-92 ~]$ sudo systemctl status httpd
● httpd.service - The Apache HTTP Server
     Loaded: loaded (/usr/lib/systemd/system/httpd.service; enabled; preset: disabled)
     Active: active (running) since Mon 2024-12-23 21:09:55 UTC; 14s ago
       Docs: man:httpd.service(8)
   Main PID: 15979 (httpd)
     Status: "Total requests: 0; Idle/Busy workers 100/0;Requests/sec: 0; Bytes served/sec:   0 B/sec"
      Tasks: 177 (limit: 1111)
     Memory: 12.9M
        CPU: 62ms
     CGroup: /system.slice/httpd.service
             ├─15979 /usr/sbin/httpd -DFOREGROUND
             ├─16087 /usr/sbin/httpd -DFOREGROUND
             ├─16091 /usr/sbin/httpd -DFOREGROUND
             ├─16092 /usr/sbin/httpd -DFOREGROUND
             └─16093 /usr/sbin/httpd -DFOREGROUND

Dec 23 21:09:55 ip-172-31-31-92.ec2.internal systemd[1]: Starting httpd.service - The Apache HTTP Server...
Dec 23 21:09:55 ip-172-31-31-92.ec2.internal systemd[1]: Started httpd.service - The Apache HTTP Server.
Dec 23 21:09:55 ip-172-31-31-92.ec2.internal httpd[15979]: Server configured, listening on: port 80
```

Figure 6.7: *Httpd Process Status*

This figure illustrates the status of the **httpd** process, which is the Apache HTTP Server daemon responsible for handling web server requests. The figure provides key details such as the process ID (PID), current state, uptime, and the number of active connections. Monitoring the status of the **httpd** process is crucial for ensuring the smooth operation of the server, diagnosing potential issues, and optimizing performance. By analyzing this data, administrators can identify bottlenecks, verify service availability, and take corrective actions when necessary.

Please use the letter q to exit this interface.

5. Stop Apache: **`sudo systemctl stop httpd`**

Creating a Custom Service File

1. **Create a Service File**: Create a custom service file, for example, **`myapp.service`** in **`/etc/systemd/system/`**: **`sudo nano /etc/systemd/system/myapp.service`**

   Example contents:

```
[Unit]
Description=My Custom Application Service
After=network.target

[Service]
ExecStart=/usr/bin/python3 /path/to/myapp.py
Restart=always
```

```
User=myuser
Group=mygroup

[Install]
WantedBy=multi-user.target
```

3. Reload the **Systemd** Daemon: **sudo systemctl daemon-reload**
4. Start the Service: **sudo systemctl start myapp**
5. Enable the Service: **sudo systemctl enable myapp**

Analyzing Boot Performance

To analyze boot times and identify slow services.

Example output: **systemd-analyze blame**

```
[ec2-user@ip-172-31-31-92 ~]$ systemd-analyze blame
30.230s update-motd.service
 3.773s dev-disk-by\x2dpartlabel-EFI\x5cx20System\x5cx20Partition.device
 3.773s dev-xvda128.device
 3.773s sys-devices-vbd\x2d51712-block-xvda-xvda128.device
 3.773s dev-disk-by\x2duuid-A012\x2dE846.device
 3.773s dev-disk-by\x2dpartuuid-83487aae\x2d6913\x2d4aba\x2da619\x2d371a54eb3168.device
 3.771s dev-xvda127.device
 3.771s dev-disk-by\x2dpartuuid-470caf5b\x2d592d\x2d4cbc\x2db3ab\x2d9e1a1d316147.device
 3.771s sys-devices-vbd\x2d51712-block-xvda-xvda127.device
 3.771s dev-disk-by\x2dpartlabel-BIOS\x5cx20Boot\x5cx20Partition.device
 3.751s dev-ttyS0.device
 3.751s sys-devices-pnp0-00:06-tty-ttyS0.device
 3.750s sys-devices-platform-serial8250-tty-ttyS3.device
 3.750s dev-ttyS3.device
 3.749s sys-devices-platform-serial8250-tty-ttyS1.device
 3.749s dev-ttyS1.device
 3.742s dev-xvda.device
 3.742s dev-disk-by\x2ddiskseq-1.device
 3.742s sys-devices-vbd\x2d51712-block-xvda.device
 3.740s sys-devices-platform-serial8250-tty-ttyS2.device
 3.740s dev-ttyS2.device
 3.729s sys-devices-vbd\x2d51712-block-xvda-xvda1.device
 3.729s dev-disk-by\x2duuid-3a8023d8\x2d2841\x2d47f7\x2d985b\x2dab4b5825ae27.device
 3.729s dev-disk-by\x2dpartuuid-e6b45c27\x2dde47\x2d44bd\x2db6d9\x2d689e61716d15.device
 3.729s dev-xvda1.device
```

Figure 6.8: *Systemd Services Analysis*

This image provides an analysis of **systemd** services, which are fundamental to managing system processes and resources on Linux. The figure highlights key details such as active and inactive services, their statuses, and dependencies. Understanding the state of these services is critical for maintaining system stability, troubleshooting errors, and ensuring seamless operation of essential functions. By analyzing this information, administrators can identify failed or misconfigured services, prioritize critical tasks, and optimize system performance.

Using Journals for Troubleshooting

Systemd utilizes **journald** for centralized logging. The key commands are listed in the following table:

No.	Command	Description
1	`journalctl`	Displays the entire system journal.
2	`journalctl -u <service>`	Filters logs for a specific systemd service.
3	`journalctl --since "2 hours ago"`	Shows logs generated within the last 2 hours.
4	`journalctl -b`	Retrieves logs from the current boot session.

Figure 6.9: *Key journalctl Commands for Troubleshooting in Systemd*

Figure 6.9 provides a concise reference to essential commands used for analyzing and diagnosing issues within systemd-managed services and the system log. It highlights practical options such as viewing recent logs, filtering by service unit, and following real-time log output, all of which are critical for quickly identifying the root cause of system errors. By consolidating these commands, the table serves as a quick-access tool for administrators, enabling efficient troubleshooting of boot issues, service failures, and runtime errors in Rocky Linux and other systemd-based environments.

Example: **`journalctl -u httpd`**

Understanding Targets

Targets represent system states and group related services together. Examples include:

- **`multi-user.target`:** Multi-user, non-graphical mode.
- **`graphical.target`:** Multi-user with GUI.
- **`rescue.target`:** Single-user mode for maintenance.

To change the default target: **`sudo systemctl set-default graphical.target`**

To switch targets:

- **`sudo systemctl isolate rescue.target`**
- **`sudo systemctl set-default graphical.target`**

Finally, press *Control* + D to return to the graphic interface.

The **`systemd`** is a powerful tool for managing services in Rocky Linux 9. Its structured approach to services, logging, and boot optimization makes it indispensable for administrators. By mastering **`systemd`,** we can effectively control and troubleshoot the Linux systems.

Monitoring System Performance

Monitoring system performance is essential for maintaining stability and ensuring optimal resource usage. Rocky Linux 9 provides various tools for this purpose, with **`ps`** and **`top`** being two of the most used commands. This guide will cover the features, usage, and practical examples of these tools to help us monitor and troubleshoot system performance effectively.

Overview of ps and top

ps Command: The **ps** command (process status) provides a snapshot of the currently running processes. It is particularly useful for scripting and analyzing specific processes.

top Command: The top command offers a real-time, dynamic view of system processes and resource usage. It provides an interactive interface for monitoring and managing processes.

Using the ps Command

Basic Syntax- ps [options]

No.	Option	Description
1	-e	Lists all processes across all sessions.
2	-f	Displays a full-format listing with extended details.
3	-u <user>	Filters and shows processes owned by a specific user.
4	-p <PID>	Displays information for a specific process ID.
5	--sort=<key>	Sorts the output by a given key (e.g., %cpu , %mem , pid).

Figure 6.10: *Commonly Used Options for the ps Command*

Figure 6.10 presents an overview of frequently applied arguments that enhance the effectiveness of process monitoring in Linux systems. These options allow administrators to list active processes with detailed information such as process IDs (PIDs), parent-child relationships, CPU and memory usage, and associated users. By mastering these options, system administrators can quickly assess system performance, identify resource-intensive tasks, and troubleshoot unresponsive applications. It serves as a practical guide, simplifying the use of ps for both routine monitoring and in-depth system diagnostics.

Examples

1. **List All Processes: ps -e**
2. **Display Detailed Information: ps -ef**

```
[cmorera@localhost ~]$ ps -ef
UID          PID    PPID  C STIME TTY          TIME CMD
root           1       0  1 01:35 ?        00:00:01 /usr/lib/systemd/systemd rhg
root           2       0  0 01:35 ?        00:00:00 [kthreadd]
root           3       2  0 01:35 ?        00:00:00 [pool_workqueue_]
root           4       2  0 01:35 ?        00:00:00 [kworker/R-rcu_g]
root           5       2  0 01:35 ?        00:00:00 [kworker/R-rcu_p]
root           6       2  0 01:35 ?        00:00:00 [kworker/R-slub_]
root           7       2  0 01:35 ?        00:00:00 [kworker/R-netns]
root           8       2  0 01:35 ?        00:00:00 [kworker/0:0-ata_sff]
root           9       2  0 01:35 ?        00:00:00 [kworker/0:0H-events_highpri
root          10       2  0 01:35 ?        00:00:00 [kworker/u512:0-events_unbou
root          11       2  0 01:35 ?        00:00:00 [kworker/R-mm_pe]
root          12       2  0 01:35 ?        00:00:00 [kworker/u512:1-netns]
root          13       2  0 01:35 ?        00:00:00 [rcu_tasks_kthre]
root          14       2  0 01:35 ?        00:00:00 [rcu_tasks_rude_]
root          15       2  0 01:35 ?        00:00:00 [rcu_tasks_trace]
root          16       2  0 01:35 ?        00:00:00 [ksoftirqd/0]
```

Figure 6.11: *Main Process Running in Rocky Linux 9*

In Rocky Linux 9, the **ps -ef** command is used to display a snapshot of all currently running processes on the system. The output provides detailed information about each process, including the user ID (UID), process ID (PID), parent process ID (PPID), CPU usage (C), start time (STIME), controlling terminal (TTY), total accumulated CPU time (TIME), and the command that initiated the process (CMD). For example, the output might show that the **systemd** process (PID 1) is running under the root user and has been running for 5 seconds, while a process such as **python3** (PID 456) initiated by the user **user1** is currently utilizing 1% of the CPU. This output is crucial for administrators to monitor and manage system processes, ensuring smooth operation and troubleshooting when necessary.

3. **Filter by User:** `ps -u` [add the username]
4. **Find a Specific Process by Name:** `ps -e | grep systemd`
5. **Sort Processes by CPU Usage:** `ps -eo pid,ppid,cmd,%mem,%cpu --sort=-%cpu`

```
[cmorera@localhost ~]$ ps -eo pid,ppid,cmd,%mem,%cpu --sort=-%cpu
    PID    PPID CMD                         %MEM %CPU
   1414       1 /usr/libexec/mysqld --based  5.9  0.6
   2761    2677 /usr/bin/gnome-shell         8.8  0.6
   3014    2741 /usr/bin/gnome-software --g  4.8  0.3
      1       0 /usr/lib/systemd/systemd rh  0.8  0.2
   2827    2677 /usr/bin/pipewire            0.6  0.2
     29       2 [kworker/u514:0-events_unbo  0.0  0.1
     55       2 [kswapd0]                    0.0  0.1
    948       1 /usr/lib/polkit-1/polkitd -  1.2  0.1
   3267    3252 /usr/libexec/ibus-extension  1.8  0.1
   3397    2677 /usr/libexec/gnome-terminal  2.9  0.1
      2       0 [kthreadd]                   0.0  0.0
      3       2 [pool_workqueue_]            0.0  0.0
      4       2 [kworker/R-rcu_g]            0.0  0.0
      5       2 [kworker/R-rcu_p]            0.0  0.0
      6       2 [kworker/R-slub_]            0.0  0.0
      7       2 [kworker/R-netns]            0.0  0.0
      9       2 [kworker/0:0H-events_highpr  0.0  0.0
     10       2 [kworker/u512:0-events_unbo  0.0  0.0
```

Figure 6.12: CPU Uses Processes

This figure presents an overview of CPU usage by various processes, highlighting their resource consumption and activity levels. The figure includes details such as process IDs (PIDs), CPU usage percentages, and associated commands. This analysis is crucial for identifying processes that may be overloading the CPU, ensuring balanced resource allocation, and optimizing overall system performance. By monitoring CPU-intensive processes, administrators can troubleshoot bottlenecks, prioritize tasks, and maintain the stability and efficiency of the system.

Using the `top` Command: Launching `top`

Run top from the terminal: **`top`.**

Interface Overview

The top interface is divided into two sections:

1. **Summary Section:** Displays overall system metrics, including load average, CPU usage, memory usage, and swap usage.

2. **Process List:** Shows running processes with metrics such as CPU and memory usage.

Key Metrics in top

In Rocky Linux 9, monitoring key system metrics is essential for maintaining performance, stability, and security across enterprise environments. These metrics provide administrators with critical insights into system health, covering areas such as CPU usage, memory consumption, disk I/O, network throughput, and active processes. By tracking and analyzing these values, administrators can quickly identify performance bottlenecks, optimize resource allocation, and ensure the system remains reliable under varying workloads. Understanding and leveraging these key metrics forms the foundation for proactive troubleshooting, capacity planning, and efficient system administration in Rocky Linux 9.

Field	Description
`PID`	Process ID. Uniquely identifies each running process on the system.
`USER`	Username of the process owner. Indicates the account under which it runs.
`PR`	Process priority. Determines scheduling precedence in the system.
`%CPU`	CPU usage percentage. Reflects how much processor time the process consumes.
`%MEM`	Memory usage percentage. Shows the proportion of RAM used by the process.
`TIME+`	Total CPU time consumed. Accumulated execution time since process start.
`COMMAND`	Initiating command. Specifies the program or script that launched the process.

Figure 6.13: *Commonly Used Terms for Processes*

It provides a glossary of essential terminology related to process management in Linux systems. It defines key concepts such as process ID (PID), parent process, child process, threads, foreground and background execution, as well as states like running, sleeping, or zombie. Understanding these terms is fundamental for interpreting system outputs, analyzing process behavior, and applying administrative commands effectively. By familiarizing themselves with this terminology, administrators and learners gain the foundational knowledge required to manage processes confidently and troubleshoot system performance issues with precision.

Interactive Commands in top

Command	Description
h	Displays help. Lists available commands and their functions.
k	Terminates a process by entering its PID.
r	Renices a process. Adjusts its scheduling priority (nice value).
q	Quits `top`. Returns to the terminal prompt.
Shift+P	Sorts processes by CPU usage. Highest consumers appear first.
Shift+M	Sorts processes by memory usage. Prioritizes RAM-intensive processes.
Shift+T	Sorts processes by total running time. Longest-running processes appear first.

Figure 6.14: *Understanding the Top Command Options*

This figure outlines the most important parameters available in the top utility, a powerful tool for real-time monitoring of system performance in Linux. The figure highlights options that allow administrators to sort processes by CPU or memory usage, adjust the refresh rate, filter results, and toggle between different display modes. These options provide flexibility in customizing the output to focus on specific performance metrics, making it easier to detect bottlenecks, identify resource-hungry processes, and maintain system stability. By mastering these options, administrators can transform top into a dynamic diagnostic tool tailored to their monitoring needs.

It helps users interact with the ***top*** command effectively for real-time process.

Customizing `top`

1. **Change Refresh Interval:** Press d and enter a new interval (in seconds).
2. **Filter by User:** Press u and type the username.
3. **Highlight Resource-Intensive Processes:** Enable highlighting by pressing z.

Practical Examples with `top`

1. **Monitor CPU-Intensive Processes: *top* -o %CPU**

   press the letter q to exit this process's interface.
2. **Monitor Memory-Intensive Processes: *top* -o %MEM**
3. **Kill a Process:**
   a. Locate the PID of the process.
   b. Press k, enter the PID, and confirm.
4. **Save Output to a File:** Run **`top`** in batch mode to save data for later analysis:
   a. **`top -b -n 1 > top-output.txt`**
   b. **`cat top-output.txt`**

Combining `ps` and `top` with Other Tools

To monitor disk activity, the **`iostat -x 1`** command can be used in combination with **`ps`** and **`top`**. The **`iostat`** command provides detailed statistics about disk I/O, helping system administrators track disk usage performance. The **-x** option gives extended output, and the 1 specifies an update interval of 1 second. This allows for real-time monitoring of disk activity and performance metrics. Note that **iostat** is part of the **sysstat** package, which may not be pre-installed on Rocky Linux 9, and must be installed manually if needed.

Monitor Disk I/O - Combine with `iostat` to monitor disk activity, `iostat -x 1`

The iostat command is part of the sysstat package, which may not be installed by default on Rocky Linux 9. To get it working, follow these steps:

Steps to Enable iostat in Rocky Linux 9:

a. **Install the `sysstat` Package**: Run the following command to install the **sysstat** package: **`sudo dnf install sysstat -y`**

b. **Enable the `sysstat` Service**: Once installed, enable and start the sysstat service for data collection: **`sudo systemctl enable --now sysstat`**

c. **Verify Installation**: Test if iostat is working: **`iostat -x 1`**

   We apply *Control* + C to exit this interface.

d. **Optional Configuration**: If needed, edit the configuration file to customize **sysstat** settings: **`sudo nano /etc/sysconfig/sysstat`**

Ensure Data Collection is Enabled: Look for the **SADC_OPTIONS** variable and ensure it is properly configured. For example:

```
# Additional options for sadc, used by cron
SADC_OPTIONS="-S DISK"
```

e. Reboot or Restart **sysstat** Service: Apply the changes by restarting the service: **`sudo systemctl restart sysstat`**

Alternative Tools for Monitoring Disk I/O:

If **iostat** is not preferred, consider these alternatives:

- **`dstat`:** Install and use dstat for monitoring disk, CPU, and memory usage in real-time:
    - `sudo dnf install dstat -y`
    - `dstat -dny`
- **`iotop`:** Install iotop for a real-time view of I/O usage by individual processes:
    - `sudo dnf install iotop -y`
    - `sudo iotop`

Monitor Specific Applications: Use **ps** and **grep** to monitor processes of a specific application: **`ps -ef | grep nginx`**

Additional monitoring tool `htop` option

- `sudo dnf install htop -y`
- `htop`

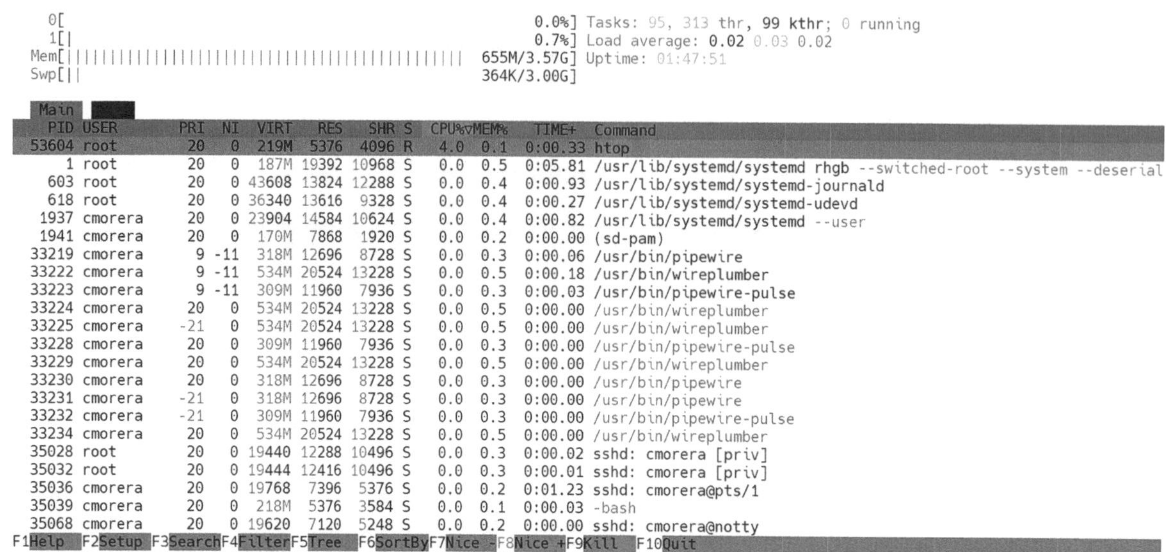

Figure 6.15: *Htop Monitoring Processes*

The **htop** utility is a powerful, interactive process viewer that provides a real-time overview of system processes and resource utilization. Unlike the traditional top command, **htop** features a more user-friendly, visually appealing interface that uses color-coded metrics to highlight system performance. It displays CPU, memory, and swap usage graphs at the top, followed by a sortable list of running processes, including details such as process ID (PID), user, priority, and CPU or memory usage. Users can easily navigate the process list using arrow keys, search for specific processes, and even kill or renice processes directly through the interface. This makes htop an indispensable tool for system administrators and developers who need to monitor and manage system performance efficiently.

Monitoring system performance in Rocky Linux 9 using tools such as **ps** and **top** is a fundamental skill for administrators. While **ps** provides a detailed snapshot of processes, top offers real-time insights and interactivity. By mastering these tools and combining them with other utilities, we can efficiently manage and troubleshoot the system.

Automating Tasks with cron

Automating repetitive tasks is a key aspect of efficient system administration. In Rocky Linux 9, the **cron** utility provides a powerful way to schedule and manage automated tasks. This guide explores how to use **cron**, including practical examples and best practices.

Overview of cron

cron is a time-based job scheduler in Unix-like operating systems. It allows users to execute commands or scripts at specified times and intervals. Jobs managed by **cron** are defined in a file called a "crontab."

Key Components

- **crond:** The daemon responsible for executing scheduled tasks.
- **crontab:** The configuration file where jobs are defined.

Managing the cron Service

Before using **cron**, ensure the **crond** service is running:

Start and Enable `crond`

- `sudo systemctl start crond`
- `sudo systemctl enable crond`

Check Service Status: `sudo systemctl status crond`

Using `crontab`

The **`crontab`** command is used to manage cron jobs. Each user can have their own crontab file.

Basic Syntax `crontab` [options]

Option	Description
`-e`	Edits the current user's crontab. Enables modification of scheduled tasks.
`-l`	Lists the current user's crontab. Displays all scheduled tasks.
`-r`	Removes the current user's crontab. Deletes the crontab file entirely.
`-u <user>`	Manages crontab for another user (requires `sudo`). Allows editing or listing.

Figure 6.16: *Crontab Command Options*

This figure summarizes the key options available when working with the crontab utility, which is used to schedule and manage recurring tasks in Linux systems. It explains common options such as listing current cron jobs, editing user-specific cron tables, removing scheduled tasks, and applying changes for different users. These options are essential for automating system maintenance, backups, monitoring scripts, and other routine operations. By understanding and applying the crontab command options effectively, administrators can streamline repetitive tasks, reduce manual intervention, and ensure consistent execution of critical processes.

Crontab File Format

The crontab file format consists of lines, where each line represents a scheduled job. Each line follows a specific structure, consisting of six fields: **`<minute> <hour> <day_of_month> <month> <day_of_week> <command>`**. The first five fields define when the job will run, specifying the minute, hour, day of the month, month, and day of the week. The sixth field is the command that will be executed at the specified time. The **`cron`** scheduler interprets these values to determine the timing and frequency of task execution, allowing users to automate repetitive tasks at specified intervals.

Field	Allowed Values
`Minute`	`0-59` – Represents the minute of the hour.
`Hour`	`0-23` – Represents the hour of the day (24-hour format).
`Day of Month`	`1-31` – Specifies the day of the month.
`Month`	`1-12` or `jan-dec` – Accepts numeric or abbreviated month names.
`Day of Week`	`0-7` or `sun-sat` – Both `0` and `7` represent Sunday. Accepts names or numbers.

Figure 6.17: *Allowed Values for Time and Frequency Fields in Cron Job Scheduling*

Note: Cron fields support wildcards (*), ranges (1-5), lists (1,3,5), and step values (/10). Use quotes when combining alpha values with special characters in scripts.*

This figure provides a detailed reference for the valid entries used in defining cron job schedules. It outlines the acceptable ranges and special characters for fields such as minute, hour, day of month, month, and day of week, which together determine when a task will execute. For example, values can be specified as exact numbers, ranges, lists, or wildcards, giving administrators fine-grained control over scheduling. It is particularly useful for ensuring accuracy when configuring recurring jobs, preventing misconfigurations that could lead to missed executions or unintended task frequency. By mastering these values, administrators can design reliable and efficient automation routines tailored to system requirements.

It provides the valid range of values that can be used when specifying the time and frequency for cron jobs.

String	Meaning
`@reboot`	Executes once at system startup.
`@yearly`	Executes once per year (`@annually`).
`@monthly`	Executes once per month.
`@weekly`	Executes once per week.
`@daily`	Executes once per day (`@midnight`).
`@hourly`	Executes once per hour.

Figure 6.18: *Special Strings for Scheduling in Crontab*

Note: These shorthand strings simplify cron scheduling. Some have aliases (example, @yearly ≈ @annually, @daily ≈ @midnight) and are ideal for system-level tasks.

This figure provides a detailed reference for the valid entries used in defining cron job highlights predefined macros that simplify the process of configuring scheduled tasks without manually specifying all time fields. These special strings, such as @reboot, @daily, @weekly, @monthly, and @yearly, provide shorthand notations for common scheduling patterns. By using these strings, administrators can quickly create cron jobs that run at startup or on a regular schedule with minimal syntax. This table serves as a practical reference, reducing complexity in cron configuration and helping ensure consistent execution of routine tasks across Linux environments.

These special strings provide a shorthand for common scheduling intervals, making it easier to set up recurring tasks, without specifying exact time fields.

Practical Examples

1. **Scheduling a Daily Backup**

   a. Edit the crontab file: **`crontab -e`**

   b. Add the following line to schedule a backup at 2:00 AM every day:

   ```
   0 2 * * * /usr/bin/rsync -a /home/user/data /backup/data
   ```

2. **Clearing Temporary Files Weekly**

To remove files **from /tmp** every Sunday at 3:00 AM:

```
0 3 * * 0 /usr/bin/find /tmp -type f -mtime +7 -exec rm -f {} \;
```

3. **Restarting a Service Monthly**

To restart the **nginx** service on the first day of every month at midnight:

```
0 0 1 * * sudo systemctl restart nginx
```

Viewing and Debugging Cron Jobs

a. **List Existing Jobs: `crontab -l`**

b. **Check Cron Logs:** Logs are often stored in /var/log/cron. View them with:
```
sudo tail -f /var/log/cron
```

c. **Test Commands Manually:** Run the scheduled command directly in the terminal to verify it works.

d. **Ensure PATH is Set Correctly:** By default, cron jobs have a limited **PATH**. Add this line at the top of the crontab to set a broader **PATH**:
```
PATH=/usr/local/sbin:/usr/local/bin:/usr/sbin:/usr/bin:/sbin:/bin
```

Security Considerations

1. **Restrict User Access:** Use **/etc/cron.allow** and **/etc/cron.deny** to control who can use **cron**.
```
echo "username" | sudo tee -a /etc/cron.allow
```
2. **Validate Commands:** Ensure that commands or scripts executed by cron are secure and tested.
3. **Limit Permissions:** Use non-root users for cron jobs whenever possible.

Best Practices for Cron Job Error Handling

Automating tasks with cron is a standard administrative responsibility in Linux systems. However, without effective error handling, failed jobs may go undetected, potentially causing critical production failures. This chapter outlines best practices for logging, monitoring, and alerting, enabling reliable task automation and fast troubleshooting.

Enable Dedicated Logging for Cron Jobs

By default, cron jobs are logged in system logs (for example, **/var/log/cron**), but this can be insufficient for specific job diagnostics. Redirecting cron output to dedicated log files enhances clarity and allows quicker troubleshooting.

Example: Redirecting Output to a Log File:

```
0 2 * * * /usr/local/bin/backup.sh >> /var/log/backup.log 2>&1
```

- '>>' appends standard output (**stdout**) to backup.log.
- '2>&1' redirects standard error (**stderr**) to the same log file.

Recommendation: Use separate log files for each critical cron job to maintain clean, organized logs.

Use the `MAILTO` Variable for Basic Alerts

The MAILTO environment variable sends any output from a cron job to a specified email address. **Example**: **`MAILTO=admin@example.com`**

```
0 3 * * * /usr/local/bin/sync.sh
```

If the script generates output or errors, it will be emailed to **`admin@example.com`**.

Note: *Ensure an MTA (Mail Transfer Agent) such as* **`mailx`**, **`postfix`**, *or* **`sendmail`** *is installed and properly configured.*

Send Alerts Only on Failure (Conditional Emails)

To avoid unnecessary emails and only be notified when a job fails, wrap our cron job in a script that checks the exit status and sends an alert if needed. Example Script:

```
#!/bin/bash
LOGFILE="/var/log/myscript.log"
ERRORLOG="/var/log/myscript_error.log"

/usr/local/bin/myscript.sh >> "$LOGFILE" 2>> "$ERRORLOG"
if [ $? -ne 0 ]; then
    mail -s "Cron Job Failed: myscript.sh" admin@example.com < "$ERRORLOG"
fi
```

Add this wrapper script to the crontab instead of the original command.

Use the System Journal for Monitoring

On **`systemd`**-based distributions such as Rocky Linux, the **`crond`** service logs all cron jobs, which can be viewed with **`journalctl`**.

Commands: **`journalctl -u crond.service`**

Filter logs by date or time range: **`journalctl -u crond.service --since "2025-05-20"`**

This centralized log access simplifies diagnosis, especially in systems using **`systemd`**.

Integrate External Monitoring Tools

For high-availability systems, external monitoring tools provide proactive alerts and dashboards:

- **Nagios, Zabbix:** Infrastructure-level cron monitoring.
- **`Healthchecks.io`, Cronitor, Dead Man's Snitch:** SaaS solutions for cron job monitoring.

Example with Healthchecks.io:

```
0 * * * * curl -fsS --retry 3 https://hc-ping.com/the-unique-uuid && /path/to/
job.sh
```

If the job fails to complete successfully and send the expected ping, Healthchecks.io will alert us.

Effective cron job error handling is essential for maintaining reliable automated processes in Linux systems. By combining redirected logging, email alerts, **`systemd`** journal access, and external monitoring services, administrators can detect issues early, respond faster, and reduce the risk of unnoticed failures in production environments. Adopting these best practices strengthens system reliability and operational resilience.

Cron is a versatile tool for automating tasks in Rocky Linux 9. By understanding its syntax, scheduling options, and best practices, administrators can efficiently manage routine jobs and improve system reliability. Always test and monitor the cron jobs to ensure they run as intended.

Rocky Linux Administration in AWS Environments

Rocky Linux is a robust, open-source enterprise operating system, well-suited for deployment in cloud environments such as Amazon Web Services (AWS). Managing Rocky Linux in AWS involves using AWS tools and features alongside Linux-specific configurations to ensure optimal performance, security, and scalability. Please note that utilizing Amazon cloud services may incur additional charges.

Setting Up Rocky Linux on AWS

1. **Launching a Rocky Linux Instance**
    a. **Log in to AWS Management Console:** Navigate to the EC2 service.
    b. **Select an AMI:**
        i. Search for "`Rocky Linux`" in the AWS Marketplace or Community AMIs.
        ii. Choose an AMI that matches the desired version (for example, Rocky Linux 9).
    c. **Choose Instance Type:** Select an instance type based on the workload (for example, `t3.micro` for testing or `m5.large` for production).
    d. **Configure Instance Details:**
        i. Set the number of instances.
        ii. Configure networking, including VPC, subnet, and security group.
    e. **Add Storage:** Choose the size and type of storage (for example, 20 GB General Purpose SSD).
    f. **Add Tags:** Add tags to organize and identify the instance (for example, `Environment:Production`).
    g. **Configure Security Group:** Define inbound rules, such as allowing SSH (port 22).
    h. **Launch Instance:**
        i. Select or create a key pair for SSH access.
        ii. Review and launch the instance.
2. **Connecting to the Instance**
    a. **Retrieve Public IP:**
        - In the AWS Console, find the instance's public IP address.
    b. **Connect via SSH:** `ssh -i /path/to/<the given key>.pem rocky@<public-ip>`
    c. **Initial Setup:**
        - Update the system: `sudo dnf update -y`
        - Install essential tools: `sudo dnf install wget curl vim -y --allowerasing`

Configuring Rocky Linux in AWS

1. **Optimizing Networking**
    a. **Enable Firewall Rules:** Configure firewalld to manage ports:
        i. `sudo firewall-cmd --add-service=ssh --permanent`
        ii. `sudo firewall-cmd --reload`
    b. **Use Elastic IPs:** Assign an Elastic IP to ensure a static IP for the instance.
    c. **Enable High Availability:** Use multiple availability zones and load balancers for redundancy.
2. **Disk Management**
    a. **Configure Auto-Mounting with `/etc/fstab`**
        i. Open the **`/etc/fstab`** file: **`sudo nano /etc/fstab`**
        ii. Add the following line for automatic mounting (ensure the correct device name **`/dev/xvda127`** is used):

```
/dev/xvda127 /data ext4 defaults,nofail 0 2
```

        iii. Save and exit the file.
    b. **Verify the Attached Volume**
        i. SSH into the EC2 instance and run: **`lsblk`**
        ii. Validation of disk and partitions:

```
[ec2-user@ip-172-31-20-219 ~]$ lsblk
NAME       MAJ:MIN RM SIZE RO TYPE MOUNTPOINTS
xvda       202:0    0   8G  0 disk
├─xvda1    202:1    0   8G  0 part /
├─xvda127  259:0    0   1M  0 part
└─xvda128  259:1    0  10M  0 part /boot/efi
```

Figure 6.19: *Output of lsblk Command on an EC2 Instance*

This figure would typically show the expected output when running the **`lsblk`** command, which lists information about block devices (such as disks) on the EC2 instance.

        iii. We should see /dev/xvda127 as the new volume in the list.
    c. **Format the Volume:** Format /dev/xvda127 with the ext4 filesystem: **`sudo mkfs.ext4 /dev/xvda127`**
    d. **Create a Mount Point:** Create a directory where the volume will be mounted: **`sudo mkdir /data`**
    e. **Mount the Volume**: Mount /dev/xvda127 to the /data directory: **`sudo mount /dev/xvda127 /data`**
    f. **Verify the Mount**
        i. Check the mounted filesystem: **`df -h`**
        ii. We should see the new volume mounted at /data.

g. **Test Auto-Mounting**

i. Unmount and remount to test the configuration:

- `sudo umount /data`
- `sudo mount -a`

ii. Verify that the volume is successfully mounted: `lsblk`.

3. **Security Best Practices**

a. **Regular Updates:** Schedule updates using dnf-automatic:

i. `sudo dnf install dnf-automatic -y`

ii. `sudo systemctl enable --now dnf-automatic.timer`

b. **Harden SSH Access:**

i. Disable root login:

- `sudo sed -i 's/#PermitRootLogin yes/PermitRootLogin no/' /etc/ssh/sshd_config`
- `sudo systemctl restart sshd`

ii. Use key-based authentication.

iii. Restrict SSH access by IP in the AWS Security Group.

c. **Install and Configure Fail2Ban:** Protect against brute-force attacks:

i. `sudo dnf install fail2ban -y`

ii. `sudo systemctl enable --now fail2ban`

Integrating with AWS Services

Integrating with AWS Services" refers to the process of connecting and utilizing various AWS cloud services, such as EC2, S3, RDS, and Lambda, within the applications or infrastructure. This integration allows for scalable, secure, and efficient management of resources and data across the AWS cloud environment.

IAM Roles and Policies

- **Attach Roles to EC2 Instances:** Use IAM roles to grant permissions without hardcoding AWS credentials. Additional resource guide
- **Example Use Case:** Grant S3 access.
  1. Create an IAM role with AmazonS3ReadOnlyAccess.
  2. Attach the role to the EC2 instance.

Before the following step, we need to click on the username in the upper right corner, then go to security credentials to configure and access key, and download the csv file with the credentials' information.

3. Verify access: `aws configure`.

Enter the following information:

- Access Key ID
- Secret Access Key

- Default region (for example, `us-east-1`)
- Output format (for example, `json`, `table`, `text`)

We execute the following command to validate the content of some cloud services: `aws s3 ls`.

CloudWatch Monitoring

1. **Install CloudWatch Agent:**
    - `sudo dnf install amazon-cloudwatch-agent -y`
    - `sudo /opt/aws/amazon-cloudwatch-agent/bin/amazon-cloudwatch-agent-config-wizard`
    - `sudo systemctl start amazon-cloudwatch-agent`
    - `sudo systemctl enable amazon-cloudwatch-agent`
    - `sudo systemctl status amazon-cloudwatch-agent`
2. **Configure Metrics and Logs:** Monitor CPU, memory, disk usage, and application logs in the AWS CloudWatch Console.

Scaling and High Availability

Scaling and High Availability refers to strategies and practices designed to ensure applications and services can efficiently handle increasing workloads while remaining accessible and resilient. By utilizing tools such as load balancing, auto-scaling, and multiple availability zones, organizations can maintain optimal system performance under fluctuating demand and ensure continuous operation, even during hardware failures or outages.

1. **Auto Scaling Groups**
    - Configure Auto Scaling Groups to add or remove instances based on demand.
    - Define policies triggered by CloudWatch alarms.
2. **Load Balancing**
    - Use an Application Load Balancer (ALB) or Network Load Balancer (NLB) for distributing traffic.
3. **Multi-AZ Deployments**
    - Deploy instances in multiple availability zones to ensure high availability.

Troubleshooting and Maintenance

Troubleshooting and Maintenance involves identifying and resolving issues within a system or application, along with performing routine upkeep to ensure optimal performance. Key activities include monitoring system health, applying updates and patches, diagnosing errors, and optimizing resources to prevent disruptions and maintain long-term reliability.

Common Issues

- **Instance Unreachable:**
    - Verify security group rules.
    - Check `firewalld` and SSH configurations.
- **Disk Full:**
    - Identify large files: `sudo du -sh /* | sort -h`
    - Clean up or resize volumes.

Automating Maintenance

- Use cron for periodic tasks:
    - `sudo yum install cronie`
    - `sudo crontab -e`

Example: Clear temp files every Sunday

```
0 3 * * 0 /usr/bin/find /tmp -type f -mtime +7 -exec rm -f {} \;
```

Finally, we use ESC key from the keyboard plus **`:wq`** to save the changes.

Administering Rocky Linux in AWS environments requires a combination of Linux expertise and familiarity with AWS tools. By optimizing system configurations, integrating with AWS services, and adhering to best practices, we can achieve a secure, scalable, and efficient cloud infrastructure.

Cloud Automation with AWS CLI and SDK

Automation is key to efficiently managing cloud infrastructure in Amazon Web Services (AWS). The AWS Command Line Interface (CLI) and Software Development Kits (SDKs) provide powerful tools for automating tasks, scaling operations, and integrating AWS services into applications.

Introduction to AWS CLI

The AWS CLI is a command-line tool that allows users to interact with AWS services programmatically. It supports all AWS services, provides an efficient way to script and automate tasks.

1. **Update the system:** `sudo dnf update -y`
2. **Install AWS CLI v2-** Download and install AWS CLI v2:
    a. `curl "https://awscli.amazonaws.com/awscli-exe-linux-x86_64.zip" -o "awscliv2.zip"`
    b. `unzip awscliv2.zip`
    c. `sudo ./aws/install`
3. **Verify Installation:** Run the following command to confirm the AWS CLI is installed correctly: **`aws --version`**

We should see something like: **`aws-cli/2.x.x Python/3.x.x Linux/5.x.x`**

4. **Common Commands**

List S3 Buckets

Listing S3 buckets refers to the process of retrieving and displaying all the Amazon S3 storage buckets associated with the AWS account. This can be done using the AWS CLI with the command **aws s3 ls,** providing an overview of available storage resources.

- `aws s3 mb s3://kasparov-server`
- `aws s3 mb s3://cesarmserver`
- `aws s3 ls`

Example output:

```
[ec2-user@ip-172-31-31-92 ~]$ aws s3 ls
2024-12-23 22:08:54 cesarmserver
2024-12-23 22:08:36 kasparov-server
```

Figure 6.20: *Listing S3 Buckets via AWS CLI*

The commands shown are used to create and list Amazon S3 buckets using the AWS CLI. The **`aws s3 mb s3://<bucket-name>`** command creates a new S3 bucket with the specified name, such as **`kasparov-server`** or **`cesarmserver`**. Afterward, the **`aws s3 ls`** command lists all the available buckets associated with the AWS account. The example output (*Figure* 6.9) displays the newly created buckets, providing a quick overview of the S3 storage resources. These commands are essential for managing and organizing data in Amazon S3.

Validation Example with AWS CLI

To automate instance launch and validation.

1. **Launch Instance from AMI:** This information is available in the dashboard of the instance.

```
aws ec2 run-instances --image-id ami-0abcd1234efgh5678 --count 1 --instance-type t2.micro --key-name MyKeyPair --security-group-ids sg-12345 --subnet-id subnet-67890
```

Example output:

```
{
    "Groups": [],
    "Instances": [
        {
            "AmiLaunchIndex": 0,
            "ImageId": "ami-01816d07b1128cd2d",
            "InstanceId": "i-0d72a88e976ee017e",
            "InstanceType": "t2.micro",
            "KeyName": "RockyLinux_9",
            "LaunchTime": "2024-12-29T06:23:08+00:00",
            "Monitoring": {
                "State": "disabled"
            },
            "Placement": {
                "AvailabilityZone": "us-east-1d",
                "GroupName": "",
                "Tenancy": "default"
            },
            "PrivateDnsName": "ip-172-31-22-111.ec2.internal",
            "PrivateIpAddress": "172.31.22.111",
            "ProductCodes": [],
:
```

Figure 6.21: *Launching an EC2 Instance Using AWS CLI*

The command shown demonstrates how to automate the launch of an EC2 instance from a specified Amazon Machine Image (AMI) using the AWS CLI. By running **`aws ec2 run-instances`**, we can specify the AMI ID, instance type, key pair, security group, and subnet for the instance. In this case, the **`--image-id`** refers to a particular AMI, while **`--instance-type`** specifies the instance type (for example, **`t2.micro`**). The example output (*Figure* 6.10) would typically display information about the newly launched instance, including its ID and other related metadata, confirming successful execution. This process is integral for automating instance management in AWS environments.

2. **Connect and Validate:** Use SSH or run Systems Manager commands.

3. **Terminate Instance:** We are going to omit this command for now.

   `aws ec2 terminate-instances --instance-ids i-0abcd1234efgh5678`

   Validating an AMI ensures it performs as expected in real-world scenarios, saving us time and resources in future deployments.

5. **Configure AWS CLI:** To interact with AWS using the credentials, configure AWS CLI with the AWS credentials.

   a. **Install the AWS SDK for Python (Boto3)**

      While the AWS CLI allows interaction through command-line commands, Boto3 is the AWS SDK for Python and provides a programmatic way to interact with AWS services.

   b. **Install Python and pip:**

      Rocky Linux 9 should come with Python pre-installed, but verify by running:

      `python3 --version`

      If not installed, run: **`sudo dnf install python3 -y`**

      a. **Install pip (Python package installer):** `sudo dnf install python3-pip -y`

      b. **Install Boto3 (AWS SDK for Python):** `pip3 install boto3`

6. **Write a Basic Python Script Using Boto3**

   Let us write a simple Python script to interact with AWS services (S3 and EC2).

   a. **Create a new Python file:** `nano aws_sdk_lab.py`

   b. Write the script to list EC2 instances and create an S3 bucket:

```
import boto3
import botocore.exceptions

# Create an EC2 client
ec2_client = boto3.client('ec2')

# Describe EC2 instances
def describe_instances():
    print("Listing EC2 Instances:")
    try:
        response = ec2_client.describe_instances()
        if len(response['Reservations']) == 0:
            print("No EC2 instances found.")
        for reservation in response['Reservations']:
            for instance in reservation['Instances']:
                print(f"Instance ID: {instance['InstanceId']} | State: 
{instance['State']['Name']}")
    except botocore.exceptions.ClientError as e:
        print(f"Error describing instances: {e}")

# Create an S3 client
s3_client = boto3.client('s3')
```

```
# List S3 buckets
def list_buckets():
    print("\nListing S3 Buckets:")
    try:
        response = s3_client.list_buckets()
        if len(response['Buckets']) == 0:
            print("No S3 buckets found.")
        for bucket in response['Buckets']:
            print(f"Bucket Name: {bucket['Name']} | Creation Date: {buck-
et['CreationDate']}")
    except botocore.exceptions.ClientError as e:
        print(f"Error listing buckets: {e}")

# Main function to run the script
if __name__ == '__main__':
    describe_instances()   # List EC2 instances
    list_buckets()         # List S3 buckets
```

a. **`describe_instances`**: This function lists all EC2 instances.

b. **`create_bucket`**: This function creates an S3 bucket with a specified name.

- Run the Python script: **`python3 aws_sdk_lab.py`**

7. **Verify Results**

   Example output:

```
[ec2-user@ip-172-31-20-219 ~]$ python3 aws_sdk_lab.py
Listing EC2 Instances:
Instance ID: i-03d4545eb4f988a37 | State: running
Instance ID: i-0d72a88e976ee017e | State: running

Listing S3 Buckets:
Bucket Name: cesarmserver | Creation Date: 2024-12-23 22:08:54+00:00
Bucket Name: kasparov-server | Creation Date: 2024-12-23 22:08:35+00:00
```

***Figure 6.22:** Verifying Running Instances with a Python Script*

The command **`python3 aws_sdk_lab.py`** runs a Python script designed to interact with AWS services, typically to list or manage EC2 instances. After executing the script, the example output (*Figure* 6.22) would display the current instances running in the AWS environment, providing details like instance IDs, states, and other relevant information. This process helps verify that the instances are active and functioning as expected, serving as a crucial step in managing and automating cloud resources.

a. **EC2 Instances:** If there are any EC2 instances running, we should see the list printed by the **`describe_instances`** function.

b. **S3 Bucket:**

   i. We can verify the bucket creation by running the following AWS CLI command:

      `aws s3 ls`

   ii. We should see the newly created bucket listed.

8. **Clean Up:** After testing, it is important to clean up the resources we have created to avoid incurring unnecessary costs.

   a. Delete the S3 Bucket (if the created one): **`aws s3 rb s3://my-unique-bucket-12345 --force`**

b. Terminate EC2 Instances (if any were created): **`aws ec2 terminate-instances --instance-ids <the-instance-id>`**

In the previous laboratory, the following steps were successfully completed:

a. AWS CLI and Boto3 were set up on a Rocky Linux 9 instance.

b. A Python script was written to interact with AWS services (EC2 and S3).

c. An S3 bucket was created, and EC2 instances were listed programmatically using the AWS SDK (Boto3).

These steps provided a foundational understanding of automating cloud operations and managing AWS resources efficiently.

Integrating Advanced AWS Security in System Administration

Section: Security Best Practices (Enhanced)

1. **Identity and Access Management (IAM)**
   - **Attribute-Based Access Control (ABAC):** Implement ABAC by assigning tags to users and resources, allowing access decisions based on these attributes. For example, tag EC2 instances and IAM users with Department=IT, and create policies that permit actions only when tags match.
   - **Emergency Access Procedures:** Define break-glass IAM roles with limited-duration permissions, monitored via AWS CloudTrail. Restrict usage to critical failure scenarios and document procedures for audit compliance.
   - **Continuous Permission Review:** Schedule quarterly reviews of IAM roles and policies using AWS Access Analyzer and AWS IAM Access Advisor to ensure minimal required permissions are in use.
2. **Data Protection Enhancements**
   - **Encrypt Data at Rest and in Transit:** Use AWS KMS for managing encryption keys. Enable default encryption on S3 buckets and EBS volumes. Enforce HTTPS on ELBs and API Gateway endpoints.
   - **Object Lock and Glacier Vault Lock:** Enable S3 Object Lock for WORM (write-once-read-many) protection in compliance-sensitive environments. Configure Glacier Vault Lock to enforce compliance retention policies.
3. **Monitoring and Threat Detection**
   - **AWS GuardDuty:** Enable GuardDuty in all AWS regions to detect anomalous or unauthorized behavior across accounts, including port scanning, data exfiltration, and API misuse.
   - **AWS Security Hub:** Aggregate findings from GuardDuty, Inspector, Macie, and third-party integrations. Use custom insights to prioritize remediation workflows.
   - **Automated Incident Response:** Use AWS Lambda and Step Functions to trigger automatic workflows in response to specific GuardDuty findings (for example, disabling access keys, quarantining EC2 instances).
4. **Infrastructure and Application Security**
   - **Zero Trust Implementation:** Enforce identity verification at every layer. Use AWS PrivateLink, AWS Cognito, and VPC Service Controls to reduce lateral movement and secure inter-service communication.

- **Secure Application Load Balancers (ALBs):** Configure HTTPS listeners with TLS 1.2 or higher, enable Web Application Firewall (WAF) integration, and define security headers (e.g., HSTS, X-Frame-Options).
- **Security in CI/CD Pipelines:** Integrate tools such as AWS CodeGuru Reviewer, Amazon Inspector, and open-source security linters in CodePipeline stages to catch vulnerabilities before deployment.

Cloud Automation with AWS CLI and SDK: Real-Life Examples for Beginners

Cloud automation simplifies repetitive tasks and makes large-scale deployments reliable and fast. Here are beginner-friendly real-life use cases using AWS CLI and Boto3 SDK:

Example 1: Automate EC2 Instance Launch with AWS CLI

Scenario: A startup wants to launch a web server every morning for 8 hours to reduce costs.

Step-by-step CLI workflow:

1. Launch instance:

```
aws ec2 run-instances \
  --image-id ami-0abcd1234efgh5678 \
  --instance-type t2.micro \
  --key-name MyKeyPair \
  --security-groups WebSG \
  --tag-specifications 'ResourceType=instance,
Tags=[{Key=Purpose,Value=DailyWebServer}]'
```

2. Schedule shutdown via cron on a local admin workstation:

```
0 16 * * * aws ec2 stop-instances --instance-ids i-0abcd1234efgh5678
```

This automates launching and stopping an instance on a schedule.

Example 2: Create and Sync a Website Backup to S3

Scenario: A small business wants to back up its website data to AWS S3 daily.

```
# Sync a local folder to S3
aws s3 sync /var/www/html s3://mybusiness-backup-bucket --storage-class
STANDARD_IA
```

Explanation:

- This command recursively copies the local website directory to an S3 bucket.
- It uses Infrequent Access (IA) storage class to save costs.

Example 3: Use Boto3 to List and Start EC2 Instances

Scenario: A sysadmin wants to start only the stopped EC2 instances every Monday morning.

```
import boto3

ec2 = boto3.resource('ec2')

# Filter stopped instances
stopped_instances = ec2.instances.filter(Filters=[{'Name': 'instance-state-
name', 'Values': ['stopped']}])

# Start them
```

```
    for instance in stopped_instances:
        print(f"Starting {instance.id}")
        instance.start()
```

Explanation:

- This script uses the EC2 resource interface.
- It finds all stopped instances and starts them automatically.

Example 4: Automated CloudWatch Alarm Setup with Boto3

Scenario: Linux administrators want to get notified if CPU usage on an EC2 instance exceeds 70% for 5 minutes.

```
import boto3
client = boto3.client('cloudwatch')
client.put_metric_alarm(
  AlarmName='HighCPUAlarm',
  MetricName='CPUUtilization',
  Namespace='AWS/EC2',
  Statistic='Average',
  Period=300,
  EvaluationPeriods=1,
  Threshold=70.0,
  ComparisonOperator='GreaterThanThreshold',
  Dimensions=[{'Name': 'InstanceId', 'Value': 'i-0abcd1234efgh5678'}],
  AlarmActions=['arn:aws:sns:us-east-1:123456789012:NotifyMe']
)
```

Explanation:

- Sets up an alarm in CloudWatch.
- Sends a notification if the CPU exceeds 70%.

Area	Updated Recommendation
IAM	Use ABAC; set up emergency roles; review and audit permissions quarterly.
Data Protection	Encrypt data at rest and in transit; enable Object Lock and Vault Lock.
Monitoring & Detection	Enable GuardDuty; use Security Hub; automate incident response with Lambda.
Infrastructure & App Security	Apply Zero Trust; secure ALBs; integrate security into CI/CD pipelines.
Cloud Automation	Use CLI and SDK to manage EC2, S3, and CloudWatch; include real-world script examples.

Figure 6.23: *Updated Best Practices Summary Table*

Figure 6.23 presents a refined set of recommendations aimed at enhancing system administration efficiency and reliability. This table consolidates key operational practices covered throughout the chapter, incorporating recent updates in system management tools and methodologies. Each best practice is aligned with specific tasks, such as service management, performance tuning, RAID configuration, and automation with cron, providing actionable guidance for real-world scenarios. Additionally, the inclusion of AWS CLI and SDK-related practices highlights the increasing relevance of hybrid and cloud-native infrastructures, offering administrators a comprehensive framework for managing both on-premises systems and cloud environments with consistency and confidence.

Best Practices

- **Use IAM Roles:** Avoid hardcoding credentials. Use IAM roles attached to EC2 instances or Lambda functions.
- **Secure Access Keys:**
  - Store keys securely using AWS Secrets Manager or environment variables.
  - Regularly rotate keys.
- **Error Handling:** Implement proper error handling in scripts and applications to ensure reliability.
- **Logging and Monitoring:** Use CloudWatch for logging and monitoring automation scripts.

AWS CLI and SDKs provide powerful tools for automating cloud operations. By scripting routine tasks and integrating AWS services into applications, organizations can reduce manual effort, improve efficiency, and scale their cloud infrastructure seamlessly. These tools also enable administrators to manage cloud resources with precision, ensuring optimized performance and cost savings across environments.

Conclusion

This chapter explored advanced administration techniques essential for managing Rocky Linux in both on-premises and cloud environments. Key topics included RAID setup and management, emphasizing redundancy and performance in data storage. The chapter introduced **`systemd`** for streamlined service control and explored performance monitoring tools such as **`ps`** and **`top`**, which assist in identifying and resolving system bottlenecks effectively. Automation was another core focus, with the use of **`cron`** for scheduling routine tasks and showcasing how scripting enhances consistency and efficiency in system operations. The discussion extended to cloud-based administration, where the **AWS CLI and SDK** were utilized to automate and manage Rocky Linux instances within scalable cloud infrastructures. These tools and practices form a vital foundation for managing hybrid and cloud-native environments, enabling the deployment, monitoring, and optimization of resources with confidence and precision. Mastery of these techniques contributes to maintaining high availability, robust performance, and adaptability across modern IT ecosystems.

In *Chapter* 7, the focus shifts to *File System Management* in Rocky Linux 9. This includes mounting and unmounting file systems, partitioning disks, and integrating with cloud storage—core tasks for maintaining data integrity and system efficiency.

Points to Remember

RAID Configuration and Management

- RAID ensures **data redundancy** and improves **performance**. Use **`mdadm`** to configure RAID levels like RAID 0, 1, 5, and 10 based on the needs for redundancy and speed.
- Regularly monitor the health of RAID arrays using **`cat /proc/mdstat`** and automate alerts with tools like **`mailx`**.

Service Management with systemd

- `systemd` simplifies managing services with commands such as **`systemctl`** start, enable, and status.
- Custom service files enhance control over application behavior, including dependency handling and automatic restarts.

System Monitoring with ps and top

- Use **`ps`** for detailed process snapshots and top for real-time monitoring.
- Combine with tools such as iostat and scripts to identify resource bottlenecks and proactively resolve performance issues.

Task Automation with cron

- Automate routine tasks such as backups, log cleanup, and service restarts with cron jobs.
- Crontab supports flexible scheduling using time fields or special strings (**`@daily`**, **`@reboot`**).

Cloud Administration in AWS

- **Rocky Linux Integration:** Launch instances using AWS Marketplace, configure VPCs, security groups, and Elastic IPs for optimal connectivity.
- Enable **high availability** with multi-AZ deployments, load balancers, and auto-scaling groups.
- Use IAM roles to securely manage permissions without embedding credentials.

Cloud Automation with AWS CLI and SDK

- The AWS CLI facilitates automating tasks such as creating EC2 instances, managing S3 buckets, and scheduling snapshots.
- SDKs like Boto3 allow for advanced scripting, enabling resource provisioning, monitoring, and data processing in AWS environments.

Best Practices for Security and Automation

- Regularly update systems with **`dnf`** and use tools such as Fail2Ban for enhanced SSH security.
- Document changes to RAID arrays and automate network monitoring using scripts and AWS CloudWatch.

Scalability and Monitoring

- Implement VPC Flow Logs for traffic analysis and troubleshoot networking issues effectively using tools such as traceroute and CloudWatch logs.
- Design for scalability by combining RAID storage, AWS scaling solutions, and robust task automation.

Multiple Choice Questions

1. Which command is used to configure and manage RAID arrays in Rocky Linux?

   a. **`fdisk`**

   b. **`mdadm`**

   c. **`lsblk`**

   d. **`parted`**

2. What is the purpose of the systemctl command in Rocky Linux?
   a. Monitor CPU and memory usage
   b. Manage system services and processes
   c. Configure network interfaces
   d. Schedule automated tasks
3. Which cron command would we use to schedule a script to run every day at midnight?
   a. **`0 0 * * * /path/to/script.sh`**
   b. **`@daily /path/to/script.sh`**
   c. Both a and b
   d. None of the above
4. In AWS, what is the primary role of IAM roles?
   a. To control inbound and outbound traffic to EC2 instances
   b. To manage permissions securely for AWS resources
   c. To monitor system performance using CloudWatch
   d. To automate the launch of EC2 instances
5. What does the **`cat /proc/mdstat`** command display?
   a. Detailed CPU usage statistics
   b. The status of all RAID arrays
   c. Active network connections
   d. Logs of failed services
6. Which AWS CLI command is used to create an EC2 snapshot?
   a. **`aws s3 sync`**
   b. **`aws ec2 describe-instances`**
   c. **`aws ec2 create-snapshot`**
   d. **`aws ec2 run-instances`**
7. What is the primary benefit of using a RAID 5 configuration?
   a. Improved performance with no redundancy
   b. Mirroring data for complete redundancy
   c. Balancing performance and redundancy with parity
   d. Dual parity for maximum fault tolerance
8. Which tool provides a dynamic, real-time view of running processes in Rocky Linux?
   a. **`ps`**
   b. **`top`**
   c. **`cron`**
   d. **`systemctl`**

9. What is the role of an Internet Gateway (IGW) in an AWS VPC?
    a. To route traffic between VPCs
    b. To provide internet access to resources in a public subnet
    c. To block all external traffic for security
    d. To monitor VPC traffic logs
10. What is the default logging tool for system services in Rocky Linux?
    a. **`journalctl`**
    b. **`syslog`**
    c. **`dmesg`**
    d. **`rsyslog`**

Answers

1. b
2. b
3. c
4. b
5. b
6. c
7. c
8. b
9. b
10. a

Questions

1. What is the purpose of configuring and managing RAID arrays in Rocky Linux?
2. Which RAID level provides both redundancy and improved performance by combining mirroring and striping?
3. How can we use **`systemd`** to enable a service to start automatically on boot?
4. What is the purpose of the **`journalctl`** command in **`systemd`**?
5. Which command in Rocky Linux is commonly used to monitor real-time system performance?
6. How can **`cron`** be used to schedule a daily system backup?
7. What is the role of AWS CLI when managing Rocky Linux in AWS environments?
8. Which AWS SDK is commonly used for Python-based cloud automation?
9. How does automating tasks with **`cron`** benefit system administrators in Rocky Linux?
10. What is the advantage of using **`systemd`** over traditional **`init`** systems on Linux?

Key Terms

- **Redundant Array of Independent Disks (RAID):** A storage virtualization technology combining multiple physical drives into one logical unit for redundancy and/or performance. Common levels include RAID 0, RAID 1, and RAID 5.
- **`mdadm`:** A Linux utility used to configure and manage RAID arrays, including creating, monitoring, and troubleshooting RAID setups.
- **`systemd`:** A Linux **`init`** system and service manager providing features such as parallel service startup, service dependency management, and advanced logging through **`journald`**.
- **`journalctl`:** A command-line tool in **`systemd`** for querying and displaying logs generated by system services and the kernel.
- **`ps`:** A Linux command that provides a snapshot of currently running processes, useful for identifying resource-intensive tasks.
- **`top`:** A real-time command-line utility to monitor system performance, displaying CPU, memory, and process information interactively.
- **`cron`:** A job scheduler in Linux used to automate repetitive tasks by scheduling commands or scripts to run at specified times.
- **AWS CLI (Command Line Interface):** A command-line tool for managing AWS services programmatically, enabling automation of tasks such as launching instances and synchronizing S3 data.
- **AWS SDK (Software Development Kit):** A collection of tools for developers to interact with AWS services programmatically in languages such as Python (Boto3), JavaScript, and Java.
- **Auto Scaling Group:** A feature in AWS that automatically adjusts the number of EC2 instances in response to changes in demand, ensuring high availability and performance.

CHAPTER 7
File System Management

Introduction

File systems are fundamental to data storage and access in any operating system, and Rocky Linux 9 is no exception. They define the structure and method by which data is stored, organized, and retrieved on storage devices, ensuring consistency, reliability, and performance. Efficient file system management is critical for both standalone systems and enterprise-grade server environments.

This chapter explores the essential aspects of file system management in Rocky Linux 9, beginning with core tasks such as disk partitioning and mounting—key processes that enable structured access to storage devices. It examines modern file systems, including **ext4**, **XFS**, and **Btrfs**, each offering distinct capabilities tailored to different operational requirements such as high performance, enhanced data integrity, and scalability.

The discussion then extends into advanced storage concepts vital for managing dynamic and high-demand environments. **Logical Volume Management (LVM)** introduces flexibility in storage allocation and resizing without service interruption, while **RAID** configurations provide redundancy and performance improvements to safeguard against data loss and hardware failures. The chapter also includes diagnostic and troubleshooting techniques for addressing common file system issues, ensuring continued stability and efficiency.

By understanding and applying these concepts, Linux administrators can implement robust, scalable, and resilient storage solutions that support both current workloads and future growth within Rocky Linux 9 environments.

Structure

This chapter covers the following topics:

- Mounting and Unmounting File Systems
- Creating and Resizing File Systems
- Disk Partitioning and Management
- File System Types
- Backup and Recovery Strategies
- Cloud Storage Integration

Mounting and Unmounting File Systems

File system management is a fundamental aspect of any operating system, as it governs how data is organized, stored, and retrieved. In Rocky Linux 9, effective file system management is critical for maintaining system stability, ensuring high performance, and safeguarding data integrity. This includes tasks such as disk partitioning, formatting storage devices, allocating space, and selecting appropriate file system types such as **ext4** and **XFS.** These modern file systems offer enhanced reliability, scalability, and performance to meet a wide range of storage needs. In addition to local storage, administrators are increasingly tasked with integrating cloud-based storage solutions and implementing robust backup strategies to protect against data loss and ensure business continuity.

One of the key operations in managing file systems is mounting, which involves attaching a storage device–such as a hard drive, USB stick, or network share–to a specific directory, known as a mount point, within the system's directory tree. This action makes the contents of the device accessible to users and applications. Conversely, unmounting detaches the device safely, ensuring all pending write operations are completed to prevent data corruption. Rocky Linux 9 provides powerful tools such as the **`mount`** and **`umount`** commands for manual management, as well as configuration files such as **`/etc/fstab`** to automate mounting at boot time. This chapter delves into these essential tools and best practices, guiding readers through critical tasks such as mounting, resizing, and integrating file systems, both on-premises and in cloud environments.

Key Concepts

- **File System Basics**
    - A file system needs to be mounted to make it accessible under a directory.
    - Unmounting detaches the file system, making it unavailable.
- **Mounting File Systems**
    - Identify available devices using **`lsblk`** or **`fdisk -l`**.
    - Create a directory for the mount point using **`mkdir /mnt/mountpoint`**.
    - Mount a device with the mount command:
      `mount /dev/device_name /mnt/mountpoint`

Example: **`mount /dev/sda1 /mnt/data`**.

- **Unmounting File Systems**
    - Check active mounts with **`df -h or mount`**.
    - Use the **`umount`** command to unmount: **`umount /mnt/mountpoint`**

Example: **`umount /dev/sda1`**.

    - For force unmounting, use: **`umount -f /mnt/mountpoint`**
- **Persistent Mounting with Fstab**
    - Use the **`/etc/fstab`** file to configure automatic mounting at boot.
    - Entry format: **<device> <mount_point> <file_system> <options> <dump> <pass>**

Example: **`/dev/sda1 /mnt/data ext4 defaults 0 2`**

    - Prefer UUIDs or labels over device names for reliability.
- **Managing Processes During Unmounting**
    - Ensure no active processes are using the file system: **`lsof | grep /mnt/mountpoint`**
    - Kill processes if necessary, using **`kill`** or **`killall`**.
- **Network File System (NFS) Mounting**
    - Install NFS utilities: **`dnf install nfs-utils`**
    - Mount an NFS share: **`mount -t nfs server:/remote/path /mnt/mountpoint`**
- **Troubleshooting Mount Issues**
    - Check kernel messages using **`dmesg`** for errors during mounting.
    - Verify and repair file system integrity using **`fsck`**.
- **Best Practices**
    - Always keep a back up of the critical data before mounting or unmounting.

- Validate **/etc/fstab** entries to prevent boot issues.
- Avoid manual unmounting of critical file systems during runtime.

The Importance of Mounting and Unmounting File Systems

Proper management of mounting and unmounting file systems is essential for:

- Accessing and organizing data efficiently across multiple storage devices.
- Ensuring data integrity by properly detaching file systems before removal or maintenance.
- Automating and simplifying storage management using persistent configurations such as **/etc/fstab**.
- Supporting dynamic storage requirements such as Network File Systems (NFS) and removable drives.

Mastering the processes of mounting and unmounting file systems enables administrators to maintain a flexible and reliable storage infrastructure, ensuring smooth operation in dynamic and demanding environments.

Mounting and Unmounting File Systems Lab Experience

Objective: By the end of this lab, participants will have a comprehensive understanding of the concepts of mounting and unmounting file systems, including hands-on experience performing these tasks. They will learn to configure persistent mounts using the **/etc/fstab** file and set up dynamic automounting using systemd, enabling efficient and automated storage management.

Prerequisites: This lab builds upon the foundational work covered in *Chapter* 6; therefore, participants should ensure that all tasks and concepts from that chapter are thoroughly understood before proceeding.

Preparing for Mounting: In this task, the disks and partitions will be identified

To identify the available disks and partitions on a Rocky Linux system, we can use commands such as **lsblk, fdisk -l**, or **parted -l**. These commands provide a list of all storage devices, their partitions, and file system types. The **lsblk** command is particularly useful for displaying a tree-like structure of block devices, showing their mount points and sizes. The **fdisk -l** and parted **-l** commands offer detailed partitioning information, including partition sizes and their labels. By using these tools, we can easily assess the system's storage configuration and ensure that the necessary disks are available for mounting or further management.

lsblk: use **lsblk** to list block devices:

```
[rockylinux@rocky9 ~]$ lsblk
NAME          MAJ:MIN RM   SIZE RO TYPE MOUNTPOINTS
sda             8:0    0   512G  0 disk
├─sda1          8:1    0     1G  0 part /boot
└─sda2          8:2    0   511G  0 part
  ├─rl-root   253:0    0    70G  0 lvm  /
  ├─rl-swap   253:1    0     2G  0 lvm  [SWAP]
  └─rl-home   253:2    0 438.9G  0 lvm  /home
sdb             8:16   0    10G  0 disk
└─sdb1          8:17   0    10G  0 part
sdc             8:32   0    20G  0 disk
sr0            11:0    1  1024M  0 rom
[rockylinux@rocky9 ~]$
```

Figure 7.1: Block Devices

This figure illustrates the output of the **lsblk** command, a standard utility in Rocky Linux and other Linux distributions for listing block devices in a structured, tree-like format. The output displays critical information such as device names (for example, **sda**, **sdb**), partition sizes, filesystem types, and mount points. It also highlights the hierarchical relationships between physical disks and their child partitions, making it easier to understand how storage is organized within the system. By using **lsblk** command, administrators can quickly assess available storage devices, verify partitioning schemes, and troubleshoot configuration issues, making it an essential tool for effective storage management.

Note the name of the target device (example: /dev/sdb1).

Now, if the **blkid /dev/sdb1** command does not return anything, it usually indicates that the partition does not exist, or it does not have a filesystem assigned to it yet. It is required to create and format the partition before it can be used.

At this moment, a step-by-step process will be presented:

1. **Verify the Disk is Detected**

Run the following command to list all detected disks and their partitions: **lsblk**

Verify that **/dev/sdb** appears in the output. If it does not, the system is not detecting the disk.

2. **Create a Partition on the Disk**

Use a partitioning tool such as **fdisk** or parted to create a new partition on **/dev/sdb.** Example of using the **fdisk** command: **sudo fdisk /dev/sdb**

Steps in **fdisk**:

a. Press **n** to create a new partition.

b. Choose the partition type (Primary or Logical).

c. Specify the partition number (default is fine).

d. Set the starting and ending sectors (default is usually fine).

e. Press **w** to write changes to the disk and exit.

3. **Format the Partition**

After creating the partition, format it with a filesystem, for example, **ext4**:

```
sudo mkfs.ext4 /dev/sdb1
```

4. **Label the Partition (Optional)**

We can assign a label to the partition for easier identification:

```
sudo e2label /dev/sdb1 our_label
```

5. **Verify with blkid**

Now, run the **blkid** command again to confirm the filesystem is recognized: **blkid /dev/sdb1**

6. **Mount the Partition**

Mount the partition to a directory:

a. `sudo mkdir -p /mnt/mydisk`

b. `sudo mount /dev/sdb1 /mnt/mydisk`

To make the mount permanent, add it to **/etc/fstab:**

```
echo "/dev/sdb1 /mnt/mydisk ext4 defaults 0 0" | sudo tee -a /etc/fstab
```

Troubleshooting: If **`fdisk`** does not work or the disk is not detected, check the **`dmesg`** logs:

```
dmesg | grep sdb
```

This can give more information about the disk.

7. **Verify the mount:**

- `mount | grep /mnt/mydisk`
- `df -h | grep /mnt/mydisk`

Evaluate access to the File System

Create a test file:

- `sudo touch /mnt/mydisk/testfile.txt`
- `ls /mnt/mydisk`

Remove the test file: **`sudo rm /mnt/mydisk/testfile.txt`**

8. **Persistent Mounting with**

Edit: Open **`/etc/fstab`** in a text editor: **`sudo nano /etc/fstab`**

Add the following entry to make the mount persistent:

```
/dev/sdb1    /mnt/mydisk    ext4    defaults    0    2
```

Test without Rebooting

Test the configuration: **`mount -a`**

Verify the mount: **`mount | grep /mnt/mydisk`**

9. **Unmounting File Systems**

Unmount the file system: **`sudo umount /mnt/mydisk`**

Verify it is unmounted: **`ls /mnt/mydisk`**

An error or empty output indicates successful unmounting.

Resolve Busy Devices (Optional)

If the device is busy, find the processes using it:

- `lsof +D /mnt/mydisk`
- `fuser -m /mnt/mydisk`

Stop the processes or services holding the file system and retry unmounting.

Automount with Task

Create Unit Files

Create a mount unit file: **`sudo nano /etc/systemd/system/mnt-mydisk.mount`**

Add the following content:

```
[Unit]
Description=Mount my disk

[Mount]
What=/dev/sdb1
Where=/mnt/mydisk
```

```
Type=ext4

[Install]
WantedBy=multi-user.target
Create an automount unit file:
nano /etc/systemd/system/mnt-mydisk.automount
Add the following content:
[Unit]
Description=Automount my disk

[Automount]
Where=/mnt/mydisk

[Install]
WantedBy=multi-user.target
```

Enable and Start Automounting

Automounting allows a system to mount a disk automatically when it is accessed, improving efficiency by eliminating the need for manual mounting. In this task, we configure **systemd** to manage automounting for the **/mnt/mydisk** directory. After creating the necessary unit files, reload the **systemd** daemon with **sudo systemctl daemon-reload**. Then, enable the automount service to start at boot using **sudo systemctl enable mnt-mydisk.automount**, and start it with **sudo systemctl start mnt-mydisk.automount**. Once set up, the disk will mount automatically when accessed, streamlining the process and optimizing resource use.

Enable the automount unit:

- `systemctl enable mnt-mydisk.automount`
- `systemctl start mnt-mydisk.automount`

Test Automounting

Access the mount point: **ls /mnt/mydisk**

The file system should mount automatically.

Verify automount status: **systemctl status mnt-mydisk.automount**

Cleanup

Disable and remove **systemd** unit files:

- `sudo systemctl disable mnt-mydisk.automount`
- `sudo rm /etc/systemd/system/mnt-mydisk.*`

The error message **"Device or resource busy"** usually indicates that the directory is currently in use or mounted, preventing its removal. By following the given steps, this issue can be resolved:

- **Check if the Directory is Mounted:** Run the following command to see if **/mnt/mydisk** is mounted: **mount | grep /mnt/mydisk**

  If it is mounted, we will see an entry like this: **/dev/sdb1 on /mnt/mydisk type ext4 (rw, ...)**

- **Unmount the Directory:** If the directory is mounted, unmount it with the following command:

  `sudo umount /mnt/mydisk`

  If the system still reports that the device is busy, we can use the **-l** (lazy) option to unmount:
  `sudo umount -l /mnt/mydisk`

- **Check for Active Processes Using the Mount:** We can check if any processes are currently using the mount by running: `lsof +D /mnt/mydisk`

If any processes are listed, consider stopping or killing those processes before attempting to remove the directory again.

- **Remove the Directory:** Once the directory is unmounted and not in use, we should be able to remove it:
  `sudo rmdir /mnt/mydisk`

If the directory is still in use and we cannot identify the process, restarting the system should release the resources, and we should be able to remove the directory after rebooting.

This laboratory provided practical experience in mounting and unmounting file systems in Rocky Linux 9, configuring persistent mounts, and implementing dynamic automounting using **`systemd`**. Consistent practice and adherence to industry's best practices will promote efficient and reliable file system management.

Sample Output for Essential Commands

`Lsblk`: List Information About Block Devices

Command: `lsblk`

Sample Output:

```
NAME    MAJ:MIN RM  SIZE RO TYPE  MOUNTPOINT
sdb     8:16    0   100G 0  disk
└─sdb1  8:17    0   100G 0  part  /mnt/data
```

Figure 7.2: *Sample lsblk Output Showing Block Device sdb and Partition sdb1 with Mount Point*

This figure displays a sample output of the **`lsblk`** command, focusing on the block device **`sdb`** and its partition **`sdb1`.** The output illustrates the hierarchical relationship between the physical disk **(`sdb`)** and its partition **(`sdb1`),** along with key attributes such as size, type, and the assigned mount point. By highlighting how partitions are linked to their respective devices and mount locations, the figure demonstrates how system administrators can quickly interpret storage layouts. Such information is critical for verifying disk configurations, managing filesystems, and ensuring that storage devices are mounted and accessible for operational use.

Explanation:

- **Purpose:** Displays all block storage devices (for example, hard drives, USBs) and their partitions.
- **`sdb`:** Represents the physical disk.
- **`sdb1`:** A partition on the **`sdb`** disk.
- **MOUNTPOINT:** Indicates where the partition is mounted in the file system, such as **`/mnt/data`**.

Usefulness: Helps identify available storage devices, how they are partitioned, and their mount points.

`df -h – Display Disk Space Usage`

Command: `df -h`

Sample Output:

```
Filesystem      Size  Used Avail Use% Mounted on
/dev/sdb1       100G   15G   80G  16% /mnt/data
```

Figure 7.3: *Sample df -h Output for /dev/sdb1 Mounted on /mnt/data*

This figure shows the output of the **df -h** command, which provides a human-readable summary of disk space usage. In this example, the partition **/dev/sdb1** has a total capacity of 100 GB, with 15 GB used and 80 GB available, resulting in 16% utilization. The partition is mounted at **/mnt/data**, making it accessible for storing files and applications. The **df -h** utility is widely used by administrators to monitor storage usage, verify available space, and ensure that partitions have sufficient capacity for system operations and user data.

Explanation:

- **Filesystem:** Device name (for example, **/dev/sdb1**).
- **Size:** Total capacity of the file system.
- **Used:** Amount of space used.
- **Avail:** Available free space.
- **Use%:** Percentage of used space.
- **Mounted on:** Directory where the file system is attached.

Usefulness: Allows monitoring of disk space usage to prevent storage-related issues.

mount: Display Mounted File Systems

Command: `mount`

Sample Output:

```
/dev/sdb1 on /mnt/data type ext4 (rw,relatime,data=ordered)
```

Figure 7.4: *Sample mount Command Output Showing /dev/sdb1 Mounted on /mnt/data*

This figure displays the output of the **mount** command, which reports how filesystems are attached to the system. In this example, the partition **/dev/sdb1** is mounted on **/mnt/data** using the **ext4** filesystem. The output also lists important mount options: **rw** (read-write access), **relatime** (relative access time updates for improved performance), and ***data=ordered*** (a journaling mode that balances consistency and speed for **ext4**). This information confirms not only that the partition is active and accessible, but also the conditions under which it operates, providing administrators with essential insight into storage reliability and performance.

Explanation:

- **/dev/sdb1:** The mounted device or partition.
- **/mnt/data:** The directory to which the device is mounted.
- **type ext4:** The file system type.
- **(rw,relatime,data=ordered):** Mount options:
  - **rw:** Mounted with read and write access.
  - **relatime:** Updates file access times efficiently.
  - **data=ordered:** Ensures file metadata is written after the data.

Usefulness: Validates which devices are mounted and the options used.

blkid: Identify Block Devices by UUID and File System Type

Command: `blkid`

Sample Output:

```
/dev/sdb1: UUID="a1b2c3d4" TYPE="ext4"
```

Figure 7.5: *Sample blkid Output Showing UUID and Filesystem Type for /dev/sdb1*

This figure illustrates the output of the **blkid** command, which is used to display block device attributes. In this example, the partition **/dev/sdb1** is identified with a unique UUID **(a1b2c3d4)** and formatted with the **ext4** filesystem type. The UUID provides a consistent identifier for the partition, ensuring reliable mounting even if device names change across reboots. This information is particularly important when configuring the **/etc/fstab** file for automatic mounting at startup, as using UUIDs minimizes the risk of misconfigured mounts and improves system stability.

Explanation:

- **UUID:** A unique identifier for the partition, independent of device name.
- **TYPE:** Indicates the file system format (for example, **ext4**, **xfs**, etc.).

Usefulness: Essential for configuring persistent mounts using UUIDs in **/etc/fstab.**

Command	Purpose	Key Output Details
lsblk	View block devices and layout	Disk, partition, mount point
df -h	Check disk usage	Size, used, available space, mount location
mount	List mounted file systems	Device, mount point, file system, options
blkid	Identify partitions uniquely	UUID and file system type

Table 7.1: *Linux Storage Inspection Commands Summary*

This table summarizes the most commonly used commands for inspecting and managing storage in Linux environments. It includes utilities such as **lsblk, blkid, df, mount,** and **fdisk,** outlining their primary functions and typical use cases. By consolidating these tools into a single reference, the table provides administrators with a quick guide for tasks like identifying block devices, checking filesystem types, monitoring disk usage, and reviewing partition layouts. This summary helps streamline storage management by ensuring that system administrators can efficiently verify configurations, diagnose issues, and maintain optimal performance across Linux systems.

Creating and Resizing File Systems

Efficient management of file systems is critical for system administrators to optimize storage and ensure data integrity. This section provides practical guidance on creating and resizing file systems in Rocky Linux 9, focusing on essential commands and use cases.

Creating File Systems

Creating a file system involves formatting a storage device or partition with a specific file system type. Common file system types in Rocky Linux include **ext4** and **xfs**.

1. **Identifying Storage Devices:** Before creating a file system, identify the target device using tools such as **lsblk**, **fdisk**, or parted.

   Display storage devices and partitions **lsblk**

   Example output:

```
[rockylinux@rocky9 ~]$ lsblk
NAME          MAJ:MIN RM   SIZE RO TYPE MOUNTPOINTS
sda             8:0    0   512G  0 disk
├─sda1          8:1    0     1G  0 part /boot
└─sda2          8:2    0   511G  0 part
  ├─rl-root   253:0    0    70G  0 lvm  /
  ├─rl-swap   253:1    0     2G  0 lvm  [SWAP]
  └─rl-home   253:2    0 438.9G  0 lvm  /home
sdb             8:16   0    10G  0 disk
└─sdb1          8:17   0    10G  0 part
sdc             8:32   0    20G  0 disk
sr0            11:0    1  1024M  0 rom
[rockylinux@rocky9 ~]$
```

Figure 7.6: *Disk and Partitions*

The previous output illustrates the logical division of a physical disk into multiple partitions, which serve as independent storage segments. Each partition can be allocated for specific purposes, such as hosting operating systems, storing data, or acting as a swap space. This structure enhances disk organization and efficiency, allowing users to manage resources and perform tasks such as backups or multi-boot configurations. The figure emphasizes the hierarchy of disk components, including the master boot record (MBR), partition table, and individual partitions. It underscores the critical role of partitioning in system performance and storage management.

2. **Creating a Partition (If Required):** If the storage device lacks partitions, create one using **`fdisk`** or parted. **Example:** Creating a Partition with **`fdisk`**

```
sudo fdisk /dev/sdb
```

Steps:

a. Press '`n`' to create a new partition.

b. Choose the partition type (primary or logical).

c. Specify the partition size.

d. Press '`w`' to write changes.

3. **Formatting the Partition**

Use the **`mkfs`** command to create a file system on the partition.

Example 1: Creating an ext4 File System

```
sudo mkfs.ext4 /dev/sdb1
```

Example 2: Creating an `xfs` File System

```
sudo mkfs.xfs /dev/sdb1
```

4. **Verifying the File System:** After formatting, confirm the file system type using the **`blkid`** command: **`blkid /dev/sdb1`**

5. **Resizing File Systems:** Resizing a file system involves increasing or decreasing its size. This process depends on the file system type and whether the underlying storage is being resized.

   a. Resizing ext4 File Systems

   Prerequisites: Unmount the file system before resizing.

b. Check current size:
   - `sudo mkdir -p /mnt/data`
   - `sudo mount /dev/sdb1 /mnt/data`
   - `df -h /mnt/data`
c. Unmount the File System: **`sudo umount /mnt/data`**
d. Resize the File System:

   To expand and resize, we use the following commands:
   - `sudo e2fsck -f /dev/sdb1`
   - `sudo resize2fs /dev/sdb1`

   To shrink (ensure data safety before shrinking): **`resize2fs /dev/sdb1 <new_size>`**
e. Remount the File System: **`sudo mount /dev/sdb1 /mnt/data`**

Best Practices

- **Backup Data:** Always back up data before resizing file systems.
- **Monitor Storage:** Use tools such as df and **`lsblk`** to monitor storage utilization.
- **Choose the Right File System:** Select a file system type based on workload and performance needs.
- **Test Changes:** Perform operations on a test environment before applying them in production.

By mastering the processes of creating and resizing file systems, administrators can ensure optimal storage management and maintain the reliability of Rocky Linux 9 environments. These skills are critical for adapting to changing storage needs, whether it is expanding existing volumes to accommodate growing data or reclaiming unused space for better resource allocation. With a deep understanding of file system operations, administrators can effectively prevent storage-related issues, minimize downtime, and enhance overall system performance and reliability.

File System Recovery with `fsck`

This section demonstrates a real-world example of file system recovery using the **`fsck`** command.

The **`fsck`** (file system check) command is a critical tool used to identify and repair file system inconsistencies and errors. It should be used **only on unmounted file systems** to prevent data corruption.

Scenario: Recovering a Corrupted File System

Assume a secondary disk **`/dev/sdb1`** is showing errors or behaving unusually slowly. Here is how to check and repair it using **`fsck`**.

Step-by-Step Guide

1. **Unmount the File System:** Before running **`fsck`**, make sure the partition is unmounted: **`sudo umount /dev/sdb1`**

   If the disk is in use, we may need to stop related services or boot into rescue mode.

2. **Run `fsck` with Force Check**

   ```
   sudo fsck -f /dev/sdb1
   ```
   - The **`-f`** option forces the check, even if the system believes the file system is clean.
   - We will be prompted to fix errors – respond with **y** (yes) to allow repairs.

Sample Output

```
fsck from util-linux 2.37.2
e2fsck 1.46.5 (30-Dec-2021)
/dev/sdb1: clean, 12345/131072 files, 67890/524288 blocks
Pass 1: Checking inodes, blocks, and sizes
Pass 2: Checking directory structure
Pass 3: Checking directory connectivity
Pass 4: Checking reference counts
Pass 5: Checking group summary information
/dev/sdb1: ***** FILE SYSTEM WAS MODIFIED *****
```

Figure 7.7: *Sample fsck Output Checking and Repairing /dev/sdb1*

This figure shows the output of the **`fsck (file system check)`** command, which is used to verify and repair Linux filesystems. In the example, the utility **`e2fsck`** runs multiple passes to check inodes, blocks, directory structures, connectivity, reference counts, and group summaries on the partition **`/dev/sdb1`**. The report indicates that the filesystem was modified during the repair process, meaning errors were detected and corrected. Running **`fsck`** is a critical maintenance task for ensuring data integrity, particularly after improper shutdowns, disk errors, or suspected corruption, helping administrators restore filesystem consistency and system stability.

Troubleshooting Tools

To investigate what might have caused the issue or triggered errors, use the following commands:

- **`dmesg | grep sdb1`**: This command shows kernel messages related to the disk, including errors or I/O problems.
- **`journalctl -xe`**: This displays detailed system logs, including any file system warnings or errors.

Additional Tips

- Always back up data before performing repairs.
- Use **`lsblk`** or **`blkid`** to confirm the correct device name.
- If a disk frequently requires fsck, consider checking for hardware failure with tools such as **`smartctl`**: **`sudo smartctl -a /dev/sdb`**.
- For automatic file system checks during boot, configure the **`/etc/fstab`** file's sixth column (**`fs_passno`**) with a value of 1 or 2 to enable auto **`fsck`**.

The **`fsck`** utility is essential for maintaining file system health. Understanding when and how to use it, along with interpreting its output, is a key skill for system administrators.

RAID Versus LVM Comparison Table

The following figure compares RAID and LVM in terms of their key features:

Feature	RAID	LVM	Snapshot Support	Primary Use Case
Redundancy	Yes (RAID 1, 5, 6, etc.)	No (unless combined with RAID)	No	Fault tolerance
Performance	High (striping improves speed)	Moderate	No	Efficient data access
Flexibility	Low (static partitioning)	High (dynamic resizing, volume management)	Yes (point-in-time copies)	Flexible volume management

Figure 7.8: *RAID vs LVM Comparison*

This figure provides a side-by-side comparison between Redundant Array of Independent Disks (RAID) and Logical Volume Manager (LVM), two essential technologies for managing storage in Linux systems. While both are used to enhance storage flexibility and reliability, they serve different purposes. RAID focuses on data redundancy and performance by combining multiple physical disks, whereas LVM provides dynamic volume management, allowing administrators to resize, create, and move partitions with ease. This figure helps clarify their differences in functionality, use cases, and configuration complexity, assisting readers in choosing the appropriate solution for their storage needs.

Disk Partitioning and Management

Efficient disk partitioning and management are essential for optimizing storage usage and ensuring data security, particularly in environments where multiple partitions are required for system stability, performance, or isolation purposes. By creating separate partitions for the operating system, data, and other critical files, system administrators can minimize the risk of data loss or corruption in case of system failure. Proper partitioning also enhances performance by reducing fragmentation and improving file system management. Additionally, partitioning allows for easier backups, disk encryption, and overall system organization. In Rocky Linux 9, tools such as **`fdisk`**, **`parted`**, and **`lsblk`** enable administrators to perform these tasks with precision and ease, offering both command-line and graphical interfaces for managing disk structures.

The **`fdisk`** tool is a classic utility for creating and modifying partitions on a hard drive, especially for Master Boot Record (MBR) partition schemes, while **`parted`** is more versatile, supporting both MBR and GUID Partition Table (GPT) partitioning styles and offering a more advanced feature set, including the ability to resize partitions and manage different file systems. Meanwhile, **`lsblk`** is a command used for listing information about all available block devices, helping users understand the current disk layout and partitions. With these powerful utilities, Rocky Linux 9 provides administrators with the flexibility to create, resize, and manage partitions based on system needs, making it easier to organize and optimize disk usage while ensuring system performance and reliability.

Introduction to Disk Partitioning

Disk partitioning divides a physical drive into logical sections. Each partition acts as an independent storage unit. In Rocky Linux, partitions are necessary for organizing data and implementing security measures.

Tools for Disk Partitioning

- **`fdisk`**: For creating and managing partitions on MBR and GPT disks.

- **parted**: A flexible tool for handling both MBR and GPT partitions.
- **lsblk**: Displays information about block devices.
- **mkfs**: Formats partitions with a file system.
- **mount**: Temporarily attaches partitions to directories.

Practical Disk Partitioning: Step-by-Step

Step 1: Viewing Available Disks

Before creating or modifying partitions, list all available disks: **lsblk**

Example output:

```
[rockylinux@rocky9 ~]$ lsblk
NAME         MAJ:MIN RM   SIZE RO TYPE MOUNTPOINTS
sda            8:0    0   512G  0 disk
├─sda1         8:1    0     1G  0 part /boot
└─sda2         8:2    0   511G  0 part
  ├─rl-root  253:0    0    70G  0 lvm  /
  ├─rl-swap  253:1    0     2G  0 lvm  [SWAP]
  └─rl-home  253:2    0 438.9G  0 lvm  /home
sdb            8:16   0    10G  0 disk
└─sdb1         8:17   0    10G  0 part /mnt/data
sdc            8:32   0    20G  0 disk
sr0           11:0    1  1024M  0 rom
```

Figure 7.9: *lsbkl Disk and Partitions*

In *Figure* 7.9, the "**lsblk**" command is used to display the disk and partition information on a Linux system. This command provides a detailed view of all block devices, including hard drives, SSDs, and partitions. Each device is listed with its name, size, type, and mount points. The output typically shows the device's hierarchy, where the disk is the parent, and its partitions are the children. The partition structure is crucial for understanding how data is organized on the disk, enabling users to manage storage, create, delete, or modify partitions, and mount file systems. The "**lsblk**" command is a powerful tool for administrators to manage storage configurations in Linux systems efficiently.

Step 2: Creating Partitions with fdisk

Creating partitions is a fundamental step in preparing storage devices for use, and the **fdisk** utility provides a straightforward way to accomplish this in Rocky Linux 9. This command-line tool allows administrators to manage disk partitions by creating, deleting, resizing, and modifying partition layouts on both MBR and GPT disks. With **fdisk,** users can define partitions that suit their storage requirements, assign appropriate partition types, and write these configurations to disk. This process is essential for structuring storage devices, ensuring they are ready for file system creation and subsequent use by the operating system. Mastery of **fdisk** ensures efficient disk utilization and prepares administrators for advanced storage configurations.

a. Launch **fdisk** for the target disk: **sudo fdisk /dev/sda**

b. Inside the interactive shell:

   - Press n to create a new partition.
   - Specify the partition type (primary or extended).
   - Set the starting and ending sectors or size.

c. Write changes to disk:
   - Press **w** to save changes.

Step 3: Verifying Partitions

After partitioning, confirm changes using: **lsblk**

Step 4: Formatting the Partition

Choose a file system (for example, **ext4** or **xfs**) and format: **sudo mkfs.ext4 /dev/sda3**

Step 5: Mounting the Partition

a. Create a mount point: **sudo mkdir /mnt/newpartition**

b. Mount the partition: **sudo mount /dev/sda1 /mnt/newpartition**

c. Make the mount permanent by editing **/etc/fstab**:
   `echo '/dev/sda1 /mnt/newpartition ext4 defaults 0 0' | sudo tee -a /etc/fstab`

Step 6. Managing Partitions with parted

a. Start parted for the disk: **sudo parted /dev/sda**

b. Create a new partition table: **mklabel gpt**

c. Create a partition with specific size: **mkpart primary ext4 1MiB 50GiB**
   - Verify partitions: **print**

Step 7. Resizing Partitions

Rocky Linux supports resizing file systems dynamically. For ext4 partitions:

a. Unmount the partition: **sudo umount /dev/sda1**

b. Resize the partition: **sudo resize2fs /dev/sda1**

c. Remount the partition: **sudo mount /dev/sda1 /mnt/newpartition**

Step 8: Practical Tips for Disk Partitioning

a. Always back up data before modifying partitions.

b. Use GPT for modern systems due to its large disk support.

c. Allocate separate partitions for **/**, **/home**, and **/var** for better organization and security.

Backup and Recovery Strategies

Backup and recovery strategies are crucial components of a comprehensive data protection plan, ensuring the integrity of critical information and minimizing downtime in the event of a disaster. Regular backups help safeguard against data loss due to hardware failure, accidental deletion, or malicious attacks such as ransomware. By implementing a well-thought-out backup strategy, businesses can ensure that they have reliable copies of their data stored securely and readily available for restoration when needed. In addition, an effective recovery process is essential to quickly restore services, maintaining business continuity, and minimizing operational disruptions. Rocky Linux 9 provides robust tools and methods to create reliable backups and facilitate quick and efficient data recovery, offering both flexibility and security.

Rocky Linux 9 offers several tools to help system administrators perform reliable backups and recovery, including utilities such as **rsync, tar,** and more advanced solutions such as *Bacula or Amanda.* For file-based backups, **rsync** is particularly useful for creating incremental backups, while

tar can be used to archive entire directories or systems. For comprehensive backup solutions, *Bacula and Amanda* provide enterprise-level features such as automated scheduling, remote backups, and multi-system support. These tools allow administrators to back up individual files, directories, or entire systems with ease. To complement these backup tools, Rocky Linux 9 also integrates recovery strategies, ensuring that in the event of a failure, data can be quickly restored with minimal effort. By combining the appropriate backup techniques and recovery tools, administrators can enhance the security and resilience of their systems while ensuring business continuity.

Bacula for Backup and Recovery in Rocky Linux 9

Bacula is an open-source, enterprise-level backup solution designed to automate the process of backing up, restoring, and verifying data across a network. It is highly configurable, allowing for the backup of files, databases, and even entire systems. Bacula's components include a Director, Storage Daemon, File Daemon, and Catalog, each with specific roles for managing backups.

Installing Bacula on Rocky Linux 9

To install Bacula, follow these steps:

1. **Add the EPEL Repository (if not already installed): `sudo dnf install epel-release`.**
2. **Install Bacula packages:**
   ```
   sudo dnf install bacula-director bacula-storage bacula-fd bacula-console
   ```
3. **Start and enable the Bacula services:**
   - `sudo systemctl enable --now bacula-director`
   - `sudo systemctl enable --now bacula-sd`
   - `sudo systemctl enable --now bacula-fd`
4. **Verify that Bacula services are running:**
   - `sudo systemctl status bacula-director`
   - `sudo systemctl status bacula-sd`
   - `sudo systemctl status bacula-fd`

Configuring Bacula for Backups

Once Bacula is installed, we need to configure its components:

- **Bacula Director**: Responsible for managing backups, defining the schedule, and interacting with clients.
- **Bacula File Daemon (FD)**: Runs on the client machine and sends files to be backed up.
- **Bacula Storage Daemon (SD)**: Manages backup storage and writes the backup data to disk or tape.
- **Bacula Catalog**: Maintains the catalog of backup information.

   a. **Configure the Bacula Director**: Edit the configuration file **`/etc/bacula/bacula-dir.conf`** to define job schedules, storage, and volumes.

   b. Example job definition:

   ```
   JobDefs {
       Name = DefaultJobDef
       Type = RestoreFiles
       FileSet="Full Set"
   ```

```
    Schedule="WeeklyCycle"
    Pool=Default
    Priority=10
}

Job {
    Name = "BackupFiles"
    Type = Backup
    FileSet="Full Set"
    Schedule="WeeklyCycle"
    Pool=Default
    Priority=10
}
```

c. **Set up backup jobs and schedule** in the Bacula Director configuration file.

d. **Run the Bacula backup job** using the Bacula console: **`bconsole`**

   `*run`

e. **Restore Files** by using the Bacula console to query the catalog and select the appropriate backup to restore.

Amanda for Backup and Recovery in Rocky Linux 9

Amanda (Advanced Maryland Automatic Network Disk Archiver) is another open-source backup solution that simplifies backup management for Linux and other operating systems. It supports backing up files, directories, and systems across multiple clients and offers features such as scheduling, encryption, and compression.

Installing Amanda on Rocky Linux 9

1. **Install the Amanda server and client packages:**

   ```
   sudo dnf install amanda-server amanda-client
   ```

2. **Start and enable the Amanda service:** `sudo systemctl enable --now amanda`

3. **Verify Amanda service status:** `sudo systemctl status amanda`

Configuring Amanda for Backups

1. **Edit Amanda Configuration Files**: The main configuration file is **`/etc/amanda/amanda.conf`**.

2. Here, define the backup schedule, storage, and the dump type. For example:

   ```
   # Backup schedule
   dumpcycle 7 days
   runspercycle 5
   # Backup storage location
   tapedev /dev/st0
   ```

3. **Configure the backup client**:

   - The client needs to be configured to connect with the Amanda server and define which directories to back up.
   - Edit the **`/etc/amanda/amanda-client.conf`** file to specify client-side settings.

4. **Run the Amanda Backup**: We can run the backup job using the following command:

   `sudo amdump`

5. This command will execute the backup process based on the configured schedule.

6. **Verify the Backup**: After the backup is complete, verify the backup status using:
   `sudo amstatus`

Restoring Files with Amanda

To restore files from a previous backup, use the following command: **`sudo amrecover`**

This interactive tool allows us to browse backups, select the files or directories to restore, and specify the destination for recovery.

Both ***Bacula and Amanda*** are powerful, open-source tools available in **Rocky Linux 9** for comprehensive backup and recovery management. Bacula is ideal for enterprise environments, offering robust configuration options for complex backup scenarios. Amanda, on the other hand, is simpler to set up and can easily manage backup tasks across multiple systems. Depending on the requirements, either tool can be a solid choice for ensuring data integrity and quick recovery in case of system failures.

Types of Backups

- **Full Backup**: A complete copy of all data; best used as the initial backup.
- **Incremental Backup**: Saves only the changes made since the last backup.
- **Differential Backup**: Copies data changed since the last full backup, requiring fewer resources than full backups.

Tools for Backup and Recovery

Rocky Linux provides several utilities to perform backup and recovery operations:

- **`rsync`**: Synchronizes files and directories efficiently.
- **`tar`**: Archives and compresses files.
- **`Timeshift`**: Manages system snapshots.
- **Bacula and Amanda**: Enterprise-level solutions for extensive backup needs.
- **dd**: Performs low-level disk cloning and imaging.

Practical Steps for Backups

Backing Up with rsync

1. To back up a directory to an external drive:
   - `sudo mkdir /mnt/backup_drive`
   - `sudo rsync -av --progress /home/user /mnt/backup_drive`
2. To synchronize and remove files in the destination not present in the source:
   - `sudo rsync -av --delete /home/user /mnt/backup_drive`

Creating Archives with tar

1. Archive and compress a directory: **`sudo tar -czvf backup.tar.gz /home/user`**
2. Extract the archive:
   - `sudo mkdir /mnt/restore_location`
   - `sudo tar -xzvf backup.tar.gz -C /restore_location`

Practical Steps for Recovery

Restoring with `rsync`: To restore files from the backup: **`sudo rsync -av --progress /mnt/backup_drive/user /home`**

Restoring a tar Archive: Extract the tar archive to its original location: `sudo tar -xzvf backup.tar.gz -C /home/user`

Advanced Recovery Scenarios

- **Disk Cloning**: Use dd to create a complete disk image:
  `sudo dd if=/dev/sda1 of=/dev/sdb1 bs=64K conv=noerror,sync`

System Recovery with Timeshift

Efficient Snapshot Restoration

When using **timeshift** in a VirtualBox VM, there could be potential issues due to **differences** in how virtual and physical systems manage snapshots. **VirtualBox** provides its own **snapshot** functionality, which **captures** the entire state of the VM, while **timeshift** focuses specifically on the file system.

Conflicts may arise if both are used together, as they manage system states in diverse ways. Additionally, virtualized hardware and disk space limitations could cause issues during snapshot creation or restoration. It is recommended to ensure the VM has adequate disk space and to avoid conflicts by choosing between VirtualBox and Timeshift snapshots.

Learn how to restore the system quickly using Timeshift, a powerful tool that allows us to take snapshots of the system and roll back to a previous state when necessary. This method is particularly useful for protecting our system against unexpected issues or mistakes.

a. **Create a Snapshot:** Before making any significant changes to the system, take a snapshot to ensure we can revert, if needed: `sudo timeshift --create`

b. **Restoring from a Snapshot:** If something goes wrong, we can easily restore our system to a previous state with the following command: `sudo timeshift --restore`.

The system prompts for the selection of the snapshot to restore, ensuring a smooth and safe recovery process. This enhanced approach highlights how Timeshift safeguards the system while maintaining a simple and user-friendly process.

Best Practices for Backup and Recovery

- Schedule regular backups using cron or automation tools.
- Test backups periodically to ensure that they work as expected.
- Store critical data off-site for disaster recovery.
- Encrypt sensitive backups to secure confidential information.

By following these strategies and using the provided tools, administrators can ensure reliable and efficient data backup and recovery processes in Rocky Linux 9.

Cloud Storage Integration

Integrating cloud storage solutions such as Amazon Elastic Block Store (EBS) and Simple Storage Service (S3) into Rocky Linux allows users to extend storage capabilities, enhance scalability, and ensure data durability. This guide outlines the steps for integrating and managing EBS and S3 with Rocky Linux.

Amazon Elastic Block Store (EBS) Integration

1. **Attaching an EBS Volume to a Rocky Linux Instance**

   a. Attach the EBS volume to our EC2 instance using the AWS Management Console.

b. Verify the new disk on our instance: **`lsblk`**

c. Create a file system on the new EBS volume (for example, **`ext4`**): **`sudo mkfs.ext4 /dev/xvda127`**

d. Mount the volume to a directory:

- `sudo mkdir /mnt/ebs`
- `sudo mount /dev/xvda127 /mnt/ebs`

e. Make the mount persistent across reboots by adding an entry to **`/etc/fstab`**:

```
echo '/dev/ xvda127 /mnt/ebs ext4 defaults,nofail 0 2' | sudo tee -a /etc/
fstab
```

2. **Resizing an EBS Volume**

   a. Modify the volume size in the AWS Management Console.

   b. On our instance, notify the OS of the size change: **`sudo growpart /dev/xvda127`**

   c. Resize the file system: **`sudo resize2fs /dev/xvda127`**

3. **Amazon S3 Integration**

   Installing the AWS CLI

   a. Install the AWS CLI on our Rocky Linux instance: **`sudo dnf install awscli -y`**

   b. Configure AWS credentials: **`aws configure`**

Provide the **Access Key ID**, **Secret Access Key**, **Default Region**, and **Output Format**.

4. **Interacting with S3 Buckets**

   a. List all S3 buckets:

   - `aws s3 mb s3://cesaralonsoserver`
   - `aws s3 mb s3://cesarrocky9`
   - `aws s3 ls`

   b. Upload a file to an S3 bucket:

   - `touch testfile123`
   - `aws s3 cp /home/ec2-user/testfile123 s3://cesarrocky9`

   c. Download a file from an S3 bucket:

   - `mkdir test123_dir`
   - `aws s3 cp s3://cesarrocky9/testfile123 /home/ec2-user/test123_dir/`

5. **Mounting S3 Buckets Locally**

The **`s3fs-fuse`** package may not be included in the default Rocky Linux repositories. However, it can still be installed on Rocky Linux 9 by enabling the necessary repositories or by building the package from source. Below are the steps to complete the installation process:

Installing `s3fs-fuse` on Rocky Linux 9

Install Required Repositories: Enable the EPEL (Extra Packages for Enterprise Linux) repository, as it often contains s3fs-fuse: **`sudo dnf install epel-release -y`.**

Install s3fs-fuse: After enabling EPEL, install s3fs-fuse: **`sudo dnf install s3fs-fuse -y`.**

Verify Installation: Check the version of s3fs-fuse to confirm it is installed: **`s3fs --version`**.

1. Create a file to store S3 credentials:
   - `echo "ACCESS_KEY_ID:SECRET_ACCESS_KEY" > ~/.s3fs_passwd`
   - `chmod 600 ~/.s3fs_passwd`
2. Mount the S3 bucket:
   - `sudo mkdir -p /mnt/s3`
   - `ls -ld /mnt/s3`
   - `sudo s3fs our-bucket-name /mnt/s3 -o passwd_file=~/.s3fs_passwd`

Cloud Storage Integration Enhancements

Cloud storage integration is a key aspect of managing infrastructure in modern hybrid or cloud-native environments. In Rocky Linux, integrating and troubleshooting Amazon Web Services (AWS) Elastic Block Store (EBS) and Simple Storage Service (S3) ensures data durability, scalability, and performance. These services allow for flexible, on-demand storage provisioning and seamless data access across multiple instances. Effective integration also supports automated backup strategies, disaster recovery planning, and optimized cost management in cloud-based deployments.

EBS Troubleshooting: EBS volumes can be dynamically resized in AWS, but after resizing, Linux systems need to recognize and expand the partition and file system.

1. **Expand the partition using growpart: `sudo growpart /dev/xvdf 1`**
   - **Purpose:** Expands partition 1 on the disk **`/dev/xvdf`** to fill the newly allocated space.
   - **Tool:** growpart is part of the **`cloud-utils-growpart`** package and handles partition growth without data loss.
2. **Resize the file system using resize2fs: `sudo resize2fs /dev/xvdf1`**
   - **Purpose:** Resizes the **`ext2/ext3/ext4`** file system to match the new partition size.
   - **Note:** Make sure the file system is not in use or is mounted as read-only during this operation (or perform it on a detached volume).

Summary: After resizing an EBS volume in AWS, these two commands are required to utilize the new capacity at the OS level.

S3 Mount Troubleshooting: Amazon S3 is an object storage service and not a native file system, but tools such as s3fs-fuse allow mounting S3 buckets like a local file system.

Unmounting an S3 bucket safely: When working with S3 buckets mounted on Rocky Linux, it is important to unmount them safely to avoid data loss or system hanging. The following command uses a lazy unmount approach, which detaches the file system immediately while allowing any ongoing processes to finish gracefully in the background:

```
sudo umount -l /mnt/s3
```

- **Purpose:** Lazily unmounts the **`/mnt/s3`** mount point, allowing the unmount to proceed even if the mount is currently busy.
- **Benefit:** Prevents hanging sessions or applications from blocking the unmount process, ensuring smoother system operations.
- **Tip:** If S3 mount commands fail or the bucket becomes inaccessible, first attempt to unmount the directory before remounting or troubleshooting credential issues.

Common Issues with S3 Mounts:

- Permission errors due to invalid or expired access credentials.
- Incorrect bucket name or region.
- Connectivity issues or missing s3fs packages.

Security Best Practices for AWS Storage Integration: Securing cloud storage access is essential to prevent data leaks, unauthorized access, or accidental deletion. The following are industry-standard security best practices.

Use IAM Roles Instead of Static Access Keys

- **Static access keys** (Access Key ID and Secret Access Key) pose a risk if exposed.
- **IAM Roles** provide temporary, automatically rotated credentials.
- **Use Case:** When running on an EC2 instance, assign an IAM role to the instance with the appropriate S3 or EBS access permissions.

Benefits:

- No hard-coded secrets.
- Simplified access management.
- Enhanced auditability.

Enable Server-Side Encryption (SSE)

- **SSE-S3:** Amazon S3 manages the encryption keys.
- **SSE-KMS:** Uses AWS Key Management Service (KMS) for more control and audit logging.

Command-line example to upload with SSE-KMS:

```
aws s3 cp file.txt s3://mybucket/ --sse aws:kms
```

This is important because:

- Data is encrypted at rest.
- Ensures compliance with data protection regulations (for example, GDPR, HIPAA).

Monitor Access Logs Using AWS CloudTrail

- **CloudTrail** records all API calls made to AWS services, including access to EBS and S3.
- **Use Case:** Detect unauthorized or unusual access patterns, such as:
  - Data exfiltration
  - Use of leaked credentials
  - Policy misconfigurations

Recommendations:

- Enable CloudTrail in all regions.
- Set up alerts using AWS CloudWatch for suspicious activities.
- Regularly review audit logs.

Summary Table

Feature	Tool/Command	Purpose
EBS Resize - Partition	`growpart /dev/xvdf 1`	Expands partition to use full volume size
EBS Resize - File System	`resize2fs /dev/xvdf1`	Resizes file system to fill expanded partition
S3 Mount Troubleshooting	`umount -l /mnt/s3`	Lazily unmounts S3 mount point

Secure Access	***Use IAM roles***	Avoids hard-coded credentials, enables role-based access
Encryption	***Enable SSE-S3 or SSE-KMS***	Encrypts data at rest in S3
Audit and Monitoring	***Enable AWS CloudTrail***	Logs and monitors storage-related activity

Table 7.2: *AWS Storage Operations and Security Summary*

This table provides an overview of key AWS storage operations alongside their associated security considerations, offering administrators a clear guide for managing cloud-based storage effectively. It highlights essential tasks such as creating and configuring S3 buckets, managing Elastic Block Store (EBS) volumes, and implementing lifecycle policies, while also emphasizing best practices in access control, encryption, and auditing. By consolidating both operational steps and security measures, the table helps readers balance functionality with protection, ensuring that storage resources are not only optimized for performance but also safeguarded against unauthorized access and data loss.

Best Practices for Cloud Storage Integration

- Use IAM roles for secure access management instead of storing credentials directly.
- Monitor storage costs and optimize usage by enabling lifecycle policies for S3.
- Regularly test backups and replication configurations.
- Ensure EBS volumes are appropriately encrypted for sensitive data.

By integrating cloud storage solutions such as EBS and S3, Rocky Linux users can achieve scalable, reliable, and cost-effective storage tailored to their needs.

Conclusion

In this chapter, we explored the essential operations involved in effective file system management on Rocky Linux. Key tasks such as mounting and unmounting file systems, creating and resizing them, and performing disk partitioning and management were thoroughly covered. We examined widely used file system types such as **ext4** and **XFS**, comparing their advantages and use cases in real-world scenarios.

We also emphasized the importance of robust **backup and recovery strategies** to safeguard data against loss or corruption. Additionally, we introduced **cloud storage integration** using AWS services such as **EBS** and **S3**, enabling administrators to scale and adapt storage solutions efficiently across hybrid environments.

These file system management skills are vital for any system administrator aiming to ensure **data integrity**, **optimal performance**, and **reliable storage** both on-premises and in the cloud. A strong grasp of these concepts lays the groundwork for managing complex, high-performance Linux infrastructures that support dynamic and evolving workloads.

In **Chapter 8: Web Server Setup and Configuration**, we will build upon this foundation by turning our focus to deploying web servers using **Apache**. We will learn how to configure **virtual hosts**, implement essential **security measures**, manage **server logs**, and **deploy scalable web applications** within cloud platforms such as AWS. This next chapter will empower us to deliver fast, secure, and resilient web services in modern IT environments.

Points to Remember

- **Mounting and Unmounting File Systems:** Proper mounting and unmounting of file systems are essential for ensuring data integrity and preventing file system corruption. Use the **`mount`** **`and umount`** commands to attach or detach file systems and ensure that **`/etc/fstab`** is configured correctly for automatic mounting.
- **Creating and Resizing File Systems:** Creating and resizing file systems is crucial for efficient disk space management. Tools such as **`mkfs`** are used to create new file systems, while **`resize2fs`** or **`xfs_growfs`** allow us to resize existing ones. Always ensure data is backed up before resizing.
- **Disk Partitioning and Management:** Disk partitioning is key for organizing data and optimizing storage. Use tools such as **`fdisk`**, parted, and **`lsblk`** to create and manage partitions. Be mindful of partition types (primary, extended, logical) and the impact of changes on data storage.
- **File System Types (ext4, `xfs`):** Different file system types offer various advantages depending on the use case. **`ext4`** is a widely used file system known for stability, while xfs is optimized for performance with large files and volumes. Choosing the right file system is essential based on the workload and system requirements.
- **Backup and Recovery Strategies:** Backup and recovery are critical for data protection. Use tools such as **`rsync`**, **`tar`**, and **`dd`** to create backups, and establish a routine schedule for system backups. Having a solid recovery strategy in place ensures minimal downtime in case of data loss or system failure.
- **Cloud Storage Integration (EBS, S3):** Integrating cloud storage with Rocky Linux can extend storage capacity and provide scalability. AWS EBS can be used for persistent block storage, while S3 is ideal for object storage. Using cloud storage efficiently allows seamless data management and backup options for cloud-based environments.
- **Disk Usage and Space Management:** Monitoring disk space is crucial to prevent system performance degradation. Tools such as **`df`**, **`du`**, and **`lsblk`** can be used to check disk usage and free space. Regularly reviewing disk usage and optimizing storage helps ensure that systems run efficiently.
- **Filesystem Permissions and Ownership:** Effectively managing file permissions and ownership is necessary for system security. Use **`chmod`**, **`chown`**, and **`chgrp`** to configure access control, ensuring that files and directories are accessible only to authorized users.

Multiple Choice Questions

1. Which command is used to create a new file system in Rocky Linux?
   a. `mkfs`
   b. `fdisk`
   c. `lsblk`
   d. `mount`
2. What is the purpose of the `/etc/fstab` file in Rocky Linux?
   a. To define the system's backup strategy
   b. To configure automatic mounting of file systems
   c. To manage network settings
   d. To store file system permissions

3. Which file system type is commonly used for high-performance file storage with large files in Rocky Linux?
   a. `ext4`
   b. `xfs`
   c. `btrfs`
   d. `ntfs`
4. What command is used to resize an ext4 file system in Rocky Linux?
   a. `resize2fs`
   b. `fsresize`
   c. `xfs_growfs`
   d. `mkfs`
5. Which tool is used to manage disk partitions in Rocky Linux?
   a. `mkfs`
   b. `parted`
   c. `mount`
   d. `tar`
6. What is the function of AWS EBS (Elastic Block Store) in cloud storage integration with Rocky Linux?
   a. To store large amounts of unstructured data
   b. To provide persistent block-level storage for EC2 instances
   c. To manage network traffic between EC2 instances
   d. To provide compute power for EC2 instances
7. Which command is used to check disk space usage in Rocky Linux?
   a. `df`
   b. `du`
   c. `lsblk`
   d. `mount`
8. What does the `xfs_growfs` command do in Rocky Linux?
   a. It creates a new `xfs` file system
   b. It expands an existing `xfs` file system
   c. It formats a disk with the `xfs` file system
   d. It resizes partitions for `xfs` file systems

9. Which of the following is a recommended practice when performing backups in Rocky Linux?
   a. Perform backups only after system failure
   b. Store backups on the same physical disk
   c. Use `rsync` or tar to create backups
   d. Disable all security features during backup
10. Which tool can be used to create backups of entire disks in Rocky Linux?
    a. `dd`
    b. `mkfs`
    c. `rsync`
    d. `mount`

Answers

1. a
2. b
3. b
4. a
5. b
6. b
7. a
8. b
9. c
10. a

Questions

1. What is the primary purpose of configuring file systems in Rocky Linux?
2. Which command is used to create a new file system in Rocky Linux?
3. What is the function of the **`/etc/fstab`** file in Rocky Linux?
4. Which file system type is commonly used for high-performance file storage with large files in Rocky Linux?
5. What command is used to resize an ext4 file system in Rocky Linux?
6. Which tool is used to manage disk partitions in Rocky Linux?
7. What is the role of AWS EBS (Elastic Block Store) in cloud storage integration with Rocky Linux?
8. Which command can be used to check disk space usage in Rocky Linux?

9. What does the **`xfs_growfs`** command do in Rocky Linux?
10. What is a recommended practice when performing backups in Rocky Linux?

Key Terms

- **File System:** A method and structure used by operating systems to organize and store data on storage devices. Common file systems include **`ext4`**, **`xfs`**, and **`btrfs`**.
- **`mkfs`:** A command used to create a new file system on a storage device in Rocky Linux. Common options include **`mkfs.ext4`** and **`mkfs.xfs`**.
- **`/etc/fstab`:** A configuration file in Linux that defines how and where disk partitions, file systems, and network file systems should be mounted automatically at boot time.
- **`ext4`:** A widely used file system in Linux that is known for its stability and performance, particularly with smaller files and general-purpose storage.
- **`xfs`:** A high-performance file system used in Linux, optimized for large files and high-performance environments, often used in enterprise-level systems.
- **`resize2fs`:** A command used to resize an ext4 file system, allowing the adjustment of the file system's size without losing data.
- **`xfs_growfs`:** A command used to expand the size of an existing XFS file system, typically after increasing the underlying partition size.
- **`Parted`:** A disk partitioning tool used in Rocky Linux for creating, resizing, and managing disk partitions.
- **`rsync`:** A command-line tool used for creating backups by synchronizing files and directories between various locations, ensuring data consistency.
- **Elastic Block Store (EBS):** A service in AWS that provides persistent block-level storage for EC2 instances, used for storing operating systems, applications, and data.

Chapter 8
Web Server Setup and Configuration

Introduction

Web servers power virtually every online service, from simple websites to complex applications. For Linux administrators and beginners, mastering Apache setup and management is a fundamental skill.

This chapter provides a clear, step-by-step guide to installing, configuring, and securing Apache web servers. It covers essential tasks as well as advanced configurations to support scalable and secure environments. This foundation enables efficient hosting of web content on Linux platforms, suitable for both traditional and cloud-based deployments.

Structure

This chapter covers the following topics:

- Installing Apache Web Server
- Configuring Virtual Hosts
- Basic Web Server Security Practices
- Managing Web Server Logs
- Setting Up PHP and MySQL for Dynamic Content
- Deploying Web Servers in AWS

Installing Apache Web Server

The Apache HTTP Server is a widely used, open-source web server renowned for its versatility and reliability. Supporting both static and dynamic content, it remains a preferred choice among developers and administrators alike. With a rich set of modules, Apache seamlessly integrates with technologies such as PHP, Python, and SSL. Installing Apache on Rocky Linux is straightforward, and the operating system offers flexible configuration options suitable for everything from personal websites to large-scale enterprise deployments. This section presents the installation process along with essential configuration guidelines designed to address a variety of deployment scenarios.

Step 1: Update System Packages

Before installing any software, ensure that the system is up to date. This helps avoid compatibility issues during the installation process. Run the following commands:

- `sudo dnf update -y`
- `sudo dnf upgrade -y`

These commands update the package lists and install available upgrades for the installed packages.

Step 2: Install Apache

To install Apache, execute the following command: **`sudo dnf install httpd -y`**

This command downloads and installs Apache and its dependencies. After installation, verify the version installed by typing: **`httpd -v`**.

Step 3: Start and Enable the Apache Service

To ensure that the Apache server runs continuously, we need to start and enable it:

```
sudo systemctl start httpd
sudo systemctl enable httpd
```

- **`start`:** Immediately starts the Apache service.
- **`enable`:** Ensures Apache starts automatically at boot.

Example output:

`[cesarmserver@localhost~]$sudo enable httpd`

Created **`symlink /etc/systemd/system/multi-user.targar.wants/httpd.service`** then **`/usr/lib/system/httpd.service`**

The status of the service can be validated with the following command: **`sudo systemctl status httpd`**

The output should indicate that Apache is running.

```
[cesarmserver@localhost ~]$ sudo systemctl status httpd
● httpd.service - The Apache HTTP Server
     Loaded: loaded (/usr/lib/systemd/system/httpd.service; enabled; preset: [illegible])
     Active: active (running) since Fri 2025-01-03 13:47:16 CST; 5min ago
       Docs: man:httpd.service(8)
   Main PID: 101501 (httpd)
     Status: "Total requests: 0; Idle/Busy workers 100/0;Requests/sec: 0; Bytes served/sec:   0 B/sec"
      Tasks: 177 (limit: 10760)
     Memory: 35.9M
        CPU: 241ms
     CGroup: /system.slice/httpd.service
             ├─101501 /usr/sbin/httpd -DFOREGROUND
             ├─101502 /usr/sbin/httpd -DFOREGROUND
             ├─101503 /usr/sbin/httpd -DFOREGROUND
             ├─101504 /usr/sbin/httpd -DFOREGROUND
             └─101505 /usr/sbin/httpd -DFOREGROUND

Jan 03 13:47:16 localhost.localdomain systemd[1]: Starting The Apache HTTP Server...
Jan 03 13:47:16 localhost.localdomain httpd[101501]: AH00558: httpd: Could not reliably determine the server's fully q>
Jan 03 13:47:16 localhost.localdomain httpd[101501]: Server configured, listening on: port 80
Jan 03 13:47:16 localhost.localdomain systemd[1]: Started The Apache HTTP Server.
lines 1-20/20 (END)
```

Figure 8.1: *Apache HTTP Server Status*

The figure displays the Apache HTTP Server's detailed status page as configured on Rocky Linux 9. This dynamic dashboard offers real-time visibility into the server's operational health and activity. Key performance indicators include the number of active connections, server uptime, CPU usage, and a detailed breakdown of current requests being processed. This status page is an essential monitoring tool for administrators, enabling proactive performance tuning and swift identification of potential issues. Access to this page requires enabling the **`mod_status`** module, which can be tailored to highlight metrics most relevant to the specific environment and workload.

Remember to use the letter **`q`** on the keyboard to exit the previously shown interface.

Step 4: Configure the Firewall

To allow web traffic, open the HTTP (port 80) and HTTPS (port 443) ports in the firewall:

- `sudo firewall-cmd --permanent --add-service=http`
- `sudo firewall-cmd --permanent --add-service=https`
- `sudo firewall-cmd --reload`

We can confirm the changes with: **sudo firewall-cmd --list-all**

```
[cesarmserver@localhost ~]$ sudo firewall-cmd --list-all
public (active)
  target: default
  icmp-block-inversion: no
  interfaces: ens160
  sources:
  services: cockpit dhcpv6-client http https ssh
  ports:
  protocols:
  forward: yes
  masquerade: no
  forward-ports:
  source-ports:
  icmp-blocks:
  rich rules:
[cesarmserver@localhost ~]$
```

Figure 8.2: *Firewall Allow Web Traffic Access*

Figure 8.2 illustrates the firewall configuration for enabling web traffic access. The active zone, **public**, is configured to allow essential services, including **http** and **https**, which facilitate web server communication over ports 80 and 443, respectively. The **ens160** network interface ensures traffic is routed through the designated network adapter. This setup guarantees secure and seamless web traffic handling while maintaining access to additional services such as **ssh** for remote management and **cockpit** for web-based system administration. Proper firewall configuration is crucial for balancing accessibility and security in a server environment.

Step 5: Test Apache Installation

Open a web browser and navigate to the server's IP address (for example, **http://your-server-ip**). We should see the default Apache welcome page, confirming that the installation was successful. To find the server's IP address, use: **ip addr show**

Step 6: Apache Directory Structure

We recommend familiarizing yourself with the Apache directory structure:

- **/etc/httpd/**: Main configuration directory.
- **/etc/httpd/conf/httpd.conf**: Primary configuration file.
- **/var/www/html/**: Default root directory for website files.
- **/var/log/httpd/**: Log files (access and error logs).

Modify the configuration as needed for the specific requirements. For instance, the default page can be replaced by editing or replacing the **index.html** file in **/var/www/html/**.

Step 7: Testing with a Custom HTML Page

Create a Simple HTML File to Test the Server

Run the following command to create a test HTML file:

```
echo "<h1>Apache is Working!</h1>" | sudo tee /var/www/html/index.html
```

Refresh the Browser

Once the file is created, refresh the browser to see the custom message. If successful, we should see a page displaying: "**Apache is Working!**"

Final Validation Step: Test the Server

Navigate to our server's IP address in the browser: **http://<your_server_ip>**

If testing locally, use one of the following URLs:

- **`http://localhost`**
- **`http://127.0.0.1`**

An image like the following should be displayed:

Figure 8.3: *Apache HTML Operational Page*

The Apache HTML operational page serves as a default landing page when the Apache web server is successfully installed and running. It confirms that the server is functioning correctly, typically displaying the text "**`It works!`**" along with basic information about the Apache installation. This page is important for verifying that the Apache HTTP server is properly configured and ready to serve content. Administrators can use this page as an initial test before deploying custom web pages or applications.

Common Troubleshooting Tips

- **Service Not Starting**: Use **`sudo journalctl -xe`** to check for detailed error logs.
- **Firewall Misconfiguration**: Ensure HTTP and HTTPS ports are open using firewall-cmd.
- **Permission Issues**: Check file permissions in **`/var/www/html/`** using **`ls -l`**.

These steps provide a solid foundation for installing Apache. With Apache running, we can proceed to more advanced configurations, such as setting up virtual hosts, in the next section.

Configuring Virtual Hosts

In a multi-website environment, Apache allows us to host multiple domains on a single server using **virtual hosts**. Virtual hosts enable us to manage different websites by specifying distinct configurations for each one. In this section, we will walk through the process of setting up and configuring virtual hosts for different domains, enabling us to efficiently host multiple websites on a single Apache web server.

Step 1: Create a Directory for the Website

Each website hosted on our Apache server requires its document root directory. Let us begin by creating a directory for our first website, example.com:

```
sudo mkdir -p /var/www/example.com/public_html
```

The **`public_html`** folder will hold the website's files. Replace **`example.com`** with the actual domain or project name.

Step 2: Assign Permissions

Set proper permissions for the new directory so that Apache can read and serve the files:

```
sudo chown -R apache:apache /var/www/example.com/public_html
```

This command gives Apache user ownership of the directory.

Step 3: Create a Simple Web Page

Create a basic HTML page to confirm our virtual host is working.

For example: echo "<h1>Welcome to example.com\!</h1>" | sudo tee /var/www/example.com/public_html/index.html

This will create an index.html page with a simple welcome message.

Step 4: Configure the Virtual Host

Apache configuration files for virtual hosts are in **/etc/httpd/conf.d/ directory.** Create a new configuration file for **example.com:**

```
sudo nano /etc/httpd/conf.d/example.com.conf
```

Add the following configuration:

```
<VirtualHost *:80>
    ServerAdmin webmaster@example.com
    DocumentRoot /var/www/example.com/public_html
    ServerName example.com
    ErrorLog /var/log/httpd/example.com_error.log
    CustomLog /var/log/httpd/example.com_access.log combined
</VirtualHost>
```

Let us break this down:

- **ServerAdmin**: Contact email for the webmaster.
- **DocumentRoot**: The root directory for the website's content.
- **ServerName**: The domain name or IP address for the website.
- **ErrorLog and CustomLog**: Log files for debugging and monitoring.

Save and exit the file.

Step 5: Edit the Hosts File

To test the virtual host locally, we need to map the domain name (example.com) to the server's IP address. Edit the **/etc/hosts** file on the local machine:

```
sudo nano /etc/hosts
```

Add the following line: **127.0.0.1 example.com**

This ensures that the domain resolves to the local machine for testing purposes.

Step 6: Restart Apache

To apply the new configuration, restart Apache: **sudo systemctl restart httpd**

Step 7: Test the Virtual Host

Open a web browser and navigate to **http://example.com.** We should see the "**Welcome to example.com!**" message, confirming that the virtual host is properly set up.

Figure 8.4: *Virtual Host Test Validation*

The Virtual Host Test Validation step ensures that the Apache web server is correctly configured to handle requests for a specific domain or subdomain. By accessing the domain associated with the virtual host, we can verify that Apache is routing traffic to the correct directory and serving the appropriate content. In this validation step, visiting the domain (example example.com) should display the custom HTML page created earlier, confirming that the virtual host is functioning as intended. Successful validation of the virtual host setup is crucial for ensuring that the Apache server is properly configured for handling multiple sites or applications on the same server.

If the page is not being displayed, check the error logs:

```
sudo tail -f /var/log/httpd/example.com_error.log
```

Step 8: Configuring Additional Virtual Hosts

To add more websites, repeat the above steps for each domain. Each new site will require:

a. A unique directory under **`/var/www/`**.

b. A corresponding configuration file in **`/etc/httpd/conf.d/`** with a distinct ServerName.

c. Appropriate entries in the **`/etc/hosts file`** (for local testing) or DNS settings (for production).

Example for another site, **`example2.com`**:

- **`sudo mkdir -p /var/www/example2.com/public_html`**
- **`sudo nano /etc/httpd/conf.d/example2.com.conf`**

Then, repeat the configuration steps and set ServerName to example2.com.

Step 9: Managing SSL for Virtual Hosts

For production websites, enabling **SSL** is essential for secure communication. We can configure SSL for each virtual host by using the following configuration:

Install SSL if not already installed:

- `sudo dnf install mod_ssl -y`
- `sudo nano /etc/httpd/conf.d/example.com.conf`

Configure SSL for a virtual host:

```
<VirtualHost *:443>
    ServerAdmin webmaster@example.com
    DocumentRoot /var/www/example.com/public_html
    ServerName example.com
    SSLEngine on
    SSLCertificateFile /etc/ssl/certs/example.com.crt
    SSLCertificateKeyFile /etc/ssl/private/example.com.key
    ErrorLog /var/log/httpd/example.com_error.log
    CustomLog /var/log/httpd/example.com_access.log combined
</VirtualHost>
```

The previous script can be ignored since this is not a production server environment. In each case scenario, it is required to generate or purchase an SSL certificate and specify the paths to the certificate and key files.

Troubleshooting

- **Site not loading**: Ensure that the virtual host configuration file is valid and Apache has been restarted.
- **Permissions issues**: Verify directory permissions and ensure that Apache has the necessary access.

- **Log file errors**: Examine error logs to diagnose specific issues with file paths, server name, or permissions.

This process, known as configuring virtual hosts, enables administrators to efficiently host multiple websites on a single Apache server instance. By assigning each site its own unique set of configurations, including its document root, domain name, access and error logs, and SSL settings–Apache provides a highly flexible and scalable solution for web hosting. This approach not only conserves server resources but also simplifies site management and enhances the ability to isolate and troubleshoot individual sites as needed.

Enhance SSL Configuration Troubleshooting (Rocky Linux 9)

Issue

The SSL configuration section currently lacks practical guidance for diagnosing and fixing HTTPS-related issues. Beginners might find it difficult to interpret SSL errors or misconfigurations without clear steps and examples.

Solution

Expand this section to include a detailed troubleshooting guide specifically tailored for Rocky Linux 9 using Apache (httpd) or Nginx, OpenSSL, and common CA providers such as Let's Encrypt.

Step-by-Step SSL Troubleshooting Guide for Rocky Linux 9

1. **Verify SSL Certificate Installation**

   Check if your certificate and key files are valid and correctly installed:

   - `sudo openssl x509 -in /etc/ssl/certs/yourdomain.crt -text -noout`
   - `sudo openssl rsa -in /etc/ssl/private/yourdomain.key -check`

   Make sure the files exist and have the right permissions:

   - `sudo ls -l /etc/ssl/certs/yourdomain.crt`
   - `sudo ls -l /etc/ssl/private/yourdomain.key`

2. **Confirm Certificate Chain (Intermediate Certificates):** If the certificate chain is incomplete, many browsers will reject the connection. Combine your certificate with the intermediate:

```
cat yourdomain.crt intermediate.crt > fullchain.crt
```

Update your configuration:

Apache:

- `SSLCertificateFile /etc/ssl/certs/fullchain.crt`
- `SSLCertificateKeyFile /etc/ssl/private/yourdomain.key`

Nginx:

- `ssl_certificate /etc/ssl/certs/fullchain.crt;`
- `ssl_certificate_key /etc/ssl/private/yourdomain.key;`

3. **Restart Web Server and Monitor Logs**

   Restart the web server and check for errors:

   - `sudo systemctl restart httpd   # Apache`
   - `sudo systemctl restart nginx   # Nginx`

- `sudo journalctl -xe | grep -i ssl`

Common messages include:

- `SSL_CTX_use_certificate:ca md too weak`
- `ssl3_read_bytes:tlsv1 alert unknown ca`

4. **Test with OpenSSL Client**

   Manually test the HTTPS response:

```
openssl s_client -connect yourdomain.com:443 -servername yourdomain.com
```

Ensure:

- The certificate chain is valid (`**Verify return code: 0 (ok)**`)
- A strong cipher is in use
- There are no self-signed or hostname mismatch errors

5. **Use External SSL Testing Tools**

   Helpful online and local tools include:

- [SSL Labs Test](**https://www.ssllabs.com/ssltest/**)
- Let us encrypt dry run: **`sudo certbot renew --dry-run`**

Error Message	Probable Cause	Suggested Solution
NET::ERR_CERT_COMMON_NAME_INVALID	The Common Name (CN) or Subject Alternative Name (SAN) does not match the requested domain.	Verify that the domain matches the CN/SAN in the certificate.
SSL_ERROR_RX_RECORD_TOO_LONG	Port 443 is not properly configured for SSL/TLS.	Ensure `SSLEngine on` is enabled in the server configuration.
ERR_CERT_DATE_INVALID	Certificate has expired or the system clock is incorrect.	Renew the certificate or correct the server's date and time.
SSL handshake failed	Cipher suite incompatibility or incorrect configuration.	Adjust supported cipher suites in the server configuration.
Self-signed certificate	Certificate authority is not trusted.	Use a certificate issued by a trusted public CA.

***Figure* 8.5:** *Common HTTPS Errors and Fixes*

Figure 8.5 presents a summary of common HTTPS-related errors that system administrators and developers may encounter when configuring SSL/TLS on Rocky Linux 9. These errors can arise due to misconfigured certificates, unsupported protocols, expired credentials, or incorrect domain bindings. For each listed error, the table identifies its most likely root cause and provides a concise, practical solution to aid in rapid diagnosis and resolution. This reference serves as a quick troubleshooting guide to ensure secure and reliable HTTPS deployment.

Best Practices for SSL Configuration

- Keep OpenSSL and CA-related packages up to date: **`sudo dnf update openssl`**
- Enforce secure TLS versions and cipher suites:

Apache:

```
SSLProtocol all -SSLv3 -TLSv1 -TLSv1.1
SSLCipherSuite HIGH:!aNULL:!MD5
```

Redirect HTTP to HTTPS with rewrite rules to enforce secure connections.

SSL/HTTPS Configuration Enhancements

Configuring SSL/HTTPS is essential for securing web servers and encrypting client-server communication. This section highlights common challenges such as certificate errors and redirection issues, offering practical solutions to help us build a reliable, secure HTTPS setup. Proper SSL configuration not only protects sensitive data but also boosts user confidence and meets modern security standards. Understanding these pitfalls early can save time and prevent vulnerabilities in production environments.

When configuring SSL, administrators may encounter a few common issues:

1. Expired or Misconfigured Certificates:
   - Use the following command to check the certificate status:
     `openssl s_client -connect yourdomain.com:443`
   - Look for lines containing `Verify return code: 0 (ok)` to confirm successful validation.
2. Incorrect Certificate File Paths: Ensure the **`SSLCertificateFile`** and **`SSLCertificateKeyFile`** paths in the configuration match the actual location of the certificate files.
3. Missing Intermediate Certificates: Some CAs require an intermediate bundle. Use the **`SSLCertificateChainFile`** directive if needed.
4. Sample Apache HTTPS Output:
   - **`httpd -M | grep ssl`**
   - **`ssl_module (shared)`**

Include documentation for enabling port 443 in firewall:

- **`sudo firewall-cmd --permanent --add-port=443/tcp`**
- **`sudo firewall-cmd -reload`**

By addressing these common issues effectively, the overall security and performance of web servers can be significantly improved. This ensures a safer browsing experience and greater trust from users and stakeholders alike.

Real-World Troubleshooting Enhancements

Effective troubleshooting is essential when deploying secure and reliable web services using Apache, especially in cloud environments such as AWS. Below are some enhanced insights into common issues and solutions:

Apache-Specific Errors

- **DocumentRoot Issues:** Misconfigured or incorrect DocumentRoot paths are a frequent source of Apache errors. Ensure that the specified directory exists and contains the necessary index.html or application files. For example, if the virtual host is pointing to **`/var/www/example.com/public_html`**, verify that this path is accurate and accessible to the Apache service.

- **`.htaccess` Permissions:** Apache may ignore or deny .htaccess files if they lack proper permissions or if the **`AllowOverride`** directive is not set in the virtual host configuration. Make sure the .htaccess file is readable:

  ```
  sudo chmod 644 /var/www/html/.htaccess
  ```

Additionally, ensure the containing directory allows overrides:

```
<Directory "/var/www/html">
    AllowOverride All
</Directory>
```

- **`VirtualHost` Conflicts:** Duplicate ServerName or overlapping **`VirtualHost`** directives can prevent Apache from serving the correct site. Always check for redundancy using:

  ```
  apachectl -S
  ```

This command will display active virtual hosts and highlight configuration conflicts.

AWS Networking Issues

- **Security Group Settings:** Apache will not be reachable from the internet unless the EC2 instance's security group permits inbound traffic on HTTP (port 80) and HTTPS (port 443). Go to the AWS Console and verify the security group rules:
  - Allow inbound TCP on port 80 (HTTP)
  - Allow inbound TCP on port 443 (HTTPS)
- **EC2 Metadata Issues:** Access to EC2 instance metadata can be crucial for dynamic configuration or cloud-aware applications. If metadata access fails, it may indicate a network misconfiguration or a missing IAM role. To test connectivity:

  ```
  curl http://169.254.169.254/latest/meta-data/
  ```

A successful response confirms metadata access; otherwise, check that the instance has appropriate permissions and that no firewall rules are blocking the request.

Apache and MySQL Performance Tuning

Apache Optimizations

- Enable caching:
  - **`sudo a2enmod cache`**
  - **`sudo a2enmod deflate`**
- Enable **`KeepAlive`**:

  ```
  KeepAlive On
  MaxKeepAliveRequests 100
  KeepAliveTimeout 5
  ```

- Adjust **`MaxRequestWorkers`** in **`/etc/httpd/conf.modules.d/00-mpm.conf`**

MySQL Optimizations

- Enable **`slow_query_log`**:

  ```
  SET GLOBAL slow_query_log = 'ON';
  ```

- Tune **`InnoDB`** in **`/etc/my.cnf`**:

  ```
  innodb_buffer_pool_size = 512M
  ```

- Use indexes on frequently queried columns.

Output Samples for Verification

Apache Version Check

```
httpd -v
Server version: Apache/2.4.57 (Rocky Linux)
```

Firewall Rules:

- `firewall-cmd --list-all`
- `services: ssh dhcpv6-client http http`

AWS CLI EC2 Instance Launch

```
aws ec2 run-instances --image-id ami-xxxxxx --instance-type t2.micro   --key-name MyKeyPair --security-groups my-sg
```

Basic Web Server Security Practices

Securing the web server is essential to prevent unauthorized access, data breaches, and service disruptions. While Apache is a robust and secure web server by default, it is important to implement additional security practices to harden the server and reduce vulnerabilities. This section will guide us through some basic security practices that can be easily applied to the Apache web server.

Step 1: Keep Apache and System Updated

Regularly updating the Apache web server and the underlying operating system is one of the most important steps in maintaining security. Security patches and updates fix known vulnerabilities and improve performance. To update Apache and the system packages, run the following commands:

- **`sudo dnf update -y`**
- **`sudo dnf upgrade -y`**

Check Apache's version after updating: **`httpd -v`**.

Ensure that the latest stable version of Apache is always installed and running.

Step 2: Disable Unnecessary Modules

Apache comes with several modules that might not be required for the use case. Disabling unused modules reduces the attack surface. We can disable a module by commenting out the corresponding **`LoadModule`** directive in the **`/etc/httpd/conf/httpd.conf` file.**

To disable the status module at this moment, open the configuration file using the following command: **`sudo nano /etc/httpd/conf/httpd.conf`**.

Find and comment out the line:

```
# LoadModule status_module modules/mod_status.so
```

If it is already commented out with the # sign, no action is necessary.

Save the file and restart Apache: **`sudo systemctl restart httpd`**.

We can also list all enabled modules with: **`httpd -M`**.

Step 3: Limit Server Information Exposure

By default, Apache includes detailed information in error messages, which can be useful for attackers. To limit this exposure, modify the **`ServerTokens`** and **`ServerSignature`** directives in the Apache configuration.

Follow these steps:

a. **Open the `httpd.conf` file**: Open the Apache configuration file in a text editor:

   `sudo nano /etc/httpd/conf/httpd.conf`

   Add the directives: Scroll to the end of the file or search for a suitable section (for example, after the **`LogLevel`** directive or within the global settings section), and add the following lines to limit server information exposure:

   - **`ServerTokens Prod`**
   - **`ServerSignature Off`**
     - **`ServerTokens` Prod:** This will reduce the version of information shown in HTTP headers to just the server's name (example "**`Apache`**").
     - **`ServerSignature` Off:** This disables the footer that includes Apache version and other details on error pages.

b. Save and close the file: After adding the directives, save the file and exit the editor. In nano, press *Ctrl*+O to save, then *Ctrl*+X to exit.

   Restart Apache: After making the changes, restart Apache to apply the new configuration: **`sudo systemctl restart httpd`**.

Step 4: Enable SELinux for Additional Security

SELinux (Security-Enhanced Linux) provides an additional layer of security by enforcing security policies that restrict processes from accessing sensitive resources. SELinux should be enabled for a production server, as it can mitigate the impact of a compromised application.

Check the status of SELinux: **`sestatus`**.

```
[cesarmserver@localhost ~]$ sestatus
SELinux status:                 enabled
SELinuxfs mount:                /sys/fs/selinux
SELinux root directory:         /etc/selinux
Loaded policy name:             targeted
Current mode:                   enforcing
Mode from config file:          enforcing
Policy MLS status:              enabled
Policy deny_unknown status:     allowed
Memory protection checking:     actual (secure)
Max kernel policy version:      33
[cesarmserver@localhost ~]$
```

Figure 8.6: *SELinux Status Output on Rocky Linux*

This figure presents the command output used to verify the status of SELinux (Security-Enhanced Linux) on a Rocky Linux 9 system. The output confirms that SELinux is enabled and operating in enforcing mode, ensuring that defined security policies are actively applied. The targeted policy is loaded, restricting enforcement to specific services to balance security with system usability. Additional details, such as the SELinux root directory, policy version, and memory protection checks, provide further insight into the system's security configuration. This verification step is essential for administrators to confirm that SELinux is functioning correctly and maintaining a hardened security posture.

To enable SELinux, if it is not already enabled, run the following command and reboot:

- `sudo setenforce 1`
- `sudo reboot`

We can configure SELinux to allow or deny specific access based on defined policies.

Step 5: Configure Apache Security Headers

HTTP security headers can protect the server against several common vulnerabilities, such as clickjacking, XSS (Cross-Site Scripting), and other attacks. We can configure these headers in Apache's virtual host configuration.

a. Open the site's configuration file (example **/etc/httpd/conf.d/example.com.conf): sudo nano /etc/httpd/conf.d/example.com.conf**).

b. Add the following directives to enable secure headers at the beginning of the current file:

```
    # Add security headers
    Header always set X-Content-Type-Options "nosniff"
    Header always set X-Frame-Options "SAMEORIGIN"
    Header always set X-XSS-Protection "1; mode=block"
    Header always set Strict-Transport-Security "max-age=31536000; include
SubDomains; preload"
    Header always set Content-Security-Policy "default-src 'self'; script-src
'self';"
```

These headers provide protections such as:

- **X-Content-Type-Options**: Prevents browsers from interpreting files as something else.
- **X-Frame-Options**: Prevents the site from being embedded in an iframe to avoid clickjacking.
- **Strict-Transport-Security**: Forces secure (HTTPS) connections to the site.
- **Content-Security-Policy**: Defines which sources are allowed to load content (useful for preventing XSS).

c. Save the file and restart Apache: **sudo systemctl restart httpd**

Step 6: Restrict Access to Sensitive Files and Directories

There are certain directories and files in the Apache configuration that should not be publicly accessible, such as .htaccess files and server configuration files. Use Apache's Require directive to restrict access to these files.

To restrict access to sensitive files and directories in Apache on Rocky Linux, we should add the necessary directives to the Apache configuration files. It can be completed as follows:

a. **Locate the Apache Configuration Files**: On Rocky Linux, Apache's main configuration file is typically located at **/etc/httpd/conf/httpd.conf.** Additional configuration files are often found in the **/etc/httpd/conf.d/** directory.

b. **Edit the Appropriate Configuration File**: It is recommended to add security directives in the main configuration file (httpd.conf) or within a specific virtual host configuration file located in **/etc/httpd/conf.d/.** This approach ensures that the directives are applied globally or to specific virtual hosts as needed.

c. **Add the Access Restriction Directives**: Within the chosen configuration file, add the following directives to deny access to **.conf**, **.log**, and **phpinfo.php** files. Any other changes will be disregarded at this point, and we will proceed directly to Step e in this section.

```
sudo nano /etc/httpd/conf/httpd.conf
<Directory "/var/www/html">
    <Files "*.conf">
        Require all denied
    </Files>
    <Files "*.log">
        Require all denied
    </Files>
```

```
    <Files "phpinfo.php">
        Require all denied
    </Files>
</Directory>
```

This configuration specifies that any requests to files matching the patterns **`*.conf`**, **`*.log`**, or **`phpinfo.php`** within the **`/var/www/html`** directory will be denied.

d. **Save and Exit the Editor**: After adding the directives, save the changes and exit the text editor.

e. **Test the Apache Configuration**: Before restarting Apache, it is important to test the configuration for syntax errors: **`sudo apachectl configtest`**

   If the output is **`Syntax OK`**, proceed to the next step.

f. **Restart Apache to Apply Changes**:

   To apply the changes, restart the Apache service: **`sudo systemctl restart httpd`**

g. **Verify the Restrictions**: After restarting Apache, verify that access to the specified files is denied by attempting to access them through a web browser. We should receive a 403 Forbidden error when trying to access these files.

Important Considerations:

- **Backup Configuration Files**: Always back up the Apache configuration files before making changes to prevent potential misconfigurations.
- **Use of `.htaccess` Files**: While **`.htaccess`** files can be used to override global settings, it is more efficient to place these directives directly in the main configuration files, especially if we have access to them.
- **Testing**: After applying these changes, thoroughly test the web server to ensure that legitimate access is not inadvertently blocked.

By following these steps, we can effectively restrict access to sensitive files and directories on the Apache web server, enhancing its security.

Step 7: Use Strong Passwords and Secure Authentication

If the web server uses authentication for administrative access, it is critical to use strong passwords. For Apache, we can use **`.htpasswd`** to secure directories. To create a password file:

a. Install the httpd-tools package (if not already installed):

```
sudo dnf install httpd-tools -y
```

b. Create a password file: **`sudo htpasswd -c /etc/httpd/.htpasswd username`**

   This will prompt us to enter a password for the specified user.

c. Edit the Apache configuration to secure the desired directory. For example, to protect **`/var/www/protected`**, add the following to the virtual host or directory configuration: **`sudo nano /var/www/protected`**.

```
<Directory "/var/www/protected">
    AuthType Basic
    AuthName "Restricted Access"
    AuthUserFile /etc/httpd/.htpasswd
    Require valid-user
</Directory>
```

Step 8: Disable Directory Listing

By default, Apache allows users to see a list of files in a directory if no index file is present. Disable this feature to prevent attackers from seeing the contents of the directories. In the Apache configuration file:

a. Open **`/etc/httpd/conf/httpd.conf: sudo nano /etc/httpd/conf/httpd.conf`**

b. Find and disable directory listing by ensuring the Options directive does not include Indexes. Add the following line to this specific file: **`Options -Indexes`**

With *Control* + V navigation to the end of the files is easier. This will prevent users from viewing a list of files if there is no index.html or another default page.

Step 9: Monitor and Analyze Logs

Regularly reviewing Apache's access and error logs is crucial for identifying potential security threats. The logs are stored in **`/var/log/httpd/`**:

- **Access logs**: **`/var/log/httpd/access_log`**
- **Error logs**: **`/var/log/httpd/error_log`**

We can use tail to continuously monitor these logs:

- **`sudo tail -f /var/log/httpd/access_log`**
- **`sudo tail -f /var/log/httpd/error_log`**

Press *Ctrl* + C to exit and return to the command prompt. Set up log rotation to ensure logs do not consume too much disk space. This can be managed with the **`logrotate`** tool.

Step 10: Set Up `Fail2Ban` to Prevent Brute Force Attacks

`Fail2Ban` is a tool that helps prevent brute force attacks by monitoring log files and blocking IP addresses that show malicious activity.

Install Fail2Ban:

- `sudo dnf install epel-release -y`
- `sudo dnf install fail2ban -y`

Enable and start the service:

- `sudo systemctl enable fail2ban`
- `sudo systemctl start fail2ban`
- `sudo systemctl status fail2ban`

Fail2Ban will now monitor Apache logs for failed login attempts and block the IP addresses of attackers.

Troubleshooting

- **Permissions Issues**: Ensure that files are owned by the correct user (apache) and that directory permissions are set correctly.
- **Access Denied Errors**: Double-check the configuration file for any incorrect paths or missing directives.
- **Security Headers Not Working**: Ensure the **`mod_headers`** module is enabled. We can do this by running **`httpd -M | grep`** headers.

These basic security practices can significantly improve the overall security of the Apache web server and ensure that the websites remain protected from common vulnerabilities and attacks. Regular monitoring and updates are essential for maintaining a secure server environment.

Managing Web Server Logs

Managing web server logs is a critical aspect of maintaining, troubleshooting, and securing a web server. Apache web server generates several types of logs that provide valuable insights into the server's performance, access patterns, and potential security issues. In this section, we will cover the basics of Apache's logging mechanism, how to configure and manage logs, and best practices for log analysis and retention.

Step 1: Understanding Apache Log Files

Apache web server primarily generates two types of log files:

- **Access Logs**: These logs capture every request made to the server, including the client's IP address, requested resource, response status, and other details about the request.
- **Error Logs**: These logs capture errors, warnings, and other important messages from the web server. These are useful for identifying problems with server configurations, missing files, or any other issues.

By default, Apache stores these logs in the following directories:

- **Access Logs**: `/var/log/httpd/access_log`
- **Error Logs**: `/var/log/httpd/error_log`

Step 2: Configuring Log Formats

Apache allows us to define the format of the logs through the `LogFormat` directive. We can customize this format to include different pieces of information about each request. The default log format typically looks like this: `LogFormat "%h %l %u %t \"%r\" %>s %b" combined`

Where:

- `%h`: Remote host (client's IP address)
- `%l`: Remote `logname` (not usually used)
- `%u`: Remote user (authenticated user)
- `%t`: Date and time of the request
- `%r`: First line of the request (example `GET /index.html HTTP/1.1`)
- `%>s`: Status code of the response
- `%b`: Size of the response in bytes

To define a custom log format, open the Apache configuration file (`/etc/httpd/conf/httpd.conf` or a `site-specific config` file) and add a new LogFormat directive. For example, to include the user agent and referrer, we can use the following format:

```
LogFormat "%h %u %t \"%r\" %>s %b \"%{Referer}i\" \"%{User-Agent}i\"" extended
```

After modifying the log format, update the CustomLog directive to use the new format: `CustomLog /var/log/httpd/access_log extended`.

Save the changes and restart Apache to apply the new logging configuration:

- `sudo systemctl restart httpd`
- `sudo systemctl status httpd.service`

Step 3: Managing Log Rotation

As web server logs can grow rapidly, it is important to manage log file sizes by rotating them regularly. Apache uses the `logrotate` utility, which is often pre-configured in most Linux distributions.

`Logrotate` is typically configured for Apache in the file **`/etc/logrotate.d/httpd`**. We can edit this file to adjust the log rotation settings, such as the frequency of rotation, the number of backups to retain, and the maximum size of the log files before rotation.

Example of a default configuration for Apache logs:

```
/var/log/httpd/*log {
    monthly
    rotate 12
    compress
    delaycompress
    notifempty
    missingok
    create 640 apache apache
    sharedscripts
    postrotate
        /bin/systemctl reload httpd.service > /dev/null 2>/dev/null || true
    endscript
}
```

Explanation:

- **`monthly`**: Rotate the logs once a month.
- **`rotate 12`**: Keep 12 months' worth of logs.
- **`compress`**: Compress old logs.
- **`delaycompress`**: Compress logs only after the next rotation.
- **`notifempty`**: Do not rotate empty logs.
- **`missingok`**: Do not throw errors if logs are missing.
- **`create 640 apache apache`**: Create new log files with 640 permissions, owned by the apache user and group.
- **`sharedscripts`**: Ensures that the postrotate block runs only once, even if multiple logs are rotated.
- **`postrotate`**: The script to reload the httpd service after rotation to ensure the service continues writing to the new log files. The **`> /dev/null 2>/dev/null || true`** suppresses any errors.

Force log rotation can be completed by running the following command:

```
sudo logrotate -f /etc/logrotate.d/httpd
```

Step 4: Analyzing Logs for Security and Performance

Apache logs can be a valuable tool for identifying security threats and server performance issues. By analyzing both access and error logs, we can spot unusual activities, such as brute-force attacks, unauthorized access attempts, and slow-performing requests.

a. **Identifying Suspicious Activity:** Look for repeated failed login attempts, especially in the error logs:

   ```
   sudo grep "authentication failure" /var/log/httpd/error_log
   ```

   In the access log, look for patterns such as unusual user-agents, multiple requests from the same IP address, or requests for nonexistent files:

   ```
   sudo grep "404" /var/log/httpd/access_log
   ```

b. **Performance Monitoring:** To analyze server performance, examine the response times and status codes in the access logs. For example, filter for 500 status codes (server errors):

```
sudo grep "500" /var/log/httpd/access_log
```

This can help identify server misconfigurations or resource issues.

b. **Using Log Analysis Tools:** There are several log analysis tools that can automate the process of log monitoring and provide detailed insights into web traffic. Some popular tools include:

- **GoAccess**: A real-time web log analyzer.
- **AWStats**: A popular log analyzer for generating reports.
- **Logwatch**: A log analysis tool for system logs.

To install GoAccess on the system: **`sudo dnf install goaccess -y`**

We can then analyze the Apache access logs using GoAccess:

```
sudo goaccess /var/log/httpd/access_log -o /var/www/html/report.html
--log-format=COMBINED
```

This command generates a detailed HTML report of the access logs that we can view in the browser.

Step 5: Implementing Log Forwarding for Centralized Logging

For large-scale deployments or environments with multiple servers, it is useful to implement centralized logging. This allows us to aggregate logs from multiple web servers into a specific location for easier analysis and monitoring.

Apache supports log forwarding through the **`syslog`** facility. To forward logs to a remote syslog server, modify the Apache configuration to use syslog:

- `sudo nano /etc/httpd/conf/httpd.conf`
- `CustomLog "|/usr/bin/logger -t apache" combined`
- `sudo systemctl restart httpd`

This forwards the logs to the system's syslog, which can then be sent to a centralized log management system (example ELK stack, Graylog, or Splunk).

Step 6: Enabling and Configuring Logwatch

Logwatch is a system log analyzer that can provide daily reports of Apache server activities. To install Logwatch: **`sudo dnf install logwatch -y`**.

Create a simple script that automates the process of updating the Logwatch configuration to resolve the issue. This script will check and fix the Service directive in the **`logwatch.conf`** file, ensuring that it is correctly set for Apache and removing any conflicting entries. Adding entries is needed for the service to work.

```
sudo nano /etc/logwatch/conf/logwatch.conf
Service = All
- http
- ssh
```

Steps to Create the Update Script:

a. **Create a new script file**, such as **`update_logwatch_conf.sh`**, which will automatically modify the Logwatch configuration file.

To do this, open the script file in a text editor:

```
sudo nano /usr/local/bin/update_logwatch_conf.sh
```

b. **Add the Script Content**: In the script, add the following content to ensure that the Service directive is properly set:

```
#!/bin/bash

# File path to the logwatch configuration
CONFIG_FILE="/etc/logwatch/conf/logwatch.conf"

# Check if the Service directive is set to 'http' and update if necessary
if grep -q "^Service = " "$CONFIG_FILE"; then
    sudo sed -i 's/^Service = .*/Service = http/' "$CONFIG_FILE"
else
    echo "Service = http" | sudo tee -a "$CONFIG_FILE" > /dev/null
fi

# Ensure there are no conflicting 'Service = All' entries
sudo sed -i '/^Service = All/d' "$CONFIG_FILE"

echo "Logwatch configuration has been updated to monitor Apache logs."
```

c. **Make the Script Executable**:

After saving the script, make it executable:

```
sudo chmod +x /usr/local/bin/update_logwatch_conf.sh
```

Run the Script: Now, we can run the script to automatically fix the Logwatch configuration:

```
sudo /usr/local/bin/update_logwatch_conf.sh
```

This script will:

Check if the **`Service = http`** entry exists and update it if necessary.

Remove any conflicting **`Service = All`** entries.

Append the correct **`Service = http`** entry if it does not exist.

Troubleshooting

- **Logs Not Appearing**: Ensure that Apache has permission to write to the log files. Check the ownership and permissions of the log directory (**`/var/log/httpd/`**) and files.
  ```
  sudo chown apache:apache /var/log/httpd/*
  ```
- **Log Rotation Not Working**: Verify that logrotate is installed and the configuration files are correct. We can manually test log rotation with:
  ```
  sudo logrotate -d /etc/logrotate.d/httpd
  ```
- **Missing Logs**: If logs are missing or empty, verify that Apache is configured to log requests. Check the CustomLog directive in the Apache configuration file to ensure it points to the correct log location.

Managing Apache web server logs effectively is crucial for system monitoring, security analysis, and troubleshooting. By configuring log formats, analyzing logs for potential issues, and implementing log rotation, we can ensure that our Apache server runs securely and efficiently. Regular log monitoring can help us spot security vulnerabilities and improve overall server performance.

Setting up PHP and MySQL for Dynamic Content

Dynamic web applications require a backend stack to process user inputs, manage data, and serve dynamic content. One of the most popular combinations is the **LAMP stack** (Linux, Apache, MySQL/

MariaDB, PHP). This lab focuses on setting up PHP and MySQL on **Rocky Linux** to create a fully functional environment for hosting dynamic websites.

By the end of this lab, a fully functional server capable of running PHP scripts and interacting with a MySQL database to serve dynamic content will be available.

Installing PHP with a graphical interface on Rocky Linux 9 can be made easier by using tools such as Cockpit or DNFDragora. Follow the next steps:

Step 1. Install Cockpit

Cockpit is a web-based server management interface that simplifies server administration tasks.

a. Install Cockpit: **`sudo dnf install cockpit -y`**.

b. Start and enable Cockpit: **`sudo systemctl enable --now cockpit.socket`**.

c. Access Cockpit:

   i. Open the browser and navigate to **`https://<your-server-ip>:9090`**.

   ii. Log in with our root or user credentials.

d. Use Cockpit to Manage Software:

   i. Navigate to the Applications or Software section.

   ii. Search for php, select the PHP packages needed (for example: **`php`**, **`php-fpm, php-mysqlnd`**), and install them.

   iii. Or use the command prompt to install the following packages:

```
sudo dnf install php php-cli php-common php-fpm php-mysqlnd
```

Step 2. Verify PHP Installation

After installing PHP, verify the installation: **`php -v`**.

To ensure the PHP module is enabled for Apache: **`sudo systemctl restart httpd`**.

Step 3. Install MySQL

MySQL is the database that will store the dynamic content.

a. Install the MySQL server: **`sudo dnf install mysql-server -y`**.

b. Enable and start MySQL:

   - `sudo systemctl enable mysqld`
   - `sudo systemctl start mysqld`

c. Secure the MySQL installation: **`sudo mysql_secure_installation`**.

d. Set a root password and follow the prompts to secure the setup.

Step 4: Verify MySQL Installation

a. Log in to MySQL: **`sudo mysql -u root -p`**

b. Verify the server is running:

```
SHOW DATABASES;
Exit MySQL:
EXIT;
```

The topic of database management will be explored in greater depth in *Chapter 9, Database Management*, of this book. This chapter provides a comprehensive guide on installing and configuring MySQL and MariaDB, implementing effective database backup and restore strategies, optimizing database performance, and introducing AWS RDS for managed database services. Additionally, it will cover approaches to scaling databases in cloud environments. Each topic is designed to cater to beginners, with clear explanations in the chapter and supplementary downloadable guides for practical learning.

Step 5: Connect PHP to MySQL

a. Install PHP-MySQL module: **`sudo dnf install php-mysqlnd -y`**.

b. Restart Apache to apply changes: **`sudo systemctl restart httpd`**.

Step 6: Create a Sample PHP-MySQL Script

a. Create a PHP file to test the connection: **`sudo nano /var/www/html/dbtest.php`**

b. Add the following code:

```
<?php
$servername = "localhost";
$username = "root";
$password = "your_root_password";

// Create connection
$conn = new mysqli($servername, $username, $password);

// Check connection
if ($conn->connect_error) {
    die("Connection failed: " . $conn->connect_error);
}
echo "Connected successfully to MySQL!";
?>
```

c. Save and close the file.

d. Access the script in the browser: **`http://<server-ip>/dbtest.php`**

In this case, the server IP address is the **`local ipv4 address`**. If successful, the following message will be displayed: "**`Connected successfully to MySQL!`**"

Step 7: Adjust Firewall and SELinux (if necessary)

a. Open HTTP and HTTPS ports:

- `sudo firewall-cmd --permanent --add-service=http`
- `sudo firewall-cmd --permanent --add-service=https`
- `sudo firewall-cmd --reload`

b. Adjust SELinux for Apache and PHP:

- `sudo setsebool -P httpd_can_network_connect on`

The setup of the PHP and MySQL environment on Rocky Linux has been effectively completed. This setup serves as a foundation for hosting dynamic websites or applications. From this point, more complex applications can be built, CMS platforms such as WordPress can be installed, or custom PHP code can be experimented with.

Scalable Web Server Deployment with ELB and Auto Scaling on AWS

In modern cloud infrastructure, scalability and high availability are critical for delivering reliable web services. AWS provides powerful tools such as Elastic Load Balancing (ELB) and Auto Scaling to help distribute traffic and adapt to changing workloads automatically. When combined with Apache web servers hosted on EC2 instances, this architecture enables seamless scaling and improved fault tolerance.

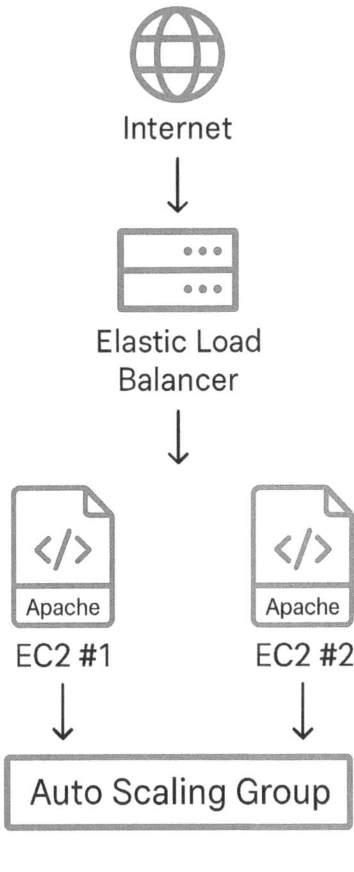

Figure 8.7: *EC2 Deployment with ELB and Auto Scaling*

This diagram illustrates the flow of web traffic in a horizontally scalable architecture on AWS. Incoming requests from users on the internet are first directed to the Elastic Load Balancer (ELB), which intelligently distributes the traffic across multiple EC2 instances running the Apache web server. These instances are part of an Auto Scaling Group, which dynamically adjusts the number of EC2 instances based on real-time demand and resource utilization. This setup ensures high availability, fault tolerance, and efficient load distribution, making it well-suited for web applications that experience variable traffic patterns.

Deploying Web Servers in AWS

Deploying a web server in AWS offers the benefits of cloud scalability, high availability, and simplified management. In this section, we will walk through the process of deploying an Apache web server on an AWS EC2 instance, setting up auto-scaling to handle varying traffic loads, and configuring an ELB to efficiently distribute incoming traffic.

Step 1: Launching an EC2 Instance

The first step in deploying a web server on AWS is to launch an EC2 instance. AWS EC2 (Elastic Compute Cloud) provides scalable compute capacity, and we can choose from a variety of instance types depending on the requirements.

a. **Log in to AWS Management Console**: Go to the AWS Management Console and log in with your credentials.

b. **Launch a New EC2 Instance**: Navigate to the EC2 dashboard, click "**`Launch Instance`**," and follow these steps:

   i. **Choose an Amazon Machine Image (AMI)**: Select an Amazon Linux 2 AMI, which is a free, stable, and secure operating system optimized for the AWS cloud.

   ii. **Choose an Instance Type**: Select a suitable instance type, such as t2.micro for low-cost testing or t2.medium for more performance.

   iii. **Configure Instance Details**: Leave the default settings or adjust them based on our needs. Ensure the network is set to the default VPC (Virtual Private Cloud) and configure the subnet.

   iv. **Add Storage**: The default 8 GB of Elastic Block Store (EBS) storage is sufficient for this basic setup.

   v. **Configure Security Group**: Create a new security group or use an existing one. Open the necessary ports:

      - HTTP (Port 80) for web traffic.
      - SSH (Port 22) for remote access to the instance.

   vi. **Launch the Instance**: Choose a key pair for SSH access and click "**`Launch`**".

c. **Access the EC2 Instance**: Once the EC2 instance is running, obtain the public IP address of the instance from the EC2 dashboard. Use SSH to connect to the instance: **`ssh -i /path/to/your-key.pem ec2-user@your-ec2-public-ip`**

Replace **`/path/to/your-key.pem`** with the path to the key pair and **`your-ec2-public-ip`** with the public IP of the instance.

Step 2: Installing Apache on the EC2 Instance

After accessing the EC2 instance, install Apache to serve web content. The Amazon Linux 2 AMI comes with the Apache HTTP Server package, but if it is not installed, we can do so with the following command:

- `sudo yum update -y`
- `sudo yum install httpd -y`

Once installed, start the Apache service and enable it to start on boot:

- `sudo systemctl start httpd`
- `sudo systemctl enable httpd`

To test the installation, open the public IP address of the instance in a browser. We should see the Apache default test page, confirming that the web server is working.

Step 3: Configuring Apache for the Website

We can now configure Apache to serve the web content. By default, Apache serves content from **`/var/www/html`**. We can upload the HTML files or web application code here.

a. **Create a simple webpage**:

   Create an index.html file in the /var/www/html directory:

   ```
   sudo nano /var/www/html/index.html
   ```

   Add some content to test our server:

   ```
   <html>
   <head>
     <title>Welcome to My Website</title>
   </head>
   <body>
     <h1>Apache Web Server on AWS EC2</h1>
     <p> This web server is successfully deployed! </p>
   </body>
   </html>
   ```

b. **Restart Apache**: After adding the content, restart Apache to ensure the changes are reflected:

   ```
   sudo systemctl restart httpd
   ```

Ensure Security Group Allows HTTP Traffic

a. Go to the **`AWS Management Console`**.

b. Navigate to **`EC2 > Instances`** and select the instance.

c. Under **`Security Groups`**, edit the **`Inbound Rules`** to include:

   i. **Type**: HTTP

   ii. **Protocol**: TCP

   iii. **Port Range**: 80

   iv. **Source**: Anywhere (0.0.0.0/0) or a specific range.

Now, if we visit the public IP address of our EC2 instance, we should see the web page we just created. Alternatively, there are several additional options for integration with the command-line interface, if needed.

- `sudo dnf install links`
- `curl http://localhost`
- `links http://<Public IP address>`

Step 4: Setting Up Auto Scaling

To ensure that the web server can handle varying levels of traffic, we can configure Auto Scaling in AWS. Auto Scaling automatically adjusts the number of EC2 instances in the application's scaling group to handle the traffic.

a. **Create an Auto Scaling Group**:

   i. **Navigate to EC2 Dashboard**: On the AWS Management Console, go to the EC2 dashboard and find the "Auto Scaling" section under "Auto Scaling Groups."

   ii. **Create Launch Configuration**: This configuration specifies how to launch new EC2 instances in the scaling group. Choose an existing AMI (Amazon Machine Image), configure instance types (such as t2.micro or larger for more traffic), and select the security group created earlier.

   iii. **Create Auto Scaling Group**: Define the Auto Scaling group, selecting the launch configuration we just created. Set the desired number of instances (example 2 instances for redundancy), minimum instances (1), and maximum instances (example 5) based on expected traffic.

vi. **Set Scaling Policies**: Define policies for scaling up and down. For example, the Auto Scaling group can be set to launch new instances when CPU usage exceeds 70% and scale down when CPU usage is below 30%.

b. **Monitor Auto Scaling**: The Auto Scaling group will automatically adjust the number of EC2 instances based on traffic. Administrators can monitor the health of instances in the group from the AWS Management Console under "**`Auto Scaling Groups`**."

Step 5: Configuring Elastic Load Balancer (ELB)

To ensure even distribution of traffic to all running instances in the Auto Scaling group, we should set up an ELB.

a. **Create an ELB**:

i. **Navigate to the EC2 Dashboard**: In the AWS Management Console, go to the EC2 dashboard and click "**`Load Balancers`**" under the "**`Load Balancing`**" section.

ii. **Create Load Balancer**: Choose an Application Load Balancer or Network Load Balancer. An Application Load Balancer is recommended for web traffic because it operates at the HTTP/HTTPS layer.

iii. **Configure Listeners**: Set up a listener on port 80 (HTTP) and link it to the Auto Scaling group.

iv. **Register Instances**: Register the EC2 instances in the Auto Scaling group with the Load Balancer. The ELB will automatically distribute traffic among them.

b. **Test Load Balancing**: Once the ELB is configured, access the DNS name of the load balancer (for example, **`my-load-balancer-123456.elb.amazonaws.com`**) in a browser. The load balancer will distribute traffic across all available EC2 instances in the Auto Scaling group.

Step 6: Configuring Auto Scaling and Load Balancer Health Checks

To ensure high availability, AWS offers health checks that monitor the health of the EC2 instances. These checks help the Auto Scaling group automatically replace any unhealthy instances.

i. **Health Checks for EC2**: Configure EC2 instance health checks in the Auto Scaling group settings. AWS will monitor the health of instances based on HTTP response codes from the web server (for example, if the EC2 instance fails to respond to HTTP requests, it will be marked as unhealthy).

ii. **Health Checks for Load Balancer**: The ELB also performs health checks on the EC2 instances it routes traffic to. Configure the health check path (for example, **`/index.html`**) to monitor if the web server is responding correctly.

Step 7: Final Testing and Monitoring

After deploying the web server, setting up Auto Scaling, and configuring the ELB, we should test the system to ensure it functions correctly under load.

a. **Simulate Traffic**: Use a tool such as Apache JMeter or LoadImpact to simulate a heavy load on the web server and observe how Auto Scaling handles the traffic.

b. **Monitor Performance**: AWS CloudWatch provides detailed metrics and logs for monitoring instance health, CPU usage, and network traffic. Set up CloudWatch alarms to notify us if any issues arise with the EC2 instances or load balancer.

By following these steps, we have successfully deployed a scalable web server infrastructure in AWS using EC2, Auto Scaling, and Elastic Load Balancing. This architecture ensures that the web application can handle varying traffic loads and remains available, even during peak traffic periods. With the flexibility of AWS, we can easily scale up or down as needed, while ensuring optimal performance and availability.

Important Note: Please be careful to add monitoring services for the network devices in the cloud, as additional charges may be incurred on the credit card by Amazon for these services, such as CloudWatch or VPC Flow Logs.

Conclusion

In this chapter, we explored the complete process of setting up a reliable web server using Apache, focusing on best practices for configuration and security. We began with the installation of Apache and the configuration of virtual hosts, allowing multiple websites to be hosted on a single server. Security was a key focus, covering essential measures such as securing sensitive files, configuring firewalls, and implementing SSL certificates to encrypt web traffic. Additionally, we examined web server logs, highlighting their importance in monitoring and troubleshooting server performance to ensure a seamless user experience.

To enhance functionality, we delved into the integration of dynamic content by installing and configuring PHP and MySQL, enabling the deployment of interactive and data-driven websites. We also explored cloud-based deployments, specifically using AWS. By leveraging AWS EC2 instances and Auto Scaling, we can ensure high availability and scalability, allowing web servers to efficiently handle varying levels of traffic. These cloud-based strategies enhance performance, reliability, and resource efficiency for production environments.

Looking ahead, the next chapter will focus on database management, covering the installation and configuration of MySQL/MariaDB, along with best practices for backup and restoration. We will also explore database performance tuning to optimize efficiency and reliability. Finally, we will examine AWS RDS as a cloud-based database solution and discuss strategies for scaling databases in cloud environments to ensure seamless performance under increasing workloads.

Points to Remember

- **Apache Web Server Installation:** Apache is one of the most widely used web servers. It can be easily installed on Linux systems (including Rocky Linux) using package managers such as dnf or yum.
- **Virtual Hosts Configuration**:
    - Virtual hosts allow hosting multiple websites on a single server. This is achieved by configuring Apache to differentiate between different domains or subdomains.
    - Important configuration files include **`httpd.conf`** and individual site configuration files in **`/etc/httpd/conf.d/`**.
- **Web Server Security Practices:**
    - Implement basic security measures, such as setting up firewalls, securing Apache configuration files, and using SSL/TLS encryption.
    - Regularly update Apache and associated software to patch known vulnerabilities.
    - Use .htaccess files for directory-level security and to manage access control.
- **Managing Web Server Logs:**
    - Apache generates log files such as access.log and error.log that track server activity and errors.

  - These logs are crucial for troubleshooting, monitoring server performance, and detecting security issues.
  - Configuration of log file locations and log levels is done in httpd.conf.
- **Setting Up PHP and MySQL for Dynamic Content:**
  - PHP allows Apache to process dynamic content. Installing PHP with Apache enables support for server-side scripting.
  - MySQL (or MariaDB) provides a database backend for dynamic content, such as user data, e-commerce systems, and content management systems (CMS).
  - Configuring Apache to work with PHP and MySQL involves installing the necessary packages and ensuring the correct configurations in Apache's httpd.conf.
- **Deploying Web Servers in AWS:**
  - AWS provides scalable infrastructure to deploy web servers using EC2 instances. Auto Scaling helps adjust the number of instances in response to traffic.
  - Use Elastic Load Balancing (ELB) to distribute incoming traffic across multiple EC2 instances for high availability.
  - For deployment, configure AWS security groups and key pairs for secure access.
- **Scalability and High Availability:**
  - Leverage AWS services such as EC2 Auto Scaling to dynamically scale web servers based on demand.
  - Implementing redundancy through multiple instances and regions can ensure high availability and minimize downtime.
- **Backup and Recovery:**
  - Regularly back up both server configurations and web content (including databases) to prevent data loss.
  - AWS offers automated backups and snapshots for EC2 instances and RDS databases.

Multiple Choice Questions

1. Which command is used to install the Apache web server in Rocky Linux?
   a. `yum install apache2`
   b. `dnf install apache2`
   c. `apt-get install apache2`
   d. `yum install httpd`
2. What file is used to configure virtual hosts in Apache on Rocky Linux?
   a. `/etc/httpd/httpd.conf`
   b. `/etc/httpd/vhosts.conf`
   c. `/etc/apache2/vhosts.conf`
   d. `/etc/httpd/conf.d/vhost.conf`
3. Which of the following is a best practice for securing an Apache web server?
   a. Disable `mod_rewrite`
   b. Enable SSL/TLS with a certificate

   c. Allow all traffic on port 80
   d. Disable server status monitoring
4. Which command is used to restart the Apache web server after making configuration changes?
   a. `systemctl stop apache2`
   b. `systemctl restart apache2`
   c. `systemctl restart httpd`
   d. `systemctl reload httpd`
5. What is the purpose of the ErrorLog directive in Apache configuration?
   a. To specify the location of access logs
   b. To define the log level for Apache errors
   c. To configure SSL certificates
   d. To set the server name for virtual hosts
6. Which PHP package is necessary to enable Apache to process PHP scripts?
   a. `php`
   b. `php-fpm`
   c. `httpd-php`
   d. `php-apache`
7. What is the function of AWS Elastic Load Balancer (ELB) when deploying a web server in AWS?
   a. To automatically provision EC2 instances
   b. To distribute incoming web traffic across multiple EC2 instances
   c. To store static content such as images and videos
   d. To provide persistent block storage for EC2 instances
8. What is the purpose of Auto Scaling in AWS?
   a. To increase the compute power of EC2 instances manually
   b. To automatically adjust the number of EC2 instances based on traffic demand
   c. To store backups of EC2 instances
   d. To configure network settings for EC2 instances
9. Which file is commonly used for configuring SSL certificates in Apache?
   a. `/etc/httpd/conf.d/ssl.conf`
   b. `/etc/apache2/sites-available/ssl.conf`
   c. `/etc/httpd/ssl/ssl.conf`
   d. `/etc/ssl/ssl.conf`

10. Which AWS service is best suited for storing static content for a web server, such as images and videos?

    a. EC2

    b. S3

    c. RDS

    d. EBS

Answers

1. d
2. d
3. b
4. c
5. b
6. a
7. b
8. b
9. a
10. b

Questions

1. What is the primary function of the Apache web server in a Linux environment?
2. Which command is used to install the Apache web server on Rocky Linux?
3. What configuration file is used to define virtual hosts in Apache on Rocky Linux?
4. What is the purpose of configuring SSL/TLS on an Apache web server?
5. Which command is used to restart the Apache web server after making changes to its configuration?
6. What is the role of the DocumentRoot directive in Apache's configuration?
7. Which PHP package is required to run PHP scripts with Apache on Rocky Linux?
8. What is the purpose of AWS Elastic Load Balancer (ELB) when deploying a web server in AWS?
9. Which AWS service can be used to automatically scale the number of EC2 instances based on traffic demand?
10. What is the recommended file format for SSL certificates in Apache on Rocky Linux?

Key Terms

- **Apache Web Server**: A widely used open-source web server software that serves content over the HTTP/HTTPS protocols. It is essential for hosting websites and can run on Linux, including Rocky Linux.
- **Virtual Hosts**: A method for configuring Apache to host multiple websites on a single server by mapping different domains or subdomains to specific directories.
- **SSL/TLS**: Protocols used to encrypt data transmitted between the server and clients. SSL certificates are essential for securing web traffic, and Apache can be configured to support HTTPS using these protocols.
- **DocumentRoot**: A directive in Apache configuration that specifies the directory where website files are stored. It is the root directory from which Apache serves web content.
- **`mod_rewrite`**: An Apache module used for rewriting URLs. It is commonly used for SEO-friendly URLs, redirects, and other URL manipulations.
- **PHP**: A server-side scripting language used to build dynamic content on websites. It is integrated with Apache to process PHP files on the web server.
- **`mod_ssl`**: An Apache module that enables SSL/TLS support, allowing the Apache web server to serve content securely over HTTPS.
- **Elastic Load Balancer (ELB)**: A service provided by AWS to distribute incoming web traffic across multiple EC2 instances, ensuring high availability and reliability of web applications.
- **Auto Scaling**: An AWS service that automatically adjusts the number of EC2 instances based on the incoming web traffic, helping maintain optimal performance and cost efficiency.
- **Elastic Compute Cloud (EC2)**: An AWS service that provides resizable compute capacity in the cloud. EC2 instances are used to run web servers such as Apache, enabling dynamic scalability based on demand.

CHAPTER 9
Database Management

Introduction

Databases are the foundation of modern applications, powering everything from small websites to large-scale enterprise systems. In this chapter, we will learn how to manage databases effectively on **Rocky Linux**, with a focus on **MySQL** and **MariaDB**—two of the most widely adopted open-source database platforms. Through practical guidance on installation, configuration, and optimization, we will develop the skills to handle data efficiently across both local and cloud environments.

But we go beyond the basics. This chapter also explores advanced topics such as **database backups**, **performance tuning**, and **cloud integration**. A special focus is placed on **Amazon RDS**, a fully managed service that simplifies deployment, scaling, and high availability in the cloud. By the end, we will be equipped not only to manage robust database systems on Rocky Linux but also to harness the power of cloud solutions for **scalable, secure, and highly available** deployments.

Structure

This chapter covers the following topics:

- Installing and Configuring MySQL/MariaDB
- Database Backup and Restore Strategies
- Performance Tuning for Databases
- Introduction to AWS RDS for Database Management
- Scaling Databases in Cloud Environments

Installing and Configuring MySQL/MariaDB

Databases are essential to modern digital infrastructure, enabling efficient storage, retrieval, and management of data. For system administrators, understanding database management is key to maintaining the reliability and performance of enterprise systems. This chapter provides practical guidance on deploying and managing MySQL and MariaDB on Rocky Linux, highlighting their stability, scalability, and open-source advantages. Through step-by-step instruction, it covers installation, configuration, user access control, performance optimization, and secure backup and recovery—emphasizing real-world scenarios that ensure data integrity and continuity.

The chapter also introduces Amazon RDS, a cloud-based service that simplifies database deployment, and offers built-in scalability, automated backups, advanced security features, and seamless integration with other AWS services to support high-availability and distributed environments. By integrating both traditional and cloud-native approaches, system administrators gain a comprehensive foundation to manage databases effectively across on-premises and cloud environments. This knowledge empowers administrators to adapt to evolving technology landscapes, and meet the demands of modern data-driven applications with confidence.

Check Available Modules

Run the following commands to confirm if the mysql module is available and the system updates were previously completed:

- `sudo dnf update -y`
- `sudo dnf module list`

Look for mysql in the list of modules. If it is not there, it indicates that the module is not included in the enabled repositories.

Enable Extra Repositories: Ensure that the necessary repositories, such as AppStream or any specific repository for MySQL, are enabled: **`sudo dnf repolist`**.

If AppStream or other required repositories are missing, enable them:

```
sudo dnf config-manager --enable appstream
```

Regenerate Metadata

Clear cached repository data and regenerate it:

- `sudo dnf clean all`
- `sudo dnf makecache`

Installing MySQL Directly

If the MySQL module is not available, MySQL can be installed either from the default Rocky Linux repository or by enabling the official MySQL repository provided by Oracle. This approach ensures access to a stable and up-to-date version of the database server.

Installation and Configuration

Installing MySQL:

- `sudo dnf install @mysql`
- `sudo systemctl enable --now mysqld`
- `sudo mysql_secure_installation`

Verifying installation: **`mysql -V`**

Sample Output:

`mysql  Ver 8.0.32 for Linux on x86_64` (Source distribution)

a. **Install MySQL from DNF:** `sudo dnf install mysql-server -y`

b. **Use the Official MySQL Repository:**

Download the MySQL repository configuration package:

- `sudo dnf install` **`https://dev.mysql.com/get/mysql80-community-release-el8-1.noarch.rpm`**

Enable the MySQL 8.0 repository:

- `sudo dnf config-manager --enable mysql80-community`

Install MySQL Server:

- `sudo dnf install mysql-community-server -y`

  It seems like we are encountering two issues:

a. **GPG check failed error:** This occurs when the system is unable to verify the authenticity of a package due to missing or incorrect GPG keys. To resolve this, we can try the following:

Clear the DNF cache: `sudo dnf clean all`

Import the correct GPG key if necessary or update the key for the repository. For example:

- `sudo rpm --import https://repo.mysql.com/RPM-GPG-KEY-mysql`
- `sudo dnf install https://dev.mysql.com/get/mysql80-community-release-el8-1.noarch.rpm`

Then try installing the package again.

b. **Incorrect MySQL Version Check Command:** The error displayed with the `mysql --versionbs` command occurs due to a typo. The correct command to check MySQL's version is: `mysql -version`

c. **Verify Installation:** After installation, verify that MySQL is installed:

- `mysql -version`
- `mysql -V`

Start and Enable MySQL Service: Start and enable the MySQL service:

- `sudo systemctl start mysqld`
- `sudo systemctl enable mysqld`

Basic Configuration

After installation, the database server is accessible, and the initial configurations can be performed.

1. Log in to the database server: `mysql -u root -p`
2. Create a new database: `CREATE DATABASE example_db;`
3. Create a new user and grant privileges:
```
CREATE USER 'example_user'@'localhost' IDENTIFIED BY 'strong_password';
GRANT ALL PRIVILEGES ON example_db.* TO 'example_user'@'localhost';
FLUSH PRIVILEGES;
```
4. Test the configuration: Exit the root account and log in as the new user: `mysql -u example_user -p`

   Verify access to the database: `SHOW DATABASES;`

The question mark (?) will display the available options. Once the `exit` command is executed, the previous Rocky Linux CLI interface will be restored.

Database Security Best Practices

User Management:

```
CREATE USER 'readonly'@'%' IDENTIFIED BY 'StrongP@ss!';
GRANT SELECT ON database.* TO 'readonly'@'%';
```

Firewall Configuration:

```
sudo firewall-cmd --permanent --add-service=mysql
sudo firewall-cmd --reload
```

Security Recommendations:

- Disable root remote login.
- Use strong passwords and rotate regularly.
- Regularly update MySQL/MariaDB packages.

Managing a Sample Database Schema

The following script creates a sample schema with tables for audit logs, database versions, employees, and more. To create the script, execute the command **`sudo nano initialize_db.sql`**, and then add the following content:

```
CREATE TABLE audit (
  modified_by_ip   VARCHAR(39)  NOT NULL DEFAULT '',
  modified_by_user VARCHAR(50)  NOT NULL DEFAULT '',
  modified_when    BIGINT(14)   NOT NULL,
  modified_from    BIGINT(14)   NOT NULL,
  modified_to      BIGINT(14)   NOT NULL,
  modified_why     VARCHAR(250) NOT NULL DEFAULT '',
  user_modified    VARCHAR(50)  NOT NULL DEFAULT '',
  PRIMARY KEY (modified_when),
  UNIQUE KEY modified_when (modified_when)
) ENGINE=MyISAM;

CREATE TABLE dbversion (
  dbversion DECIMAL(5, 1) NOT NULL DEFAULT '0.0',
  PRIMARY KEY (dbversion)
) ENGINE=MyISAM;

INSERT INTO dbversion VALUES ('1.4');

CREATE TABLE employees (
  empfullname     VARCHAR(50) NOT NULL DEFAULT '',
  tstamp          BIGINT(14) DEFAULT NULL,
  employee_passwd VARCHAR(25) NOT NULL DEFAULT '',
  displayname     VARCHAR(50) NOT NULL DEFAULT '',
  email           VARCHAR(75) NOT NULL DEFAULT '',
  user_groups     VARCHAR(50) NOT NULL DEFAULT '', -- Renamed to user_groups
  office        VARCHAR(50) NOT NULL DEFAULT '',
  admin           TINYINT(1)  NOT NULL DEFAULT '0',
  reports         TINYINT(1)  NOT NULL DEFAULT '0',
  time_admin      TINYINT(1)  NOT NULL DEFAULT '0',
  disabled        TINYINT(1)  DEFAULT NULL,
  PRIMARY KEY (empfullname)
) ENGINE=MyISAM;

INSERT INTO employees VALUES ('admin', NULL, 'xy.RY2HT1QTc2', 'administrator',
'', '', '', 1, 1, 1, NULL);

CREATE TABLE user_groups ( -- New table for user groups
  groupname VARCHAR(50) NOT NULL DEFAULT '',
  groupid   INT(10)     NOT NULL AUTO_INCREMENT,
  officeid  INT(10)     NOT NULL DEFAULT '0',
  PRIMARY KEY (groupid)
) ENGINE=MyISAM;

CREATE TABLE info (
```

```
  fullname  VARCHAR(50) NOT NULL DEFAULT '',
  status    VARCHAR(50) NOT NULL DEFAULT '', -- Renamed from inout to status
  timestamp BIGINT(14) DEFAULT NULL,
  notes     VARCHAR(250) DEFAULT NULL,
  ipaddress VARCHAR(39) NOT NULL DEFAULT '',
  KEY fullname (fullname)
) ENGINE=MyISAM;

CREATE TABLE metars (
  metar     VARCHAR(255) NOT NULL DEFAULT '',
  timestamp TIMESTAMP    NOT NULL,
  station   VARCHAR(4)   NOT NULL DEFAULT '',
  PRIMARY KEY (station),
  UNIQUE KEY station (station)
) ENGINE=MyISAM;

CREATE TABLE offices (
  officename VARCHAR(50) NOT NULL DEFAULT '',
  officeid   INT(10)     NOT NULL AUTO_INCREMENT,
  PRIMARY KEY (officeid)
) ENGINE=MyISAM;

CREATE TABLE punchlist (
  punchitems VARCHAR(50) NOT NULL DEFAULT '',
  color      VARCHAR(7)  NOT NULL DEFAULT '',
  in_or_out  TINYINT(1) DEFAULT NULL,
  PRIMARY KEY (punchitems)
) ENGINE=MyISAM;

INSERT INTO punchlist VALUES ('in', '#009900', 1);
INSERT INTO punchlist VALUES ('out', '#FF0000', 0);
INSERT INTO punchlist VALUES ('break', '#FF9900', 0);
INSERT INTO punchlist VALUES ('lunch', '#0000FF', 0);
```

This script demonstrates how to create tables, insert data, and manage the structured data in a relational database. Next, ensure that the correct permissions are assigned to the file by running the following command: **`sudo chmod 755 initialize_db.sql`**

Check MySQL/MariaDB Connection

Make sure the administrators have MySQL or MariaDB installed and running. We can check the MySQL service status by running: **`sudo systemctl status mysqld`**

If it is not running, start it using: ***sudo systemctl start mysqld***

Run the Script

Since the script is in the home directory, we can run it by following these steps:

Method 1: Using MySQL Command Line

Log in to MySQL as a superuser or root with appropriate permissions to the target database: **`sudo mysql -u root -p`**

a. **Verify User Existence**

   Run the following query to check if the user exists:

   ```
   SELECT user, host FROM mysql.user WHERE user = 'username';
   ```

If no entry is found for **'localhost'**, Linux administrators need to create the user.

b. **Create the User**

If the user does not exist, create it with the desired password by executing the following command:

```
CREATE USER 'username'@'localhost' IDENTIFIED WITH mysql_native_password BY
'NewStrongP@ssw0rd!';
FLUSH PRIVILEGES;
```

Replace **'username'** with the desired account name, and '**NewStrongP@ssw0rd!**' with a secure password. The **FLUSH PRIVILEGES;** command ensures that the changes take effect immediately.

Clarifications:

- Added single quotes around localhost ip address, which is the current IP address for our local Rocky Linux virtual machine, to ensure proper syntax.
- Provided context for the **FLUSH PRIVILEGES;** command.

c. **Grant Privileges to the User**

Once the user is created, grant the necessary privileges:

```
GRANT ALL PRIVILEGES ON *.* TO 'username'@'localhost' WITH GRANT OPTION;
```

d. **Reload Privileges**

Apply the changes by reloading the privileges:

```
FLUSH PRIVILEGES;
```

Configuring MySQL for Remote Access and Ensuring Proper Permissions

- Ensure that MySQL is configured to allow remote connections. Modify the configuration file **sudo nano/etc/my.cnf** and set the **bind-address** as follows: **bind-address = 0.0.0.0**
- Ensure that no firewall rules are blocking access from the **localhost** IP address. Adjusting firewall settings may be necessary to permit **external connections.**

Log in to MySQL as a regular user with appropriate permissions to the target database:

```
sudo systemctl restart mysqld mysql -u your_user -p
```

After entering the password, select the appropriate database to ensure that the script can be executed on the correct target. Use the **USE** command followed by the database name to switch to the desired database.

```
SHOW DATABASES;
USE your_database_name;
```

Then, execute the script: `source /home/username/initialize_db.sql;`

Replace **/home/username/initialize_db.sql** with the correct path if it is different. This should execute the script and create the tables as defined.

Method 2: Running the Script Directly from the Command Line

Alternatively, we can run the script directly from the terminal without entering the MySQL client. Use the following command:

```
mysql -u your_user -p your_database_name < /home/username/initialize_db.sql
```

Make sure to replace **your_user** with the actual MySQL username and **your_database_name** with the name of the database desired. This ensures the script runs under the correct user and operates on the specified database.

Verify Execution

a. **List Available Databases:** First, confirm access to the relevant database by listing all available databases. This helps verify that the target database exists and can be accessed:

SHOW DATABASES;

This will display all available databases. For example:

```
mysql> SHOW DATABASES;
+--------------------+
| Database           |
+--------------------+
| example_db         |
| information_schema |
| my_database        |
| mysql              |
| performance_schema |
| sys                |
+--------------------+
6 rows in set (0.01 sec)
```

Figure 9.1: *Database's Information*

Figure 9.1 illustrates the structure and contents of the database, showcasing key tables such as audit, dbversion, employees, user_groups, and info. Each able fulfills a distinct role in supporting database functionality: the audit table records changes and activities, while the dbversion table maintains the current schema version. The employees and user_groups tables manage organizational and access-related data, and the *info* table stores general information. This visualization provides a structured overview of the database, emphasizing how these interconnected tables support data management and operational integrity.

Select a Database: Before running **`SHOW TABLES`**, select a database. For example, if the current database is named **`my_database`**, use: **`USE my_database;`**

This will set **`my_database`** as the active database.

Show Tables

Now that a database is selected, we can run the **`SHOW TABLES`** command to list its tables: **`SHOW TABLES;`**

Complete Example:

```
mysql> USE my_database;
Database changed
mysql> SHOW TABLES;
+----------------------+
| Tables_in_my_database |
+----------------------+
| audit                |
| dbversion            |
| employees            |
| info                 |
| metars               |
| offices              |
| punchlist            |
| user_groups          |
+----------------------+
8 rows in set (0.00 sec)
```

Figure 9.2: *Use a Database and Display the Tables*

Figure 9.2 demonstrates the process of selecting a database and viewing its tables using MySQL commands. The USE command activates the specified database, making it the current working context for subsequent operations. Once the database is active, the SHOW TABLES command lists all tables contained within it, providing an overview of its structure and available data. This step is fundamental for database navigation, enabling administrators and developers to confirm table availability before performing queries or modifications.

This section explored the installation and configuration of MySQL and MariaDB on Rocky Linux, two widely adopted and reliable database systems. Covered topics included initial setup, user permission management, performance tuning, and backup and recovery strategies. With these foundations, readers are now prepared to administer MySQL and MariaDB in local environments, establishing the skills needed to advance toward more complex database management and optimization tasks.

Troubleshooting Tips

If the database service fails to start, check the status and logs:

- `sudo systemctl status mysqld`
- `sudo journalctl -xe`

Ensure the firewall allows database connections (if applicable):

- `sudo firewall-cmd --add-service=mysql -permanent`
- `sudo firewall-cmd --reload`

Database Backup and Restore Strategies

Data is the backbone of modern applications, and ensuring its availability is crucial for business continuity. Database backup and restore operations are essential to protect against risks such as hardware failures, software corruption, or accidental deletions. These processes not only provide peace of mind but also form the cornerstone of a solid disaster recovery plan. Regular backups and verified restoration procedures ensure that critical data can be quickly recovered, minimizing downtime and mitigating potential financial or reputational losses. This section explores strategies for managing MySQL and MariaDB backups and restorations on Rocky Linux, covering built-in tools, advanced solutions, and cloud-based integration. With this guide, administrators will gain the knowledge needed to implement reliable, customized backup strategies for their database systems.

Understanding Backup Types

Before implementing a backup strategy, it is essential to understand the various types of backups:

- **Full Backup:** Captures the entire database, providing a complete snapshot. Recommended critical points in time.
- **Incremental Backup:** Captures only the changes made since the last backup, reducing storage requirements.
- **Differential Backup:** Backs up changes made since the last full backup, balancing storage and recovery time.

Select the backup type based on the specific requirements for the recovery time objective (RTO) and available storage capacity. Consider how quickly data needs to be recovered and how much storage space can be allocated for backups.

Backing Up Databases

Using `mysqldump`

To modify the lab using **example_db** for the backups, please kindly follow the steps with the **example_db**:

1. Log in to MySQL as root:

   ```
   sudo mysql -u root -p
   ```

   This command is correct. We will be prompted for the MySQL root user password.

2. Show databases:

   ```
   SHOW DATABASES;
   ```

   This SQL command is correct and will list all available databases in MySQL.

3. Use a specific database (replace **example_db** with the desired database name): **USE example_db;**

   This command is correct. It switches to the **example_db** database, allowing us to work within it. Make sure the database exists; otherwise, an error might be displayed.

4. Create a new table with columns:

   ```
   CREATE TABLE example_table (
       id INT AUTO_INCREMENT PRIMARY KEY,
       name VARCHAR(255) NOT NULL
   );
   ```

   This SQL command is also correct. It creates a table named **example_table** with two columns:

   a. **id**: An integer that auto-increments and is the primary key.

   b. **name**: A string of up to 255 characters that cannot be **NULL**.

Summary of corrections:

- Ensure that the database exists before using the **USE** statement.
- The SQL syntax looks good for the **CREATE TABLE** command.

Comprehensive and Updated Lab Guide: MySQL Backup and Restoration Using **example_db**

Objective: This guide provides updated step-by-step instructions for performing MySQL backups and restoration using the **example_db** database.

a. **Log in to MySQL**: Log in to MySQL using the root user (or the appropriate user): **mysql -u root -p**

b. **Use the Database:** Switch to the **example_db** database: **USE example_db;**

c. **Verify Tables in example_db**: Check the tables in **example_db** to ensure they exist:

   ```
   SHOW TABLES;
   ```

d. **Backup the Entire Database**: To create a full backup of **example_db**, use the following command:

   ```
   mysqldump -u root -p example_db > example_db_backup.sql
   ```

5. Backup Multiple Databases

   To back up both **example_db** and another database, for instance **my_database**, use:

   ```
   mysqldump -u root -p --databases example_db my_database > multiple_databases_backup.sql
   ```

6. Backup All Databases: To back up all databases, use:
   `mysqldump -u root -p --all-databases > all_databases_backup.sql`
7. Backup Database Structure Only: To back up just the structure (without the data) of **example_db**, use:
   `mysqldump -u root -p --no-data example_db > example_db_structure.sql`
8. Backup Specific Tables - To back up specific tables, such as **table1** and **table2**, use:
   `mysqldump -u root -p example_db table1 table2 > example_db_tables_backup.sql`
9. Return to the Main Menu

   Press *Ctrl* + C to return to the main menu. To validate if **table1** and **table2** exist, list all tables in the **example_db** database: **SHOW TABLES IN example_db;**
10. Exit MySQL:

    After completing tasks, type the following to exit MySQL: **exit**
11. Ensure Backup Creation on Rocky Linux - From the Rocky Linux interface, run:
    `mysqldump -u root -p example_db > example_db_backup.sql 2>&1`
    This ensures the backup process is initiated correctly.
12. Check the Backup Files: After creating the backups, list the backup files to verify their existence:
    - `ls -lh example_db_backup.sql`
    - `ls -lh multiple_databases_backup.sql`
13. Restoring from Backups - To restore from the backup, use the following command:
    `mysql -u root -p example_db < example_db_backup.sql`

Important Notes:

- *Ensure that the tables to be backed up (for example,* ***table1***, ***table2****) exist in the* ***example_db*** *database.*
- *Verify that sufficient disk space is available for large databases.*
- *Always confirm the integrity of backup files by checking their size or opening them to inspect their contents.*
- *Regularly test the backup process to ensure it runs smoothly and data can be restored successfully.*

With these updated steps, users can confidently backup and restore the **example_db** database, ensuring that all critical elements are handled correctly, from verifying backup commands to checking MySQL permissions and available disk space. For any persistent issues, further assistance is available to ensure a seamless backup and restoration process.

Backup and Disaster Recovery

Ensuring data integrity and continuity of operations is a core responsibility of any database administrator. In the context of Rocky Linux and MySQL/MariaDB, implementing an effective backup and disaster recovery (DR) strategy is crucial for minimizing downtime and data loss in the event of failures.

Full Database Backup

A full backup creates a snapshot of the entire database at a specific point in time. This backup includes all databases, user privileges, and system tables. It is especially useful for disaster recovery or for migrating databases.

Command Example:

```
mysqldump --all-databases --single-transaction --quick --lock-tables=false > /
backups/full_backup.sql
```

Explanation:

a. **all-databases:** Dumps all databases on the server.

b. **single-transaction:** Ensures the backup is consistent without locking tables (ideal for InnoDB).

c. **quick:** Reduces memory usage by retrieving rows one at a time.

d. **lock-tables=false:** Avoids locking tables during the dump, which is helpful in high-availability environments.

It is recommended to store backups in a dedicated, versioned directory such as `**/backups/YYYY-MM-DD/full_backup.sql**`.

Restoration Process

In the event of a failure or data corruption, restoring from a full backup is straightforward.

Command Example: **mysql < /backups/full_backup.sql**

Step-by-Step Procedure:

a. Start the MySQL Server (if not already running): **sudo systemctl start mysqld**

b. Verify the Backup File Exists: **ls -lh /backups/full_backup.sql**

c. Run the Restore Command: **mysql -u root -p < /backups/full_backup.sql**

d. Enter the password when prompted.

e. Verify Restoration: After the command completes without errors, verify the restoration: **mysql -u root -p**

Then inside the MySQL shell:

```
SHOW DATABASES;
```

Verify restoration by logging into the MySQL shell and checking the list of databases.

Point-In-Time Recovery (PITR)

Point-in-Time Recovery allows restoration of a database to a specific moment just before a failure or unwanted transaction occurred. This process depends on the use of binary logs.

Requirements: Binary logs must be enabled in the MySQL configuration file (`**my.cnf**`):

```
ini
  [mysqld]
  log-bin=mysql-bin
```

A full backup from a well-known state.

The set of binary logs recorded after the backup.

Recovery Steps:

Restore the full backup: **mysql < /backups/full_backup.sql**

Apply binary logs up to the desired recovery point:

```
mysqlbinlog --stop-datetime="2025-06-02 12:45:00" /var/lib/mysql/mysql-
bin.000001 | mysql
```

We can use `**--start-datetime**` and `**--stop-datetime**` to narrow down the exact time range of changes.

Automating Backups with Cron

Automating backups helps ensure consistency and reduce the risk of human error. Cron jobs can be scheduled for daily or weekly backups.

Example: Daily Full Backup at 2 AM:

```
0 2 * * * /usr/bin/mysqldump --all-databases > /backups/$(date +\%F)_full_
backup.sql
```

Always verify that backup jobs are completing successfully and consider setting up alerting mechanisms in case of failures.

Real-World Case Study: Retail Company Recovery

A retail company experienced a critical hardware failure that caused its main MySQL server to crash in the middle of a business day. Fortunately, the company had a solid backup and recovery strategy in place.

Actions Taken: A new Rocky Linux server was provisioned using an infrastructure-as-code template.

- MySQL was installed and configured to mirror the original setup.
- A recent full backup was restored using the **mysqldump** file.
- Binary logs were applied using point-in-time recovery to restore the last hour of transactions.
- Total time to full restoration: 47 minutes.

This timely recovery minimized financial loss, preserved customer trust, and demonstrated the value of proper disaster planning.

Best Practices for Backup and Recovery

- Store backups in multiple locations, including offsite or cloud-based storage (for example, Amazon S3, Azure Blob).
- Regularly test backup restoration procedures to verify integrity.
- Encrypt backups to ensure data confidentiality.
- Maintain a schedule that includes weekly full backups and daily binary logs.
- Implement automated monitoring of backup scripts and log output.

Recommended Tools and Utilities

- **mysqldump:** Ideal for logical backups.
- **mysqlpump:** Faster alternative to **mysqldump,** supports parallel processing.
- **mysqlbinlog:** Used to parse and apply binary logs for PITR.
- **Percona XtraBackup:** Enables hot, physical backups for InnoDB.
- **Mydumper/Myloader:** High-speed multithreaded backup and restore tool.

Automating processes with crontab

The first step is to start the crond process:

- `sudo systemctl start crond`
- `sudo systemctl enable crond`

Then, open the crontab editor: **`crontab -e`**

Add the following cron job:

```
0 2 * * * mysqldump -u root -p example_db > /path/to/backup/example_db_$(date
+\%F).sql
```

On the keyboard, escape and: **`wq`** is required to save these changes successfully.

Restoring Databases

a. **Restoring from Backup Files**

   Restore a Single Database: **`mysql -u root -p example_db < example_db_backup.sql`**

   Restore All Databases: **`mysql -u root -p < all_databases_backup.sql`**

b. **Verifying Restoration**

   Post-restoration, verify data integrity: **`mysql -u root -p`**

```
SHOW DATABASES;
USE example_db;
SHOW TABLES;
```

Best Practices for Backup and Restore

- **Encrypt Backups:** Use tools such as `**gpg**` to encrypt backups for security.
- **Store Backups Securely:** Maintain multiple copies in secure locations, including offsite or cloud storage (for example, AWS S3).
- **Regular Testing:** Periodically test restoration processes to ensure data integrity.
- **Automate Processes:** Use scripts and scheduling tools to reduce human error.
- **Monitor Backup Logs:** Check logs to confirm successful completion of scheduled backups.

Advanced Backup Tools

Percona XtraBackup is an essential open-source tool used for performing hot backups of MySQL and MariaDB databases without disrupting ongoing operations. It allows for efficient, non-blocking backups, making it ideal for high-availability environments where downtime must be minimized. XtraBackup provides a reliable and consistent backup solution, ensuring that data can be restored accurately without corruption. Its importance lies in its ability to create full backups, incremental backups, and support point-in-time recovery, all while maintaining minimal impact on system performance. For businesses and organizations relying on large-scale, high-performance databases, Percona XtraBackup is a critical tool to ensure data protection, disaster recovery, and business continuity.

It is now recommended to follow the steps outlined below to complete the process.

Step 1: Add the Percona repository

First, the administrators need to add the Percona repository to the system. We can do this by downloading and installing the Percona YUM repository configuration package:

```
sudo dnf install -y https://repo.percona.com/yum/percona-release-latest.
noarch.rpm
```

Step 2: Install Percona XtraBackup

The Percona XtraBackup package is still not found, which means the repository configuration is not correct or the specific version we are trying to install is not available in the repository.

Let us go through a more detailed troubleshooting and solution process:

a. **Check that the Percona repository is enabled:** Ensure that the Percona repository is enabled and properly configured. We can list all enabled repositories with the following command: **`sudo dnf repolist enabled`**

   Look for **Percona** on the list. If it is not listed, try enabling it explicitly:

   ```
   sudo percona-release setup ps80
   ```

   This sets up the repository for Percona XtraBackup compatible with MySQL 8.0. Afterward, try installing the package again: **`sudo dnf install -y percona-xtrabackup-80`**

b. **Check the package availability:** Sometimes, specific versions of packages might not be available immediately after the installation of a repository. We can search for the available packages in the Percona repository using: **`sudo dnf search percona-xtrabackup`**

   This will show all versions of **`XtraBackup`** available. If we find the package listed, try installing it with the exact version name.

Step 3: Verify the installation

a. After the installation is complete, we can verify it by checking the version of Percona **`XtraBackup: xtrabackup --version`**

b. Cloud-Based Backup Solutions

   Cloud storage solutions provide reliable offsite backups. For example, using AWS S3:

   1. Install and configure AWS CLI. This step has been guided in previous chapters.
      - `mkdir -p /home/cmorera/backup_file`
      - `touch /home/cmorera/backup_file/backup_data.txt`
   2. Upload backups to S3:

      ```
      aws s3 cp /home/cmorera/backup_file/backup_data.txt s3://cesarrocky9/
      ```
   3. Use lifecycle policies to automate the retention and deletion of old backups.

By implementing these database backups and restoring strategies, data can be effectively safeguarded, ensuring business continuity. These practices are particularly critical in production environments where high availability and reliability are essential. From basic **`mysqldump`** commands to advanced tools such as Percona XtraBackup and AWS S3 integration, Rocky Linux administrators have a diverse set of options to address their specific requirements.

Replication and High Availability in MySQL/MariaDB and AWS RDS

In today's always-on digital world, database uptime and reliability are non-negotiable. Replication and high availability (HA) are the backbone of resilient database systems, ensuring continuous service and data protection. This section explores two popular approaches: the traditional MySQL/MariaDB asynchronous master-slave replication, and AWS RDS Multi-AZ–a cloud-native, fully managed solution with automatic failover and synchronous replication. We will break down their differences in complexity, reliability, and performance to help us choose the right strategy for the environment.

MySQL/MariaDB Replication: Asynchronous master-slave setup using binlog.

AWS RDS Multi-AZ:

- Automatic failover.
- Synchronous replication across availability zones.

Feature	MySQL/MariaDB Replication	AWS RDS Multi-AZ
Type	Asynchronous	Synchronous
Failover Time	Manual	Automatic
Setup Complexity	High	Low
Maintenance	Manual	AWS Managed

***Figure* 9.3:** *Feature Comparison: MySQL/MariaDB Replication versus AWS RDS Multi-AZ*

Figure 9.3 resents a comparative overview of MySQL/MariaDB asynchronous replication and AWS RDS Multi-AZ synchronous replication. The table contrasts critical aspects such as replication type, failover behavior, setup complexity, and ongoing maintenance responsibilities. By outlining these differences, it provides a practical reference for selecting the most appropriate replication strategy, depending on infrastructure requirements, operational expertise, and desired availability.

Performance Tuning for Databases

Efficient database performance is vital for ensuring the reliability and speed of modern applications, particularly in environments with high data volumes and frequent transactions. Optimizing performance helps databases meet user demands without bottlenecks or failures, which is essential for providing a seamless user experience and achieving business goals. This guide provides practical insights and step-by-step instructions for optimizing MySQL and MariaDB databases on Rocky Linux. By focusing on key areas such as configuration tuning, query optimization, and resource management, administrators can create a robust and scalable database infrastructure that supports growing operational needs.

Understanding Database Performance Metrics

Database performance is influenced by multiple factors. Understanding key metrics helps identify and address bottlenecks effectively:

- **Query Response Time:** Measures the time taken to execute queries. High response times often indicate inefficient queries or system constraints.
- **CPU and Memory Usage:** Elevated usage may point to inadequate hardware resources or poorly optimized queries.
- **Disk I/O:** Since databases depend heavily on disk operations, high latency in disk I/O can significantly degrade performance.

Steps to Monitor Metrics

1. **Check Server Status:**
   - `sudo systemctl status mysqld   # For MySQL`
   - `sudo systemctl status mariadb  # For MariaDB`

2. Install Monitoring Tools: **`sudo dnf install sysstat -y`**
3. Use System-Level Commands:
   - **`top`**: Monitors running processes.
   - **`iostat`**: Observes CPU, memory, and disk usage.

Optimizing MySQL/MariaDB Configuration

The MySQL/MariaDB configuration file (**`/etc/my.cnf`**) contains critical parameters for database performance. Adjusting these settings can yield substantial improvements.

1. **Backup the Configuration File**

Before making any changes, back up the current configuration:

```
sudo cp /etc/my.cnf /etc/my.cnf.backup
```

2. **Key Performance Tuning Parameters**

Edit the configuration file to include the following optimized parameters:

```
sudo nano /etc/my.cnf
```

3. **Add or modify** the following in the **`[mysqld]`** section one line at the time restarting the service per line edited:

```
[mysqld]
innodb_buffer_pool_size = 2G
max_connections = 300
join_buffer_size = 2M
tmp_table_size = 128M
max_heap_table_size = 128M
slow_query_log = 1
slow_query_log_file = /var/log/mysql/mysql-slow.log
long_query_time = 2
```

4. **Save and close the file:**
   - **Nano**: Press *Ctrl*+O, then *Enter*, followed by *Ctrl*+X.
   - **Vi**: Press *Esc*, type **`:wq`**, and hit *Enter*.

5. **Restart the MySQL/MariaDB Service**

   Apply the changes by restarting the database server:

```
sudo systemctl restart mysqld   # For MySQL
```

6. **Verify Configuration Changes**

Log in to the MySQL/MariaDB shell and confirm the updates: **`sudo mysql -u root -p`**

Run these commands to verify the applied changes:

```
SHOW VARIABLES LIKE 'innodb_buffer_pool_size';
SHOW VARIABLES LIKE 'max_connections';
SHOW VARIABLES LIKE 'tmp_table_size';
SHOW VARIABLES LIKE 'max_heap_table_size';
```

7. **Monitor Performance**

Monitor MySQL performance and logs for stability:

```
sudo journalctl -xeu mysqld.service
```

8. **Optimize Tables**

Reclaim unused space and defragment data files to improve performance by running the following SQL command for each table:

```
mysql> show DATABASES;
mysql> Use my_database
mysql> show TABLES;
mysql> OPTIMIZE TABLE offices;
```

This last command optimized the table and improved its performance.

9. **Analyze and Optimize Queries**

- **Enable Slow Query Log**: Capture and review slow queries by enabling the slow query log. Use the command: ***sudo tail -f /var/log/mysql/mysql-slow.log***
- **Analyze Queries Using EXPLAIN**: Identify inefficient queries with the **`EXPLAIN`** statement. For example:
  ```
  SELECT * FROM employees;
  ```

This is a basic filter to find information regarding the employees of the company in the table.

10. **Test the Configuration**

Test database performance under load to ensure the settings are optimized. Use **`sysbench`** to benchmark: **`sudo dnf install sysbench -y`.**

Running Other Benchmarks: For other types of benchmarks, such as CPU, memory, or fileio, the new syntax is also different. Here is how to use a CPU benchmark as an example: **`sysbench cpu --cpu-max-prime=20000 run`**

Similarly, for memory benchmarking: **`sysbench memory --memory-block-size=8K --memory-total-size=10G run`**

11. **Regular Maintenance**

- **Schedule Routine Optimization**: Regularly optimize tables and review queries for potential inefficiencies.
- **Update MySQL/MariaDB**: Keep the database up to date by running the following command:
  ```
  sudo dnf update -y
  ```

12. **Optional: Upgrade Hosting**

If the current hardware cannot meet performance demands, consider upgrading to high-performance cloud VPS services, such as **`Shape.host`**, which provide SSD storage and expert support for optimal MySQL performance.

Monitoring with Open-Source Tools

Effective monitoring of database services is essential to ensure performance, availability, and scalability. In Rocky Linux environments, open-source tools such as Prometheus and Grafana are widely used to collect, store, and visualize real-time metrics. This section explores how to implement a monitoring system using **`mysqld_exporter`** to collect MySQL/MariaDB metrics and configure visualizations using Grafana.

Prometheus and Exporters

Prometheus is a monitoring and metrics collection tool that uses a pull model, and a query language called PromQL. To integrate Prometheus with services such as MySQL, exporters are used to expose metrics in a format Prometheus can scrape.

Installing mysqld_exporter

Steps to install **mysqld_exporter** on Rocky Linux:

a. `sudo useradd -rs /bin/false mysqld_exporter`

b. `wget https://github.com/prometheus/mysqld_exporter/releases/download/v0.15.0/mysqld_exporter-0.15.0.linux-amd64.tar.gz`

c. `tar xvf mysqld_exporter-0.15.0.linux-amd64.tar.gz`

d. `sudo cp mysqld_exporter-0.15.0.linux-amd64/mysqld_exporter /usr/local/bin/`

e. `sudo chown mysqld_exporter:mysqld_exporter /usr/local/bin/mysqld_exporter`

MySQL Access Configuration

Create a MySQL user for the exporter:

```
CREATE USER 'exporter'@'localhost' IDENTIFIED BY 'exporter_password' WITH MAX_
USER_CONNECTIONS 3;
GRANT PROCESS, REPLICATION CLIENT, SELECT ON *.* TO 'exporter'@'localhost';
```

Then create a configuration file:

```
echo "DATA_SOURCE_NAME='exporter:exporter_password@(localhost:3306)/'" > /etc/
default/mysqld_exporter
```

systemd Service Configuration

Create the service file: **sudo nano /etc/systemd/system/mysqld_exporter.service**

Paste the following content:

```
[Unit]
Description=Prometheus MySQL Exporter
After=network.target

[Service]
User=mysqld_exporter
EnvironmentFile=/etc/default/mysqld_exporter
ExecStart=/usr/local/bin/mysqld_exporter
Restart=always

[Install]
WantedBy=multi-user.target
```

Enable and start the service:

- `sudo systemctl daemon-reexec`
- `sudo systemctl enable --now mysqld_exporter`

Collected Metrics

Useful metrics provided by `**mysqld_exporter**` include:

mysql_global_status_threads_connected: Number of active connections.

mysql_global_status_slow_queries: Number of slow queries.

mysql_global_status_innodb_data_reads / writes: Disk I/O operations.

mysql_uptime_seconds: MySQL server uptime.

Grafana Dashboards: Grafana enables interactive dashboards to visualize data from Prometheus.

Integrating Prometheus

Steps:

a. Log into **`Grafana`** (default: http://localhost:3000).

b. Navigate to **`Configuration`** > **`Data Sources`**.

c. Add Prometheus as a data source.

d. Use **`URL: http://localhost:9090`**

Creating Specific Panels

Examples of PromQL queries:

- CPU usage: **`rate(node_cpu_seconds_total{mode!="idle"}[1m])`**
- Active MySQL connections: **`mysql_global_status_threads_connected`**
- Slow queries: **`increase(mysql_global_status_slow_queries[5m])`**
- Uptime: **`mysql_uptime_seconds`**

Alert Rules

Example rules:

- More than 100 active connections: **`mysql_global_status_threads_connected > 100`**
- Sudden spike in slow queries:
  `increase(mysql_global_status_slow_queries[1m]) > 10`

Continuous monitoring is vital for identifying and resolving issues before they impact users. With Prometheus, **`mysqld_exporter`**, and Grafana, system administrators gain full visibility into database health. Proactive alerting and customized dashboards help ensure availability and performance.

Introduction to AWS RDS for Database Management

Amazon Relational Database Service (RDS) is a fully managed cloud database solution provided by Amazon Web Services (AWS). It simplifies the setup, operation, and scaling of relational databases, enabling organizations to focus on application development and innovation rather than database maintenance. AWS RDS supports multiple database engines, including MySQL, MariaDB, PostgreSQL, Oracle, and SQL Server, making it versatile for a variety of workloads.

Key Features of AWS RDS

- **Automated Backups and Snapshots:** One of the core features of AWS RDS is its automated backup system. By default, RDS performs daily backups of the database during a predefined backup window, ensuring data safety and recovery options. Additionally, users can take manual snapshots to create specific recovery points. These backups can be retained for up to 35 days, providing flexibility for different business needs.

  Example: A retail company uses RDS automated backups to recover data after a transaction system crash during peak shopping hours. By restoring from a snapshot taken minutes before the incident, the company avoids significant downtime.

- **Multi-AZ Deployments:** Multi-AZ (Availability Zone) deployments enhance database availability and reliability. In this configuration, RDS automatically replicates the database to a standby instance in a different availability zone. This ensures automatic failover in case of maintenance or hardware failures, minimizing disruption to critical applications.
- **Read Replicas:** To handle read-intensive workloads, AWS RDS offers read replicas for engines like MySQL, MariaDB, and PostgreSQL. Read replicas distribute query load, reducing strain on the primary database and improving performance. They also support horizontal scaling, making them ideal for large-scale applications.
- **Scalability:** AWS RDS provides flexible scaling options:
    - **Vertical Scaling:** Adjust instance sizes to increase CPU, memory, or storage capacity without downtime.
    - **Storage Scaling:** Dynamically increase storage or IOPS (Input/Output Operations Per Second) as application demands grow.
    - **Example:** An e-commerce platform uses RDS to scale up during Black Friday sales, ensuring high availability and quick response times despite increased traffic.
    - **Security:** AWS RDS integrates robust security features, including:
    - **Encryption at Rest and In Transit:** Protects sensitive data using AWS Key Management Service (KMS).
    - **Access Control:** Employs AWS Identity and Access Management (IAM) to define fine-grained user permissions.
    - **Monitoring and Metrics:** RDS integrates seamlessly with Amazon CloudWatch, enabling real-time monitoring of key database metrics such as CPU utilization, memory usage, and query performance. Administrators can set up alerts to proactively address issues before they escalate.

Setting Up an AWS RDS Instance

Step-by-Step Guide

1. **Log in to AWS Management Console:** Navigate to the RDS dashboard.
2. **Select Database Engine:** Choose from supported engines such as MySQL or PostgreSQL.
3. **Choose Deployment Options:** Opt for "`Multi-AZ Deployment`" for high availability or a single instance for development purposes.
4. **Configure Instance Settings:** Specify instance class, storage type (SSD or provisioned IOPS), and Virtual Private Cloud (VPC).
5. **Set Up Credentials:** Define a master username and password for secure database access.
6. **Configure Connectivity:** Enable public or private access and adjust security group rules to allow specific IP addresses or EC2 instances.
7. **Review and Launch:** Confirm configurations and create the database. The instance will be ready for use within minutes.

Best Practices: For production environments, always enable Multi-AZ deployments and configure automatic backups.

Performance Monitoring

Monitoring is essential for maintaining optimal database performance. Use Amazon CloudWatch to track:

- **CPU Utilization:** High values may indicate inefficient queries or resource constraints.
- **Database Connections:** Ensure sufficient connections to handle user traffic.
- **Free Storage Space:** Prevent disruptions by monitoring available storage.

Automated Backups and Restore

To restore a database from a snapshot:

1. Navigate to the RDS dashboard.
2. Select a snapshot.
3. Click "`Restore Snapshot`" to create a new instance with the same data.

Scaling Database Instances: Adjust the instance size or storage as needed via the RDS dashboard. Scaling operations are seamless and can be performed with minimal downtime.

Applying Maintenance Updates: AWS RDS schedules maintenance during a preferred window. Updates include minor version upgrades, patching, and hardware replacements. Plan maintenance windows during low-traffic periods to minimize impact.

Advantages of AWS RDS

- **Ease of Use:** Simplifies database deployment and management with an intuitive interface.
- **Cost-Effective:** `Pay-as-you-go` pricing accommodates small startups and large enterprises alike.
- **Scalability:** Dynamically adjusts resources to match workload requirements.
- **Reliability:** Multi-AZ deployments ensure high availability and fault tolerance.
- **Security:** Robust encryption and access controls protect sensitive data.

Common Use Cases for AWS RDS

- **Web Applications:** AWS RDS is ideal for hosting dynamic web applications requiring scalable, reliable databases.

  Example: A social media platform uses MySQL on RDS to store user data, handling millions of transactions daily.
- **E-Commerce Platforms:** RDS supports secure storage and management of transactional data for online shopping systems.
- **Data Warehousing:** Read replicas enable efficient data analysis without impacting the primary database.
- **Development and Testing:** Quickly deploy isolated database environments for development and testing purposes.

  By leveraging AWS RDS, organizations can focus on innovation and application development while AWS handles the complexities of database management. From automated backups to advanced security features, RDS offers tools to deploy scalable, reliable database solutions effortlessly. This fully managed service empowers businesses to meet their database needs efficiently in both local and global environments.

Cloud Deployment with AWS RDS

Launching RDS via CLI:

```
aws rds create-db-instance \
--db-instance-identifier mydb \
--db-instance-class db.t3.micro \
--engine mysql \
--allocated-storage 20 \
--master-username admin \
--master-user-password Secure123 \
--backup-retention-period 7
Sample Output:
{
  "DBInstance": {
    "DBInstanceIdentifier": "mydb",
    "DBInstanceStatus": "creating"
  }
}
```

- **Scaling considerations:**
  - **Vertical scaling:** switch instance class.
  - **Horizontal scaling:** read replicas.

Cost Optimization Case: A startup switched from **`db.t3.large`** to **`db.t3.medium`** and optimized queries, cutting monthly costs by 40%.

Troubleshooting Common Issues

Check service logs: **`journalctl -u mysqld`**

Cannot connect to database:

  - Ensure port 3306 is open.
  - Check **`bind-address`** in **`my.cnf`**.

Data corruption: Use **`mysqlcheck`** and **`innodb_force_recovery`** as needed.

Scaling Databases in Cloud Environments

Database scaling is a cornerstone of modern application architecture. As application usage and data volume grow, scaling ensures consistent performance and high availability. Cloud environments simplify database scaling by offering flexible and scalable infrastructure. Scaling can be categorized into two primary approaches:

- **Vertical Scaling (Scaling Up):** Adding more resources (CPU, RAM, or storage) to an existing database instance.
- **Horizontal Scaling (Scaling Out):** Adding more database instances to distribute the workload across multiple nodes.

Cloud providers such as AWS offer tools and services to streamline database scaling, enabling applications to handle increased traffic efficiently.

Vertical Scaling in Cloud Databases: Vertical scaling upgrades the resources of a single database instance, making it a straightforward solution for improving performance, especially in read-heavy or compute-intensive workloads.

Key Features in Cloud Environments:

- AWS RDS: Supports instance type modifications with minimal downtime.
- Dynamic Storage Scaling: Allows seamless storage expansion without service interruption.

Advantages:

- Simple to implement.
- No changes required to the application architecture.

Limitations:

- Constrained by the maximum capacity of a single machine.
- Ineffective for addressing performance issues caused by high traffic.

Horizontal Scaling in Cloud Databases

Horizontal scaling adds more database instances and distributes the load across them, making it ideal for applications with intensive read/write operations.

Key Approaches in Cloud Environments:

- **Read Replicas**: AWS RDS enables creating multiple read-only replicas for scaling read operations.
- **Sharding**: Divides the database into smaller shards based on a key (for example, user ID or region).
- **Auto Scaling Groups**: Amazon Aurora supports auto-scaling for both compute and storage, dynamically adjusting capacity as needed.

Advantages:

- Seamless scalability for growing workloads.
- Enhanced fault tolerance and high availability.

Challenges:

- Increased management complexity.
- May require modifications to application logic to support replication or sharding.

Load Balancing for Scaled Databases

In horizontally scaled environments, load balancers ensure traffic is evenly distributed across database instances. AWS provides tools such as:

- **Amazon Route 53:** Offers DNS-based load balancing for database endpoints.
- **Elastic Load Balancer (ELB):** Manages traffic to multiple database servers.

Effective load balancing minimizes latency and ensures resource utilization is optimized.

Scaling Databases with Amazon Aurora

Amazon Aurora is a cloud-native database service designed for scalability and performance. It provides advanced features to meet modern application needs:

- **Storage Auto-scaling:** Automatically adjusts storage up to 128 TB as data grows.
- **Aurora Serverless:** Dynamically scales compute capacity based on application demand, eliminating manual scaling.
- **Global Databases:** Replicates data across multiple AWS Regions for low-latency global access and disaster recovery.

Use Case: A global e-commerce platform can leverage Aurora's global databases to ensure low-latency user experiences across regions while maintaining consistent data integrity.

Scaling a Database on AWS RDS: In this lab, we will scale a database instance both vertically and horizontally using AWS RDS.

Objective: Learn to upgrade an RDS MySQL instance and create read replicas for scaling.

Prerequisites:

- An AWS account.
- An existing RDS MySQL database instance.

Steps:

1. **Vertical Scaling:**
    a. Log in to the AWS Management Console and navigate to RDS.
    b. Select the MySQL instance and click on Modify.
    c. Choose a higher instance type (for example, from `db.t3.medium` to `db.m6g.large`).
    d. Save the changes and wait for the upgrade to complete.
2. **Horizontal Scaling:**
    a. Select the same RDS instance and choose Create Read Replica from the Actions dropdown.
    b. Configure the replica settings, such as instance type and storage.
    c. Launch the read replica and wait for its creation.
3. **Verification:**
    a. Check instance metrics under the Monitoring tab to confirm improved performance.
    b. Test the read replica by connecting and running read queries.
4. **Clean-up:** Delete the read replica to avoid unnecessary costs.

Scaling databases in cloud environments is vital for ensuring performance and availability in growing applications. Leveraging AWS tools such as RDS and Aurora, along with best practices for vertical and horizontal scaling, organizations can efficiently handle dynamic workloads. Selecting the appropriate scaling strategy depends on the application's specific requirements and growth trajectory.

Conclusion

In this chapter, we provided an in-depth exploration of database management on Rocky Linux, with a focus on MySQL and MariaDB, two key open-source database systems. We learned the process of installing, configuring, and optimizing these databases, as well as techniques for backing up and restoring data. These practices, including tuning query performance and configuring storage, are essential for maintaining efficient and secure databases, whether in local or cloud-based environments. We also examined the role of Amazon Web Services (AWS) Relational Database Service (RDS) in modern database management, highlighting its scalability, availability, and managed solutions. This foundation will help us integrate cloud-based databases into the infrastructure seamlessly.

In the next chapter, we will build on these concepts by delving into advanced database management techniques. We will cover topics such as database replication, high availability, and disaster recovery strategies. By mastering these advanced practices, we will enhance our ability to manage and scale fault-tolerant, highly available database systems, whether deployed locally or in the cloud, ensuring they can meet the growing demands of modern applications.

Points to Remember

- **Installing and Configuring MySQL/MariaDB:**
  - MySQL and MariaDB are two popular relational database management systems that can be easily installed on Rocky Linux using package managers such as dnf or yum.
  - Proper configuration is essential to ensure database security, performance, and functionality. Configuration files such as `my.cnf` are in `/etc/my.cnf.d/` and should be adjusted according to system requirements.
- **Database Backup and Restore Strategies:**
  - Regular database backups are critical for preventing data loss. Tools such as mysqldump for MySQL/MariaDB or automated backup solutions in cloud environments should be used for creating reliable backups.
  - Restoring databases involves using backup files to return the database to a previous state. Ensure that backup strategies cover both full and incremental backups to minimize downtime and data loss.
- **Performance Tuning for Databases:**
  - Optimizing database performance is essential for high-traffic applications. Key aspects of performance tuning include adjusting query cache sizes, buffer pool sizes, and optimizing index strategies.
  - Monitoring tools such as MySQLTuner or `performance_schema` in MySQL/MariaDB can help identify performance bottlenecks and suggest optimizations.
- **Introduction to AWS RDS for Database Management:**
  - AWS Relational Database Service (RDS) is a managed service that simplifies database setup, operation, and scaling. It supports MySQL, MariaDB, and other databases.
  - With RDS, users can focus on application development while AWS manages maintenance tasks such as patching, backups, and scaling, providing a high level of automation and availability.
- **Scaling Databases in Cloud Environments:**
  - Cloud databases can scale horizontally or vertically. Horizontal scaling involves distributing data across multiple instances, while vertical scaling involves increasing the resources of a single instance.
  - AWS services such as Amazon RDS and Amazon Aurora offer built-in scaling options and replication features that allow databases to manage increased load while maintaining high availability and fault tolerance.

Multiple Choice Questions

1. Which command is used to install MySQL or MariaDB on Rocky Linux?
   a. `dnf install mysql`
   b. `yum install mariadb`
   c. `dnf install mariadb-server`
   d. `apt-get install mysql-server`

2. What file contains the default configuration settings for MySQL or MariaDB?
   a. `/etc/mysql/my.cnf`
   b. `/etc/my.cnf`
   c. `/etc/mysql.conf.d/mysqld.cnf`
   d. `/etc/my.cnf.d/mysql.conf`
3. Which tool is used to back up a MySQL or MariaDB database?
   a. `mysqldump`
   b. `mysql-backup`
   c. `backup-mysql`
   d. `mariadb-backup`
4. What is the purpose of the **`performance_schema`** in MySQL/MariaDB?
   a. To store all database backups
   b. To monitor and improve database performance
   c. To configure SSL/TLS encryption
   d. To define database tables
5. Which of the following is a recommended practice for securing MySQL or MariaDB?
   a. Disable SSL encryption
   b. Use the default root password for easier access
   c. Restrict remote root access
   d. Store backups in the same location as the database
6. Which AWS service allows us to manage MySQL or MariaDB databases without handling server administration?
   a. AWS RDS
   b. AWS EC2
   c. AWS Lambda
   d. AWS S3
7. What is the primary function of Amazon RDS for MySQL or MariaDB?
   a. To provide a managed database service with automated backups and scaling
   b. To offer high-performance virtual machines for database installation
   c. To serve as a storage solution for database backups
   d. To offer object storage for database files
8. Which method can be used to scale a database in a cloud environment such as AWS?
   a. Increasing the size of the database instance
   b. Adding more storage to the local disk

   c. Configuring read replicas for horizontal scaling
   d. Removing indexes from tables
9. Which of the following backup strategies is commonly used for MySQL or MariaDB databases?
   a. Cold backups with database shutdown
   b. Incremental backups only
   c. Full backups and incremental backups
   d. Backup only database configuration files
10. What is the purpose of database replication in a cloud environment such as AWS?
   a. To automatically increase storage space
   b. To ensure high availability and fault tolerance by copying data across multiple servers
   c. To optimize query performance by merging data
   d. To create a backup of the database configuration

Answers

1. d
2. d
3. b
4. c
5. b
6. a
7. b
8. b
9. a
10. b

Questions

1. What is the primary function of MySQL or MariaDB in a Linux environment?
2. Which command is used to install MySQL or MariaDB on Rocky Linux?
3. What configuration file is used to set up MySQL or MariaDB on Rocky Linux?
4. What is the purpose of using the mysqldump command?
5. Which tool is recommended for optimizing the performance of MySQL or MariaDB databases?
6. What is the role of replication in MySQL/MariaDB for cloud environments?
7. Which AWS service provides managed MySQL and MariaDB database instances with automated backups?
8. What is the purpose of configuring read replicas in MySQL or MariaDB?

9. What is the benefit of using Amazon Aurora for MySQL or MariaDB in AWS?
10. What is a common backup strategy for MySQL or MariaDB databases in cloud environments?

Key Terms

- **MySQL**: A popular open-source relational database management system (RDBMS) used for managing data in a structured format. It is commonly used in web applications and can be installed on Linux, including Rocky Linux.
- **MariaDB**: A fork of MySQL that offers enhanced performance, security, and features. It is fully compatible with MySQL, making it an alternative for database management.
- **mysqldump**: A command-line utility used to create backups of MySQL and MariaDB databases. It exports the database structure and data into a file for easy restoration.
- **Replication**: A process in MySQL and MariaDB that allows data from one database server to be copied to one or more other servers, ensuring high availability and load balancing.
- **Performance Schema**: A feature in MySQL and MariaDB that provides detailed performance metrics to help diagnose and optimize database performance.
- **AWS RDS (Relational Database Service)**: A managed service by AWS that simplifies the setup, operation, and scaling of relational databases such as MySQL and MariaDB, providing automated backups and scaling.
- **Amazon Aurora**: A high-performance, MySQL-compatible relational database engine offered by AWS. Aurora is designed for cloud applications, providing scalability and fault tolerance.
- **Backup Strategies**: Techniques for ensuring that database data is safely stored and recoverable, including full backups, incremental backups, and point-in-time restores.
- **Read Replicas**: A type of database replication that allows for the creation of read-only copies of a database to distribute query load and improve performance in high-traffic environments.
- **Scaling**: The process of adjusting the database resources to manage changes in workload. This can be achieved through vertical scaling (increasing instance size) or horizontal scaling (adding more instances or read replicas).

CHAPTER 10
Mail Server Setup

Introduction

In today's interconnected world, email stands as a core pillar of communication and collaboration. This chapter will guide us through configuring a secure, reliable, and scalable mail server on Rocky Linux 9, with notes on compatibility for earlier versions. Using Postfix, we will gain hands-on experience managing mail domains, users, and essential configurations. To support clarity and troubleshooting, expected outputs are provided for commands such as **`postfix check`**, **`mailq`**, **`tail -f /var/log/maillog`**, and **`firewall-cmd --list-all`**. Configuration annotations highlight critical areas like firewall rules and virtual hosts, while SSL certificate setup is simplified with practical step-by-step guidance. **SPF/DKIM** implementation and AWS SES policies are aligned with the latest security standards to ensure proper mail authentication and delivery.

Beyond local deployment, this chapter introduces advanced cloud integration using AWS *Simple Email Service* (SES), demonstrating how to build scalable and resilient email infrastructure. Visual diagrams illustrate the interaction between EC2 instances, Load Balancers, and Auto Scaling Groups in dynamically managing traffic. The chapter also addresses essential performance tuning strategies for Apache and MySQL. Whether serving as a Linux administrator or a developer, readers will gain practical insights for building enterprise-grade email systems on Rocky Linux–suitable for both on-premises environments and cloud platforms.

Structure

This chapter covers the following topics:

- Setting Up and Configuring Mail Servers and Integration with AWS Services
- Installing and Configuring Postfix
- Managing Mail Domains and Users
- Basic Mail Server Security
- Monitoring and Troubleshooting
- Integration with AWS SES for Scalable Email Management

Setting Up and Configuring Mail Servers and Integration with AWS Services

Email is the backbone of modern communication, powering everything from business correspondence to automated notifications. For system administrators, mastering the art of configuring and managing mail servers is not just a technical necessity, it is a gateway to ensuring seamless communication across organizations. In this chapter, we dive into the intricacies of setting up and managing mail servers using Postfix on Rocky Linux, a robust and versatile platform for handling email delivery with precision and reliability.

Beyond traditional setups, we will explore how to enhance the mail server's capabilities by integrating it with AWS Simple Email Service (SES). This powerful cloud-based service allows us to leverage the scalability, security, and cost-efficiency of AWS for sending and receiving emails at scale. From configuring mail domains and managing users to implementing essential security features and troubleshooting, this chapter offers a step-by-step guide to building secure, scalable, and cloud-enabled email solutions.

Lab1: Creating Users and Groups in AWS IAM Identity Center

Prerequisites

- **Administrator Access**: Ensure we have administrative permissions in AWS.
- **IAM Identity Center Enabled**: Verify that AWS IAM Identity Center (formerly AWS SSO) is enabled in our AWS account.

Step 1: Access AWS IAM Identity Center

a. Log in to the **`AWS Management Console`**.

b. Navigate to **`IAM Identity Center`**.

c. In the **`AWS Management Console`**, search for **`IAM Identity Center`** in the search bar and select it.

Step 2: Add Users

a. In the left-hand menu, select **`Users`**.

b. Click on the **`Add User`** button.

c. Fill in the following details:

`First Name`*: Enter the user's first name.*

`Last Name`*: Enter the user's last name.*

`Email`*: Enter the email address for the user (for example, user@example.com).*

`Username`*: Enter the username (this can be the email address or another unique name).*

`Temporary Password`*: Provide a temporary password (users will reset it at first login).*

(Optional)* `Add tags` *to the user for better organization.

Click* `Add User` *to complete the process.

Repeat this process for each email address required.

Step 3: Create Groups

a. In the left-hand menu, select **`Groups`**.

b. Click on the **`Create Group`** button.

c. Enter the Group Name (example, Admins, Developers, Finance Team).

d. (Optional) Add a description to explain the group's purpose.

e. Click Create Group to finalize.

Step 4: Assign Users to Groups

a. Navigate to the **`Groups`** section.

b. Select the group to which we want to add users.

c. Click **Add Users**.

d. From the list, select the users we created earlier.

e.Click **Add** to assign them to the group.

Step 5: Assign Permissions to Groups

a. In the left-hand menu, go to **Permission Sets**.

b. **Permission Sets** define access policies for users and groups.

c. Create a new permission set or use an existing one:

d. Click **Create Permission Set** and choose a predefined policy (for instance, **AdministratorAccess**, **PowerUserAccess**) or create a custom policy.

e. Assign the permission set to the group:

f. Navigate to **Assignments** and click **Assign Users or Groups**.

g. Select the group and the appropriate permission set, then click **Assign**.

Step 6: Verify and Share Login Details

a. Locate the **IAM Identity Center** User Portal URL:

b. This URL can be found in the Dashboard tab under User portal URL.

c. Example: **https://<our-aws-sso-domain>.awsapps.com/start**.

d. Share the login details with the users:

e. Email: Their registered email address.

f. Temporary Password: The one provided during user creation.

g. Instruct users to log in, reset their password, and start using their assigned permissions.

Example Email Addresses

If we are creating users for these emails:

a. alice@example.com; bob@example.com; charlie@example.com;

b. Add them as users in Step 2.

c. Assign them to groups in Step 4.

d. Ensure their permissions are set according to their roles in Step 5.

Lab2: Setting Up and Managing Users and Groups in AWS IAM Identity Center

Objective: By completing this lab, we will learn how to:

1. Create users and groups in AWS IAM Identity Center.
2. Assign users to groups.
3. Apply permissions to groups to control access.

Prerequisites

- AWS Management Console access with administrative privileges.
- IAM Identity Center enabled in the AWS account.

Lab Steps

Step 1: Create Users

a. Log in to the **`AWS Management Console`**.

b. Navigate to **`IAM Identity Center`** by searching for it in the console's search bar.

c. Click **`Users`** in the left-hand menu.

d. Click **`Add User`** and fill in the following details for at least two users:

`First Name:` example, Alice

`Last Name:` example, Smith

`Email:` example, alice@example.com

`Username:` example, alice@example.com

`Temporary Password:` Set a password that Alice will update upon first login.

e. Click **`Add User`** to save.

f. Repeat the steps to create another user, for instance, Bob (bob@example.com).

Step 2: Create Groups

a. In the **`IAM Identity Center`** menu, select **`Groups`**.

b. Click **`Create Group`** and name it, for example, **`Developers`**.

c. Add a description, such as '**`Group for development team members`**.'

d. Click **`Create Group`** to save.

Step 3: Assign Users to Groups

a. Navigate back to **`Groups`** and select the **`Developers`** group.

b. Click **`Add Users`** and select the users we created (example, Alice and Bob).

c. Click **`Add to confirm`**.

Step 4: Assign Permissions to Groups

a. Click **`Permission Sets`** in the left-hand menu.

b. Create a new permission set or use an existing one:

   i. Click **`Create Permission Set`**.

   ii. Choose a policy such as **`PowerUserAccess`**.

   iii. Click **`Create`** to finalize.

c. Assign the permission set to the **`Developers`** group:

   i. Go to **`Assignments`**.

   ii. Click **`Assign Users`** or **`Groups`**.

iii. Select the **Developers** group and the permission set, then click **Assign**.

Step 5: Verify Access

a. Locate the **IAM Identity Center User Portal URL** from the **Dashboard** tab.

b. Share the following details with the users:

   - User portal URL.
   - Their email address and temporary password.

c. Have the users log in to the portal, reset their passwords, and verify they can access AWS services based on their permissions.

Challenge Task (Optional)

1. Create a second group, for example, Finance Team, and add a new user.
2. Assign a custom permission set that allows access only to AWS Billing and Cost Management services.

Installing and Configuring Postfix

Postfix is a powerful and flexible ***Mail Transfer Agent* (MTA)** designed to route and deliver emails. Known for its high performance, security, and ease of configuration, it is widely used in Linux environments. Its efficient and versatile design makes it ideal for managing email communications on modern servers.

On Rocky Linux, Postfix is a popular choice due to its simple setup and strong community support. Additionally, it is the default MTA in many Linux distributions and integrates seamlessly with tools like Dovecot and AWS SES, enabling scalable email management.

1. **Installing Postfix**

a. Update the system packages: **sudo dnf update -y**

b. Install Postfix: **sudo dnf install postfix -y**

c. Start and enable Postfix:

```
sudo systemctl start postfix
sudo systemctl enable postfix
```

Verify the Postfix installation: **sudo systemctl status postfix**

2. **Configuring Postfix**

Basic Configuration: The main Postfix configuration file is located at **/etc/postfix/main.cf**. The following are the key configurations to set up a simple Postfix server:

a. **Set the hostname:** Edit **/etc/postfix/main.cf** and configure the following:

```
# hostname information
myhostname = mail.example.com
mydomain = example.com
myorigin = $mydomain
```

b. **Configure the relay host:** If using an external SMTP relay like AWS SES, add:

```
# relayhost
relayhost = [email-smtp.us-east-1.amazonaws.com]:587
smtp_sasl_auth_enable = yes
smtp_sasl_password_maps = hash:/etc/postfix/sasl_passwd
```

```
smtp_sasl_security_options = noanonymous
smtp_use_tls = yes
```

c. **Create the password file for SMTP relay:**

```
echo "[email-smtp.us-east-1.amazonaws.com]:587 username:password" | sudo tee /
etc/postfix/sasl_passwd
```

- `sudo postmap /etc/postfix/sasl_passwd`
- `sudo chmod 600 /etc/postfix/sasl_passwd /etc/postfix/sasl_passwd.db`

d. **Restart Postfix:** `sudo systemctl restart postfix`

3. **Testing Postfix**

Configuring Thunderbird for Email Testing: Install Thunderbird, if Thunderbird is not installed, download it from the official site or install it using: **`sudo dnf install thunderbird -y`**.

a. Set Up **`Email Accounts`**

b. Open Thunderbird in the graphical interface of Rocky Linux and set up the test email accounts:

c. **`Email 1: user1@educate.com`**

d. Add a **`New Email Account`**

In the **`Account Settings`** window, scroll to the bottom of the left sidebar and click **`Account Actions`**.

a. Select **`Add Mail Account...`** from the dropdown menu.

b. Email 2: user2@educate.com

Use the following settings:

```
Incoming Server: IMAP or POP3 (choose based on the prefer option).
Outgoing Server (SMTP): Should match the email provider's configuration.
Authentication: SMTP Username and Password (from SES credentials).
Send a Test Email: Use Thunderbird to send a test email:
Subject: Testing email Rocky Linux 9
Body: "This is a test email sent via Postfix and Rocky Linux 9."
```

Kindly use both email test addresses to complete this step.

4. **Verifying the Configuration**

a. Check Email Delivery.

b. Confirm that the test email is delivered successfully by checking the inbox of user1@educate.com.

c. Review the AWS SES dashboard for email activity logs.

Troubleshooting

a. Check the Postfix logs for errors: ***sudo tail -f /var/log/maillog.***

b. Common issues include incorrect SES credentials or missing DNS records.

Final Steps

1. **Implement Email Security**: Add **SPF, DKIM, *and* DMARC *records*** to the DNS to improve email deliverability, and protect against spoofing.

2. **Monitor Mail Server Activity**: Use tools like **`postfix-logwatch`** to analyze logs and monitor email traffic.

3. **Optimize Thunderbird Usage**: Configure folders, filters, and signatures for efficient email management.

Mastering the installation and configuration of Postfix is a significant milestone in building a reliable and efficient mail server on Rocky Linux. Through this chapter, we have learned to deploy Postfix, a robust and versatile Mail Transfer Agent, and configure it to handle both incoming and outgoing emails. By understanding the critical components of Postfix, such as its main configuration files, transport mechanisms, and relay settings, we are now equipped to create a functional and secure mail server that can cater to the organization's communication needs. These skills form the foundation for managing mail domains, users, and messages with precision and scalability.

With Postfix successfully set up and configured, we are prepared to tackle additional challenges in mail server management such as implementing enhanced security measures and monitoring tools to maintain optimal performance. The knowledge gained in this chapter will enable us to integrate the mail server with advanced cloud-based services like AWS Simple Email Service (SES), allowing the system to scale seamlessly as demand grows. By leveraging these capabilities, we can ensure that our email infrastructure remains a cornerstone of efficient and secure communication in both local and cloud-enabled environments.

Managing Mail Domains and Users

Effective management of mail domains and users is fundamental to establishing a secure and efficient email infrastructure. Mail domains define the scope of email services within an organization, serving as the foundation for communication. Configuring essential DNS records, such as **MX** and **SPF**, ensures reliable email delivery and robust authentication, reducing the risk of spam and unauthorized access.

Equally important is the administration of users. This involves creating, modifying, and deactivating accounts as organizational needs evolve, as well as implementing user quotas to manage resources efficiently. Secure access protocols, including **IMAP**, **SMTP**, and **POP3**, ensure seamless and protected communication. Additionally, measures such as spam filtering, enforcement of security policies, and diligent monitoring of mail logs contribute to a resilient email environment.

By maintaining well-structured domains and user management practices, organizations can ensure scalability, compliance, and uninterrupted operations. Let us explore the strategies and tools required to achieve these objectives in detail.

Managing Mail Domains

A mail domain refers to the part of an email address that comes after the '@' symbol (e.g., user@example.com). Configuring and managing mail domains on the server allows us to manage who can send and receive emails from the server.

Configuring the Mail Server for Multiple Domains

Postfix can be configured to handle emails for multiple domains by editing the destination parameter in the main.cf configuration file. This parameter specifies the domains that the mail server will manage locally, allowing for efficient handling of email services across multiple domains.

For example, if we want to handle emails for example.com and example.net, we will edit the main.cf file as follows: `sudo nano /etc/postfix/main.cf`.

Then, modify the `mydestination` line:

```
mydestination = $myhostname, localhost.$mydomain, localhost, example.com,
example.net
```

This configuration will ensure that Postfix accepts email for both example.com and example.net and routes it accordingly.

Adding New Domains

Adding new domains to a mail server requires updating the **`Postfix configuration`** by including the domains in the **`mydestination`** field. This ensures the mail server recognizes and processes these domains locally.

For managing multiple domains, **virtual mail domains** can be configured. This approach allows the server to efficiently handle emails for several domains on the same system, maximizing resource efficiency and eliminating the need for additional physical infrastructure.

Managing Users on a Mail Server

Managing users on a mail server involves creating, modifying, and deleting user accounts, as well as assigning appropriate mailboxes and permissions.

Adding New Users

In most Linux distributions, we can create a user account with the **`useradd`** command. For example, to create a user named john, use the following command:

- `sudo useradd john`
- `sudo passwd john`

This will create a user account for john, and we can assign a password for the account. Each user on the system will have their own mailbox, typically stored in the **`/var/mail/`** directory.

Creating Mail Aliases

Mail aliases allow us to forward emails from one address to another. For example, we might want to forward all emails sent to sales@example.com to sales@example.net.

To create an alias, edit the /etc/aliases file: **`sudo nano /etc/aliases`**

Add the following line for the alias: **`sales: sales@example.net`**

After saving the file, run the following command to update the aliases database:

- `sudo newaliases`

This will ensure that emails sent to sales@example.com are forwarded to **`sales@example.net`**.

Managing User Permissions

In addition to managing user accounts, we should also manage permissions for accessing mailboxes. Postfix typically uses the local user system to handle mailboxes. By default, each user has a mailbox in **`/var/mail/username`**. The permissions for this directory need to be set correctly to ensure proper access.

To check or modify permissions for a mailbox, use the **`chmod`** and **`chown`** commands. For example, to give the user john read/write access to their mailbox, use the following command:

- `sudo chown john:john /var/mail/john`
- `sudo chmod 660 /var/mail/john`

These commands ensure that only the user and root have access to the mailbox.

Configuring Mailbox Formats

Postfix supports different types of mailbox formats, such as the traditional **mbox** format and the **Maildir** format. The **Maildir** format is recommended for its performance and scalability benefits, especially on high-traffic mail servers.

To configure Postfix to use the **Maildir** format, we need to modify the **/etc/postfix/main.cf** file: **sudo nano /etc/postfix/main.cf**.

To make navigation easier, use the '*Ctrl + W*' keyboard shortcut. Let us review the grammar and clarify the ideas. Add or modify the following line: **home_mailbox = Maildir/.**

This configuration ensures that each user's email is stored in a **Maildir** directory within their home directory (for example, **/home/john/Maildir/**).

Setting Up Virtual Users and Domains

For managing email across multiple domains and users without corresponding Linux accounts, Postfix can be configured to use virtual users and domains. This setup allows for the management of email accounts independently of the Linux user system. Virtual users can be set up by creating a database file, such as MySQL or PostgreSQL, to store essential user information like email addresses, passwords, and delivery destinations. This method ensures flexibility in handling email services for large numbers of users across various domains.

To configure Postfix for virtual users, follow these steps:

a. Install the required packages for MySQL/PostgreSQL support in Postfix.

b. Modify the **main.cf** file to enable virtual alias maps and virtual mailboxes:

   - `virtual_alias_maps = mysql:/etc/postfix/mysql-aliases.cf`
   - `virtual_mailbox_maps = mysql:/etc/postfix/mysql-mailboxes.cf`

c. Create the necessary configuration files for MySQL (**mysql-aliases.cf**, **mysql-mailboxes.cf**).

d. Create the database and tables to store the virtual users and domains.

Monitoring and Troubleshooting

Proper monitoring and troubleshooting are essential for maintaining the health of the mail server. Regularly check the mail logs to identify potential issues. Mail logs are typically located in the **/var/log/** directory and can be monitored using the following commands:

- `tail -f /var/log/mail.log`

This will display real-time updates to the mail log file. In case of any issues, review the logs to identify common problems, such as incorrect DNS configuration, missing MX records, or issues with user permissions.

Backup and Recovery

To ensure the continuity of email services, regularly back up mail domains, user configurations, and mailbox data. We can use tools like **rsync** or **tar** to back up the **/etc/postfix/** directory and the **/var/mail/** directory. Additionally, consider using automated backup solutions in the cloud for extra security and reliability.

Basic Mail Server Security

Securing a mail server is critical to protecting sensitive email communication, ensuring that confidential information remains private, and safeguarding against various security threats such as spam, malware, and phishing attacks. Mail servers, often exposed to the internet, are prime targets for attackers seeking unauthorized access or to exploit vulnerabilities. These threats can result in compromised accounts, data breaches, and disruptions in service, making it essential to implement a robust security strategy that mitigates risks and enhances the integrity of email systems.

To effectively secure a mail server, administrators should adopt a combination of security best practices and technologies. Basic measures such as configuring firewalls, using encryption for both stored and transmitted data, and implementing strong authentication methods are essential for preventing unauthorized access. Additionally, integrating anti-spam and anti-malware tools, along with enforcing policies like email filtering and domain-based authentication (for example, **SPF, DKIM, and DMARC**), can reduce the chances of successful phishing attacks and other malicious activities. By addressing these risks proactively, organizations can maintain a secure and reliable mail server environment.

Securing Postfix

Postfix is a powerful and flexible mail server, but its configuration needs to be secured to prevent misuse. To begin securing the Postfix server, start by restricting the types of relays allowed. By default, Postfix accepts mail from any source. However, it is recommended to limit incoming connections only from trusted IPs. Modify the main.cf file to configure this:

- `sudo nano /etc/postfix/main.cf`

Add the following line to restrict access: **`mynetworks = 127.0.0.0/8, [::1]/128`**.

This will limit the connections to the local machine only. We can add trusted IPs by specifying them in the **`mynetworks`** parameter.

Another important step is enabling TLS (Transport Layer Security) encryption for email communication. Add these lines to the **`main.cf`** file to enable TLS encryption:

```
#Adding lines for encryption
smtpd_use_tls = yes
smtpd_tls_cert_file = /etc/ssl/certs/your_domain_cert.pem
smtpd_tls_key_file = /etc/ssl/private/your_domain_key.pem
```

This ensures that emails sent to and from our server are encrypted during transmission, adding an extra layer of security.

Protecting Against Spam

Spam is a major concern for mail servers, and Postfix offers several ways to reduce spam and prevent unwanted email traffic. One method is to use **`SpamAssassin`**, a popular anti-spam tool. Install **`SpamAssassin`** on the server and configure Postfix to use it as a filter for incoming emails. To install **`SpamAssassin`**, use the following command:

```
sudo dnf install spamassassin -y
sudo systemctl enable --now spamassassin
```

Once installed, we can integrate it with Postfix by adding the following to the **`main.cf`** file:

- `sudo nano /etc/postfix/main.cf`
- `content_filter = smtp:[127.0.0.1]:10024`

Postfix must be configured to use a filter such as **amavisd-new**, to interact with **SpamAssassin**, and check emails for spam.

Using Fail2Ban for Brute Force Protection

Fail2Ban is a tool that monitors logs for suspicious activity and can block IP addresses that show signs of malicious intent such as repeated failed login attempts. This is particularly useful for preventing brute force attacks on the mail server.

To install **Fail2Ban**, use the following command:

- `sudo dnf install epel-release`
- `sudo dnf install fail2ban`

After installing Fail2Ban, configure it by editing the **/etc/fail2ban/jail.local** file. To protect against brute force attacks on SMTP, add a block for Postfix with the following configuration:

```
[postfix]
enabled  = true
port     = smtp,ssmtp
filter   = postfix
logpath  = /var/log/mail.log
maxretry = 5
bantime  = 3600
```

1. **enabled:** Activates the jail for Postfix.
2. **port:** Specifies the ports for SMTP services.
3. **filter:** Refers to the filter configuration for Postfix.
4. **logpath:** Points to the Postfix log file.
5. **maxretry:** Sets the maximum number of failed login attempts before banning.
6. **bantime:** Defines the duration of the ban in seconds.

A final step to validate the service is to execute the following commands:

- `sudo systemctl restart fail2ban`
- `sudo systemctl status fail2ban`

This setup helps mitigate brute force attacks by temporarily banning IP addresses that exceed a specified number of failed login attempts.

Using DKIM and SPF for Email Authentication

DomainKeys Identified Mail (DKIM) and Sender Policy Framework (SPF) are essential techniques for authenticating email and preventing spoofing. DKIM works by adding a cryptographic signature to email headers which allows the recipient to verify the authenticity of the sender. To implement DKIM with Postfix, we will need to install **OpenDKIM** and configure it to sign outgoing mail.

To install **OpenDKIM** on Ubuntu, use the following command:

- `sudo apt-get install opendkim opendkim-tools`

Once installed, configure OpenDKIM by editing the **/etc/opendkim.conf** file and adding our domain's DKIM signing key. SPF is used to specify which mail servers are authorized to send emails on behalf of our domain. To set up SPF, add a DNS record for our domain with a policy such as this: **v=spf1 mx a ~all**

This policy will authorize mail servers listed in our domain's MX records and prevent unauthorized servers from sending emails on behalf of our domain.

Regular Software Updates

Keeping the mail server software up to date is one of the most effective ways to prevent security vulnerabilities. Regularly check for and install updates to the operating system, Postfix, and other associated mail server tools.

Use the following commands to check for updates on a Debian-based system:

- `sudo apt-get update`
- `sudo apt-get upgrade`

This ensures that our server remains protected against known vulnerabilities.

Backup and Recovery

Mail server data, including configurations, user data, and email archives, should be regularly backed up. Consider using tools like **`rsync`** or **`tar`** to back up the relevant directories, such as **`/etc/postfix`** and **`/var/mail`**.

In addition, implement a disaster recovery plan that ensures, we can quickly restore mail services in case of failure.

Integrating Security in a Real-World Case Study on Mail Server Vulnerabilities

Mail servers are a critical communication component in any organization, and their security must not be underestimated. Misconfigurations can lead to spoofing, phishing, unauthorized access, and data leakage. While protocols such as **SPF, DKIM, and DMARC** are designed to authenticate and protect email communications, they are often misconfigured or entirely omitted.

To illustrate the impact of poor email server security, this section includes a real-world-style case study demonstrating how improper configuration of email authentication protocols can lead to serious consequences.

Case Study: Spoofing Attack Due to Misconfigured SPF and DKIM

In April 2023, an internal user from a mid-sized financial consulting firm reported suspicious emails appearing to come from the firm's HR department. The emails requested the recipients to verify their credentials via a third-party link, cleverly disguised as a corporate login portal. The link led to a phishing website designed to harvest usernames and passwords. Although the emails looked genuine on the surface–with correct logos, signatures, and sender names–IT security analysts quickly flagged them as suspicious upon closer inspection of the email headers.

Initial Clues:

- The sender's address was **`"[hr@company.com](mailto:hr@company.com)"`** (an internal address).
- Recipients noted the email lacked the usual internal warning banner.
- The domain had no DMARC policy enforced.

Technical Analysis: Email Header Examination

Security analysts examined the email headers, and identified the following authentication results:

```
Authentication-Results: mail.company.com;
   spf=fail (sender IP is not authorized)
   dkim=none (no DKIM signature)
   dmarc=fail (SPF not aligned; policy not enforced)
```

The header analysis revealed multiple issues:

SPF Failure: The sending IP address was not listed in the domain's SPF record.

DKIM Missing: The message lacked a DKIM signature entirely.

DMARC Misconfigured: The DMARC policy was either missing or set to "**none**," allowing unauthorized messages to pass without rejection or quarantine.

As a result, the spoofed email bypassed basic security checks and was delivered to users' inboxes.

Implications and Damages

The lack of proper SPF, DKIM, and DMARC enforcement allowed attackers to impersonate internal users easily. In this case:

Five employees entered their credentials on the phishing site.

- The attackers used these credentials to access internal systems and attempted to initiate a fraudulent payroll transfer.
- The organization had to reset all compromised accounts, conduct a full forensic analysis, and notify potentially affected stakeholders.

Estimated cost of response and remediation: **`$25,000 USD`.**

Lessons Learned and Preventive Measures: This incident highlights the critical importance of implementing and testing proper email authentication protocols. The following best practices were enforced after the breach:

Implementing a strict SPF policy: The organization updated its DNS with an accurate SPF record listing all authorized mail servers.

- `v=spf1 ip4:192.0.2.0/24 include:_spf.google.com -all`

Enabling DKIM for all outbound mail: All outgoing mail is now signed with a DKIM key to verify integrity and authenticity. Keys are rotated periodically.

Enforcing a DMARC policy:

DMARC was updated to a strict policy:

- `v=DMARC1; p=reject; rua=mailto:dmarc-reports@company.com; aspf=s;`

Daily reports are reviewed to monitor alignment and anomalies.

User Awareness Training

Regular phishing simulations and cybersecurity awareness workshops were introduced to reduce the success of future attacks.

This case study underscores how even basic misconfigurations in SPF, DKIM, and DMARC can expose organizations to severe threats. Email remains a primary vector for cyberattacks, and security measures must be proactive, layered, and continuously monitored. Organizations that fail to implement proper mail server security invite significant risks–not just technical but also reputational and financial.

Mail server administrators must treat SPF, DKIM, and DMARC as essential, not optional. These tools–combined with vigilant monitoring and educated users–form a strong defense against modern email-based threats.

Relay Access Control

When configuring a mail server, one of the most critical aspects is *relay access control.* Misconfigurations can result in the server becoming an *open relay* which spammers can exploit to send unauthorized emails. This not only degrades our server's reputation but can also get our IP blacklisted globally.

This section clarifies how to *securely configure relaying* using *Postfix* on *Rocky Linux* 9, with simple, practical examples to help beginners avoid common mistakes.

Understanding Mail Relaying

Mail relaying refers to the process of one mail server forwarding email to another server for delivery. This is legitimate if:

- The sender is from within our network (internal user).
- The recipient is part of our domain or an allowed domain.
- The server is explicitly authorized to relay messages.

However, if our server relays mail from **any source to any destination** without restriction, it becomes an **open relay** – a severe security issue.

Example of a Misconfigured Open Relay

Let us explore a *dangerous configuration* example often made by beginners:

Example: Open Relay (Insecure)

```
ini
relay_domains = *
```

Challenges in the Current Setup

The asterisk `*` tells Postfix to allow *relaying for any domain*, which effectively means:

- Any user from anywhere can send emails **through our server.**
- Spammers will exploit our server to send bulk or malicious emails.
- The IP address may get blacklisted on DNS blocklists like *Spamhaus* or *Barracuda.*

Resulting Effects

- Massive outgoing spam.
- IP blacklisting.
- Server resource abuse (CPU, RAM, disk space).
- Legal implications in some cases.

Proper Relay Configuration (Secure Setup)

To secure the Postfix server, we should explicitly define:

- **Which domains are allowed to relay.**

- **Which hosts/networks are trusted.**

Secure Example: Accept Only Local Mail and Specific Domains

Here is a basic but secure configuration:

```
ini
relay_domains = example.com
smtpd_recipient_restrictions = permit_mynetworks, reject_unauth_destination
```

Explanation:

```
relay_domains = example.com
  This limits relaying **only for the domain `example.com`
 smtpd_recipient_restrictions = permit_mynetworks, reject_unauth_destination
```

This line tells Postfix:

- Allow relaying *only from trusted networks* (defined in `**mynetworks**`).
- For all others, *reject any mail not destined for local domains* (`**reject_unauth_destination**`).

Define the Trusted Network:

Make sure we have a correct **mynetworks** entry:

```
ini
mynetworks = 127.0.0.0/8, [::1]/128
```

Optionally, include internal IP ranges if we are running a local mail relay.

Testing the Configuration

We can verify that our server is **not an open relay** by using the command:

```
postconf | grep relay_domains
postconf | grep smtpd_recipient_restrictions
```

Also, we can test using tools like:

- **[MXToolbox Relay Test](https://mxtoolbox.com/diagnostic.aspx)**
- Telnet-based manual testing (for advanced users).

Best Practices

- **Never use relay_domains =** unless we are building a custom trusted internal-only relay system.
- Use **authentication (smtpd_sasl_auth_enable = yes)** if we allow remote clients to send mail.
- Monitor mail logs in **/var/log/maillog** for suspicious activity.
- Ensure firewall rules block unwanted external SMTP access unless needed.

Relay access control is a **vital security setting** in Postfix. By avoiding dangerous configurations like **relay_domains = *** and enforcing correct recipient restrictions, we can protect the server, maintain our domain reputation, and provide reliable email services on Rocky Linux 9. Always test and validate the configuration, especially in production environments.

Monitoring and Troubleshooting

Monitoring and troubleshooting are essential for maintaining a healthy and secure mail server. Effective monitoring involves using tools to track performance metrics such as CPU usage, memory, disk space, and network bandwidth, as well as monitoring email traffic for unusual patterns, spam, or unauthorized access attempts. Security monitoring is crucial to detect threats like brute force attacks and malware infections. Real-time alerts and log analysis help administrators address issues before they escalate. Troubleshooting requires a systematic approach to identify and resolve problems, including reviewing log files for errors, checking mail queues, and diagnosing issues such as DNS misconfigurations or authentication failures. By combining proactive monitoring with efficient troubleshooting, administrators can quickly detect and resolve issues, ensuring the server remains secure, reliable, and fully operational.

Monitoring Mail Server Health

Monitoring the health of a mail server is critical to ensure efficient and reliable operation. Key metrics that should be regularly monitored include server load, disk usage, mail queue size, and network traffic. Postfix offers built-in tools for monitoring mail queues and server performance. For instance, the **`postqueue -p`** command can be used to view the mail queue and identify any backlogs.

For more comprehensive monitoring, tools like **Nagios** and **Zabbix** can be employed. These platforms provide real-time alerts on system health, disk space usage, and mail traffic, ensuring that administrators are immediately notified of any emerging issues.

Using Log Files for Troubleshooting

Logs play a crucial role in troubleshooting mail server issues by providing detailed information about errors, failures, and unusual activity. Both **Postfix logs** and **system logs** contain valuable data that help diagnose problems effectively.

Postfix logs are typically found in files such as **`/var/log/mail.log`** or **`/var/log/mail.err`**. These logs include important details like error messages, delivery attempts, and spam filtering results. This information is essential for identifying issues and maintaining smooth mail server operation.

To view Postfix logs, live, use this command: **`sudo tail -f /var/log/mail.log`**

On Linux systems, using **`systemd`**, logs can also be accessed with the **`journalctl`** tool, which provides a comprehensive view of all Postfix-related logs: **`sudo journalctl -u postfix`**

Regular monitoring of these logs allows administrators to quickly detect and resolve problems, ensuring the mail server remains efficient and reliable.

Analyzing logs helps pinpoint the root cause of issues such as:

- Email delivery failures
- Security breaches
- Performance problems

Troubleshooting Common Mail Server Issues

Several common issues may arise when running a mail server, including problems with email delivery, mail queues, or server connectivity. Here are some basic troubleshooting steps:

- **Email Delivery Failures:** If emails are not being delivered, check the Postfix logs for error messages like "451 *Temporary Failure*" or "550 *Relaying Denied*." These errors often indicate issues with server configuration or DNS settings. Ensure that the mail server has proper DNS records (MX, SPF, DKIM) and is not blacklisted.
- **Mail Queue Backlog:** If the mail queue is full, we can view the queue with the postqueue command. A large mail queue may indicate that the server is overwhelmed or there are issues with mail routing. Try to flush the queue with the following command: **`sudo postqueue -f`**

- **Server Connectivity:** If the mail server is not responding, check the firewall settings and ensure that the appropriate ports (25, 587, 465) are open. Use the telnet command to test connectivity to the mail server's SMTP port: **`telnet mail.example.com 25`**
- **Spam Filtering Problems:** If legitimate emails are being marked as spam or vice versa, review the configuration of the spam filters and adjust the settings in **`SpamAssassin`** or other filtering tools. Ensure that our spam filters are not overly aggressive.

Performance Tuning and Optimization

Performance issues can arise due to resource limitations, improper configuration, or high mail traffic. To optimize the performance of the mail server, consider the following steps:

1. **Optimize Mail Queue Processing**: Adjust Postfix's configuration to optimize mail queue processing. We can change the values of parameters like **`maximal_queue_lifetime`** or **`minimal_backoff_time`** to control the speed at which emails are processed and retry attempts are made.
2. **Limit Connection Rates**: To prevent overload, set limits on the number of simultaneous connections Postfix will accept. Adjust the following parameters in the main.cf file:

```
smtpd_client_connection_rate_limit = 10
smtpd_client_connection_count_limit = 20
```

3. **System Resource Optimization**: Monitor the server's CPU, memory, and disk usage. If necessary, add more resources (CPU, RAM) or tune the system's settings for better performance. Use tools such as **`top`**, **`htop`**, or **`vmstat`** to monitor resource usage in real time.

Automating Monitoring and Alerts

To ensure the continuous operation of a mail server, automating monitoring and alerting is essential. Automated systems can quickly notify administrators when an issue arises, allowing for rapid response and minimizing downtime. One effective approach is to implement a monitoring tool like Prometheus, which collects performance metrics from the mail server and triggers alerts when predefined thresholds are surpassed. These alerts can be configured to send notifications via email, SMS, or integrate with services such as Slack or PagerDuty, ensuring timely awareness of potential issues.

Another option for monitoring server performance is using the Postfix status command, which can be regularly executed to check key server metrics. Administrators can schedule cron jobs to monitor the mail queue size, disk space, and system load. If any of these metrics exceed predefined limits, email alerts can be automatically sent, enabling quick corrective action before problems escalate.

Regular Backup and Recovery Testing

Routine backups are essential for ensuring the availability and integrity of mail server data. Backups should include mail data, user configurations, and server settings. It is not enough to just back up the data—testing the recovery process is just as important.

To ensure that we can recover from a disaster, perform regular recovery drills to test the backup process, and make sure it works. Additionally, regularly verify the integrity of backups to prevent data loss in case of server failure.

Troubleshooting Common Mail Server Issues

Several common issues may arise when running a mail server, including problems with email delivery, mail queues, server connectivity, or authentication mechanisms such as SPF, DKIM, and DMARC. The following is a systematic guide to identifying and resolving these problems effectively.

Email Delivery Failures

When emails are not being delivered, it is essential to check the Postfix logs for specific error messages such as:

- `451 Temporary Failure`
- `550 Relaying Denied`
- `554 Message rejected: Email address is not verified`
- `550 5.7.1 SPF check failed`
- `DKIM verification failed`

These errors often indicate issues with server configuration, DNS records, or domain authentication.

Key Areas to Check:

1. DNS Records for Domain Authentication:

    SPF: Ensure the domain includes Amazon SES in its SPF policy.

    `dig TXT yourdomain.com +short`

    Expected Output:

    `v=spf1 include:amazonses.com ~all`

    DKIM: Verify that the public key for DKIM is published and correctly formatted.

    `dig TXT selector._domainkey.yourdomain.com +short`

    Replace `**selector**` with the actual DKIM selector provided by SES.

    DMARC: Ensure that a DMARC record is configured.

    `dig TXT _dmarc.yourdomain.com +short`

    Example Output:

    `v=DMARC1; p=none; rua=mailto:admin@yourdomain.com"`

2. Mail Server Blacklisting: Use tools like `**mxtoolbox.com**` or `**dnsbl.info**` to ensure the mail server is not on a blocklist.

3. Verify Mail Server Identity and Routing:
    - Confirm the domain's MX record points to the correct host.
    - Validate that the domain's reverse DNS (PTR record) resolves properly.

Mail Queue Backlog

If the mail queue is full, it may be due to undelivered emails piling up, often caused by routing issues or downstream mail server delays.

To view the queue: **`mailq`**

Sample Output:

```
A1B2C3D4E5      12345 Tue Jun  8 09:30:00  sender@example.com
                                            recipient@example.net
                (connect to smtp.example.net[1.2.3.4]:25: Connection timed out)
```

Alternatively, use: **`postqueue -p`**

Sample Output:

```
-Queue ID-  --Size-- ----Arrival Time---- -Sender/Recipient-------
A1B2C3D4E5     12345 Tue Jun  8 09:30:00  sender@example.com
                                           recipient@example.net
```

To attempt re-delivery of all queued mail: **`sudo postqueue -f`**

Server Connectivity

If the mail server is not responding, check local and network firewall rules to ensure the required ports are open:

- **Port 25 (SMTP)**
- **Port 465 (SMTPS)**
- **Port 587 (Submission)**

To test SMTP access: **`telnet mail.example.com 25`**

Expected Output:

```
220 mail.example.com ESMTP Postfix
```

If the server does not respond, check:

- Local firewall **(`iptables`, `ufw`, `firewalld`)**
- Cloud provider security groups (for example, AWS EC2 security groups)

Spam Filtering Problems

If legitimate emails are marked as spam, or spam is not being filtered properly:

1. Review the configuration of the spam filtering software (for example, **`SpamAssassin`**).
2. Ensure the spam threshold is appropriate: **`sudo nano /etc/spamassassin/local.cf`**

   Set: **`required_score 5.0`**

   Lowering this score makes filtering more aggressive; increasing it makes it more permissive.
3. Examine message headers for **`SpamAssassin`** scores and **`DKIM/SPF`** status.

Reviewing Logs for Deeper Insight

Logs are critical for diagnosing mail server problems.

To view Postfix-specific logs: **`sudo tail -f /var/log/mail.log`**

For **`systemd`**-based systems: **`sudo journalctl -u postfix`**

Sample Output:

```
Jun 08 09:30:00 mailserver postfix/smtp[1234]: connect to smtp.example.
net[1.2.3.4]:25: Connection timed out
Jun 08 09:30:05 mailserver postfix/qmgr[5678]: A1B2C3D4E5: from=<sender@
example.com>, size=12345, nrcpt=1 (queue active)
Jun 08 09:30:10 mailserver postfix/smtp[1234]: A1B2C3D4E5: to=<recipient@
example.net>, relay=none, delay=10, status=deferred
```

These logs help identify delivery issues, authentication failures, DNS resolution problems, and server load delays.

Understanding expected output for key postfix mail queue commands in Rocky Linux 9

For system administrators and learners managing *mail servers with Postfix on Rocky Linux 9*, interpreting the output of diagnostic commands like **`mailq`**, **`postqueue -p`**, and **`journalctl`** is essential. This section breaks down these commands and highlights ***understanding success and errors displayed***, helping us quickly identify and resolve mail issues.

`mailq`: View the Mail Queue

The **`mailq`** command shows pending email messages in the Postfix mail queue.

Successful Output (Queue Has Mail)

```
$ mailq
-Queue ID- --Size-- ----Arrival Time---- -Sender/Recipient-------
1234ABCD     1024  Mon Jun 10 12:00:00  admin@example.com
                                        user@example.com

-- 1 Kbytes in 1 Request.
```

Exploring the Meaning

Queue ID: Unique ID for the email.

Size: Size in bytes.

Arrival Time: When the mail was queued.

Sender/Recipient: From and to addresses.

The last line shows total queued size and number of messages.

Problematic Output (Empty Queue)

```
$ mailq
```

Mail queue is empty

This is not necessarily a problem. It means there are **`no pending messages`** – useful to confirm successful delivery.

`postqueue -p` – Postfix Mail Queue (Same as `**mailq**`)

This is identical in function to **`mailq`** and produces the same output:

```
$ postqueue -p
-Queue ID- --Size-- ----Arrival Time---- -Sender/Recipient-------
9F5F2ABC     5120  Tue Jun 11 08:34:20  webmaster@domain.com
                                        client@example.org

-- 5 Kbytes in 1 Request.
```

Use **`postqueue`** if scripting Postfix tools (for example, with `**-f**` to flush the queue).

`journalctl -u postfix` : Check Postfix Logs for Errors

This command shows **`systemd journal logs`** for the Postfix service.

Filtered for Errors Only

```
$ journalctl -u postfix -p err --no-pager
Jun 11 10:12:47 mailserver postfix/smtp[10234]: connect to smtp.example.
com[192.0.2.25]:25: Connection timed out
Jun 11 10:12:48 mailserver postfix/smtp[10234]: 9F5F2ABC: to=<client@example.
org>, relay=smtp.example.com[192.0.2.25]:25, delay=301, status=deferred
(connect to smtp.example.com[192.0.2.25]:25: Connection timed out)
```

Navigating This Section

Connection timed out: Could mean network issues, DNS errors, or the SMTP server being unreachable.

`status=deferred`: Postfix will retry sending later.

Healthy Service Output

```
$ journalctl -u postfix -p info --no-pager | tail -n 3
Jun 11 10:15:03 mailserver postfix/qmgr[1243]: 9F5F2ABC: removed
Jun 11 10:15:03 mailserver postfix/smtp[1250]: 9F5F2ABC: to=<client@example.
org>, relay=mail.example.org[198.51.100.23]:25, delay=2, status=sent (250 OK)
Jun 11 10:15:03 mailserver postfix/qmgr[1243]: 9F5F2ABC: removed from queue
```

This means:

- Mail was sent successfully.
- Message was **`removed from queue`**.

Command	Purpose	Success Output	Problem Indicator
`mailq`	Show mail queue	Messages listed with IDs and size	"Mail queue is empty" or no messages listed when expected
`postqueue -p`	Same as `mailq`	Same as above	Same
`journalctl -u postfix -p err`	Show Postfix errors only	No output or normal info logs	Connection errors, "deferred" status, timeouts

Figure 10.1: *Command Reference for Mail Server Administration in Rocky Linux*

Figure 10.1 provides a practical overview of essential commands for configuring and managing mail servers in Rocky Linux. It functions as a quick reference guide, outlining the purpose, basic syntax, and common usage scenarios of each command. The figure covers key tasks such as installing and configuring Postfix, managing mail queues, and integrating with cloud-based services like AWS SES. By consolidating this information, the table streamlines the learning process and enables administrators to execute critical tasks securely and efficiently, whether in on-premises or cloud environments.

Tip for Beginners

If mail is not being delivered, follow this workflow:

1. *Check the queue:* ***`mailq`***
2. *Inspect errors:* ***`journalctl -u postfix -p err`***
3. *Flush the queue (if needed):* ***`postqueue -f`***
4. *Restart the service (as a last resort):* ***`systemctl restart postfix`***

Integration with AWS SES for Scalable Email Management Introduction

Amazon Simple Email Service (Amazon SES) is a flexible, scalable, and cost-effective cloud-based email platform that enables businesses to send and receive emails using their own domains or email addresses. Designed with high deliverability in mind, Amazon SES includes robust features such as domain authentication, dedicated IP addresses, reputation dashboards, and email feedback loops. These capabilities make it well-suited for integration with on-premises mail servers like **Postfix**, enhancing email deliverability and reducing reliance on local infrastructure.

This section focuses on how to configure Postfix to relay outgoing emails through Amazon SES, leveraging AWS's infrastructure to improve scalability, security, and deliverability while minimizing operational overhead.

Amazon SES supports a wide range of email use cases, including transactional messages (for example, password resets), marketing campaigns, and system alerts. By integrating SES with a mail server like Postfix, organizations can benefit from AWS's globally distributed, highly available infrastructure, while keeping their on-premises environment lightweight and easy to manage.

Setting Up AWS SES

Before integrating AWS SES with Postfix, we need to set up an SES account. Follow these steps to get started:

1. **Sign up for AWS SES**: First, we need an AWS account. Once logged in, navigate to the SES service in the AWS Management Console.
2. **Verify the Email Address or Domain**: AWS requires that we verify the email address or domain we are planning to use for sending emails. This ensures that we own the domain and helps prevent unauthorized use.
3. **Request Production Access**: Initially, the SES account will be in the sandbox environment, which limits the number of emails we can send. To increase this limit and start sending production-level emails, we must request production access from the AWS SES console.
4. **Get SMTP Credentials**: AWS SES provides SMTP credentials, which we will use to authenticate Postfix when sending emails. These credentials are separate from our AWS access keys and can be generated in the SES console under ***SMTP Settings.***

Configuring Postfix to Use AWS SES

Once the AWS SES account is set up, we can configure Postfix to use AWS SES as an outbound SMTP server. Here are the steps we will follow:

1. **Install Postfix and Dependencies**: Ensure Postfix is installed and running on the server. We will also need the ca-certificates package to ensure that SSL/TLS certificates are validated correctly.
2. **Configure Postfix to Use AWS SES SMTP Server**: Edit the **`main.cf`** configuration file to include the SES SMTP server settings. We will need to add the following lines to the main.cf file:

```
relayhost = email-smtp.us-east-1.amazonaws.com:587 smtp_sasl_auth_enable = yes
smtp_sasl_password_maps = hash:/etc/postfix/sasl_passwd smtp_sasl_security_
options = noanonymous
smtp_tls_security_level = encrypt
smtp_tls_CAfile = /etc/ssl/certs/ca-certificates.crt
```

   Replace **`email-smtp.us-east-1.amazonaws.com`** with the SES SMTP server region specific to the setup. Ensure that the port 587 is used for TLS encryption.

3. Configure SMTP Authentication: Create the `/etc/postfix/sasl_passwd` file and add the SES SMTP credentials:

```
[email-smtp.us-east-1.amazonaws.com]:587
AWS_ACCESS_KEY_ID:AWS_SECRET_ACCESS_KEY
```

Replace **`AWS_ACCESS_KEY_ID`** and **`AWS_SECRET_ACCESS_KEY`** with the SES SMTP credentials. Then, run the following command to hash the password file and update Postfix's configuration: **`sudo postmap /etc/postfix/sasl_passwd`**.

Reload Postfix Configuration: After making the changes, reload Postfix to apply the new configuration: **`sudo systemctl reload postfix.`**

Testing the Integration

After configuring Postfix to use AWS SES, it is important to test the integration to ensure everything is working as expected. We can test the setup by sending a test email using the mail command or a script.

To send a test email using the **`mail`** command:

```
echo 'Test Email from Postfix using AWS SES' | mail -s 'Test Email' recipient@
example.com
```

Check the SES dashboard and email inbox for confirmation of the email delivery. If the email is successfully sent, we will see it in the **AWS SES Sent** section.

AWS SES Integration and Troubleshooting (SMTP Focus)

Amazon Simple Email Service (SES) provides a scalable platform for sending transactional, marketing, or notification emails. While integration with SES is straightforward, SMTP-based delivery can face challenges related to authentication, delivery errors, and permissions. This section offers an in-depth guide to properly configuring and debugging SES SMTP connections.

1. **Setting Up SMTP with Amazon SES:** To use Amazon SES with SMTP, follow these steps:
    1. **Generate SMTP credentials** via the AWS Management Console.
    2. **Use an SMTP client** like swaks or openssl for testing.
    3. **Ensure correct IAM permissions** are configured.
2. **SMTP Testing with `swaks`:** **`swaks`** is a powerful command-line tool for testing SMTP servers. Install it on our Linux system with:
    a. `sudo apt install swaks    # Debian/Ubuntu`
    b. `sudo yum install swaks    # RHEL/Rocky Linux`
    c. `sudo dnf install swaks    # RHEL/Rocky Linux`

To test SES with SMTP using **`swaks`**:

```
swaks --to recipient@example.com \
      --from admin@yourdomain.com \
      --server email-smtp.us-east-1.amazonaws.com \
      --port 587 \
      --auth LOGIN \
      --auth-user YOUR_SMTP_USERNAME \
      --auth-password YOUR_SMTP_PASSWORD \
      --tls
```

Parameters:

- **`--server`**: Region-specific SMTP endpoint (e.g., **`email-smtp.us-east-1.amazonaws.com`**)
- **`--auth-user` and `--auth-password`:** Use the SMTP credentials generated from the SES console.
- **`--tls`:** Enforces **`STARTTLS`** encryption.

3. **Understanding SES SMTP Errors:** SES may return specific SMTP status codes. Understanding these can speed up resolution:

SMTP Code	Error Meaning	Explanation / Action
554	**Transaction Failed**	Email was rejected – check domain verification or reputation issues.
530	**Authentication Required**	SMTP credentials missing or invalid.
535	**Authentication Credentials Invalid**	Username/password are incorrect.
421	**Temporary Service Issue**	Retry later; Amazon might be throttling.
550	**Message Rejected**	Could be blacklisted or invalid recipient.
451	**Throttling or Temporary**	Delay sending or check sending quota.

Table 10.1: SES SMTP Errors

Tip: *Check the full response from the SES server for specific error strings.*

4. **Required IAM Policy for Sending Email**

To authorize SES sending via API or SMTP, the IAM user or role must have the following permissions:

```
{
  "Version": "2012-10-17",
  "Statement": [
    {
      "Effect": "Allow",
      "Action": [
        "ses:SendEmail",
        "ses:SendRawEmail"
      ],
      "Resource": "*"
    }
  ]
}
```

- **`ses:SendEmail`:** For sending emails via the SES API.
- **`ses:SendRawEmail`:** Required for custom headers or MIME-type messages.
- **Resource: "*":** We can narrow this to specific identities like **`arn:aws:ses:us-east-1:123456789012:identity/yourdomain.com`**.

5. **Domain Verification and DKIM Configuration**

To avoid authentication failures or 554 errors, make sure:

- Our **domain or email address is verified** in SES.
- We have added the required **DKIM and SPF records** to the DNS:
  - **SPF**: **`v=spf1 include:amazonses.com ~all`**
  - **DKIM**: Amazon provides CNAME records to be added.
- **`Mail from domain`** settings are optionally configured for better DMARC alignment.

Best Practices for SES Troubleshooting

Step	Recommendation
Verify SMTP Credentials	Recreate if authentication fails repeatedly.
Confirm Domain Verification	Must be complete in the SES console.
Monitor SES Console Logs	Use CloudWatch for delivery and rejection logs.
Review Sending Limits	Check the daily sending quota and rate.
Use Test Emails	Use Amazon's provided test addresses (`success@simulator.amazonses.com`) to verify setup without delivery.

***Table 10.2**: SES Troubleshooting*

Advanced Debugging Tips

- **Using `openssl` for manual SMTP handshake:**

```
openssl s_client -starttls smtp -crlf -connect email-smtp.us-east-1.amazonaws.
com:587
```

Use this to view SSL/TLS certificate exchange and debug handshake issues.

- **Using CloudWatch Logs:**
  - Enable sending logs from SES.
  - Use metrics such as Delivery, Reject, and Bounce.

Sample Use Case

Suppose our application running on EC2 needs to send alert emails. We should:

1. Create an IAM role with **`ses: SendEmail`** permissions.
2. Attach it to the EC2 instance or Lambda.
3. Configure the application (for example, Postfix, Python, and so on) to use SES SMTP credentials or API.
4. Test with **`swaks`**, and confirm message delivery via SES logs.

Monitoring and Managing Email Delivery

Automating monitoring and alerting is a critical step to maintaining the reliability of a mail server. By setting up automated systems, administrators can be promptly alerted to potential issues, ensuring faster response times and minimizing service disruption. Tools like Prometheus can be used to collect metrics from the mail server such as server load, mail queue size, and delivery times. Prometheus can be configured to send alerts through various channels, including email, SMS, or third-party services like Slack or PagerDuty, making it easier to track issues in real time.

Additionally, Postfix provides a built-in status command that can be utilized to monitor server performance. Administrators can automate checks of essential system parameters, such as disk space, mail queue size, and system load, by scheduling regular cron jobs. If any of these parameters exceed set thresholds, the system can send immediate email alerts, allowing administrators to act before issues impact mail delivery or server functionality.

Best Practices for AWS SES Integration

Here are some best practices when integrating Postfix with AWS SES:

1. **Ensure Proper Authentication**: Use DKIM, SPF, and DMARC to authenticate our emails and improve deliverability. These records should be set up for our domain in AWS SES.
2. **Monitor Bounce and Complaint Rates**: Regularly monitor the bounce and complaint rates to avoid being flagged as a spammer. If our rates are too high, AWS may limit or suspend the SES usage.
3. **Send in Small Batches**: If we are sending marketing emails or large volumes of messages, consider sending emails in smaller batches to avoid overwhelming the email system or SES.
4. **Use a Dedicated IP Address**: For better control over our email reputation, we can request a dedicated IP address from AWS SES for sending emails.

Cost Considerations

Using AWS SES for sending emails is cost-effective compared to maintaining our own email infrastructure. AWS SES charges based on the number of emails sent and the amount of data transferred. However, be sure to track the usage to avoid unexpected charges. AWS provides a free tier for SES usage, but once we exceed the free tier limits, additional charges may apply.

Conclusion

This chapter provided an in-depth exploration of mail server setup and configuration on Rocky Linux, focusing on the installation and configuration of Postfix, a widely used Mail Transfer Agent (MTA). We learned the step-by-step process to install Postfix, configure essential parameters, and test its functionality to ensure successful email routing and delivery. This foundational knowledge enables us to handle basic mail server requirements and troubleshoot common issues effectively.

Advanced topics were also covered, including setting up secure email communication using TLS/SSL encryption, configuring virtual domains for multi-domain email management, and integrating user authentication mechanisms. These techniques provide robust tools for building a secure and scalable mail server infrastructure.

Additionally, the role of cloud services in modern email management was examined, with a focus on Amazon Web Services (AWS) Simple Email Service (SES). By integrating SES with Postfix, we can leverage a scalable, reliable, and cost-effective email delivery service for large-scale environments. This chapter equips us with essential skills to manage and secure mail servers in both local and cloud-based infrastructures, ensuring that they meet the demands of modern enterprise communication.

In the next chapter, we will explore virtualization with KVM on Rocky Linux, covering its installation, configuration, and virtual machine management. Additionally, we will discuss key concepts related to networking in virtualized environments and compare on-premises virtualization with cloud-based solutions like AWS EC2.

Points to Remember

- **Installing and Configuring Postfix:**
  - Postfix is a powerful Mail Transfer Agent (MTA) used for routing and delivering emails. It can be easily installed on Rocky Linux, using package managers like `dnf`.

  - Proper configuration is crucial for secure and efficient email delivery. Key configuration files include `/etc/postfix/main.cf` where essential parameters like **myhostname**, **mydomain**, and **myorigin** are set.
- **Managing Mail Domains and Users:**
  - Postfix supports multiple mail domains and virtual users, allowing administrators to manage emails for different domains on a single server.
  - Configuring virtual domains and using aliases in **/etc/aliases** can streamline mail management for enterprise environments.
- **Basic Mail Server Security:**
  - Securing mail servers is critical to prevent unauthorized access and spam. Postfix can be configured to use TLS/SSL for encrypting email traffic by setting up certificates in **/etc/postfix**.
  - Implementing user authentication with SASL (Simple Authentication and Security Layer) ensures that only authorized users can send emails through the server.
- **Monitoring and Troubleshooting:**
  - Monitoring tools like **mailq**, **postqueue**, and log files in **/var/log/maillog** help administrators identify and resolve email delivery issues.
  - Common troubleshooting techniques include verifying DNS records (e.g., MX and SPF records) and using the postfix check command to identify configuration errors.
- **Integration with AWS SES for Scalable Email Management:**
  - Amazon Simple Email Service (SES) is a cost-effective cloud solution for scalable and reliable email delivery. It integrates seamlessly with Postfix for sending large volumes of emails.
  - AWS SES handles email reputation management, bounces, and complaints, enabling administrators to focus on core server functions, while benefiting from a robust email infrastructure.

Multiple Choice Questions

1. Which command is used to install Postfix on Rocky Linux?
   a. `dnf install postfix`
   b. `yum install mail-server`
   c. `apt-get install postfix`
   d. `dnf install smtp-server`
2. What is the purpose of the `/etc/postfix/main.cf` file?
   a. To store email logs
   b. To configure Postfix settings
   c. To manage user authentication
   d. To define domain aliases
3. Which of the following is used to send a test email with Postfix?
   a. `smtp-test`
   b. `echo` and `mail`

   c. `postfix-sendmail`

   d. `smtp-cli`

4. Which parameter in the Postfix configuration specifies the domain from which emails originate?

   a. `mydomain`

   b. `myorigin`

   c. `inet_interfaces`

   d. `smtpd_tls_cert_file`

5. What is the purpose of TLS/SSL in Postfix?

   a. To compress email attachments

   b. To encrypt email traffic for secure communication

   c. To log email delivery details

   d. To enhance server performance

6. Which tool can be used to monitor Postfix Logs for troubleshooting?

   a. `mailq`

   b. `logcheck`

   c. `systemctl`

   d. `tail`

7. What is the function of AWS Simple Email Service (SES)?

   a. To manage virtual mail domains locally

   b. To provide a scalable and reliable cloud-based email service

   c. To monitor Postfix server logs

   d. To enable offline email backup solutions

8. Which parameter is configured in Postfix for multi-domain email management?

   a. `virtual_alias_maps`

   b. `relay_domains`

   c. `myhostname`

   d. `smtpd_use_tls`

9. What is the purpose of the postfix check command?

   a. To send a test email

   b. To verify the syntax and correctness of Postfix configurations

   c. To restart the Postfix service

   d. To view the Postfix mail queue

10. Which security measure is commonly recommended for Postfix servers?
    a. Disable TLS/SSL encryption for performance
    b. Restrict mail relay to authorized users
    c. Allow open relay for increased flexibility
    d. Disable logging for email activity

Answers

1. a
2. b
3. b
4. b
5. b
6. a
7. b
8. c
9. c
10. b

Questions

1. What is the role of email communication in modern organizations, and why is mastering mail server configuration essential?
2. Which mail transfer agent is recommended in this chapter for setting up a mail server on Rocky Linux?
3. What are the key steps involved in installing and configuring Postfix on Rocky Linux?
4. How can we manage mail domains and users effectively when setting up a mail server?
5. What are the primary security measures to implement on a mail server to safeguard communication channels?
6. How can monitoring and troubleshooting be effectively handled in a mail server setup?
7. What are the benefits of integrating AWS Simple Email Service (SES) with our mail server?
8. How does AWS SES enable scalability for email management in an enterprise environment?
9. What are the basic steps to configure Postfix for secure email transmission?
10. What are some common challenges faced during mail server configuration, and how can they be resolved?

Key Terms

- **Mail Transfer Agent (MTA):** A software responsible for the routing and delivery of email messages between servers. Postfix is an example of an MTA used for setting up mail servers.
- **Postfix:** A widely used open-source Mail Transfer Agent (MTA) for routing and delivering email on Unix-based systems, including Rocky Linux.
- **Mail Domains:** Domains used to route emails where the domain name typically represents the organization's email system (for example, user@domain.com).
- **Mail Users:** Individual email accounts created under a domain, allowing users to send, receive, and manage their emails.
- **Secure Socket Layer (SSL)/Transport Layer Security (TLS):** Protocols used to encrypt email communications, ensuring security during transmission.
- **Simple Mail Transfer Protocol (SMTP):** The protocol used for sending email messages between servers or from email clients to mail servers.
- **IMAP (Internet Message Access Protocol):** A protocol used for retrieving emails from a mail server, allowing users to access and manage their messages from any device.
- **POP3 (Post Office Protocol 3):** A protocol used for retrieving emails from a server to a local device, typically used for downloading and removing messages from the server.
- **Spam Filtering:** The process of identifying and blocking unwanted or malicious emails (spam) from reaching a user's inbox.
- **AWS Simple Email Service (SES):** A scalable and cost-effective email-sending service offered by Amazon Web Services, allowing seamless integration for sending and receiving emails at scale.
- **Mail Server Security:** A set of practices and tools, such as SPF (Sender Policy Framework) and DKIM (DomainKeys Identified Mail), used to protect mail servers from unauthorized access and abuse.
- **Email Queue:** A temporary storage area where outgoing emails are placed before being processed and sent by the mail server.
- **DNS (Domain Name System) Records:** DNS entries used for email services, including MX (Mail Exchange) records that direct email traffic to the correct mail server.
- **Virtual Mail Domains:** The use of multiple domain names on a single mail server, allowing different domains to be managed within a single server setup.
- **Greylisting:** A method used to block spam emails by temporarily rejecting them, forcing the sending server to retry after a delay which helps to identify legitimate servers.

CHAPTER 11
Virtualization with KVM

Introduction

Virtualization has revolutionized the way IT infrastructure is designed, enabling efficient utilization of resources, enhanced scalability, and reduced operational costs. Kernel-based Virtual Machine (KVM) is a robust, open-source virtualization solution that seamlessly integrates with Rocky Linux, transforming it into a powerful hypervisor capable of hosting diverse workloads. By leveraging KVM, organizations can create and manage multiple Virtual Machines (VMs) on a single physical host, ensuring optimal resource utilization and operational flexibility.

This chapter explores the implementation and management of virtualization on Rocky Linux using KVM, with a focus on installation, configuration, and integration with cloud-based solutions. Additional topics include networking with virtual machines, a comparison of the benefits and challenges of on-premises virtualization with AWS EC2, and an introduction to hybrid cloud environments for modern IT operations.

Structure

This chapter covers the following topics:

- Installing and Configuring KVM
- Creating and Managing Virtual Machines
- Networking with Virtual Machines
- Comparing On-premises Virtualization with AWS EC2
- Introduction to Hybrid Cloud Environments

Installing and Configuring KVM

Kernel-based Virtual Machine (KVM) is a powerful and open-source virtualization technology integrated directly into the Linux kernel. It enables Linux-based systems to function as full-featured hypervisors, offering high performance, scalability, and flexibility for managing Virtual Machines (VMs) across a wide range of use cases.

Rocky Linux, with its enterprise-grade stability and compatibility with modern hardware, serves as an ideal platform for deploying KVM. Its robust ecosystem supports both development and production environments, making it suitable for administrators at various experience levels.

This section presents a clear, step-by-step guide for installing and configuring KVM on Rocky Linux. Real-world lab scenarios are included to reinforce practical skills and support hands-on learning in environments that reflect typical IT infrastructure challenges.

Disclaimer. *For best results, use a physical machine or dedicated partition running Rocky Linux 9 with internet access. Virtual machines may not fully support all configurations, especially those involving hardware recognition and network performance. A physical setup ensures a realistic environment for advanced practice and troubleshooting.*

Prerequisites

Before beginning the installation, verify that the system meets the following requirements:

- A 64-bit processor with hardware virtualization support (Intel VT-x or AMD-V)
- Root (administrator) access to a Rocky Linux system
- Virtualization enabled in BIOS/UEFI

To check for virtualization support, run: **`egrep -c '(vmx|svm)' /proc/cpuinfo`**

A result greater than 0 indicates that virtualization is supported.

Step 1: Install Required Packages

Install KVM and its dependencies, using the dnf package manager:

- `sudo dnf install -y qemu-kvm libvirt virt-install bridge-utils`

These packages include:

- **`qemu-kvm`:** The main hypervisor
- **`libvirt`:** A toolkit to manage virtualization platforms
- **`virt-install`:** A tool to create new VMs
- **`bridge-utils`:** For configuring network bridges

Step 2: Enable and Start the Libvirt Service

Once the packages are installed, start the libvirt daemon and enable it to start on

```
sudo systemctl enable --now libvirtd
```

To confirm the service is active, use:

```
sudo systemctl status libvirtd
```

Step 3: Configure Bridged Networking (Optional but Recommended)

To allow VMs to communicate with external networks as if they were physical machines, configure bridged networking. We can use nmcli or manually edit network configuration files. Example with **`nmcli`**:

- `sudo nmcli connection add type bridge autoconnect yes con-name br0 ifname br0 ("KVM VM on bridge to host not getting IP address")`
- `sudo nmcli connection modify br0 bridge.stp no`
- `sudo nmcli connection add type bridge-slave autoconnect yes con-name br0-slave ifname <Your-eth-device> master br0`
- `sudo nmcli connection up br0`

Final Notes

This setup ensures that the Rocky Linux system is ready to create and manage virtual machines efficiently. It lays the groundwork for more advanced use cases, such as:

- Virtual network management
- Cloud integration (for example, OpenStack, AWS, and so on)
- Hybrid cloud deployments
- Virtualized lab environments for education or testing

Configuring Networking for Virtual Machines

Networking configuration is crucial for VMs to interact with each other and external systems. This lab shows how to configure network interfaces for the VM.

Scenario: We will configure the VM to use a **bridged network** to allow it to access the internet.

Steps:

- **Check the available network interfaces**: `sudo ip address`

  Identify the network interface to bridge (typically ens33 or eth0).

- **Create a bridge network**: To allow the VM to connect to the same network as the host, we will set up a bridge interface.

1. **Edit the Network Configuration:**

   Open the network configuration file for the active interface. For example:

   ```
   sudo nano /etc/sysconfig/network-scripts/virbr0
   ```

2. **Modify the Configuration:** Change the settings to create a bridge:

   ```
   DEVICE=virbr0
   ONBOOT=yes
   BRIDGE=br0
   ```

   Save and close the file.

3. **Create the Bridge Interface:** Create a new configuration file for the bridge:

   ```
   sudo nano /etc/sysconfig/network-scripts/virbr0
   ```

   Add the following content:

   ```
   DEVICE=virbr0
   TYPE=Bridge
   BOOTPROTO=dhcp
   ONBOOT=yes
   ```

   Save and close the file.

4. Restart Networking: `sudo systemctl restart NetworkManager`

   The bridge should now be active, and we can verify it using:

   ```
   ip addr show virbr0
   ```

Creating our First Virtual Machine

Once KVM is installed and networking is configured, we can create our first virtual machine. Follow these steps:

Steps to download the Ubuntu Desktop ISO on Rocky Linux 9 with Firefox

1. **Open Firefox:** Open the Firefox web browser.

   a. Click the **`Activities`** menu in the top left corner of the desktop.

   b. Type Firefox in the search bar and select the Firefox application to open it.

2. **Navigate to the Ubuntu Official Website**

   a. In the Firefox address bar, type the following URL: **https://ubuntu.com/download/desktop**

   b. Press **`Enter`** to access the Ubuntu download page.

3. **Select the Ubuntu Desktop Version**

   On the Ubuntu Desktop download page:

   a. Locate the "**`Download Ubuntu Desktop`**" section.

   b. Click on the download button for the latest version of Ubuntu Desktop. (for example, "*Ubuntu* 22.04 LTS")

4. **Confirm the Download:** A pop-up dialog will appear asking if we want to save the file.

   a. Ensure that the selected option is "**`Save File.`**"

   b. Click **`OK`** to start the download.

5. **Monitor the Download:** Firefox will display a download progress bar: Click on the **`download`** icon (a downward arrow) in the top-right corner of the Firefox window to view progress.

6. **Verify the Download:** Once the download is complete:

   a. Go to the default downloads directory (for example, **`~/Downloads`**).

   b. Verify the presence of the ISO file. It will typically be named something like: ubuntu-22.04-desktop-amd64.iso

7. **(Optional) Verify the ISO File Checksum**

   a. Download the checksum file from the Ubuntu website (available on the download page).

   b. Open a terminal and navigate to the download location: **`cd ~/Downloads`**

   c. Verify the checksum: **`sha256sum ubuntu-24.04.1-desktop-amd64.iso`**

   d. Compare the output with the checksum provided on the Ubuntu website. ("How to Download Ubuntu 24.04 LTS ISO File - YouTube")

8. **Ready to Use the ISO:** The downloaded ISO will be used to create a bootable USB drive or for virtualization purposes.

Troubleshooting KVM Networking (Bridged and NAT)

Networking issues are among the most common problems when working with virtual machines. The following are examples of common networking problems in KVM with solutions for bridged and NAT configurations:

1. **VM has no IP address**

   Symptom: The VM shows 127.0.0.1 or no IP via 'ip a'.

   Fix:

   - `sudo systemctl restart NetworkManager`
   - `sudo virsh net-autostart default`
   - `sudo virsh net-start default`

2. **Bridge network not working**

   Symptom: The VM cannot access external networks.

   Fix:

   - `sudo nmcli connection show`
   - `sudo nmcli connection modify br0 ipv4.method auto`

- `sudo systemctl restart NetworkManager`

3. **NAT not forwarding packets**

   Symptom: Internet unreachable from VM (ping fails).

   Fix:

   - `cat /proc/sys/net/ipv4/ip_forward`
   - `sudo sysctl -w net.ipv4.ip_forward=1`
   - `sudo firewall-cmd --zone=libvirt --list-all`

4. **DNS issues inside VM**

   Symptom: Ping to domain fails, but IPs work.

   Fix: Check **`/etc/resolv.conf`** inside VM

   Try **`pinging 8.8.8.8`** and compare with **`ping google.com`**

Creating and Managing Virtual Machines in Rocky Linux 9

Creating and managing virtual machines (VMs) in this environment begins with setting up KVM, allowing a single physical system to host multiple isolated VMs. Once the virtualization framework is in place, virtual machines can be configured with specific resources such as CPU cores, memory, disk storage, and network interfaces. Installation of operating systems within these VMs mirrors the process on physical hardware, offering a familiar workflow for system administrators.

An essential part of this setup includes configuring networking to allow communication between VMs and external systems. Whether for internal testing environments or production deployments, properly defined virtual networking ensures reliable data flow and system integration.

Beyond creation, managing VMs involves monitoring their performance, allocating resources dynamically, and ensuring each virtual instance runs efficiently. Maintenance tasks such as system updates, backups, and troubleshooting are integral to sustaining a high-performing virtual environment. Well-managed VMs contribute to system stability and scalability across various workloads.

This guide introduces a series of hands-on labs designed to reinforce practical skills in virtualization. These scenarios replicate real-world challenges, providing valuable experience in setting up, configuring, and managing virtual machines within Rocky Linux 9. Through structured learning and application, administrators can build confidence and proficiency in handling virtual infrastructures effectively.

Installing and Configuring KVM on Rocky Linux 9

Before we begin creating virtual machines, let us ensure that **KVM** is professionally installed and configured on our Rocky Linux 9 system.

Steps to create the virtual machine.

1. Create a Virtual Machine:

   - **`cd Downloads`**
   - **`sudo mkdir -p /var/lib/libvirt/images`**
   - **`sudo chmod 755 /var/lib/libvirt/images`**
   - **`sudo chmod +x ubuntu-24.04.1-desktop-amd64.iso`**

- **`sudo setfacl -m u:qemu:x /home/username`**

2. Adding the network interfaces:
   - `sudo nmcli connection add type bridge con-name br0 ifname br0 ("Linux as WiFi AP Bridge | Steely Wing Note")`
   - `sudo nmcli connection add type ethernet con-name br0-port1 ifname enp4s0 master br0`
   - `sudo nmcli connection up br0`
3. Use the **`virt-install`** command to create a virtual machine:

```
sudo virt-install \
  --name ubuntu24.04 \
  --ram 2048 \
  --vcpus 2 \
  --disk path=/var/lib/libvirt/images/ubuntu24.04.qcow2,size=20 \
  --os-variant ubuntu20.04 \
  --network bridge=br0 \
  --graphics none \
  --cdrom /home/username/Downloads/ubuntu-24.04.1-desktop-amd64.iso
```

4. **Monitor the Installation**: Follow the prompts to complete the OS installation. Once finished, the virtual machine will be ready to use.

Additional Lab Scenarios

Issue: "`Domain to Clone Must Be Shutoff`"

The error message **"`Domain to clone must be shutoff`"** occurs because the original virtual machine (ubuntu24.04) is still running. The virt-clone command requires the source VM to be powered off before it can proceed with cloning.

Solution:

1. **Shut down the original VM:** First, shut down the ubuntu24.04 by using **`virsh`**: **`sudo virsh shutdown ubuntu-vm`**

   If the VM does not shut down immediately (in case it is unresponsive), We can forcefully stop it with: **`sudo virsh destroy ubuntu-vm`**

2. **Clone the VM:** Once the original VM is powered off, we can run the virt-clone command again:
   `sudo virt-clone --original ubuntu-vm --name ubuntu-vm-clone --file /var/lib/libvirt/images/ubuntu-vm-clone.qcow2`
3. **Start the cloned VM:** After cloning, we can start the cloned VM:
   `sudo virsh start ubuntu-vm-clone`
4. **Snapshot Management:** Take snapshots of a VM to preserve its state before making changes:
   `sudo virsh snapshot-create-as ubuntu-vm snapshot1 "Initial setup snapshot"`

List and restore snapshots as needed:

- `sudo virsh snapshot-list ubuntu-vm`
- `sudo virsh snapshot-revert ubuntu-vm snapshot1`

With the next set of commands turning off, the virtual machine clone should be done:

- `sudo virsh shutdown ubuntu-vm-clone`
- `sudo virsh destroy ubuntu-vm-clone`

Finally, there is a command to confirm the service is enabled and which is the status of the virtual machines:

- `sudo systemctl enable --now libvirtd`
- `sudo virsh list --all`

This lab offers a thorough guide to downloading the Ubuntu Desktop ISO and managing virtual machines (VMs) on Rocky Linux 9. By following the detailed steps provided, users will gain the skills to effectively set up and manage virtual environments, whether for testing, development, or production purposes. The ability to create and clone VMs on a Linux-based system enhances flexibility and efficiency in handling various computing tasks.

Networking with Virtual Machines in Rocky Linux 9

In this chapter, we will focus on setting up and configuring networking for VMs running on **Rocky Linux 9**. We will explore various network setups, such as **bridged**, **NAT**, and **host-only** networking. Networking is a vital aspect of virtualization as it allows VMs to communicate with each other, the host system, and the outside world.

1. **Checking Network Interfaces**

To ensure the interfaces are up and properly configured, we can use the following commands:

- **`ip a` or `ip address`:** Shows all network interfaces and their current IP addresses.

  `ip a`

- **`ifconfig`:** If We still have this older command installed, it will also show the status of network interfaces.
  `ifconfig`
- **`nmcli` device status:** Displays the status of network devices managed by **`NetworkManager`**.
  `nmcli device status`

2. **Testing Connectivity**

- **`ping`:** Test connectivity to other devices or the internet.
  - **`ping google.com`**
  - **`ping 192.168.122.1`**
- **`ping6`:** To test IPv6 connectivity.
  - **`ping6 google.com`**

If this test fails, IPv6 is not enabled and internet; a request will need to be made with the ISP or service provider to have this option available.

- **`traceroute`**: Shows the path taken by packets to reach a destination. Useful for identifying network bottlenecks.
  - **`sudo dnf install traceroute -y  # Install if not available`**
  - **`traceroute google.com`**

3. **Route and Gateway Information**

- **`ip route`:** Displays the routing table for the system.
  - **`ip route`**

- `route`: Older but still useful, shows the routing table.
  - `route -n`
- `nmcli connection show`: To verify the current routing information for the active connections.
  - `nmcli connection show`

4. **DNS Troubleshooting**
   - `dig`: To query DNS servers for a specific domain.
     - `dig google.com`
   - `nslookup`: Another DNS lookup tool.
     - `nslookup google.com`
   - `cat /etc/resolv.conf`: Shows the DNS resolver settings.
     - `cat /etc/resolv.conf`
5. **Network Service Validation**
   - `systemctl status NetworkManager`: To check the status of NetworkManager.
     - `systemctl status NetworkManager`
   - `journalctl -xe | grep NetworkManager`: Shows logs related to NetworkManager for troubleshooting.
     - `journalctl -xe | grep NetworkManager`
6. **Firewall Rules and Ports**
   - `firewalld` **status**: If we are using `firewalld`, check its status.
     - `sudo systemctl status firewalld`
   - `iptables -L`: Lists iptables firewall rules.
     - `sudo iptables -L`
   - `nft list ruleset`: If using `nftables`, it shows the current ruleset.
     - `sudo nft list ruleset`
7. **Checking Network Interface Status**
   - `nmcli`: Useful to check and troubleshoot network interfaces.
     - `sudo nmcli`
8. **Network Diagnostics**
   - `ss`: Shows socket statistics which can help troubleshoot network services.
     - `ss -tuln  # List open ports and services`
   - `netstat`: Another tool for network statistics (use ss as a replacement on newer systems).
     - `netstat -tuln`
9. **Checking the Network Configuration**
   - `cat /etc/networks`: To view networks configured in the rocky linux 9 machine.
     - `cat /etc/networks`
   - `nmcli connection show <connection_name>`: View detailed configuration of a specific connection managed by `NetworkManager`.
     - `nmcli connection show <connection_name>`

10. **Testing Network Speed and Latency**
    - **`iperf`:** To measure network bandwidth between systems.
        - **`sudo dnf install iperf3 -y`**
        - **`iperf3 --version`**

    ```
    iperf -s  # On server
    iperf -c <server_ip>  # On client
    ```

11. **Checking Active Connections**
    - **`lsof -i`:** Lists all open network connections and related processes.
        - **`sudo lsof -i`**

12. **System Logs for Network Events**
    - **`dmesg | grep eth`:** Check for interface-related messages in the kernel logs.
        - **`dmesg | grep eth`**
    - **`journalctl -xe | grep network`:** Check logs for network-related errors.
        - **`journalctl -xe | grep network`**

Summary of Useful Commands:

- **Interface information**: `ip a`, `nmcli device status`
- **Connectivity tests**: `ping`, `traceroute`, `ping6`
- **Route and gateway**: `ip route`, `route -n`, `nmcli` connection show
- **DNS checks**: `dig`, `nslookup`, `cat /etc/resolv.conf`
- **Network service status**: `systemctl status NetworkManager`
- **Firewall status**: `firewalld status`, `iptables -L`, `nft list ruleset`
- **Network diagnostics**: `ss`, `netstat`
- **Networks troubleshooting**: `nmcli`
- **Speed and latency testing**: `iperf`
- **Active connections**: `lsof -i`
- **Logs**: `dmesg`, `journalctl`

This chapter has provided a comprehensive overview of configuring **virtual machine networking** in Rocky Linux 9. The primary networking models–**bridged, NAT, and host-only**–were analyzed in detail, each offering distinct advantages for connectivity, security, and isolation. Together, these models enable flexible configurations that can adapt to diverse deployment scenarios.

Through the **hands-on lab exercises**, readers gained practical experience in setting up and managing VM networking. These exercises reinforced core concepts by demonstrating real-world applications, from creating isolated test environments to enabling external connectivity and secure internal communication.

Armed with this knowledge, administrators can approach virtual machine networking with confidence, applying **best practices** to both small-scale setups and enterprise-level infrastructures. This chapter concludes by establishing a solid foundation for advancing into more complex virtualization and cloud integration tasks in the chapters ahead.

Securing KVM Virtualization Environments

Security is a fundamental aspect of any virtualization environment, particularly in enterprise or hybrid cloud setups. Kernel-based Virtual Machine (KVM), while robust and efficient, must be properly secured to prevent unauthorized access, data breaches, and cross-VM attacks. This section outlines the best practices for securing KVM on Rocky Linux, focusing on access control, encryption, virtual machine isolation, and firewall configuration.

1. **Access Control and User Privileges**

Proper access control ensures that only authorized users can manage virtual machines or modify critical configurations.

Create a dedicated user group for virtualization:

- `sudo groupadd kvmadmins`
- `sudo usermod -aG libvirt,kvm kvmuser`

This approach limits administrative rights and prevents users outside the group from modifying VM configurations.

Restrict socket permissions:

Ensure that **`/var/run/libvirt/libvirt-sock`** is only accessible to trusted groups:

- `sudo chgrp libvirt /var/run/libvirt/libvirt-sock`
- `sudo chmod 770 /var/run/libvirt/libvirt-sock`

2. **Encrypting Virtual Machine Disk Images**

Use LUKS to encrypt virtual disk images:

Create an empty disk image:

```
qemu-img create -f raw /var/lib/libvirt/images/encrypted.img 10G
```

Encrypt it using LUKS:

- `sudo cryptsetup luksFormat /var/lib/libvirt/images/encrypted.img`
- `sudo cryptsetup open /var/lib/libvirt/images/encrypted.img encrypted_vm`

Format and use the volume:

```
sudo mkfs.ext4 /dev/mapper/encrypted_vm
```

Assign to a VM as a block device.

3. **Virtual Machine Isolation and Network Segmentation**

Ensuring that VMs are isolated from each other (and the host) reduces the attack surface.

Use **`SELinux`** or **`AppArmor`**:

These kernel-level security modules provide Mandatory Access Control (MAC):

- `sestatus  # Check SELinux status`
- `sudo setenforce 1  # Enforce SELinux policies`

Isolate networks using firewalld zones:

- **`sudo firewall-cmd --zone=trusted --add-interface=virbr0 --permanent`**
- **`sudo firewall-cmd --reload`**

4. **Monitoring and Logging**

Continuous monitoring helps detect unusual behavior or attacks.

Enable and monitor **`libvirt`** logs:

- `sudo journalctl -u libvirtd`
- `sudo tail -f /var/log/libvirt/qemu/ubuntu24.log`

Install and use **`auditd`**:

- `sudo dnf install audit`
- `sudo systemctl enable --now auditd`

Configure audit rules for KVM-related binaries:

```
sudo auditctl -w /usr/bin/virsh -p x -k kvm-access
```

5. **Hardening Network Services**

Only expose the **`libvirt`** service where necessary and always protect remote access.

Disable remote TCP access unless using TLS or SSH:

```
sudo nano /etc/libvirt/libvirtd.conf
```

Make sure these lines are present and correctly set:

```
listen_tls = 1
listen_tcp = 0
auth_tls = "none"
```

Use SSH tunneling for remote management: **`ssh -L 5900:localhost:5900 user@host`**

6. **Keep KVM and Dependencies Updated**

Always patch vulnerabilities by ensuring the system is up to date:

```
sudo dnf update qemu-kvm libvirt virt-manager -y
```

Securing a KVM-based virtualization environment requires a multi-layered approach that combines system hardening, effective user management, and proactive monitoring. Within Rocky Linux 9, robust security can be achieved by enforcing encryption standards, applying strict access controls, and isolating virtual machines to prevent lateral movement and unauthorized access.

Network security plays a critical role in this process. Implementing firewall rules, using secure communication protocols, and segmenting networks contribute to minimizing exposure to potential threats. Each layer of protection strengthens the overall integrity of the virtual infrastructure, ensuring that virtual machines operate within a secure and controlled environment.

When properly configured, KVM can serve as a secure foundation for hosting production workloads. The combination of well-established Linux security mechanisms and best practices in virtualization results in a resilient platform capable of withstanding a wide range of attack vectors.

Comparing On-Premises Virtualization with AWS EC2

In this chapter, we will compare on-premises virtualization with cloud-based solutions like **AWS EC2**. By focusing on practical differences, we will explore factors such as performance, scalability, cost, and management complexity. We will also see how **KVM (Kernel-based Virtual Machine)** on **Rocky Linux 9** can be used for on-premises virtualization, and how this compares to AWS EC2 for scalable, cloud-based virtual machine deployments.

Firstly, all existing virtual machines should be deleted, using the graphical interface of the Virtual Machine Manager to clear the work environment.

Installing Ubuntu in `Virt Manager` on Rocky Linux 9

Objective: This lab will guide We through the process of installing Ubuntu on a virtual machine (VM) using Virt Manager on Rocky Linux 9. We will create a new virtual machine, allocate resources, and perform the installation, using the Ubuntu ISO image.

The steps to complete this event will now be shared:

Step 1: Launch Virt Manager

To begin with, open Virt Manager: **`sudo virt-manager`**

This will launch a graphical interface for managing virtual machines.

Step 2: Delete Existing Virtual Machines

Before creating a new VM, it is good practice to delete any previously created virtual machines to ensure a clean environment.

a. In Virt Manager, right-click on any existing VM.

b. Select "**`Delete`**" to remove it from the list of available virtual machines.

c. Confirm deletion if prompted, making sure to also delete associated disk images (if desired).

Step 3: Create a New Virtual Machine

To create a new virtual machine, follow these steps:

a. Click on "**`Create a New Virtual Machine`**"

   In Virt Manager, click the "**`Create a new virtual machine`**" button.

b. Select **`Local Install Media`** **(ISO image or CDROM)**

   Choose the option "**`Local install media (ISO image or CDROM)`**" and click **`Forward`**.

c. **Select the ISO Image**

   i. In the next window, click **`Browse`** and navigate to the location of the Ubuntu ISO image file (for example, **`ubuntu-20.04.iso`**).

   ii. Select the Ubuntu ISO image and click **`Forward`**.

d. **Choose Operating System and Version**

   i. Virt Manager will automatically detect the operating system. Confirm that **`Ubuntu`** is selected as the OS type and version.

   ii. Click **`Forward`**.

Step 4: Set Memory and CPU Resources

Next, configure the virtual machine's memory and CPU settings:

a. **Memory:** Assign memory to the virtual machine. A recommended amount for Ubuntu would be **2 GB**.

b. **CPU:** Assign at least **2 CPUs** for better performance.

c. Click **`Forward`**.

Step 5: Set Disk Storage

a. **Disk Space:**

   i. For storage, set a disk size of **25 GB** for the VM.

   ii. We can leave the default options for disk type and storage format (usually `qcow2` is fine).

b. Click `Forward`.

Step 6: Finalize the Configuration

At this point, we will see a summary of the VM configuration. We can review the settings:

- **CPU**: 2 CPUs
- **Memory**: 2 GB
- **Disk**: 25 GB

   a. Click "`Finish`" to create the virtual machine.

   b. The VM will be created and listed in Virt Manager, but it has not yet started.

Step 7: Start the VM and Begin Ubuntu Installation

Now that the VM is created, let us start the installation process:

a. Select the newly created virtual machine from the Virt Manager main window.

b. Click the "`Play`" button to start the VM.

c. The system will boot from the ISO image, and the Ubuntu installation process will begin.

Step 8: Follow the Ubuntu Installation Wizard

Once the VM starts, follow the Ubuntu installation wizard:

a. Select `Language and Region Preferences`.

b. **Choose installation type:**

   - Select "`Install Ubuntu.`"

c. **Update options:** Choose "`Download updates while installing`".

d. **Select installation type (Erase disk and install Ubuntu):**

   - Since this is a fresh install on a virtual machine, choose "`Erase disk and install Ubuntu.`"

e. **Continue and set the timezone, keyboard laWet, and user credentials.**

f. Click `Install Now` and follow the remaining prompts to complete the installation process.

This process may take some time, so it is important to be patient.

Step 9: Finish Installation and Reboot

After the installation is completed:

a. The installer will prompt us to **remove the installation media (ISO image)**. Virt Manager can automatically do this when we shut down the VM.

b. Click `Reboot Now`.

Step 10: Log In to Ubuntu

Once the system reboots, we will be greeted with the Ubuntu login screen. Log in using the credentials We created during the installation process.

Step 11: Verify the Installation

To ensure that Ubuntu is installed, check the status of the VM:

a. Open a terminal in the VM and verify the system's status.
    - `sudo apt update`
b. Confirm the VM's IP address (use ip a or ifconfig if networking is set up) to ensure it is connected properly.
c. From the host system (Rocky Linux 9), verify the VM's status using Virt Manager or the following virsh commands:
    - To list all VMs: **`sudo virsh list --all`**
    - To check the status of the VM: **`sudo virsh domstate <vm-name>`**

Lab Summary

These steps should now be completed in the laboratory environment:

1. Created a new Ubuntu virtual machine using Virt Manager.
2. Configured resources such as memory, CPU, and storage for the VM.
3. Installed Ubuntu using the installation wizard.
4. Verified the status and connectivity of the virtual machine after installation.

Creating a Virtual Machine using Virt-Manager

1. **Create a Virtual Machine using Virt-Manager:** Using **`Virt-Manager`**, we will create a new virtual machine for our on-premises environment. First, launch **Virt-Manager**: **`sudo virt-manager`**

    Choose the **New Virtual Machine** option, then follow the wizard to specify resources (RAM, CPU, disk space) and select the installation media (e.g., a **Rocky Linux 9** ISO).

    Please ensure that the **Network Interface** is connected to the **bridge**, in accordance with the guidelines provided for bridged networking previously in this chapter.

2. **Manage the Virtual Machine:** After the VM is installed, we can manage it directly from **Virt-Manager** or use **`virsh`** for command-line management:

    ```
    sudo virsh list --all
    ```

Updating all packages in ubuntu 24 virtual machine

Objective: This tutorial will guide us through updating all packages in the Ubuntu 24 Virtual Machine (VM). We will also cover how to access the Command Line Interface (CLI) inside the VM.

Access the command cine interface (CLI) in the virtual machine

Option 1: Using the VM's Console (Graphical Interface)

a. **Open the Virtual Machine Manager (Virt Manager, VMware, VirtualBox, etc.)** where the Ubuntu 24 VM is running.
b. **Start the Ubuntu 24 VM,** if it is not already running.

c. Once the VM boots up, log in to Ubuntu using the username and password.

d. After logging in, open the terminal: In the **GNOME** desktop environment, click on **"Activities"** at the top left, search for "**Terminal**", and open it.

Option 2: Access the VM via SSH (Remote Access)

If We have set up SSH on the Ubuntu VM, we can access the CLI remotely from the host machine or another system.

a. Ensure SSH is installed on Ubuntu 24 (if not already installed):

```
sudo apt install openssh-server
```

b. Find the IP address of the Ubuntu VM: We can find the IP address by running: `ip a`

c. Use **SSH to connect** to the Ubuntu VM: **ssh <username>@<VM-IP-address>**

d. Enter the password when prompted.

Step 2: Update Package Repositories

Now that We are in the CLI, it is time to update the package repository information. This ensures that the system can download the latest updates.

Run the following command: **`sudo apt update`**

Explanation: This command fetches the latest package information from the repositories.

Step 3: Upgrade All Installed Packages

To upgrade all installed packages, run the following command: **`sudo apt upgrade`**

Explanation: This command will upgrade all installed packages to the latest available versions. We may be prompted to confirm the upgrade; type Y and press *Enter* to proceed.

Step 4: Perform a Full System Upgrade (Optional)

To upgrade the entire system, including those packages that require new dependencies or removal of unused ones, use the following command:

```
sudo apt full-upgrade
```

Explanation: This command will perform a more comprehensive upgrade, which might involve installing new dependencies or removing old packages.

Step 5: Clean Up Unused Packages

After upgrading, it is a good practice to remove unnecessary packages that are no longer required. Use this command: **`sudo apt autoremove -y`**

Explanation: This command removes packages that were installed as dependencies but are no longer needed.

Step 6: Verify the Update

Finally, verify that all packages are up to date by running: **`sudo apt list --upgradable`**

Explanation: If no packages are listed, it means that the system is fully updated.

Summary: Key learning points in this tutorial:

- Access the Command Line Interface (CLI) inside our Ubuntu 24 Virtual Machine.
- Update the package repositories.
- Upgrade all installed packages.

- Perform a full system upgrade (optional).
- Clean up unused packages.

Monitor Performance

To monitor the performance of the KVM virtual machine, use tools such as **`htop`** and **`virt-top: sudo virt-top`**

The CPU, memory, and disk usage of VMs using the **virsh** can be validated with this command: **`sudo virsh domstats ubuntu24.04`**

Launching a Virtual Machine in AWS EC2

In this lab, we will explore how to launch a virtual machine in AWS EC2, which provides scalable computing resources in the cloud. AWS EC2 allows us to easily create virtual instances based on the requirements for computer power, memory, and storage.

Scenario: We will launch an EC2 instance, using the **AWS Management Console** and the **AWS CLI**, and then compare it to our on-premises KVM VM.

Steps:

1. **Create an AWS Account and Set Up AWS CLI:** If we have not already, create an **AWS account** at **`https://aws.amazon.com/`**
2. Then, install the AWS CLI on the local machine or Rocky Linux server:

It looks like the **`aws-cli`** package is not found in the current repository. We might need to enable the AWS CLI repository or install it using an alternative method.

Installing AWS CLI on Rocky Linux

- **Install via pip (Python package manager):**

Now install AWS CLI via **`pip`**:

```
sudo dnf install python3-pip
pip3 install awscli --upgrade --user
```

- **Install using the official AWS CLI bundle**:

  It is necessary to manually download and install AWS CLI version 2:

  - `sudo curl "https://awscli.amazonaws.com/awscli-exe-linux-x86_64.zip" -o "awscliv2.zip"`
  - `sudo unzip awscliv2.zip`
  - `sudo ./aws/install`

At this point, we can begin the following configuration process in the Rocky Linux CLI console: **`aws configure.`** The AWS configuration procedure has been covered in previous chapters.

3. **Launch an EC2 Instance from the AWS Management Console:**
   a. Log into the **AWS Management Console,** and navigate to **EC2**.
   b. Click **Launch Instance**, and choose an Amazon Machine Image (AMI) like **Amazon Linux 2** or **Rocky Linux 9**.
   c. Select an instance type (example, **t2.micro** for small workloads) and configure instance details (network, storage, security group).
   d. After the instance is created, it will be automatically assigned an IP address.

4. **SSH into the EC2 Instance:** Once the EC2 instance is running, use SSH to connect to it:
```
cd ~
cd Downloads
chmod 400 "Current key created"
ssh -i /path/to/your-key.pem ec2-user@<instance-public-ip>
```
5. **Install Software and Configure Networking:**
   a. The httpd service can be enable with the following commands:
      - `sudo dnf install httpd`
      - `sudo systemctl start httpd`
      - `sudo systemctl enable httpd`
      - `sudo systemctl status httpd`
6. **Verify Performance and Scaling:**
   a. AWS EC2 instances are highly scalable. The instance type or resize can change the instance as the workload grows. Scaling can be achieved easily through the AWS Management Console or using the AWS CLI:
```
aws ec2 modify-instance-attribute --instance-id <instance-id> --in-
stance-type <new-instance-type>
```

Example: `aws ec2 modify-instance-attribute --instance-id i-1234567890abcdef0 --instance-type t3.medium`

Comparing Performance: On-Premises KVM vs Rocky Linux Machine

Scenario: In this lab, we will compare the performance of an on-premises KVM virtual machine (Ubuntu 24) and a Rocky Linux 9 machine (either virtual or physical). The goal is to assess how hardware and virtualization affect system performance based on CPU performance, memory usage, disk I/O, and network latency. We will run several benchmarks on both systems to compare their performance in a real-world scenario.

Objectives:

- Benchmark CPU performance, memory usage, disk I/O, and network latency on both systems.
- Compare the results to understand the impact of virtualization and hardware resources.

Prerequisites:

- An **on-premises KVM virtual machine** running Ubuntu 24.
- A **Rocky Linux 9 machine**, either virtualized or physical.
- Internet access to install benchmarking tools.

Benchmarking On-Premises KVM Virtual Machine (Ubuntu 24)

The following steps will now be followed:

Step 1: Install Benchmarking Tools

On the **Ubuntu 24 KVM virtual machine**, open a terminal and install **sysbench**:
```
sudo apt-get update
sudo apt-get install sysbench
```

Step 2: Run CPU Benchmark

To benchmark CPU performance, run the following command:
```
sysbench --test=cpu --cpu-max-prime=20000 run
```

Note: *This command will calculate prime numbers, and the process may take a few minutes depending on the machine's CPU performance. It will output results, including the time taken and events per second which are key metrics for evaluating CPU performance.*

Step 3: Run Memory Benchmark

To benchmark memory performance, use the following command:

```
sysbench --test=memory run
```

This command will test the system's memory read and write capabilities, providing data such as the total time taken for memory operations.

Step 4: Run Disk I/O Benchmark

- To benchmark disk I/O, prepare the system by creating test files:
  `sysbench --test=fileio --file-total-size=10G prepare`
- This command creates 10GB of test files on the disk. After preparing, run the following to measure disk I/O performance:
  `sysbench --test=fileio --file-total-size=10G --file-test-mode=rndrd run`
- This will test random read operations on the disk. We can change the test mode to **`rndwr`** for random write operations.

Benchmarking Rocky Linux 9

New steps will now be completed:

Step 1: Install Benchmarking Tools

On the **Rocky Linux 9 machine**, open a terminal and install **`sysbench`**:

- `sudo dnf install epel-release -y`
- `sudo dnf install sysbench -y`
- `sysbench --version`

This will install **`sysbench`**, and check its version to confirm successful installation.

Step 2: Run CPU Benchmark

To benchmark CPU performance, run the following command:

```
sysbench --test=cpu --cpu-max-prime=20000 run
```

Like the Ubuntu KVM VM, this command will calculate prime numbers and provide CPU performance metrics, including execution time and events per second.

Step 3: Run Memory Benchmark

a. To benchmark memory performance, run: **`sysbench --test=memory run`**

b. This test measures memory throughput, including read and write speeds.

Step 4: Run Disk I/O Benchmark

a. To benchmark disk I/O, prepare the disk with the following command:
   `sysbench --test=fileio --file-total-size=10G prepare`

b. After preparing, run the disk test:
   `sysbench --test=fileio --file-total-size=10G --file-test-mode=rndrd run`

This test measures random read operations on the disk. If we would like to measure write performance, use the **`rndwr`** mode instead of **`rndrd`**.

c. To conclude this laboratory, the next commands are required:
   - `mkdir backup_disk`
   - `mv test_file* backup_disk`

Compare Results

Now that We have run benchmarks on both the **KVM VM (Ubuntu 24)** and the **Rocky Linux 9 machine**, it is time to compare the results.

CPU Performance Comparison

- **Metric:** The key metric for CPU performance is the execution time and events per second.
- **Interpretation:**
  - A **lower execution time** indicates better CPU performance.
  - Higher **events per second** indicate better CPU performance as the system can handle more calculations within a given period.

Memory Performance Comparison

- **Metric:** The key metric for memory performance is the time taken for memory read and write operations.
- **Interpretation:** Faster memory performance means lower time and higher throughput (MB/s) for read and write operations.

Disk I/O Performance Comparison

- **Metric:** The key metrics for disk performance are the read and write speeds (in MB/s) and IOPS (Input/Output Operations Per Second).
- **Interpretation:**
  - **Higher read/write speeds** and **higher IOPS** indicate better disk performance.
  - The KVM VM might show different disk performance based on its virtualization configuration and underlying physical hardware.

Network Latency Comparison

- If network latency is a concern in our environment, we can use tools like ping or iperf to measure network performance between the two machines.
- **Metric:** The key metric is latency in milliseconds (ms).
- **Interpretation:** Lower latency indicates better network performance, with faster data transmission.

By completing this lab, we should now have a better understanding of how an **on-premises KVM virtual machine** compares to a **Rocky Linux 9 machine** in terms of performance. The virtual machine's performance depends on the host machine's hardware, while Rocky Linux dynamically allocates resources, causing performance to vary with instance type and hardware.

Key Takeaways:

- On-premises KVM machines offer dedicated resources but are limited by the server's capacity.
- Rocky Linux virtual machines provide dynamic resource allocation but may experience performance variations depending on the underlying infrastructure.

This comparison can help We determine which environment is best suited for several types of workloads, whether it is CPU-intensive, memory-bound, or I/O-heavy tasks.

Cost Comparison between On-Premises Virtualization and AWS EC2

Cost is a critical factor in deciding between on-premises and cloud-based virtualization solutions. Let us compare the cost of running on-premises virtual machines using KVM and cloud instances on AWS EC2.

Scenario: We will calculate the cost of running a KVM virtual machine on-premises and compare it to the cost of running an EC2 instance for a similar workload.

Choosing between on-premises virtualization with KVM and cloud-based virtualization with AWS EC2 involves weighing factors such as initial costs, scalability, and maintenance. The following table outlines the key differences:

`AWS EC2 vs On-Premises KVM`

Feature	AWS EC2	KVM On-Premises
Initial Cost	None (Pay-as-you-go model)	High (Upfront hardware investment)
Maintenance	Fully managed by AWS	Manual (cooling, hardware support, replacements)
Scalability	Instant and elastic	Requires purchasing and configuring new hardware
Billing Model	Hourly or Monthly	One-time purchase + ongoing power and maintenance
Control Level	Limited (runs on shared infrastructure)	Full administrative and hardware control
Example Cost	t3.medium: $37/month ≈ $444/year	$3,000 server for 10 VMs ≈ $300/VM/year
Best Use Case	Short-term, elastic workloads	Long-term, stable and predictable workloads
Data Transfer Costs	Charged per GB (e.g., to/from internet)	Free (within local network/LAN)

Figure 11.1: *Cost Comparison: AWS EC2 vs On-Premises KVM*

This figure provides a side-by-side cost comparison between cloud-based virtualization using **AWS EC2 (Elastic Compute Cloud)** and **on-premises virtualization using KVM (Kernel-based Virtual Machine)**. It outlines key financial and operational factors such as initial investment, scalability, maintenance responsibilities, billing models, and data transfer costs. The comparison highlights that while AWS EC2 offers flexibility, rapid deployment, and a pay-as-We-go model suitable for dynamic workloads, KVM on-premises provides greater control and cost efficiency for long-term and predictable workloads. This table serves as a practical reference for organizations evaluating virtualization strategies based on budget, workload patterns, and administrative preferences.

Steps:

1. **On-Premises KVM Costs:**
    - The cost of on-premises KVM includes hardware expenses (initial purchase, maintenance, electricity), network infrastructure, and administrative overhead.

- **Example calculation**: Assume the cost of a physical server is **$3000**, and it can run 10 VMs. The annual cost of running each VM will be:

  `$3000 / 10 VMs = $300 per VM per year`

2. **AWS EC2 Costs:**
   - AWS charges based on instance type, storage, and data transfer. The cost for a **t2.micro** instance is approximately **$8.47/month** (varies by region).
   - We can calculate the cost for running an EC2 instance for a year:

     `$8.47 * 12 = $101.64 per year`

3. **Compare Costs:**
   - On-premises KVM virtualization may be cheaper overall for large-scale operations, but it requires upfront investment in hardware.
   - AWS EC2 is more cost-effective for small-scale or short-term use due to its pay-as-We-go model, with the flexibility to scale as needed.

In this chapter, we have explored and compared three distinct types of virtualization models: **local machines**, **virtual machines (VMs)**, and **cloud-based machines**. Local machines, also known as on-premises machines, are physical hardware owned and managed by the business. When using **on-premises virtualization**, such as KVM on Rocky Linux 9, businesses have complete control over the hardware, allowing for highly customizable and potentially cost-effective solutions for large-scale, long-term operations. However, this approach requires upfront investment in hardware and the ongoing maintenance of the infrastructure, making it less flexible than cloud solutions.

On the other hand, **cloud-based machines**, such as **AWS EC2**, offer scalability, flexibility, and ease of management, with the ability to scale up or down based on demand. Cloud platforms manage the underlying hardware, so businesses can focus on running their applications without worrying about hardware maintenance or resource limitations. While cloud services come with recurring costs, they provide unmatched agility and are well-suited for dynamic workloads or businesses that require rapid scaling. By understanding the benefits and trade-offs of each model, organizations can make informed decisions about which solution best fits their needs, whether for development, testing, or production environments.

Introduction to Hybrid Cloud Environments

A Hybrid Cloud environment seamlessly integrates on-premises data centers with cloud-based infrastructure, enabling organizations to bridge traditional systems with modern, scalable cloud solutions. This model offers the best of both world flexibility, scalability, and cost-efficiency—while maintaining control over sensitive data and meeting compliance requirements.

In this chapter, we will delve into the fundamentals of hybrid cloud architecture and examine practical strategies for integrating Rocky Linux 9 systems within such environments. Our focus will include the interoperability between on-premises infrastructure and cloud platforms such as Amazon Web Services (AWS), providing a clear roadmap for deploying hybrid workloads effectively.

Understanding Hybrid Cloud Architecture

In a hybrid cloud setup, organizations can strategically distribute workloads across local infrastructure and cloud services to maximize performance, minimize latency, and optimize costs. We will begin by exploring the key components of hybrid cloud architecture and how they interconnect to support dynamic and secure IT environments.

Scenario: We will begin by understanding the basic components of a hybrid cloud system, focusing on the interaction between **local virtualization (KVM)**, **AWS EC2**, and **AWS S3** for hybrid storage.

Components of Hybrid Cloud

- **On-Premises Data Center (Private Cloud):** This is the local infrastructure where We can deploy and manage our own virtual machines, networking, and storage using solutions like **KVM** on **Rocky Linux 9**.
- **Public Cloud (AWS):** AWS offers a wide array of services for virtual machines (EC2), storage (S3), and networking (VPC) that we can scale up or down based on our needs.
- **Cloud Management Platforms:** To manage hybrid environments, cloud management platforms such as **AWS Outposts** or **OpenStack** can be used to orchestrate workloads across on-premises and cloud systems.
- **Hybrid Cloud Network:** A hybrid cloud network connects on-premises and cloud environments, allowing seamless data transfer. For AWS, use **AWS Direct Connect** or **VPN connections**.

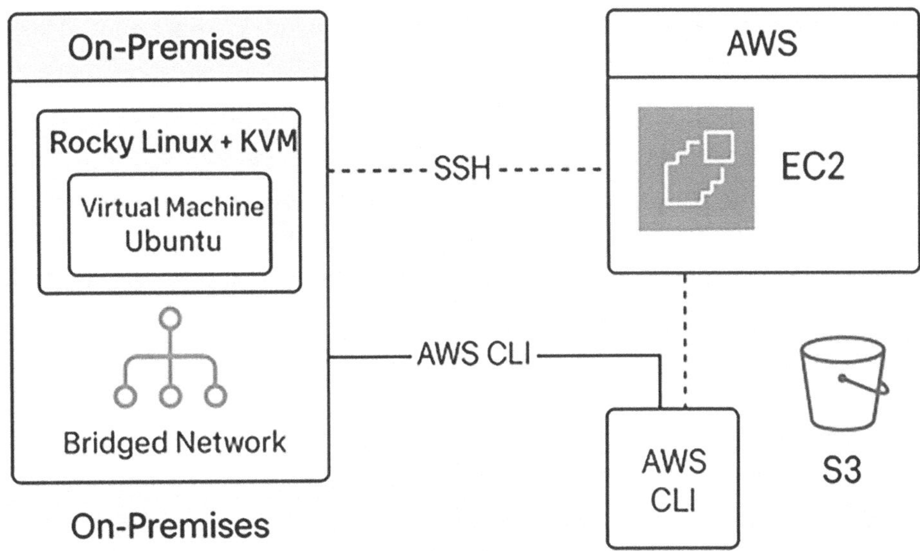

Figure 11.2: *A Hybrid Cloud Architecture*

This illustration seamlessly integrates on-premises virtual machines managed by **Kernel-based Virtual Machine (KVM)** with cloud resources in **AWS**, specifically **EC2** instances and **S3 storage**. In this architecture, the on-premises infrastructure, typically hosted in a local data center, runs virtualized workloads using KVM. These virtual machines can securely communicate with AWS EC2 instances over a **VPN or Direct Connect**, enabling workload extension, backup, or migration to the cloud. Simultaneously, the architecture allows the on-premises systems to access **Amazon S3** for scalable object storage, supporting tasks such as offsite backups, data archiving, and cloud-based analytics. This hybrid setup provides organizations with flexibility, scalability, and improved resource utilization while maintaining control over sensitive workloads within their local environment.

Setting Up Hybrid Cloud with AWS EC2 and On-Premises Virtualization

In this lab, we will configure a basic hybrid cloud environment by connecting a **KVM virtual machine** on **Rocky Linux 9** to an **AWS EC2 instance**, enabling the exchange of data between both environments.

Scenario: We will set up an on-premises KVM VM and link it to an AWS EC2 instance using a **VPN** connection to simulate a hybrid cloud environment.

Steps:

1. **Install and Configure KVM on Rocky Linux 9:** If not already installed, install **KVM** on the local **Rocky Linux 9** machine as explained in earlier chapters.

2. **Launch an EC2 Instance:**

   a. Go to the **AWS Management Console**, navigate to **EC2**, and create a **t2.micro** instance.

   b. Make sure to assign a **public IP address** for the EC2 instance.

   c. Configure the instance's **security group** to allow SSH and ICMP (ping) access.

3. **Set Up an SSH Connection to the EC2 Instance:** Instead of setting up a VPN connection, we will use the standard method to connect to our EC2 instance via SSH. This process is simpler, and does not require additional software installation like OpenVPN.

   a. **Prepare the SSH Key Pair:** If We have not already, ensure We have an SSH key pair created for the EC2 instance.

      i. Generate an SSH key pair (if not already created):

      ```
      ssh-keygen -t rsa -b 2048 -f ~/.ssh/my-ec2-key
      ```

      ii. Download the private key: when connecting to a newly created EC2 instance, make sure to download the private key file (`.pem`) from the AWS Management Console when We create the EC2 instance.

   b. **Modify Security Group for EC2:** Ensure the security group associated with the EC2 instance allows SSH access (default port 22) from the local machine's IP address.

      i. In the AWS Management Console, go to EC2 → Security Groups.

      ii. Select the security group associated with the EC2 instance.

      iii. Edit the inbound rules and ensure We have a rule that allows SSH access (port 22) from the IP or the range of IPs that should have access.

   c. **SSH into the EC2 Instance**: To connect to the EC2 instance via SSH, use the following command, replacing <ec2-public-ip> with the public IP of the EC2 instance, and <path-to-private-key> with the path to the .pem file:

      ```
      ssh -i <path-to-private-key>/my-ec2-key.pem ec2-user@<ec2-public-ip>
      ```

      Example: `ssh -i ~/.ssh/my-ec2-key.pem ec2-user@3.18.200.100`

      - `ec2-user` is the default username for Amazon Linux or RHEL-based instances (for Ubuntu, it is ubuntu).
      - Replace `` `<ec2-public-ip>` `` with the EC2 instance's actual public IP address.

   d. **Verify the Connection**: Once connected, we should be able to run commands on the EC2 instance remotely. To test the connection: `whoami`

This should be returned to `ec2-user` (or the appropriate user for the EC2 instance).

Final Notes:

- No VPN setup required: Unlike the previous VPN method, we do not need to configure additional services on the EC2 instance.

- Security Considerations: Always make sure to secure the SSH keys and only allow SSH from trusted IP addresses in the EC2 security group.

This is the regular and most common way to connect to an EC2 instance, making the process much simpler compared to setting up a VPN.

Lab 3: Using AWS S3 for Hybrid Cloud Storage

Hybrid clouds often use **cloud storage** solutions to store and manage data across both on-premises and cloud environments. In this lab, we will integrate **AWS S3** storage into our hybrid cloud, allowing both the on-premises and cloud-based systems to share data efficiently.

Scenario: We will configure **AWS S3** as a central storage solution, where both the **KVM virtual machine** on **Rocky Linux 9** and the **AWS EC2 instance** can upload, download, and synchronize data.

Steps:

1. **Create an S3 Bucket:**
   a. Log into the **`AWS Management Console`** and navigate to **`S3`**.
   b. Click on **`Create Bucket`** and follow the wizard to create a new S3 bucket. Choose an appropriate name and region.
2. **Install AWS CLI on Rocky Linux 9:**

   Install the **`AWS CLI`** on the **`Rocky Linux 9`** machine:
   ```
   sudo dnf install aws-cli
   aws configure  # Set up access keys, region, and output format
   ```
3. **Sync Data with S3 Bucket:**
   a. To upload a file from the KVM VM to AWS S3, use the **`aws s3 cp`** command:
   ```
   aws s3 ls
   touch myfile.txt
   aws s3 cp /path/to/local/file s3://<bucket-name>/<object-key>
   ```
   b. Similarly, we can download files from S3 to the KVM VM:
   ```
   aws s3 cp s3://<bucket-name>/<object-key> /path/to/local/destination
   ```
4. **Set Permissions for Hybrid Cloud Access:** Configure the **IAM roles** and **S3 bucket policies** to ensure secure access to S3 from both the EC2 instance and on-premises servers. Create an IAM role with the appropriate permissions and assign it to the EC2 instance.
5. **Automating Data Sync**: Automate data sync between the on-premises KVM VM and AWS EC2 instance using AWS CLI scripts and **`cron jobs`** can be done. Example:
   ```
   crontab -e  # Edit the cron jobs
   0 * * * * aws s3 sync /local/folder s3://<bucket-name>/backup/
   ```

Lab 4: Managing Hybrid Cloud Security with AWS IAM

Security is a critical concern in hybrid cloud environments. **IAM (Identity and Access Management)** plays a key role in controlling access to cloud resources and managing identities across both on-premises and cloud systems.

Scenario: We will configure **AWS IAM** to manage access to AWS services, ensuring that both the on-premises system and cloud services are secure.

Steps:

1. **Create IAM Roles and Policies:**

   a. Create a new **IAM role** for the EC2 instance that allows access to the S3 bucket and other services. Assign appropriate **`permissions`** to the role using IAM policies.

   b. Example IAM policy to allow full access to S3:

   ```
   {
     "Version": "2012-10-17",
     "Statement": [
       {
         "Effect": "Allow",
         "Action": "s3:*",
         "Resource": "arn:aws:s3:::<bucket-name>/*"
       }
     ]
   }
   ```

2. **Assign IAM Role to EC2 Instance:** Attach the IAM role to the **EC2 instance** that needs access to S3 storage or other AWS resources.

3. **Use IAM for On-Premises Systems:**

   a. On the **Rocky Linux 9** machine, we can use **`AWS CLI`** with **`IAM credentials`** to interact with AWS resources securely.

   b. Ensure that our AWS credentials are stored in the **`~/.aws/credentials`** file or set up using environment variables.

4. **Best Practices for Security in Hybrid Environments:**

   a. **Encryption:** Always encrypt sensitive data both in transit (using VPNs) and at rest (using S3 encryption).

   b. **Multi-Factor Authentication (MFA):** Enable MFA for IAM users and roles that access critical cloud resources.

In this chapter, we have explored the concept of **Hybrid Cloud Environments**, focusing on integrating **on-premises infrastructure (using KVM on Rocky Linux 9)** with **cloud resources (AWS EC2 and S3)**. Hybrid cloud models offer businesses flexibility and scalability, allowing them to optimize workloads, manage costs, and securely integrate on-premises systems with cloud-based resources.

Key takeaways include:

- **Hybrid Cloud Architecture** integrates private (on-premises) and public (cloud) clouds for optimal performance and cost-efficiency.
- The **VPN** connection enables seamless communication between on-premises and cloud systems.
- **AWS S3** provides a scalable storage solution accessible from both on-premises and cloud systems.
- **IAM** roles and policies help secure hybrid environments and manage access to cloud services.

By understanding and implementing these practices, organizations can leverage the power of both on-premises and cloud-based resources in a hybrid model, ensuring that they are well-prepared for future scalability and efficiency.

This concludes the chapter on *Introduction to Hybrid Cloud Environments*.

Conclusion

Virtualization with KVM offers a powerful and flexible framework for optimizing IT infrastructure, making it a cornerstone for modern data centers and cloud solutions. By transforming Rocky Linux into a hypervisor, KVM enables efficient resource allocation, cost savings, and operational scalability. Throughout this chapter, we explored the fundamental steps to install and configure KVM, demonstrating how to set up and manage virtual machines effectively. The integration of virtual networking further enhances connectivity and ensures seamless communication between VMs and physical or cloud-based networks, a critical aspect for deploying robust virtualization solutions.

Additionally, this chapter provided a comparative analysis of on-premises KVM virtualization and AWS EC2, shedding light on their unique advantages and use cases. This comparison offers insights into how organizations can choose the best approach based on their needs. Finally, the introduction to hybrid cloud environments underscored the potential of combining on-premises and cloud-based solutions, providing the flexibility to leverage the strengths of both. Mastering KVM on Rocky Linux equips readers with the knowledge to deploy versatile and scalable virtualization solutions, paving the way for efficient IT management and innovative cloud strategies.

In the next chapter, we shift our focus to containerization with Docker, a lightweight and efficient alternative to traditional virtualization. We will explore how to deploy and manage containers on Rocky Linux, integrate them with AWS services, and leverage Docker Compose for multi-container applications, setting the stage for scalable and portable cloud-native solutions.

Points to Remember

- **Installing and Configuring KVM**
    - Kernel-based Virtual Machine (KVM) is a built-in feature of the Linux kernel that allows Rocky Linux to function as a hypervisor for hosting virtual machines (VMs). Installing KVM involves using package managers like dnf to install necessary packages such as **`qemu-kvm`**, **`libvirt`**, and **`virt-manager`**.
    - Important configuration files are **`/etc/libvirt/qemu.conf`** and **`/etc/libvirt/libvirtd.conf`**, which define virtualization networking and storage pools. Enabling and starting the libvirtd service ensures the hypervisor operates correctly.
- **Creating and Managing Virtual Machines**
    - KVM enables administrators to create and manage VMs using tools like virt-manager for graphical interfaces or **`virsh`** for command-line operations. VMs can run different operating systems and be customized with CPUs, memory, and storage.
    - Snapshots and backups provide flexibility for managing VM states, enabling administrators to revert changes or replicate configurations.
- **Networking with Virtual Machines**
    - KVM virtual networking uses bridging or NAT. Bridged networking connects VMs directly to the host's physical network, while NAT allows VMs to communicate internally or access external networks through the host.
    - Use the **`virsh`** tool or edit network XML files in **`/etc/libvirt/qemu/networks/`** to manage virtual networks.
- **Comparing On-Premises Virtualization with AWS EC2**
    - On-premises KVM virtualization provides full control over infrastructure and can be more cost-effective for predictable workloads, while AWS EC2 offers scalability and elasticity for dynamic needs.

  - AWS EC2 simplifies infrastructure management by handling hardware provisioning, scaling, and updates, while KVM allows for customized environments tailored to specific organizational requirements.

- **Introduction to Hybrid Cloud Environments**
  - Hybrid cloud environments combine the benefits of on-premises infrastructure with cloud resources, offering flexibility and redundancy.
  - Using KVM in conjunction with cloud platforms like AWS enables organizations to create a hybrid setup, where local VMs interact seamlessly with cloud-based services for enhanced scalability and resilience.

Multiple Choice Questions

1. Which command is used to install KVM on Rocky Linux?
   a. `dnf install kvm-qemu`
   b. `dnf install qemu-kvm`
   c. `yum install kvm-tools`
   d. `apt-get install qemu-kvm`
2. What is the purpose of the `/etc/libvirt/libvirtd.conf` file?
   a. To store VM logs
   b. To configure the `libvirt` daemon
   c. To manage virtual machine snapshots
   d. To define network interfaces for VMs
3. Which tool is commonly used to create and manage virtual machines via a command-line interface in KVM?
   a. `virt-manager`
   b. `virsh`
   c. `kvm-cli`
   d. `qemu-tools`
4. What does a bridged network in KVM allow?
   a. Internal VM communication only
   b. Direct connection of VMs to the host's physical network
   c. VM access to the internet through the host
   d. Isolated communication within virtual machines
5. What is the role of snapshots in KVM?
   a. To encrypt VM disk images
   b. To create backups of the host system
   c. To save the current state of a VM for future restoration
   d. To monitor VM performance in real time

6. Which command starts the libvirt service on Rocky Linux?
   a. `service libvirt start`
   b. `systemctl enable libvirt`
   c. `systemctl start libvirtd`
   d. `libvirt --start`
7. What is the key advantage of AWS EC2 compared to on-premises KVM virtualization?
   a. Full control over the hardware infrastructure
   b. Simplified hardware provisioning and scalability
   c. Lower initial cost for predictable workloads
   d. Advanced support for virtual networking
8. Which parameter in KVM virtual network configuration defines the network type as NAT or bridged?
   a. `<forward mode>`
   b. `<network type>`
   c. `<bridge name>`
   d. `<host interface>`
9. What is a hybrid cloud environment?
   a. A setup that only uses cloud-based virtual machines.
   b. A system combining local VMs and cloud resources for flexibility.
   c. An on-premises KVM setup with no external integrations.
   d. A network configuration exclusive to AWS EC2.
10. Which tool is used for graphical management of virtual machines in KVM?
    a. `virt-manager`
    b. `qemu-gui`
    c. `kvm-console`
    d. `libvirt-dashboard`

Answers

1. a
2. b
3. b
4. b
5. b
6. a
7. b
8. a
9. b
10. a

Questions

1. What is the significance of virtualization in modern IT infrastructure, and how does KVM contribute to its effectiveness?
2. Which virtualization technology is highlighted in this chapter for use with Rocky Linux?
3. What are the key steps involved in installing and configuring KVM on Rocky Linux?
4. How can virtual machines be effectively created and managed using KVM?
5. What are the primary networking options available for virtual machines in KVM, and how do they differ?
6. What are the advantages and limitations of on-premises KVM virtualization compared to AWS EC2?
7. How does a hybrid cloud environment benefit organizations, and what role does KVM play in such setups?
8. What tools are commonly used to monitor and troubleshoot virtual machines in a KVM environment?
9. What steps are necessary to configure KVM virtual networks for seamless communication between VMs and external networks?
10. What are some challenges faced during KVM virtualization deployment, and how can they be addressed?

Key Terms

- **Kernel-based Virtual Machine (KVM):** An open-source virtualization technology built into the Linux kernel, allowing Rocky Linux to function as a hypervisor for hosting Virtual Machines (VMs).
- **Hypervisor:** Software that enables the creation, management, and operation of virtual machines by abstracting hardware resources. KVM is an example of a hypervisor.
- **Virtual Machine (VM):** A software-based emulation of a physical computer that runs an operating system and applications independently on a host system.
- **Libvirt:** A toolkit and API used for managing virtualization platforms like KVM, offering a unified way to create and control virtual machines and networks.
- **virt-manager:** A graphical user interface for managing virtual machines and virtualization configurations, commonly used with KVM.
- **virsh:** A command-line tool for interacting with KVM and libvirt, allowing administrators to manage VMs, networks, and storage.
- **Bridged Networking:** A network configuration where virtual machines are connected directly to the host's physical network, enabling them to communicate as independent devices on the network.
- **NAT (Network Address Translation):** A virtual network configuration where VMs access external networks through the host, typically used for isolating virtual machines.
- **Snapshot:** A saved state of a virtual machine that can be restored later, used for backups, testing, and recovering from errors.
- **Hybrid Cloud:** A computing environment that combines on-premises infrastructure with cloud services, enabling organizations to leverage the benefits of both.

CHAPTER 12
Containerization with Docker

Introduction

Containerization has transformed modern IT operations by providing lightweight, portable, and efficient application environments. Docker, one of the most widely used containerization platforms, enables developers and system administrators to package applications and their dependencies into isolated units, ensuring consistency across different environments. By leveraging Docker, Rocky Linux users can deploy and manage applications seamlessly, reducing overhead compared to traditional virtualization.

This chapter explores the implementation and management of containers, using Docker on Rocky Linux, focusing on installation, configuration, and integration with cloud-based solutions. Additional topics include container networking and storage, using Docker Compose for multi-container applications, and leveraging AWS services such as Amazon ECS and EKS for large-scale container orchestration.

Structure

In this chapter, we will cover the following topics:

- Installing Docker on Rocky Linux
- Creating and Managing Docker Containers
- Container Networking and Storage
- Docker Compose for Multi-Container Applications
- AWS ECS and EKS for Container Orchestration in the Cloud

Installing Docker on Rocky Linux

Docker is a powerful containerization platform that enables developers and system administrators to package applications and their dependencies into lightweight, portable containers. In cloud and hybrid environments, Docker plays a crucial role in simplifying application deployment and management.

Rocky Linux, as a robust enterprise-grade operating system, provides a stable foundation for running Docker containers. This guide details the step-by-step process to install Docker on Rocky Linux, configure essential settings, and verify its proper functionality.

Prerequisites

Before installing Docker, ensure that our system meets the following requirements:

- Rocky Linux 9 (or an earlier supported version) installed.

- Root or **sudo** privileges to perform administrative tasks.
- Internet connectivity to download Docker packages.
- The system is updated with the latest security patches and package updates.

To update the system, run: `sudo dnf update -y`

Step 1: Enable the Docker Repository

Docker is not included in the default Rocky Linux repositories. To install it, we need to enable the official Docker repository by running the following command in a single line on the CLI interface:

```
sudo dnf config-manager --add-repo https://download.docker.com/linux/centos/
docker-ce.repo
```

Note: *It is important to use the CentOS repository because Rocky Linux is binary-compatible with RHEL. Docker provides CentOS packages that work seamlessly on Rocky Linux.*

Verify the repository: `sudo dnf repolist | grep docker`

Step 2: Install Docker

Once the repository is added, install Docker with:

```
sudo dnf install -y docker-ce docker-ce-cli containerd.io
```

Confirm the installation: `docker --version`

Step 3: Enable and Start Docker

Enable and start the service: `sudo systemctl enable --now docker`

Check the status: `sudo systemctl status docker`

Step 4: Add the User to the Docker Group (Optional)

To allow a non-root user to execute Docker commands without using sudo, add the user to the **docker** group by running:

- `sudo usermod -aG docker $USER`
- `sudo newgrp docker`

After running this command, log out and log back in for the changes to take effect.

Note: *In this step, the local user must be added to the docker group to ensure they can run Docker commands without requiring elevated privileges.*

Step 5: Test Docker Installation

Run a test container to verify the installation: `docker run hello-world`

For running services: `docker ps -a`

Step 6: Running an Nginx Container (Example)

To verify that Docker is installed correctly, run an Nginx web server using the following command: `docker run -d --name mynginx -p 8080:80 nginx`

Once the container is running, we can access the Nginx web server in the browser at: **http://localhost:8080**

Note: *For easier navigation and access, this step should be performed using the graphical interface of Rocky Linux with Firefox.*

Step 7: Security Best Practices

To maintain security:

- Use non-root users for containers.
- Enable firewall rules.
- Regularly update Docker.
- Monitor logs: **`journalctl -u docker`**.
- Limit privileged containers.

By completing these steps, the docker is successfully installed and configured on Rocky Linux. This setup enables seamless container deployment and management, providing a more efficient and flexible environment for running applications.

The next section will cover the creation and management of Docker containers, including running applications inside containers, working with Docker images, and understanding essential container management commands.

Creating and Managing Docker Containers

Docker containers provide a lightweight, portable, and efficient way to deploy applications. Unlike traditional virtual machines, containers share the host operating system's kernel, making them more resource efficient. This section covers the fundamental concepts of creating, running, and managing Docker containers on Rocky Linux.

Understanding Docker Containers

A Docker container is a runnable instance of an image. It contains everything needed to execute an application, including the code, runtime, libraries, and dependencies. Containers are isolated environments that can be started, stopped, moved, and deleted without affecting the host system.

Step 1: Pulling a Docker Image

Before creating a container, it is necessary to pull an image from Docker Hub or another repository. The following command retrieves the latest official Nginx image:

```
sudo docker pull nginx
```

To verify that the image has been downloaded, list all available images:

```
sudo docker images
```

Step 2: Running a Docker Container

To delete the previous container and create a new container based on the Nginx image, the following set of commands should be applied:

- `sudo docker ps -a | grep mynginx`
- `sudo docker rm -f mynginx`
- `sudo docker run -d --name mynginx -p 8080:80 nginx`
- `sudo docker ps -a | grep mynginx`

Explanation:

- **`-d`:** Runs the container in detached mode (in the background).
- **`--name mynginx`:** Assigns a custom name to the container.
- **`-p 8080:80`:** Maps port **8080** on the host to port **80** in the container.

- **nginx:** Specifies the image to use.

To check if the container is running: sudo docker ps

Visit **http://localhost:8080** in a browser to see the Nginx welcome page.

Step 3: Listing and Inspecting Containers

- To list all running containers: **sudo docker ps**
- To view both running and stopped containers: **sudo docker ps -a**
- To get detailed information about a specific container: **sudo docker inspect mynginx**

Step 4: Managing Containers

a. Restarting a Container

   To restart a stopped container: **sudo docker restart mynginx**

   To validate the running docker: **sudo docker ps -a | grep mynginx**

b. Stopping a Container

   To stop a running container, use: **sudo docker stop mynginx**

c. **Removing a Container**

   To remove a container, first stop it (if running), then delete it: **sudo docker rm mynginx**

   To remove all stopped containers: **sudo docker container prune**

Step 5: Running Interactive Containers

For interactive containers, such as an Ubuntu-based shell session:

```
sudo docker run -it ubuntu
```

This process may take a few minutes depending on the internet connection.

Explanation:

- **-it:** Runs in interactive mode with a terminal.
- **ubuntu:** Specifies the Ubuntu image.
- **:** Opens a shell inside the container.

Exit the interactive session with exit. The **exit** command is now executed: It is essential at this point to exit the current location´s interface from the CLI hierarchy.

Step 6: Managing Container Logs

Finally, it is required to install the **sudo** command in this specific CLI and location:

```
apt update && apt install -y sudo
```

The next set of commands is used one more time to download the nginx image and add functionality to this service:

- `sudo docker pull nginx`
- `sudo docker run -d --name mynginx -p 8080:80 nginx`

Docker allows monitoring of container logs, using: **sudo docker logs mynginx**

To follow logs in real-time: sudo docker logs -f mynginx

Note: *To exit the real-time log view in Docker, we can simply press Ctrl + C. This will stop the log-following process but will not stop the container itself.*

This section covered the essential Docker commands and concepts for creating, running, managing, and removing containers. Mastering these fundamental operations is crucial for deploying and managing applications in containerized environments. These basic commands enable users to work with containers effectively, ensuring that applications are packaged with their dependencies for consistent deployment across different systems.

The next section will focus on more advanced topics, including **Container Networking** and **Storage**. It will explain how containers communicate with each other and how to efficiently manage persistent data, both critical aspects for building scalable and reliable applications. Understanding these concepts is the key for creating more complex, production-ready systems, using Docker.

Adding Expected Command Outputs

To improve clarity and help readers verify successful command execution, include expected outputs for critical commands such as ***docker compose up***, ***docker info***, and ***aws ecs describe-clusters.*** This section provides steps to integrate these outputs into *Chapter* 12.

1. **Identify Key Commands:** Review Chapter 12 to identify commands where expected outputs would enhance understanding. Focus on:
   - **docker compose up:** Shows the startup of multi-container applications.
   - **docker info:** Displays system-wide Docker configuration details.
   - **aws ecs describe-clusters:** Provides ECS cluster details.
   - **docker ps:** Lists running containers.
   - **docker logs mynginx:** Displays container logs.
2. **Execute Commands in a Test Environment:** Sct up a Rocky Linux 9 environment with Docker installed. Run each command and capture the output. For example:

   ```
   $ sudo docker compose up -d [+] Running 2/2
   -  redis Pulled
   -  web Pulled
   [+] Building 0.0s (0/0) [+] Running 2/2
   -  redis Running
   -  web   Running
   ```

   Listing 1: Expected Output for docker compose up

   Listing 1 shows the expected terminal output after running the `docker compose up` command in a configured Rocky Linux 9 environment. This command initializes and starts all services defined in the `docker-compose.yml` file. The output provides real-time logs indicating that Docker is creating containers, networks, and volumes (if not already present), followed by status messages from each running service. This listing helps users verify that their multi-container application is launching correctly and that all services are starting without errors.
3. **Integrate Outputs into the Chapter:** Add a subsection titled "`Expected Output`" after each command explanation. Use a code block to display the output, ensuring it is formatted clearly with the `lstlisting` environment in LaTeX or a similar formatting tool in our authoring software.
4. **Explain the Output:** Provide a brief description of what the output indicates. For example, for docker compose up `-d`, note that the output confirms the pulling and running of the Redis and Nginx containers in detached mode.
5. **Validate Outputs:** Test commands on Rocky Linux 9 with the latest Docker version (for example, Docker 27.3.1 as of June 2025) to ensure that outputs reflect current behavior. Update the chapter to specify the tested Docker version.

Container Networking and Storage

Container networking and storage are fundamental aspects of containerized environments, enabling efficient communication between containers and persistent data management. Unlike traditional virtualization, where virtual machines operate with dedicated network interfaces and persistent storage, containers rely on lightweight networking solutions and external storage systems to achieve portability and scalability.

This section explores key concepts in container networking and storage, covering network modes, storage options, and best practices for optimizing performance and security in containerized deployments.

Container Networking

Networking in containers allows them to communicate with each other and external services. Docker provides multiple networking options to accommodate different use cases. These include:

Bridge Network

The bridge network is the default networking mode for Docker containers. It enables communication between containers on the same host, using an internal virtual network, while isolating them from external networks unless explicitly exposed.

Key Features:

- Containers on the same bridge network can communicate using their container names.
- By default, containers on different bridge networks cannot communicate.
- Port mapping is required to expose container services to the host.

Example:

```
# Create a custom bridge network
docker network create my_bridge_network
# Run a container attached to the network
docker run -d --name web_container --network my_bridge_network nginx
```

Host Network

The host network mode allows a container to share the host's network stack. This eliminates the need for port mapping but removes network isolation between the container and the host.

Key Features:

- Direct access to the host's network interface.
- Reduced latency since traffic does not go through Docker's virtual network.
- Containers cannot be isolated from the host network.

To validate the existing containers, we run the next command: **`sudo docker ps -a`**

Overlay Network

Overlay networking is used in multi-host docker swarm deployment, enabling communication between containers running on different hosts.

Key Features:

- Requires a Swarm cluster to function.

- Provides built-in service discovery.
- Ensures encrypted communication between nodes.

Example:

```
# Initialize a Docker Swarm cluster
docker swarm init
# Create an overlay network
docker network create -d overlay my_overlay_network
```

Macvlan Network

Macvlan allows containers to appear as physical devices on a network by assigning unique MAC addresses.

Key Features:

- Containers can communicate directly with the external network.
- Suitable for legacy applications requiring Layer 2 network access.
- Each container gets its own IP address from the external network.

Example:

```
docker network create -d macvlan --subnet=192.168.1.0/24 my_macvlan_network
```

Macvlan networking is particularly useful in scenarios where containers need to be treated as separate physical devices on the network. This approach eliminates the need for NAT (Network Address Translation), allowing direct communication between containers and external devices while maintaining network isolation. It is ideal for environments where applications require direct Layer 2 network access such as legacy systems, network appliances, or specific security configurations. However, proper network configuration is essential, as Macvlan relies on the underlying host's physical network interface which may require adjustments to avoid conflicts with existing network settings.

Container Storage

Unlike traditional applications, containers are ephemeral by default. This means that any data generated inside a container is lost when it stops. To persist data, Docker provides several storage options:

Volumes

Volumes are the preferred storage solution for Docker containers. They are managed by Docker, and stored outside the container's filesystem, ensuring data persistence across container restarts.

Key Features:

- Independent of the container's lifecycle.
- Can be shared between multiple containers.
- Stored in /var/lib/docker/volumes/on the host.

Example:

```
# Create a volume
docker volume create my_volume
# Run a container with the volume
docker run -d --name db_container -v my_volume:/var/lib/mysql mysql
```

Bind Mounts

Bind mounts allow containers to access files and directories from the host system. Unlike volumes, bind mounts are tied to specific host paths.

Key Features:

- Direct access to host files and directories.
- Changes on the host are reflected in the container immediately.
- Security risks due to direct host system access.

Example:

```
docker run -d --name app_container -v /host/path:/container/path nginx
```

`tmpfs` Mounts

A **`tmpfs`** mount is an in-memory storage option that does not persist after a container stops. It is ideal for storing temporary runtime data.

Key Features:

- Fast, as data is stored in RAM.
- Data is lost when the container stops.
- Useful for session storage or caching.

Example:

```
docker run -d --name cache_container --tmpfs /tmp:rw,size=64m,mode=1777 nginx
```

Storage Drivers

Docker uses different storage drivers to manage container file systems. The choice of a driver impacts performance and compatibility.

Common storage drivers include:

- **OverlayFS:** Default for most Linux distributions, supports copy-on-write.
- **AUFS:** Legacy driver, used in older Docker versions.
- **Device Mapper:** Ideal for high-density workloads requiring performance isolation.

Checking the Storage Driver: `docker info | grep "Storage Driver"`

Choosing the right storage driver is crucial for optimizing Docker's performance and ensuring compatibility with the underlying operating system. Each driver has its strengths, and is suited for different workloads. OverlayFS is preferred for its efficiency and minimal overhead, while Device Mapper provides strong isolation for high-density deployments. AUFS, though once widely used, is now largely deprecated. Understanding the characteristics of each driver allows for better resource management and stability, particularly when running containers in production environments. Regularly verifying the active storage driver with docker info helps ensure optimal performance and troubleshooting, when necessary.

Best Practices for Networking and Storage

To optimize container performance, follow these best practices:

- **Networking Best Practices:**
  - Use **bridge networks** for internal container communication.

  - Leverage **overlay networks** for multi-host container deployments.
  - Minimize the use of the **host network** to reduce security risks.
  - Secure network traffic using **firewall rules and encryption**.
- **Storage Best Practices:**
  - Use **volumes** for persistent data instead of bind mounts.
  - Regularly back up volumes to prevent data loss.
  - Optimize performance by choosing the right **storage driver**.
  - Secure sensitive data with **encryption and access controls**.

Container networking and storage are crucial for ensuring efficient, scalable, and secure deployments. By selecting the appropriate network mode and storage solution, organizations can enhance the reliability of their containerized applications. Following the best practices for security and performance further strengthens containerized environments, ensuring seamless operation in both on-premises and cloud infrastructures.

Docker Compose for Multi-Container Applications

Docker Compose is a powerful tool that simplifies the management of multi-container applications. It allows developers to define and run applications with multiple interconnected services, using a single YAML configuration file. This chapter will explore how to effectively use Docker Compose on Rocky Linux 9, providing practical examples and insights into its capabilities.

Understanding Docker Compose

Docker Compose enables us to define all our application's services, networks, and volumes in a single **`docker-compose.yml`** file. This eliminates the need to run multiple docker run commands, streamlining the deployment process, and making it easier to manage complex applications. By using Docker Compose, developers can focus on building their applications, rather than managing the underlying infrastructure.

Installing Docker and Docker Compose on Rocky Linux 9

Before using Docker Compose, Docker must be installed on a Rocky Linux 9 system. The following steps outline the installation process:

1. **Install Docker**: First, ensure the system is **up-to-date**, and install the necessary packages:
   - `sudo dnf update -y`
   - `sudo dnf install -y yum-utils`
   - `sudo dnf config-manager --add-repo https://download.docker.com/linux/centos/docker-ce.repo`
   - `sudo dnf install docker-ce docker-ce-cli containerd.io`
2. **Start Docker**: After installation, start the Docker service, and enable it to run at boot:
   - `sudo systemctl start docker`
   - `sudo systemctl enable docker`

3. **Install Docker Compose**: Docker Compose can be installed, using the following command in a single line:
    - `sudo curl -L "https://github.com/docker/compose/releases/latest/download/docker-compose-$(uname -s)-$(uname -m)" -o /usr/local/bin/docker-compose`
    - `sudo chmod +x /usr/local/bin/docker-compose`
4. **Verify Installation**: Check if Docker Compose is installed correctly:
    - `docker compose version`

Creating a Multi-Container Application

Let us create a simple multi-container application, using Docker Compose. We will set up a web application, using Nginx and a Redis database for caching.

1. **Create a Project Directory**:
    - **`mkdir myapp`**
    - **`cd myapp`**
2. **Create a `docker-compose.yml` File**: This file will define our services. Create a file named **`docker-compose.yml`**, and add the following content:
    - **`touch docker-compose.yml`**

```
version: "3.8"

services:
  web:
    image: nginx:latest
    ports:
      - "8080:80"
    volumes:
      - ./html:/usr/share/nginx/html
    depends_on:
      - redis

  redis:
    image: redis:latest
```

In this configuration:

- The web service uses the Nginx image and maps port 8080 on the host to port 80 on the container.
- The redis service uses the Redis image.
- The **`depends_on`** directive ensures that the Redis service starts before the web service.

3. **Create HTML Content**: Create a directory named html, and add an **`index.html`** file:
    - `mkdir html`
    - `echo "<h1>Hello from Nginx and Redis\!</h1>" > html/index.html`

    a. **Start the Application**: Run the following command to start our multi-container application:

    b. **Troubleshooting scenario:** It is possible that **`docker-compose`** is not in the correct system **`PATH`**, even though the installation has been successfully validated (Docker Compose version v2.32.4). To resolve this issue, follow these steps:

    c. Check if **`docker-compose`** is installed.

Run: `which docker-compose or find / -name docker-compose 2>/dev/null`

`If the binary exists at /usr/local/bin/docker-compose, try running: /usr/local/bin/docker-compose up`

d. Use the new Docker Compose command format.

In recent Docker versions, **`docker-compose`** is now integrated as a subcommand. Instead of **`docker-compose`**, use: docker compose up

Note: *there is no hyphen - between docker and compose.*

e. Add **`docker-compose`** to the PATH

Which docker-compose returns a valid path but the command is still not recognized, add it to this **`PATH: export PATH="/usr/local/bin:$PATH"`**

f. To make this change permanent, run:

- `echo 'export PATH="/usr/local/bin:$PATH"' >> ~/.bashrc`
- `source ~/.bashrc`

g. Restart the session

If **`docker-compose`** still does not work, try logging out and back in or restart our system:

- `reboot`
- `docker-compose up`

This command will pull the necessary images, and start the containers as defined in the **`docker-compose.yml`** file. The output indicates that both services are running should now be displayed. At the end, *Control* + C is required to exit the previously entered interface.

Ensuring that Docker Compose is correctly installed and accessible is essential for managing multi-container applications efficiently. Misconfigurations related to the system **`PATH`** can prevent the command from being recognized, even when the installation is valid. By verifying the binary location and adjusting the **`PATH`** if necessary, users can avoid common execution errors. Additionally, since newer Docker versions integrate Compose as a subcommand (**`docker compose`** instead of **`docker-compose`**), adapting to this change ensures compatibility with modern setups. Regularly updating Docker, and reviewing system configurations help maintain a stable and functional development environment.

4. **Access the Application**: Open the web browser and navigate to **`http://localhost:8080`**. We should see the message "**`Hello from Nginx and Redis!`**".

Managing the Application

Docker Compose provides several commands to manage our application effectively:

Stopping the Application: To stop the running containers, use:

- `cd myapp`
- `docker-compose down`

Starting the Application: To start the running containers, use:

- `sudo docker compose up -d`

In case there is a warning shown, this happens because the **`docker-compose.yml`** file contains the obsolete version field. Some additional steps will be completed to mitigate any new error message.

Fixing the Warning:

1. Remove the version field from **docker-compose.yml**: Open the file with **nano /home/username/myapp/docker-compose.yml**
   a. Find and delete this line (or something similar): **version: '3.8'**
   b. Save and exit (CTRL+X, then Y, then *Enter*).
2. **Verify the fix**: It is recommended to run: **docker compose logs**

The warning should no longer appear.

Additional troubleshooting procedures:

Now, there are some additional steps required:

1. To check if the container´s services are, run this command: **sudo docker ps**.

   If the containers are not running, this explains the absence of logs.
2. Start the Containers if necessary. If no containers are running, start them with: **sudo docker compose up -d**

   Then check the logs again: **sudo docker compose logs**
3. Check for Errors in the Compose File. If the containers will not start, validate the docker-compose.yml file: **sudo docker compose config**
4. Verify Log Command, the correct command is: **sudo docker compose logs**
   - **Viewing Logs:** To view the logs of the services, run:
   - **Scaling Services:** We can scale services by specifying the number of instances. For example, to run two instances of the web service: **docker-compose up --scale web=2**

Networking and Volumes

Docker Compose automatically creates a network for the application, allowing containers to communicate with each other using their service names. We can also define custom networks and volumes in the **docker-compose.yml** file.

For example, to create a custom network and a volume for persistent data, modify the **docker-compose.yml** as follows: **sudo nano docker-compose.yml**

```
#yaml
#version: '3.8'

services:
  web:
    image: nginx:latest
    ports:
      - "8080:80"
    volumes:
      - ./html:/usr/share/nginx/html
    networks:
      - my_network
    depends_on:
      - redis
  redis:
    image: redis:latest
    networks:
      - my_network
```

```
    volumes:
      - redis_data:/data

networks:
  my_network:

volumes:
  redis_data:
```

In this configuration:

- A custom network named **`my_network`** is created for the services.
- A volume named **`redis_data`** is defined for the Redis service to persist data.

Defining custom networks and volumes in a **`docker-compose.yml`** file enhances both the connectivity and data persistence of containerized applications. By creating a dedicated network, services can communicate seamlessly using their service names, improving organization, and reducing reliance on manual network configurations. Persistent storage, managed through named volumes, ensures that data remains intact even if a container is restarted or removed. This setup is particularly beneficial for databases and stateful services like Redis, preventing data loss and enabling consistent application behavior. Proper network and volume management contribute to a more scalable, maintainable, and resilient containerized environment.

Best Practices for Using Docker Compose

Here are some best practices to follow when working with Docker Compose to improve organization, security, and reliability:

- **Keep the YAML File Organized:** Use comments and structure the **`docker-compose.yml`** file clearly to enhance readability and maintainability.
- **Use Environment Variables:** For sensitive information such as passwords or API keys, consider using environment variables or a **`.env`** file to keep the configuration secure.
- **Version Control:** Store the **`docker-compose.yml`** file in a version control system (such as Git) to track changes and collaborate with others effectively.
- **Testing**: Regularly test the Docker Compose setup in a staging environment before deploying to production to ensure everything works as expected.

Docker Compose is an invaluable tool for managing multi-container applications, especially on platforms such as Rocky Linux 9. By defining our application in a single YAML file, we can easily deploy, manage, and scale the services. This chapter provided a practical example of setting up a simple web application with Nginx and Redis, demonstrating the ease of use and flexibility that Docker Compose offers.

As we continue to explore Docker Compose, consider integrating it with CI/CD pipelines for automated deployments or expanding our applications with additional services to meet our needs. The possibilities are vast, and Docker Compose is a key component in modern application development and deployment.

Incorporating a CI/CD Integration Section

To enhance the practicality of *Chapter* 12, include a section on integrating Docker with a CI/CD pipeline using GitHub Actions. This section provides a sample workflow to build, test, and deploy a Dockerized application.

1. **Define the Section Objective:** Add a new subsection titled "*Integrating Docker with CI/CD*

Pipelines" after the *Docker Compose* section (Page 18). The objective is to demonstrate how to automate Docker image building and deployment.

2. **Create a Sample Application:** Use the existing Nginx and Redis example from the Docker Compose section. Ensure the **docker-compose.yml** file is stored in a GitHub repository.

3. **Write a GitHub Actions Workflow:** Create a workflow file to build and push a Docker image to Docker Hub. Below is a sample workflow:

```
name: CI/CD Pipeline for Docker on:
push:
branches:
-      main
jobs:
build-and-push:
runs-on: ubuntu-latest steps:
-      name: Checkout code
uses: actions/checkout@v4
-      name: Log in to Docker Hub uses: docker/login-action@v3 with:
username: ${{ secrets.DOCKER_USERNAME }} password: ${{ secrets.DOCKER_PASSWORD
}}
-      name: Build and push Docker image uses: docker/build-push-action@v6
with:
context: .
file: ./Dockerfile push: true
tags: user/myapp:latest
-      name: Run tests
run: docker-compose -f docker-compose.yml up -d && docker-compose -f docker-
compose.yml logs
-      name: Clean up
run: docker-compose -f docker-compose.yml down
```

Listing 2: GitHub Actions Workflow for Docker CI/CD

Listing 2 showcases a GitHub Actions workflow file designed to automate the CI/CD process for a Dockerized application. This workflow is triggered on code pushes to the main branch and performs a series of steps, including checking out the repository, logging into Docker Hub, building the Docker image, tagging it appropriately, and pushing it to a remote Docker registry. By leveraging GitHub Actions, this setup ensures that latest changes are automatically containerized and published, promoting consistent deployments and reducing manual intervention. This integration forms a critical part of modern DevOps pipelines, enhancing efficiency, traceability, and reliability in application delivery.

4. **Add the Workflow to the Chapter:** Include the above YAML file in a code block within the new subsection. Explain each step:

   - **Checkout code:** Clones the repository.
   - **Log in to Docker Hub:** Authenticates, using secrets.
   - **Build and push:** Builds and pushes the Docker image.
   - **Run tests:** Starts containers and checks logs.
   - **Clean up:** Stops containers to free resources.

5. **Provide Setup Instructions:** Instruct readers to:

   - Create a GitHub repository with the **docker-compose.yml** and **Dockerfile**.
   - Add Docker Hub credentials as GitHub Secrets (**DOCKER_USERNAME**, **DOCKER_PASSWORD**).
   - Create a **.github/workflows/docker-ci.yml** file with the workflow.

6. **Test the Workflow:** Validate the workflow in a test repository to ensure it builds and deploys correctly. Include a screenshot of a successful GitHub Actions run in the chapter.

AWS ECS and EKS for Container Orchestration in the Cloud

Container orchestration is a critical aspect of modern cloud computing, enabling organizations to manage and scale containerized applications efficiently. AWS offers two primary services: Amazon ECS and Amazon EKS. This guide explores both services, and their integration with Rocky Linux 9.

Note: *Using AWS services may incur charges. Ensure that we review AWS pricing details before proceeding.*

Both Amazon ECS (Elastic Container Service) and Amazon EKS (Elastic Kubernetes Service) provide robust solutions for deploying and managing containers at scale. ECS offers a simplified, AWS-native approach to container orchestration, while EKS provides a managed Kubernetes environment for greater flexibility and portability. When integrating these services with Rocky Linux 9, organizations can leverage the operating system's stability and security to build resilient, cloud-native applications. Understanding the key differences between ECS and EKS, along with their use cases, helps in selecting the right orchestration tool based on workload requirements, operational complexity, and cost considerations.

- **Amazon ECS:** Amazon ECS is a fully managed container orchestration service that simplifies deploying, managing, and scaling containerized applications. It allows running applications in Docker containers on EC2 instances or AWS Fargate.
- **Amazon EKS:** Amazon EKS is a managed Kubernetes service that simplifies running Kubernetes on AWS. It allows users to leverage Kubernetes' extensive ecosystem, while benefiting from AWS's scalability.

The following table highlights the key differences between Amazon ECS and Amazon EKS, helping users understand their distinct features, and determine the best fit for their container orchestration needs.

Feature	AWS ECS	AWS EKS
Management	Native AWS integration with simplified setup	Requires Kubernetes proficiency and cluster management
Complexity	Lower operational overhead	Steeper learning curve due to Kubernetes architecture
Vendor Lock-in	Tightly coupled to AWS ecosystem	Supports multi-cloud and hybrid deployments
Flexibility	Limited to AWS-native services	Extensible via Kubernetes tools and third-party plugins
Networking	Seamless integration with AWS networking stack	Manual configuration of networking components
Use Case	Ideal for lightweight, AWS-centric workloads	Suited for scalable, containerized applications with complex orchestration needs

Figure 12.1: *Key Differences between ECS and EKS*

This figure compares Amazon Elastic Container Service (ECS) and Amazon Elastic Kubernetes Service (EKS), highlighting their distinct roles in container orchestration on AWS. ECS is a fully managed solution tightly integrated with AWS services, offering simplicity and built-in support for AWS Fargate, which enables serverless container execution without managing underlying infrastructure. It emphasizes ease of use and seamless security with AWS Identity and Access Management (IAM). Conversely, EKS is a managed Kubernetes service that provides flexibility and portability, supporting both AWS-hosted and on-premises deployments via Amazon EKS Anywhere. By leveraging the open-source Kubernetes ecosystem, EKS allows the use of Kubernetes-native tools, configurations, and community-driven innovations. While ECS streamlines operations for teams preferring AWS-native workflows, EKS appeals to organizations that require Kubernetes-specific features, multi-environment deployments, and broader customization. The decision between ECS and EKS depends on factors such as complexity tolerance, scalability goals, and alignment with Kubernetes standards.

Setting Up AWS ECS on Rocky Linux 9

Prerequisites:

- AWS CLI installed
- Docker installed
- IAM role with ECS permissions

To set up AWS ECS on Rocky Linux 9, follow these steps to create and configure the ECS cluster, and ensure that it is ready for deploying containerized applications.

1. **Create an ECS Cluster**
   a. Log in to the **`AWS Management Console`** and navigate to ECS.
   b. Click on **`'Clusters'`** → '**`Create Cluster`**'.
   c. Choose '**`EC2 Linux + Networking`**' or '**`AWS Fargate`**'.
   d. Configure the cluster settings.
2. **Define a Task Definition**
   a. Go to '**`Task Definitions`**' → '**`Create new Task Definition`**'.
   b. Choose launch type: EC2 or Fargate.
   c. Specify Docker image, CPU, memory, networking, and IAM role.
3. **Run a Task**
   a. Navigate to **`'Clusters'`** → **`'Tasks'`** → '**`Run new Task`**'.
   b. Select the created task definition and specify the number of tasks.

After completing these steps, the ECS cluster will be set up and ready to deploy containerized applications on Rocky Linux 9. By defining a task and running it within the cluster, we can efficiently manage container workloads on a scale. We can further customize the deployment by configuring networking, security, and resource settings according to the application's needs. ECS offers flexibility with EC2 and Fargate options, enabling us to choose the best method based on the infrastructure and scalability requirements. As our containerized applications grow, we can monitor and manage them through the AWS Management Console, ensuring smooth and efficient operations.

Setting Up AWS EKS on Rocky Linux 9

Prerequisites:

- AWS CLI installed
- `kubectl` installed
- IAM role with EKS permissions

To set up AWS EKS on Rocky Linux 9, follow these steps to create and configure the EKS cluster, enabling us to manage and deploy Kubernetes-based containerized applications.

1. **Create an EKS Cluster**

    a. Open **`AWS Management Console`** → **`EKS`** → **`Create Cluster`**.

    b. Specify cluster name, Kubernetes version, and VPC settings.

    c. Create worker nodes using AWS Managed Node Groups.

2. **Configure `kubectl`**

    ```
    aws eks --region <region> update-kubeconfig --name <cluster_name>
    ```

3. **Deploy Applications**

    Create a Kubernetes deployment YAML file:

    ```
    apiVersion: apps/v1
    kind: Deployment
    metadata:
      name: my-app
    spec:
      replicas: 3
      selector:
        matchLabels:
          app: my-app
      template:
        metadata:
          labels:
            app: my-app
        spec:
          containers:
            - name: my-app
              image: my-docker-image:latest
              ports:
                - containerPort: 80
    ```

    Apply the deployment: **`kubectl apply -f deployment.yaml`**

4. **Expose the Application**

    ```
    apiVersion: v1
    kind: Service
    metadata:
      name: my-service
    spec:
      type: LoadBalancer
      ports:
        - port: 80
      selector:
        app: my-app
    kubectl apply -f service.yaml
    ```

Once we have completed these steps, the EKS cluster on Rocky Linux 9 will be fully configured to manage and deploy Kubernetes-based applications. By defining and applying Kubernetes deployment YAML files, we can easily scale the applications and manage them within the EKS environment. Exposing the application through a LoadBalancer service ensures that it is accessible to external traffic. With kubectl configured to interact with the EKS cluster, we can continue to deploy, manage, and monitor applications in a highly scalable and secure Kubernetes environment. EKS simplifies the management of containerized applications, enabling seamless integration with AWS services for enhanced performance and flexibility.

Creating a Decision Matrix for AWS ECS Versus EKS

To help readers choose between AWS ECS and EKS, add a decision matrix to the AWS ECS and EKS section. The matrix will compare key factors like cost, scalability, learning curve, and portability.

1. **Identify Comparison Criteria:** Based on the existing table (Page 20), expand the comparison to include:
    - **Cost:** ECS is cheaper; EKS incurs node and control plane costs.
    - **Scalability:** Both scale well, but ECS is simpler for smaller workloads.
    - **Learning Curve:** ECS requires less expertise; EKS demands Kubernetes knowledge.
    - **Portability:** ECS is AWS-specific; EKS supports multi-cloud.
    - **Use Case Suitability:** ECS for simple apps; EKS for complex, Kubernetes-native apps.
2. **Design the Decision Matrix:** Create a table in LaTeX to present the comparison clearly:

Criteria	AWS ECS	AWS EKS
Cost	Lower cost, especially with Fargate. No control plane fees.	Higher cost due to control plane and node fees.
Scalability	Simple scaling with AWS Auto Scaling and Fargate.	Highly scalable with Kubernetes features like Horizontal Pod Autoscaling.
Learning Curve	Easier for AWS users; minimal Kubernetes knowledge needed.	Requires Kubernetes expertise; steeper learning curve.
Portability	AWS-specific; limited multi-cloud support.	Kubernetes-native; supports multi-cloud and on-premises.
Use Case Suitability	Ideal for simple applications and tight AWS integration.	Best for complex, Kubernetes-native, or multi-cloud applications.

Table 12.1: *Decision Matrix- AWS ECS vs. EKS*

Table 12.1 presents a decision matrix that compares AWS Elastic Container Service (ECS) and Elastic Kubernetes Service (EKS) across key criteria to assist in selecting the most suitable orchestration platform for a given workload. The matrix evaluates factors such as ease of use, operational complexity, flexibility, integration with AWS services, support for Kubernetes-native tools, and cost considerations. By laying out these dimensions side by side, the table provides a practical reference for architects, developers, and DevOps teams to make informed decisions based on their specific technical requirements and organizational goals.

3. **Integrate the Matrix:** Insert the table after the existing comparison table (page 20). Reference it in the text, explaining that it helps readers decide based on their project needs.

4. **Add Decision Guidance:** Include a paragraph explaining how to use the matrix. For example: *"If cost and simplicity are priorities, choose ECS with Fargate. For complex, multi-cloud applications requiring Kubernetes, opt for EKS."*
5. **Validate with Real-World Scenarios:** Add a brief example for each service:
    - **ECS:** Deploying a simple web app with Nginx and Redis.
    - **EKS:** Managing a microservices-based application with multiple Kubernetes namespaces.

Adding Visual Diagrams for Docker Compose Architecture

To enhance understanding of Docker Compose, include a visual diagram illustrating the architecture of the Nginx and Redis multi-container application.

1. **Design the Diagram:** Create a diagram showing:
    - **Two containers:** web (Nginx) and redis.
    - **A custom network (`my_network`):** connecting the containers.
    - **A volume (`redis_data`):** for Redis persistence.
    - **Port mapping (`8080:80`):** for the web service.
2. **Integrate the Diagram:** Add the diagram to the Docker Compose section, after the **`docker-compose.yml`** example.

Docker Compose Architecture for Nginx and Redis Application

The Docker Compose architecture for an Nginx and Redis application demonstrates how multi-container environments can be efficiently orchestrated using a single configuration file. By defining services, networks, and volumes declaratively, Docker Compose simplifies the deployment and management of interconnected applications. In this case, the architecture integrates a web service powered by Nginx and a Redis service for in-memory data storage. The setup ensures seamless communication between containers through a custom network, while persistent volumes maintain data consistency across restarts. This approach highlights the advantages of container-based microservices, including modularity, portability, and ease of scaling, making it ideal for modern application development and testing workflows.

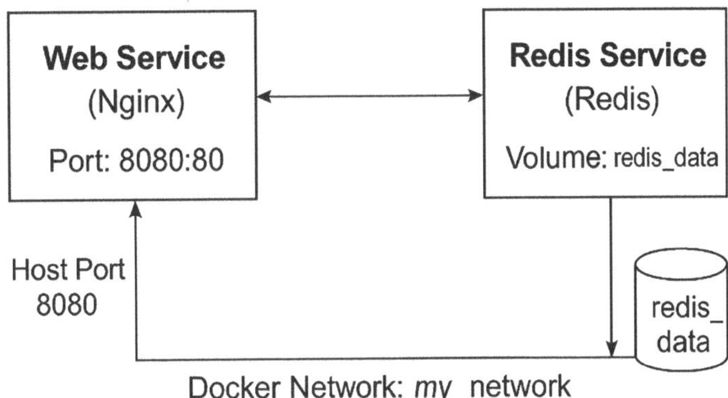

Figure 12.2: *Docker Compose Architecture for Nginx and Redis Application*

This figure depicts the architecture of a Docker Compose deployment that integrates two key services: a web service powered by Nginx and a Redis service for in-memory data storage. Both containers are orchestrated within a custom Docker network named **`my_network`**, enabling seamless inter-service communication through their service names. The web service exposes port 8080 on the host, mapped to port 80 inside the container, allowing external access to the application. The Redis service is linked to a persistent named volume, **`redis_data`**, which ensures data durability and continuity even when the container restarts. By combining networking, storage, and multi-service orchestration into a single configuration file, this architecture highlights how Docker Compose simplifies the management of complex containerized applications while maintaining scalability and resilience.

3. **Explain the Diagram:** Add a paragraph describing the components:
   - **web service:** Hosts the Nginx server, accessible via port 8080.
   - **`redis` service:** Runs the Redis database, connected to the web service via **`my_network`**.
   - **`redis_data` volume:** Persists Redis data across container restarts.
   - **`my_network`:** Facilitates communication between services.
4. **Ensure Compatibility:** Verify that the diagram aligns with the **`docker-compose.yml`** configuration previously shared. Test the setup on Rocky Linux 9 to confirm accuracy.

Integrating with AWS Cloud Services

Monitoring and Logging:

- **Amazon CloudWatch**: Monitor ECS and EKS containers.
- **CloudWatch Logs:** Log application errors and debugging information.

```
aws logs describe-log-groups --log-group-name /aws/ecs/container-insights/
```

Security Best Practices:

- **IAM Roles:** Assign least privilege policies.
- **AWS WAF:** Protect against common web attacks.
- **AWS Secrets Manager:** Store environment variables securely.

Best Practices for Implementation

To ensure the improvements are effective and maintain the chapter's quality:

- **Test All Changes:** Validate all commands, workflows, and diagrams in a Rocky Linux 9 environment with Docker 27.3.1, Docker Compose v2.32.4, and the latest AWS CLI.
- **Simplify Explanations:** Ensure latest content is beginner-friendly by using plain language and avoiding jargon where possible.
- **Version Control:** Store updated chapter files, diagrams, and workflow files in a version control system (e.g., Git) to track changes.
- **Review for Consistency:** Ensure the latest content aligns with the existing tone and structure of *Chapter* 12.
- **Seek Feedback:** Share the updated chapter with beta readers or technical reviewers to confirm improvements address the feedback from the questionnaire.

Finally, recommendations:

AWS ECS and EKS provide powerful solutions for container orchestration in the cloud, each with its strengths and use cases:

- ECS offers a simpler AWS-native experience.
- EKS provides the flexibility and extensibility of Kubernetes.

Both AWS ECS and EKS cater to different operational needs, with ECS being ideal for users seeking simplicity and tight integration with AWS services, while EKS appeals to those who need the flexibility and robust ecosystem offered by Kubernetes. When deciding between the two, organizations should consider factors such as the complexity of their workloads, their familiarity with Kubernetes, and the level of customization required for their container orchestration needs. By integrating these services with Rocky Linux 9, users can benefit from a stable and secure environment for running cloud-native applications, ensuring high performance and scalability in production environments.

By leveraging these services on Rocky Linux 9, organizations can efficiently deploy, manage, and scale their containerized applications.

Conclusion

By implementing these enhancements, Chapter 12 transforms into a more practical, visually engaging, and beginner-friendly guide. Including expected command outputs empowers readers to confidently verify their setups, while the addition of a CI/CD section demonstrates real-world application and workflow automation. The ECS vs. EKS decision matrix provides clear guidance for choosing the right orchestration tool, and the Docker Compose diagram simplifies the understanding of complex multi-container configurations.

Together, these improvements elevate the chapter's quality, making it an invaluable resource for professionals and students alike, who are working with Docker on Rocky Linux. With this comprehensive approach, readers will gain not only theoretical knowledge but also actionable insights to streamline containerization workflows and accelerate cloud-native development.

In the following chapter, we will build on this foundation by exploring automation with Ansible – diving into system administration, cloud infrastructure management, and scalable deployment strategies that further enhance the Rocky Linux environment.

Points to Remember

- **Installing Docker on Rocky Linux**
  - Docker is a containerization platform that enables applications to run in isolated environments with all dependencies bundled together. Installing Docker on Rocky Linux involves using the **`dnf`** package manager to install **`docker-ce`**, **`docker-ce-cli`**, and **`containerd.io`**.
  - Important configuration files include **`/etc/docker/daemon.json`** for custom runtime settings and **`/var/lib/docker/`** for container storage. Enabling and starting the Docker service ensures proper operation.
- **Creating and Managing Docker Containers**
  - Docker containers are lightweight, portable, and efficient alternatives to virtual machines, running applications with minimal overhead. Docker commands such as docker run, docker ps, and docker stop help manage container lifecycles.
  - Docker images, essential for container creation, can be pulled from Docker Hub or built using Dockerfiles, which define the dependencies and execution environment.
- **Container Networking and Storage**

  Docker supports several networking modes:
  - Bridge mode (default) allows isolated communication between containers.
  - Host mode provides direct network access for performance-sensitive applications.
  - Overlay networks enable communication across multiple hosts in Docker Swarm or Kubernetes setups.

    - Docker Volumes (docker volume create) offer persistent storage, ensuring data is retained across container restarts. Bind mounts allow direct file system access between the host and container.

- **Docker Compose for Multi-Container Applications**
    - Docker Compose simplifies multi-container deployment using a **`docker-compose.yml`** file, which defines services, networks, and volumes in a single place. Running docker-compose up automates container orchestration, making it easier to deploy and scale microservices-based applications.

- **AWS ECS and EKS for Container Orchestration in the Cloud**

  AWS provides two powerful solutions for container orchestration:

    - Amazon ECS offers a fully managed service for running Docker containers, with options for using AWS Fargate (serverless) or EC2 instances.
    - Amazon EKS enables Kubernetes-based container orchestration, offering scalability and high availability for cloud-native applications.

Integrating Docker with AWS ECS or EKS enables efficient deployment, scaling, and management of containerized applications in cloud environments, leveraging AWS's automation and scalability features.

Multiple Choice Questions

1. Which command is used to install Docker on Rocky Linux?
    a. `dnf install docker`
    b. `dnf install docker-ce docker-ce-cli containerd.io`
    c. `yum install docker-engine`
    d. `apt-get install docker`
2. What is the default Docker network mode?
    a. Host
    b. None
    c. Bridge
    d. Overlay
3. Which command is used to list all running containers?
    a. `docker ps`
    b. `docker list`
    c. `docker show`
    d. `docker containers -running`
4. What is the purpose of a Dockerfile?
    a. To execute Docker containers
    b. To define and build a custom container image
    c. To store logs for running containers
    d. To monitor container resource usage

5. Which Docker command removes a container permanently?
    a. `docker delete <container_id>`
    b. `docker stop <container_id>`
    c. `docker rm <container_id>`
    d. `docker halt <container_id>`
6. Which networking mode should be used to allow a container to share the host machine's network namespace?
    a. Bridge
    b. Host
    c. Overlay
    d. None
7. Which of the following tools is used for managing multi-container applications?
    a. Kubernetes
    b. Docker Compose
    c. Docker Swarm
    d. All of the above
8. Which command is used to build a Docker image from a Dockerfile?
    a. `docker run -f Dockerfile`
    b. `docker build -t <image_name> .`
    c. `docker create --image <Dockerfile>`
    d. `docker compile Dockerfile`
9. What is the primary function of AWS ECS?
    a. Running Docker containers at scale in the AWS cloud
    b. Managing virtual machines in AWS
    c. Providing Kubernetes-based container orchestration
    d. Storing container images securely
10. Which command starts a new container from an existing image?
    a. `docker launch <image_name>`
    b. `docker create <image_name>`
    c. `docker run <image_name>`
    d. `docker start <image_name>`

Answers

1. b
2. c
3. b
4. b
5. c
6. b
7. b
8. b
9. a
10. c

Questions

1. What is the significance of containerization in modern IT infrastructure, and how does Docker contribute to its effectiveness?
2. Which containerization platform is highlighted in this chapter for use with Rocky Linux?
3. What are the key steps involved in installing and configuring Docker on Rocky Linux?
4. How can containers be effectively created and managed using Docker?
5. What are the primary networking options available for containers in Docker, and how do they differ?
6. What are the advantages and limitations of using Docker containers compared to virtual machines?
7. How does Docker Compose help manage multi-container applications, and what benefits does it provide?
8. How can AWS ECS and EKS be integrated with Docker for large-scale container orchestration?
9. What are the steps necessary to configure Docker containers for persistent storage and seamless data management?
10. What are some common challenges faced during Docker container deployment, and how can they be addressed?

Key Terms

- **Containerization**: A lightweight form of virtualization that packages applications and their dependencies into isolated units, called containers, which can run consistently across different environments.
- **Docker**: An open-source platform for automating the deployment, scaling, and management of containerized applications.
- **Docker Image**: A read-only template used to create containers, containing the application and its dependencies.

- **Docker Container**: A running instance of a Docker image that encapsulates an application and its environment, providing portability and consistency across environments.
- **Dockerfile**: A text file that contains instructions to build a Docker image, specifying dependencies, configuration, and commands.
- **Docker Compose**: A tool used to define and manage multi-container applications in Docker, allowing users to configure and run multiple containers with a single command.
- **Docker Hub**: A cloud-based registry service that stores and distributes Docker images, providing access to both public and private repositories.
- **Container Orchestration**: The process of managing the deployment, scaling, and networking of containers, often using tools such as Docker Swarm, AWS ECS, or Kubernetes.
- **AWS ECS (Elastic Container Service)**: A fully managed container orchestration service provided by AWS for deploying, managing, and scaling Docker containers.
- **AWS EKS (Elastic Kubernetes Service)**: A managed Kubernetes service by AWS, allowing users to run and scale containerized applications using Kubernetes on AWS infrastructure.
- **Container Networking**: The configuration of networking in Docker allows containers to communicate with each other and the outside world, supporting bridge, host, and overlay network modes.
- **Persistent Storage**: The concept of managing and storing data outside of containers to ensure data durability and consistency, typically using Docker Volumes.

CHAPTER 13
Automation with Ansible

Introduction

Automation plays a critical role in efficiently managing modern IT infrastructure, and Ansible offers a robust, agentless framework for streamlining administrative operations. This chapter delves into how Ansible enhances configuration management, application deployment, and infrastructure provisioning within Rocky Linux environments, both in local data centers and cloud platforms. The key topics discussed in this chapter include the installation and configuration of Ansible, the development of structured playbooks, and the automated deployment of Rocky Linux instances on AWS. The chapter also introduces Ansible Tower as an enterprise-grade solution for managing large-scale automation workflows, improving system reliability, and operational efficiency. With Ansible's modular and declarative approach, system consistency is maintained, manual errors are minimized, and infrastructure processes are significantly accelerated, making it an indispensable asset in cloud-centric Linux administration.

Structure

This chapter covers the following topics:

- Installing and Configuring Ansible
- Writing Ansible Playbooks
- Managing Infrastructure with Ansible
- Automating Rocky Linux Deployments in AWS
- Ansible Tower for Large-Scale Automation

Installing and Configuring Ansible

Automation has become a cornerstone of modern IT operations, enabling organizations to streamline processes, reduce human error, and enhance efficiency. Ansible, a powerful open-source automation tool, simplifies the management of systems and applications through its agentless architecture and easy-to-understand playbooks. This chapter focuses on automating system administration tasks using Ansible, with a particular emphasis on managing cloud infrastructure, specifically in AWS environments. We will cover the installation and configuration of Ansible, writing playbooks, managing infrastructure, automating Rocky Linux deployments in AWS, and utilizing Ansible Tower for large-scale automation.

Installing and Configuring Ansible

To get started with Ansible, the first step is to install it on the administrator's control machine. Ansible can be installed on various Linux distributions, including Rocky Linux 9. Here is how to install and configure Ansible:

Prerequisites:

- Ensure that the administrator system is updated: **`sudo dnf update -y`**

- **Ansible Version:** Install Ansible 2.9 or later, as it supports Rocky Linux 9 and modern AWS modules.
- **Python Version:** Ensure Python 3.6 or later is installed, as required by Ansible.
- **Boto/Boto3:** Install **`boto3>=1.18.0`** for AWS integration.

1. **Install Ansible:**

   The administrators can install Ansible using the following command:

   - `sudo dnf install ansible -y`
   - `sudo dnf install python3-y`
   - `pip install ansible>=2.9 boto3>=1.18.0`

2. **Verify Installation:**

   After installation, verify that Ansible is installed correctly by checking its version: `ansible -version`

Expected Output:

```
ansible [core 2.15.3]
  config file = /etc/ansible/ansible.cfg
  configured module search path = ['/home/user/.ansible/plugins/modules', '/
usr/share/ansible/plugins/modules']
  ansible python module location = /usr/lib/python3.9/site-packages/ansible
  python version = 3.9.16 (default, Jan 11 2024, 15:30:00) [GCC 11.4.1
20230605 (Red Hat 11.4.1-3)]
```

This output confirms that Ansible is installed, displays the installed version, and provides relevant configuration paths. Seeing this output indicates that Ansible is ready for use.

Important note: *"Verify that Ansible 2.9 or later, and boto3 1.18.0 or later are installed to ensure compatibility with Rocky Linux 9 and AWS modules."*

1. **Configure Ansible Inventory**: Ansible uses an inventory file to manage the hosts it will automate. The default inventory file is located at **`/etc/ansible/hosts`**. The administrators can edit this file to add the administrator managed nodes:

   ```
   [webservers]
   web1 ansible_host=local ip address ansible_user=admin username
   web2 ansible_host=local ip address ansible_user=admin username

   [dbservers]
   db1 ansible_host=local ip address ansible_user=admin username

   [all_servers:children]
   webservers
   ```

2. **Set Up SSH Key Authentication:** SSH keys are required for Ansible to connect to remote hosts. To manage SSH keys and set up password-less authentication, follow these steps:

   a. **Generate SSH Keys:** If the administrators do not have an SSH key pair yet, generate one using the following command. Press Enter when prompted for a passphrase (leave it empty if the administrators do not want to use a passphrase).

      `ssh-keygen -t rsa -b 4096`

The keys will be stored in the following files:

- **Private key:** `~/.ssh/id_rsa`
- **Public key:** `~/.ssh/id_rsa.pub`

b. **Copy Public Key to Remote Hosts:** To enable password-less login, use the **ssh-copy-id** command to copy the administrator SSH public key to each remote host. Replace the IP addresses below with the administrator's actual host IPs:

```
ssh-copy-id admin@172.17.0.1
ssh-copy-id admin@172.18.0.1
ssh-copy-id admin@172.19.0.1
```

The first time, the administrators will be prompted to enter the password for each remote server.

Note: *Some of the IP addresses configured in the previous chapter for Docker containers are used here.*

3. **Verify SSH Key Authentication:** After copying the key, test the SSH connection to each remote host to confirm that password-less login is working correctly:

```
ssh admin@172.17.0.1
ssh admin@172.18.0.1
ssh admin@172.19.0.1
```

If login happens without entering a password, SSH key authentication is set up correctly.

- **dbserversTesting Connectivity**: Use the **ping** module to test connectivity to the administrator managed nodes: **ansible all -m ping**

```
web2 | SUCCESS => {
    "ansible_facts": {
        "discovered_interpreter_python": "/usr/bin/python3"
    },
    "changed": false,
    "ping": "pong"
}
```

Figure 13.1: *Successful Ping Connectivity*

This figure demonstrates a successful connection between the control machine and remote hosts using Ansible. The result confirms that SSH key-based authentication is properly configured, allowing Ansible to communicate with the target servers without requiring manual password entry. The use of the ping module—an Ansible command designed to test connectivity—returns a positive response, indicating that the remote servers are reachable. This validation ensures that the infrastructure is correctly set up and ready for executing more complex automation tasks with Ansible.

Expected Output:

```
server1 | SUCCESS => {
    "changed": false,
    "ping": "pong"
}

server2 | SUCCESS => {
    "changed": false,
    "ping": "pong"
}
```

This output shows that Ansible successfully connected to the target machines and executed the ping module. A response of **"ping": "pong"** means the communication is working as expected.

Writing Ansible Playbooks: Ansible playbooks are YAML files that define the tasks to be executed on the managed nodes. Playbooks allow the administrators to automate complex workflows and configurations. Here is how to write a simple playbook:

1. **Creating a Playbook:**

   Create a new YAML file, for example, **`setup-webserver.yml`**:

   ```
   ssh-copy-id cmorera@web2
   sudo nano setup-webserver.yml
   yaml
   ---
   - name: Setup Web Server
     hosts: webservers
     become: yes
     tasks:
       - name: Install Nginx
         yum:
           name: nginx
           state: present

       - name: Start Nginx
         service:
           name: nginx
           state: started
           enabled: yes
   ```

2. **Running the Playbook:** Execute the playbook using the following command:

   `ansible-playbook setup-webserver.yml --ask-become-pass`

3. **Understanding Playbook Structure:** Each playbook consists of one or more plays which define the hosts to target and the tasks to execute. Tasks can include installing packages, managing services, copying files, and many more.

Managing Infrastructure with Ansible

Ansible can be used to manage not only applications but also the underlying infrastructure. This includes provisioning servers, configuring networking, and managing cloud resources.

1. **Provisioning AWS Resources:**

   - Ansible can interact with AWS services using the boto library. Ensure the administrators have the necessary AWS credentials configured in the administrator environment.
   - Example of provisioning an EC2 instance:

     ```
     yaml
     ---
     - name: Provision EC2 Instance
       hosts: localhost
       tasks:
         - name: Launch EC2 Instance
           ec2:
             key_name: my-key
             instance_type: t2.micro
             image: ami-0abcdef1234567890
             wait: yes
             region: us-west-2
             group: my-security-group
             count: 1
           register: ec2
     ```

2. **Managing Configuration:** Use Ansible to ensure that the administrator servers are configured consistently. For example, the administrators can enforce specific package installations, firewall rules, and user accounts across the administrator infrastructure.

3. **Idempotency:** One of the key features of Ansible is idempotency, meaning that running the same playbook multiple times will not change the system state if it is already in the desired configuration.

Automating Rocky Linux Deployments in AWS

Automating deployments on Rocky Linux in AWS can significantly reduce the time and effort required to set up and manage the administrator infrastructure. Here is how to automate a deployment:

1. **Creating a Deployment Playbook:** Create a playbook that installs necessary packages and configures the server:

```
yaml
- name: Deploy Rocky Linux Application
  hosts: rocky_servers
  become: yes
  tasks:
    - name: Install Required Packages
      yum:
        name:
          - httpd
          - git
        state: present

    - name: Start Apache
      service:
        name: httpd
        state: started
        enabled: yes
```

2. **Running the Deployment:** Execute the playbook to deploy the administrator application:

```
ansible-playbook deploy-rocky-app.yml
```

3. **Integrating with CI/CD:** Ansible can be integrated into CI/CD pipelines to automate deployments further. For example, the administrators can trigger Ansible playbooks from Jenkins or GitLab CI after code changes are pushed to a repository.

Ansible Tower for Large-Scale Automation

Ansible Tower is a web-based interface for managing Ansible automation at scale. It provides a user-friendly dashboard, role-based access control, and job scheduling capabilities.

1. **Installing Ansible Tower:** Ansible Tower can be installed on a dedicated server or virtual machine. Follow the official installation guide to set it up.

2. **Creating Projects and Inventories:** In Ansible Tower, the administrators can create projects that link to the administrator playbooks stored in version control systems. The administrators can also define inventories to manage the administrator hosts.

3. **Job Templates**: Create job templates in Tower to define how playbooks should be executed. The administrators can specify parameters, inventory, and credentials for each job.

4. **Monitoring and Reporting**: Ansible Tower provides real-time monitoring of job execution

and detailed reporting, allowing the administrators to track the status of the administrator automation tasks.

Ansible is a powerful tool for automating system administration tasks, particularly in cloud environments like AWS. By mastering Ansible, system administrators can streamline their workflows, reduce manual errors, and ensure consistent configurations across their infrastructure. This chapter covered all the necessary aspects of using Ansible, from installation and playbook creation to managing infrastructure and leveraging Ansible Tower for large-scale automation. As organizations continue to embrace automation, Ansible will remain a vital component of their IT operations, enabling them to adapt quickly to changing demands, and improve overall efficiency.

Writing Ansible Playbooks

Ansible playbooks are at the core of Ansible's automation capabilities. They provide a structured way to define a series of tasks that Ansible should execute on managed nodes, enabling system administrators to automate configuration management, application deployment, and orchestration of services. This section will delve into the fundamentals of writing Ansible playbooks, including syntax, best practices, and practical examples to illustrate their use.

Understanding the Playbook Structure

Ansible playbooks are written in YAML (YAML Ain't Markup Language), a human-readable data serialization language. This choice of format makes playbooks easy to read and write, even for those who may not be deeply technical. A typical playbook consists of a list of plays where each play maps to a group of hosts and specifies the tasks to be executed.

Basic Components of a Playbook:

- **Name:** A descriptive name for the playbook or task.
- **Hosts:** The target hosts or groups defined in the inventory file.
- **Tasks:** A list of actions to be performed on the specified hosts.
- **Variables** (optional): Customizable parameters that can be used within tasks.
- **Handlers** (optional): Special tasks that are executed only when notified by other tasks.

Here is a simple example of a playbook structure:

```
yaml
- name: Install and start Nginx
  hosts: webservers
  become: yes
  tasks:
    - name: Install Nginx
      yum:
        name: nginx
        state: present

    - name: Start Nginx
      service:
        name: nginx
        state: started
        enabled: yes
```

Introducing Ansible Galaxy: Community-Powered Automation

Ansible Galaxy is an ***online hub for finding, sharing, and reusing Ansible roles***—predefined sets of tasks, templates, and variables that simplify automation. Think of it like an "**`app store`**" for Ansible roles where system administrators and DevOps professionals around the world contribute and download useful automation building blocks.

We can visit Ansible Galaxy at: Ansible Galaxy

Ansible Role and Functionalities

In Ansible, a ***role*** is a structured way of organizing playbooks into reusable components. A role typically includes:

- **Tasks:** The actions we want to perform (for example, installing software)
- **Handlers:** Notifications that respond to changes (such as restarting a service)
- **Variables:** Custom inputs for the tasks
- **Templates:** Configuration files that adapt based on variables
- **Files and defaults:** Static resources or default values

Roles make it easier to reuse code, enforce standards, and share with others.

Reasons for Using Ansible Galaxy

Ansible Galaxy provides a practical solution for automating infrastructure tasks by offering a vast collection of reusable roles. These roles are created and maintained by the community, making it easier to implement reliable and consistent automation across systems.

By using Ansible Galaxy, administrators can:

- Reduce development time by downloading ready-to-use roles, instead of creating everything from scratch.
- Ensure quality and reliability by leveraging roles that are widely adopted and frequently updated by trusted contributors.
- Standardize automation practices across teams and environments, using roles that follow recommended structures.

Promote collaboration and sharing, allowing teams to build on each other's work efficiently.

For example, installing a well-known role like **`geerlingguy.nginx`** simplifies web server deployment. The command: **`ansible-galaxy install geerlingguy.nginx`**.

This command downloads the `geerlingguy.nginx` role, and places it in our local role's directory.

Using a Galaxy Role in a Playbook

Once installed, the role can be easily included in a playbook to set up a web server, as shown below:

```
yaml
- name: Setup Web Server with Galaxy Role
  hosts: webservers
  become: yes
```

```
    roles:
      - geerlingguy.nginx
```

This playbook tells Ansible to apply the tasks defined in the **geerlingguy.nginx** role to all the servers in the `**webservers**` group.

Benefits for Beginners and Teams

- **Reusability:** Roles save time by providing repeatable solutions.
- **Collaboration:** Teams can share and improve roles over time.
- **Best Practices:** Many community roles follow industry standards.
- **Community Support:** Thousands of roles are available for various tools and platforms.

Thus, whether we are setting up a database, configuring a firewall, or deploying applications, Ansible Galaxy gives us a head start with reliable, ready-made automation content.

Updated Playbook with Error Handling

```
- name: Deploy Rocky Linux Application
  hosts: rocky_servers
  become: yes
  tasks:
    - name: Install Required Packages
      yum:
        name:
          - httpd
          - git
        state: present
      register: yum_result
      ignore_errors: yes

    - name: Log package installation failure
      debug:
        msg: "Failed to install packages: {{ yum_result.msg }}"
      when: yum_result.failed

    - name: Start Apache
      service:
        name: httpd
        state: started
        enabled: yes
      register: service_result
      failed_when: service_result.state != 'started'

    - name: Notify on service failure
      debug:
        msg: "Apache failed to start: {{ service_result.msg }}"
      when: service_result.failed

  handlers:
    - name: Reload httpd
      service:
        name: httpd
        state: reloaded
```

Listing 1: Updated Playbook with Error Handling

This updated Ansible playbook introduces vital error-handling mechanisms to ensure reliable and predictable deployments in Rocky Linux environments. It begins by installing key packages such as Apache (httpd) and Git, using the **yum** module, along with the **ignore_errors** directive which allows the playbook to continue execution even if the installation fails. To maintain visibility into such failures, a **debug** task is included to log any installation errors. The playbook then attempts to start the Apache service and uses the **failed_when** directive to explicitly define what constitutes a failure, ensuring that unexpected conditions are properly captured. If the service fails to start, a helpful debug message provides context for troubleshooting. This structured approach helps beginners learn how to manage errors gracefully within automation workflows, enabling the creation of more resilient and maintainable infrastructure automation scripts.

Adding Logging Configuration

Add the following configuration to **/etc/ansible/ansible.cfg** to enable detailed logging:

```
[defaults]
log_path = /var/log/ansible.log
```

Listing 2: Ansible Logging Configuration

This listing demonstrates how to configure Ansible's logging capabilities to improve traceability and auditing during automation tasks. By specifying a custom log file in the Ansible configuration file (**ansible.cfg**), administrators can capture detailed execution output for every playbook run. This logging feature is especially valuable in production environments where maintaining a historical record of changes and diagnosing failures is critical. With logging enabled, teams can review task outcomes, error messages, and variable states–providing a robust mechanism for troubleshooting and continuous improvement in automated infrastructure management.

Writing Playbooks: Best Practices

To write effective Ansible playbooks, consider the following best practices:

- **Use Descriptive Names:** Each playbook and task should have a clear and descriptive name to make the playbooks self-documenting. This helps anyone reading the playbook understand its purpose quickly.
- **Organize Playbooks into Roles:** For complex applications, consider organizing tasks into roles. Roles provide a way to do group related tasks, handlers, files, and variables into a structured format, making playbooks more modular and reusable.
- **Leverage Variables:** Use variables to parameterize the administrator playbooks, making them flexible and adaptable to different environments. Variables can be defined in the playbook, inventory file, or external files.
- **Implement Error Handling:** Include error handling in the administrator playbooks by using the **ignore_errors** keyword or the **failed_when** directive to manage task failures gracefully.
- **Use Handlers for Service Management:** Define handlers to manage services that should only restart when configuration changes occur. This avoids unnecessary restarts and conserves resources.
- **Document the administrator Playbooks:** Include comments within the playbook to explain complex tasks or decisions, making it easier for others to understand the logic behind the administrator automation.

Advanced Playbook Features

Ansible playbooks also support advanced features that enhance their usability and functionality:

- **Conditionals:** Conditionals can be applied to control task execution based on specific conditions. For instance, to validate if a package is already installed before attempting to install it:

```
yaml
- name: Install httpd only if not already installed
  yum:
    name: httpd
    state: present
  when: ansible_os_family == "RedHat"
```

- **Loops**: Ansible allows the administrators to execute tasks in a loop, making it easy to perform repetitive actions. For example, installing multiple packages:

```
yaml
- name: Install multiple packages
  yum:
    name: "{{ item }}"
    state: present
  loop:
    - httpd
    - git
    - curl
```

- **Templates:** Use Jinja2 templating to create dynamic configuration files. Templating allows the administrators to substitute variable values into files during deployment. For example:

```
yaml
- name: Deploy configuration file
  template:
    src: myconfig.j2
    dest: /etc/myapp/config.conf
```

- **Include and Import Statements**: The administrators can break down large playbooks into smaller, more manageable files, using include or import statements. This promotes reusability and better organization.

Example Playbook: Automating Rocky Linux Setup

To illustrate the concepts discussed, let us create a more comprehensive playbook that automates the setup of a web server on Rocky Linux, including the installation of necessary packages, configuration of services, and deployment of a sample application.

```
yaml
---
- name: Setup Rocky Linux Web Server
  hosts: rocky_servers
  become: yes
  vars:
    my_app_version: "1.0.0"
    my_app_name: "myapp"

  tasks:
    - name: Install required packages
      yum:
        name:
          - httpd
```

```
          - git
          - firewalld
        state: present

    - name: Start and enable httpd service
      service:
        name: httpd
        state: started
        enabled: yes

    - name: Configure firewall
      firewalld:
        service: http
        permanent: yes
        state: enabled

    - name: Reload firewall
      command: firewall-cmd --reload

    - name: Clone application repository
      git:
        repo: 'https://github.com/example/myapp.git'
        dest: /var/www/html/{{ my_app_name }}
        version: "{{ my_app_version }}"

    - name: Deploy application configuration
      template:
        src: templates/myapp.conf.j2
        dest: /etc/httpd/conf.d/{{ my_app_name }}.conf

    - name: Restart httpd service
      service:
        name: httpd
        state: restarted
      notify: Reload httpd

  handlers:
    - name: Reload httpd
      service:
        name: httpd
        state: reloaded
```

In this example, the playbook performs the following tasks:

1. Installs required packages (**httpd**, **git**, **firewalld**).
2. Starts and enables the Apache web server.
3. Configures the firewall to allow HTTP traffic.
4. Clones a sample application from a Git repository.
5. Deploys a configuration file using a Jinja2 template.
6. Restarts the Apache service if the configuration changes.

By following these practices and leveraging the advanced features of Ansible playbooks, the administrators can effectively automate complex workflows and ensure consistent deployments across the administrator infrastructure.

Writing Ansible playbooks is a fundamental skill for anyone looking to automate system administration tasks effectively. By understanding the structure, best practices, and advanced features of playbooks, the administrators can create robust automation scripts that simplify the management of the administrator infrastructure. As the administrators gain experience with Ansible, the administrators will discover that playbooks can not only help streamline repetitive tasks but also enhance collaboration and consistency across the administrator teams. With the knowledge gained from this section, the administrators are now equipped to start writing the administrator own playbooks, paving the way for efficient automation in the administrator environment.

Managing Infrastructure with Ansible

Ansible provides a powerful framework for managing infrastructure as code, enabling organizations to automate the provisioning, configuration, and orchestration of their IT resources. With its agentless architecture, Ansible simplifies the management of infrastructure across various platforms, including physical servers, virtual machines, and cloud environments. This section will explore how to effectively manage infrastructure using Ansible, focusing on key concepts, strategies, and practical examples.

Infrastructure as Code (IaC) Concept

The concept of Infrastructure as Code (IaC) is central to modern infrastructure management. It allows teams to define and manage their infrastructure using code, enabling version control, reproducibility, and automation. Ansible plays a significant role in implementing IaC by allowing users to write playbooks that describe the desired state of their infrastructure.

Benefits of IaC

- **Version Control:** Infrastructure definitions can be stored in version control systems (for instance, Git), enabling tracking of changes and collaboration among team members.
- **Consistency:** IaC ensures that environments are provisioned consistently, reducing configuration drift and mitigating risks associated with manual configurations.
- **Automation:** By automating the provisioning and management of infrastructure, organizations can save time, reduce human error, and improve operational efficiency.

Ansible's Role in IaC

Ansible allows users to define their infrastructure, using human-readable YAML playbooks. These playbooks can describe everything from server provisioning to application deployment, making it easy to manage complex environments.

Provisioning Infrastructure with Ansible

Ansible can provision infrastructure on various platforms, including cloud providers such as AWS, Azure, Google Cloud, and on-premises environments. The following are the steps to provision infrastructure using Ansible.

1. **Setting Up Inventory:** The inventory file in Ansible specifies the hosts that will be managed. This file can be static (defined in a file) or dynamic (generated from cloud providers). For example, an inventory for AWS might look like this:

   ```
   ini
   [webservers]
   ec2-203-0-113-25.compute-1.amazonaws.com
   ec2-203-0-113-26.compute-1.amazonaws.com
   ```

```
[databases]
ec2-203-0-113-27.compute-1.amazonaws.com
```

2. **Using Modules for Provisioning**: Ansible includes a variety of modules specifically designed for provisioning resources in different environments. For example, the ec2 module can be used to launch EC2 instances in AWS:

```
yaml
- name: Launch EC2 Instance
  ec2:
    key_name: my-key
    instance_type: t2.micro
    image: ami-0abcdef1234567890
    wait: yes
    region: us-west-2
    group: my-security-group
    count: 1
  register: ec2
```

3. **Cloud Modules**: In addition to EC2, Ansible provides modules for other cloud services, allowing users to manage compute resources, storage, and networking. For example, the administrators can use the **gcp_compute_instance** module to manage Google Cloud instances or the **azure_rm_virtualmachine** for Azure VMs.

Configuration Management with Ansible

Once the infrastructure is provisioned, Ansible can be used to ensure that the servers are configured according to the desired state. This involves installing packages, configuring services, and managing files.

1. **Installing Packages**: Ansible can install packages using the appropriate package manager for the target operating system. For instance, on a Rocky Linux server, the administrators can use the yum module:

```
yaml
- name: Install required packages
  yum:
    name:
      - httpd
      - git
    state: present
```

2. **Configuring Services**: After installing packages, the administrators can manage services such as starting, stopping, and enabling them to run at boot. For instance:

```
yaml
- name: Start and enable Apache
  service:
    name: httpd
    state: started
    enabled: yes
```

3. **Managing Configuration Files**: Use the template module to deploy configuration files derived from Jinja2 templates. This allows the administrators to dynamically generate configuration files based on variables defined in the administrator playbooks:

```
yaml
- name: Deploy application configuration
  template:
    src: templates/myapp.conf.j2
    dest: /etc/httpd/conf.d/myapp.conf
```

Orchestration with Ansible

Ansible excels in orchestration, allowing the administrators to coordinate multiple tasks across different servers and services. This is particularly useful for deploying complex applications that require multiple components to work together seamlessly.

1. **Defining Roles:** Organize tasks related to specific components into roles. Each role can include its own tasks, handlers, variables, and templates. This modularity promotes reusability, and simplifies playbook structure.

   ```
   yaml
   roles:
     - webserver
     - database
   ```

2. **Sequential Execution:** Ansible executes tasks in the order they are defined in the playbook. This sequential execution makes it easy to manage dependencies, and ensure that tasks are completed in the correct sequence.

3. **Asynchronous Tasks:** For long-running tasks, Ansible supports asynchronous execution. This allows the administrators to run tasks in the background, while continuing to execute subsequent tasks. For example:

   ```
   yaml
   - name: Long-running task
     command: /path/to/long_running_script.sh
     async: 600
     poll: 0
   ```

Example: Managing a Web Application Infrastructure

Let us consider a practical example where we manage a web application infrastructure using Ansible. This example will cover provisioning EC2 instances, configuring a web server, and deploying a sample application.

```
yaml
---
- name: Manage Web Application Infrastructure
  hosts: localhost
  gather_facts: no
  tasks:
    - name: Launch EC2 Instances
      ec2:
        key_name: my-key
        instance_type: t2.micro
        image: ami-0abcdef1234567890
        region: us-west-2
        group: my-security-group
        count: 2
      register: ec2_instances

    - name: Wait for instances to be up
      wait_for:
        host: "{{ item.public_ip }}"
        port: 22
        delay: 10
        timeout: 300
      loop: "{{ ec2_instances.instances }}"
```

```
- name: Configure Web Servers
  hosts: "{{ ec2_instances.instances | map(attribute='public_ip') | list }}"
  become: yes
  tasks:
    - name: Install and start Nginx
      yum:
        name: nginx
        state: present

    - name: Start Nginx service
      service:
        name: nginx
        state: started
        enabled: yes

    - name: Deploy application code
      git:
        repo: 'https://github.com/example/myapp.git'
        dest: /usr/share/nginx/html/myapp
```

In this example, the playbook performs the following steps:

1. Launches two EC2 instances in AWS.
2. Waits for the instances to be accessible over SSH.
3. Configure the web servers by installing and starting Nginx.
4. Deploys the application code from a Git repository.

Managing infrastructure with Ansible allows organizations to automate the entire lifecycle of their IT resources, from provisioning to configuration and orchestration. By embracing the principles of Infrastructure as Code, teams can achieve greater consistency, reliability, and efficiency in their operations. Ansible's powerful modules and flexible playbook structure empower administrators to define their infrastructure systematically, ensuring that environments can be recreated and managed with ease. As the administrators continue to explore Ansible's capabilities, the administrators will find that it can significantly enhance the administrator infrastructure management practices, enabling the administrators to focus on delivering value, rather than managing complexity.

Automating Rocky Linux Deployments in AWS

Automating the deployment of Rocky Linux in AWS using Ansible is a powerful way to streamline the process of provisioning and configuring servers in the cloud. By combining Ansible's agentless infrastructure management capabilities with AWS's scalable and reliable platform, organizations can rapidly deploy, configure, and manage Rocky Linux instances. This section explores the complete workflow for automating Rocky Linux deployments in AWS, from provisioning EC2 instances to post-deployment configuration.

Automating Rocky Linux Deployments in AWS

Rocky Linux is a popular enterprise-grade Linux distribution known for its stability and compatibility with Red Hat Enterprise Linux (RHEL). Deploying Rocky Linux in AWS provides the benefits of cloud scalability and reliability, while Ansible ensures deployments are consistent, repeatable, and efficient. Key benefits of automating deployments include:

- **Faster Deployments:** Automating server provisioning and configuration reduces deployment time.

- **Consistency:** Ensures that all Rocky Linux instances are configured identically.
- **Scalability:** Easily scale deployments to match workload demands.
- **Reduced Errors:** Eliminate manual configuration errors through automation.
- **Cost Efficiency:** Optimize infrastructure provisioning and usage in AWS.

Prerequisites

Before automating Rocky Linux deployments in AWS, ensure that the following prerequisites are met:

- **AWS Account:**
  - We need an active AWS account with sufficient permissions to create and manage EC2 instances, security groups, and other resources.
  - Use IAM roles, instead of storing AWS credentials directly for security best practices.
- **Ansible Installed:**
  - Install Ansible on the control machine (for example, Rocky Linux or another Linux distribution): **`sudo dnf install ansible -y`**
- **AWS CLI Installed:**
  - Install and configure the AWS CLI with the credentials (or IAM role if running on an AWS instance):
    1. `sudo dnf install aws-cli -y`
    2. `aws configure`
- **IAM Role:** Ensure the AWS account has an IAM role or user with permissions to manage EC2, VPC, and related services.
- **SSH Key Pair:** Create an AWS key pair or ensure, we have an existing one. This key will allow us to SSH into our Rocky Linux instances.

Provisioning Rocky Linux Instances with Ansible

The first step in automating Rocky Linux deployments is provisioning EC2 instances in AWS. Ansible provides modules like **`amazon.aws.ec2_instance`** to automate this process.

Playbook for Provisioning Rocky Linux EC2 Instances

Create a playbook named **`provision_rocky_linux.yml`:**

```
- name: Provision Rocky Linux EC2 Instances
  hosts: localhost
  gather_facts: no
  tasks:
    - name: Launch Rocky Linux EC2 instances
      amazon.aws.ec2_instance:
        key_name: my-key
        instance_type: t2.micro
        image_id: ami-0abcdef1234567890  # Replace with the Rocky Linux AMI ID
for your region
        wait: yes
        region: us-west-2
        security_group: rocky-linux-sg
        count: 2
        tags:
          Name: "RockyLinuxInstance"
      register: ec2_instances

    - name: Display instance information
```

```
        debug:
          msg: "Launched instance with ID: {{ item.id }} and public IP: {{ item.
public_ip }}"
        loop: "{{ ec2_instances.instances }}"
```

Running the Playbook

Run the playbook to provision the instances: **`ansible-playbook provision_rocky_linux.yml`**

Configuring Rocky Linux Instances

After provisioning the EC2 instances, the next step is configuring them to meet the requirements. This includes installing necessary packages, setting up services, configuring users, and ensuring security.

Playbook for Configuring Rocky Linux

Create a playbook named **`configure_rocky_linux.yml`**:

```
- name: Configure Rocky Linux Instances
  hosts: rocky_servers
  become: yes
  tasks:
    - name: Update all packages
      yum:
        name: "*"
        state: latest

    - name: Install necessary packages
      yum:
        name:
          - httpd
          - git
          - firewalld
        state: present

    - name: Start and enable Apache
      service:
        name: httpd
        state: started
        enabled: yes

    - name: Configure firewall for HTTP
      firewalld:
        service: http
        permanent: yes
        state: enabled

    - name: Reload firewall
      command: firewall-cmd --reload

    - name: Create a deployment user
      user:
        name: deploy
        groups: wheel
        state: present
        shell: /bin/bash
```

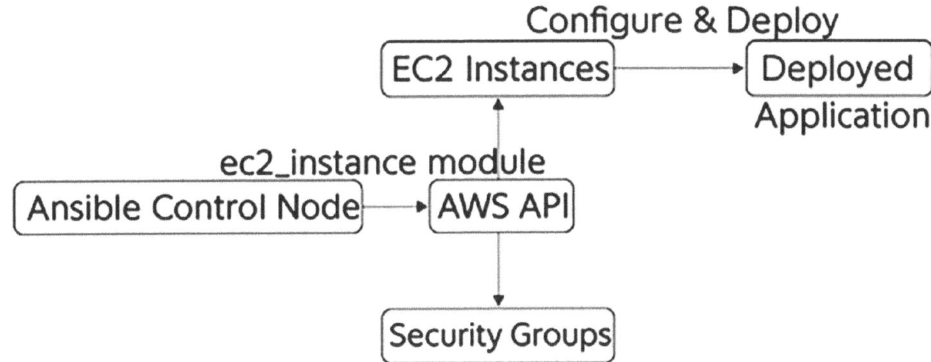

Figure 13.2: *AWS EC2 Orchestration with Ansible*

Figure 13.2 illustrates the orchestration process of AWS EC2 instances using Ansible. The diagram showcases how Ansible communicates with AWS using dynamic inventory plugins and API calls. Playbooks are executed from a control node—typically a local machine or a management server—that contains the necessary Ansible configurations and credentials. The dynamic inventory script retrieves real-time information about EC2 instances, allowing Ansible to target and manage them efficiently. Tasks such as provisioning, configuration, software deployment, and instance lifecycle management are automated using YAML-based playbooks. This orchestration model ensures scalable, repeatable, and consistent deployments across cloud environments, streamlining infrastructure management in AWS.

Deploying an Application on Rocky Linux

Once the instances are provisioned and configured, the last step is deploying our application or workload on Rocky Linux. This can be done, using Ansible's git and template modules.

Playbook for Deploying an Application

Create a playbook named **deploy_app.yml**:

```
- name: Deploy Application on Rocky Linux
  hosts: rocky_servers
  become: yes
  tasks:
    - name: Clone application repository
      git:
        repo: 'https://github.com/example/myapp.git'
        dest: /var/www/html/myapp

    - name: Deploy application configuration
      template:
        src: templates/myapp.conf.j2
        dest: /etc/httpd/conf.d/myapp.conf

    - name: Restart Apache to apply configuration
      service:
        name: httpd
        state: restarted
```

Dynamic Inventory for AWS Instances

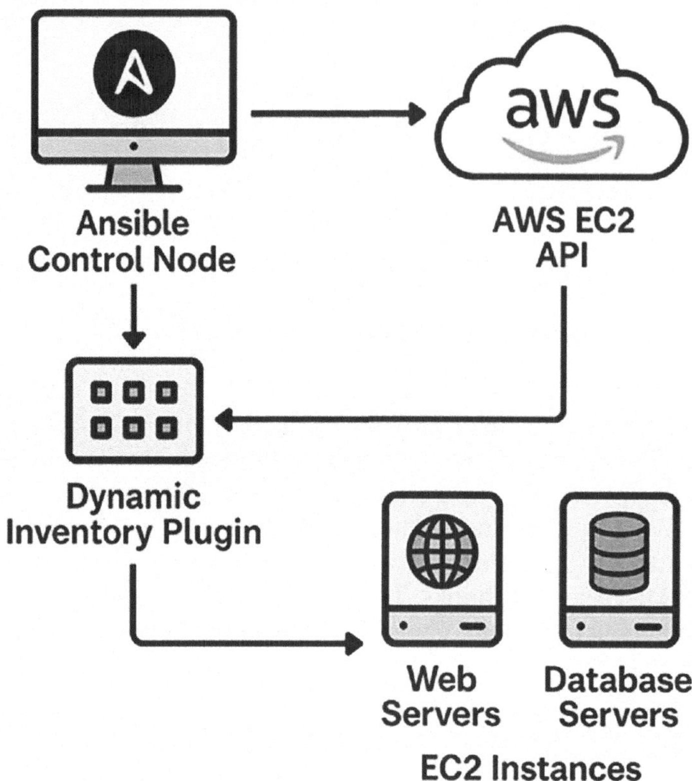

Figure 13.3: *Dynamic Inventory for AWS Instances*

This figure depicts how Ansible leverages dynamic inventory to manage AWS EC2 instances. Unlike static inventory files that require manual updates, dynamic inventory plugins or scripts query AWS APIs in real time to collect instance details such as IP addresses, tags, regions, and availability zones. The retrieved metadata is then organized into groups based on predefined filters or tags, enabling Ansible to accurately target hosts. This approach ensures scalability and consistency in automation workflows, especially in cloud environments where resources are continuously created, terminated, or reconfigured.

Instead of manually defining the inventory, use Ansible's dynamic inventory plugin for AWS. This plugin fetches the list of EC2 instances dynamically.

Enable the Dynamic Inventory Plugin:

1. Install the required plugin: **`pip install boto boto3`**
2. Create a configuration file for AWS inventory (**`aws_ec2.yml`**):

   `plugin: amazon.aws.aws_ec2`
3. regions: **`- us-west-2`**
4. filters: **`tag:Name: RockyLinuxInstance`**
5. Run the playbooks, using the dynamic inventory:

   ```
   ansible-playbook -i aws_ec2.yml configure_rocky_linux.yml
   ```

Automating Rocky Linux deployments in AWS, using Ansible is a reliable and efficient way to manage cloud infrastructure. From provisioning EC2 instances to configuring and deploying applications,

Ansible's powerful modules and playbooks simplify complex workflows. By leveraging dynamic inventory and modular playbook design, we can scale deployments, ensure consistency, and reduce manual errors. This approach accelerates deployments and enables seamless management of Rocky Linux in AWS, allowing organizations to focus on delivering value, rather than managing infrastructure.

Dynamic Inventory Flow

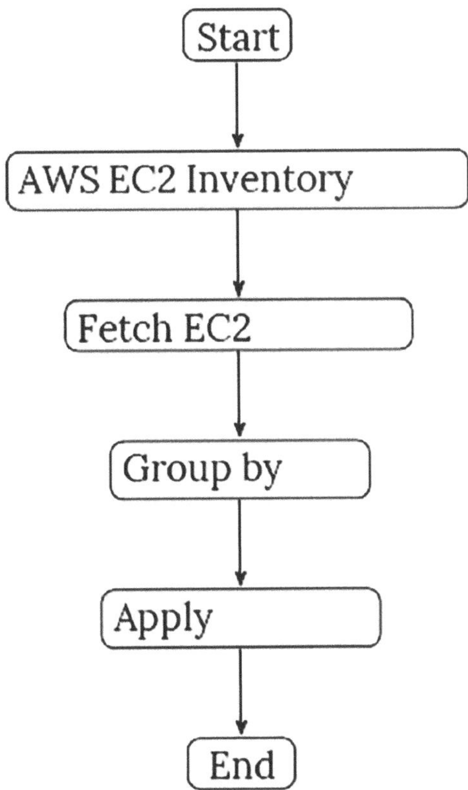

Figure 13.4: *Dynamic Inventory Flow for* AWS EC2

This figure illustrates how Ansible leverages dynamic inventory to interact with AWS EC2. Unlike static inventories, which rely on predefined host lists, dynamic inventory allows Ansible to query the AWS API in real time. The process begins when Ansible invokes a dynamic inventory plugin or script, which authenticates with AWS using IAM credentials or roles. AWS responds with up-to-date metadata about EC2 resources—such as instance IDs, private and public IP addresses, tags, and regions. Ansible then parses this information to determine the appropriate hosts and groups for playbook execution. This dynamic approach ensures scalability, automation accuracy, and adaptability to frequent infrastructure changes, making it especially valuable in cloud-native and elastic environments.

Ansible Tower for Large-Scale Automation

Ansible Tower is a powerful web-based interface and API for managing Ansible automation tasks. Designed for organizations that require centralized control over their automation processes, Ansible Tower provides features that enhance collaboration, scalability, and security. This platform enables administrators to streamline complex deployments, monitor automation in real time, and enforce role-based access control to strengthen security practices. In this section, we will explore the key features of Ansible Tower, its benefits for large-scale automation, and practical examples of how it can be implemented effectively within enterprise infrastructures.

AWS EC2 Orchestration with Ansible

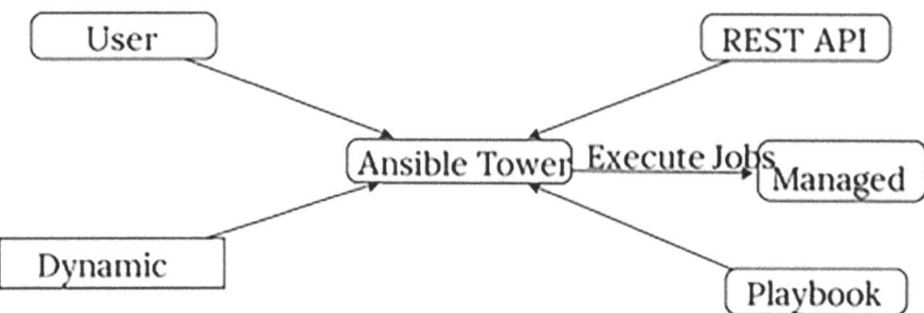

Figure 13.5: *Ansible Tower Architecture*

This figure illustrates how Ansible Tower enhances automation management by offering a centralized, user-friendly platform for controlling and monitoring Ansible operations. The architecture integrates users, projects, and inventories into structured workflows, enabling secure, scalable, and consistent deployments across on-premises and cloud environments. Features such as visual CI/CD dashboards, role-based access control, job scheduling, and real-time status updates simplify complex automation tasks, making them accessible even to users with minimal programming experience.

Key Components of Ansible Tower

- **Dashboard:** A visual overview of the automation landscape, displaying job statuses, recent activity, and system health.
- **Job Templates:** Reusable configurations for executing playbooks, allowing users to define parameters such as inventory, credentials, and verbosity levels.
- **Inventories:** Centralized management of hosts and groups which can be imported dynamically from cloud providers or other sources.
- **Credentials:** Secure storage of sensitive data such as SSH keys and API tokens, allowing for secure connections to managed nodes.
- **Notifications:** Integration with various notification systems (for example, email, Slack, and so on.) to alert teams about job statuses and events.
- **API Access:** RESTful API for programmatic access to Tower's features, enabling integration with other systems and automation frameworks.

Benefits of Using Ansible Tower

Implementing Ansible Tower in an organization can provide several significant benefits:

- **Centralized Management:** Ansible Tower centralizes the management of automation tasks, allowing teams to view and control automation processes from a single interface. This reduces the complexity of managing multiple playbooks across different environments.
- **Role-Based Access Control (RBAC):** Tower supports role-based access control, allowing administrators to define user roles and permissions. This ensures that only authorized personnel can access specific resources, enhancing security and compliance.
- **Job Scheduling and Workflow Automation:** Tower enables users to schedule jobs to run at specific times or events, automating routine tasks and reducing the need for manual intervention. Additionally, workflows can be created to define complex job sequences, ensuring that tasks are executed in the correct order.

- **Scalability:** Ansible Tower is designed for large-scale environments with the ability to manage thousands of nodes across multiple geographic locations. It can oversee job scaling, load balancing, and clustering for high availability.
- **Enhanced Visibility and Reporting:** The dashboard and reporting features provide visibility into job performance, success rates, and resource usage. This data helps teams identify bottlenecks, and optimize their automation strategies.
- **Integration with CI/CD Pipelines:** Ansible Tower can be integrated with Continuous Integration and Continuous Deployment (CI/CD) tools, allowing for automated deployments and testing within a DevOps framework.

Setting Up Ansible Tower

Setting up Ansible Tower involves several steps, including installation, configuration, and integration with existing Ansible playbooks and inventories.

Installation Prerequisites

Before installing Ansible Tower, ensure that the environment meets the following prerequisites:

- **Supported Operating Systems:** Ansible Tower can be installed on Red Hat Enterprise Linux (RHEL) or CentOS.
- **Hardware Requirements:** Minimum recommended hardware includes 4 GB of RAM and 2 CPUs for small deployments, with additional resources for larger environments.
- **Database:** Ansible Tower uses a PostgreSQL database for storing configurations, job statuses, and inventories. This can be installed as part of the Tower installation or as a separate service.

Installation Steps

1. **Download the Ansible Tower Installer:** Obtain the latest version of the Ansible Tower installer from the official Ansible website.
2. **Run the Installation Script:** Execute the installation script as a superuser: `sudo ./setup.sh`
3. **Access the Web Interface:** Once installed, access the Tower web interface by navigating to `http://<tower_server_ip>/` in a web browser.
4. **Initial Configuration:** Set up the initial admin user and configure the basic settings, including the database connection and SMTP settings for notifications.

Creating Job Templates and Inventories

Once Ansible Tower is installed and configured, the next step is to create job templates and inventories to manage automation tasks.

Creating an Inventory

1. **Navigate to the Inventories Section:** In the Tower dashboard, go to the "`Inventories`" tab to create a new inventory.
2. **Add Hosts:** Define hosts manually or import from external sources (for example, cloud providers), using dynamic inventory scripts.
3. **Group Hosts:** Organize hosts into groups for easier management and targeting in job templates.

Creating a Job Template

1. **Navigate to the Job Templates Section:** Go to the "`Job Templates`" tab to create a new job template.
2. **Define Job Parameters:**

   Specify the following parameters:

   a. **`Name`:** A descriptive name for the job template.

   b. **`Inventory`:** Select the inventory containing the target hosts.

   c. **`Playbook`:** Choose the Ansible playbook to execute.

   d. **`Credentials`:** Select the credentials for accessing the hosts.
3. **Set Additional Options:** Configure other options such as verbosity levels, job tags, and job limits.
4. **Save the Job Template:** Once all parameters are set, save the job template for future use.

Executing Jobs and Monitoring: Executing jobs in Ansible Tower is straightforward. Users can launch jobs from job templates with a few clicks, monitor their progress, and view detailed logs.

1. **Launching a Job:** Select the desired job template and click the "`Launch`" button. Administrators can specify additional parameters such as job tags or job limits if needed.
2. **Monitoring Job Progress:** The job dashboard provides real-time updates on job execution, including success and failure notifications. Users can view logs to troubleshoot issues, or verify task completion.
3. **Handling Job Failures:** If a job fails, logs provide detailed error messages. Administrators can configure automatic retries, or use failure notifications to take corrective actions.

Integrating Ansible Tower with CI/CD

Ansible Tower can be integrated into CI/CD pipelines to enhance deployment automation. This integration allows teams to trigger Ansible jobs, based on events in their version control systems or CI/CD tools.

Enhancing CI/CD Integration: To address the need for CI/CD integration, we will include a sample workflow using GitHub Actions to trigger an Ansible playbook for deploying a web application on Rocky Linux.

GitHub Actions Workflow for Ansible Deployment

```
# Listing 1: GitHub Actions Workflow for Ansible Deployment

name: Deploy with Ansible

on:
  push:
    branches:
      - main

jobs:
  deploy:
    runs-on: ubuntu-latest
    steps:
      - name: Checkout repository
```

```
        uses: actions/checkout@v3

      - name: Set up Python
        uses: actions/setup-python@v4
        with:
          python-version: '3.x'

      - name: Install Ansible and Boto3
        run: |
          pip install ansible boto3

      - name: Configure AWS credentials
        uses: aws-actions/configure-aws-credentials@v2
        with:
          aws-access-key-id: ${{ secrets.AWS_ACCESS_KEY_ID }}
          aws-secret-access-key: ${{ secrets.AWS_SECRET_ACCESS_KEY }}
          aws-region: us-west-2

      - name: Run Ansible Playbook
        run: ansible-playbook -i aws_ec2.yml deploy_app.yml
```

Listing 1: GitHub Actions Workflow for Ansible Deployment

This workflow demonstrates how to automate Ansible-based deployments, using GitHub Actions. Triggered on every push to the **main** branch, the pipeline runs in a Ubuntu-based GitHub runner. It begins by checking out the repository code, and setting up the appropriate Python environment. Ansible and Boto3 (required for AWS interaction) are then installed via **pip.** The workflow securely injects AWS credentials using GitHub Secrets, allowing Ansible to interact with AWS resources. Finally, it executes an Ansible playbook (**deploy_app.yml**) against a dynamic inventory file (**aws_ec2.yml**). This integration provides a streamlined CI/CD approach for infrastructure automation, enabling consistent and repeatable deployments in AWS environments.

- **Webhook Integration:** Use webhooks from services such as GitHub or GitLab to trigger Ansible jobs automatically when code is pushed to the repository.
- **Integration with Jenkins:** Ansible Tower can be integrated with Jenkins to automate deployment pipelines. Use the Ansible Tower plugin for Jenkins to trigger jobs, and manage job statuses.
- **Creating a CI/CD Workflow:** Define a workflow in Tower that includes multiple job templates (e.g., test, build, deploy, and so on) to create a complete CI/CD pipeline.

Thus, by following these guidelines, administrators can successfully implement Ansible Tower, streamlining automation, and improving operational efficiency within their organizations.

Conclusion

Automating administrative tasks with Ansible optimizes infrastructure management, reducing time and human errors in system configurations. This chapter covered everything from installing and configuring Ansible to writing playbooks, and managing Rocky Linux deployments on AWS. Additionally, Ansible Tower was introduced as a solution for large-scale automation, enabling centralized management of complex environments. With these tools, system administrators can enhance operational efficiency, and ensure consistent and secure deployments.

The next chapter explores deploying Rocky Linux in cloud environments, focusing on AWS. It covers essential cloud computing concepts, configuring Rocky Linux instances, and implementing best security practices in hybrid and multi-cloud environments.

Points to Remember

- **Installing and Configuring Ansible:**
    - Ansible is an open-source automation tool that streamlines system administration, allowing for agentless management across servers.
    - Installation on Rocky Linux can be achieved using the **`dnf`** package manager or pip, with key configuration in **`/etc/ansible/ansible.cfg`** to customize behavior and environment settings.
- **Writing Ansible Playbooks:**
    - Playbooks are YAML files that define a series of tasks (plays) executed on target hosts, ensuring idempotency and reproducibility.
    - Essential components include plays, tasks, modules, and variables; using roles can further organize and reuse common automation patterns across projects.
- **Managing Infrastructure with Ansible**
    - Ansible modules enable direct interaction with various systems and cloud platforms, automating tasks such as software installation, configuration management, and service orchestration.
    - Leveraging inventory files–both static and dynamic–ensures accurate host management, allowing targeted and flexible deployments.
- **Automating Rocky Linux Deployments in AWS**
    - Ansible streamlines the provisioning and configuration of Rocky Linux instances on AWS, reducing manual intervention through automation.
    - AWS-specific modules (for example, **`ec2`** and **`cloudformation`**) can be incorporated in playbooks to facilitate tasks like instance creation, network configuration, and resource scaling.
- **Ansible Tower for Large-Scale Automation**
    - Ansible Tower provides a centralized web interface and REST API, making it easier to manage, schedule, and monitor automation tasks across large environments.
    - Features such as role-based access control, job templates, and integrated notifications help streamline enterprise-grade automation workflows.

Multiple Choice Questions

1. Which command is used to install Ansible on Rocky Linux?
    a. `dnf install ansible`
    b. `apt-get install ansible`
    c. `yum install ansible`
    d. `pip install ansible`
2. Which file contains the default configuration settings for Ansible?
    a. `/etc/ansible/ansible.cfg`
    b. `/etc/ansible.cfg`
    c. `/etc/ansible/inventory`
    d. `/usr/local/etc/ansible.cfg`

3. What is the primary purpose of an Ansible playbook?
   a. To manually execute commands on remote servers
   b. To automate tasks, using a series of YAML-defined instructions
   c. To install Ansible Tower
   d. To create container images for deployment
4. In an Ansible playbook, which keyword specifies the target hosts for tasks?
   a. tasks
   b. hosts
   c. roles
   d. modules
5. What does idempotency in Ansible playbooks ensure?
   a. Tasks run only once per host.
   b. Tasks can be executed multiple times without causing unintended changes.
   c. Playbooks always produce random outcomes.
   d. Manual intervention is required after each run.
6. Which file is used to define the managed nodes in Ansible?
   a. `ansible.cfg`
   b. `inventory`
   c. `playbook.yml`
   d. `roles.yml`
7. Which Ansible module is typically used for managing AWS EC2 instances during automated deployments?
   a. `azure_rm`
   b. `ec2`
   c. `gcp_compute`
   d. `digital_ocean`
8. What is a key feature of Ansible Tower?
   a. It provides a command-line tool for ad-hoc tasks.
   b. It offers a graphical user interface and centralized job management.
   c. It replaces the need for playbooks.
   d. It is used solely for inventory management.
9. How does Ansible manage remote systems without requiring additional software on those systems?
   a. Through a custom agent installed on each node
   b. By leveraging SSH and Python for communication

   c. By directly accessing the system hardware
   d. Through a proprietary remote access protocol
10. Which command is used to execute an Ansible playbook?
   a. `ansible playbook run playbook.yml`
   b. `ansible-playbook playbook.yml`
   c. `ansible execute playbook.yml`
   d. `ansible-run playbook.yml`

Answers

1. a
2. a
3. b
4. b
5. b
6. b
7. b
8. b
9. b
10. b

Questions

1. What is the significance of automation in modern IT infrastructure, and how does Ansible contribute to its effectiveness?
2. Which automation tool is highlighted in this chapter for managing Rocky Linux deployments?
3. What are the key steps involved in installing and configuring Ansible on Rocky Linux?
4. How can infrastructure be effectively managed using Ansible playbooks?
5. What are the primary components of an Ansible playbook, and how do they work together to execute tasks?
6. What are the advantages and limitations of using Ansible for automating system administration compared to traditional manual methods?
7. How does Ansible Tower facilitate large-scale automation, and what benefits does it provide to administrators?
8. How can Ansible be integrated with AWS to automate the deployment and management of Rocky Linux instances?
9. What are the steps necessary to maintain and update inventory files in Ansible for accurate host management?

10. What are some common challenges faced during the implementation of Ansible automation, and how can they be addressed?

Key Terms

- **Automation:** The process of using software tools to perform tasks with minimal human intervention, streamlining system administration and configuration management.
- **Ansible:** An open-source, agentless automation tool that simplifies configuration management, application deployment, and infrastructure provisioning, particularly in Rocky Linux environments.
- **Ansible Playbook:** A YAML-based file that defines a sequence of tasks to be executed on target hosts, enabling the automation of complex workflows in a repeatable and consistent manner.
- **Task:** The fundamental unit of work in an Ansible playbook that performs a single action, such as installing software or modifying configuration files.
- **Module:** A reusable, standalone script used within Ansible playbooks to conduct specific operations, including system management, cloud provisioning, and service orchestration.
- **Inventory:** A file or dynamic source that lists the target hosts and groups for Ansible automation, ensuring accurate and flexible management of infrastructure.
- **Idempotence:** A core principle in Ansible ensuring that running the same playbook multiple times results in the same system state, preventing unintended changes.
- **Role:** A method for organizing playbooks into reusable components that encapsulate tasks, variables, files, and templates to simplify complex automation setups.
- **Handler:** A specialized task in an Ansible playbook that is triggered by notifications from other tasks, typically used to restart services or apply changes after configuration updates.
- **Ansible Tower:** An enterprise solution that provides a centralized web-based interface, role-based access control, and job scheduling for managing and scaling Ansible automation across large environments.
- **Agentless:** A characteristic of Ansible where automation is executed over standard protocols like SSH, eliminating the need for additional software agents on target hosts.
- **AWS Integration:** The use of Ansible modules and playbooks to automate the provisioning, configuration, and management of Rocky Linux deployments on AWS, enabling seamless cloud infrastructure management.

CHAPTER 14
Rocky Linux in Cloud Environments

Introduction

As cloud computing continues to reshape modern IT, mastering Linux in the cloud has become a gateway to building resilient and future-ready infrastructures. This book provides a practical and inspiring guide to deploying, securing, and optimizing **Rocky Linux 9** on **Amazon Web Services (AWS)**, covering automation with Terraform and Ansible, IAM and Security Groups, hybrid cloud strategies, and performance tuning. With hands-on labs and troubleshooting techniques aligned with industry standards of mid-2025, it equips both seasoned administrators and beginners to thrive in today's cloud-driven landscape, where Rocky Linux now stands as the trusted enterprise-grade successor to CentOS.

Structure

This chapter covers the following topics:

- Understand fundamental cloud computing concepts and models.
- Deploy Rocky Linux instances on AWS, using Amazon Machine Images (AMIs) and EC2.
- Configure and manage Rocky Linux servers in AWS.
- Implement security best practices, using IAM and Security Groups.
- Explore Rocky Linux in hybrid and multi-cloud environments.

Understanding Fundamental Cloud Computing Concepts and Models

Cloud computing provides scalable and cost-efficient IT resources–such as servers, storage, databases, networking, and software–delivered over the internet through providers like AWS, allowing organizations to dynamically adjust capacity without maintaining extensive on-premises infrastructure. Supporting rapid innovation, high availability, and global access, it is structured around service models (IaaS, PaaS, SaaS) and deployment models (public, private, hybrid). Rocky Linux 9, with its enterprise stability, AWS compatibility, and long-term support, serves as a reliable foundation for secure and flexible cloud deployments.

Key Characteristics of Cloud Computing

- **On-Demand Self-Service:** Users can provision computing resources automatically, without requiring direct interaction with service providers.
- **Broad Network Access:** Cloud services are accessible over the internet from a wide range of devices, including laptops, smartphones, and tablets.

- **Resource Pooling:** Providers use a multi-tenant model to dynamically allocate computing resources, maximizing efficiency and scalability across clients.
- **Rapid Elasticity:** Resources can be quickly scaled up or down based on current demand, supporting flexible workload management.
- **Measured Service:** Resource usage is continuously monitored, controlled, and billed based on consumption, promoting cost transparency and accountability.

Service and Deployment Models

Cloud services are commonly delivered through three main service models:

- **Infrastructure as a Service (IaaS):** Offers fundamental computing resources such as virtual machines, storage, and networking (for example, Amazon EC2).
- **Platform as a Service (PaaS):** Provides a managed development environment with tools and frameworks that abstract infrastructure complexities (for instance, AWS Elastic Beanstalk).
- **Software as a Service (SaaS):** Delivers fully managed software applications via the internet, requiring no local installation or maintenance (for example, Google Workspace).

Deployment models define how cloud services are made available:

- **Public Cloud:** Services hosted by third-party providers, and shared among multiple customers (for example, AWS, Azure, and so on).
- **Private Cloud:** Infrastructure operates solely for a single organization, offering enhanced security and control.
- **Hybrid Cloud:** Combines public and private cloud environments to optimize flexibility and resource allocation.
- **Community Cloud:** Shared infrastructure among organizations with common goals or compliance requirements (for instance, government or healthcare entities).

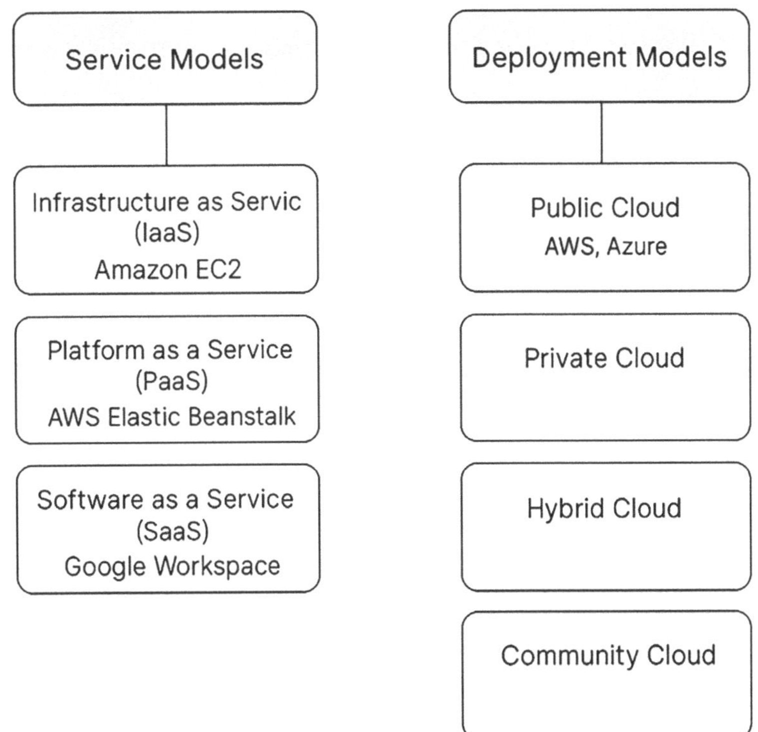

Figure 14.1: *Cloud Service and Deployment Models*

This figure illustrates the two core dimensions of **cloud computing architecture**. On the left, it presents the **service models**–Infrastructure as a Service (IaaS), Platform as a Service (PaaS), and Software as a Service (SaaS)–with examples such as **Amazon EC2**, **AWS Elastic Beanstalk**, and **Google Workspace**. On the right, it highlights the **deployment models**, including **Public, Private, Hybrid, and Community Cloud**, showcasing the diverse ways cloud environments can be structured and delivered. Together, these perspectives simplify the conceptual understanding of how cloud services are consumed and deployed, helping readers grasp the balance between scalability, control, and flexibility.

Benefits and Challenges

Benefits

- **Cost Efficiency:** Pay-as-you-go pricing reduces capital expenditure on physical infrastructure.
- **Scalability:** Resources can be scaled automatically to meet fluctuating workload demands.
- **Global Accessibility:** Services are accessible from anywhere with internet connectivity, supporting distributed teams.
- **Enhanced Security:** Leading providers implement encryption, identity management, and regulatory compliance.
- **Automatic Maintenance:** Providers handle updates and backups, minimizing manual effort and downtime.
- **Business Continuity:** Cloud storage and disaster recovery solutions improve resilience against data loss or system failure.

Challenges

- **Security and Privacy:** Data stored offsite raises concerns about breaches and unauthorized access.
- **Regulatory Compliance:** Industries such as finance or healthcare face strict data governance requirements.
- **Latency and Downtime:** Service reliability depends on internet connectivity and provider uptime.
- **Vendor Lock-in:** Proprietary tools or APIs can complicate migration between cloud platforms.
- **Data Governance:** Managing data ownership, access, and location across cloud environments requires careful planning.

Future Trends

Several emerging technologies are shaping the future of cloud computing, such as:

- **Edge Computing:** Brings computation closer to data sources, reducing latency for applications like IoT and real-time analytics.
- **AI Integration:** Cloud-based machine learning and AI services enhance automation, prediction, and data-driven decision-making.
- **Serverless Computing:** Enables developers to deploy code without managing infrastructure (for example, AWS Lambda, and Google Cloud Functions).
- **Multi-Cloud Strategies:** Organizations adopt multiple cloud providers to improve redundancy, avoid lock-in, and optimize costs.
- **Quantum Computing:** Though in initial stages, cloud-based quantum services offer potential for solving complex computational problems.

As digital transformation continues to accelerate, cloud computing will remain a cornerstone of IT innovation, delivering scalability, agility, and new opportunities for Rocky Linux and other enterprise platforms.

Rocky Linux on AWS: AMIs and EC2 Deployment

Rocky Linux is a stable, enterprise-grade Linux distribution engineered for reliability, performance, and long-term support, making it a strong successor to CentOS and an excellent choice for cloud environments. On Amazon Web Services (AWS), official Rocky Linux 9 Amazon Machine Images (AMIs)—such as *ami-0a2b7ef1b* in the *us-east-1* region—enable administrators to quickly launch secure and fully compatible EC2 instances with minimal setup. Amazon EC2 provides scalable, flexible virtual machines designed to support workloads ranging from simple applications to complex enterprise systems. When paired with Rocky Linux, EC2 instances gain the benefits of enhanced stability, robust security, and high availability, creating a reliable foundation for cloud operations. Deployments can be performed manually using the EC2 console or fully automated through Infrastructure-as-Code (IaC) tools such as AWS CloudFormation and Terraform. This integration ensures deployments are not only fast and consistent but also repeatable, maintainable, and scalable, aligning perfectly with modern DevOps practices and cloud-native strategies.

Reasons to Choose Rocky Linux on AWS

- **Enterprise-Grade Stability:** Rocky Linux delivers long-term support, including a 10-year lifecycle for each release, making it ideal for production environments that demand reliability.
- **Seamless AWS Integration:** It integrates effortlessly with core AWS services such as Amazon S3 (object storage), RDS (relational databases), and IAM (access control), supporting cloud-native workflows and automation.
- **Security and Performance:** Regular security patches and system-level optimizations ensure that instances remain secure, efficient, and aligned with best practices for cloud deployment.

Deploying a Rocky Linux Instance on AWS

Deploying a Rocky Linux instance on AWS provides a scalable and cost-effective solution for running applications in the cloud. Rocky Linux, a downstream, community-supported alternative to CentOS, offers long-term stability and enterprise-grade performance. In this guide, we will walk through the process of launching a Rocky Linux instance using Amazon EC2. The walkthrough covers key steps such as selecting an official Amazon Machine Image (AMI), configuring instance details, and securing access with SSH key pairs. By the end, we will have a reliable virtual server ready to support application hosting, development, or automation workflows in a cloud-native environment.

Selecting and Launching a Rocky Linux AMI

To deploy a Rocky Linux instance, follow these steps:

1. **Log into the `AWS Management Console`:** Access the AWS account by navigating to AWS Console and entering the credentials.
2. **Navigate to the `EC2 Dashboard`:** From the AWS Console, go to the **EC2** service, which provides virtual server instances in the cloud.
3. **Click on "`Launch Instance`.":** This option allows us to create and configure a new virtual machine in AWS.
4. **Search for Rocky Linux in the `Amazon Machine Image` (AMI) section:** AWS provides a list of available AMIs (pre-configured OS images). Search for "Rocky Linux" to find the latest official version.

5. **Choose the latest official Rocky Linux AMI:** Select the most recent, stable release published by the Rocky Linux community.
6. **Select an instance type**
   - If using AWS Free Tier, choose **`t2.micro`** for cost-free eligibility.
   - For better performance, consider a **`t3.medium`** or higher.
7. **Configure network settings (VPC, subnet, Elastic IP):** Configure instance settings (for example, network, VPC, subnet, Elastic IP, IAM role, and storage) to match our deployment requirements.
8. **Add security rules:** Ensure that the instance's security group allows **port 22 (SSH)** for remote access. We may also define additional rules based on the application requirements.
9. **Launch the instance and download the private key file (`.pem`):** When prompted, create or select an existing key pair. This private key will be required for SSH authentication, when accessing our instance.

Once the instance is running, we can connect to it via SSH and begin configuring the Rocky Linux environment to support the desired workloads.

Command Example: Launch via AWS CLI

```
aws ec2 run-instances \
  --image-id ami-0a2b7ef1b \
  --count 1 \
  --instance-type t2.micro \
  --key-name mykey \
  --security-groups my-sg
Expected Output:
{
  "Instances": [
    {
      "InstanceId": "i-1234567890abcdef0",
      "InstanceType": "t2.micro",
      "State": {
        "Name": "pending"
      }
    }
  ]
}
Accessing the Instance:
ssh -i mykey.pem ec2-user@<instance-public-ip>
sudo dnf update -y
Expected Output:
Last metadata expiration check: 0:00:01 ago on Tue Jul 2 20:45:21 2025.
Dependencies resolved.
Nothing to do.
Complete!
```

Accessing and Configuring the Instance

1. Open a terminal and connect to the instance, using SSH:

   ```
   ssh -i your-key.pem ec2-user@your-instance-ip
   ```

2. Update the system:

   ```
   sudo dnf update -y
   ```

3. Create additional users, if needed:

```
sudo useradd -m newuser
sudo passwd newuser
```

4. Verify system information:

```
uname -a
df -h
```

Customizing and Creating a Custom AMI

Installing Essential Packages

1. Install utilities and necessary tools:
   - `sudo dnf install -y nano wget curl git unzip`
2. (Optional) Set up a web server:
   - `sudo dnf install -y httpd`
   - `sudo systemctl start httpd`
   - `sudo systemctl enable httpd`
3. Stop the instance and create an AMI from the AWS EC2 dashboard.

Automating Deployment with CloudFormation and Terraform

Manually deploying instances can be time-consuming, especially when managing multiple environments or ensuring consistent configurations. Automation tools such as AWS CloudFormation and Terraform help streamline this process by defining infrastructure as Code (IaC). These tools allow us to deploy and manage Rocky Linux instances efficiently, ensuring repeatability, scalability, and reducing configuration drift.

Automating with CloudFormation

AWS CloudFormation enables us to define and provision AWS infrastructure, using code. By writing a YAML template, we can specify the Rocky Linux AMI, instance type, security groups, and other configurations in a structured format. This approach ensures that deployments remain consistent, repeatable, and manageable.

Steps to Automate Deployment with CloudFormation

1. **Create a YAML Template**

Define the necessary infrastructure components, including:

- **`ImageId`:** Specifies the Rocky Linux AMI.
- **`InstanceType`:** Defines the compute resources allocated to the instance.
- **`SecurityGroups`:** Controls access rules (for example, allowing SSH on port 22).

2. **Deploy the CloudFormation stack, using AWS CLI**

Use the following command to create a new stack:

```
aws cloudformation create-stack --stack-name rocky-linux-stack --template-body
file://rocky-linux-template.yml
```

This command instructs AWS CloudFormation to read the **`rocky-linux-template.yml`** file, and provision the required resources automatically.

Once deployed, AWS CloudFormation ensures that the infrastructure adheres to the defined specifications, making it easier to manage multiple environments (for instance, development, testing, and production) with minimal manual intervention.

3. **Automating with Terraform**

Terraform is another powerful IaC tool that allows us to define AWS infrastructure, using HashiCorp Configuration Language (HCL). Terraform is cloud-agnostic, making it a flexible choice for managing infrastructure across multiple providers.

Steps to Automate Deployment with Terraform

Create a Terraform configuration file (**`main.tf`**), define the AWS provider and instance details:

```
     terraform {
  required_providers {
    aws = {
      source  = "hashicorp/aws"
      version = "~> 5.0"
    }
  }
}

provider "aws" {
  region = "us-east-1"
}

resource "aws_instance" "rocky_linux" {
  ami           = "ami-0bb84b8ffd87024d8"  # Example Rocky Linux AMI
  instance_type = "t2.micro"
  key_name      = "your-key"               # Ensure this key exists in AWS

  tags = {
    Name        = "rocky-linux-instance"
    Environment = "dev"
  }
}
```

Deploy with Terraform

To deploy infrastructure with Terraform, begin by initializing the working directory and applying the configuration:

- terraform init
- terraform apply -auto-approve
- **`terraform init`:** Prepares the working directory by downloading the necessary provider plugins and setting up the backend configuration.
- **`terraform apply -auto-approve`:** Applies the configuration and provisions the resources automatically, without requiring manual approval.

After execution, Terraform provisions the defined Rocky Linux instance on AWS. It also generates and maintains a state file that tracks the current state of the infrastructure. This file allows for efficient updates and consistent infrastructure management over time.

Both AWS CloudFormation and Terraform are robust tools for automating Rocky Linux deployments on AWS. CloudFormation, being AWS-native, uses YAML or JSON templates and integrates deeply with other AWS services. In contrast, Terraform uses its own declarative language (HCL) and supports multi-cloud deployments, offering greater flexibility. The choice between the two depends on the organization's infrastructure strategy, cloud provider dependencies, and preferred tooling ecosystem.

Security and IAM Integration

Setting Up IAM Roles:

1. Create an IAM role with Amazon EC2 permissions.
2. Attach the role to the Rocky Linux instance.
3. Verify IAM role access within the instance: `aws s3 ls`.

Configuring Security Groups:

- Allow only necessary inbound and outbound traffic.
- Restrict SSH access to known IP addresses.
- Implement firewall rules for application security.

Practical Labs

Lab 1: Launching and Configuring a Rocky Linux Instance

Objective: Deploy a Rocky Linux instance, and perform basic configurations.

1. Launch an EC2 instance with the latest Rocky Linux AMI.
2. Connect via SSH and update the system.
3. Install Apache and verify its functionality.

Lab 2: Automating Deployment with Terraform

Objective: Use Terraform to deploy a Rocky Linux instance.

1. Install Terraform on our local machine.
2. Write a Terraform configuration file.
3. Deploy the instance, using Terraform commands.

Lab 3: Security Best Practices

Objective: Secure an EC2 instance with IAM roles and Security Groups.

1. Create a custom IAM role, and attach it to an EC2 instance.
2. Configure Security Groups to limit SSH access.
3. Verify that unauthorized access is blocked.

Lab 4: Configuring Automated Backups

Objective: Implement automated backups for Rocky Linux instances.

1. Create a snapshot of an EC2 instance manually.
2. Configure an AWS Lambda function to automate snapshots.
3. Test recovery, using the snapshot.

Deploying Rocky Linux on AWS EC2 is both straightforward and effective–particularly when enhanced through automation tools such as AWS CloudFormation and HashiCorp Terraform. These tools simplify the provisioning and management of EC2 instances by enabling infrastructure as code (IaC). CloudFormation provides a native, declarative approach optimized for AWS environments, whereas Terraform offers cross-platform compatibility, allowing infrastructure to be managed consistently across different cloud providers. Through predefined configurations, Rocky Linux instances can be deployed and customized with precision and repeatability.

Security remains a critical component of any cloud-based deployment. Implementing IAM best practices–such as the principle of least privilege and role-based access control–helps ensure that access is limited to authorized users and services. Additionally, configuring security groups and firewall rules minimizes exposure to external threats by restricting unnecessary network traffic.

This chapter features **practical labs** focused on deploying, configuring, and securing Rocky Linux instances on AWS. These exercises provide hands-on experience in automating infrastructure, and applying cloud security standards in a controlled environment.

Configuring Rocky Linux Instances in AWS

Configuring Rocky Linux instances in AWS ensures optimal performance, security, and automation. This guide covers key aspects such as networking, storage, security, and automation tools to efficiently manage Rocky Linux environments in the AWS cloud.

- **Instance Initialization and System Updates**
  - Log in to the AWS Management Console and launch a Rocky Linux instance.
  - Connect via SSH using **ssh -i my-key.pem ec2-user@<instance-public-ip**.
  - Update the system with **sudo dnf update -y**.
  - Set **hostname** and enable required services.
- **Configuring Networking and Security**
  - Assign a static private IP address if necessary.
  - Configure firewall rules using **firewall** or **iptables**.
  - Set up security groups to allow only necessary inbound traffic.
  - Enable SSH key-based authentication and disable password authentication.
- **Storage and Disk Management**
  - Attach additional EBS volumes and format them, using **mkfs.xfs**.
  - Mount and configure automatic mounting, using **/etc/fstab**.
  - Optimize disk performance, using `**tuned**` profiles.
- **User Management and Access Control**
  - Create and manage users with **useradd** and **passwd**.
  - Configure **sudo** permissions for administrative tasks.
  - Set up SSH access restrictions, using **/etc/ssh/sshd_config**.
- **Automation with Ansible and Terraform**
  - Use Ansible to automate package installations and configuration.
  - Deploy instances with Terraform defining security groups and AMIs.
  - Schedule automated maintenance tasks, using **cron** or **systemd timers**.

- **Monitoring and Logging**
  - Install and configure CloudWatch Agent for instance monitoring.
  - Set up log rotation, using **`logrotate`.**
  - Use **`journalctl`** for **`systemd`** logs and troubleshooting.

Final chapters' recommendations

- Properly configuring Rocky Linux on AWS improves security and performance.
- Automation with Ansible and Terraform streamlines instance management.
- Monitoring and logging help maintain system health and reliability.

Best Practices for Cloud Security: IAM and Security Groups

Cloud security is essential for safeguarding infrastructure, applications, and data against unauthorized access and cyber threats. Identity and Access Management (IAM) and Security Groups are foundational components of cloud security, providing controlled access to resources and network segmentation. This guide expands on best practices for IAM and Security Groups, emphasizing security strategies, monitoring, and automation to strengthen cloud security.

Identity and Access Management (IAM) Best Practices

IAM is a crucial security mechanism that ensures only authorized users and services can access cloud resources. The following best practices enhance IAM security:

Principle of Least Privilege (PoLP)

The Principle of Least Privilege ensures users, applications, and services receive only the permissions necessary for their tasks. This minimizes the risk of privilege escalation and accidental exposure.

1. Use IAM policies with fine-grained permissions.
2. Assign permissions at the role or group level, instead of the user level.
3. Regularly review IAM policies to remove excessive permissions.

Use IAM Roles Instead of Long-Term Credentials: IAM roles provide temporary security credentials, reducing the risk of credential leaks and unauthorized access.

- Use IAM roles for applications and services that need AWS resource access.
- Avoid hard-coding access keys in code or configuration files.
- Rotate IAM credentials frequently, and enforce strict lifecycle management.

Enable Multi-Factor Authentication (MFA): MFA strengthens access security by requiring additional authentication factors.

- Enforce MFA for all privileged users, including administrators and service accounts.
- Utilize hardware or virtual MFA tokens for improved security.
- Use conditional access policies to mandate MFA based on user roles and locations.

Audit IAM Policies and Access Logs: Regular audits help detect misconfigurations and potential security threats.

- Use AWS IAM Access Analyzer to assess policies and identify overly permissive access.

- Monitor IAM access logs with AWS CloudTrail to track account activity.
- Automate IAM policy enforcement using AWS Config Rules.

Avoid Using Root Account Credentials for Daily Operations: The AWS root account has unrestricted access and should only be used for essential administrative tasks.

- Create separate IAM accounts for day-to-day operations.
- Store root credentials securely, and enable MFA for root access.
- Monitor root account usage through CloudTrail logs.

Security Groups Best Practices: Security Groups function as virtual firewalls for instances, controlling inbound and outbound traffic. Adopting best practices for Security Groups enhances network security.

Apply the Principle of Least Privilege: Limit Security Group rules to only necessary traffic to minimize exposure.

- Restrict inbound and outbound traffic based on specific application needs.
- Avoid using overly permissive rules such as allowing all traffic (0.0.0.0/0).
- Regularly review and update Security Group rules.

Restrict SSH (Port 22) Access: Unrestricted SSH access increases the risk of brute-force attacks.

- Limit SSH access to trusted IP addresses, using CIDR blocks.
- Implement AWS Systems Manager Session Manager for secure remote access.
- Use key-based authentication, instead of passwords.

Use Separate Security Groups for Different Workloads: Segmentation enhances isolation, and minimizes the attack surface.

- Assign separate Security Groups to different applications, environments (dev, test, prod), and teams.
- Restrict cross-communication between Security Groups, unless explicitly required.

Monitor Security Group Changes: Unauthorized changes to Security Groups can indicate potential security threats.

- Use AWS CloudTrail to track Security Group modifications.
- Enable AWS Config to audit Security Group rules, and enforce compliance.

Clean Up Unused Security Groups and Rules: Unused Security Groups and excessive rules increase security risks.

- Regularly audit Security Groups, and remove unnecessary ones.
- Use AWS Trusted Advisor to identify overly permissive security configurations.

Network Security and Encryption: Ensuring network segmentation and encryption further enhances security.

Virtual Private Cloud (VPC) Best Practices

- Use VPCs with private and public subnets to separate workloads.
- Restrict access between subnets, using Network ACLs and Security Groups.
- Implement VPC Peering or AWS PrivateLink for secure cross-VPC communication.

Encrypt Data in Transit and at Rest

- Use AWS Key Management Service (KMS) to encrypt sensitive data.

- Enforce TLS encryption for all data transmissions.
- Enable server-side encryption for S3, EBS, and RDS.

Monitoring and Logging for Security: Continuous monitoring and logging help detect and mitigate security threats in real time.

Enable AWS CloudTrail: AWS CloudTrail provides an audit trail for AWS account activity.

- Track user actions, resource changes, and security incidents.
- Integrate CloudTrail logs with Amazon CloudWatch for real-time monitoring.

Use Amazon GuardDuty for Threat Detection

GuardDuty provides intelligent threat detection for AWS environments.

- Detect unauthorized access, compromised credentials, and anomalous activities.
- Enable GuardDuty alerts to receive real-time notifications of security threats.

Monitor Security Metrics with AWS Security Hub: AWS Security Hub aggregates security findings across multiple AWS services.

- Continuously assess security configurations.
- Automate security compliance checks, using AWS Config.

Automated Security and Compliance: Automation reduces the risk of human error, and ensures adherence to security best practices.

Use AWS Config for Compliance Enforcement: AWS Config continuously monitors AWS resource configurations.

- Detect non-compliant IAM policies, and Security Group settings.
- Automate remediation with AWS Config Rules.

Implement Patch Management with AWS Systems Manager

- Automate OS and application patching for EC2 instances.
- Use maintenance windows to schedule security updates.

Use Infrastructure as Code (IaC) Security Checks

- Validate security configurations in Terraform and AWS CloudFormation.
- Enforce security policies, using tools like Checkov and AWS Config Rules.

Cloud security is an ongoing process requiring continuous monitoring and adherence to the best practices. Implementing robust IAM policies and well-structured Security Groups enhances cloud security posture. Regular audits, automation, and security monitoring tools help mitigate risks, and ensure compliance in cloud environments. Thus, by following these best practices, organizations can achieve a more secure and resilient cloud infrastructure.

Customizing and Creating AMIs: A Rocky Linux instance can be customized by installing necessary packages, and enabling required services. Once configuration is complete, an Amazon Machine Image (AMI) may be created for reuse in future deployments.

Install packages, and create a custom AMI:

- `sudo dnf install -y nano wget curl git httpd`
- `sudo systemctl start httpd`
- `sudo systemctl enable httpd`

After the configuration steps are completed, the instance must be stopped and the AMI created through the EC2 Dashboard.

Automating Deployments with CloudFormation and Terraform

Infrastructure as Code (IaC) enables consistency and repeatability across deployments. Tools such as AWS CloudFormation and Terraform are commonly used to manage infrastructure programmatically.

CloudFormation

The following YAML template defines a basic EC2 instance configuration:

```
Resources:
  RockyInstance:
    Type: AWS::EC2::Instance
    Properties:
      ImageId: ami-0a2b7ef1b
      InstanceType: t2.micro
      KeyName: mykey
      SecurityGroupIds:
        - sg-1234567890
Deployment via AWS CLI:
aws cloudformation create-stack --stack-name rockylinuxstack --template-body
file://template.yaml
```

Expected output:

```
{
  "StackId": "arn:aws:cloudformation:us-east-1:123456789012:stack/rockylinux-
stack/..."
}
```

Terraform: The following Terraform configuration file defines the same infrastructure:

```
provider "aws" {
  region = "us-east-1"
}

resource "aws_instance" "rocky_linux" {
  ami           = "ami-0a2b7ef1b"
  instance_type = "t2.micro"
  key_name      = "mykey"
  security_group_ids = ["sg-1234567890"]
}
```

To deploy:

```
terraform init
terraform apply -auto-approve
```

Expected Output:

```
Apply complete! Resources: 1 added, 0 changed, 0 destroyed.
```

Outputs:

```
instance_id = "i-1234567890abcdef0"
```

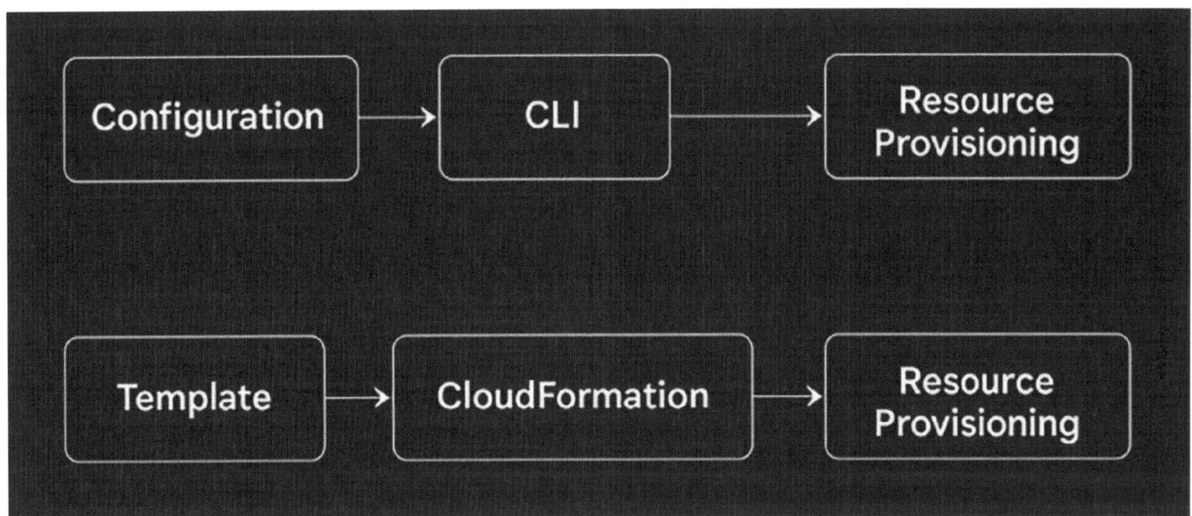

Figure 14.2: *Terraform vs. CloudFormation Workflow*

This figure provides a side-by-side view of the **deployment workflows** for two leading Infrastructure as Code (IaC) tools—**Terraform** and **AWS CloudFormation**. The top sequence depicts Terraform's process, starting with configuration files written in **HashiCorp Configuration Language (HCL)**, executed through the **command-line interface (CLI)**, and resulting in the provisioning of cloud resources across multiple platforms. The lower sequence illustrates CloudFormation's workflow, beginning with declarative templates in **JSON or YAML**, which are directly interpreted by the **CloudFormation service** to create and manage AWS resources. This comparison highlights Terraform's **platform-agnostic, CLI-driven automation** versus CloudFormation's **AWS-native, fully managed orchestration model**, helping readers understand the strengths of each approach.

Criteria	CloudFormation	Terraform
AWS Integration	Native and tightly integrated with AWS services	Compatible with AWS but less seamless than CloudFormation
Multi-Cloud Support	Limited to AWS	Supports AWS, Azure, Google Cloud, and other providers
Configuration Language	YAML or JSON	HCL (HashiCorp Configuration Language)
State Management	Automatically managed by AWS	Requires manual setup; supports local and remote backends
Learning Curve	Moderate; easier for AWS-focused teams	Moderate to high; steeper for multi-cloud environments

Figure 14.3: *CloudFormation vs. Terraform Comparison*

This figure presents a side-by-side comparison of **AWS CloudFormation** and **HashiCorp Terraform**, two leading Infrastructure as Code (IaC) tools. CloudFormation, tightly integrated with the AWS ecosystem, offers native support and streamlined state management through AWS services. Terraform, on the other hand, provides multi-cloud flexibility and infrastructure portability, making it ideal for heterogeneous environments. Key differences in configuration languages, state handling, and learning complexity are highlighted to guide administrators in selecting the most suitable tool for their deployment, scalability, and cross-platform needs.

Security and IAM Integration

Security is critical for cloud deployments. IAM and Security Groups ensure controlled access and network protection.

IAM Best Practices

- **Least Privilege:** Assign minimal permissions via policies.
- **IAM Roles:** Use roles for temporary credentials.
- **MFA:** Enforce for privileged users.
- **Audits:** Use IAM Access Analyzer and CloudTrail.
- **Avoid Root:** Use IAM users for daily operations.

Example IAM Policy:

```
{
  "Version": "2012-10-17",
  "Statement": [
    {
      "Effect": "Allow",
      "Action": "s3:ListBucket",
      "Resource": "arn:aws:s3:::mybucket"
    }
  ]
}
```

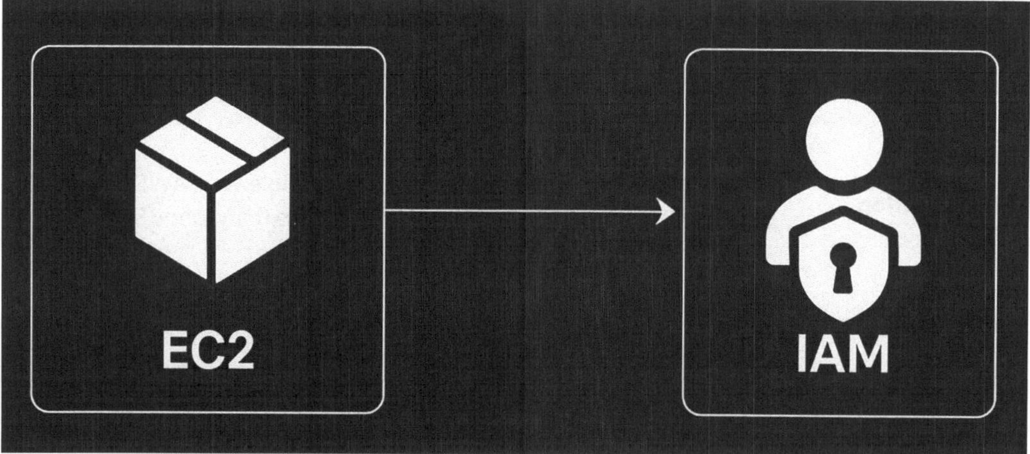

***Figure 14.4**: AWS EC2 and IAM Integration*

This figure illustrates how AWS Identity and Access Management (IAM) integrates with EC2 instances to enforce secure access control across services. It demonstrates the use of IAM roles attached to EC2 instances via instance profiles, allowing the instances to obtain temporary credentials for accessing other AWS resources such as S3, DynamoDB, or CloudWatch. By eliminating the need for hardcoded credentials, this integration enhances security, and aligns with best practices for identity management. The figure also emphasizes how policies define the scope of access, ensuring that EC2 instances operate under the principle of least privilege.

Security Groups

- Restrict traffic to necessary ports (for example, SSH on 22).
- Limit SSH to trusted IPs (for example, 192.168.1.0/24).
- Use separate groups for different workloads.

- Monitor changes with CloudTrail.

Cost Optimization and Autoscaling

Optimize costs and performance, using AWS Trusted Advisor and Auto Scaling Groups (ASGs).

Cost Optimization with Trusted Advisor:

- Identify underutilized EC2 instances.
- Use Reserved Instances or Savings Plans for predictable workloads.
- Monitor costs with AWS Cost Explorer.

Aspect	On-Premises	AWS EC2
Upfront Cost	High — includes hardware and licensing	Low — pay-as-you-go pricing model
Scalability	Limited and requires manual intervention	Automatic scaling via Auto Scaling Groups
Maintenance	Fully managed by internal IT teams	Managed by AWS infrastructure
Cost Example	Approx. $10,000 per physical server	As low as $0.01/hour for t2.micro instance

***Figure 14.5**: Cost Comparison: On-Premises vs. AWS EC2*

This figure illustrates the financial and operational contrasts between traditional **on-premises infrastructure** and **cloud-based deployments with AWS EC2**. It highlights key factors such as upfront capital investment, scalability, maintenance responsibilities, and ongoing operational costs. On-premises environments often demand significant initial spending on hardware, licensing, and in-house IT support, with scalability requiring manual intervention. By contrast, AWS EC2 enables a **pay-as-you-go model**, automated scalability through **Auto Scaling Groups**, and reduced administrative overhead by leveraging AWS-managed services. This comparison helps decision-makers weigh economic trade-offs and identify opportunities when considering **migration or hybrid cloud strategies**.

Auto Scaling: Auto Scaling Groups (ASGs) allow instances to scale based on defined metrics. An example command:

```
aws autoscaling create-auto-scaling-group \
  --auto-scaling-group-name rockyasg \
  --launch-configuration-name mylaunchconfig \
  --min-size 1 \
  --max-size 5 \
  --desired-capacity 2 \
  --vpc-zone-identifier subnet-xxxxxxxx
```

CI/CD Integration with GitHub Actions: Infrastructure deployments can be automated using GitHub Actions integrated with Terraform:

```
name: Deploy Rocky Linux
on: [push]
jobs:
  deploy:
    runs-on: ubuntu-latest
    steps:
```

```
        - uses: actions/checkout@v4
        - uses: hashicorp/setup-terraform@v3
          with:
            terraform_version: 1.9.8
        - run: terraform init
        - run: terraform apply -auto-approve
      env:
        AWS_ACCESS_KEY_ID: ${{ secrets.AWS_ACCESS_KEY_ID }}
        AWS_SECRET_ACCESS_KEY: ${{ secrets.AWS_SECRET_ACCESS_KEY }}
```

Hybrid and Multi-Cloud Environments

Rocky Linux supports hybrid and multi-cloud setups, integrating on-premises infrastructure with AWS, Azure, or GCP.

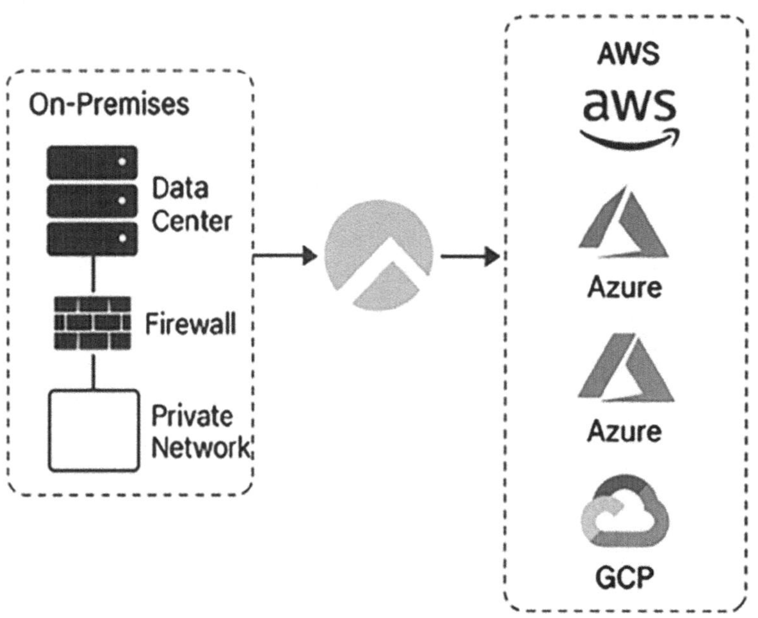

Figure 14.6: Hybrid Cloud Network Setup

This figure illustrates how on-premises infrastructure integrates with multiple cloud providers to create a flexible and resilient environment. Rocky Linux systems deployed locally connect securely to public cloud resources across AWS, Azure, and GCP using VPN or Direct Connect links. Core services–including identity management, storage, and databases–are distributed between private datacenters and cloud platforms to ensure workload portability and redundancy. By adopting this hybrid model, administrators can optimize costs, strengthen disaster recovery, and scale applications dynamically while maintaining compliance and control over sensitive data. The setup also supports multi-cloud strategies, reducing vendor lock-in and enabling organizations to select the most suitable services from each provider.

Lab: Backup and Recovery with AWS Backup

1. Create a backup plan in AWS Backup.
2. Assign EC2 instances to the plan.

3. Test recovery by restoring an EBS snapshot.

Troubleshooting Common Issues

Issue	Fix
IAM permission denied	Verify policy ARN and role attachment
Terraform state lock	Use `terraform force-unlock`
SSH connection refused	Check Security Group rules for port 22

Figure 14.7: *Common AWS Deployment Issues and Fixes*

This figure highlights frequent challenges that arise during **AWS deployments** and provides practical solutions to resolve them quickly. Common issues include incorrect IAM permissions, misconfigured security groups, insufficient instance limits, and missing key pairs. Each entry outlines the **symptoms, root causes, and recommended fixes**, serving as a quick troubleshooting reference for administrators. By understanding these recurring problems and their resolutions, teams can ensure smoother deployments, minimize downtime, and maintain stronger security and reliability across cloud environments.

Rocky Linux in Hybrid and Multi-Cloud Environments: Practical Laboratories

Rocky Linux is an enterprise-grade Linux distribution designed as a stable and secure alternative to RHEL (Red Hat Enterprise Linux). It is widely utilized in hybrid and multi-cloud environments due to its reliability, compatibility with enterprise applications, and cost-effectiveness. This document focuses on deploying, managing, and securing Rocky Linux within AWS, using practical laboratories to provide hands-on experience.

Lab 1: Deploying Rocky Linux on AWS

Objective: Deploy a Rocky Linux instance on AWS, configure networking, and establish secure access.

Requirements

- AWS account with permissions to launch EC2 instances
- SSH key pair for secure access
- Rocky Linux AMI available in AWS Marketplace

Steps

1. **Launch an `EC2 Instance`**
   a. Navigate to the **`AWS EC2 Dashboard`**.
   b. Click on **`Launch Instance`**.
   c. Select **`Rocky Linux AMI`** from the AWS Marketplace.
   d. Choose an instance type (for example, **`t2.micro`** for testing).
   e. Configure network settings:
      i. Select a **`VPC`** and **`subnet`**.
      ii. Attach an **`Elastic IP`** for external access.

iii. Create a **`security group`** allowing only necessary inbound traffic (e.g., SSH on port 22 from trusted IPs).

f. Launch the instance and connect via SSH.

2. **Secure Access**

   a. Disable root SSH login: Edit **`/etc/ssh/sshd_config and set PermitRootLogin no.`**

   b. Configure a non-root user with sudo privileges:

   ```
   sudo adduser admin
   sudo usermod -aG wheel admin
   ```

   c. Implement SSH key authentication and disable password login:

   ```
   sudo nano /etc/ssh/sshd_config
   PasswordAuthentication no
   ```

   d. Restart SSH service: **`sudo systemctl restart sshd`**

3. **Verify Deployment**

   a. Run system updates:

   ```
   sudo dnf update -y
   ```

   b. Check system logs:

   ```
   journalctl -xe
   cat /var/log/messages
   ```

   c. Confirm internet connectivity:

   ```
   ping -c 4 google.com
   curl -I https://www.centos.org/
   ```

Lab 2: Hybrid Cloud Networking between AWS and Azure

Objective: Establish a secure communication channel between Rocky Linux instances running on AWS and Azure.

Steps

1. **Set Up an IPsec VPN Tunnel**

   a. Deploy a **`VPN gateway`** on AWS and Azure.

   b. Configure a **`site-to-site VPN connection`** between both clouds.

   c. Ensure **`routing policies`** allow internal traffic between instances.

2. **Secure SSH Key Exchange**

   a. Generate SSH key pairs for inter-instance authentication:

   ```
   ssh-keygen -t rsa -b 4096 -C "admin@rockylinux"
   ```

   b. Deploy **`AWS Secrets Manager`** to store and retrieve private keys securely.

Lab 3: Deploying Containers on Rocky Linux in AWS

Objective: Deploy and manage Docker containers on Rocky Linux in AWS.

Steps

1. **Install Docker**

   a. Install Docker: **`sudo dnf install -y docker`**

   b. Start and enable Docker:

   ```
   sudo systemctl start docker
   sudo systemctl enable docker
   ```

   c. Verify installation: `docker --version`

2. **Deploy a Web Application Container**

   a. Pull and run a sample **`Nginx`** container:

   ```
   docker pull nginx
   docker run -d -p 80:80 nginx
   ```

   b. Confirm accessibility via public IP.

3. **Set Up Load Balancing Using AWS ELB**

   a. Deploy an AWS **Elastic Load Balancer (ELB)**.

   b. Register **Rocky Linux instances** running Nginx as targets.

   c. Configure **auto-scaling** for workload management.

Lab 4: Implementing Centralized Logging and Monitoring

Objective: Configure Prometheus and Grafana for monitoring Rocky Linux instances in AWS.

Steps

1. **Install Prometheus**

   a. Download and install Prometheus: `sudo dnf install -y prometheus`

   b. Configure Prometheus to monitor system metrics.

2. **Deploy Grafana**

   a. Install Grafana: `sudo dnf install -y grafana`

   b. Configure Grafana to fetch `Prometheus metrics`.

   c. Set up dashboards to monitor **CPU, memory, and network activity**.

3. **Enable AWS CloudWatch Logging**

   a. Install and configure `AWS CloudWatch Agent`.

   b. Create log groups and define retention policies.

Lab 5: Automating Deployments with Ansible

Objective: Use Ansible to automate Rocky Linux instance configuration and package installation.

Steps

1. **Install Ansible**

   a. Install Ansible: ***sudo dnf install -y ansible***

   b. Verify installation: ***ansible --version***

2. **Create an Ansible Inventory File**

   a. Define Rocky Linux instances in `/etc/ansible/hosts`:

   ```
   [servers] 192.168.1.100
   ```

   b. Ensure connectivity: **`ansible all -m ping`**

3. **Run a Playbook to Install Nginx**

   a. Create an Ansible playbook (**`nginx.yml`**):

```
- hosts: servers
  become: yes
  tasks:
    - name: Install Nginx
      dnf:
        name: nginx
        state: present
```

   b. Execute the playbook: **`ansible-playbook nginx.yml`**

   c. Verify installation via the server's public IP.

These practical laboratories demonstrate how to deploy, secure, and manage Rocky Linux efficiently within hybrid and multi-cloud environments, with a primary focus on AWS. By leveraging **automation tools, secure networking configurations, and monitoring solutions**, organizations can enhance operational efficiency and security in cloud deployments.

Conclusion

Rocky Linux proves to be a powerful and versatile operating system for cloud deployments, offering stability, security, and flexibility across various cloud environments. This chapter has explored key aspects of deploying and managing Rocky Linux in AWS, from provisioning instances with Amazon Machine Images (AMIs) to implementing security best practices with IAM and Security Groups.

Furthermore, the discussion on hybrid and multi-cloud strategies highlights the importance of flexibility in modern enterprise infrastructure. Thus, by leveraging automation tools such as Terraform and Ansible, organizations can streamline their cloud operations, ensuring efficiency and scalability.

As cloud adoption continues to evolve, mastering Rocky Linux in cloud environments will be essential for IT professionals and organizations aiming to optimize performance, security, and cost-efficiency in their deployments.

In the next chapter, we will explore performance tuning techniques to optimize Rocky Linux for both on-premises and cloud environments. The salient topics in this chapter will include system monitoring, resource optimization, and network tuning to enhance efficiency and scalability.

Points to Remember

- **Optimized Deployment on AWS**
  - **Preconfigured AMIs:** Rocky Linux provides official Amazon Machine Images (AMIs), ensuring a streamlined EC2 instance deployment.
  - **Scalability and High Availability:** Supports AWS Auto Scaling Groups (ASG) and Elastic Load Balancing (ELB) to maintain performance and uptime.
  - **Infrastructure as Code (IaC):** Tools such as Terraform and AWS CloudFormation enable automated provisioning of Rocky Linux instances.
- **Security Best Practices in the Cloud**
  - **Identity and Access Management (IAM):** Implementing least-privilege access with IAM roles and policies prevents unauthorized access.

- **Network Security:** Security Groups and Network ACLs define strict inbound and outbound traffic rules for enhanced protection.
- **Data Encryption:** AWS Key Management Service (KMS) enables encryption of data at rest and in transit to ensure security.
- **Logging and Monitoring:** Integration with AWS CloudWatch, AWS CloudTrail, and third-party tools (for example, Splunk) provides real-time security insights.

- **Optimized Configuration for Cloud Environments**
  - **Automated Instance Setup:** Cloud-init and Ansible allow for automated configuration and post-deployment customization.
  - **Storage Management:** Supports Amazon EBS for persistent storage and S3 for scalable object storage solutions.
  - **Performance Optimization:** Fine-tuning CPU, memory, and I/O parameters ensures cost-effective and efficient instance operation.
- **Hybrid and Multi-Cloud Compatibility**
  - **Cross-Cloud Deployment:** Rocky Linux can run on AWS, Azure, and Google Cloud, offering flexibility for multi-cloud strategies.
  - **Hybrid Integration:** Tools such as AWS Direct Connect and VPN enable seamless connectivity between on-premises data centers and cloud infrastructure.
  - **Containerization and Orchestration:** Kubernetes and Docker allow for efficient deployment and management of Rocky Linux workloads in cloud-native applications.

Multiple Choice Questions

1. Which command is used to launch a Rocky Linux instance on AWS, using the AWS CLI?
   a. `aws ec2 run-instances --image-id ami-xxxxx --count 1 --in stance-type t2.micro`
   b. `aws start-rocky-linux-instance`
   c. `aws deploy rocky-linux --instance t2.micro`
   d. `aws create-instance rocky-linux`
2. Which AWS service provides virtual servers to run Rocky Linux in the cloud?
   a. Amazon RDS
   b. Amazon Lambda
   c. Amazon EC2
   d. AWS Fargate
3. Which tool can be used to automate the provisioning of Rocky Linux instances in AWS?
   a. AWS CloudFormation
   b. Kubernetes
   c. Docker Compose
   d. Prometheus

4. Which AWS security feature helps control inbound and outbound traffic to Rocky Linux instances?
   a. IAM Policies
   b. AWS WAF
   c. Security Groups
   d. AWS Shield
5. What is the primary function of IAM roles in AWS when working with Rocky Linux?
   a. Restrict SSH access to EC2 instances
   b. Provide temporary permissions for AWS services to interact securely
   c. Encrypt EBS volumes automatically
   d. Assign static IP addresses to instances
6. Which command can be used to connect to a Rocky Linux instance via SSH on AWS?
   a. ssh -i my-key.pem ec2-user@public-ip
   b. connect rocky-linux --aws-ssh
   c. aws ssh rocky-linux-instance
   d. remote-login rocky-linux
7. Which cloud storage service can be used to store backups of Rocky Linux system logs?
   a. Amazon RDS
   b. Amazon S3
   c. AWS Lambda
   d. AWS DynamoDB
8. What is the key benefit of using Rocky Linux in a hybrid cloud setup?
   a. Requires a proprietary hypervisor for cloud compatibility
   b. Provides seamless integration between on-premises and cloud environments
   c. Supports only AWS, and no other cloud providers
   d. Eliminates the need for security configurations
9. Which monitoring tool can be integrated with Rocky Linux on AWS for performance tracking?
   a. AWS CloudWatch
   b. AWS GuardDuty
   c. AWS Config
   d. AWS CloudTrail
10. Which feature of Rocky Linux enhances security when deployed in the cloud?
    a. Built-in SELinux policies
    b. Automatic root access for all users
    c. Default unrestricted inbound traffic
    d. Disabling all firewall rules by default

Answers

1. a
2. c
3. a
4. c
5. b
6. a
7. b
8. b
9. a
10. a

Questions

1. What are the key differences between public, private, and hybrid cloud environments, and how do they impact the deployment of Rocky Linux?
2. How do Amazon Machine Images (AMIs) simplify the deployment process of Rocky Linux on AWS, and what factors should be considered when selecting an AMI?
3. What steps are involved in configuring network settings such as VPC and subnets, when deploying Rocky Linux on AWS EC2?
4. How can EC2 instance types impact the performance and cost of Rocky Linux deployments on AWS?
5. What are the best practices for managing access to AWS resources when working with Rocky Linux, specifically, using IAM roles and policies?
6. How do AWS Security Groups enhance the security of Rocky Linux instances, and what rules should be applied for secure access?
7. What is the significance of using Elastic Load Balancing (ELB) for distributing traffic across multiple Rocky Linux instances in the cloud?
8. How does Amazon S3 integrate with Rocky Linux deployments for backup and storage management?
9. What are the advantages of using Ansible for automating the deployment and management of Rocky Linux instances in AWS, and how does it integrate with cloud services?
10. In what ways can Rocky Linux be deployed in multi-cloud environments to maximize flexibility, and avoid vendor lock-in?

Key Terms

- **Cloud Computing:** The delivery of computing services over the internet, including servers, storage, databases, networking, and software, enabling scalable and on-demand infrastructure management.
- **Rocky Linux AMI:** An Amazon Machine Image (AMI) specifically designed for deploying Rocky Linux 9 instances on AWS, providing a pre-configured system for cloud environments.
- **Amazon EC2:** A cloud service that provides scalable virtual machines for running Rocky Linux 9 instances, allowing flexible deployment and management.
- **Infrastructure as Code (IaC):** The practice of managing and provisioning cloud infrastructure through machine-readable scripts such as Ansible playbooks, ensuring consistency and automation.
- **Security Groups:** AWS firewall rules that control inbound and outbound traffic for Rocky Linux 9 instances, enhancing security in cloud deployments.
- **IAM (Identity and Access Management):** AWS service that manages access permissions and authentication for users and services interacting with Rocky Linux 9 instances.
- **Ansible Cloud Modules:** A set of modules within Ansible used for automating cloud operations, including provisioning, scaling, and configuring Rocky Linux 9 instances in AWS.
- **Hybrid Cloud:** A cloud computing model that integrates on-premises infrastructure with public cloud services, enabling Rocky Linux 9 to operate across multiple environments.
- **Auto Scaling:** A feature that automatically adjusts the number of Rocky Linux 9 instances in AWS based on demand, ensuring efficiency and cost optimization.
- **AWS CLI (Command Line Interface):** A tool that allows users to manage AWS resources, including Rocky Linux 9 instances through command-line commands and automation scripts.
- **Amazon S3 (Simple Storage Service):** An object storage service used for storing backups, logs, and other data related to Rocky Linux 9 cloud deployments.
- **AWS CloudFormation:** An AWS service that automates infrastructure provisioning using templates, allowing Rocky Linux 9 deployments to be defined and managed as code.
- **CloudWatch:** An AWS monitoring service that collects performance metrics and logs from Rocky Linux 9 instances, ensuring system health and optimization.
- **Elastic Load Balancer (ELB):** An AWS service that distributes incoming traffic across multiple Rocky Linux 9 instances, improving scalability and reliability.
- **AWS Systems Manager:** A management service that provides automation, patching, and compliance tracking for Rocky Linux 9 instances in AWS.

CHAPTER 15
Performance Tuning in Rocky Linux 9

Introduction

Performance tuning is essential to ensuring Rocky Linux operates efficiently across diverse environments, from on-premises infrastructure to cloud platforms. By continuously monitoring system resources, administrators can identify and resolve bottlenecks through targeted optimization of CPU, memory, storage, and networking. Rocky Linux offers a robust set of tools for performance analysis and fine-tuning, enabling responsive, stable, and scalable systems, whether deployed on physical servers, virtual machines, or cloud instances. Real-world tuning practices, including profiling and diagnostics, support early issue detection and proactive adjustments tailored to workload demands. These strategies help maximize resource utilization, reduce latency, and sustain consistent throughput, making them critical in mission-critical environments where uptime and efficiency are paramount.

Structure

This chapter covers the following topics:

- System Monitoring and Profiling
- Optimizing CPU, Memory, and Disk Usage in Rocky Linux 9
- Tuning Networking for Performance in Rocky Linux 9
- Performance Optimization in Cloud Environments

Version Compatibility

The content in this chapter has been tested on Rocky Linux 9.3. While many instructions will work on Rocky Linux 8, some tools may differ slightly in version, syntax, or output format.

Tool	Tested Version (Rocky Linux 9)	Notes on Rocky Linux 8 Compatibility
`perf`	v5.14	Available via `perf` package; syntax may differ slightly
`fio`	v3.28	Fully compatible; may require enabling the EPEL repository
`tuned`	v2.18	Profiles and default settings may vary slightly
`aws-cli`	v2.15.33	Version 1 differs in command structure; migration may be required
`iostat`	sysstat v12.5.6	Available; output formatting may differ slightly

Figure 15.1: *Tool Versions and Compatibility Across Rocky Linux Versions*

This figure summarizes the versions of performance and monitoring tools referenced throughout this chapter, verified on Rocky Linux 9.3. It also includes compatibility notes for Rocky Linux 8, highlighting differences in syntax, functionality, or package availability that administrators may encounter. By providing this side-by-side comparison, it helps ensure smoother transitions when working across different Rocky Linux releases. Readers can quickly identify which tools are supported, what adjustments may be required, and how to maintain consistent performance monitoring practices in mixed environments.

System Monitoring and Profiling

System monitoring and profiling are necessary for identifying and resolving performance issues in Rocky Linux. Administrators use these techniques to track resource usage, analyze bottlenecks, and optimize system performance. Effective monitoring enables proactive detection of anomalies before they impact production workloads. By continuously observing system behavior, administrators can ensure that the system runs efficiently, and meets performance expectations.

System monitoring and profiling are essential for identifying performance bottlenecks. Tools like **`top`**, **`htop`**, **`sar`**, **`iostat`**, **`vmstat`**, **`pidstat`**, **`netstat/ss`**, and **`dstat`** provide insights into CPU, memory, disk, and network performance.

Tool	Key Metrics	Primary Use Case
`perf`	CPU cycles, cache misses, instruction counts	Diagnose CPU bottlenecks
`mpstat`	CPU utilization, per-core statistics	Monitor multi-core performance
`fio`	I/O throughput, latency, IOPS	Benchmark disk performance
`iostat`	Disk I/O rates, CPU wait time, utilization	Identify I/O bottlenecks

Figure 15.2: *Comparison of Performance Tuning Tools*

This figure provides a detailed comparison of widely used monitoring and diagnostic utilities in Rocky Linux, highlighting the system metrics they measure, their primary functionalities, and the scenarios where they are most effective. The goal is to help system administrators quickly identify the right tool for specific performance tuning tasks, whether monitoring CPU load, tracking memory usage, measuring disk throughput, or analyzing network latency. Tools such as **`top`**, **`iostat`**, and **`vmstat`** offer quick, command-line visibility into real-time system health, while more advanced utilities like **`perf`** and **`tuned-adm`** deliver deeper insights into performance profiling and automated optimization. By aligning the choice of tool with the performance objective, administrators can improve troubleshooting accuracy, reduce overhead, and apply targeted optimizations that fit both workload demands and infrastructure constraints.

Monitoring Tools in Rocky Linux

Rocky Linux provides a variety of tools for system monitoring and profiling. Each tool offers unique insights into various aspects of system performance:

- **`top`:** Provides real-time CPU and memory usage. It displays a dynamic view of system processes, sorted by resource consumption.
- **`htop`:** A more user-friendly alternative to top, with an interactive interface that allows sorting, filtering, and managing processes more efficiently.

- **`vmstat`:** Reports system performance metrics, including CPU, memory, and disk activity, providing snapshots of system performance.
- **`iostat`:** Monitors disk I/O activity, helping to identify heavily loaded disks that may cause performance bottlenecks.
- **`sar`:** Collects and reports system activity data over time, aiding in historical performance analysis and trend identification.
- **`pidstat`:** Tracks CPU usage per process, offering granular insights into individual process performance.
- **`netstat/ss`:** Displays network connections and statistics, helping to diagnose network-related performance issues.
- **`dstat`:** Combines multiple resource usage statistics into one output, offering a comprehensive performance overview of CPU, memory, disk, and network utilization.

Lab 1: Using `top` and `htop` for Process Monitoring

Objective: Learn how to monitor real-time CPU and memory usage, using top and htop.

Steps:

1. Open a terminal and run **`top`.**
2. Observe CPU and memory usage, load average, and running processes. Note that processes are sorted by CPU usage by default.
3. Press **`q`** to exit the top.
4. Install **`htop`** after updating and upgrading the current packages:
    - `sudo dnf update`
    - `sudo dnf upgrade`
    - `sudo dnf install htop -y`
5. Run **`htop`**, and explore interactive options such as sorting processes by memory usage, killing processes, and searching for specific processes.
6. Exit **`htop`**, using **`q`** or F10.

```
top - 10:55:01 up 1 day, 2:30, 1 user, load average: 0.10, 0.15,
   0.20
Tasks: 120 total, 1 running, 119 sleeping, 0 stopped, 0 zombie
%Cpu(s): 2.0 us, 1.0 sy, 0.0 ni, 96.5 id, 0.5 wa, 0.0 hi, 0.0 si
MiB Mem: 3924.3 total, 1500.2 used, 2424.1 free, 100.5 buff/cache
MiB Swap: 2048.0 total, 0.0 used, 2048.0 free

PID USER PR NI VIRT RES SHR %CPU %MEM TIME+ COMMAND
1234 user 20 0 500m 200m 180m 1.0 5.1 0:10.45 process_name
```

Listing 15.1: *Sample Output of top Command*

The **`top`** and **`htop`** commands provide administrators with real-time insights into system performance by displaying running processes and their resource utilization. While **`top`** delivers a detailed, text-based view of CPU, memory, and process activity, **`htop`** enhances usability with an intuitive, interactive interface that simplifies process management tasks such as killing or renicing processes. Both tools are indispensable for quickly identifying resource-intensive workloads, troubleshooting performance bottlenecks, and maintaining system stability during live operations.

Lab 2: System Activity Monitoring with sar

Objective: Use sar to collect and analyze system performance metrics over time.

Steps:

1. Install the **sysstat** package, if not already installed:

   `sudo dnf install sysstat -y && systemctl enable --now sysstat`

2. Start the **sysstat** service:

   `systemctl enable --now sysstat`

   `systemctl status sysstat`

3. Monitor CPU usage, every 5 seconds for 10 iterations: **`sar -u 5 10`**
4. Monitor memory usage: **`sar -r 5 10`**
5. Analyze the results to identify trends and potential performance bottlenecks.

```
Linux 5.14.0-362.8.1.el9_3.x86_64 (localhost) 07/01/2025 _x86_64_
    (4 CPU)
10:55:10 %user %nice %system %iowait %steal %idle
10:55:15 2.50 0.00 1.25 0.50 0.00 95.75
Average: 2.50 0.00 1.25 0.50 0.00 95.75
```

Listing 15.2: *Sample CPU Usage Output from sar*

The **sar** command is a powerful utility for historical performance analysis, enabling administrators to monitor CPU usage and other system metrics over time. By collecting and storing performance data at regular intervals, it helps identify long-term trends such as recurring CPU spikes, memory leaks, or periods of underutilization. This historical perspective supports proactive performance management, accurate capacity planning, and informed decision-making for scaling or optimizing system resources.

Lab 3: Disk I/O Monitoring with iostat

Objective: Monitor disk performance, using **iostat**.

Steps:

1. Ensure that **sysstat** is installed.
2. Run the following command to view **disk utilization**, and response time:
   `iostat -x 5 10`
3. Identify disks with high utilization or long response times which may indicate bottlenecks.

```
Linux 5.14.0-362.8.1.el9_3.x86_64 (localhost) 07/01/2025
avg-cpu: %user %nice %system %iowait %steal %idle
2.50 0.00 1.25 0.50 0.00 95.75
Device r/s w/s rkB/s wkB/s rrqm/s wrqm/s %rrqm %wrqm r_await
   w_await aqu-sz rareq-sz wareq-sz svctm %util
nvme0n1 10.0 5.0 400.0 200.0 0.0 0.0 0.0 0.0 1.50 2.00 0.1 40.0
   40.0 0.5 3.60
```

Listing 15.3: *Sample iostat Output for Disk Utilization*

Disk I/O performance is a key factor in the efficiency of data-intensive applications. The **iostat** command provides detailed statistics on disk activity, including read and write rates, queue lengths, and response times. These metrics help administrators diagnose storage bottlenecks, evaluate the effectiveness of existing hardware, and determine whether optimizations or upgrades are required. By monitoring disk utilization trends, **iostat** supports informed decision-making for capacity planning and ensures that storage systems can sustain application performance under varying workloads.

System monitoring and profiling are crucial for performance tuning in Rocky Linux. By using tools such as **top, htop, sar**, and **iostat**, administrators can proactively track system health, identify inefficiencies, and optimize system performance. These tools provide valuable insights into distinct aspects of system performance, allowing administrators to make informed decisions to improve efficiency, and ensure reliability.

In the next section, we will focus on optimizing CPU, memory, and disk usage for improved system efficiency. This will involve techniques such as tuning system parameters, optimizing application performance, and implementing best practices for resource management.

Expected Outputs and Functionalities

For clarity and verification, this section provides sample outputs for essential system performance tools. These examples are intended to assist Linux administrators and unaccustomed users in understanding expected behavior, and identifying key metrics when commands are executed in a typical Rocky Linux 9 environment.

Including these outputs helps establish a baseline for performance and facilitates troubleshooting by making it easier to compare actual results against standard reference values. Each command is presented, along with a representative output and explanatory notes that highlight important metrics relevant to system monitoring and optimization.

First, we will proceed to install the package with the following command:

```
sudo dnf install perf -y
```

perf stat: CPU Performance Metrics

Command: **perf stat -d sleep 1**

```
[cesarmserver@localhost ~]$ perf stat -d sleep 1

 Performance counter stats for 'sleep 1':

              3.10 msec task-clock:u                     #    0.003 CPUs utilized
                 0      context-switches:u               #    0.000 /sec
                 0      cpu-migrations:u                 #    0.000 /sec
                61      page-faults:u                    #   19.650 K/sec
                 0      cycles:u                                                          (36.09%)
                 0      stalled-cycles-frontend:u                                         (65.58%)
                 0      stalled-cycles-backend:u
                 0      instructions:u                                                    (63.91%)
                 0      branches:u                       #    0.000 /sec                  (34.42%)
     <not counted>      branch-misses:u                                                   (0.00%)
     <not counted>      L1-dcache-loads:u                                                 (0.00%)
     <not counted>      L1-dcache-load-misses:u                                           (0.00%)
   <not supported>      LLC-loads:u
   <not supported>      LLC-load-misses:u

       1.007823662 seconds time elapsed

       0.001012000 seconds user
       0.003333000 seconds sys


Some events weren't counted. Try disabling the NMI watchdog:
        echo 0 > /proc/sys/kernel/nmi_watchdog
        perf stat ...
        echo 1 > /proc/sys/kernel/nmi_watchdog
```

Figure 15.3: *Detailed Performance Statistics for sleep 1, using perf stat*

This figure presents software and hardware performance counters collected by running the command perf stat -d sleep 1 in user mode. The results show that the process consumed only 3.10 milliseconds of CPU time during a total elapsed time of 1.0078 seconds, indicating minimal resource usage and an effective CPU utilization of just 0.003. This output highlights how perf stat can provide precise insights into system behavior, even for lightweight processes.

Key Points: Context switches and CPU migrations: Both zero, confirming no task rescheduling occurred.

- **Page faults:** Sixty-one, caused by memory mapping of shared libraries.
- **Hardware events (cycles, instructions, cache accesses):** Not recorded or unsupported in user-mode profiling under the current kernel settings.
- **Branch and cache metrics:** Also not counted or unavailable, due to the active Non-Maskable Interrupt (NMI) watchdog.

To obtain full hardware counter data, the NMI watchdog can be temporarily disabled:

```
echo 0 > /proc/sys/kernel/nmi_watchdog
perf stat -d sleep 1
echo 1 > /proc/sys/kernel/nmi_watchdog
```

Key metrics include CPU utilization (`task-clock`), instruction-per-cycle ratio, and number of context-switches.

Now, we will proceed to install the package with the following command:

- `sudo systemctl start tuned`
- `sudo systemctl enable tuned`

`tuned-adm active`: Current Tuned Profile

Command: **`tuned-adm active`**

```
[cesarmserver@localhost ~]$ tuned-adm active
Current active profile: virtual-guest
```

Figure 15.4: *Confirming the Active Tuned Performance Profile*

This figure verifies which **`tuned`** performance profile is currently active–such as **`balanced`**, **`throughput-performance`**, or **`virtual-guest`**–to ensure that system-level optimizations are applied in line with workload requirements. Confirming the active profile allows administrators to validate that the intended tuning strategy is in effect, helping maintain consistent performance, efficient resource utilization, and predictable system behavior across different environments.

Then, we will proceed to install the package with the following command:

- `sudo dnf install fio -y`

`fio`: Disk I/O Benchmark

Command:

```
fio --name=test --rw=randread --bs=4k --size=512M --numjobs=1 --time_based
--runtime=10s --group_reporting
```

```
test: (g=0): rw=randread, bs=(R) 4096B-4096B, (W) 4096B-4096B, (T) 4096B-4096B, ioengine=psync, iodepth=1
fio-3.35
Starting 1 process
test: Laying out IO file (1 file / 512MiB)
Jobs: 1 (f=1): [r(1)][100.0%][r=15.1MiB/s][r=3869 IOPS][eta 00m:00s]
test: (groupid=0, jobs=1): err= 0: pid=34556: Tue Jul  1 22:41:44 2025
  read: IOPS=3891, BW=15.2MiB/s (15.9MB/s)(152MiB/10001msec)
    clat (usec): min=96, max=1838, avg=254.09, stdev=104.08
     lat (usec): min=96, max=1838, avg=254.33, stdev=104.14
    clat percentiles (usec):
     |  1.00th=[  119],  5.00th=[  137], 10.00th=[  147], 20.00th=[  167],
     | 30.00th=[  188], 40.00th=[  210], 50.00th=[  231], 60.00th=[  258],
     | 70.00th=[  289], 80.00th=[  330], 90.00th=[  388], 95.00th=[  441],
     | 99.00th=[  578], 99.50th=[  644], 99.90th=[  906], 99.95th=[ 1074],
     | 99.99th=[ 1336]
   bw (  KiB/s): min=15049, max=16502, per=100.00%, avg=15649.74, stdev=385.78, samples=19
   iops        : min= 3762, max= 4125, avg=3912.37, stdev=96.43, samples=19
  lat (usec)   : 100=0.04%, 250=57.60%, 500=39.91%, 750=2.20%, 1000=0.19%
  lat (msec)   : 2=0.06%
  cpu          : usr=0.82%, sys=10.00%, ctx=38862, majf=0, minf=8
  IO depths    : 1=100.0%, 2=0.0%, 4=0.0%, 8=0.0%, 16=0.0%, 32=0.0%, >=64=0.0%
     submit    : 0=0.0%, 4=100.0%, 8=0.0%, 16=0.0%, 32=0.0%, 64=0.0%, >=64=0.0%
     complete  : 0=0.0%, 4=100.0%, 8=0.0%, 16=0.0%, 32=0.0%, 64=0.0%, >=64=0.0%
     issued rwts: total=38922,0,0,0 short=0,0,0,0 dropped=0,0,0,0
     latency   : target=0, window=0, percentile=100.00%, depth=1

Run status group 0 (all jobs):
   READ: bw=15.2MiB/s (15.9MB/s), 15.2MiB/s-15.2MiB/s (15.9MB/s-15.9MB/s), io=152MiB (159MB), run=10001-10001msec

Disk stats (read/write):
    dm-0: ios=38276/10, merge=0/0, ticks=7943/9, in_queue=7952, util=99.17%, aggrios=38922/9, aggrmerge=0/1, aggrticks=7887/4,
aggrin_queue=7890, aggrutil=99.02%
  nvme0n1: ios=38922/9, merge=0/1, ticks=7887/4, in_queue=7890, util=99.02%
You have new mail in /var/spool/mail/cesarmserver
```

Figure 15.5: *Sample Output from FIO Random Read Performance Test*

This figure displays the results of a random read performance test conducted with **fio**, using a 4K block size, a 512MB file, and a single job executed over 10 seconds. The output highlights key performance metrics: bandwidth (BW) averaging **15.2 MiB/s**, IOPS averaging **3,912**, and latency measurements showing most read operations completing in under **500 microseconds**, indicating minimal delay. Disk utilization data further confirms near-saturation of the device during the test, reflecting conditions of sustained high I/O load. Together, these metrics provide valuable insight into storage subsystem behavior under random read workloads, making them essential for capacity planning and performance tuning.

`iostat`: CPU and Disk Utilization

Command: `iostat -x 1 1`

```
Linux 5.14.0-427.42.1.el9_4.x86_64 (localhost.localdomain)      07/01/2025      _x86_64_        (2 CPU)

avg-cpu:  %user   %nice %system %iowait  %steal   %idle
           1.23    0.12    3.69    0.49    0.00   94.46

Device            r/s     rkB/s   rrqm/s  %rrqm r_await rareq-sz     w/s     wkB/s   wrqm/s  %wrqm w_await wareq-sz     d/s     dkB/s   drqm/s
 %drqm d_await dareq-sz     f/s f_await  aqu-sz  %util
dm-0            56.52    754.91     0.00   0.00    0.42    13.36    6.53    524.84     0.00   0.00    2.57    95.74    0.00      0.00     0.00
  0.00    0.00     0.00    0.00    0.00    0.04   3.55
dm-1             0.31      2.76     0.00   0.00    0.44     9.04    3.95     20.98     0.00   0.00    6.38     5.31    0.00      0.00     0.00
  0.00    0.00     0.00    0.00    0.00    0.03   0.03
nvme0n1         57.03    805.73     0.08   0.14    0.36    14.13    6.10    647.61     4.90  44.57    4.24   106.21    0.00      0.00     0.00
  0.00    0.00     0.00    0.00    0.00    0.05   3.60
```

Figure 15.6: *Extended I/O Statistics Snapshot Using iostat*

This figure presents detailed I/O statistics collected with the command iostat -x over a single interval, offering device-level performance insights on a two-CPU system. Reported metrics include read and write operations per second (**`r/s`**, **`w/s`**), throughput in kilobytes per second (**rkB/s**, **wkB/s**), average request size (**`rareq-sz`**, **`wareq-sz`**), and average wait times (**`r_await`**, **`w_await`**). The **`%util`** field highlights device utilization, with the primary device (**nvme0n1**) showing approximately **`3.6% utilization`** during the sample period. These statistics are essential for identifying potential storage bottlenecks, evaluating device efficiency, and characterizing workload behavior in real-world environments.

Understanding the Output:

- **`%iowait`:** Indicates the percentage of time the CPU spends waiting for I/O operations to complete.
- **`%util`:** Measures disk usage, and values near 100% may indicate a storage bottleneck.

Optimizing CPU, Memory, and Disk Usage in Rocky Linux 9

Optimizing CPU, memory, and disk usage is crucial for ensuring Rocky Linux 9 performs efficiently. By applying tuning techniques, administrators can reduce resource contention, improve responsiveness, and maximize system throughput.

CPU Optimization Techniques

Process Scheduling and CPU Affinity

To optimize CPU performance, we can manage process scheduling and CPU affinity, using the following commands:

- Install necessary tools: **`sudo dnf install kernel-tools -y`**
- Assign specific CPUs to processes: **`taskset -c 0,1 <PID>`**
- Adjust scheduling policies for real-time priority tuning: **`chrt -r -p 99 <PID>`**

Optimizing resource usage improves system efficiency. This section covers CPU affinity, memory tuning, and disk I/O optimization with practical examples.

CPU Optimization

Example: Assigning CPU Affinity

- **`sudo dnf install kernel-tools -y`**
- **`sudo taskset -cp 0,1 1234`**

Expected Output:

```
taskset -p 1234
pid 1234's current affinity mask: 3
```

Listing 15.4: *Verifying CPU Affinity with taskset*

The **`taskset`** command allows administrators to view and control the CPU affinity of processes, determining which CPU cores a given process is permitted to run on. By restricting or distributing processes across specific cores, administrators can optimize performance for workloads that benefit from dedicated CPU resources or reduce contention in multi-core systems. Verifying CPU affinity with **`taskset`** helps ensure that critical applications receive the necessary processing power, supports performance tuning in high-demand environments, and provides greater control over system resource allocation.

Memory Optimization Tuning `Swappiness`:

- `sudo sysctl -w vm.swappiness=10`
- `echo "vm.swappiness=10" | sudo tee -a /etc/sysctl.conf`
- `sudo sysctl -p`

Enabling Transparent Huge Pages (THP):

- `echo always | sudo tee /sys/kernel/mm/transparent_hugepage/enabled`
- `cat /sys/kernel/mm/transparent_hugepage/enabled`

Expected Output:

```
[always] madvise never
```

Listing 15.5: *Verifying THP Setting*

Transparent Huge Pages (THP) is a Linux kernel feature designed to improve memory management and system performance by using larger memory pages. While THP can enhance throughput for some workloads, it may introduce latency in others, such as database servers. Verifying the THP setting in Rocky Linux 9 ensures administrators can confirm whether the feature is enabled, disabled, or set to "**madvise**," depending on the workload requirements. Properly tuning THP, alongside CPU scheduling with tools like **taskset** and real-time priority adjustments with **chrt**, helps reduce resource contention, improve responsiveness, and maximize system throughput.

Optimizing CPU, memory, and disk usage is crucial for ensuring Rocky Linux 9 performs efficiently. Tuning techniques help reduce resource contention, improve responsiveness, and maximize system throughput.

To optimize CPU performance, manage process scheduling and CPU affinity with commands like **taskset** to assign CPUs and **chrt** for real-time priority tuning, using tools like **kernel-tools.**

Configuring CPU Performance in VMware

When using the VMware Workstation or ESXi, enhance CPU performance through advanced settings:

- Open the **VM settings** in VMware Workstation/ESXi.
- Navigate to the "**Processors**" section.
- Enable the "Virtualize CPU Performance Counters" option.
- Increase the number of virtual CPUs assigned if possible.
- Save the changes and restart the VM.

Verifying CPU Model and Frequency Configuration

Before making advanced configurations, it is crucial to verify the processor architecture to ensure compatibility with the desired optimizations. Verifying the CPU model and frequency configuration helps administrators understand the hardware capabilities and limitations, ensuring that any tuning aligns with the system's specifications. Using commands such as **lscpu** and **cat /proc/cpuinfo**, administrators can gather the necessary details about the CPU model, core count, and frequency settings. This information is vital for determining the most effective performance tuning strategies, whether adjusting CPU scaling, enabling specific features, or configuring power management options to enhance system performance.

- Retrieve the model of the processor in use: **lscpu | grep "Model name"**

Example output: `Model name: AMD Ryzen 5 5500`

- Check CPU frequency management settings in the kernel:
  grep CONFIG_CPU_FREQ /boot/config-$(uname -r)

Example output:

```
CONFIG_CPU_FREQ=y
CONFIG_CPU_FREQ_DEFAULT_GOV_PERFORMANCE=y
```

This output indicates that CPU frequency scaling is supported, and the default frequency governor is set to performance.

Manage System-Wide Performance Tuning in Rocky Linux

List the available tuning profiles to see all available tuning profiles, run: **`tuned-adm list`**

This will display profiles such as:

- balanced (default)
- powersave (for energy efficiency)
- latency-performance (for low-latency optimization)
- network-latency (for network-intensive workloads)
- throughput-performance (for high-throughput workloads)

Understanding the CPU model and frequency settings, along with available tuning profiles, allows administrators to make informed decisions about optimizing system performance. By leveraging tools like **`tuned-adm`** and kernel configurations, they can tailor the system to meet specific workload demands, whether prioritizing energy efficiency, low latency, or high throughput. Ensuring that the correct tuning strategy aligns with the hardware capabilities is key to achieving optimal performance in Rocky Linux environments.

Tuning Profiles with Tuned

Tuned is a dynamic tuning daemon that helps optimize system performance based on workload characteristics. It provides preconfigured profiles that adjust kernel parameters, power settings, and scheduler behavior. *Figure* 15.7 summarizes the commonly used profiles, and their typical impacts.

In addition to its predefined profiles, **tuned** allows administrators to create custom profiles tailored to specific performance requirements. For example, a database server might benefit from tuning parameters that prioritize I/O throughput, while a virtualized host could be optimized for CPU scheduling and memory allocation. Profiles can be switched dynamically without rebooting, making it easy to adapt the system to changing workload demands. This flexibility ensures that Rocky Linux environments can maintain efficiency, stability, and responsiveness across a wide range of use cases, from energy saving on laptops to performance tuning in enterprise data centers.

Profile	**Key Parameters**	**System Impact**	**Typical Use Case**
`virtual-guest`	Low swappiness; balanced CPU governor	Optimized I/O performance on virtual machines	Virtual machines
`throughput-performance`	Aggressive CPU governor; power-saving features disabled	Maximized throughput and CPU utilization	High-performance workloads
`latency-performance`	Low-latency CPU settings; power-saving features disabled	Reduced latency; faster system response	Real-time applications

Figure 15.7: *Common Tuned Profiles and Their Impacts*

This figure summarizes the most frequently used tuned performance profiles available in Rocky Linux. It highlights each profile's key configuration parameters, the resulting system behavior, and the types of workloads for which the profile is best suited. Choosing the appropriate profile allows administrators to fine-tune system performance in alignment with workload demands, whether for virtualized environments, high-throughput applications, or latency-sensitive services.

Applying a Profile

To apply a **`tuned`** profile on Rocky Linux:

- `sudo systemctl enable --now tuned`
- `sudo tuned-adm profile latency-performance`
- `tuned-adm active`

Expected Output

```
[cesarmserver@localhost ~]$ tuned-adm active
Current active profile: latency-performance
```

Figure 15.8: *Current Active Profile: Throughput-performance*

This figure shows the output of the **`tuned-adm`** active command, confirming that the **throughput-performance** profile is applied. This profile is optimized to maximize system throughput by enabling aggressive CPU frequency scaling and disabling power-saving features. It is particularly well-suited for workloads requiring sustained high performance, such as large-scale data processing, file servers, and I/O-intensive applications. Verifying the active profile ensures that system tuning aligns with performance objectives and that the intended optimizations are correctly in effect.

Apply a High-Performance Profile

The maximum performance, apply the latency-performance profile which will be displayed:

`sudo tuned-adm profile latency-performance`

This profile:

- Disables power-saving mechanisms
- Prioritizes CPU performance
- Lowers system latency

Verify the Active Profile

To confirm that the profile has been applied correctly, use:

- `tuned-adm active`

Expected output:

Current active profile: `latency-performance`

Ensure Tuned Service is Running

To make sure the tuned is running, and will persist after reboots, enable it:

- **`sudo systemctl enable --now tuned`**
- To check its status: **`systemctl status tuned`**

The "**`active (running)`**" status should be displayed now.

Applying a high-performance profile ensures that the system operates at its maximum potential by reducing latency, and prioritizing CPU performance. Verifying the active profile, and enabling the

tuned service guarantees that these optimizations persist across reboots, maintaining consistent system efficiency and responsiveness in demanding workloads.

Make the Changes Persistent

The profile remains active even after reboots, but the next will allow us to reset it:

- **sudo tuned-adm profile balanced**

This returns the system to default settings.

In virtualized environments, hypervisors often impose restrictions on CPU frequency scaling, which can prevent performance tuning tools such as **tuned-adm** from applying changes effectively. Understanding these limitations helps administrators adjust their expectations, and explore alternative optimizations such as configuring CPU pinning or adjusting hypervisor settings to enhance performance within the given constraints.

To validate the **troubleshooting** section in relation to the lab, let us break down each point and provide verification steps:

Virtualized Environment Limitations (for example, VMware)

If tuned-adm does not apply performance settings correctly, it may be due to virtualization restrictions.

To check if CPU frequency scaling is available in the VM, run:

- **lscpu | grep "Hypervisor vendor"**

If the output shows **VMware**, **KVM**, or another hypervisor, CPU frequency control might be limited by the virtualization platform.

Thus, by recognizing the impact of virtualization on performance tuning, administrators can make informed decisions about optimizing their Rocky Linux systems. Whether running on bare metal or within a virtualized environment, verifying hardware capabilities, and applying appropriate tuning profiles ensures that the system operates efficiently, and meets workload demands.

Final Recommendations

- If tuned-adm does not work, check CPU scaling support in **/sys/devices/system/cpu/cpu*/cpufreq/**.
- Virtualized environments may require enabling CPU performance counters.
- Ensure correct power management drivers are loaded.

Monitoring CPU Utilization

- Use **mpstat** to analyze CPU usage per core.
- Track high CPU-consuming processes with **top** and **htop.**

  Now, another package will be installed: **sudo dnf install -y perf**

  Profile system performance with these commands: **perf stat -a sleep 10**

This command will take about 10 seconds to be successfully applied. The following output will be shown:

```
[root@localhost cmorera]# perf stat -a sleep 10

 Performance counter stats for 'system wide':

         80,023.48 msec cpu-clock                 #    8.000 CPUs utilized
             3,868      context-switches          #   48.336 /sec
                44      cpu-migrations            #    0.550 /sec
               615      page-faults               #    7.685 /sec
       534,622,437      cycles                    #    0.007 GHz
       202,839,133      stalled-cycles-frontend   #   37.94% frontend cycles idle
        85,847,207      instructions              #    0.16  insn per cycle
                                                  #    2.36  stalled cycles per insn
        21,732,042      branches                  #  271.571 K/sec
         2,673,191      branch-misses             #   12.30% of all branches

      10.002601035 seconds time elapsed
```

Figure 15.9: *Profile System Performance*

This figure illustrates the use of the **`perf stat`** command in system-wide mode (-a), which monitors key performance metrics across all CPUs while the system remains idle for 10 seconds. Once executed, the command produces an output similar to that shown previously, detailing hardware and software performance counters such as CPU cycles, instructions, context switches, and cache references. Running **`perf stat`** in this mode provides administrators with a baseline snapshot of system activity, helping differentiate between idle behavior and workload-driven performance changes.

Figure 15.9, displaying various CPU performance counters, including:

- **CPU Clock:** Total CPU time utilized during the sampling period.
- **Context Switches:** Number of times the CPU switched between tasks.
- **Page Faults:** Memory access operations requiring additional processing.
- **CPU Cycles & Instructions:** Metrics on executed instructions and processor cycles.
- **Branch Misses:** Failed branch predictions that impact execution efficiency.

These metrics help in diagnosing potential bottlenecks, such as high context switching, low instruction-per-cycle (IPC) values, or excessive branch mispredictions. If inefficiencies are detected, further investigation using perf record or perf top can provide deeper insights into system performance.

Now, there are some final commands regarding performance monitoring which are:

- `perf record -a -g -- sleep 10`
- `perf report`

Performance monitoring with perf provides valuable insights into system behavior and resource utilization. By recording and analyzing performance data, administrators can identify bottlenecks, optimize workloads, and ensure the system is running efficiently under various conditions.

Memory Management

Tuning Swap Usage:

- Adjust swappiness: **`sysctl -w vm.swappiness=10`**
- Make it persistent, and add these commands:
  `echo "vm.swappiness=10" >> /etc/sysctl.conf && sysctl -p`

Reducing the swappiness value helps prioritize RAM usage over swap space, minimizing unnecessary disk swapping and improving overall system performance. Making this adjustment persistent ensures that memory management remains optimized across reboots, enhancing system responsiveness for workload demands.

Optimizing Memory Allocation:

- Use free-m and vmstat to monitor memory consumption.
- Enable Transparent Huge Pages (THP):
  `sudo echo always > /sys/kernel/mm/transparent_hugepage/enabled`
- Verify with the other command:
  `cat /sys/kernel/mm/transparent_hugepage/enabled`

Optimizing memory allocation with monitoring tools and Transparent Huge Pages (THP) improves system efficiency by reducing memory fragmentation, and enhancing performance for memory-intensive applications. Ensuring these settings are correctly applied helps maintain optimal resource utilization and system stability.

Disk I/O Optimization

Monitoring Disk Performance:

- Analyze read/write operations: **`iostat -x 5`**
- Measure latency: **`sudo dnf install fio -y`**

```
fio --name=test --rw=randread --bs=4k --size=1G --numjobs=4 --runtime=60
--time_based
```

The fio command provided is used to perform a **random read I/O test** on a storage device or filesystem. Let us break it down:

Command Breakdown:

```
fio --name=test --rw=randread --bs=4k --size=1G --numjobs=4 --runtime=60
--time_based
```

Explanation of each option:

- **fio:** Runs the **Flexible I/O Tester** (fio), a tool used for benchmarking disk I/O performance.
- **`name=test`:** Names the test "**`test`**" (purely for identification).
- **`rw=randread`:** Performs **random read** operations (instead of sequential read/write).
- **`bs=4k`:** Uses a **block size of 4 KB** for each read operation (common for storage benchmarks).
- **`size=1G`:** The total **data set size is 1 GB** (each job will read from this pool).
- **`numjobs=4`:** Runs **4 parallel jobs** (simulating 4 threads/processes performing I/O simultaneously).
- **`runtime=60`:** Runs the test for **60 seconds**.
- **`time_based`:** Ensures the test **runs for the full 60 seconds**, instead of stopping after reading 1 GB.

Functionality: This command performs a **random read test**, using **4 KB block size**, with **4 parallel jobs** running for **60 seconds**. The results help evaluate the **read performance** of a storage device (for example, SSD, HDD, and so on) under concurrent load.

Storage performance testing with **fio** provides critical insights into read efficiency and the ability of a device to manage concurrent workloads. By analyzing the results, administrators can assess storage bottlenecks, optimize configurations, and ensure that the system meets the demands of high-performance applications.

Performance Optimization Labs for Rocky Linux 9

By fine-tuning these critical system components, administrators can enhance application performance, reduce bottlenecks, and ensure stability under varying workloads. Effective performance tuning involves optimizing CPU scheduling, managing memory allocation, and improving disk I/O operations to achieve a balanced and efficient system. Proper configuration of these elements helps prevent resource contention, and ensures that applications run smoothly, even under heavy load conditions.

These exercises will cover practical techniques such as adjusting kernel parameters, managing process scheduling, optimizing memory usage, and configuring network settings for improved throughput. By applying these methods in real-world scenarios, users will develop a deeper understanding of how system tuning impacts performance. Through hands-on experimentation, they will learn the best practices for analyzing system behavior, and implementing adjustments to maximize efficiency in Rocky Linux 9.

Analyzing and Optimizing CPU Usage

Objective: Optimize CPU performance, using CPU affinity and scheduling.

Steps:

1. Identify high CPU-consuming processes: `top`
2. Assign a process to specific CPU cores: `taskset -c 0,1 <PID>`
3. Change scheduling priority: `chrt -r -p 99 <PID>`
4. Verify optimization:
   a. Check CPU affinity: `taskset -p <PID>`
   b. Confirm priority: `chrt -p <PID>`

Optimizing CPU usage through process affinity and scheduling ensures efficient workload distribution and system responsiveness. By assigning processes to specific cores and adjusting their priority, administrators can prevent resource contention, enhance performance for critical applications, and maintain overall system stability.

Optimizing Memory Management

Objective: Improve memory usage by tuning swappiness and THP.

Steps:

1. Check current swappiness value: `cat /proc/sys/vm/swappiness`
2. Reduce swap usage: `sudo sysctl -w vm.swappiness=10`

To improve the process of making the system changes persistent, let us break down the steps in a more efficient and structured way. Here is how we can achieve both:

Make `vm.swappiness=10` persistent: This can be added to /etc/sysctl.conf to ensure that it is applied at every boot.

Steps:

1. Open /etc/sysctl.conf for editing: `sudo nano /etc/sysctl.conf`
2. Add the following line to the file: `vm.swappiness=10`

3. Save and close the file (Press *Ctrl*+O, then *Enter*, and *Ctrl*+X to exit).
4. Apply the changes immediately: **`sudo sysctl -p`**

This will apply the swappiness setting immediately, and make it persistent for future reboots.

Ensuring system changes persist across reboots helps maintain performance optimizations without manual intervention. By properly configuring system files like **`/etc/sysctl.conf`**, administrators can enforce consistent tuning parameters, improving system efficiency and reliability over time.

Make the Transparent Hugepage Setting Persistent: Instead of modifying **`/etc/rc.local`**, which is not always available or enabled on all systems, it is better to use a sysctl configuration for the Transparent Hugepage setting.

Steps:

1. **Modify `/etc/rc.local` (if still preferred):** If we want to keep using **`/etc/rc.local`** for the Transparent Hugepage setting, follow these steps:
   a. Open **`/etc/rc.local`** for editing:
      ```
      sudo nano /etc/rc.local
      ```
   b. Add the following line **before exit 0:**
      ```
      echo always | sudo tee /sys/kernel/mm/transparent_hugepage/enabled
      ```
   c. Make sure /etc/rc.local is executable:
      ```
      sudo chmod +x /etc/rc.local
      ```

   This will set Transparent Hugepages to "*always*" on every reboot.
2. **Alternative: Use a `sysctl` configuration**: Since the /sys file system is not designed to persist changes across reboots, it is a better practice to make such changes through sysctl.
   a. Create a new file in **`/etc/sysctl.d/`** (if it is not already done):
      ```
      sudo nano /etc/sysctl.d/99-transparent-hugepage.conf
      ```
   b. Add the following line to set Transparent Hugepages to "always":
      ```
      vm.transparent_hugepage.enabled = always
      ```
   c. Save and close the file (Press *Ctrl*+O, then *Enter*, and *Ctrl*+X to exit).
   d. Apply the changes:
      ```
      sudo sysctl --system
      ```

   This method is more consistent and effective, as changes to **`/etc/sysctl.d/`** files are automatically applied at boot.
3. **Verify the Changes:** After rebooting or applying the changes, we can verify both settings:
   - **Swappiness:** `sysctl vm.swappiness`
   - **Transparent Hugepage setting:** `cat /sys/kernel/mm/transparent_hugepage/enabled`

Summary of Changes:

- **`vm.swappiness=10`** will be added to **`/etc/sysctl.conf`** for persistence.
- Transparent Hugepages can either be managed in **`/etc/rc.local`** (if desired) or with sysctl settings by adding **`vm.transparent_hugepage.enabled = always`** to a .conf file in **`/etc/sysctl.d/`**.

Tuning Networking for Performance in Rocky Linux 9

Advanced Network Configuration in a Virtualized KVM Environment

In this lab, we will explore network configuration in a virtualized KVM environment. It is essential to understand that in such environments, traditional physical Ethernet interfaces are often abstracted. Instead, virtualized network interfaces and Software-Defined Networking (SDN) play a crucial role in connectivity.

1. **Identifying Network Interfaces:** To analyze the available network interfaces, use the following command:

    - `ip a`

These are some of the multiple interfaces, including:

- **`lo`:** (Loopback interface)
- **`ens160`:** (The primary network interface assigned to the virtual machine)
- **`br`:** (Bridge interfaces used for managing virtual network traffic)
- **`docker0 and docker_gwbridge`:** (Docker-created network interfaces facilitating container networking)

These interfaces allow both internal and external connectivity depending on the network configuration of the host machine and its virtual network settings.

2. **Setting Up a Virtual Network Bridge**

To provide enhanced networking for virtual machines, we utilize a network bridge. This allows multiple virtual machines to communicate as if they were on a physical network. First, ensure that the necessary utilities are installed:

```
sudo dnf install -y bridge-utils
```

Now, create and configure a new bridge:

- `sudo nmcli connection add type bridge con-name br0 ifname br0`
- `sudo nmcli connection modify br0 ipv4.addresses 192.168.119.1/24 ipv4.method manual`
- `sudo nmcli connection up br0`

This configuration assigns the bridge br0 a static IP address (192.168.119.1/24), ensuring that virtual machines, using this bridge can communicate within this subnet.

3. **Attaching the Network Bridge to a Virtual Machine**

Once the bridge is properly configured, it needs to be associated with a virtual machine for seamless network access. This can be done, using the following command:

```
sudo virsh attach-interface --domain my_vm --type bridge --source br0 --model
virtio --config --live
```

This step connects the virtual machine **`my_vm`** to the bridge br0, enabling it to interact with other networked devices in the virtual environment.

4. **Testing and Verifying Network Connectivity**

To confirm proper configuration, execute the following commands inside the virtual machine:

- `ip a`

- `ping -c 4 192.168.119.1`

If correctly set up, the ping command should return responses from the br0 bridge, verifying network connectivity.

In this lab, we successfully configured advanced virtual networking in a KVM-based environment. By leveraging virtual bridges such as br0, we enabled seamless interconnectivity between virtual machines, while ensuring compatibility with the existing interfaces such as **docker0** and **docker_gwbridge**. Understanding these network components is necessary for administrators working with virtualized infrastructure and containerized environments.

- `sudo nmcli connection delete br0`
- `sudo nmcli connection up <connection name>`

It might take a few minutes to return to the previous network connection, and grant us "**ssh**" access, once again.

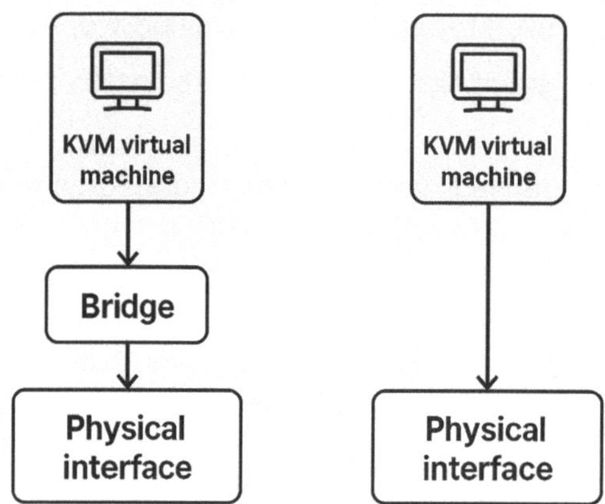

Figure 15.10: *KVM Network Bridge vs. Physical Interface*

This figure compares two networking approaches in KVM virtualization: using a network bridge versus relying solely on the host's physical interface. In the bridged configuration, virtual machines connect through a virtual bridge (e.g., **br0**), which is bound to the host's physical network card. This enables VMs to obtain IP addresses directly from the external network, allowing seamless communication with other devices as if the VMs were physical hosts on the same subnet. In contrast, the physical interface configuration shows a host-only or NAT-based connection, where VM traffic is routed through the host system. While this provides isolation, it limits direct external accessibility. The diagram highlights how bridging enhances flexibility and integration, making it the preferred choice for scenarios requiring full VM-to-network connectivity, such as running servers or testing distributed applications.

Lab: Setting Up a KVM Network Bridge

```
sudo dnf install -y bridge-utils
sudo nmcli connection add type bridge con-name br0 ifname br0
sudo nmcli connection modify br0 ipv4.addresses 192.168.119.1/24
   ipv4.method manual
sudo nmcli connection up br0
sudo virsh attach-interface --domain my_vm --type bridge --source
    br0 --model virtio --config --live
```

Figure 15.11: *Setting up a KVM Network Bridge*

This figure illustrates the configuration of a network bridge (**br0**) on a Rocky Linux host for use with KVM virtual machines. A bridge enables VMs to function as full participants on the network, allowing them to communicate with external systems or other devices on the same subnet. The process begins by installing the necessary bridge utilities with **sudo dnf install -y bridge-utils**. Next, a new bridge connection named **br0** is created using **nmcli**, and a static IP address (e.g., 192.168.119.1/24) is manually assigned. The bridge is then activated with nmcli connection up br0. Finally, a virtual machine is connected to the bridge using **virsh attach-interface**, specifying the domain name, interface type (**bridge**), source (**br0**), and model (**virtio**) for optimal performance. This setup allows VMs to access services such as SSH, DNS, and the internet as though they were physical hosts, supporting seamless integration into existing network environments.

Performance Optimization in Cloud Environments

Optimizing cloud environments is vital for ensuring efficiency, cost savings, and high performance. This document explores strategies for enhancing AWS EC2 instances, auto scaling, load balancing, and storage/network performance, with a focus on Rocky Linux 9.

Step-by-Step Guide: Optimizing EC2 Instances

1. **Enable Enhanced Networking (ENA):** Enhanced Networking improves network performance and reduces latency. First, ensure our instance type supports ENA (for example, **t3**, **c5**, **m5**, and so on).

   - `sudo modprobe ena`
   - `aws ec2 modify-instance-attribute --instance-id i-1234567890abcdef0 --ena-support`

   Run this AWS CLI command from a workstation with appropriate IAM permissions.

2. **Configure NVMe Storage:** Many EC2 instance types use NVMe for EBS volumes. Format and mount the disk:

```
lsblk
sudo mkfs.ext4 /dev/nvme1n1
sudo mount /dev/nvme1n1 /mnt
```

Figure 15.12: *Storage Volumes*

This figure demonstrates the process of configuring and mounting storage volumes on an Amazon EC2 instance using NVMe-based EBS devices. The workflow begins with the lsblk command, which lists the block devices attached to the instance, such as **/dev/nvme1n1**. Once the correct volume is identified, it is formatted with the **mkfs.ext4** command to create a Linux-compatible file system. The formatted device is then mounted to a directory–commonly **/mnt**–using the mount command. To ensure persistence across reboots, an entry must be added to the **/etc/fstab** file, allowing the system to automatically remount the volume during startup. This configuration provides reliable and high-performance storage for applications and services running on the instance.

3. **Set CPU Affinity for Web Server:** Pin the `**httpd**` process (Apache) to specific CPU cores (for example, CPU 0 and 1):

   `taskset -c 0,1 $(pidof httpd)`

   Only use CPU affinity if we are troubleshooting performance bottlenecks or tuning for multi-core balancing.

4. **Scenario: Tuning for Database (for instance, MySQL):** Use `tuned` to apply performance profiles, and manually adjust MySQL parameters.
   - `sudo tuned-adm profile throughput-performance`
   - `echo "innodb_buffer_pool_size=2G" | sudo tee -a /etc/my.cnf`

Adjust `innodb_buffer_pool_size` *based on RAM size. Restart MySQL after* **config** *changes.*

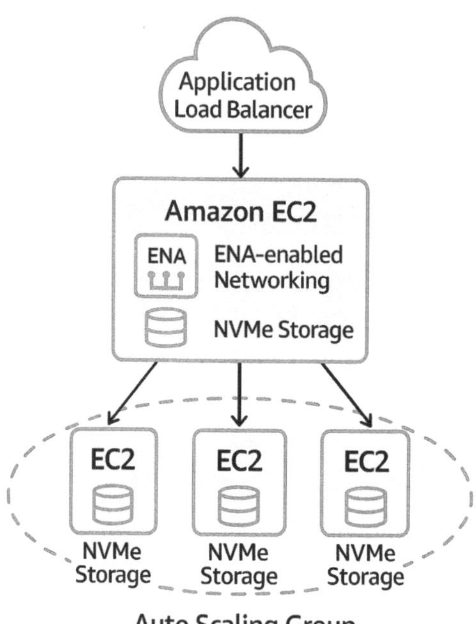

Figure 15.13: *Optimizing EC2 Instances with Enhanced Networking and Scalable Architecture*

This diagram illustrates an optimized Amazon EC2 architecture designed for high performance and scalability. At the core, EC2 instances are equipped with **Elastic Network Adapters (ENA)** to deliver enhanced networking capabilities, reducing latency and increasing throughput for demanding workloads. Storage is provisioned using **NVMe-based EBS volumes**, providing fast read/write operations essential for data-intensive applications. To handle traffic efficiently, an **Application Load Balancer (ALB)** distributes incoming requests evenly across multiple instances, ensuring high availability and fault tolerance. The infrastructure is further supported by an **Auto Scaling Group**, which dynamically adjusts the number of EC2 instances in response to workload demands, maintaining performance while optimizing costs. The directional flow of data–from the ALB to EC2 instances and then to storage–emphasizes how the components interact to create a resilient, scalable, and efficient cloud environment.

AWS EC2 Performance Tuning Strategies

Choosing the Right Instance Type: Selecting an appropriate instance type is essential for maximizing performance while maintaining cost-effectiveness. EC2 instances are categorized based on workload needs:

- **Compute-Optimized:** Suitable for CPU-intensive applications such as scientific modeling and machine learning.

- **Memory-Optimized:** Ideal for applications handling large datasets such as databases and in-memory analytics.
- **Storage-Optimized:** Designed for workloads that require high-speed disk access, including data warehousing and NoSQL databases.

By selecting the right EC2 instance type based on workload requirements, administrators can ensure that cloud resources are aligned with performance needs, while controlling costs. Tailoring instance choices for specific applications enhances efficiency, and provides a solid foundation for optimized cloud environments on Rocky Linux 9.

CPU and Memory Optimization

Performance tuning can significantly enhance efficiency:

- **Enable CPU Credits:** For burstable T-series instances, enabling CPU credits allows higher CPU usage during peak loads.
- **NUMA Awareness:** Applications that are NUMA-aware can take advantage of memory locality for better performance.
- **HugePages:** Large memory allocations can benefit from HugePages, reducing processing overhead, and improving efficiency.

Optimizing Virtual CPUs (vCPUs): Proper allocation and scaling of vCPUs based on workload demands can lead to better performance. Ensuring that the number of vCPUs matches the workload's parallel processing requirements avoids over-provisioning, which can waste resources, or under-provisioning that can throttle performance.

Disk and I/O Performance

Storage plays a key role in performance:

- **GP3 Volumes:** A cost-effective option with adjustable IOPS and throughput.
- **Provisioned IOPS:** Useful for latency-sensitive applications such as transactional databases.
- **Benchmarking:** Using tools such as fio to measure disk performance ensures optimal storage configurations.

Elastic File System (EFS): For scalable and shared storage, using Amazon EFS provides high availability and durability. It automatically scales as data grows, and allows multiple EC2 instances to access the same storage, making it ideal for applications requiring shared file systems without the overhead of managing physical hardware.

CPU Scheduling and Kernel Tuning

Kernel-level optimizations can improve overall system responsiveness:

- **Performance Profiles:** Utilize tuned-adm to apply appropriate performance profiles.
- **CPU Frequency Scaling:** Adjusting CPU frequency settings helps maximize efficiency.

Auto Scaling and Load Balancing Techniques

Auto scaling ensures applications remain available and responsive:

- **Launch Templates:** Enable consistent and dynamic instance configurations.
- **Scaling Policies:** Adjust based on CPU usage, network traffic, or request count.
- **Monitoring:** AWS CloudWatch alarms can trigger scaling actions when thresholds are exceeded.

Load Balancing

Load balancers distribute traffic efficiently:

- **Application Load Balancer (ALB):** Best for web applications requiring content-based routing.
- **Network Load Balancer (NLB):** Optimized for high-throughput and low-latency applications.
- **Session Persistence:** Sticky sessions ensure user requests are directed to the same instance.
- **TLS Offloading:** Reduces encryption overhead on application servers.

Storage and Network Performance Considerations

Optimizing storage and network performance requires a balance between throughput, latency, and cost. For storage, choosing the right volume type such as SSD for high-performance workloads or HDD for infrequent access can significantly impact both speed and cost-efficiency. In terms of networking, enabling enhanced networking features such as Elastic Network Adapter (ENA) for EC2 instances, improves data transfer rates and reduces latency, which is crucial for performance-sensitive applications. Additionally, ensuring that storage is properly provisioned to match network bandwidth ensures a seamless flow of data without bottlenecks, leading to overall system efficiency.

Efficient storage management reduces costs, and improves performance:

- **Elastic File System (EFS):** A scalable and managed file system for multiple instances.
- **S3 Intelligent Tiering:** Automatically moves infrequently accessed data to lower-cost storage tiers.
- **FS-Cache:** Speeds up file access in NFS environments.

Network Performance Tuning

Network performance can be enhanced by leveraging features such as Enhanced Networking with Elastic Network Adapter (ENA) or Intel 82599 Virtual Function (VF) interfaces which provide higher bandwidth, lower latency, and reduced jitter. Additionally, utilizing placement groups in AWS ensures that instances are physically closer to one another, optimizing inter-instance communication. Implementing Quality of Service (QoS) settings and traffic shaping can further prioritize critical traffic, reducing congestion and ensuring consistent performance for high-demand applications. These optimizations, combined with proper network monitoring, ensure efficient and reliable network communication across cloud environments.

Network optimizations improve connectivity, and reduce latency by:

- **Elastic Network Adapters (ENA):** Provides higher bandwidth and better performance.
- **TCP Stack Tuning:** Adjust kernel parameters to enhance network performance.
- **MTU Jumbo Frames:** Enabling larger packets can improve data transfer efficiency.
- **DNS Caching:** Reducing DNS resolution times enhances responsiveness.

Hands-On Labs

Lab 1: Choosing the Right Instance Type

- Identify workload type, and select the best instance category.
- Launch an instance, and monitor performance using CloudWatch.

Lab 2: CPU and Memory Optimization

- Enable CPU credits for burstable instances.

- Optimize memory with HugePages for better application performance.

Lab 3: Disk and I/O Tuning

- Configure GP3 volumes for cost-effective storage.
- Benchmark disk performance with fio to validate improvements.

Lab 4: Auto Scaling and Load Balancing

- Set up Auto Scaling Groups (ASG) with appropriate scaling policies.
- Configure an Application Load Balancer (ALB) to distribute traffic efficiently.

Lab 5: Network Performance Tuning

- Enable ENA for enhanced networking.
- Adjust TCP stack settings, and enable Jumbo Frames for improved data transmission.

By implementing these optimization techniques, AWS EC2 instances running Rocky Linux 9 can achieve better efficiency, stability, and cost-effectiveness. Regular monitoring and fine-tuning ensure cloud environments remain optimized for evolving workloads.

Conclusion

Optimizing the performance of Rocky Linux is essential for ensuring efficiency, reliability, and scalability across various environments. This chapter covered key strategies, including system monitoring and profiling techniques, CPU and memory tuning, disk I/O optimization, and network performance enhancements. Additionally, we explored cloud-specific optimizations for AWS EC2, leveraging Auto Scaling to maintain performance under varying workloads. By applying these techniques, Rocky Linux systems can achieve optimal resource utilization and responsiveness, whether deployed on-premises or in the cloud.

In the next chapter, we will explore real-world deployment scenarios for Rocky Linux, covering best practices for server configurations, high availability setups, and scaling applications, using load balancers and AWS deployment strategies.

Multiple Choice Questions

1. Which of the following techniques is used to optimize CPU usage in Rocky Linux?
   a. Enabling hyper-threading
   b. Adjusting CPU governor settings
   c. Disabling the swap space
   d. Configuring jumbo frames
2. How can memory usage be optimized in Rocky Linux for better performance?
   a. Decreasing the swappiness value
   b. Increasing the size of swap partitions
   c. Disabling the huge pages feature
   d. Reducing the cache pressure

3. Which disk I/O scheduler is recommended for optimizing performance on SSDs in Rocky Linux?

   a. `noop`

   b. `cfq`

   c. `deadline`

   d. `anticipatory`

4. What is the benefit of using sysctl parameters for network tuning in Rocky Linux?

   a. Enhances system security

   b. Optimizes network performance and latency

   c. Increases system memory allocation

   d. Modifies disk partitioning schemes

5. What is the role of irqbalance in networking performance optimization?

   a. Distributes interrupts across multiple processors to balance CPU load

   b. Controls the flow of network traffic to virtual machines

   c. Adjusts the transmission rate of network interfaces

   d. Provides encryption for network packets

6. Which AWS service can be used to automate the scaling of instances based on load?

   a. AWS Auto Scaling

   b. AWS CloudFormation

   c. AWS Lambda

   d. AWS RDS

7. In Rocky Linux, which of the following commands can be used to measure disk I/O performance?

   a. `df`

   b. `iostat`

   c. `free`

   d. `top`

8. Which feature in AWS helps distribute network traffic across multiple EC2 instances for high availability?

   a. AWS CloudWatch

   b. AWS Elastic Load Balancer (ELB)

   c. AWS Route 53

   d. AWS Direct Connect

9. Which feature in AWS helps improve network performance by providing low-latency, high-bandwidth connections between on-premise data centers and AWS?

   a. AWS CloudFront

   b. AWS Direct Connect

   c. AWS VPN

   d. AWS Transit Gateway

10. In Rocky Linux, which tool can be used to monitor real-time memory and CPU usage for performance analysis?

    a. `vmstat`

    b. `iostat`

    c. `htop`

    d. `dstat`

Answers

1. b
2. a
3. a
4. b
5. a
6. a
7. b
8. b
9. b
10. c

Questions

1. What are the key metrics to monitor for evaluating system performance in Rocky Linux?
2. How can you use top and htop to profile CPU and memory usage in Rocky Linux?
3. What steps should be taken to optimize disk usage, and reduce I/O bottlenecks in Rocky Linux?
4. How can adjusting the swappiness value impact memory performance in Rocky Linux?
5. What tools can be used to monitor network traffic, and optimize networking performance in Rocky Linux?
6. How do you configure and optimize CPU governor settings for performance in Rocky Linux?
7. What role do tuned profiles play in optimizing system performance on a Rocky Linux server?
8. How can sysctl parameters be tuned to improve network performance, and reduce latency in Rocky Linux?

9. What are the main factors to consider when choosing the appropriate disk I/O scheduler for different workloads in Rocky Linux?

10. How can AWS EC2 Auto Scaling be leveraged to automatically adjust Rocky Linux instances for optimal performance under varying loads?

Key Terms

- **System Monitoring:** The process of tracking system performance and resource utilization (CPU, memory, disk, and network) to ensure optimal operation.
- **Profiling:** The practice of analyzing system resources, and identifying performance bottlenecks for further optimization.
- **CPU Governor:** A tool or setting used to manage CPU frequency scaling, optimizing CPU usage based on system demand.
- **Swappiness:** A kernel parameter that controls how much the system uses swap space relative to RAM, affecting memory performance.
- **Tuned Profiles:** Pre-configured system settings designed to optimize performance for specific workloads, such as high-performance or power-saving modes.
- **Sysctl Parameters:** Kernel parameters in Linux that can be adjusted to tune system behavior, especially for network performance.
- **Disk I/O Scheduler:** A component that controls how disk I/O operations are handled, optimizing for performance or fairness, depending on the workload.
- **Noop Scheduler:** A disk I/O scheduler that minimizes latency by applying a "no operation" approach, ideal for SSDs.
- **Auto Scaling:** AWS service that automatically adjusts the number of instances based on real-time load, optimizing cost and performance.
- **Elastic Load Balancer (ELB):** A service in AWS that distributes incoming traffic to multiple instances, improving application availability and scalability.
- **CloudWatch:** AWS service for monitoring and managing logs and performance metrics from instances, helping ensure optimal performance and troubleshooting.
- **Performance Bottleneck:** Any factor or component that limits system performance, requiring optimization for improved efficiency.

CHAPTER 16
Common Deployment Scenarios

Introduction

Rocky Linux offers a dependable, enterprise-ready platform for deploying servers in both on-premises and cloud environments. For physical setups, success starts with selecting the right hardware, configuring RAID for data protection, and optimizing network performance. Tools like Ansible simplify installation, and help standardize environments, making system maintenance and scaling far more manageable.

In cloud deployments, automation takes center stage. Solutions such as Terraform or CloudFormation accelerate infrastructure provisioning, while enforcing consistency. Security remains paramount—firewalls, IAM roles, and controlled access are vital. When paired with Docker and Kubernetes, Rocky Linux becomes an agile foundation for containerized workloads, while monitoring tools like Prometheus and Grafana.

Structure

This chapter covers the following topics:

- Standard Server Deployments
- High Availability Setups
- Scaling Applications with Load Balancers
- Rocky Linux Deployment Strategies in AWS

Deploying Rocky Linux 9 requires thoughtful preparation to achieve reliable and scalable results across various infrastructures. This chapter introduces strategies for rolling out Rocky Linux—whether on a single server, across high-availability clusters, or through cloud-based deployments in AWS. It walks administrators and DevOps teams through practical scenarios that highlight the power of tools such as Ansible, Terraform, HAProxy, Nginx, and AWS services (including ECS, ELB, and Auto Scaling).

With real-world examples, visual diagrams, and proven best practices, readers will gain actionable insights into optimizing Rocky Linux environments. Hence, whether you are building a containerized platform with Docker or orchestrating resources through Infrastructure-as-Code, this guide provides the roadmap for deploying with confidence and efficiency.

Key considerations include:

- **On-Premises:** Hardware selection, RAID configuration, network optimization, and automation with Ansible.
- **Cloud:** Infrastructure as Code (IaC) with Terraform, security with IAM and firewalls, and container orchestration with AWS ECS.
- **Monitoring:** Tools such as Prometheus, Grafana, and AWS CloudWatch for performance tracking.

Standard Server Deployments

A single-server deployment is the most straightforward approach for hosting applications and services, where all components run on a single Rocky Linux 9 machine. It is commonly used for development environments, small business applications, or standalone services that do not require high availability or scalability. This section outlines the key technical considerations, best practices, and validation steps for implementing a standard server deployment.

By consolidating resources into one system, administrators can reduce infrastructure complexity and streamline maintenance tasks. However, this simplicity comes with trade-offs, as hardware limitations and the absence of redundancy may introduce risks in production scenarios. To mitigate these challenges, careful configuration of security, performance optimization, and regular backups are essential for ensuring reliability and sustainability in single-server environments.

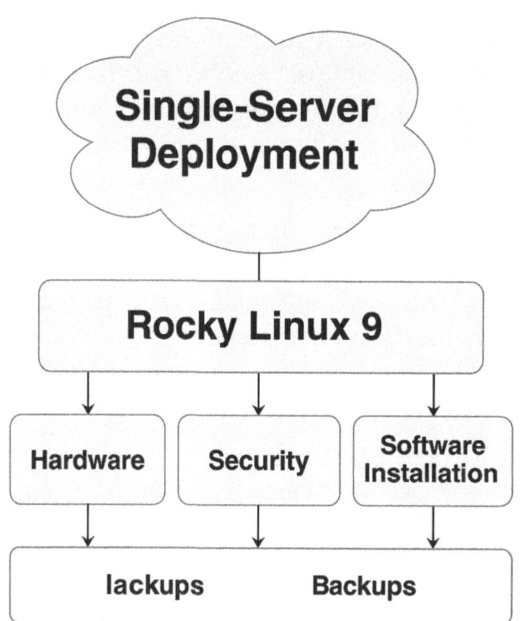

***Figure 16.1:** Single-server Deployment Architecture Overview*

This figure presents the architecture of a single-server deployment running Rocky Linux 9. All core functions—hardware configuration, software installation, security controls, storage, and backups—are consolidated within one system. Such a model is best suited for small environments or development scenarios, where rapid setup, simplified management, and minimal resource overhead are priorities. The diagram underscores how different operational layers integrate seamlessly under a single server to deliver a complete, self-contained platform for hosting basic applications and services without the complexity of distributed infrastructure.

Key Considerations:

- **Hardware and Resource Allocation:** Ensure that the server has adequate CPU, memory, and storage.
- **Security Configuration:** Implements firewalls (`iptables`, `firewalld`, and so on) and SELinux policies.
- **Software Installation:** Use package managers such as `dnf` to install the required applications.
- **Backup and Recovery:** Configure automatic backups, using `rsync` or **Bacula.**

Best Practices

Consider using **`firewalld`** to open **HTTP(S)** ports:

Example Commands:

- `sudo firewall-cmd --permanent --add-service=http`
- `sudo firewall-cmd --permanent --add-service=https`
- `sudo firewall-cmd -reload`

There are some additional commands required:

- `sudo systemctl stop nginx`
- `sudo systemctl disable nginx`

Verify Apache is running with this set of new commands:

- `sudo dnf install -y httpd`
- `sudo systemctl enable httpd`
- `sudo systemctl start httpd`
- `sudo systemctl status httpd`
- `sudo systemctl stop httpd`

Implementation Steps

1. **Install Apache Web Server**
   a. Use the following commands to install and start Apache:
      - `sudo dnf install httpd -y`
      - `sudo systemctl enable --now httpd`

   b. Verify the status of the Apache service: `sudo systemctl status httpd`

Expected Output:

```
[cmorera@localhost ~]$ sudo systemctl status httpd
● httpd.service - The Apache HTTP Server
     Loaded: loaded (/usr/lib/systemd/system/httpd.service; enabled; preset: disabled)
     Active: active (running) since Mon 2025-07-07 22:34:51 CST; 11s ago
       Docs: man:httpd.service(8)
   Main PID: 9692 (httpd)
     Status: "Total requests: 0; Idle/Busy workers 100/0;Requests/sec: 0; Bytes served/sec:   0 B/sec"
      Tasks: 177 (limit: 10741)
     Memory: 38.1M
        CPU: 94ms
     CGroup: /system.slice/httpd.service
             ├─9692 /usr/sbin/httpd -DFOREGROUND
             ├─9773 /usr/sbin/httpd -DFOREGROUND
             ├─9774 /usr/sbin/httpd -DFOREGROUND
             ├─9775 /usr/sbin/httpd -DFOREGROUND
             └─9776 /usr/sbin/httpd -DFOREGROUND

Jul 07 22:34:51 localhost.localdomain systemd[1]: Starting The Apache HTTP Server...
Jul 07 22:34:51 localhost.localdomain httpd[9692]: AH00558: httpd: Could not reliably determine the server's fully qualified domain>
Jul 07 22:34:51 localhost.localdomain systemd[1]: Started The Apache HTTP Server.
Jul 07 22:34:51 localhost.localdomain httpd[9692]: Server configured, listening on: port 80
lines 1-20/20 (END)
```

Figure 16.2: *sudo systemctl status httpd*

This command checks the status of the Apache HTTP Server (httpd) service on a Rocky Linux system. When executed, it provides detailed output indicating whether the service is active (running), inactive, or failed. It also displays the process ID, memory usage, uptime, and any recent log entries related to the service. This information is necessary for verifying that the Apache web server is operational, and for troubleshooting issues. *Figure* 16.3 visually represents a sample output of this command, helping administrators confirm that the web server is correctly configured, and running as expected.

2. **Configure `firewalld` for HTTP/HTTPS**
   a. Allow HTTP and HTTPS traffic through the firewall:
      - `sudo firewall-cmd --permanent --add-service=http`
      - `sudo firewall-cmd --permanent --add-service=https`
      - `sudo firewall-cmd --reload`
   b. Check the current firewall configuration: `sudo firewall-cmd --list-all`

Expected Output:

```
[cmorera@localhost ~]$ sudo firewall-cmd --list-all
public (active)
  target: default
  icmp-block-inversion: no
  interfaces: ens160
  sources:
  services: cockpit dhcpv6-client http https ssh
  ports:
  protocols:
  forward: yes
  masquerade: no
  forward-ports:
  source-ports:
  icmp-blocks:
  rich rules:
```

Figure 16.3: *sudo firewall-cmd --list-all*

This figure shows the output of the **`firewall-cmd --list-all`** command on a Rocky Linux system. The command reveals the active firewall zone along with its configuration, including associated interfaces, allowed services (such as HTTP, HTTPS, and SSH), open ports, and related rules. Reviewing this output enables administrators to confirm which services are permitted and verify that the firewall is aligned with security and accessibility requirements.

Best Practices

Regularly update packages:

Keep the system updated to patch security vulnerabilities: **`sudo dnf update -y`**

Enable SELinux in enforcing mode:

Check SELinux status: **getenforce**

To enforce SELinux, edit the configuration: **`sudo nano /etc/selinux/config`**

```
 Set:
 SELINUX=enforcing
Reboot to apply changes: sudo reboot
```

Schedule automated backups using **`rsync`** and **`crontab`:**

Open the crontab: **`crontab -e`**

Add a daily backup job (e.g., at 2 AM):

```
0 2 * * * /usr/bin/rsync -av /var/www/html/ /backup/web_backup/
```

Multi-Server Deployment

In a multi-server deployment, services run on several different machines instead of just one. This helps the system work faster, share the workload evenly, and keep running even if one machine fails. This setup is great for websites or applications that get a lot of users and need to stay reliable. For Linux administrators, it means managing multiple servers that work together to manage tasks efficiently and avoid downtime.

Common Configurations:

- **Application Server + Database Server:** Separates web applications from databases for performance optimization.
- **File Server + Application Server:** Centralizes file storage while keeping applications isolated.
- **Proxy Server Setup:** Uses Nginx or Apache as a reverse proxy to improve performance and security.

Implementation Steps

Install and configure Nginx as a reverse proxy:

1. Install Nginx: `sudo dnf install nginx -y`

   Enable and start Nginx service:

   - `sudo systemctl enable nginx`
   - `sudo systemctl start nginx`
2. Edit **`/etc/nginx/nginx.conf`** to set up load balancing:
3. Open the config file: **`sudo nano /etc/nginx/nginx.conf`**
4. Add or modify the following sections to include the backend servers:

```
nginx
  http {
      upstream backend {
          server 192.168.1.10:80;
          server 192.168.1.11:80;
      }

      server {
          listen 80;

          location / {
              proxy_pass http://backend;
          }
      }
  }
```

Save and close the file.

Validate and restart Nginx:

Test the configuration syntax: `sudo nginx -t`

If the test passes, restart Nginx to apply changes: `sudo systemctl restart nginx`

Expected Output:

```
[cmorera@localhost ~]$ sudo nginx -t
nginx: the configuration file /etc/nginx/nginx.conf syntax is ok
nginx: configuration file /etc/nginx/nginx.conf test is successful
```

Figure 16.4: *sudo nginx -t command*

This figure displays the result of the **sudo nginx -t** command, which validates the Nginx configuration file for syntax errors and overall correctness before changes are applied. By running this test, administrators can detect misconfigurations early and prevent service startup failures. A successful validation confirms that the syntax is correct and the test has passed, providing assurance that it is safe to reload or restart the Nginx service.

Troubleshooting Tips

Solution: Stop the Conflicting Service (Apache)

1. Run the following commands:
   ```
   sudo systemctl stop httpd
   sudo systemctl disable httpd
   ```
2. Then try starting Nginx again:
   ```
   sudo systemctl start nginx
   ```
3. Check its status:
   ```
   sudo systemctl status nginx
   ```

Issue: Nginx fails to start due to port conflict.

Solution: Check for services using port 80: **sudo netstat -tulnp | grep :80**

Issue: Backend servers not responding.

Solution: Verify backend server availability:

- **curl http://192.168.1.10:80**
- **curl http://192.168.1.11:80**

Virtualized Deployments with KVM

Kernel-based Virtual Machine (KVM) enables efficient virtualization on Rocky Linux 9 by allowing multiple virtual machines (VMs) to run on a single physical host. This virtualization technology provides robust performance and flexibility, making it ideal for testing, development, and production environments.

Implementation Steps

1. **Install KVM and related packages**: Begin by installing essential packages for virtualization:
   ```
   sudo dnf install virt-install libvirt-daemon libvirt-daemon-kvm libvirt-client
   virt-manager -y
   ```
   This command installs KVM, libvirt (the virtualization management service), and Virt-Manager, a graphical tool for managing virtual machines.
2. **Start and enable the libvirt service**: Enable and start the **libvirt** daemon to manage virtual machines:
   ```
   sudo systemctl enable --now libvirtd
   ```

3. **Configure the libvirt URI environment variable**: Set the default URI to connect to the local QEMU system:

```
export LIBVIRT_DEFAULT_URI="qemu:///system"
echo 'export LIBVIRT_DEFAULT_URI="qemu:///system"' >> ~/.bashrc
source ~/.bashrc
```

   This ensures that the user environment is set up to interact with libvirt properly.

4. **Verify KVM support**

   Check if the processor supports hardware virtualization extensions:

   `egrep -c '(vmx|svm)' /proc/cpuinfo`

   A non-zero output means the CPU supports KVM.

Using Virt-Manager to Create and Manage Virtual Machines

Virt-Manager provides an easy-to-use graphical interface to create, configure, and control virtual machines.

Open Virt-Manager from our applications menu or by running: **`virt-manager`**

Click **`Create a new virtual machine`**, and follow the wizard to specify:

- VM name
- Memory and CPU allocation
- Disk size and storage location
- Network settings (using either NAT or bridge mode)
- Installation media (ISO image or network install)

Virt-Manager simplifies complex configurations, allowing Linux administrators to manage virtualized environments with minimal effort.

Best Practices:

1. Verify if the system supports KVM:

   `egrep -c '(vmx|svm)' /proc/cpuinfo.`
2. List available network bridges before using virbr0:

   `sudo virsh net-list --all`
3. Use virt-manager (GUI) for easier VM management:

   `sudo dnf install virt-manager -y`

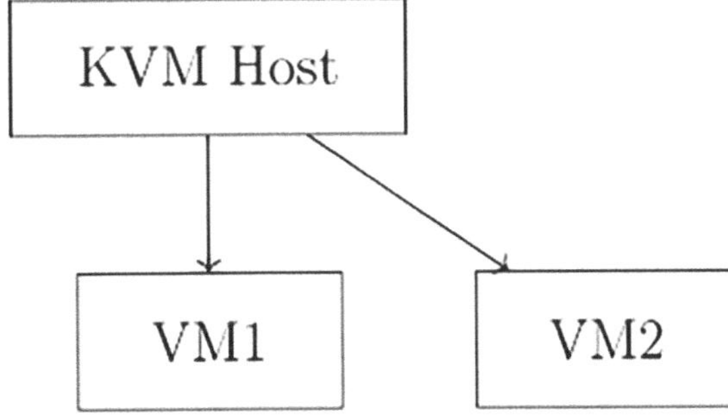

Figure 16.5: *KVM Virtualization Architecture*

This figure illustrates how Kernel-based Virtual Machine (KVM) extends Rocky Linux into a full-featured hypervisor. By enabling hardware virtualization extensions such as Intel VT-x or AMD-V, the Linux kernel gains the ability to host multiple isolated virtual machines (VMs) simultaneously. Each VM is provisioned with its own virtualized CPU, memory, storage, and network interfaces, while resource allocation and lifecycle management are orchestrated through the `libvirt` service. This architecture balances strong isolation with efficient hardware utilization, making KVM an ideal platform for creating flexible, scalable, and high-performance virtualized environments.

Container-Based Deployment

Using containers such as Docker or Podman simplifies application deployment and management.

Deployment Steps:

1. Install Podman: `sudo dnf install podman -y`
2. Pull and run a Rocky Linux container:
   - `podman pull docker.io/rockylinux/rockylinux:9`
   - `podman run -it rockylinux/rockylinux:9 /bin/bash`
3. Manage container networking and persistent storage.

Uses of These Commands:

- **`dnf install podman -y`:** Running this command will help us, installing Podman on Rocky Linux.
- **`podman pull rockylinux/rockylinux:9`:** Execute this command, for pulling the latest Rocky Linux 9 image.
- **`podman run -it rockylinux/rockylinux:9 /bin/bash`:** In conclusion, running an interactive Rocky Linux container.

Best Practices:

List of downloaded images: `podman images`

List running containers: `podman ps`

Use `--rm` to automatically remove the container when stopped:

```
podman run --rm -it rockylinux/rockylinux:9 /bin/bash
```

If root access is required, use:

```
sudo podman run -it rockylinux/rockylinux:9 /bin/bash
```

Automated Deployment with Ansible

Ansible helps automate server provisioning, and configuration management.

Steps for Automating Rocky Linux Deployment:

To start, we validate the ansible install was completed before:

- `sudo dnf install ansible -y`

Steps to Correct the Issue:

1. **Ensure the Playbook Exists:** First, verify that the `apache_setup.yml` file is in the directory running the `ansible-playbook` command from. Kindly check the current directory with: `ls`

   If the file does not exist, create it in the current directory, or specify the correct path to the playbook.

2. **Create the Apache Playbook:** If the playbook file is missing, we can create it by running: **`nano apache_setup.yml`**

   Then add the following content to the file:

   ```
   yaml
      - name: Install Apache on Rocky Linux
        hosts: rocky_servers
        become: yes
        tasks:
          - name: Install httpd
            dnf:
              name: httpd
              state: present
   ```

   Save and exit the editor (*Ctrl* + X, Y, *Enter*).

3. **Verify the Inventory File:** Ensure that the **`/etc/ansible/hosts`** file contains the correct IPs of the target servers. It should look something like:

   ```
   [rocky_servers]
   172.19.0.1 ansible_user=root
   172.20.0.1 ansible_user=root
   ```

4. **Run the Playbook Again:** After ensuring that the playbook file exists, and our inventory is correctly set, run the following command: **`sudo -E ansible-playbook apache_setup.yml`**

This should successfully run the playbook, and install Apache on the specified servers.

These methods provide flexibility and scalability for different deployment needs. Hence, by understanding these standard deployment strategies, administrators can build robust Rocky Linux environments tailored to their specific use cases.

High Availability Setups

Ensuring High Availability (HA) is critical for enterprise deployments. HA configurations minimize downtime, and ensure that services remain accessible during failures.

Load Balancing with HAProxy

HAProxy is a widely used open-source load balancer for distributing network traffic across multiple servers.

Installation and Configuration:

- `sudo dnf install haproxy -y`
- `sudo nano /etc/haproxy/haproxy.cfg`
- `sudo systemctl enable --now haproxy`

Uses of These Commands:

- **`dnf install haproxy -y`:** This will help us to install the HAProxy.
- **`nano /etc/haproxy/haproxy.cfg`:** This is the path to the file location for HAProxy configuration.
- **`systemctl enable --now haproxy`:** This is the proper manner to start HAProxy and enabling it at boot.

Sample Configuration:

```
frontend http_front
    bind *:80
    default_backend web_servers
```

```
backend web_servers
    balance roundrobin
    server web1 192.168.1.10:80 check
    server web2 192.168.1.11:80 check
```

Validation

- **`bind *:80`**: Listens for incoming connections on port 80.
- **`balance roundrobin`**: Distributes traffic evenly among backend servers.
- **`server web1 192.168.1.10:80 check`**: Ensures HAProxy checks web1's availability.

Best Practices:

After editing the config file, assess HAProxy syntax before restarting:

```
sudo haproxy -c -f /etc/haproxy/haproxy.cfg
```

Restart HAProxy only if syntax check passes:

```
sudo systemctl restart haproxy
```

Monitor HAProxy logs for troubleshooting:

```
sudo journalctl -u haproxy --no-pager
```

Clustering with Pacemaker and Corosync

Steps for Cluster Setup:

1. Install required packages:
   ```
   sudo dnf install pacemaker corosync pcs -y
   ```
2. Enable and start the services:
   ```
   sudo systemctl enable --now pcsd
   ```
3. Configure cluster nodes and define resources.

Validation

- **`dnf install pacemaker corosync pcs -y`**: installs required packages.
- **`systemctl enable --now pcsd`**: Enables and starts the cluster management service.

Cluster Node Authentication

The command must be conducted:

```
sudo pcs cluster auth node1 node2 -u hacluster -p password
```

Validation

- **`pcs cluster auth`**: Correct for authenticating nodes in the cluster.

Cluster Setup

The next command will be completed:

```
sudo pcs cluster setup --name mycluster node1 node2
sudo pcs cluster start -all
```

Validation

- **`pcs cluster setup`**: Creates a cluster named mycluster.
- **`pcs cluster start --all`**: Starts the cluster on all nodes.

Best Practices:

- Check cluster status: **`sudo pcs status`**
- Enable the cluster to start on boot: **`sudo pcs cluster enable -all`**
- If needed, add a floating virtual IP for failover:
  ```
  sudo pcs resource create virtual_ip ocf:heartbeat:IPaddr2 ip=192.168.1.100
  cidr_netmask=24 op monitor interval=30s
  ```

Testing Failover Scenarios

Simulating a node failure:

```
sudo pcs cluster stop node1
```

Ensure that node2 takes over services.

Restarting a failed node:

```
sudo pcs cluster start node1
```

Ensure that the cluster rebalances correctly.

Best Practices

Use **pcs status** to check failover behavior:

- **`sudo pcs status`**

Enable **`logging and alerts`** to monitor cluster health:

- **`sudo journalctl -u pacemaker --no-pager`**

Scaling Applications with Load Balancers

Vertical Scaling

- Involves increasing system resources (CPU, RAM, Storage) for better performance.
- Use tuned-adm to optimize system performance:
  ```
  sudo tuned-adm profile throughput-performance
  ```

Validation

- **`tuned-adm` profile throughput-performance:** Correct for optimizing CPU performance.

Best Practices:

Check available tuning profiles:

```
sudo tuned-adm list
```

View current system tuning profile:

```
sudo tuned-adm active
```

Apply changes persistently to maintain performance after reboots.

Horizontal Scaling

- Distributes load across multiple instances.
- Uses HAProxy, Nginx, or cloud load balancers.
- Example: Adding new servers to a web farm.

Load Balancing with HAProxy

Commands to verify:

- `sudo dnf install haproxy -y`
- `sudo nano /etc/haproxy/haproxy.cfg`
- `sudo systemctl restart haproxy`

Validation

- **`dnf install haproxy -y`:** Correct for installing HAProxy.
- **`nano /etc/haproxy/haproxy.cfg`:** Correct configuration file path.
- **`systemctl restart haproxy`:** Correct command to apply changes.

HAProxy Configuration for Load Balancing

The following procedure is not mandatory, and it is recommended to ignore it for now.

The following script can be implemented:

```
frontend http_front
    bind *:80
    default_backend web_servers

backend web_servers
    balance roundrobin
    server web1 192.168.1.10:80 check
    server web2 192.168.1.11:80 check
```

Load balancing is a crucial technique in horizontal scaling, ensuring that incoming traffic is efficiently distributed across multiple servers. By using HAProxy, we can improve the availability, reliability, and scalability of web applications. The round-robin algorithm evenly distributes requests, preventing any single server from becoming overloaded. Proper configuration of HAProxy, combined with system tuning profiles, helps optimize performance, and maintain system stability, making it an essential component in high-traffic environments.

Validation

- **`bind *:80`:** Listens on port 80.
- **`balance roundrobin`:** Evenly distributes traffic.
- **`server web1 192.168.1.10:80 check`:** Ensures HAProxy monitors web1's availability.

Best Practices:

Verify HAProxy syntax before restarting:

```
sudo haproxy -c -f /etc/haproxy/haproxy.cfg
```

Use **`sticky sessions`** for session persistence:

```
backend web_servers
    balance roundrobin
    cookie SERVERID insert indirect nocache
    server web1 192.168.1.10:80 check cookie A
    server web2 192.168.1.11:80 check cookie B
Rocky Linux Deployment Strategies in AWS
Load Balancing with Nginx
```

Commands to verify:

- `sudo dnf install nginx -y`
- `sudo nano /etc/nginx/nginx.conf`
- `sudo systemctl restart nginx`

Validation

- **`dnf install nginx -y`:** Correct for installing Nginx.
- **`nano /etc/nginx/nginx.conf`:** Correct configuration file path.
- **`systemctl restart nginx`:** Correct for applying changes.

Nginx Configuration for Load Balancing

The following procedure is not required, and it is recommended to ignore it for now.

The following script will be used:

```
http {
    upstream backend {
        server 192.168.1.10;
        server 192.168.1.11;
    }

    server {
        listen 80;
        location / {
            proxy_pass http://backend;
        }
    }
}
```

Validation

- **`upstream backend`:** Defines backend servers.
- **`proxy_pass http://backend;`:** Routes requests to backend servers.

Best Practices:

Verify configuration syntax: **`sudo nginx -t`**

Reload instead of restarting for minimal downtime: **`sudo systemctl reload nginx`**

Scaling in AWS with Auto Scaling and Load Balancers

AWS provides Auto Scaling Groups (ASG) and Elastic Load Balancer (ELB) for high availability.

Auto Scaling with AWS CLI

```
aws autoscaling create-auto-scaling-group \
    --auto-scaling-group-name rocky-asg \
    --launch-template LaunchTemplateName=my-template \
    --min-size 1 --max-size 5
```

Validation

- **`aws autoscaling create-auto-scaling-group`:** Creates an ASG.
- **`--launch-template`:** Uses an existing launch template.
- **`--min-size 1 --max-size 5`:** Defines minimum and maximum instances.

Best Practices:

Check ASG status:

```
aws autoscaling describe-auto-scaling-groups
```

Manually trigger scaling for testing:

```
aws autoscaling set-desired-capacity --auto-scaling-group-name rocky-asg --de-
sired-capacity 3
```

AWS Elastic Load Balancer (ELB) Setup

Commands to verify:

```
aws elb create-load-balancer \
    --load-balancer-name my-load-balancer \
    --listeners "Protocol=HTTP,LoadBalancerPort=80,InstanceProtocol=HTTP,
InstancePort=80"
```

Validation

- **`aws elb create-load-balancer`:** Correct for creating an ELB.
- **`--listeners`:** Configures HTTP forwarding.

Best Practices:

List all ELBs: **`aws elb describe-load-balancers`**

Register EC2 instances with the ELB:

```
aws elb register-instances-with-load-balancer --load-balancer-name
my-load-balancer --instances i-0123456789abcdef0
```

Enable **health checks** for automatic failover:

```
aws elb configure-health-check --load-balancer-name my-load-balancer --health-
check Target=HTTP:80/index.html,Interval=30,UnhealthyThreshold=2,HealthyTh-
reshold=2,Timeout=5
```

Deploying on AWS EC2

a. Choose the appropriate instance type (**`t3.micro`**, **`m5.large`**, and so on).

b. Use the Rocky Linux AMI available in AWS Marketplace.

c. Configure security groups for SSH and HTTP/HTTPS access.

Auto Scaling for Rocky Linux

- Use AWS Auto Scaling Groups to dynamically adjust the number of instances based on load.

Example CLI Commands:

- `aws autoscaling create-auto-scaling-group --auto-scaling-group-name rocky-asg \`
- `--launch-template LaunchTemplateName=my-template --min-size 1 --max-size 5`

Using AWS Elastic Load Balancer (ELB)

- Distributes incoming traffic across multiple EC2 instances.

Example CLI Command:

```
aws elb create-load-balancer --load-balancer-name my-load-balancer --listeners
"Protocol=HTTP,LoadBalancerPort=80,InstanceProtocol=HTTP,InstancePort=80"
```

Rocky Linux offers flexibility for various deployment scenarios, from single-server setups to enterprise-scale high availability and cloud-based deployments. By leveraging best practices in server management, load balancing, and AWS cloud solutions, administrators can ensure optimal performance and reliability for their workloads.

High Availability Setups in Rocky Linux 9 and AWS

High Availability (HA) refers to the ability of a system to remain operational and accessible even in the event of hardware or software failures. HA minimizes downtime, and ensures continuous service availability.

Key Concepts of HA

- **Redundancy:** Having backup systems ready to take over in case of failure.
- **Fault Tolerance:** The ability to continue functioning despite hardware or software issues.
- **Failover:** Automatic switching to a standby system in case of failures.
- **Load Balancing:** Distributing traffic across multiple servers to optimize performance and reliability.

Common Use Cases

- Web and database servers requiring minimal downtime.
- Cloud-based applications needing auto-scaling and redundancy.
- Mission-critical enterprise services requiring 24/7 uptime.

High Availability Components and Techniques

Load Balancing

Load balancing is essential for distributing traffic across multiple nodes.

- **HAProxy:** A widely used open-source load balancer.
  - Supports HTTP, TCP, and SSL termination.
  - Provides health checks and failover mechanisms.
- **AWS Elastic Load Balancer (ELB):** Automatically distributes traffic across multiple AWS instances.
  - **Application Load Balancer (ALB)** for HTTP/HTTPS traffic.
  - **Network Load Balancer (NLB)** for TCP traffic.

Failover Mechanisms

- **Pacemaker and Corosync:**
  - Pacemaker manages resources and detects failures.
  - Corosync provides cluster communication.
- **`Keepalived`:** Uses VRRP (Virtual Router Redundancy Protocol) to provide automatic failover of a virtual IP.

Data Replication and Storage HA:

- **Distributed Replicated Block Device (DRBD):** Real-time block-level replication between two nodes.
- **GlusterFS:** Distributed file system ensuring redundancy and scalability.

Implementing HA on Rocky Linux 9

Setting Up a Two-Node HA Cluster

1. **Install Required Packages:**

   ```
   sudo dnf install -y pacemaker corosync pcs
   ```

2. **Enable and Start Cluster Services:**

   ```
   sudo systemctl enable --now pcsd
   ```

3. **Authenticate Nodes:**

   ```
   sudo pcs cluster auth node1 node2 -u hacluster -p password
   ```

4. **Create and Start the Cluster:**

   - `sudo pcs cluster setup --name mycluster node1 node2`
   - `sudo pcs cluster start --all`

Configuring HAProxy for Load Balancing

1. **Install HAProxy:**

   ```
   sudo dnf install -y haproxy
   ```

2. **Configure `/etc/haproxy/haproxy.cfg`:**

   ```
   frontend http_front
       bind *:80
       default_backend web_servers
   backend web_servers
       balance roundrobin
       server web1 192.168.1.10:80 check
       server web2 192.168.1.11:80 check
   ```

3. **Restart HAProxy:**

   ```
   sudo systemctl restart haproxy
   ```

Testing Failover Scenarios:

- Shut down one node, and check if the service continues running on the second node.
- Use pcs status to monitor cluster status.

High Availability in AWS

High Availability (HA) in AWS ensures minimal downtime and continuous operation by distributing resources across multiple Availability Zones (AZs). AWS services such as Elastic Load Balancing (ELB), Auto Scaling, and Multi-AZ deployments for databases (RDS, Aurora) help maintain redundancy and fault tolerance. Thus, by leveraging these features, applications can automatically recover from failures, providing a reliable and resilient infrastructure.

AWS Services for HA

- **AWS Auto Scaling:** Automatically adjusts the number of EC2 instances based on demand.
- **Elastic Load Balancing (ELB):** Distributes traffic among healthy instances.
- **Multi-AZ Deployments:** Ensures high availability for databases such as RDS, MySQL, and PostgreSQL.

Example: Setting Up a Highly Available Web Application

1. **Deploy EC2 instances in multiple Availability Zones.**

2. **Create an Application Load Balancer (ALB).**
   a. Navigate to **`AWS EC2 Dashboard`** > **`Load Balancers`**.
   b. Select **`Application Load Balancer`**.
   c. Attach instances across different AZs.
3. **Configure Route 53 for DNS failover.**
   a. Use health checks to monitor server status.
   b. Set up a failover routing policy.

Best Practices for HA Deployments

Monitoring and Alerting

- **Prometheus and Grafana** for real-time system monitoring.
- **AWS CloudWatch** for tracking performance metrics.

Backup and Disaster Recovery

- Regular **snapshot backups** for critical data.
- **AWS Backup** for automated recovery.

Security Considerations

- **Firewalls and SELinux** to protect HA clusters.
- **IAM roles and policies** for AWS HA resources.

This guide provides a structured, step-by-step approach to setting up high availability in **Rocky Linux 9** and **AWS**, ensuring minimal downtime and maximum reliability.

Scaling Applications with Load Balancers in Rocky Linux

Load balancing involves distributing incoming network traffic across multiple servers to prevent any single server from becoming overloaded. This improves performance, reliability, and availability.

Benefits of Load Balancing:

- **Performance Optimization:** Distributes traffic evenly to prevent overload on a single node.
- **High Availability:** Ensures application uptime even if one server fails.
- **Scalability:** Allows applications to scale by adding more backend servers.

Types of Load Balancers:

- **Layer 4 (Transport Layer):** Routes traffic based on IP address and port.
- **Layer 7 (Application Layer):** Routes traffic based on application-level data (e.g., HTTP headers, cookies).

Load Balancer Technologies in Rocky Linux: Rocky Linux supports various load balancing technologies to distribute network traffic efficiently and enhance system availability. HAProxy is a widely used open-source solution that provides high-performance load balancing for HTTP, TCP, and other protocols. Nginx, another powerful option, offers reverse proxy and load balancing capabilities with advanced caching features. Additionally, Keepalived can be used for high availability by managing virtual IP failover. These technologies help ensure optimal resource utilization, fault tolerance, and scalability in enterprise environments.

HAProxy (High Availability Proxy):

- Open-source, high-performance TCP/HTTP load balancer.
- Provides health checks, SSL termination, and failover mechanisms.

NGINX Load Balancer:

- Functions as a reverse proxy with load balancing.
- Supports Layer 7 load balancing, caching, and security controls.

`Keepalived`:

- Implements Virtual Router Redundancy Protocol (VRRP) for high availability.
- Ensures failover between active and standby load balancers.

AWS Elastic Load Balancer (ELB):

- Cloud-based managed load balancer.
- Supports multiple availability zones for redundancy.

Firsthand Lab: Deploying HAProxy Load Balancer

Scenario: Load balancing traffic between two Rocky Linux web servers, using HAProxy.

Steps:

1. **Install HAProxy**: `sudo dnf install -y haproxy`
2. **Configure HAProxy** (**`/etc/haproxy/haproxy.cfg`**):

```
frontend http_front
    bind *:80
    default_backend web_servers

backend web_servers
    balance roundrobin
    server web1 192.168.1.10:80 check
    server web2 192.168.1.11:80 check
```

3. **Restart HAProxy**: `sudo systemctl restart haproxy`
4. **Test Load Balancing**:
   - Access the HAProxy IP in a browser.
   - Refresh the page to see requests served by different backend servers.

Direct Lab: Configuring AWS Elastic Load Balancer (ELB)

Scenario: Scaling a Rocky Linux-based web application, using AWS ELB.

We start with the following steps:

1. **Launch Two EC2 Instances** (Rocky Linux), and install a web server:
   - `sudo dnf install -y httpd`
   - `sudo systemctl enable --now httpd`

2. **Create an Application Load Balancer (ALB):**
    a. Navigate to **`AWS EC2 Dashboard`** > **`Load Balancers`**.
    b. Select "**`Application Load Balancer`**", and configure listeners for HTTP/HTTPS.
    c. Attach EC2 instances across different Availability Zones.
3. **Test Load Balancing:**
    a. Access the ALB DNS name in a browser.
    b. Observe traffic distribution across instances.

Best Practices for Scaling Applications

Optimizing Load Balancer Performance:

- Enable **connection pooling** to manage large volumes of requests.
- Use **gzip compression** to reduce bandwidth usage.

Monitoring and Logging Traffic

- **Prometheus and Grafana:** Monitor system metrics in real time.
- **AWS CloudWatch:** Track ELB performance metrics.

Security Considerations:

- Implement **`firewall rules`** to restrict access.
- Use **`AWS Web Application Firewall (WAF)`** for DDoS protection.

This guide provides a comprehensive approach to scaling applications with load balancers in Rocky Linux and AWS, ensuring performance, availability, and security.

Rocky Linux Deployment Strategies in AWS

Deploying Rocky Linux in AWS provides scalability, flexibility, and security for enterprise workloads. This section explores various deployment strategies, best practices, and automation techniques to optimize Rocky Linux instances in AWS.

Key Benefits of Deploying Rocky Linux in AWS:

- **Scalability:** Easily scale compute resources based on demand.
- **High Availability:** Deploy applications across multiple Availability Zones (AZs).
- **Security:** Utilize AWS security tools like IAM, Security Groups, and WAF.
- **Cost Optimization:** Use reserved instances and auto-scaling strategies.

Deployment Strategies

Single Instance Deployment (Basic Setup)

Use Case: Development environments, small-scale applications.

Steps:

1. Launch an EC2 instance using the official Rocky Linux AMI.
2. Configure security groups to allow necessary traffic (e.g., SSH, HTTP/HTTPS).

3. Attach an Elastic IP for persistent public access.
4. Configure IAM roles for secure access to AWS services.

High Availability of Deployment

Use Case: Production workloads requiring minimal downtime.

Steps:

1. Deploy multiple Rocky Linux EC2 instances in separate AZs.
2. Use Elastic Load Balancing (ALB/NLB) to distribute traffic.
3. Configure Auto Scaling Groups to manage instance availability.
4. Enable Amazon CloudWatch for monitoring and alerts.

Infrastructure as Code (IaC) with Terraform

Use Case: Automated and repeatable deployments.

Steps:

1. Define infrastructure as code, using Terraform.
2. Use AWS Provider in Terraform to manage EC2 instances, VPCs, and security groups.
3. Deploy configurations, using terraform apply.
4. Maintain version control with Git.

Containerized Deployment with AWS ECS

Use Case: Running containerized workloads.

Steps:

1. Install Docker and containerize the application.
2. Push the container image to Amazon Elastic Container Registry (ECR).
3. Deploy Rocky Linux-based containers in Amazon ECS with Fargate or EC2.
4. Configure load balancing and service discovery.

Hybrid Cloud Deployment

Use Case: Integrating on-premises and AWS environments.

Steps:

1. Establish a site-to-site VPN or AWS Direct Connect.
2. Deploy Rocky Linux workloads across on-premises and AWS.
3. Use AWS Systems Manager for centralized management.
4. Implement AWS Backup for disaster recovery.

Best Practices

Security Considerations:

- Enable SSH key-based authentication, and disable password logins.
- Apply the principle of least privilege, using IAM roles.

- Use AWS Security Groups and Network ACLs for traffic control.
- Regularly update Rocky Linux packages, and apply security patches.

Performance Optimization:

- Use Amazon EBS with proper volume types (gp3 for general-purpose, io1 for high-performance needs).
- Optimize instance sizes based on workload requirements.
- Enable AWS CloudWatch and AWS X-Ray for performance monitoring.

Cost Optimization:

- Use Reserved or Spot Instances for cost savings.
- Enable Auto Scaling to match resource demand.
- Utilize AWS Compute Savings Plans for long-term deployments.

Deploying Rocky Linux in AWS offers a robust, scalable, and secure platform for workloads of any size. By leveraging automation, high availability strategies, and best practices, organizations can optimize their cloud infrastructure efficiently. Implementing Infrastructure as Code (IaC), containerized deployments, and hybrid cloud integration further enhances flexibility and operational efficiency in AWS environments.

Rocky Linux Deployment Strategies in AWS Validation

This section ensures optimal deployment of Rocky Linux on AWS using **EC2, Terraform, ECS,** and **Hybrid Cloud setups**.

Single Instance Deployment (Basic Setup): A single **EC2** instance is suitable for development and small-scale applications.

Commands to Verify:

```
aws ec2 run-instances \
    --image-id ami-0abcdef1234567890 \
    --count 1 \
    --instance-type t3.micro \
    --key-name my-key-pair \
    --security-groups my-security-group
```

Validation:

- **`aws ec2 run-instances`:** Correct command to launch an EC2 instance.
- **`--image-id`:** Specifies the Rocky Linux AMI ID. (Ensure we use the correct **AMI ID** for our AWS region.)
- **`--instance-type t3.micro`:** Defines the instance size.
- **`--key-name my-key-pair`:** Uses a key pair for SSH access.
- **`--security-groups my-security-group`:** Ensures security rules are applied.

Best Practices:

- **Find the latest Rocky Linux AMI** before launching:

  ```
  aws ec2 describe-images --owners 679593333241 --filters "Name=name,
  Values=Rocky-9-*" --query 'Images[*].[ImageId,Name]' --output table
  ```

- **Check running instances:**

  ```
  aws ec2 describe-instances --query 'Reservations[*].Instances[*].
  [InstanceId,State.Name,PublicIpAddress]'
  ```

- **Connect via SSH** (once the instance is running):
  ```
  ssh -i my-key-pair.pem ec2-user@public-ip
  ```

High Availability Deployment: For production, deploy multiple **EC2** instances across different **Availability Zones (AZs).**

Steps to Implement:

1. **Launch multiple EC2 instances** (Repeat aws ec2 run-instances with different AZs).
2. Configure AWS Elastic Load Balancer (ELB) to distribute traffic.
3. Set up Auto Scaling for dynamic resource allocation.

Best Practices:

- Use **Multi-AZ Auto Scaling Groups**:
  ```
  aws autoscaling create-auto-scaling-group \
      --auto-scaling-group-name rocky-ha-asg \
      --launch-template LaunchTemplateName=my-template \
      --min-size 2 --max-size 6 \
      --availability-zones us-east-1a us-east-1b
  ```
- Monitor EC2 instances with **AWS CloudWatch:**
  ```
  aws cloudwatch describe-alarms
  ```

Infrastructure as Code (IaC) with Terraform

Terraform automates AWS deployments using declarative configuration.

```
Terraform Configuration (main.tf)
provider "aws" {
  region = "us-east-1"
}

resource "aws_instance" "rocky" {
  ami           = "ami-0abcdef1234567890"
  instance_type = "t3.micro"
  key_name      = "my-key-pair"
  security_groups = ["my-security-group"]
  tags = {
    Name = "RockyLinux-Server"
  }
}
```

Validation:

- Defines an **`EC2 instance`** with Rocky Linux.
- Uses a **`provider block`** for AWS region configuration.
- Applies **`tags`** for better resource management.

Commands to Verify:

- **`terraform init`**
- **`terraform apply -auto-approve`**

Validation:

- **`terraform init`:** Initializes Terraform modules.
- **`terraform apply -auto-approve`:** Deploys infrastructure **without requiring manual approval**.

Best Practices:

- Use **version control** for Terraform files (git).
- **Destroy infrastructure when not needed** to save costs:

```
terraform destroy -auto-approve
```

Containerized Deployment with AWS ECS: Using AWS Elastic Container Service (ECS) for deploying Rocky Linux containers provides a scalable and efficient alternative to traditional EC2 instances. By leveraging ECS, applications can be containerized, making them easier to manage, deploy, and scale. With options like Fargate for serverless execution and EC2 for more control, ECS ensures flexibility based on workload requirements. Defining task configurations, registering them, and running containerized applications simplifies deployment, while maintaining high availability and resource optimization in cloud environments.

Steps to Deploy Rocky Linux Containers in ECS:

1. Create an ECS Cluster.
2. Register a Task Definition (Docker container).
3. Run the containerized app on Fargate or EC2.

Commands to verify:

```
aws ecs create-cluster --cluster-name rocky-ecs-cluster
```

Validation

- **`aws ecs create-cluster`**: Creates an ECS cluster.

Task Definition Example (`task-def.json`)

```
{
  "family": "rocky-linux-task",
  "containerDefinitions": [
    {
      "name": "rocky-container",
      "image": "rockylinux/rockylinux:9",
      "memory": 512,
      "cpu": 256,
      "essential": true
    }
  ]
}
```

Validation:

- Defines a container running **Rocky Linux 9**.

Register Task Definition

```
aws ecs register-task-definition --cli-input-json file://task-def.json
```

Validation:

- Registers the **ECS task** to deploy the container.

Run a Container Task:

```
aws ecs run-task --cluster rocky-ecs-cluster --task-definition rocky-linux-task
```

Validation:

- Runs the **containerized Rocky Linux workload**.

Best Practices:

List running containers in ECS:

```
aws ecs list-tasks --cluster rocky-ecs-cluster
```

Use **AWS Fargate** for serverless container execution:

```
aws ecs update-service --cluster rocky-ecs-cluster --service rocky-service
--desired-count 2
```

Implementing high availability and load balancing in Rocky Linux and AWS ensures optimized performance, fault tolerance, and scalability for modern applications. By leveraging technologies like HAProxy, Nginx, and AWS ECS, organizations can efficiently distribute workloads, minimize downtime, and enhance resource utilization. Containerized deployments further streamline management and deployment, offering flexibility and automation. Adopting these best practices strengthens infrastructure reliability, making it well-suited for both on-premises and cloud-based environments.

Hybrid Cloud Deployment (On-Prem + AWS): Hybrid Cloud deployments allow Rocky Linux to **integrate with on-premise environments**.

Connect On-Prem Rocky Linux to AWS:

1. Establish a Site-to-Site VPN or AWS Direct Connect.
2. Use AWS Systems Manager for hybrid management.

Commands to Verify:

```
aws ssm create-document \
    --name "HybridConfig" \
    --document-type "Command" \
    --content file://hybrid-config.json
```

Validation:

- Creates an **AWS Systems Manager (SSM) document** for hybrid management.

Best Practices:

- Monitor hybrid servers with AWS CloudWatch Logs:
  `aws logs describe-log-groups`
- Set up AWS Backup for disaster recovery:
- aws backup create-backup-plan --backup-plan-name hybrid-backup

Deploying Rocky Linux in AWS allows organizations to build scalable, secure, and available infrastructures. This chapter explored various deployment strategies, from single-instance setups to high-availability architectures using load balancers and Auto Scaling. We covered automation with Terraform and Ansible, along with containerized deployments using ECS for flexibility and scalability. Additionally, hybrid cloud integration ensures seamless connectivity between on-premises and cloud environments. By following best practices in security, resource optimization, and automation, administrators can effectively deploy and manage Rocky Linux workloads in AWS, ensuring reliability, performance, and operational efficiency in diverse enterprise environments.

Conclusion

This chapter covered the essential deployment scenarios for Rocky Linux, from standard server setups to high-availability configurations. By leveraging best practices, such as automation tools, load balancers, and cloud deployment strategies, administrators can ensure their Rocky Linux environments are secure, scalable, and dependable. Proper planning for hardware, failover mechanisms, and cloud integrations, especially in AWS, is key to optimizing performance and minimizing downtime.

The next *Chapter 17* provides a direct project that guides readers through deploying a complete application on Rocky Linux in AWS. It covers everything from launching an EC2 instance to setting up a web server, configuring security, and ensuring scalability. This practical approach helps solidify the concepts learned in earlier chapters, and gives readers the experience needed to deploy applications effectively in a cloud environment.

Points to Remember

- **Standard server deployments** require configuring networking, storage, and security settings to ensure optimal performance, and reliability.
- **High availability setups** enhance uptime by utilizing clustering, failover mechanisms, and redundancy techniques.
- **Load balancing** efficiently distributes network traffic to prevent bottlenecks, optimize resource utilization, and improve scalability.
- **AWS deployment strategies** leverage Infrastructure as Code (IaC), Auto Scaling Groups, and manage services for flexibility and resilience.
- **Automating deployments** with AWS tools enhances efficiency, strengthens security, and optimizes resource management.

Multiple Choice Questions

1. What is a key benefit of high availability setups in Rocky Linux deployments?
   a. Improved security
   b. Continuous uptime and fault tolerance
   c. Faster file transfers
   d. Lower hardware costs
2. Which tool is typically utilized for load balancing in Rocky Linux?
   a. `iptables`
   b. `HAProxy`
   c. `rsync`
   d. `systemd`
3. What is the primary purpose of AWS Auto Scaling Groups?
   a. Automating instance resizing based on demand
   b. Encrypting network traffic
   c. Managing DNS records
   d. Monitoring CPU temperatures
4. Which AWS service is best suited for distributing traffic among multiple instances?
   a. AWS CloudWatch
   b. AWS S3
   c. AWS Elastic Load Balancer (ELB)
   d. AWS Lambda

5. What is the main advantage of using Infrastructure as Code (IaC) in cloud deployments?
    a. Manual server provisioning
    b. Automated and repeatable deployments
    c. Reduced need for monitoring
    d. Higher energy consumption
6. Which feature ensures Rocky Linux remains available in case of a server failure?
    a. High availability clustering
    b. Disabling firewall rules
    c. Increasing swap memory
    d. Running processes as root
7. What is the role of a reverse proxy in load balancing?
    a. Managing database queries
    b. Distributing client requests among backend servers
    c. Encrypting disk storage
    d. Disabling network interfaces
8. How does AWS Systems Manager help in Rocky Linux deployments?
    a. Provides remote management and automation capabilities
    b. Replaces the need for SSH access
    c. Acts as a replacement for the Linux kernel
    d. Reduces server costs by 50%
9. What is an example of a high availability storage solution for Rocky Linux?
    a. NFS without replication
    b. GlusterFS or Ceph
    c. Using only a local SSD
    d. Disabling RAID configurations
10. Why is monitoring important in cloud-based deployments?
    a. To increase manual intervention
    b. To proactively detect and address performance issues
    c. To disable firewalls automatically
    d. To prevent all system failures completely

Answers

1. b
2. b
3. a
4. c
5. b

6. a
7. b
8. a
9. b
10. b

Questions

1. What are the key considerations for deploying a standard Rocky Linux server?
2. How can high availability be implemented in Rocky Linux environments?
3. What is the function of load balancers in scaling applications?
4. What are the benefits of using AWS Auto Scaling for Rocky Linux instances?
5. How does Infrastructure as Code improve cloud deployments?
6. What tools can be used for monitoring Rocky Linux performance in AWS?
7. How does AWS Systems Manager enhance system administration?
8. What best practices should be followed for securing cloud-based Rocky Linux deployments?
9. How can redundancy be ensured in a high availability cluster?
10. What are the differences between deploying Rocky Linux on-premises, and in AWS?

Key Terms

- **Standard Server Deployment:** The process of configuring a Linux server with essential services and security settings.
- **High Availability (HA):** Techniques to ensure system uptime and fault tolerance.
- **Load Balancer:** A tool that distributes network traffic across multiple servers to enhance scalability.
- **Infrastructure as Code (IaC):** The use of automation tools like Terraform to manage cloud deployments.
- **Auto Scaling Groups (ASG):** AWS feature that adjusts server instances based on workload demand.
- **Reverse Proxy:** A server that routes client requests to backend services for improved performance and security.
- **AWS Systems Manager:** A cloud-based service that automates configuration management and monitoring.
- **GlusterFS/Ceph:** Distributed storage solutions for high availability.
- **Elastic Load Balancer (ELB):** AWS service for managing network traffic distribution.
- **CloudWatch:** AWS monitoring service for tracking performance metrics and logs.

Chapter 17
End-to-End Cloud Deployment Project

Introduction

Deploying applications in the cloud is essential for system administrators and DevOps engineers. It enables scalability, high availability, and cost efficiency in modern IT environments. Rocky Linux, known for its stability and compatibility with Red Hat-based systems, is well-suited for cloud deployments.

This chapter offers a practical, step-by-step guide to deploy a complete application on AWS, using Rocky Linux. The key topics include EC2 instance provisioning, web server and database setup, and security configuration. Monitoring strategies and automation tools, such as Terraform and CodePipeline are also introduced.

The guide is designed to support both beginners and experienced Linux administrators through hands-on learning. Best practices in cloud security, scalability, and deployment automation are emphasized throughout. Through this chapter, readers will gain practical experience in launching and managing applications in AWS.

Visual aids, troubleshooting tips, and real-world scenarios help bridge theory and implementation. The goal is to ensure reliable, secure, and efficient application deployment in the cloud.

Structure

This chapter covers the following topics:

- Launching a Rocky Linux EC2 Instance
- Setting up a Web Server and Database
- Configuring Security Groups, Scaling, and Monitoring
- Deploying the Application in a Cloud Environment
- Hands-on Project: A Complete End-to-End Cloud Deployment, using AWS

Rocky Linux Version Compatibility

To ensure clarity and prevent confusion across different environments, this chapter standardizes examples, using Rocky Linux 9. However, most instructions and configurations are also compatible with Rocky Linux 8, with minor adjustments noted where applicable.

System administrators and DevOps professionals working in hybrid or legacy environments can adapt the steps with confidence, provided they verify package versions and CLI tool compatibility as needed.

Version	Compatibility Notes	Operational Considerations
Rocky Linux 9	Fully supported. Core commands (`dnf`, `systemctl`) and AWS integrations verified.	Use latest stable packages. Confirm AWS CLI v2 is installed and functional.
Rocky Linux 8	Broadly compatible. Minor limitations with AWS CLI features may occur.	Check `dnf` module streams. Upgrade to AWS CLI v2 if using cloud services.

***Figure 17.1**: Rocky Linux Version Compatibility*

This figure provides a reference for evaluating how the chapter's examples and procedures apply across different Rocky Linux versions. While Rocky Linux 9 serves as the primary platform for testing and validation, compatibility with Rocky Linux 8 is also considered. The table highlights important differences, including variations in command availability, AWS CLI version requirements, and package management behavior. By using this reference, readers working with earlier releases can make the necessary adjustments to ensure consistent functionality and reliable deployments across supported versions.

Launching a Rocky Linux EC2 Instance

Amazon Elastic Compute Cloud (EC2) is a key AWS service that provides scalable computing capacity in the cloud. Businesses and individuals can launch virtual machines (instances) on demand, adjusting computing resources as required. EC2 enables cost-effective and flexible deployments, making it a preferred choice for cloud-based applications.

Rocky Linux, an enterprise-grade, community-supported operating system, is widely adopted for its stability, security, and compatibility with Red Hat Enterprise Linux (RHEL). It is commonly used to host web applications, databases, and cloud-based services.

Prerequisites for Deployment

Before launching a Rocky Linux EC2 instance, ensure that we have:

- An **active AWS account** with permissions to create EC2 instances.
- Basic understanding of **AWS EC2 and cloud networking** (VPCs, subnets, and security groups).
- An **SSH key pair** for secure remote access.
- **Familiarity with AWS regions and availability zones** for optimized performance.

Step-by-Step Guide to Launching a Rocky Linux EC2 Instance

Step 1: Access the AWS Management Console

a. Log into the **`AWS account`** at AWS Console.

b. Navigate to the **`EC2 Dashboard`** by searching for **`'EC2'`** in the AWS search bar.

c. Click **`'Launch Instance`**' to begin the deployment process.

Step 2: Choose the Rocky Linux AMI

a. In the **`Amazon Machine Image`** **(AMI)** selection, search for '**`Rocky Linux`**'.

b. Choose the latest **official Rocky Linux AMI**, usually maintained by AWS or the Rocky Linux project.

c. Click **'Select'** to proceed.

Step 3: Configure Instance Details

a. **Select an instance type** based on our needs:

- **t2.micro (1 vCPU, 1GB RAM):** Free tier eligible, ideal for testing.
- **t3.medium (2 vCPUs, 4GB RAM):** Suitable for web hosting.
- **c5.large (2 vCPUs, 4GB RAM):** Optimized for compute-intensive tasks.

b. Define the **number of instances,** and enable **auto-scaling** if required.

c. Assign the instance to a **Virtual Private Cloud (VPC)** and **subnet**.

d. Attach an **IAM role** for secure access to AWS services.

Step 4: Configure Security Groups

a. Create a **new security group**, or select an existing one.

b. Set up **inbound rules**:

- Allow **SSH (port 22)** only from trusted IPs.
- If hosting a web server, allow **HTTP (port 80)** and **HTTPS (port 443)**.

c. Apply **security best practices** to minimize exposure.

Step 5: Configure SSH Key Pair

a. Choose an **existing SSH key pair,** or create a new one.

b. **Download and store the private key** (`.pem` file) securely.

c. Set appropriate permissions, using: **`chmod 400 your-key.pem`**

Step 6: Configure Additional Storage

a. In the **Storage Configuration** section, we can add additional Amazon Elastic Block Store (EBS) volumes.

b. Define the size of the root volume (default: 8 GiB, recommended: 20 GiB for production).

c. Click **'Add New Volume'** to attach extra storage.

   i. Choose **General Purpose SSD (gp3)** or **Provisioned IOPS SSD (io1/io2)** for high-performance workloads.

   ii. Define the size (for example, 50 GiB for applications, 100 GiB for databases).

   iii. Set **Delete on Termination** to false to persist data.

d. Attach an existing EBS volume if needed.

Step 7: Review and Launch

a. Carefully review all configurations.

b. Click **'Launch'**, and confirm our settings.

c. Wait for the instance to initialize. Its **status should change to 'running'**.

Connecting to our Rocky Linux EC2 Instance

Once the instance is running, use SSH to connect:

For **Linux/macOS:** `ssh -i your-key.pem ec2-user@<public-ip-address>`

For **Windows (using `PuTTY`):**

1. Convert the `.pem key` to `.ppk` format, using `PuTTYgen`.
2. Use PuTTY to establish an SSH connection.

Attaching and Mounting Additional Storage

Step 1: Verify Attached Disks

Once logged in, list the available disks: `lsblk`

The additional volume should appear as `/dev/xvdb` or a similar name.

Step 2: Format the New Volume

If the volume is new, format it using `ext4: sudo mkfs.ext4 /dev/xvdb`

Step 3: Mount the Volume

a. Create a mount point: `sudo mkdir /mnt/data`

b. Mount the volume: `sudo mount /dev/xvdb /mnt/data`

Step 4: Persist Mount on Reboot

To ensure that the volume is automatically mounted on reboot:

a. Get the UUID: `sudo blkid /dev/xvdb`

b. Add an entry in `/etc/fstab`:

```
echo 'UUID=<your-uuid> /mnt/data ext4 defaults,nofail 0 2' | sudo tee -a /etc/
fstab
```

Post-Deployment Configurations

After successfully connecting, follow these best practices:

1. Update the system: `sudo dnf update -y`
2. Install essential utilities: `sudo dnf install nano wget curl -y`
3. Set up time synchronization: `sudo systemctl enable --now chronyd`
4. Create a new user for security: `sudo useradd -m adminuser`
5. **Disable root SSH access:**

   a. **`Edit /etc/ssh/sshd_config`.**

   b. Set `PermitRootLogin no.`

   c. Restart SSH: `sudo systemctl restart sshd`

Monitoring and Maintenance

- Enable `CloudWatch Logs and Alarms` for tracking performance.
- Use `htop` and `iostat` for resource monitoring.

- Implement **fail2ban** to block unauthorized access attempts.

Scalability and High Availability

- Utilize **Auto Scaling Groups** to handle variable workloads.
- Deploy instances across **multiple Availability Zones** for redundancy.
- Integrate **Elastic Load Balancing (ALB/NLB)** for traffic distribution.

Best Practices and Security Considerations

To ensure a secure and efficient setup:

- Restrict **SSH access**, using **Security** groups.
- Use **IAM roles**, instead of hardcoded credentials.
- Enable **CloudWatch monitoring** to track performance.
- Automate backups with **AWS Backup** or **snapshots**.
- Consider **AWS Systems Manager** for managing instances **without direct SSH access**.

By following these guidelines, we can efficiently deploy and secure a Rocky Linux EC2 instance with additional storage, ensuring optimal performance and security for cloud workloads.

Setting up a Web Server and Database

Deploying a web server and database is a fundamental step in setting up a functional cloud-based application. In cloud environments such as AWS, using Rocky Linux to host a web server (Apache or Nginx) and a database (MariaDB or MySQL) ensures stability, security, and scalability.

A web server is responsible for serving web content to users, while a database stores dynamic information required for applications. Together, they form the backbone of many modern applications, including websites, e-commerce platforms, and SaaS products. This section provides a step-by-step guide to installing, configuring, and securing a web server and database on Rocky Linux.

Prerequisites

Before setting up a web server and database, ensure the following:

1. A running Rocky Linux EC2 instance with SSH access.
2. Updated system packages using: **sudo dnf update -y**.
3. A properly configured security group allowing HTTP (port 80) and HTTPS (port 443).
4. Firewall configured to allow web traffic.
5. An SSH key pair to securely access the instance.

Installing and Configuring Apache/Nginx Web Server

1. **Installing Apache:** Apache is one of the most widely used web servers due to its stability and flexibility. To install Apache on Rocky Linux, follow these steps:
   a. Install Apache, using the following command: **sudo dnf install httpd -y**.
   b. Start and enable Apache to ensure that it runs on boot:
      - `sudo systemctl start httpd`
      - `sudo systemctl enable httpd`

c. Adjust the firewall to allow web traffic:
   - `sudo firewall-cmd --permanent --add-service=http`
   - `sudo firewall-cmd --permanent --add-service=https`
   - `sudo firewall-cmd --reload`

d. **Installing Nginx (Alternative Web Server):** Alternatively, we can use Nginx, known for its high performance in serving static files, and managing concurrent connections efficiently.

e. Install Nginx, using: **`sudo dnf install nginx -y`**

f. Start and enable Nginx:
   - `sudo systemctl start nginx`
   - `sudo systemctl enable nginx`

g. Configure the firewall similarly to Apache, using the same firewall commands.

Installing and Configuring MariaDB/MySQL Database

1. **Installing MariaDB:** MariaDB is a popular open-source database server that offers reliability and performance. To install and configure MariaDB:

   a. Install MariaDB, using: `sudo dnf install mariadb-server -y`

   b. Start and enable MariaDB:
      - `sudo systemctl start mariadb`
      - `sudo systemctl enable mariadb`

   c. Secure the installation by running: **`sudo mysql_secure_installation`**

Follow the prompts to set a root password, and remove unnecessary access.

1. **Creating a Database and User:** To create a new database and user for a web application:

   a. Access MariaDB: **`sudo mysql -u root -p`**

   b. Create a new database: **`CREATE DATABASE webapp_db;`**

   c. Create a user and grant privileges:
      - `CREATE USER 'webuser'@'localhost' IDENTIFIED BY 'securepassword';`
      - `GRANT ALL PRIVILEGES ON webapp_db.* TO 'webuser'@'localhost';`
      - `FLUSH PRIVILEGES;`

   d. Exit MariaDB:
      - **`EXIT;`**

Testing and Verifying the Setup

After installing the web server and database, follow these steps to ensure everything is working:

1. Check if the web server is running:
   - `sudo systemctl status httpd  # for Apache`
   - `sudo systemctl status nginx  # for Nginx`
2. Create a test HTML file in /var/www/html/:
   ```
   echo '<h1>Welcome to Rocky Linux</h1>' | sudo tee /var/www/html/index.html
   ```

3. Open a browser, and enter the public IP of our instance to check if the web page loads.

Best Practices for Security and Performance

- **Restrict database access** to specific IPs or applications.
- **Enable automatic updates** for security patches.
- **Use SSL certificates** (Let us encrypt) for secure HTTPS connections.
- **Monitor server logs**, using `journalctl` and log files in `/var/log/`.
- **Implement a Web Application Firewall (WAF)** for added security.
- **Regularly back up databases,** and web server configurations.
- **Optimize Apache/Nginx settings** to improve performance and scalability.

By following these steps and best practices, we can successfully deploy a secure and scalable web server and database on Rocky Linux in an AWS cloud environment.

Configuring Security Groups, Scaling, and Monitoring in AWS

Configuring Security Groups in AWS

Security Groups function as virtual firewalls for AWS EC2 instances, defining rules to allow or deny traffic based on IP addresses, ports, and protocols. Unlike traditional firewalls, Security Groups are stateful, meaning that if an incoming request is allowed, the corresponding outbound response is automatically permitted.

Steps to Configure Security Groups

1. **Access AWS Management Console:** Navigate to the EC2 Dashboard, and click on Security Groups under Network and Security.
2. **Create a New Security Group:** Provide a name and description, as well as select the Virtual Private Cloud (VPC) where it will be applied.
3. **Define Inbound and Outbound Rules:**
    - Inbound rules specify which incoming traffic is allowed.
    - Outbound rules define the traffic permitted to leave the instance.
4. **Apply the Security Group to an EC2 Instance:** Attach the configured Security Group to our running EC2 instances.

Lab: Configuring Security Groups for a Web Server

Objective: Secure an EC2 instance running a web server by configuring Security Groups.

Steps:

1. **Launch an EC2 Instance with Rocky Linux**:
    a. Choose the appropriate instance type, and operating system.
    b. Assign a key pair for SSH access.
2. **Create and Attach a Security Group**:
    a. Allow inbound traffic on port 22 (SSH) for administrative access.

   b. Open port 80 (HTTP) or 443 (HTTPS) for web traffic.

3. **Verify Configuration**:
   a. Connect via SSH to confirm access.
   b. Deploy a web server, and test connectivity, using a browser.

Scaling with AWS Auto Scaling: Auto Scaling ensures that the right number of EC2 instances are running based on demand. It dynamically adjusts capacity to maintain performance, while optimizing costs.

Setting Up an Auto Scaling Group

1. **Create a Launch Template:** Define instance details such as AMI, instance type, and security settings.
2. **Create an Auto Scaling Group:**
   a. Set the desired, minimum, and maximum number of instances.
   b. Configure load balancing if required.
3. **Enable Health Checks:** Ensure that unhealthy instances are replaced automatically.

Lab: Creating an Auto Scaling Group

Objective: Configure an Auto Scaling Group to manage increased traffic efficiently.

Steps:

1. **Create a Launch Template:** Define instance settings, and specify the Security Group.
2. **Create an Auto Scaling Group:** Configure scaling policies based on CPU utilization or traffic load.
3. **Test Auto Scaling:**
   a. Generate artificial CPU load, using stress.
   b. Observe the automatic scaling of instances in response.

Setting Up CloudWatch Monitoring: Amazon CloudWatch provides real-time monitoring of AWS resources and applications, enabling proactive management of infrastructure.

Steps to Configure CloudWatch Monitoring

1. **Enable CloudWatch Metrics and Monitoring:** Collect system-level metrics such as CPU usage, memory consumption, and network traffic.
2. **Set Up CloudWatch Alarms:** Define threshold values for triggering alerts.
3. **Create a CloudWatch Dashboard:** Visualize key performance indicators.

Lab: Monitoring an EC2 Instance with CloudWatch

Objective: Configure CloudWatch alarms to track CPU utilization, and ensure optimal performance.

Steps:

1. **Enable Detailed Monitoring:** Activate detailed instance monitoring via the AWS Console.
2. **Create a CPU Utilization Alarm:** Set an alarm to trigger when CPU usage exceeds a defined threshold.

3. **Test the Alarm:**
   - Use stress to simulate high CPU usage.
   - Observe the alarm triggering, and any associated automated responses.

By following these labs and configurations, AWS administrators can effectively secure instances, scale applications dynamically, and monitor performance for optimal cloud resource management.

Deploying the Application in a Cloud Environment

Cloud computing has revolutionized how applications are built, deployed, and maintained. Deploying applications in a cloud environment not only provides scalability and high availability but also streamlines the process of continuous integration, delivery, and operational management. This guide dives deep into the key areas required for successful deployment, covering everything from setting up the cloud infrastructure to automating deployment workflows using modern practices like Infrastructure as Code (IaC) and CI/CD pipelines.

Introduction to Cloud Application Deployment

Cloud deployment is a transformative approach that leverages the flexibility of cloud services to run applications reliably and efficiently. By using cloud-based services, organizations can:

- **Scale resources dynamically** in response to traffic changes.
- **Improve reliability and availability** with redundancy and global distribution.
- **Optimize costs** by paying only for the resources used.
- **Implement continuous integration/continuous deployment (CI/CD)** to quickly adapt to market changes.

In this guide, we focus on AWS as the primary cloud provider. AWS offers a robust suite of tools and services that automate most aspects of deployment, thereby enabling developers and operation teams to focus on delivering value through the application, rather than managing infrastructure.

Setting Up the Cloud Environment

Choosing the Right AWS Services: A cloud environment on AWS is composed of diverse services that support several aspects of application deployment:

- **Amazon EC2 (Elastic Compute Cloud):** EC2 is used for hosting application servers. It provides scalable computing capacity, and allows us to choose the operating system, instance type, and even integrate with auto scaling for elasticity.
- **Amazon RDS (Relational Database Service):** RDS simplifies database management by automating tasks such as backups, patching, and scaling. It supports several database engines, including MySQL, PostgreSQL, and MariaDB.
- **Amazon S3 (Simple Storage Service):** S3 is used for storing static assets, backups, logs, and other unstructured data. It offers high durability and scalability with straightforward cost management.
- **Elastic Load Balancer (ELB):** ELB distributes incoming application traffic across multiple EC2 instances. It improves fault tolerance, and ensures that no single instance becomes a bottleneck.
- **Auto Scaling Groups (ASG):** ASG allows our application to automatically scale out or in based on demand. It ensures high availability and optimal performance by adding or removing instances as required.

Launching and Configuring an EC2 Instance

When deploying our application, the first step is to set up an EC2 instance that serves as our application server. The following is a detailed breakdown of the process:

Selecting the Operating System

- **Rocky Linux AMI:** Many organizations choose Rocky Linux for its enterprise-grade stability and open-source nature. Start by selecting the appropriate Amazon Machine Image (AMI) that suits our project's needs.

Instance Type and Configuration

- **Instance Type Example:** A t3.medium instance may be ideal for moderate workloads, offering a balance between cost and performance.
- **Networking and Security:**
  - Configure the Virtual Private Cloud (VPC) settings to ensure our instance is part of a secure network.
  - Attach the necessary IAM roles to grant access to AWS resources (like S3 and RDS) securely.
- **Connecting to our Instance:** After launching the instance, connect via SSH:
  `ssh -i your-key.pem ec2-user@your-instance-ip`

This command requires that we have our private key and the public IP address of the instance ready.

Software Installation and Environment Configuration

Once connected, configure our instance by updating the OS, and installing the necessary software:

  - `sudo dnf update -y`
  - `sudo dnf install -y httpd php mysql`
- **Apache Web Server:** Install and enable Apache to serve our web application:
  - `sudo systemctl enable --now httpd`
- **Additional Tools:** Install any additional tools, such as version control systems, application dependencies, or monitoring agents.

Deploying Infrastructure as Code (IaC)

Infrastructure as Code (IaC) transforms the way infrastructure is managed. By using tools such as Terraform, we can define, provision, and manage AWS resources with versioned configuration files.

Installing Terraform

Terraform is a popular IaC tool that allows us to create and manage AWS infrastructure reliably: **`sudo dnf install -y terraform`**

Ensure that we have the latest version to support new AWS services and features.

Creating a Terraform Configuration File (main.tf)

The following is an example of a basic Terraform configuration that sets up an EC2 instance:

```
provider "aws" {
  region = "us-east-1"
}

resource "aws_instance" "web" {
  ami           = "ami-0abcdef1234567890"  # Replace with your chosen AMI ID
```

```
    instance_type = "t3.micro"
    key_name      = "your-key"

    tags = {
      Name = "WebServerInstance"
    }
  }
```

Explanation:

a. The provider block sets the region.

b. The **aws_instance** resource creates a new EC2 instance with the specified AMI, instance type, and key.

c. Tags are added to help with resource management and identification.

Applying the Terraform Configuration

Initialize and apply our Terraform configuration:

a. **`terraform init`**

b. **`terraform apply -auto-approve`**

- **Terraform Init:** Downloads necessary plugins, and prepares the working directory.
- **Terraform Apply:** Provisions the resources as defined in our configuration file. The -auto-approve flag bypasses interactive approval.

Advanced Terraform Concepts

To ensure a production-grade deployment, consider the following Terraform practices:

- **State Management:** Store Terraform state files securely (for example, using AWS S3 with encryption and versioning).
- **Modules and Reusability:** Create reusable modules for common infrastructure components (such as VPCs, security groups, and databases).
- **Environment Segregation:** Use separate state files or workspaces for development, staging, and production environments.

Automating Deployment with AWS CodePipeline

Automation is key to reducing manual overhead, and minimizing errors during deployment. AWS CodePipeline is a fully managed continuous delivery service that helps automate build, test, and deployment phases.

Creating a Source Repository

The first step in setting up CodePipeline is to define our source code repository:

- **AWS CodeCommit:** A fully managed source control service that integrates directly with AWS.
- **GitHub:** A widely used platform with robust community support and integration capabilities.

Summarizing Tools per Deployment Phase

Problem

This chapter would benefit from a consolidated view of the AWS services and tools utilized at each deployment phase. This would serve as a quick reference to reinforce the reader's understanding, and aid in troubleshooting as well as design decisions.

Additionally, there is currently no table summarizing common deployment issues which can help anticipate and resolve frequent errors during the DevOps process.

Error	Possible Cause	Solution
Terraform apply fails with "access denied"	Insufficient IAM permissions	Verify IAM role includes `ec2:CreateInstance`, `s3:PutObject`.
CodePipeline fails at build stage	Incorrect `buildspec.yml` syntax	Check YAML formatting; ensure required dependencies are installed.
EC2 instance not accessible via SSH	Security group blocks port 22	Update security group to allow SSH from your IP (`--cidr your-ip/32`).
RDS backup not initiating	Automated backups disabled	Enable automated backups in RDS Console; set backup window.

Figure 17.2: *Troubleshooting Common Deployment Issues*

Deployment workflows often encounter errors that can disrupt or slow down application delivery. These challenges commonly arise from misconfigurations, missing IAM permissions, syntax errors in configuration files, or restrictive security settings. This table summarizes the most frequent issues, their likely causes, and recommended solutions, providing engineers with a quick diagnostic tool during infrastructure provisioning, application setup, and CI/CD automation. By using this reference, teams can proactively resolve problems, minimize downtime, and maintain reliable, repeatable deployment processes.

Solution

To address this, the following enhancements are proposed:

1. Add a reference table in the "**`Deploying the Application`**" section.
2. Map key AWS and system tools to each deployment phase, including provisioning, application setup, automation, monitoring, and security.
3. Include a troubleshooting table to document common deployment issues, their causes, and recommended solutions.

Phase	Tools and Services
Provisioning	AWS EC2, Terraform, Rocky Linux AMI, IAM Roles
Application Setup	Apache/Nginx, MariaDB, PHP, AWS RDS, S3
Automation	AWS CodePipeline, CodeBuild, CodeDeploy, Terraform
Monitoring	AWS CloudWatch, `htop`, `iostat`, `fail2ban`
Security	Security Groups, IAM Policies, MFA, CloudTrail, AWS Backup

Figure 17.3: *AWS and Third-Party Tools Aligned by Deployment Phase*

Effective cloud deployments rely on using the right tools at the right stage of the process. This table aligns core AWS services and complementary third-party tools with each deployment phase, covering provisioning, application setup, automation, monitoring, and security. By presenting tools in the context of their roles, the table clarifies how they contribute to building a reliable and scalable pipeline. This structured mapping helps DevOps teams select and integrate the most suitable solutions, ensuring consistency, efficiency, and control throughout the entire application lifecycle.

Adding Expected Command Outputs

Problem

Many critical commands used throughout the chapter—such as `terraform apply`, `aws ec2 describe-instances`, and CodePipeline setup commands—lack expected output examples. This absence can create uncertainty for readers, as they have no reference to confirm whether the command has executed successfully or returned the correct results.

Solution

To enhance clarity and confidence during deployment, expected outputs will be added for key commands in their respective sections. These examples help readers recognize successful command execution, and troubleshoot deviations.

Command outputs will be formatted, using the ***listings*** package for consistent presentation in code blocks, ensuring readability across formats.

Example: Terraform Apply Output

```
$ terraform apply -auto-approve
aws_instance.web: Creating...
aws_instance.web: Creation complete after 30s [id=i-0abcdef1234567890]

Apply complete! Resources: 1 added, 0 changed, 0 destroyed.
```

Listing 17.1: *Expected Output for Terraform Apply*

This listing demonstrates the standard output produced by the terraform apply command after a successful run. The output confirms that the declared infrastructure resources have been created or modified according to the configuration. A summary at the end shows the number of resources added, changed, or destroyed, while any defined output variables—such as the public IP address of a newly provisioned instance—are displayed for reference. Providing this expected output enables readers to validate that their deployment was applied correctly and that the infrastructure matches the intended state described in the chapter.

Example: AWS CLI EC2 Describe Instances

```
$ aws ec2 describe-instances --instance-ids i-0abcdef1234567890
{
    "Reservations": [{
        "Instances": [{
            "InstanceId": "i-0abcdef1234567890",
            "InstanceType": "t3.micro",
            "State": {"Name": "running"},
            "PublicIpAddress": "203.0.113.10"
        }]
    }]
}
```

Listing 17.2: *Expected Output for aws ec2 describe-instances*

This listing presents a sample output from the **`aws ec2 describe-instances`** command, which returns detailed metadata about EC2 instances in an AWS environment. The output includes attributes such as instance IDs, instance types, public and private IP addresses, availability zones, and current state (e.g., *running*). By reviewing this information, readers can confirm that their instances have been successfully provisioned and are operating as intended. Providing this expected output allows users to validate their setup against the chapter's deployment instructions and ensures alignment with the defined infrastructure.

Visual Aids for Cloud Infrastructure and Deployment Processes

Incorporating Visual Aids: To enhance understanding of complex processes such as deployment topologies, AWS CodePipeline workflows, and Terraform configurations, this chapter includes placeholders for diagrams and tables. These visual aids will illustrate the key interactions and workflows, making the concepts more accessible. Each placeholder includes a detailed description to guide the creation of the diagrams externally.

Deployment Architecture: The deployment architecture diagram illustrates the interactions between AWS services within a Virtual Private Cloud (VPC). It provides a high-level view of a scalable and secure application infrastructure.

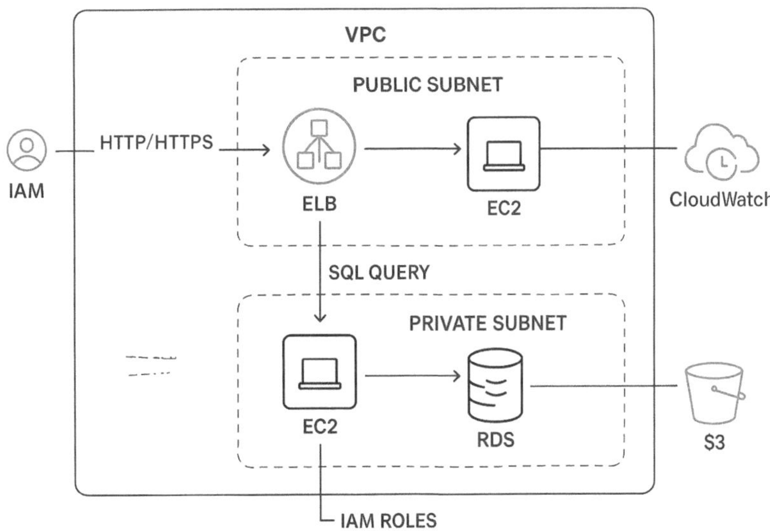

Figure 17.4: *Deployment Architecture* (EC2, RDS, S3, ELB, IAM, *and* CloudWatch)

This diagram illustrates a cloud-based deployment architecture built on AWS. The environment is organized within a VPC, divided into public and private subnets. An **Elastic Load Balancer (ELB)** in the public subnet distributes incoming HTTP/HTTPS requests to **EC2 instances** running in the private subnet. These instances handle application workloads while connecting to an **RDS database** for relational data management and an **S3 bucket** for storing and retrieving static or user-generated content. **IAM roles** enforce secure, role-based access control across services, ensuring that permissions align with the principle of least privilege. **CloudWatch** continuously monitors system performance, collecting metrics and logs for observability. Data flow is represented by directional arrows: client traffic through the ELB, application queries to RDS, file interactions with S3, and monitoring data streaming to CloudWatch.

Component	Role
AWS CodeCommit	Source code repository
AWS CodeBuild	Compiles application code, runs tests, prepares build artifacts
AWS CodeDeploy	Automates deployment of build artifacts
AWS CodePipeline	Orchestrates the CI/CD workflow
Amazon EC2	Compute capacity
Elastic Load Balancing (ELB)	Provides scalability
Amazon RDS	Provides database capability

Figure 17.5: *Roles of AWS Components in the Deployment Architecture*

This figure summarizes the functions of key AWS services within the deployment architecture. Each component contributes to automating, managing, and scaling application delivery. **`AWS CodeCommit`** provides a secure, version-controlled repository for source code and team collaboration. **`AWS CodeBuild`** compiles the code, executes tests, and generates build artifacts, while **`AWS CodeDeploy`** automates artifact deployment across environments such as Amazon EC2 or AWS Lambda. **`AWS CodePipeline`** orchestrates the CI/CD workflow, integrating source, build, test, and deployment stages into a streamlined process. Complementing these are infrastructure services such as **Amazon EC2** for compute capacity, **Elastic Load Balancing (ELB)** for traffic distribution and high availability, and **Amazon RDS** for reliable database management. Together, these services establish a cohesive and scalable deployment framework that enables continuous delivery and aligns with DevOps best practices on AWS.

Component Roles

CodePipeline Workflow: The AWS CodePipeline workflow visualizes the continuous integration and continuous deployment (CI/CD) process, showing the progression from source code to deployment.

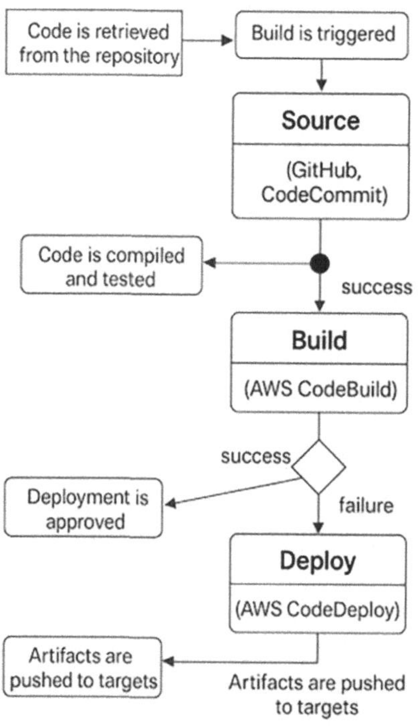

Figure 17.6: *CodePipeline Workflow*

This UML activity diagram illustrates the CodePipeline stages: Source, Build, and Deploy. The Source stage retrieves code from a repository (for example, GitHub or CodeCommit). The Build stage uses AWS CodeBuild to compile the code and run tests, producing artifacts. The Deploy stage uses AWS CodeDeploy to push artifacts to EC2 instances or other targets. Transitions between stages are shown with arrows, and decision nodes indicate success or failure paths. Annotations highlight key actions, such as code commits, build triggers, and deployment approvals.

Pipeline Stages

Stage Description: Terraform Configuration Flow

The Terraform configuration flow diagram clarifies the process of defining, managing, and applying infrastructure as code.

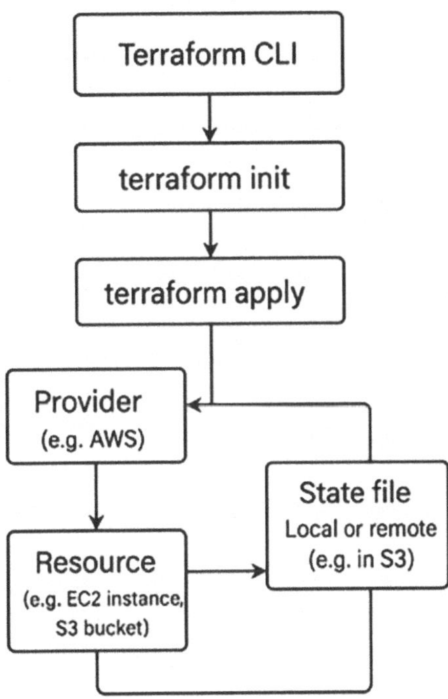

Figure 17.7: *Terraform Configuration Flow*

This UML diagram shows the Terraform workflow, including the provider, resource, and state management components. The provider block (for example, AWS) authenticates with the cloud provider. Resource blocks define infrastructure components (for example, EC2 instances, S3 buckets). The state file tracks the current infrastructure state, stored locally or remotely (for example, in S3). The diagram illustrates the sequence: `terraform init` initializes the provider, terraform plan previews changes, and terraform apply provisions resources. Arrows show data flow between the Terraform CLI, provider APIs, and state storage.

Terraform Commands

`Terraform init` Initializes provider and modules terraform plan Previews infrastructure changes terraform apply Provisions or updates resources.

Command	Purpose
`terraform init`	Initializes provider and modules
`terraform plan`	Previews infrastructure changes
`terraform apply`	Provisions or updates resources

Figure 17.8: *Key Terraform Commands and Their Purposes*

These placeholders and tables provide a framework for incorporating visual aids into the chapter. The diagrams, to be created externally, will enhance the reader's understanding of deployment topologies, CI/CD workflows, and infrastructure as code. The accompanying tables summarize critical components and processes, ensuring clarity and conciseness.

Defining the Build Process with AWS CodeBuild

AWS CodeBuild compiles our source code, runs tests, and produces deployable artifacts. The build process is defined in a **`buildspec.yml`** file:

```
version: 0.2

phases:
  install:
    commands:
      - echo "Installing dependencies..."
      - dnf install -y httpd php mysql
  pre_build:
    commands:
      - echo "Running pre-build tasks..."
  build:
    commands:
      - echo "Building the application..."
  post_build:
    commands:
      - echo "Build completed."

artifacts:
  files:
    - '**/*'
```

- **Phases:**
  a. **`Install`:** Installs all necessary software and dependencies.
  b. **`Pre_build`:** Prepares the environment.
  c. **`Build`:** Contains the compilation or build commands.
  d. **`Post_build`:** Executes any finalization tasks.
- **Artifacts:** Define what files to output for subsequent deployment steps.

Deployment Strategies: EC2 and ECS

After building our application, deployment can target either EC2 instances or containerized environments such as Elastic Container Service (ECS).

- **Using AWS CodeDeploy for EC2:** CodeDeploy automates the deployment process to EC2 instances with support for blue-green and rolling deployments, reducing downtime and risk.
- **Deploying with ECS:** For containerized applications, ECS provides orchestration and management of Docker containers, integrating seamlessly with CodePipeline and CodeBuild.

Best Practices for Cloud Deployment

Successful cloud deployments require more than just setting up infrastructure; they demand ongoing maintenance, monitoring, and adherence to best practices. Here are some key practices:

Security and IAM

- **IAM Roles and Policies:** Use the principle of least privilege when assigning IAM roles. Ensure that each service or instance only has the permissions necessary to perform its tasks.
- **Secure Access:** Utilize SSH keys and multi-factor authentication (MFA) for accessing instances and managing AWS resources.

Monitoring and Logging

- **CloudWatch Integration:** Set up CloudWatch to monitor logs, performance metrics, and system events. Configure alarms to notify us of potential issues.
- **Centralized Logging:** Aggregate logs using AWS CloudWatch Logs or third-party services like ELK Stack (Elasticsearch, Logstash, Kibana) for comprehensive analysis and troubleshooting.

Backup and Disaster Recovery

- **Regular Backups:** Automate backups of our databases and static assets using AWS Backup or native RDS backup features.
- **Multi-AZ Deployments:** Ensure high availability by deploying resources across multiple availability zones (AZs). This minimizes downtime in case of an AZ failure.
- **Disaster Recovery (DR) Plans:** Develop and test DR strategies, including failover procedures and data recovery plans, to quickly restore operations in the event of a catastrophic incident.

Cost Optimization

- **Auto Scaling:** Leverage Auto Scaling Groups to match our resource usage with demand, avoiding over-provisioning.
- **Spot Instances:** Use spot instances for non-critical workloads to reduce costs, while balancing against the risk of interruptions.
- **Right-Sizing:** Regularly review and adjust instance sizes and storage capacities based on performance metrics and utilization.

Additional Considerations for Production-Grade Deployment

Deploying an application in a production environment requires a holistic view that goes beyond initial setup and deployment. Consider these additional topics:

Continuous Integration/Continuous Delivery (CI/CD)

- **Pipeline Integration:** Integrate AWS CodePipeline with other CI/CD tools (such as Jenkins, GitLab CI, or CircleCI) for a seamless development-to-deployment workflow.

- **Automated Testing:** Incorporate unit, integration, and end-to-end tests in our pipeline to catch issues early and maintain code quality.
- **Rollback Strategies:** Define clear rollback strategies and automated triggers in the event of a failed deployment to minimize downtime and disruption.

Performance and Load Testing

- **Stress Testing:** Simulate high loads using tools like Apache JMeter or AWS's own testing services to ensure our system can handle peak traffic.
- **Benchmarking:** Continuously monitor performance and compare it against benchmarks to identify and address bottlenecks.

Containerization and Microservices Architecture

- **Containers:** For applications built as microservices, consider containerization using Docker. AWS ECS and EKS (Elastic Kubernetes Service) provide robust orchestration and scaling solutions.
- **Service Mesh:** Implement a service mesh such as AWS App Mesh to manage communication between microservices, providing observability and security across the entire architecture.

Documentation and Process Automation

- **Runbooks and SOPs:** Develop runbooks for routine tasks and incident management. Document the entire deployment process to ensure consistency and knowledge transfer.
- **Infrastructure Automation:** Beyond Terraform, consider using AWS CloudFormation or Ansible for automating additional aspects of infrastructure management.

Future-Proofing our Architecture

- **Serverless Options:** Explore serverless architectures (for example, AWS Lambda, API Gateway) for parts of our application that can benefit from event-driven scaling.
- **Hybrid Architectures:** Consider a hybrid approach that leverages both traditional EC2 instances and managed services to optimize cost, performance, and management overhead.

Deploying an application in a cloud environment such as AWS offers significant advantages in terms of scalability, availability, and cost optimization. By combining well-planned infrastructure setup with automated deployment practices like Terraform and AWS CodePipeline, we can achieve a robust, production-ready environment. Adopting best practices–ranging from strict IAM policies to comprehensive monitoring and backup strategies–further enhances the resilience and security of our application.

This comprehensive guide has explored:

- The critical steps for setting up and configuring cloud resources.
- The use of IaC to ensure consistency and repeatability.
- Automation strategies for continuous integration and delivery.
- Best practices to secure, monitor, and optimize our cloud deployment.

Implementing these strategies will not only streamline our deployment process but also empower our team to build, manage, and scale applications effectively in a dynamic cloud landscape.

Hands-on Project: Complete an End-to-End Cloud Deployment Using AWS

Securing cloud deployments is crucial to ensuring data integrity, protecting infrastructure, and preventing unauthorized access. AWS provides a variety of security mechanisms to enhance the protection of cloud-based applications. This section expands on key security best practices, detailing their implementation and importance in a real-world deployment.

Restrict SSH Access

Unrestricted SSH access can expose our cloud infrastructure to brute-force attacks and unauthorized access attempts. Restricting SSH access ensures that only trusted IP addresses can connect to the server.

Implementation Steps

1. **Use Security Groups:**
   a. Navigate to the **`AWS EC2 Console`**.
   b. Select the instance and go to the **`Security Groups`** tab.
   c. Edit the **`Inbound Rules`** and limit SSH (port 22) to specific IP addresses.

      Example command to modify **`Security Group`** rules:

      ```
      aws ec2 authorize-security-group-ingress --group-id sg-123456 --protocol tcp
      --port 22 --cidr 203.0.113.0/32
      ```
   d. Replace 203.0.113.0/32 with our trusted IP address.
2. **Use AWS Systems Manager Session Manager**:
   a. Instead of allowing direct SSH access, use AWS Session Manager, which allows secure access without opening inbound ports.
   b. Install the SSM agent on our instance and configure IAM roles accordingly.

Best Practices

- Use key-based authentication instead of passwords.
- Regularly rotate SSH keys.
- Disable root login and enforce user-based SSH authentication.

Enable Multi-Factor Authentication (MFA)

MFA adds an extra layer of security to AWS accounts by requiring an additional authentication factor (such as a mobile device), along with a password.

Implementation Steps

1. Navigate to **`AWS IAM Console`**.
2. Click on **`Users`**, select the user, and go to the **`Security credentials`** tab.
3. Click **`Manage MFA`** and follow the instructions to enable virtual MFA (for instance, using Google Authenticator).

Best Practices

- Enforce MFA for all IAM users with administrative privileges.
- Use hardware MFA devices for added security.
- Regularly audit MFA-enabled accounts.

Use IAM Roles and Policies

IAM roles and policies follow the principle of least privilege, ensuring that users and services only have access to the resources necessary for their tasks.

Implementation Steps

- **Create IAM Roles:**
  a. Navigate to **`AWS IAM Console`** > **`Roles`**.
  b. Click **`Create Role`** and choose the appropriate AWS service (for example, EC2, Lambda).
  c. Attach predefined policies or create custom ones with JSON policies.

Example of a least privilege policy for accessing an S3 bucket:

```
{
  "Version": "2012-10-17",
  "Statement": [
    {
      "Effect": "Allow",
      "Action": "s3:ListBucket",
      "Resource": "arn:aws:s3:::my-secure-bucket"
    }
  ]
}
```

Simplifying Complex Concepts

Problem

Certain AWS services such as **IAM Roles**, **Auto Scaling**, and **CodePipeline** can be intimidating to beginners due to their technical depth and configuration complexity. These topics often introduce a steep learning curve for those new to cloud deployment.

Solution

To make these concepts more accessible:

- **Provide introductory summaries** before delving into technical details.
- **Use visual aids** such as decision trees to explain dynamic behaviors like Auto Scaling.
- **Present simplified comparison tables**, such as distinguishing IAM Roles from IAM Policies, to aid comprehension.

IAM Roles vs. Policies Summary

Understanding the difference between **`IAM Roles`** and **`IAM Policies`** is fundamental to managing AWS permissions. The following table clarifies the distinctions:

Aspect	IAM Role	IAM Policy
Purpose	Assign permissions to AWS services or users	Define specific permissions (actions, resources)
Example	EC2 role for S3 access	`s3:ListBucket` permission
Attachment	Attached to EC2 instance or Lambda	Attached to roles, users, or groups

Figure 17.9: *IAM Roles vs. Policies*

This table highlights the key differences between IAM roles and IAM policies in AWS Identity and Access Management. IAM **`roles`** function as identities with defined permissions that can be temporarily assumed by users, services, or applications to access AWS resources in a controlled manner. IAM **`policies`**, on the other hand, are JSON-based documents that explicitly define permissions by specifying which actions are allowed or denied on particular resources. Policies are attached to roles, users, or groups, providing the rules that govern access. Understanding the distinction between these two elements allows administrators to implement secure, scalable, and least-privilege access models that align with organizational needs and compliance requirements.

Auto Scaling Policy Decision Tree

To better understand when and how **`Auto Scaling`** triggers scale-out or scale-in actions, the following decision tree offers a visual representation.

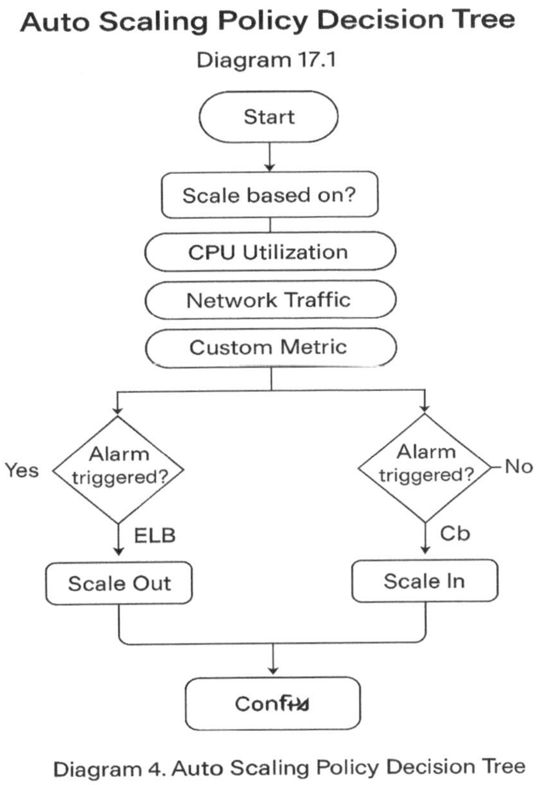

Diagram 4. Auto Scaling Policy Decision Tree

Figure 17.10: *Auto Scaling Policy Decision Tree*

This diagram illustrates the logical flow behind AWS Auto Scaling decisions. It begins with selecting the appropriate scaling metric–CPU utilization, network traffic, or a custom-defined CloudWatch metric. Based on this input, the system checks for triggered alarms. If an alarm is activated, Auto Scaling initiates a scale-out action, often coordinated with Elastic Load Balancing (ELB) to distribute traffic efficiently. If no alarm is triggered, the system evaluates the need to scale in, reducing resources to optimize cost and performance. This visual aid simplifies the decision-making process and helps users understand the conditions under which scaling actions are executed automatically.

This flowchart guides administrators in choosing appropriate scaling actions based on monitored metrics:

a. CPU Utilization

b. Network Traffic

c. Custom CloudWatch Metrics

It illustrates how Auto Scaling works in conjunction with ***Elastic Load Balancing* (ELB)** and ***CloudWatch alarms*** to manage resource demand dynamically.

Case Study: Deploying a Production Web Application on AWS

This real-world case study walks through the deployment of a production-grade ***e-commerce web application*** using AWS services and ***Rocky Linux*** on EC2. It is tailored for ***beginner-level cloud engineers and Linux administrators***, providing both conceptual understanding and practical implementation steps.

Scenario

We are tasked with deploying an e-commerce website that must be **highly available, scalable,** and **cost-effective**. The stack consists of:

- **Front-end and backend:** Apache + PHP on Rocky Linux EC2 instances.
- **Database:** MariaDB hosted on Amazon RDS.
- **Static content:** Images, CSS, and JavaScript hosted in S3.
- **Traffic Management:** Load balancing with ELB.
- **High availability:** Auto Scaling Group with min 2, max 4 EC2 instances.
- **Monitoring:** CloudWatch for system metrics and alarms.

Component	Description
EC2	Hosts Apache and PHP web server on Rocky Linux (`t3.medium`)
RDS MariaDB	Managed relational database for product and customer data
S3 Bucket	Stores static content such as images and stylesheets
Elastic Load Balancer (ELB)	Distributes HTTP traffic across instances
Auto Scaling Group (ASG)	Automatically scales EC2 instances based on load
CloudWatch	Monitors system metrics like CPU; triggers alarms

Figure 17.11: *Architecture Components*

This table summarizes the core AWS and application-level components that support the deployment of the e-commerce web application. Each element is defined by its role within the overall architecture, highlighting how these services integrate to deliver scalability, availability, and performance. Compute resources are provided by **Amazon EC2** instances running Rocky Linux with Apache and PHP, while **Amazon RDS (MariaDB)** ensures reliable and consistent database management. **Amazon S3** serves as a cost-effective solution for hosting static assets, and the **Elastic Load Balancer (ELB)** distributes incoming requests across servers to maintain responsiveness. The **Auto Scaling Group** dynamically adjusts server capacity based on demand, ensuring efficient resource utilization. Finally, **Amazon CloudWatch** provides monitoring, logging, and alerting to maintain operational visibility. Together, these components form a resilient, production-ready cloud architecture tailored for modern e-commerce applications.

Step-by-Step Deployment

Step 1: Provision Infrastructure with Terraform

As a best practice, use **IaC** with Terraform.

`main.tf snippet` (simplified for clarity):

```
hcl
provider "aws" {
  region = "us-east-1"
}

resource "aws_instance" "web" {
  ami           = "ami-xxxxxxxx" # Rocky Linux AMI ID
  instance_type = "t3.medium"
  key_name      = "your-key"

  user_data = file("setup.sh") # Installs Apache + PHP

  tags = {
    Name = "RockyLinux-Web"
  }
}
```

Ensure our key pair is created in advance and SSH access (port 22) is allowed in our security group.

Step 2: Set Up Apache and PHP on EC2

Create a **`setup.sh`** script for provisioning:

```
#!/bin/bash
yum install -y httpd php php-mysqlnd
systemctl enable httpd
systemctl start httpd
echo "<?php phpinfo(); ?>" > /var/www/html/index.php
```

Security note: *Harden our server by disabling unnecessary PHP modules and keeping system packages updated (`**yum update -y**`).*

Step 3: Configure MariaDB on Amazon RDS

Use the AWS Console or Terraform to provision an RDS instance:

a. **Engine**: MariaDB

b. **Public access**: No (private subnet)

c. **Create database**: **`ecommerce_db`**

Example connection from EC2 instance in PHP:

```
$mysqli = new mysqli("rds-endpoint", "username", "password", "ecommerce_db");
```

Use IAM roles and Security Groups to allow EC2 access to RDS securely without exposing ports to the public.

Step 4: Store Static Content in S3

Upload our assets:

```
aws s3 cp ./assets/ s3://your-bucket-name/ --recursive --acl public-read
```

In our PHP code, reference static files like:

```
<img src="https://your-bucket-name.s3.amazonaws.com/images/logo.png">
```

Use S3 Lifecycle Rules to archive or delete old assets automatically and reduce costs.

Step 5: Set Up Load Balancer and Auto Scaling

a. Create a **Launch Template** with the EC2 configuration.

b. Define an **Auto Scaling Group:**

  i. **Min:** 2 instances

  ii. **Max:** 4 instances

c. Scaling policy: Based on CPU > 70%

d. Attach the **Application Load Balancer (ALB)** to the group.

Monitor the **/var/log/httpd/access_log** *and error logs for load testing and performance tuning.*

Step 6: Enable CloudWatch Monitoring and Alarms

Set up metrics and alarms:

- `CPU Utilization > 70%** → trigger scale-out`
- `CPU Utilization < 30%** → trigger scale-in`

We can also create alarms for:

- Disk usage (`**df -h**`)
- Memory usage (with **CloudWatch** agent)

Install the CloudWatch Agent to send custom metrics:

a. `sudo yum install amazon-cloudwatch-agent`

b. `sudo /opt/aws/amazon-cloudwatch-agent/bin/amazon-cloudwatch-agent-config-wizard`

Validation Steps

1. **Access** the web app via the ALB DNS name: **http://<load-balancer-dns>**

2. **Test Scaling:**

Use a load testing tool like ApacheBench:

```
ab -n 1000 -c 50 http://<load-balancer-dns>/index.php
```

Monitor CloudWatch to observe scale-out events.

3. **Verify Monitoring:** Navigate to **CloudWatch** > **Alarms**.

Ensure alarms are triggered as expected.

Final Notes for Administrators

- **Regularly patch** Rocky Linux and PHP packages (`**yum update**`).
- **Use IAM Roles** to avoid hardcoding AWS credentials.
- **Apply security group rules** for the principle of least privilege.
- **Back up RDS data with** automated snapshots.
- **Log all access with CloudTrail** and enable **AWS Config** for compliance.

Best Practices

- Regularly review IAM policies for over-permissioned users.
- Use IAM Groups to manage permissions, instead of assigning permissions to individual users.
- Enable **`AWS IAM Access Analyzer`** to identify unused permissions.

4. **Enable HTTPS for Secure Communication**

Using HTTPS encrypts data in transit, preventing attackers from intercepting sensitive information. AWS provides **AWS Certificate Manager (ACM)** to manage SSL/TLS certificates.

Implementation Steps

a. Navigate to **`AWS Certificate Manager`** and request a new certificate.

b. Validate the certificate, using email or DNS records.

c. Attach the certificate to an **`Application Load Balancer`** **(ALB)** or **`CloudFront distribution`**.

d. Enforce HTTPS by redirecting HTTP requests to HTTPS.

Best Practices

- Use **`let us encrypt`** as an alternative for free SSL certificates.
- Implement **HSTS (HTTP Strict Transport Security)** to enforce HTTPS.
- Regularly renew and rotate SSL/TLS certificates.

Monitor Logs and Security Events with AWS CloudTrail and CloudWatch

Continuous monitoring helps detect and mitigate security threats in real-time.

Implementation Steps

a. **Enable AWS CloudTrail:**

   i. Navigate to **`CloudTrail Console`**, and create a new trail.

   ii. Store logs in **`Amazon S3`** for long-term retention.

b. **Enable CloudWatch Alarms for Security Events:**

```
aws cloudwatch put-metric-alarm --alarm-name UnauthorizedLoginAttempt \
--metric-name FailedLogins --namespace AWS/CloudTrail \
--statistic Sum --threshold 5 --comparison-operator GreaterThanOrEqual
ToThreshold \
--evaluation-periods 1 --alarm-actions arn:aws:sns:us-east-1:123456789012:
SecurityAlerts
```

Best Practices

- Enable AWS GuardDuty for threat detection.
- Use Amazon Detective for deeper investigation of security anomalies.
- Regularly review IAM access logs and CloudTrail logs.

Implement Backup Strategies

Backup strategies ensure business continuity and data protection in case of system failures, accidental deletions, or cyberattacks.

Implementation Steps

a. **Enable Automated Backups for RDS:** Navigate to **`RDS Console`**, and modify the instance to enable automated backups.

b. **Configure S3 Lifecycle Policies for Log Retention:**

```
{
  "Rules": [
    {
      "ID": "DeleteOldLogs",
      "Status": "Enabled",
      "Prefix": "logs/",
      "Expiration": { "Days": 30 }
    }
  ]
}
```

c. Use AWS Backup for EC2 Snapshots:

   i. Navigate to **AWS Backup Console** and create a backup plan.

   ii. Define retention policies, and enable cross-region backups.

Best Practices

- Test backups periodically by restoring them to a separate environment.
- Use **AWS KMS** for encrypting backup data.
- Enable **Cross-Region Replication (CRR)** for disaster recovery planning.

By implementing these security best practices, organizations can significantly reduce risks associated with cloud deployments. AWS offers a comprehensive set of tools to enhance security, monitor threats, and ensure compliance with best practices. Regular security audits, proactive monitoring, and adherence to the principle of least privilege will help maintain a secure and resilient cloud environment.

Conclusion

In this chapter, we successfully deployed a complete application, using Rocky Linux on AWS, covering necessary steps such as launching an EC2 instance, configuring a web server and database, and implementing security measures. Through this hands-on project, we gained practical experience in deploying cloud-based applications, while understanding scalability and monitoring strategies. This end-to-end deployment serves as a foundation for real-world cloud infrastructure management, reinforcing best practices in security, automation, and resource optimization.

Looking Ahead to Chapter 18: As cloud computing continues to evolve, the role of Rocky Linux in enterprise and cloud-native environments becomes increasingly significant. In the next chapter, we will explore the future of server management, emerging innovations in cloud technology, and the essential skills required for modern system administrators to stay ahead in this rapidly changing landscape.

Points to Remember

- Deploying a Rocky Linux server on AWS requires configuring networking, storage, and security settings for optimal performance and reliability.
- Setting up a web server and database ensures a functional and scalable cloud-based application.

- Security groups and IAM roles play a crucial role in controlling access, and protecting cloud resources.
- Auto Scaling and monitoring enhance system availability, ensuring resilience against traffic fluctuations.
- Automating deployments, using AWS tools improve efficiency, security, and resource management in cloud environments.

Multiple Choice Questions

1. What is a key benefit of deploying Rocky Linux on AWS with high availability?
   a. Improved security
   b. Continuous uptime and fault tolerance
   c. Faster file transfers
   d. Lower hardware costs
2. Which tool is commonly used for load balancing in a Rocky Linux cloud deployment?
   a. `iptables`
   b. `HAProxy`
   c. `rsync`
   d. `systemd`
3. What is the primary purpose of AWS Auto Scaling Groups in cloud deployments?
   a. Automating instance resizing based on demand
   b. Encrypting network traffic
   c. Managing DNS records
   d. Monitoring CPU temperatures
4. Which AWS service is best suited for distributing traffic among multiple EC2 instances?
   a. AWS CloudWatch
   b. AWS S3
   c. AWS Elastic Load Balancer (ELB)
   d. AWS Lambda
5. What is the main advantage of using Infrastructure as Code (IaC) in cloud-based Rocky Linux deployments?
   a. Manual server provisioning
   b. Automated and repeatable deployments
   c. Reduced need for monitoring
   d. Higher energy consumption

6. Which feature ensures that Rocky Linux remains available in case of an EC2 instance failure?
   a. High availability clustering
   b. Disabling firewall rules
   c. Increasing swap memory
   d. Running processes as root
7. What is the role of a reverse proxy in a cloud-based load balancing setup?
   a. Managing database queries
   b. Distributing client requests among backend servers
   c. Encrypting disk storage
   d. Disabling network interfaces
8. How does AWS Systems Manager help in managing Rocky Linux deployments?
   a. Provides remote management and automation capabilities
   b. Replaces the need for SSH access
   c. Acts as a replacement for the Linux kernel
   d. Reduces server costs by 50%
9. What is an example of a high availability storage solution for a Rocky Linux cloud environment?
   a. NFS without replication
   b. GlusterFS or Amazon EFS
   c. Using only a local SSD
   d. Disabling RAID configurations
10. Why is monitoring crucial in cloud-based Rocky Linux deployments?
    a. To increase manual intervention
    b. To proactively detect and address performance issues
    c. To disable firewalls automatically
    d. To prevent all system failures completely

Answers

1. b
2. b
3. a
4. c
5. b
6. a
7. b

8. a
9. b
10. b

Questions

1. What are the key considerations when configuring networking for a Rocky Linux instance on AWS?
2. How does AWS Auto Scaling help manage traffic during high-demand periods for Rocky Linux applications?
3. What are the differences between AWS Elastic Load Balancer (ELB), and a traditional load balancer in terms of functionality and setup?
4. How does AWS CloudWatch integrate with Rocky Linux to monitor server performance and resource utilization?
5. What are the benefits of using Infrastructure as Code (IaC) in the deployment of cloud-based applications on AWS?
6. What are the best practices for setting up security groups in AWS for a Rocky Linux-based web server?
7. How does a reverse proxy improve the performance and scalability of web applications deployed on Rocky Linux?
8. What are the steps involved in creating a high availability setup, using Rocky Linux on AWS?
9. How does AWS Systems Manager help automate administrative tasks on a Rocky Linux instance?
10. What are some common challenges when deploying a Rocky Linux application in a cloud environment, and how can they be mitigated?

Key Terms

- **Standard Server Deployment:** The process of configuring a Rocky Linux server with essential services, networking, and security settings on AWS.
- **High Availability (HA):** Techniques to ensure continuous uptime and fault tolerance for applications deployed on Rocky Linux, including clustering and failover mechanisms.
- **Load Balancer:** A tool that distributes network traffic across multiple instances to prevent bottlenecks, and improve scalability in cloud deployments.
- **Infrastructure as Code (IaC):** The practice of automating server provisioning and deployment, using tools such as Terraform for managing cloud-based infrastructure.
- **Auto Scaling Groups (ASG):** AWS feature that automatically adjusts the number of Rocky Linux instances based on real-time demand, ensuring scalability and reliability.
- **Reverse Proxy:** A server that routes incoming client requests to backend services, optimizing performance and adding a layer of security for cloud applications.
- **AWS Systems Manager:** A cloud-based service that helps automate tasks such as configuration management, patching, and monitoring for Rocky Linux instances.

- **GlusterFS/Ceph:** Distributed storage solutions used to provide high availability and scalability for cloud applications on Rocky Linux.
- **Elastic Load Balancer (ELB):** An AWS service designed to manage traffic distribution across multiple EC2 instances, enhancing performance and availability in Rocky Linux deployments.
- **CloudWatch:** AWS service used for monitoring the performance of cloud applications, including tracking logs, resource utilization, and system health for Rocky Linux instances.

CHAPTER 18

The Future of Rocky Linux and Server Management

Introduction

The world of server management and cloud computing is evolving, with **automation**, **containerization**, and **cloud-native technologies** becoming standard. As businesses shift towards **hybrid** and **multi-cloud** strategies, operating systems such as **Rocky Linux** provide **stability**, **security**, and **enterprise-level performance**.

Rocky Linux has positioned itself as a reliable, community-driven replacement for **CentOS**, offering long-term support and compatibility with **Red Hat Enterprise Linux (RHEL)**. This chapter explores the future of **Rocky Linux** and server administration, detailing innovations in **cloud computing**, **virtualization**, and **open-source development**. With the adoption of **edge computing** and **AI-driven automation**, system administrators must evolve their skill sets.

Structure

This chapter covers the following topics:

- The Role of Rocky Linux in the Cloud-Native World
- Innovations in Server and Cloud Technology
- Skills for Future System Administrators
- Future Roadmap of Rocky Linux and its Ecosystem

The Role of Rocky Linux in the Cloud-Native World

Rocky Linux, a community-driven, RHEL-compatible operating system, is pivotal in cloud-native environments due to its stability, security, and support for containerization (Docker, Kubernetes), CI/CD pipelines (Jenkins, GitHub Actions), and cloud platforms (AWS, Azure, GCP). It supports hybrid and multi-cloud strategies, edge computing, and AI-driven automation, making it ideal for modern IT infrastructures.

Practical Examples

Docker Installation:

- `sudo dnf install docker-ce`
- `sudo systemctl enable -now docker`
- `docker run hello-world`

Kubernetes Deployment:

- `sudo dnf install -y`
- `kubeadm kubelet kubectl`
- `sudo kubeadm init.`

AWS EC2 Integration

Launch Rocky Linux instances, and deploy containerized applications.

In today's dynamic IT landscape, the shift towards **cloud-native technologies** is driving businesses to modernize their infrastructures. "*Cloud-native*" refers to a design philosophy and approach that leverages the cloud's elasticity, flexibility, and scalability. This approach primarily involves using **containers**, **microservices**, **DevOps**, and **orchestration platforms** such as Kubernetes to build, deploy, and manage applications.

Rocky Linux, a community-driven enterprise operating system, plays a significant role in this transformation. Originally developed as an alternative to Red Hat Enterprise Linux (RHEL), it offers a stable, secure, and open-source environment suitable for cloud-native workloads.

Advantages of Rocky Linux

- **Stability and Compatibility:** As a binary-compatible fork of RHEL, Rocky Linux benefits from its enterprise-level stability, which makes it ideal for critical production environments.
- **Security and Long-Term Support:** With Long-term Support (LTS), Rocky Linux ensures continuous security updates and patches, a crucial feature for cloud-native systems where security is paramount.
- **Containerized Workloads:** As containerization gains ground, Rocky Linux's compatibility with Docker and Kubernetes makes it an excellent choice for deploying and managing containerized applications.

Cloud-Native Infrastructure

Cloud-native infrastructure emphasizes scalability, automation, and flexibility. For system administrators, managing cloud-native environments involves orchestrating **containers** with platforms like Kubernetes, ensuring high availability, and automating deployment pipelines, using CI/CD tools.

Practical Benefits of Rocky Linux in Cloud-Native Environments

As organizations increasingly migrate their workloads to the cloud, the choice of a stable, secure, and community-supported operating system becomes critical to ensuring performance, scalability, and long-term support. Rocky Linux has rapidly emerged as a reliable alternative in enterprise environments, especially after CentOS shifted away from its traditional support model. Its compatibility with Red Hat Enterprise Linux (RHEL), combined with strong community backing, makes it particularly attractive for cloud-native deployments. This section explores the **practical benefits of using Rocky Linux in cloud-native environments,** highlighting how it meets the evolving demands of modern infrastructure.

Containerization with Docker

Docker is a pivotal technology for cloud-native environments, enabling developers to build, ship, and run applications in containers. **Rocky Linux** integrates seamlessly with Docker, ensuring users can easily build containers and deploy them in production environments.

Practical Example:

Install Docker on Rocky Linux:

- `sudo dnf install docker-ce`
- `sudo systemctl enable --now docker`

Run a test container:

- `docker run hello-world`

Create a Docker container for a web application:

```
# Dockerfile for a simple web app
FROM rockylinux:8
RUN dnf install -y httpd
COPY index.html /var/www/html/
CMD ["httpd", "-D", "FOREGROUND"]
```

Build and run the container:

- `docker build -t web-app`
- `docker run -d -p 8080:80 web-app`

This demonstrates how **Rocky Linux** can be leveraged to create and run containers, offering portability and consistency across environments.

Kubernetes and Orchestration

In modern cloud-native environments, orchestrating containerized applications at scale is a key requirement. Kubernetes, the leading container orchestration platform, is widely used for managing clusters of containers.

Practical Example:

Deploy Kubernetes on Rocky Linux, using `kubeadm`:

- `sudo dnf install -y kubeadm kubelet kubectl`
- `sudo systemctl enable --now kubelet`

Initialize a Kubernetes cluster:

- `sudo kubeadm init`

Rocky Linux provides the necessary environment for running Kubernetes, allowing organizations to deploy, manage, and scale applications across a cluster.

Integration with Cloud Platforms

In today's rapidly evolving IT landscape, seamless integration with major cloud platforms is no longer a luxury, it is a necessity. Organizations demand flexibility, automation, and interoperability to deploy, manage, and scale applications across diverse cloud environments. Operating systems such as Rocky Linux are increasingly being adopted for their ability to integrate effectively with public, private, and hybrid cloud infrastructures. This section delves into the **integration capabilities of Rocky Linux with leading cloud platforms,** illustrating how it supports efficient cloud-native operations and infrastructure-as-code practices.

Cloud-Native Integration with AWS

Rocky Linux is optimized for integration with cloud platforms such as **AWS**, enabling users to take advantage of cloud-native features such as Auto Scaling, Elastic Load Balancing, and Amazon S3.

Practical Example:

Launching an EC2 instance with Rocky Linux:

- Choose **Rocky Linux** from the EC2 instance marketplace.
- Select instance type, configure network settings, and launch.

Once the instance is running, we can deploy a **containerized** application or manage services in the cloud.

Continuous Integration and Deployment (CI/CD)

Cloud-native applications demand automated and continuous delivery pipelines to ensure rapid and safe deployments. Rocky Linux integrates well with popular CI/CD tools like Jenkins, GitLab CI, and GitHub Actions.

Practical Example:

Install Jenkins on Rocky Linux:

1. `sudo dnf install java-1.8.0-openjdk`
2. `sudo dnf install wget`
3. `wget -q -O - https://pkg.jenkins.io/jenkins.io.key | sudo tee /etc/yum.repos.d/jenkins.repo`
4. `sudo dnf install jenkins`
5. `sudo systemctl enable --now jenkins`

Set up Jenkins to automatically build and deploy containers to our Kubernetes or Docker-based infrastructure.

Rocky Linux, being a stable and robust platform, ensures our CI/CD pipelines are seamless and efficient.

Future of Rocky Linux in Cloud-Native Environments

As the demand for cloud-native technologies continues to grow, **Rocky Linux** is poised to remain a key player in **hybrid cloud** and **edge computing** environments.

Edge Computing

Edge computing extends cloud capabilities to the edge of the network, closer to where data is generated. As industries such as manufacturing, healthcare, and retail move towards edge computing, Rocky Linux can be deployed in lightweight, distributed edge environments to manage tasks such as data processing, storage, and analytics.

Practical Example:

Deploying Rocky Linux in an edged environment, using containers ensures applications run closer to the source of data, reducing latency and bandwidth usage. With **Docker** and **Kubernetes**, administrators can deploy containerized workloads in edge environments with ease.

AI and Automation:

The future of cloud-native technologies will also be driven by **AI-driven automation**. As AI tools and services become more integrated with cloud platforms, system administrators must adapt by leveraging automation for tasks, such as scaling, fault tolerance, and predictive maintenance.

Rocky Linux's stability and support for automation tools like **Ansible**, **Chef**, and **Puppet** make it an ideal choice for managing complex cloud-native infrastructures. Additionally, AI tools integrated into platforms such as **AWS**, **Google Cloud**, and **Azure** can be used to manage cloud resources based on predicted demand, further enhancing automation.

Rocky Linux in Hybrid and Multi-Cloud Environments

In hybrid and multi-cloud architectures, where workloads span across on-premises infrastructure and multiple cloud providers, **Rocky Linux** provides the necessary support to ensure portability and consistent behavior across environments.

Hybrid Cloud

Hybrid cloud enables businesses to combine the best of on-premises and public cloud infrastructures. **Rocky Linux** plays a critical role in hybrid environments by ensuring that workloads can seamlessly move between public clouds, private data centers, and edge environments.

Practical Example:

Rocky Linux can be deployed both on-premises and in **AWS** or **Azure** to provide a unified operating environment, allowing businesses to run mission-critical applications locally, while leveraging the cloud for scalability.

Multi-Cloud

In multi-cloud environments, businesses distribute workloads across multiple cloud platforms to avoid vendor lock-in and enhance redundancy. **Rocky Linux** facilitates this by offering consistent performance and compatibility with multiple cloud providers.

Practical Example:

Rocky Linux can be used in **Google Cloud** for machine learning workloads, and in **AWS** for data storage and web hosting, ensuring consistency in operations across platforms.

Hence, **Rocky Linux** is an essential component of the cloud-native world, offering stability, security, and flexibility to businesses adopting modern IT strategies. Its seamless integration with **Docker**, **Kubernetes**, and cloud platforms like **AWS**, as well as automation tools like **Ansible** positions it as a reliable operating system for managing complex cloud-native infrastructures. As businesses continue to adopt **hybrid cloud**, **multi-cloud**, and **edge computing** strategies, **Rocky Linux** will play a pivotal role in ensuring that cloud-native workloads remain secure, efficient, and scalable.

By supporting the evolving needs of cloud-native technologies, **Rocky Linux** provides the foundation for enterprises to innovate and scale efficiently, while maintaining high standards of security and reliability. As the world of cloud computing and IT infrastructure continues to evolve, **Rocky Linux** remains at the forefront of providing solutions that meet the demands of tomorrow's technologies.

Rocky Linux, an enterprise-grade, community-supported operating system, is widely adopted for its stability, security, and compatibility with Red Hat Enterprise Linux (RHEL). It is commonly used to host web applications, databases, and cloud-based services.

Innovations in Server and Cloud Technology

Innovations such as containerization, serverless computing, edge computing, and AI-driven automation are transforming IT. Rocky Linux supports these through compatibility with Docker, Kubernetes, AWS Lambda, and tools like Ansible and Terraform, enabling scalable, efficient, and secure deployments.

Serverless and Edge Computing

- **Serverless:** AWS Lambda automates scaling, reducing infrastructure management.
- **Edge Computing:** Rocky Linux deploys lightweight containers for low-latency IoT applications.

The landscape of **server and cloud technologies** is evolving rapidly, transforming how businesses manage their infrastructure and deliver services. Innovations such as **containerization**, **serverless computing**, **edge computing**, and **AI-driven automation** are reshaping the IT world. These advances allow organizations to be more agile, efficient, and scalable, ensuring that they can meet the demands of modern workloads and emerging technologies. The rise of cloud platforms and hybrid architectures continues to push the boundaries of what is possible in terms of **scalability**, **performance**, and **security**.

Containerization and Microservices

Containerization is one of the most significant advancements in modern computing. It enables applications to be bundled with all their necessary dependencies and libraries, allowing them to run seamlessly across different environments. With **Kubernetes** and **Docker** taking the lead, **container orchestration** has become a critical aspect of managing large-scale distributed applications. Containers provide a high degree of flexibility, making them ideal for **cloud-native applications**.

In the realm of **microservices**, containerization plays an essential role. Microservices architecture breaks down applications into smaller, loosely coupled services that can be independently developed, deployed, and scaled. Each service can run in its own container, interacting with other services over APIs.

Practical Benefits:

- **Portability:** Containers ensure that applications behave the same way across development, testing, and production environments.
- **Scalability:** As demand grows, additional containers can quickly be spun up, allowing for rapid scaling.
- **Efficiency:** Containers share the same operating system kernel, which results in lower overhead compared to virtual machines, making them lightweight and fast.

Therefore, by deploying containers in the cloud, organizations can achieve greater efficiency in resource utilization. Kubernetes, as the most prominent orchestration platform, allows organizations to automate deployments, scale applications efficiently, and ensure high availability. This flexibility provides a seamless experience when scaling cloud-native applications on platforms such as **AWS**, **Azure**, or **Google Cloud**.

Serverless Computing: Simplifying Infrastructure Management

Serverless computing represents a dramatic shift in how cloud applications are built and deployed. With serverless architectures, developers are relieved from the burden of managing servers and infrastructure. Rather than provisioning and managing servers, developers can write functions that execute in response to specific events. Serverless platforms such as **AWS Lambda** and **Azure Functions**, oversee all aspects of execution, scaling, and resource management.

The fundamental difference between traditional cloud infrastructure and serverless computing is that with serverless, we pay only for the execution time of our code, not for idle server time. This model significantly reduces costs for applications with variable workloads.

Key Advantages:

- **Cost Efficiency:** Serverless allows businesses to pay only for the actual compute time used, making it a highly cost-effective solution for unpredictable workloads.
- **Simplified Management:** Serverless abstracts infrastructure management completely, enabling developers to focus on writing and deploying code.
- **Automatic Scaling:** Serverless platforms automatically scale in response to demand, ensuring that applications can manage high traffic volumes without manual intervention.

Real-world Use Case: Imagine a real-time image processing application where users upload images for analysis. With a serverless architecture, an image could trigger an AWS Lambda function that processes it, and stores the result in **Amazon S3**. The beauty of this approach is that as demand fluctuates, the serverless platform automatically scales to accommodate traffic spikes without any manual configuration.

Edge Computing: Powering Real-Time Applications

Edge computing is changing the way data is processed and analyzed by moving computation closer to the source of data generation, rather than relying solely on centralized data centers. This shift is necessary for applications that demand low latency and high bandwidth, such as in **Internet of Things (IoT)** devices, autonomous vehicles, and **real-time analytics**.

Practical Benefits:

- **Reduced Latency:** By processing data closer to the source, edge computing significantly reduces the time it takes to transfer data to centralized servers, enabling real-time decision-making.
- **Bandwidth Optimization:** Edge computing reduces the need to send all collected data to the cloud, minimizing bandwidth consumption and associated costs.
- **Enhanced Resilience:** Edge computing ensures that local devices continue to function even if the central cloud server is down, providing more reliable and resilient systems for mission-critical applications.

Edge in Action: Consider a **smart manufacturing facility** where IoT sensors monitor production lines. Rather than sending every data point to a cloud server for analysis, data can be processed on local edge devices to detect issues in real time. If a machine shows signs of malfunctioning, an immediate alert can be triggered to minimize downtime, all without needing to send data back to the cloud.

AI-Driven Automation in Cloud Systems

AI and machine learning technologies are beginning to permeate every aspect of server and cloud management. **AI-driven automation** is transforming how cloud resources are allocated, monitored, and optimized. AI can predict resource demand, automate scaling, and identify potential system issues before they become problems.

For instance, **predictive scaling** can anticipate traffic spikes and automatically scale cloud resources up or down, ensuring optimal performance and cost efficiency. **Machine learning algorithms** are also being used for security purposes, automatically detecting anomalies in system behavior and potential threats.

Key Benefits:

- **Efficiency:** Automating routine tasks and resource management ensures that IT teams can focus on more strategic work.
- **Cost Savings:** By predicting and optimizing resource usage, AI-driven automation reduces the likelihood of over-provisioning, saving on cloud costs.
- **Security:** AI can identify abnormal patterns in network traffic, providing an additional layer of security to detect potential intrusions early.

Practical Example:

Cloud providers like **Google Cloud** and **AWS** already integrate AI-driven services like **AWS Auto Scaling** and **Google Cloud's AI tools** that analyze usage patterns to automatically optimize cloud resource allocation.

Cloud-Native Databases: The Future of Data Management

As more businesses migrate to the cloud, **cloud-native databases** are emerging as the go-to solution for managing large-scale, distributed data. These databases are designed to take full advantage of the **cloud's scalability** and **elasticity**, enabling businesses to manage growing amounts of data, while ensuring high availability and reliability.

Cloud-native databases such as **Amazon Aurora**, **Google Cloud Spanner**, and **Azure Cosmos DB** are optimized for use in cloud environments. They offer features like **auto-scaling**, **multi-region replication**, and **automated backups**, which are essential for modern cloud applications.

Benefits of Cloud-Native Databases:

- **Scalability:** These databases are built to scale horizontally, allowing them to oversee vast amounts of data across multiple geographic regions.
- **High Availability:** With built-in replication, cloud-native databases provide high availability by automatically replicating data across multiple locations.
- **Performance Optimization:** Cloud-native databases are optimized to take advantage of cloud infrastructure, improving performance for large-scale applications.

The Future of Cloud and Server Technologies

The innovations in **server and cloud technology** continue to drive transformation across industries. With **containerization**, **serverless computing**, **edge computing**, and **AI-driven automation**, businesses can now build, deploy, and manage applications with greater speed, flexibility, and cost-effectiveness. These technologies are not only enhancing operational efficiency, but also laying the groundwork for future innovations in cloud computing.

Looking ahead, businesses must continue to adapt to these advancements by adopting cloud-native solutions, integrating **AI-driven automation**, and leveraging **hybrid and multi-cloud strategies**. These approaches will ensure that companies can meet the growing demands of modern workloads and remain competitive in a fast-evolving technological landscape.

As these technologies mature, they will reshape the way businesses manage infrastructure, improve performance, and enhance security. The future of cloud and server technologies holds exciting possibilities for building more intelligent, efficient, and scalable systems.

Comparison of Deployment Environments

To clarify the distinctions between on-premises, hybrid, and multi-cloud deployments, the following diagram illustrates their architectures and characteristics. The following diagram highlights the progression from on-premises to hybrid and multi-cloud setups, emphasizing trade-offs in control, complexity, and scalability.

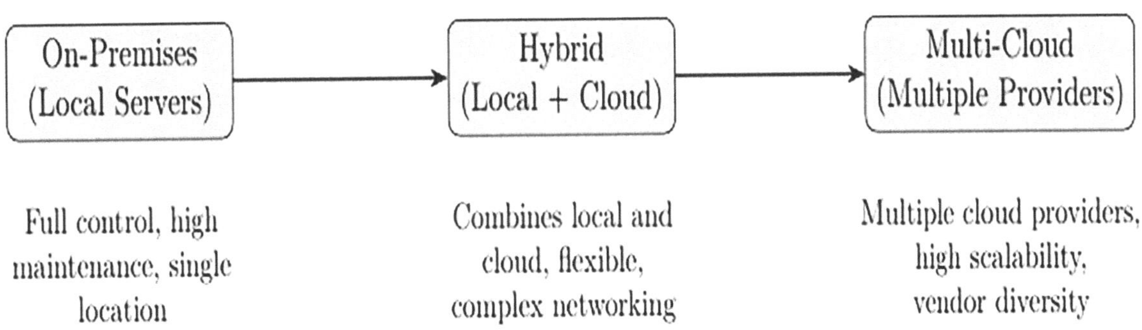

Figure 18.1: *Comparison of Deployment Environments*

Figure 18.1 visualizes the progression of deployment environments from **on-premises infrastructure** to **cloud**, **hybrid**, and **multi-cloud** models. The diagram highlights how each environment differs in terms of **control, scalability, and complexity**. On-premises deployments provide the highest level of control and security but are constrained by physical resource limits. Public cloud platforms expand scalability and flexibility but reduce direct control. Hybrid environments integrate on-premises with cloud services, balancing performance, compliance, and elasticity. Multi-cloud strategies extend this approach further by leveraging multiple providers, mitigating vendor lock-in, and enhancing resilience. This comparison illustrates the trade-offs organizations face when aligning infrastructure choices with operational requirements and long-term growth strategies.

Skills for Future System Administrators

Future sysadmins need expertise in cloud platforms **(AWS, Azure)**, automation **(Ansible, Terraform)**, container orchestration **(Kubernetes)**, and security **(IAM, SELinux)**. Soft skills like collaboration and problem-solving are equally critical.

The role of a **System Administrator** has significantly evolved over the years, transforming from traditional server management and network configuration to encompass a broader range of technical and soft skills. With the rapid advancement of technologies, such as cloud **computing**, **automation**, **containerization**, and **artificial intelligence**, system administrators must continuously adapt and refine their skills to remain relevant. As businesses increasingly adopt **cloud-based infrastructure** and **hybrid environments**, the demand for **skilled system administrators** is higher than ever.

This chapter explores the essential skills that future system administrators will need to succeed in the ever-changing IT landscape, with a focus on **cloud technologies**, **automation tools**, **security practices**, and **soft skills**. A comprehensive understanding of these areas will enable system administrators to manage complex infrastructures efficiently, and ensure systems remain secure, scalable, and reliable.

Cloud Computing and Virtualization Skills

Cloud computing has transformed the way businesses operate, offering scalability, flexibility, and cost-effectiveness. Future system administrators must have a deep understanding of **cloud platforms** such as **Amazon Web Services (AWS)**, **Microsoft Azure**, and **Google Cloud Platform**

(GCP). The ability to **design**, **deploy**, and **manage cloud infrastructure** is crucial for maintaining modern IT systems.

Key skills include:

- **Cloud Deployment Models:** Understanding the differences between public, private, and hybrid clouds and being able to deploy applications accordingly.
- **Cloud Storage and Networking:** Mastering services such as **AWS S3**, **Azure Blob Storage**, and **Google Cloud Storage** for efficient data management and transfer, as well as configuring cloud networking, using **Virtual Private Clouds (VPCs)**.
- **Cloud Security:** Knowledge of securing cloud resources is critical. Future system administrators need to be proficient in identity management, encryption, and multi-factor authentication (MFA) to protect sensitive data in the cloud.
- **Virtualization Technologies:** Proficiency in tools like **VMware**, **Hyper-V** and **KVM** are still important as businesses continue to leverage virtual machines for resource allocation, load balancing, and fault tolerance.

Practical Example:

A system administrator working in a hybrid cloud environment must be able to integrate on-premises systems with cloud-based services, ensuring seamless operation between both infrastructures.

Automation and Scripting

With the increase in infrastructure complexity, automation has become necessary. The future of system administration lies in the ability to automate routine tasks, manage configurations, and deploy applications quickly and efficiently. This is where **scripting** and **automation tools** come into play.

System administrators must become proficient in scripting languages like **Bash**, **Python**, and **PowerShell**. These tools allow administrators to automate system maintenance, configuration management, and deployments. Popular automation frameworks such as **Ansible**, **Puppet**, and **Chef** are also crucial for managing large-scale infrastructures efficiently.

Key skills include:

- **Infrastructure as Code (IaC):** Mastering IaC tools such as **Terraform** enables administrators to define infrastructure in a declarative way, and automate the provisioning of resources.
- **Configuration Management:** Tools like **Ansible** help automate the installation, configuration, and management of systems across thousands of machines.
- **Continuous Integration/Continuous Deployment (CI/CD):** Understanding the principles of CI/CD pipelines, and how to implement them is essential for automating code deployment and ensuring that systems are continuously updated.

Practical Example:

A system administrator could use **Ansible** to automate the configuration of web servers across multiple virtual machines, ensuring that all machines are deployed with the latest patches and software.

Security Skills and Cybersecurity Awareness

As cyber threats continue to evolve, system administrators must possess a strong understanding of security practices to safeguard their systems from attacks. Future administrators need to be well-versed in both **network security** and **system security**, focusing on securing infrastructures in cloud and hybrid environments.

Essential security skills include:

- **Firewalls and VPNs:** Configuring and managing firewalls, VPNs, and intrusion detection/ prevention systems (IDS/IPS) to ensure network security.
- **Encryption:** Knowing how to implement encryption for data at rest and in transit, as well as how to manage encryption keys securely.
- **Identity and Access Management (IAM):** Future administrators must be skilled in **IAM** solutions such as **AWS IAM**, **Azure AD**, and **LDAP** to manage user permissions and secure cloud resources.
- **Incident Response:** Knowledge of incident response protocols, such as logging, monitoring, and troubleshooting security breaches, is critical for minimizing potential damage.

Practical Example:

A system administrator working in a cloud environment must configure and monitor cloud firewalls, enable logging for suspicious activity, and set up automated alerts to respond to potential security breaches.

Containerization and Orchestration

As **containerization** becomes a key part of the software development lifecycle, system administrators need to develop proficiency in managing containerized applications. **Docker** and **Kubernetes** have emerged as the dominant tools in this space, enabling organizations to run applications in isolated environments while achieving greater portability and scalability.

Key skills include:

- **Docker**: Understanding how to build, deploy, and manage containerized applications using **Docker** is crucial for future administrators. This includes writing Dockerfiles, managing images, and running containers.
- **Kubernetes**: Kubernetes, the leading container orchestration platform, automates deployment, scaling, and management of containerized applications. System administrators must be skilled in managing Kubernetes clusters and configuring networking between containers.
- **Service Mesh**: Familiarity with service meshes such as **Istio** allows system administrators to manage service-to-service communication in containerized environments, including monitoring, security, and traffic management.

Practical Example:

A system administrator responsible for deploying applications across a Kubernetes cluster must ensure that the cluster is configured for auto-scaling, self-healing, and high availability. Additionally, managing updates and ensuring that containers are running with the correct versions are critical tasks.

Soft Skills and Collaboration

In addition to technical expertise, **soft skills** are becoming increasingly important for system administrators. As IT environments become more collaborative, administrators must collaborate closely with developers, security teams, and operations staff. Effective communication, **problem-solving**, and **collaboration** skills are essential for fostering a productive working environment.

Key soft skills include:

- **Team Collaboration:** System administrators often work in cross-functional teams. Being able to collaborate effectively with other IT professionals ensures smoother operations and faster problem resolution.
- **Problem Solving:** The ability to quickly identify issues, troubleshoot, and apply solutions is vital for minimizing downtime and ensuring system reliability.
- **Adaptability:** As technology continues to evolve, system administrators must be flexible and open to learning new tools and technologies.

Practical Example:

A system administrator may need to collaborate with the development team to troubleshoot an issue in a web application deployed in a Kubernetes cluster. The ability to communicate effectively with developers and understand their concerns is crucial to quickly resolving the issue.

The Path Forward

The future of system administration will require a diverse skill set encompassing both technical expertise and soft skills. As cloud technologies, automation, and containerization continue to evolve, system administrators must stay up to date with the latest tools and methodologies. Security, **cloud infrastructure management**, and **automation tools** will be at the core of IT administration, while **collaboration** and **problem-solving** will continue to play a crucial role in ensuring smooth operations.

For system administrators to succeed in the future, they must continuously adapt to modern technologies, develop their skills, and stay agile in a constantly changing IT landscape. Thus, by investing in training and development, system administrators will not only enhance their own capabilities, but also contribute to the success of their organizations in the digital age.

Skill Matrix for Future System Administrators

The following table maps essential tools and technologies evolving sysadmin tasks, providing a clear guide for skill development. This matrix ensures sysadmins prioritize skills aligned with modern IT demands. We will cover this information later within this chapter.

Future Roadmap of Rocky Linux and Its Ecosystem

Rocky Linux will enhance support for cloud-native technologies, automation, security (SELinux, compliance), and edge computing, driven by its community and long-term support **(LTS)** model.

The future of **Rocky Linux** is intrinsically tied to the changing landscape of open-source software, enterprise Linux distributions, and cloud-native technologies. As a **community-driven project** that serves as a **stable, RHEL-compatible replacement** for CentOS, Rocky Linux has quickly become a central player in the enterprise Linux space. Given its origins as a response to the shift in Red Hat's CentOS strategy, Rocky Linux is positioned to continue providing long-term support and stability for organizations relying on **enterprise-grade Linux systems**.

As technology continues to advance, particularly with the growing use of **cloud computing**, **automation**, **containerization**, and **edge computing**, Rocky Linux is evolving to meet the needs of modern IT infrastructures. This chapter delves into the future roadmap of Rocky Linux, highlighting its key developments, the direction of its ecosystem, and how it plans to integrate emerging technologies to remain competitive and relevant in the fast-paced IT world.

Key Developments in the Rocky Linux Ecosystem

Since its inception, **Rocky Linux** has been built with the goal of maintaining compatibility with **Red Hat Enterprise Linux (RHEL)**, ensuring that enterprises, using RHEL or its derivatives can migrate without disruption. However, to stay competitive and continue providing value to the open-source community, **Rocky Linux** will need to expand its ecosystem beyond just being a "*clone*" of RHEL. Below are some key areas where **Rocky Linux** is likely to develop further:

Cloud-Native Technologies and Integration with Cloud Platforms

The increasing adoption of **cloud technologies** will influence the future of Rocky Linux. As cloud platforms like **AWS**, **Microsoft Azure**, and **Google Cloud** continue to dominate the IT landscape, the role of **Rocky Linux** will extend into cloud-native technologies.

- **Kubernetes Integration**: With the growing importance of containerization, **Kubernetes** has become the go-to solution for orchestrating containers at scale. Rocky Linux's ecosystem is likely to prioritize better integration with Kubernetes, ensuring that it can support applications running in containers across multi-cloud and hybrid cloud environments.
- **Support for Cloud Platforms**: Rocky Linux will continue improving support for cloud platforms, offering easy deployment on popular platforms like AWS EC2, Azure, and Google Cloud. By optimizing its packages and configurations for these environments, Rocky Linux can provide an efficient, reliable OS for cloud workloads.

Practical Example:

In the future, system administrators deploying applications on Rocky Linux will benefit from seamless support for Kubernetes clusters, allowing for smoother scaling of cloud-native applications and the automation of deployment workflows across multiple cloud environments.

Automation and DevOps Tools

As businesses increasingly adopt **DevOps** methodologies, **automation** will become a central aspect of managing **Rocky Linux** systems. The roadmap for **Rocky Linux** includes enhancing compatibility with popular **automation tools** and integrating with **CI/CD pipelines**.

- **Integration with Ansible, Puppet, and Chef**: These **automation frameworks** will be fully supported to ensure that system administrators can easily automate the configuration and management of systems running Rocky Linux.
- **Enhanced Support for Containers**: As more enterprises adopt **Docker** and **Podman** for containerized applications, the **Rocky Linux** ecosystem will expand to ensure smooth container management with container orchestration platforms like Kubernetes.

Practical Example:

A **DevOps engineer** working with **Rocky Linux** could set up automated pipelines to deploy updates, monitor performance, and roll back problematic changes automatically, thereby enhancing operational efficiency and minimizing downtime.

Security and Compliance Features

With **cybersecurity** becoming a top priority for organizations globally, **security features** will be a major focus for the Rocky Linux ecosystem. Over the next few years, **Rocky Linux** will introduce enhanced security capabilities and tools to make it more attractive to enterprises focused on meeting strict **compliance standards**.

- **SELinux Improvements**: **Security-Enhanced Linux (SELinux)**, a security layer for managing access control, will continue to play a key role in securing **Rocky Linux**. The roadmap will include improvements to SELinux policies and better integration with automated security monitoring tools.
- **Automated Patch Management**: The system will support automated security patch management, ensuring that Rocky Linux instances are continuously protected against vulnerabilities without requiring manual intervention.
- **Compliance Tools**: **Rocky Linux** will integrate with compliance frameworks such as **PCI-DSS**, **HIPAA**, and **GDPR**, making it easier for businesses in regulated industries to meet their security and compliance requirements.

A financial institution using **Rocky Linux** can automatically apply security patches with **Red Hat Satellite**, keeping the system updated and compliant with industry standards.

Rocky Linux Roadmap

The following timeline outlines expected milestones for Rocky Linux, focusing on cloud, automation, and edge computing integrations. This roadmap highlights Rocky Linuxs commitment to staying relevant in cloud-native and edge environments.

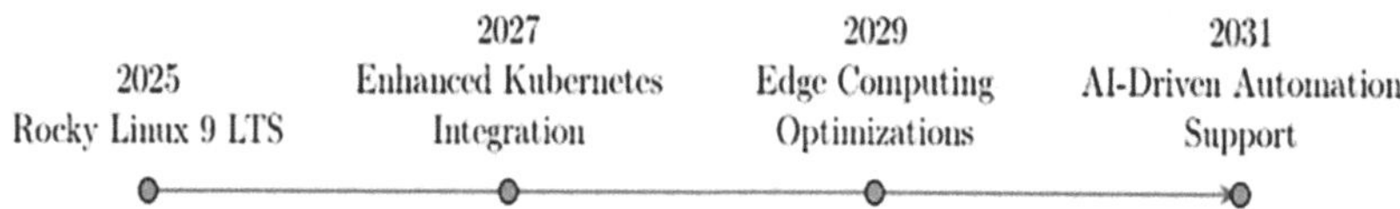

Figure 18.2: *Rocky Linux Development Timeline*

Figure 18.2 illustrates the evolution of Rocky Linux, charting significant milestones from its founding in late 2020 to its present development. The timeline begins with the **community-led initiative** launched in response to the discontinuation of CentOS Linux, followed by the release of **early beta versions**, the **first stable release (Rocky Linux 8.4, June 2021)**, and subsequent minor and major updates. It also highlights the introduction of **long-term support commitments**, integration with enterprise-ready features, and expanding community governance. Each marker in the timeline reflects Rocky Linux's mission to provide a **stable, transparent, and open-source alternative** for enterprise environments. By tracking these milestones, the figure underscores the rapid adoption and growing trust in Rocky Linux as a reliable foundation for modern infrastructure.

Category	Tools / Technologies	Key Tasks & Applications
Cloud Computing	AWS, Azure, GCP, Terraform	Provisioning and managing cloud instances, VPCs, and Infrastructure as Code (IaC)
Containerization	Docker, Kubernetes, Podman	Building, deploying, and orchestrating containerized environments
Automation	Ansible, Puppet, Chef, Jenkins	Automating system configurations and CI/CD pipeline workflows
Security	SELinux, IAM, Firewalls, MFA	Enforcing access controls, securing cloud assets, and implementing multi-factor authentication
Edge Computing	Lightweight containers, IoT frameworks	Deploying low-latency, distributed applications near data sources
AI / Machine Learning	AWS SageMaker, Google AI Platform	Predictive scaling, anomaly detection, and intelligent resource optimization
Soft Skills	Slack, Jira (Collaboration Tools)	Facilitating cross-functional communication and collaborative problem-solving

Figure 18.3: *Future Sysadmin Skill Matrix*

Figure 18.3 presents a comprehensive framework of the skill sets expected from system administrators in the coming years. The matrix organizes competencies into five key domains: **automation**, **cloud computing**, **cybersecurity**, **containerization**, and **DevOps practices**. Within each domain, both foundational and advanced skills are highlighted—for example, scripting and Linux administration under core knowledge, alongside advanced tools such as **Ansible**, **Kubernetes**, and **CI/CD pipelines**. It emphasizes the shift toward hybrid and cloud-native environments, where expertise in infrastructure-as-code, monitoring, and security hardening is critical. By mapping technical and strategic capabilities, the skill matrix functions as both a **career development roadmap** and a **training guide**, helping sysadmins remain adaptable and aligned with evolving industry demands.

Tools and Skills by Technology Area

The following table summarizes the tools and skills for key future areas, enhancing the chapter's clarity.

Area	Tools / Frameworks	Core Skills & Capabilities
Edge Computing	Docker, Kubernetes, IoT frameworks	Deploying lightweight containers; optimizing low-latency, distributed applications
CI/CD	Jenkins, GitHub Actions, GitLab CI	Designing automated pipelines; managing continuous integration and deployment workflows
Serverless Computing	AWS Lambda, Azure Functions	Writing event-driven functions; configuring auto-scaling and resource-efficient execution
AI-Driven Automation	AWS SageMaker, TensorFlow	Implementing predictive scaling; anomaly detection; scripting intelligent automation

Figure 18.4: *Tools and Skills for Future Technology Areas*

Figure 18.4 highlights the critical tools and competencies that system administrators and DevOps professionals must master to remain competitive in the era of rapidly evolving IT infrastructure. It categorizes these technologies into **artificial intelligence, edge computing, cloud-native development, infrastructure as code, and observability**. Each domain pairs specific tools with the practical skills required to leverage them effectively—for example, **AI-driven analytics platforms**, **serverless frameworks**, **Terraform for IaC automation**, and **Prometheus for monitoring and metrics collection**. The emphasis is on adaptability, cross-domain expertise, and a mindset of continuous learning, as these areas are reshaping how systems are deployed, secured, and optimized. By aligning with these future-focused technology areas, professionals can strategically plan their upskilling efforts to drive innovation and resilience in modern IT operations.

Performance Optimizations and Scalability

As IT environments continue to grow in complexity, performance and scalability will remain key considerations for any enterprise operating system. Rocky Linux is expected to continually improve its **performance optimizations** to support larger infrastructures, from **data centers** to **edge computing** deployments.

- **Edge Computing Support:** As edge computing becomes more prevalent, Rocky Linux will evolve to provide enhanced support for edge devices, offering **lightweight containers**, optimized performance for smaller systems, and **better integration** with IoT (Internet of Things) devices.

- **Resource Management and Virtualization:** With the rise of **virtualized environments** and **multi-tenant systems**, Rocky Linux will continue to enhance **resource management** capabilities, ensuring it can scale efficiently in virtualized and containerized environments.

Practical Example:

A large retail organization could deploy a **Rocky Linux** cluster across its **edge devices**, allowing data from remote locations to be processed locally before sending relevant information back to the central cloud-based systems.

Community and Ecosystem Growth

The future of **Rocky Linux** will also be shaped by its growing **community**. As a **community-driven** project, the involvement of developers, system administrators, and users is crucial to its ongoing success. The **Rocky Linux Foundation** is expected to continue fostering **community participation**, encouraging open-source contributions, and ensuring transparency in the development process.

- **Collaboration with Other Projects:** To enhance its ecosystem, **Rocky Linux** will collaborate more with other **open-source projects**. By joining forces with communities like **Fedora**, **CentOS Stream**, and **openSUSE**, Rocky Linux can provide a more comprehensive, multi-faceted approach to **enterprise Linux**.
- **Enterprise Support:** The roadmap for **Rocky Linux** will include partnerships with organizations providing **enterprise support**, ensuring that businesses that rely on Rocky Linux can receive the professional assistance they need for mission-critical systems.

Practical Example: Through its growing **community** and ecosystem, Rocky Linux could facilitate the integration of **open-source monitoring tools** like **Prometheus** and **Grafana**, enabling administrators to manage performance across large clusters of machines.

Focus on Long-Term Support (LTS)

One of the key factors that differentiate **Rocky Linux** from other Linux distributions is its **Long-Term Support (LTS)** model. As organizations demand stable, secure, and reliable operating systems, Rocky Linux will continue to deliver **enterprise-grade support** for extended periods. The roadmap will emphasize providing **updates** and **security patches** for at least 10 years, offering businesses the stability they require without having to worry about frequent, disruptive upgrades.

Practical Example:

A large financial organization could rely on **Rocky Linux** for its **core server infrastructure**, confident that the system will receive regular security patches and updates for many years, ensuring uninterrupted operations and compliance with industry regulations.

Case Study: Rocky Linux in a Future-Oriented Enterprise

This case study illustrates Rocky Linux application in a modern enterprise leveraging edge computing, serverless architectures, and AI.

Scenario: Smart Retail Chain

A global retail chain deploys Rocky Linux across its edge devices, cloud infrastructure, and serverless functions to optimize operations.

- **Edge Computing:** IoT sensors in stores run Rocky Linux containers to process real-time inventory data, reducing latency. `docker run -d rockylinux:9 inventory-app` deploys the application.

- **Serverless:** AWS Lambda functions, triggered by sensor data, update inventory databases in Amazon RDS, using Rocky Linux EC2 instances for backend processing.
- **AI Integration:** AWS SageMaker models predict demand, scaling EC2 instances via Terraform scripts.
- **CI/CD:** GitHub Actions automates deployment of updates to edge and cloud environments.

Implementation

1. Deploy Rocky Linux on edge devices using lightweight Docker containers.
2. Configure AWS Lambda for serverless processing, integrated with RDS on Rocky Linux.
3. Use Terraform for IaC to manage EC2 and SageMaker resources.
4. Set up GitHub Actions for continuous deployment of application updates.

Outcomes: This setup reduces latency by 30%, cuts cloud costs via serverless scaling, and improves inventory accuracy with AI predictions, showcasing Rocky Linux versatility.

A Bright Future for Rocky Linux

Therefore, the future of **Rocky Linux** is filled with exciting opportunities and developments. With its strong focus on **cloud-native technologies**, **automation**, **security**, and **community-driven support**, **Rocky Linux** is well-positioned to continue serving as a reliable, scalable, and secure platform for enterprises around the world.

By embracing emerging trends such as **edge computing**, **containerization**, and **AI-driven automation**, Rocky Linux will remain an essential part of the open-source ecosystem, providing both businesses and developers with the tools they need to succeed in the modern IT world. As the demand for open-source, **RHEL-compatible alternatives** grows, **Rocky Linux** will undoubtedly continue to thrive, offering stability and innovation to its growing community and user base.

Conclusion

As the landscape of server management and cloud computing continues to evolve, **Rocky Linux** is poised to play an even more pivotal role in ensuring stability, security, and flexibility within enterprise IT environments. The increasing adoption of **cloud-native technologies**, **containerization**, and **automation** has reshaped how system administrators approach both traditional infrastructure and **hybrid cloud** environments. Rocky Linux, with its open-source roots and compatibility with **RHEL**, remains a reliable and adaptable operating system, capable of meeting the demands of modern businesses.

Looking to the future, the **Rocky Linux ecosystem** will continue to grow, embracing innovative technologies such as **edge computing** and **AI-driven automation**. Thus, system administrators should be ready to evolve their skills to stay ahead of industry trends and ensure they are equipped to manage the challenges that come with increasingly complex IT environments. As **Rocky Linux** aligns itself with the broader open-source community, its role as a trusted platform for both on-premises and **cloud-based** solutions will only strengthen. In conclusion, the future of **Rocky Linux** is bright, with its continued innovation, ensuring that it remains a critical tool for those managing tomorrow's server and cloud infrastructures.

Points to Remember

- **The role of Rocky Linux in the cloud-native world** is evolving, as it adapts to recent technologies such as containerization, automation, and hybrid cloud strategies.

- **The future roadmap of Rocky Linux** includes increased focus on edge computing and AI-driven automation, aligning with modern IT trends.
- Skills for future system administrators will need to expand beyond traditional server management to include cloud technologies, container orchestration, and automation tools like Ansible and Docker.
- **Rocky Linux continues to provide a stable, secure, and adaptable foundation** for both traditional and cloud-based environments.
- **Ongoing open-source collaboration and community-driven development will ensure Rocky Linux's relevance and scalability in the long term**, supporting businesses in achieving high availability and cost-efficiency.

Multiple Choice Questions

1. What is one key role of Rocky Linux in the cloud-native ecosystem?
   a. Hosting only legacy applications
   b. Providing a stable and cost-effective alternative to other Linux distributions
   c. Managing traditional bare-metal servers
   d. Exclusively supporting proprietary software solutions
2. Which emerging server technology is most likely to influence the future management of Rocky Linux?
   a. Virtualization
   b. Containerization and microservices
   c. Bare-metal provisioning
   d. Monolithic architectures
3. Which skills are most important for system administrators managing cloud-based Rocky Linux environments in the future?
   a. Basic shell scripting
   b. Advanced networking protocols
   c. Knowledge of automation, cloud platforms, and container orchestration
   d. Manual configuration of hardware
4. How does Kubernetes enhance the management of applications on Rocky Linux in cloud-native environments?
   a. It simplifies hardware provisioning
   b. It automates network routing between containers
   c. It integrates serverless computing
   d. It provides a user interface for server management
5. What impact does serverless computing have on system administration for Rocky Linux?
   a. It requires administrators to manage hardware manually
   b. It reduces the need for administrators to manage server infrastructure

   c. It eliminates the need for cloud-based deployments
   d. It focuses on improving physical server configurations

6. Which of the following is expected to play a significant role in disaster recovery and high availability in Rocky Linux cloud deployments in the future?
   a. Traditional RAID configurations
   b. Multi-cloud architectures and global load balancing
   c. Physical server redundancy
   d. Manual backup processes

7. How will the growth of open-source communities like those around Rocky Linux, impact future server management practices?
   a. They will focus only on proprietary solutions.
   b. They will foster innovation and collaboration on cloud-native technologies.
   c. They will reduce the need for community-driven tools.
   d. They will focus solely on legacy hardware management.

8. Which tool is expected to become increasingly essential for automating deployments in Rocky Linux cloud environments?
   a. Manual configuration scripts
   b. Terraform and Ansible
   c. FTP servers
   d. Local text editors

9. What is a potential benefit of using Artificial Intelligence (AI) and Machine Learning (ML) in server management on Rocky Linux?
   a. Reduced need for network security protocols
   b. Enhanced performance optimization, and predictive maintenance
   c. Automated physical hardware provisioning
   d. Decreased reliance on cloud platforms

10. What is a major challenge in deploying Rocky Linux in future cloud environments?
   a. The absence of cloud integration tools.
   b. Lack of support for virtual machines.
   c. Balancing automation with manual intervention for complex deployments.
   d. Limited community-driven innovations.

Answers

1. b
2. b
3. a
4. c
5. b

6. a
7. b
8. a
9. b
10. b

Questions

1. What role does Rocky Linux play in the cloud-native ecosystem, and how does it compare to other Linux distributions like Ubuntu or CentOS in this context?
2. How are innovations in server technology such as containerization and microservices, transforming the way we manage and deploy applications on Rocky Linux?
3. What are the key challenges faced by system administrators in a cloud-native world, and how can the skills required to manage cloud environments evolve in the coming years?
4. What technologies or tools are emerging in the realm of server management that may become essential for future administrators working with Rocky Linux in cloud environments?
5. What are the advantages and disadvantages of serverless computing, and how does it impact the role of system administrators managing Rocky Linux servers?
6. How does Kubernetes integrate with Rocky Linux for cloud-native application deployments, and what are its primary benefits and challenges for system administrators?
7. What are the expected advancements in high availability (HA) and disaster recovery techniques for Rocky Linux in cloud environments over the next five years?
8. How will the role of open-source communities, such as those surrounding Rocky Linux, contribute to the ongoing development of cloud technologies and server management practices?
9. What impact will automation tools, such as Terraform and Ansible, have on the future of system administration for cloud-based deployments of Rocky Linux?
10. What is the potential impact of artificial intelligence (AI) and machine learning (ML) on server management, particularly for performance optimization and system monitoring in cloud environments using Rocky Linux?

Key Terms

- **Cloud-Native:** Refers to building and running applications that fully exploit cloud environments. This involves practices such as microservices, containerization (using Docker), and orchestrating these containers (using Kubernetes), all of which are integral to modern server management.
- **Containerization:** A lightweight form of virtualization that packages software and its dependencies into a standardized unit for development, shipment, and deployment. Docker is a popular platform for containerization, widely used in cloud-native architectures.
- **Kubernetes:** An open-source container orchestration platform designed to automate the deployment, scaling, and management of containerized applications. It is often paired with Linux distributions such as Rocky Linux for cloud-native deployments.

- **DevOps:** A set of practices that combines software development (Dev) and IT operations (Ops) to shorten the systems development life cycle, and provide continuous delivery with high software quality. It requires deep automation and collaboration.
- **Serverless Computing:** A cloud-computing model in which the cloud provider manages the infrastructure for application deployment. In this setup, the cloud provider dynamically allocates resources as needed, and users are only charged for actual resource usage.
- **Edge Computing:** A distributed computing framework that brings computation and data storage closer to data sources, reducing latency and bandwidth use. Edge computing will play a role in the future of server management, especially in IoT and real-time data processing.
- **Infrastructure as Code (IaC):** The practice of automating and managing cloud infrastructure using code and configuration files instead of manual processes. Tools like Terraform and Ansible are used for managing the infrastructure that supports server management on platforms such as AWS, Azure, or Google Cloud.
- **Microservices Architecture:** A method of designing software applications as a collection of loosely coupled services that can be independently developed, deployed, and scaled. This architecture is often cloud-native and runs efficiently on platforms like Rocky Linux.
- **Automation Tools:** Software such as Ansible, Chef, and Puppet that help automate the configuration, management, and monitoring of systems. These tools are vital for managing complex cloud environments, reducing the risk of human error, and speeding up deployment cycles.
- **CI/CD (Continuous Integration/Continuous Deployment):** Development practices where code changes are automatically built, tested, and deployed into production environments. CI/CD pipelines are fundamental for the future of system administration, enabling frequent reliable software updates.
- **Cloud-Native Security:** The evolving practices around securing cloud environments, applications, and data. This includes container security, identity, and access management (IAM), as well as securing microservices, all crucial for maintaining the integrity and safety of systems.
- **Rocky Linux Ecosystem:** The community-driven ecosystem surrounding Rocky Linux, including its developers, users, and contributors. The ecosystem plays a key role in shaping the future of Rocky Linux, particularly in areas such as cloud computing, security, and containerization.
- **Open-Source Software (OSS):** Software that is publicly available for anyone to use, modify, and distribute. Rocky Linux is part of the broader open-source movement which drives innovation and community collaboration in the development of recent technologies.
- **Hybrid Cloud:** A cloud computing environment that uses a mix of on-premises, private cloud, and public cloud services with orchestration between the platforms. Hybrid cloud setups are increasingly common in enterprise environments.
- **Cloud Management Platforms (CMPs):** Software solutions that provide a unified approach to managing and orchestrating cloud resources across different providers (for example, AWS, Azure, Google Cloud). CMPs are critical for administrators to oversee large-scale cloud deployments.
- **High Availability (HA):** Ensures that a system remains operational even in the event of hardware or software failure. HA systems often involve redundancy, failover mechanisms, and load balancing to guarantee uptime for the mission-critical services.
- **AI Workloads:** Computing tasks and applications that use artificial intelligence (AI) technologies, such as machine learning models, data analysis, and real-time decision-making. AI workloads are expected to become a key focus area in the future of server management.

Index

A

D

S

T

U

V

W

Z